Valerie & Walter's

BEST BOOKS FOR CHILDREN

Valerie & Walter's

BEST BOOKS FOR CHILDREN

A Lively, Opinionated Guide

**VALERIE V. LEWIS
and WALTER M. MAYES**

AVON BOOKS ◆ NEW YORK

AVON BOOKS, INC.
1350 Avenue of the Americas
New York, New York 10019

Copyright © 1998 by Walter M. Mayes and Valerie Lewis
Interior design by Rhea Braunstein
Back cover and inside cover authors photograph by Kate Nelson
Published by arrangement with the authors
Visit our website at **http://www.AvonBooks.com**
ISBN: 0-380-79438-1

Library of Congress Cataloging in Publication Data:

Lewis, Valerie V. (Valerie Valentine)
   [Best books for children]
   Valerie & Walter's best books for children: a lively, opinionated
guide / Valerie V. Lewis and Walter M. Mayes.
     p.   cm.
   Includes index.
   1. Children's literature—Bibliography.   2. Children—United
States—Books and reading.   I. Mayes, Walter M.   II. Title.
Z1037.L58   1998   98-7711
011.62—dc21   CIP

First Avon Books Trade Printing: August 1998

AVON TRADEMARK REG. U.S. PAT. OFF. AND IN OTHER COUNTRIES, MARCA
REGISTRADA, HECHO EN U.S.A.

Printed in the U.S.A.

QPM   10   9 8 7 6 5 4 3 2 1

Acknowledgments

The authors wish to acknowledge the patience, assistance, and advice of the following:

George Nicholson, agent extraordinaire . . .

Susan Coyle, Don Hall, the staff of Hicklebees, Monica Holmes, Laura Mancuso, Melissa Mytinger, Sandra Lewis Nisbet, The Pod, Dian Curtis Regan, The Rexrode family, Kay Van Hest, Joan Vigliotta, Nancy Werlin, Janet Zarem, The Boston, Pasadena, and San Francisco Public Libraries . . .

Special appreciation for "Creative charges under the gun" to Peggy Rathmann, Kelly McCoy and Kate Nelson . . .

and our deepest appreciation to our editor and champion, Elise Howard.

Walter's Dedication

Three who made a difference:

Robin Bradley Subelsky, my fourth-grade teacher and lifelong friend, who did not blink when I wrote a book report on *The Caine Mutiny* and knew not to squelch a motivated reader . . .

Rachel Semco, who shepherded me and an unruly class of ninth graders through *The Lord of the Flies* and who held my hand and massaged my brain when the light bulb switched on, revealing reading to be much more than words on a page . . .

and **Helen Howard,** formidable head librarian at Poway High, who respected the reader in me enough to give him the books she could not put out on the shelves.

And to the memory of **Sybil Mary Burgum Mayes,** my foundation, and the future of **Anthony Marshall Mayes,** my purpose.

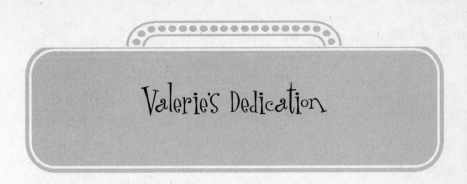

Valerie's Dedication

for **Pauline Grace Kamehameha Smith Lewis**
and **Owen Valentine Lewis**

and to my daughters Laura and Kaela Mancuso for providing the stories; to Don Hall for his endless support; and to my brother and sisters, Paul Lewis, my booster; Sandra Lewis Nisbet, my mentor; Daphne Lewis, my courage; and Monica Lewis Holmes, my partner who has worked twice as hard to provide me with the gift of time.

Contents

Introduction   1

Part One: Books for All Ages   7

Part Two: Books for Very Young Children   61

Part Three: Books for Children of Reading Age   241

Part Four: Books for Children in Middle
Elementary Grades   433

Part Five: Books for Middle School Readers and Young Adults   537

Appendix One: Tricky Situations and Frequently
Asked Questions   556

Appendix Two: Themes   561

Index   677

Introduction

Here we are, writing an introduction—and wondering who reads them, anyway. Most of you will want to get to the heart of the matter, getting books into the hands and minds of children. You chose this book because you want information about how to pick books for some child or children in your life.

People are often reluctant to choose books for children:

"Oh, I don't know her reading level."

"I don't know what he's read."

"He's so physical . . ."

"What if she doesn't like it?"

"Kids don't get excited about books as gifts."

We know these reasons and have heard dozens more. Read this and boost your confidence about choosing books on your own. Start here if you'd like to know more about us and how this book works, or in the back if you know you're looking for a particular kind of book that our extensive thematic appendix can help you find, or go straight to the title listings, more than 2000 of them (cross-referenced to death), and find a wealth of recommendations you can rely on—even if you don't yet know quite what it is you're looking for.

Why can you rely on us? We have tons of experience in doing exactly what we are telling you how to do: putting books into the hands of children.

We are writing about books we've used with children. We've read them aloud. We've whispered them at bedtime. We've performed them with large audiences. We are in the trenches. We love books. We love what books do. We believe in their power, their mystery and their magic.

Our Personal Introduction

INTRODUCING: WALTER

I don't remember learning to read. My mother tells me that I was always interested in books and that, as a kindergartner, I had a tendency to read aloud anything I saw. One day I was glancing at the things on my teacher's desk when she heard me read aloud the address on an envelope. I remember a big deal being made out of the fact that I could read. Soon after, I was sent to first grade in the afternoons to practice reading. I stayed in kindergarten for the morning, but left my friends after lunch and went off to the world of readers.

By the time I was in fourth grade, the principal asked me to visit the kindergarten during recess once a week and read stories to the little kids. That was probably a clever effort on his part to channel my aggressively outgoing personality into an acceptable medium. I have always wanted an audience, always wanted accolade and applause, and have always been willing to risk looking foolish to attain them.

My love of books and reading, my compulsive need to perform, along with the belief that we all must do what we can to make the world a better place, have inspired me, after more than twenty years as a bookseller and publisher's sales representative to create the personality known as Walter the Giant Storyteller. I travel the country making appearances in schools, libraries, bookstores, and auditoriums speaking to children, parents, teachers, and civic groups. I bring a sense of joy to my reading experience and try to instill that joy in others.

INTRODUCING: VALERIE

I grew up in a house bulging with books. Reading began first thing in the morning with the newspaper. On Sundays, newsprint was spread across the table and floor as we vied for our favorite sections: my younger sister and I for the "funnies," my brother the sports section, and my two older sisters for the magazine sections and Ann Landers.

But don't think we sat around reading all the time. Five children plus our friends added up to an active household. There were plays to rehearse, cheerleading practice, capture the flag and street softball. The TV (when we got one) was not often on, except for "Ed Sullivan" on Sunday nights.

The point is, books were not "special." They were a basic part of our life. We didn't think much about reading. It was always there.

Mom and Dad were steeped in reading, but their approaches to books were very different. Mom's books always had pencil notes in the margins—often eyebrow pencil. If a piece of writing inspired a poem or a thought or a remembered dentist appointment, she'd just jot it down. I suppose with her five kids, she needed to capture the idea at the moment. Who knew what interruptions would send it off for good?

Mom spent hours in used bookstores finding jewels about dreams or being a woman, or life in Vietnam. Or she'd pick up a book about none of those things just because a face on the cover was intriguing. When Mom died we found valuable insights, verses, and thoughts left behind in the margins.

Dad has first-edition Hemingways on his shelf along with Shakespeare, James Joyce, Dylan Thomas, and Winston Churchill. He would just as soon have his hands removed as to write in a book. He treats them as valued gifts. Mom treated books as a necessity of life—toothbrush, sweater, a book in case you wait in line or find yourself in a quiet spot. From the two of them, I learned there is more than one way to value a book. Books are a necessity. And they are a valued gift. And I learned that each one of us holds the power to help children love reading—to feel the passion of a good story.

In college I was an art major who was enchanted by books—by the words, the rhythms and the print on the page. In 1979, with partners, I opened Hicklebee's Children's Bookstore in San Jose, California. It came from my desire to be first in line to see the newest gems published each season—to read aloud pages to strangers, to boast about illustrations as though I had created them myself. My storytelling side—I can't remember not being told to "get to the point"— has been satisfied with programs for large groups of adults as well as one-on-one stories with children. After all this time, there is still nothing for me that matches the sight of a child settled on the floor of our store, lost in the magic of a book.

Walter and I have worked together since 1981. When a new book catches my attention, I save a copy to show him. We read passages aloud to anyone who will listen—each of us enjoying our own dramatic telling. Most of the time we agree on shared selections, and when we don't, I figure his judgment is slipping. I don't know anyone with his grasp on which books work best for children. Except, of course, for me.

INTRODUCING: VALERIE AND WALTER'S BEST BOOKS FOR CHILDREN

When we first sat down to write, our aim was to include every one of our favorite books and to build a fact-filled resource covering all sorts of possibilities for reading with children. After reviewing huge lists of our own, hundreds of publishers' catalogues and mountains of books, we agreed on about 8,000 titles. Whoops—it was time to get practical: we wanted to write a manageable guide. To slim the list down, we voted on which books we couldn't live without. We have included only titles we think are good and have tried not to review negatively. That doesn't mean a book that *isn't* there is one we don't like. We like a lot of books (at least 8,000!), but just could not include them all.

How This Book Is Organized

Our book is divided into several parts according to the most important feature to begin with when selecting a book for a child: its listening or interest level. This represents the age of the child to whom the book may be read or who will be interested in the book's subject matter, theme, or style of presentation. We begin our book, for instance, with books of interest to children of all ages. Those listings are followed by books of interest to babies through preschoolers, followed by books of interest to a mixed listenership of preschoolers and elementary readers, and so on. Within each interest level, books are further categorized by their reading levels. For instance, in the middle-grade category (don't worry! we're coming to definitions of all these terms!), we subdivide listings: those books easily read by a child reading at the elementary level, followed by those that will be read by a child reading at the middle-grade level, etc.

Definitions (or, About Those Levels)

Because a child's readiness for a book is not determined by chronological age, we will use general ranges represented as follows:

All = listeners of all ages
P = from babies to preschoolers
E = Early elementary (grades K-3)
M = Middle elementary (grades 3-6)
Y = Young adult/Teen (grades 6 and up)

Remember, reading readiness cannot clearly be attached to an age or grade. We recommend a range of listening and reading levels to help you choose books that best fit the needs of your child, student, or family.

In the listening/interest level area, multiple entries indicate that the book will appeal to a group that spans more than one age range.

A dual heading for reading level, such as E/M indicates that a book straddles these two levels; it will challenge an E level reader but will also satisfy a middle-level reader.

Frankly, these levels have been chosen more from gut reaction and experience than from standard reading level "recipes." Remember: There is no such thing as a perfect book for all children of a particular age.

Of course, your knowledge of the children for whom you are choosing and their individual interests and abilities should always be the determining factor when you're selecting a book. Our goal is to aim you in the right direction and to help you narrow your path through the forest of choices.

Title Listings

Within each readership category, books are organized alphabetically by title. Here is a sample title listing:

★ *Soda Jerk*   POETRY COLLECTION

AUTHOR: **Cynthia Rylant** • ILLUSTRATOR: Peter Catalanotto
HC: Orchard • PB: Beechtree
THEMES: coming of age; jobs; yearning; secrets; fitting in; wisdom; gentle boys; towns

How Rylant knows what she knows about adolescent males is beyond me, but she is dead-on accurate in her portrait of teen yearnings. A novel in prose poems of the life of a seventeen-year-old boy in Cheston, Virginia. This is my favorite of her books and I read it aloud to teens and adults when I get the chance.

I want to make it clear that this is not just a "boy" book. It's great reading and girls will recognize the soda jerk—it will give them some idea of how he thinks. And while we're at it, this goes for Bruce Brooks' Boys Will Be, *too!*

Each title listing will include some and possibly all of the following:
Title (A star ★ is used to identify standouts/gems/the best of the best in our mutual opinion.)
Author (**Boldface** indicates a "spotlight" author, one we feel has shown a consistently high level of excellence in writing for a diverse range of audiences.)
Illustrator (where applicable)
Hardcover publisher
Paperback publisher
Format: fiction; picture book; poetry; nonfiction—a basic guide to what kind of book it is.
Themes: Each title includes a list of themes, cross-referenced with the appendix at the back of the book, to offer a multitude of options when matching a child's interests with a book.

Comments: Each entry concludes with our comments, which highlight the distinctive qualities that earned a book its place in our listings. The bulk of the comments come from both of us, written separately, discussed, and revised together until we often cannot tell who wrote what initially.

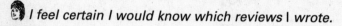 *I feel certain I would know which reviews I wrote.*

Yeah, all the reviews with the word "critter" in them are yours.

From time to time, as above, one of us will have something to say that is in addition to the review we wrote—sometimes responding to the other writer's slightly different take on a book, sometimes recounting an experience linked to a book. You'll also find some reviews identified as either Valerie ( ) or Walter's ( ) alone, as in the sample title listing. This occurs when one of us felt strongly enough about a title and the other one agreed that those feelings pretty much summed it up.

A Note on Finding the Books
We have made every effort to choose books still available from publishers and to list paperback editions, usually less expensive, if available. Find them in your library, or go to your local bookstore to buy the books. Never hesitate to ask a bookseller to special order a title if you do not see it in the store. As this guide goes into publication, some of our favorites will go "out of print"; that is, they will no longer be available for sale. In those cases look for them in the library or in used bookstores.

PART ONE

Books for All Ages

Here is a collection of books that we feel will interest listeners across the divide of, say, a three year old, a six year old and a nine year old. The best part is that early readers can join in by reading aloud with older readers in the family.

★ 17 Kings & 42 Elephants
PICTURE BOOK

AUTHOR: Margaret Mahy • ILLUSTRATOR: Patricia MacCarthy
HC: Dial • PB: Puffin
THEMES: elephants; journeys; kings; jungles; math; rhythm

A magical collaboration and an example of the best kind of picture-book storytelling. Mahy's evocative poetry, telling of a journey full of mystery, is complimented by MacCarthy's beautiful batik paintings; together they make a masterpiece. This story raises more questions than it answers. Where are the kings going? Where are they from? What do 17 kings need with 42 elephants, anyway? There is plenty of opportunity for discussion long after the reading ends.

Annie Bananie
PICTURE BOOK

AUTHOR: Leah Komaiko • ILLUSTRATOR: Laura Cornell
HC/PB: HarperCollins
THEMES: friendship; moving; loss

Anyone who has had a best friend move away will understand Annie Bananie. Komaiko, who has a talent for rhythm and for understanding true friendship, has captured the feelings in her words. Cornell has echoed the feelings in her art. Check out the beginning readers featuring Annie's further adventures: *Annie Bananie Moves to Barry Avenue*, *Annie Bananie: Best Friends to the End*, and *Annie Bananie and the People's*

Court. Her hilarious adventures continue, with the reading level just right to help her fans make the transition to reading chapter books!

Anno's Journey   PICTURE BOOK

AUTHOR/ILLUSTRATOR: Mitsumasa Anno
HC: Putnam • PB: Paperstar
THEMES: wordless; Europe; geography; social studies; journeys

Float invisibly from one perspective to another in this wordless journey through northern Europe. Anno's stunning watercolors offer details as an antidote to geography-shy readers. Anno puts this device to terrific use in many books. The geographic and historical richness makes *Anno's Britain, Anno's USA,* and *Anno's Italy* not only fascinating but great introductions to these places. Don't miss these other titles by this inventive artist: *Anno's Alphabet: An Adventure in Imagination* and *Anno's Counting Book* (HC/PB: HarperCollins).

> ### MOMENTS IN A FAMILY'S DAY TO INCORPORATE READING
>
> Bedtime is not the only time to read with a child. Have books handy at home, and pack some with you when you leave. Books can be helpful in the following situations:
>
> •Preparing for new experiences
> •Relieving stress
> •Comforting fears
> •Offering reassurance
> •Getting silly
> •During an illness
> •During time-outs
> •On the bus
> •In the car: Yes, stories on tape are a great way to share tales. A road trip also can be a time for passengers to read aloud to drivers.

The Christmas Alphabet   POP-UP

AUTHOR/ILLUSTRATOR: Robert Sabuda
HC: Orchard
THEMES: Christmas; guessing

Each letter of the alphabet is placed on its own door, concealing a pop-up prize. Perfect for the entire family, this Christmas alphabet is both a guessing game and an engineering feat. Guess what is behind each door, and marvel at all twenty-six dazzling paper creations. A Christmas treasure. Also look for Sabuda's *Twelve Days of Christmas,* another three-dimensional gem.

The Cinder-Eyed Cats   PICTURE BOOK

AUTHOR/ILLUSTRATOR: Eric Rohmann
HC: Crown
THEMES: cats; imagination; magic; sea animals; fish; dance; night; rhyme; boats; journeys; mystery

Imaginations soar with a boy and a flying boat to a faraway land where "cats like velvet shadows move, their coal-fire eyes ablaze . . ." A wondrous achievement in visual storytelling, this book's breathtaking art will take the reader on a moonlit dance and home again.

Dawn   PICTURE BOOK

AUTHOR/ILLUSTRATOR: Uri Shulevitz
HC/PB: Farrar Straus & Giroux
THEMES: night; daylight; grandfathers and grandsons; boats; morning; comparisons

Simple and exquisite. From deep darkness to stunning color, here is the beginning of day as seen by a grandfather and grandson on a fishing trip. Art and text match perfectly. A treasure.

The Dead Bird   PICTURE BOOK

AUTHOR: Margaret Wise Brown • ILLUSTRATOR: Remy Charlip
HC/PB: HarperCollins
THEMES: death; rituals; birds; problem-solving

A look at a child's first encounter with death. Children find a dead bird, examine it, bury it, sing a song for it, honor it, and finally forget about it. Simple text on white pages alternates with Charlip's unaffected art, making this a profoundly moving book and one that will serve as a snapshot of a nearly universal moment of childhood.

Everett Anderson's Goodbye   PICTURE BOOK

AUTHOR: Lucille Clifton • ILLUSTRATOR: Ann Grifalconi
PB: Holt
THEMES: death; loss; fathers; anger; denial; African American

Everett Anderson's father has died. This quiet, sensitive story shows the stages of grief he experiences before being able to say, "I knew my daddy loved me through and through, and whatever happens when people die, love doesn't stop, and neither will I." Although Everett is a very young boy, any age child will understand the emotions experienced in this treasure. Other stories about Everett Anderson, dealing with less traumatic topics, include: *Everett Anderson's 1 2 3, Everett Anderson's Friend,* and *Everett Anderson's Year.*

Free Fall   PICTURE BOOK
AUTHOR/ILLUSTRATOR: David Wiesner
HC: Lothrop • PB: Mulberry
THEMES: wordless; dreams; adventure; connections

No words are necessary. Wiesner's adventure comes to life as the pages of a sleeping boy's book break loose and sweep away into new forms connecting and changing from page to page. Let your child enjoy this one at his own pace.

George and Martha   PICTURE BOOK
AUTHOR/ILLUSTRATOR: James Marshall
HC/PB: Houghton Mifflin
THEMES: friendship; humor; relationships

The perfect expression of friendship in picture book form. Two hippos, lovingly but hilariously rendered in Marshall's droll, minimalist style (both pictures and words), star in a series of adventures that will have everyone laughing. The limits of being a friend are tested time and again in these books, but nothing can keep George and Martha apart for long. Underneath all the fun, there are some valuable lessons about trust, loyalty, and maintaining a sense of humor. There are seven George and Martha titles in all including a one-volume omnibus edition.

Though Marshall never comes right out and says it, it seems clear to the adult eye that G & M are more than just friends. I have always felt that these books should be given as a set to any couple about to embark upon a long-term relationship. George and Martha are role models for us all!

Good Times on Grandfather Mountain   PICTURE BOOK
AUTHOR: Jacqueline Briggs Martin • ILLUSTRATOR: Susan Gaber
HC/PB: Orchard
THEMES: optimism; perseverance; farms; music; woodworking

Old Washburn is as relentlessly optimistic a character as one could find, considering that he has more than his share of trials and tribulations. When his animals run away, his crops get eaten by pests, and the wind blows down his house, he calls upon his skill as a whittler and his music making to make the best of a bad deal. With his own resources and the help of his neighbors, his farm gets rebuilt, his animals return, and Old Washburn is looking mighty smart by the end of the book. A lovely testament to the value of a positive outlook.

Guess What?   PICTURE BOOK

AUTHOR: Mem Fox • ILLUSTRATOR: Vivienne Goodman
HC: Gulliver • PB: Voyager
THEMES: witches; guessing game; spooky stories

Guess what? This is a zany, ridiculous book. The bizarre illustrations are more adult than childlike. So, why do we recommend it? It's funny. The details take zillions of re-reads to find. And the story? It's an "ask a question and get the child to roar a response" book. "Has she got a cat that's really sleek and black? Guess!" (turn the page) "Yes!" "Does she sometimes wear a hat? . . ." And children do respond!

Handsigns: A Sign Language Alphabet   PICTURE BOOK

AUTHOR/ILLUSTRATOR: Kathleen Fain
HC/PB: Chronicle
THEMES: sign language; communication; alphabet; deafness

An alphabet book for the fourth most used language in the United States—American Sign Language. On each page there is a full color, bold picture of an animal, a letter of the alphabet—upper and lower case—and the corresponding sign for that letter in American Sign Language. This colorful picture book, read a few times, could give a child the gift of another alphabet to carry for a lifetime.

Handtalk: An ABC of Finger Spelling and Sign Language   PICTURE BOOK

AUTHOR: Remy Charlip and Mary Beth Miller
ILLUSTRATOR: George Ancona
HC: Simon & Schuster • PB: Aladdin
THEMES: deafness; sign-language; alphabet; spelling; language; communication

Remy Charlip is a master of mime, and it shows here. Photographs on every page clearly demonstrate the language of signing with dramatic, exaggerated expression. This gem works for the whole family. Also *Handtalk Birthday: A Number and Story Book in Sign Language* (additional theme: numbers).

The Happy Hocky Family   PICTURE BOOK

AUTHOR/ILLUSTRATOR: Lane Smith
HC: Viking • PB: Puffin
THEMES: humor; zany; family; parodies

A dead-on parody of primers is just the thing you'd expect from the
warped mind of Lane Smith, illustrator of *Math Curse* and *The Stinky
Cheese Man*. Perfect for that fourth-grader who is into puns and dumb
jokes. You can't help but laugh.

Hippos Go Berserk   PICTURE BOOK

AUTHOR/ILLUSTRATOR: Sandra Boynton
HC: Simon & Schuster • PB: Aladdin
THEMES: counting; humor

A counting book featuring 45 hippos and an unidentified creature romp-
ing out of control! Funny, and the kind of book that begs to be read again
and again.

If . . .   PICTURE BOOK

AUTHOR/ILLUSTRATOR: Sarah Perry
HC: Paul Getty Museum and Children's Library Press
THEMES: imagination; fantasy; possibilities

"If toes were teeth . . . If caterpillars were toothpaste . . ." Striking illustrations demand attention as you venture from one page to the next in
this visual stretch of the imagination from one absurd possibility to the
next. A perfect choice for the entire family.

Is That You, Winter?   PICTURE BOOK

AUTHOR/ILLUSTRATOR: Stephen Gammell
HC: Silver Whistle
THEMES: winter; snow; imagination; dolls; love; change

He makes the snow, but wonders, "Who do I make it snow for?" Grumpy
Old Man Winter goes about his work in Gammell's stunning, expressive
paintings, which form a kind of meditation on the colors blue and white.
But when a little girl is revealed to be the source of the story, Old Man
Winter is reminded of just how special he is, and the reader is given a
lesson in love that will warm the heart despite all the snow.

James Marshall's Mother Goose   PICTURE BOOK

AUTHOR/ILLUSTRATOR: James Marshall
HC/PB: Farrar Straus & Giroux
THEMES: Mother Goose; rhyme

There are many collections of Mother Goose, and each illustrator brings
a particular sensibility to any new version, not only in the illustrations
they create but in the selection of rhymes as well. Marshall's choices
and how he draws them are a study in the droll humor that became his
trademark. Sly touches abound, making this a collection as much for
adults as children.

Jeremy's Decision   PICTURE BOOK

AUTHOR: Ardyth Brott • ILLUSTRATOR: Michael Martchenko
HC: Kane/Miller
THEMES: music; jobs; orchestras; siblings; fathers and sons; individual-
ity; dinosaurs; choices

Jeremy has gotten tired of everyone asking if he's going to be like his
father, a famous symphony conductor, when he grows up. He has his
own interests—dinosaurs—but has endured the well-meaning questions
out of politeness. With a satisfying and surprising conclusion, here is a
book for every child who fears living up to adult expectations.

Mike Mulligan and His Steam Shovel   PICTURE BOOK

AUTHOR/ILLUSTRATOR: Virginia Lee Burton
HC/PB: Houghton Mifflin
THEMES: machines; buildings; digging; jobs; change; towns; problem
solving; resourcefulness; performing

Sweetly old-fashioned, it's the story of a man and his beloved steam shovel,
Mary Ann. They dig themselves into a hole, and it takes the ingenuity of
a small boy to come up with a surprising and satisfying conclusion.

My Grandma Has Black Hair   PICTURE BOOK

AUTHOR: Mary Hoffman • ILLUSTRATOR: Joanna Burroughes
HC: Dial
THEMES: grandmothers; humor; family; individuality

The day of the white-haired granny is rapidly passing, and this delightfully funny account of a grandma who simply cannot behave like the
stereotypical grannies in stories deserves a wide readership.

Noah's Ark

AUTHOR/ILLUSTRATOR: Peter Spier

HC: Doubleday • PB: Dell

THEMES: Bible stories; floods; animals; faith; courage; wordless

Winner of the Caldecott Medal, this wordless retelling of the story of Noah will captivate children, allowing them to tell the story in their own fashion.

Old MacDonald Had a Farm

AUTHOR/ILLUSTRATOR: Glen Rounds

HC/PB: Holiday House

THEMES: farms; farmers; animals; songs

Rounds' illustrations strike us as the sort that were drawn by a cowboy atop his horse and the durn thing won't hold still. Jangly and edgy, they add a rustic, real-farm feel to this traditional song.

Old Turtle

AUTHOR: Douglas Wood • ILLUSTRATOR: Cheng-Khee Chee

HC: Pfeifer Hamilton

THEMES: fables; God; the Earth; nature; environment; peace; turtles; hope

When all the beings of the world began to understand one another, they argued about what God was. "God is a swimmer, in the dark blue depths of the sea. 'She is a hunter,' roared the lion. 'God is gentle,' chirped the robin." And then Old Turtle spoke. He spoke of what God is and of what was to come. When you search for a treasure, a gift for a whole family, one that celebrates life, nature, peace, beauty, find this one.

One to Ten Pop-Up Surprises!

AUTHOR/ILLUSTRATOR: Chuck Murphy

HC: Little Simon

THEMES: numbers

Bold numbers hiding brilliantly colored, cleverly engineered creatures will get any reader's attention.

Pancakes for Breakfast

AUTHOR/ILLUSTRATOR: Tomie dePaola

PB: Voyager

THEMES: wordless; cooking; pets, eggs; neighbors; recipes; milk; meals; pancakes

Old Mother Hubbard is not the only old lady with an empty cupboard. The one in this tale wakes up yearning for pancakes but has to go to the source for the ingredients she needs. This simple, wordless story will fill youngsters up with words. Particularly if you allow non-readers to "read" this one to you.

R.E.M.
PICTURE BOOK

AUTHOR/ILLUSTRATOR: Istvan Banyai

HC: Viking

THEMES: imagination; dreams; optical illusions; change; journeys; wordless

No words. Beginning with a dark spot, figures emerge and change from page to page. This is the kind of book we would have loved as children. We're intrigued by it as adults. It's fantasy, art and imagination with endless possibilities.

The Rain
PICTURE BOOK

AUTHOR: Michael Laser • ILLUSTRATOR: Jeffrey Greene

HC: Simon & Schuster

THEMES: rain; storms; family; weather; memories

Two children, a businessman, a teacher, and an old man have differing responses to a sudden shower. Striking art enhances the tale. Another look at rain can be found in *Peter Spier's Rain*.

Rats on the Range and Other Stories
EARLY READER

AUTHOR/ILLUSTRATOR: James Marshall

HC: Dial • PB: Puffin

THEMES: animals; humor

Laugh-out-loud funny and easy to read, here is a collection of stories that will delight fans of *George and Martha* and *The Stupids*. Though we have always known this, here Marshall proves that he is as great a writer as he is an illustrator. See also *Rats on the Roof and Other Stories*.

Red Riding Hood
PICTURE BOOK

AUTHOR/ILLUSTRATOR: James Marshall

HC: Dial • PB: Puffin

THEMES: fairy tales; wolves; grandmothers; forests; consequences; disobeying; folklore

A retelling of the classic tale with just the right touches to delight a fan of Marshall's work. Classic Marshall retellings include: *Hansel & Gretel,*

Old Mother Hubbard and Her Wonderful Dog, The Three Little Pigs, and *Goldilocks and the Three Bears.* Each is a marvelous example of why Marshall is one of the most beloved creators in all children's books.

The Rolling Store   PICTURE BOOK

AUTHOR: Angela Johnson • ILLUSTRATOR: Peter Catalanotto
HC: Orchard
THEMES: African American; stores; grandfathers; friendship

A young girl recounts the tale of her grandfather's childhood, when a big truck would come out to the country, a store on wheels with something for everyone. As the girl tells of her grandfather's special memory, artist Catalanotto shows us the girl and a friend readying their own version, all in time for grandpa's return home at the end of the day. With help from the artistry of his creators, his past and his present converge and the rolling store rolls once more. This is an example of how the pairing of an author and an illustrator can be a testament to the vision of a book's editor, who sees how one can bring out the best work in another.

> While critical to building brains, reading is equally important to building trusting and close relationships. That's why many of us remember the warm embrace or the comfortable lap that cradled us when we read books as children. And that's why reading should not be viewed solely as an intellectual proposition, particularly in the era in which we now live.
> —Hillary Rodham Clinton,
> Time magazine, Feb. 2, 1997

Shoes Shoes Shoes   PICTURE BOOK

AUTHOR: Ann Morris • ILLUSTRATOR: Ken Heyman (photographs)
HC: Lothrop
THEMES: cultural diversity; shoes

This sparkling photo-essay, which uses footwear around the world to point out our differences and similarities, is typical of Ann Morris' outstanding work. With photographer Ken Heyman, Morris has given us a treasure trove of books on a variety of topics, all suitable for use with children from the very young up to middle school. These make us look at things we take for granted and really see them, and the conversations with children that result from viewing her books are full of insight. Highly recommended! Other titles include *Bread Bread Bread, Hats Hats Hats, Houses and Homes, Loving, On the Go* (about transportation) and *Tools.*

Sisters   PICTURE BOOK

AUTHOR/ILLUSTRATOR: David McPhail
HC/PB: Harcourt Brace
THEMES: sisters; comparisons; family; siblings; individuality

They aren't very much alike. They don't agree about baseball, or what to wear, or when to wake up. But there is something they have in common: each one loves her sister.

★ So Much   PICTURE BOOK

AUTHOR: Trish Cooke • ILLUSTRATOR: Helen Oxenbury
HC/PB: Candlewick
THEMES: family; relatives; babies; love; birthdays; fathers; mothers; aunts; uncles; cousins; grandmothers; birthday parties; surprises

Sitting at home, doing "nothing really," Mom and the baby are joined by Auntie Bibba, Uncle Didi, Nannie and Gran-Gran, Cousin Kay-Kay and Big Cousin Ross. Each family member makes a big deal over the baby, showing affection for him in a variety of ways, always ending in "so much!" As they gather together and wait for the next visitor, the cumulative effect of this story is the deep love they all feel for the baby. When Daddy comes home—it is his birthday that has caused them all to gather—he, too, loves the baby and the party gets into full swing. Cooke's repetitive, demands-to-be-read-aloud text is full of Anglo-Caribbean rhythms and Helen Oxenbury's art adds the right touches to this testament to unconditional love, making it a must for all families to share.

There's a Party at Mona's Tonight   PICTURE BOOK

AUTHOR: Harry Allard • ILLUSTRATOR: James Marshall
HC: Doubleday • PB: Dell
THEMES: parties; disguises; anger; friendship

Potter Pig tries every trick in the book to crash Mona's party, not realizing that an unkind comment about the largeness of her feet—and they *are* big—has resulted in her angry behavior. Very funny.

Time Flies   PICTURE BOOK

AUTHOR/ILLUSTRATOR: Eric Rohmann
HC: Crown
THEMES: wordless; dinosaurs; birds; museums

Inspired by the theory that birds are the modern relatives of dinosaurs, Rohmann's oversized oil paintings lead the reader from page to page on a wordless journey into a museum, through the dinosaur exhibit and through time.

Toad
PICTURE BOOK

AUTHOR/ILLUSTRATOR: Ruth Brown
HC: Dutton
THEMES: nature; toads; natural defenses; predators

Get eye to eye with a toad—"a muddy, mucky, clammy, sticky toad" being stalked by a giant lizard. You may not see it right away, but your child will. Great art, simple story, and fun to read aloud.

Tuesday
PICTURE BOOK

AUTHOR/ILLUSTRATOR: David Wiesner
HC/PB: Clarion
THEMES: wordless; frogs; imagination; fantasy; adventure

Except for the day and time, this book has no words. It is a flying-frog fantasy adventure that will keep you turning the pages. The art is stunning. The story is mysterious. Truly original.

★ Voyage to the Bunny Planet: First Tomato, Moss Pillows, The Island Light
PICTURE BOOK BOXED SET

AUTHOR/ILLUSTRATOR: **Rosemary Wells**
HC: Dial
THEMES: self-respect; dreams; imagination; comfort; bad days

We treasure this set and have probably given it to as many adults as children. Each of the stories in Wells' three-book box tells of the beginning of a difficult day. And then (ta dah!): "Far beyond the moon and stars, Twenty light-years south of Mars, Spins the gentle Bunny Planet, And the Bunny Queen is Janet." And Janet's role? To give the child "the day that should have been." Here's the perfect way to show your child that you do understand. Though published as a boxed set, you may be able to find individual editions of the three stories in your library.

When Stories Fell Like Shooting Stars
PICTURE BOOK

AUTHOR: Valiska Gregory • ILLUSTRATOR: Stefano Vitale
HC: Simon & Schuster
THEMES: peace; truth; folklore; respect

Two original folktales provide much food for thought. The author asks you to consider which story is true, and raises issues of peace, war and responsibility that will have you discussing this book long after you've read it. It took us several readings before we came to appreciate the wisdom of master storyteller Gregory's construction.

★ Where the Wild Things Are   PICTURE BOOK
AUTHOR/ILLUSTRATOR: Maurice Sendak
HC/PB: HarperCollins
THEMES: mischief; fantasy; monsters; adventure; journeys

Max causes so much trouble at home that he is sent to bed without supper. When his room becomes a forest from which he magically sails away, he finds himself in a land dominated by huge, grotesque beasts—wild things! Quite a bit wild himself, Max is more than a match for these creatures, and he tames them. When the fun is over, he longs for a place "where someone loved him best of all," so he returns home to find the loving gift of his supper waiting for him . . ." and it was still hot." In this simple yet never simplistic story, a child's fantasy life moves to center stage, allowing him to achieve mastery over feelings and fears through Sendak's stunning, award-winning illustrations. A classic that begs to be read again and again.

Who Says a Dog Goes Bow-Wow?   PICTURE BOOK NONFICTION
AUTHOR: Hank DeZutter • ILLUSTRATOR: Suse MacDonald
HC: Doubleday • PB: Dell
THEMES: language; animals; word play; cultural diversity; discussion

When I taught English as a second language there were fifteen countries represented. A favorite game was, "What kind of sound does _____ make?" We'd laugh hysterically at the similarities and differences in our responses. This book would have been a perfect addition. It introduces the sounds of an international zoo. Have fun! There are great opportunities for inventing new words and new spelling.

★ Wilfred Gordon McDonald Partridge   PICTURE BOOK
AUTHOR: Mem Fox • ILLUSTRATOR: Julie Vivas
HC/PB: Kane/Miller
THEMES: elderly and children; aging; memory; wisdom; friendship; gifts; diversity; memories

A small boy, "who isn't very old either," shows wisdom beyond his years in this perfectly paced tale. Lovingly presented, this book has such reverence for age and the common bonds between the very young and very old that it is difficult to read it without a lump in the throat. How Wilfred assists Miss Nancy in reclaiming her lost memories is a story you won't soon forget.

Will's Mammoth   PICTURE BOOK

AUTHOR: Rafe Martin • ILLUSTRATOR: Stephen Gammell
HC: Putnam • PB: Paperstar
THEMES: imagination; snow; mammoths; storytelling; adventure; wordless; prehistoric animals

Nearly wordless—a flight of fancy about a boy and his imaginary mammoth, made real by Gammell's impressionistic paintings. A triumph of visual storytelling.

Wombat Stew   PICTURE BOOK

AUTHOR: Marcia K. Vaughan • ILLUSTRATOR: Pamela Lofts
HC: Silver Burdett
THEMES: Australia; dingos; wombats; emus; platypus; rescue; koalas; cleverness

"One day, on the banks of a billabong, a very clever dingo caught a wombat and decided to make wombat stew . . ." and so we follow dingo as he prepares to cook and eat the wombat. Other residents of the outback have their own ideas about what belongs in such a yummy stew, and as emu, koala, platypus and the others convince dingo to add their special ingredients, we find that dingo is not as clever as he thought. A good way to introduce Australian animals to young readers and an absolute delight to read aloud.

This book has a refrain that needs to be sung and the tune is in the back of the book.

OK, Walter, I too love a jaunty tune, but nothing stifles me more than when I'm told it "needs to be sung." I do not find encouragement from the tune at the back because I don't read music (I'll someday learn, sigh). I have lots of fun with this just rapping away to the natural rhythm.

Worksong   PICTURE BOOK

AUTHOR: **Gary Paulsen** • ILLUSTRATOR: Ruth Wright Paulsen
HC: Harcourt Brace
THEMES: jobs; careers; cultural diversity; comparisons

A celebration of work, perfect for reading aloud. Paulsen's poem sings praises to the worker, illuminating the dignity of the jobs of "people here and people there, making things for all to share; all the things there are to be, and nearly all there is to see."

Yummers!   PICTURE BOOK

AUTHOR/ILLUSTRATOR: James Marshall
HC/PB: Houghton Mifflin
THEMES: food; exercise; humor

An ode to overeating! Emily the pig, concerned that she keeps gaining weight, goes for a walk with her best friend, Eugene the turtle. Along the way she consumes enough food to feed a family of four, frequently punctuated by her squeals of "Yummers!" Laugh-out-loud funny.

Zoom   PICTURE BOOK

AUTHOR/ILLUSTRATOR: Istvan Banyai
HC: Viking
THEMES: wordless; art; infinity; perspective; point of view

Zoom takes the reader into infinity. Each page moves you back farther and farther from the previous image. Just when you think you know where you are, back you go. There isn't a single word, but you won't put it down until you see how it ends. A sequel, *Re-Zoom*, examines the process in reverse.

Listening/Interest Level: All. Reading Level: Early and Middle Elementary (E/M).

Perfect for family read alouds, these books allow a wide age span of children to listen at once. Confident E readers and those in the M range can participate.

Alison's Zinnia
                                                                    PICTURE BOOK

AUTHOR/ILLUSTRATOR: Anita Lobel
HC: Greenwillow
THEMES: gardening; alphabet; alliteration; connections; names

ABC alliterations, full-page flower paintings, and a clever girl-verb-flower link from one page to the next keep the interest blooming for the whole family. "Alison acquired an amaryllis for Beryl. Beryl bought a begonia for Crystal. Crystal cut a chrysanthemum for Dawn." A vocabulary stretcher, guessing game and flower primer all in one!

And So They Build
                                                            PICTURE BOOK NONFICTION

AUTHOR/ILLUSTRATOR: Bert Kitchen
HC: Candlewick
THEMES: animals; architects; homes; habitats

Fascinating! Kitchen's stunning artwork shows off the real architects in nature—birds, spiders, frogs and others. See also *When Hunger Calls*.

Annie and the Wild Animals
                                                                    PICTURE BOOK

AUTHOR/ILLUSTRATOR: Jan Brett
HC/PB: Houghton Mifflin
THEMES: animals; winter; hunger; friendship

A sweet encounter between a young girl and the hungry animals of the wintry forest. Annie's corn cakes are delicious, and every day there are more animals outside that are hungry, until things get out of hand. Brett's precious illustrations lend a charming air, and her skill at visual narrative is evident when the observant reader notices the story going on in the margins of every page.

The Best of Michael Rosen
POETRY COLLECTION

AUTHOR: Michael Rosen • ILLUSTRATOR: Quentin Blake
HC: RDR Books
THEMES: humor; rhyme; wordplay

A fun collection of poems featuring nonsense, wordplay, and humor as well as a couple of pieces that will make you think. Rosen has a gift for light verse and this collection is a must for lovers of the poetry of Jack Prelutsky and Shel Silverstein.

Blueberries for Sal
PICTURE BOOK

AUTHOR/ILLUSTRATOR: Robert McCloskey
HC: Viking • PB: Puffin
THEMES: fruit; bears; mothers and daughters; eating; comparisons; repetition

Two mothers go picking blueberries with their respective offspring. Each child wanders off in search of berries of her own to eat, and they inadvertently switch places. That one of the mothers is a bear makes the mix-up more interesting, but McCloskey's gentle, repetitive prose and lovely blue and white illustrations never let the story become threatening.

The Butterfly Jar
POETRY COLLECTION

AUTHOR: Jeff Moss • ILLUSTRATOR: Chris Demarest
HC: Bantam
THEMES: humor; self-respect; friendship; wordplay; loss; rhyme

Jeff Moss used to write songs for "Sesame Street", including such childhood standards as *Rubber Ducky* and *I Love Trash*. In this, his first collection of poetry for children, he covers the gamut from the ridiculously silly to the serious. A terrific collection that can stand beside the best light children's verse.

Captain Snap & the Children of Vinegar Lane
PICTURE BOOK

AUTHOR: Roni Schotter • ILLUSTRATOR: Marcia Sewall
HC/PB: Orchard
THEMES: solitude; creativity; crafts; taking action; collecting

Everyone was afraid of Captain Snap. "He was thin and mean and bent and bitter." This is the story of the children of Vinegar Lane who bravely shout their "hellos" at Captain Snap's backdoor, until one day they peek through the window to find him lying, like a "pat of melted butter, droopy and yellow, on a stack of old brown mattresses." They take action and so does Captain Snap. Use this book to show how words paint pictures. There is a craft tie-in here for those of you looking for an activity in school clubs, or with your child at home.

Chicken Little   PICTURE BOOK
AUTHOR/ILLUSTRATOR: Steven Kellogg
HC: Morrow
THEMES: folktale variations; misunderstanding

The classic story of Henny Penny, Turkey Lurkey, and the rest of the feathered friends of Chicken Little, all destined to be one gigantic meal for Foxy Loxy, who masquerades as a police officer to gain their trust. In Kellogg's hands however, the sky DOES fall in the person of sky patrol pilot Officer Hippo Hefty, who thwarts the plans of the fox and saves the day. A terrific version by one of our most gifted children's writers/illustrators.

Chicken Sunday   PICTURE BOOK
AUTHOR/ILLUSTRATOR: Patricia Polacco
HC: Philomel
THEMES: neighbors; friendship; African American; Russian American; hats; rituals; family; gifts; religion; eggs; grandmothers; cultural diversity

This tender story of a Russian-American girl who, in a solemn backyard ceremony, pledges to be friends for life with her African American neighbor, comes from Polacco's own childhood. Young readers will see the wealth in a community where neighbors who are not the same race or religion can join in each other's traditions and in the joy of friendship.

The Christmas Tree Tangle.   PICTURE BOOK
AUTHOR: Margaret Mahy • ILLUSTRATOR: Anthony Kerins
HC: McElderry
THEMES: Christmas; Christmas trees; rhyme; animals; rescue; pigs; dogs; goats; cats

A rhythmic read-aloud for the Christmas holidays. A kitten gets up into the tree, and all the other animals try to save it: "Goodness gracious, what do you see? The goat is climbing the Christmas tree!" As they all get stuck, it is revealed that the kitten was tricking them all along, and as she scampers down over the back of the bleating, oinking, bow-wowing menagerie it is up to the child narrator to save the day.

The Complete Nonsense of Edward Lear   POETRY COLLECTION

AUTHOR/ILLUSTRATOR: Edward Lear
PB: Dover
THEMES: rhyme; humor; limericks

From the master of the limerick, this collection is essential for all who love silly rhyme.

Earthdance   PICTURE BOOK

AUTHOR: Joanne Ryder • ILLUSTRATOR: Norman Gorbaty
HC: Henry Holt
THEMES: earth; poem; environment; imagination

Ryder celebrates Earth with rhythmic text images that asks the reader to imagine they are Earth: "Spinning around, you are round wrapped in a quilt of bright colors—blue flowing seas, dark green woods, and deserts of golden sand." Joyful art adds to this book's value as one for the whole family to enjoy. When it comes to writing about nature, Ryder is in a class by herself. We love her enthusiasm for her subjects, and the joy she produces in readers is its direct result. Other books by Ryder not to be missed: *My Father's Hands, Under Your Feet, Winter Whale, Where Butterflies Grow* and *Without Words.*

Edward and the Pirates   PICTURE BOOK

AUTHOR/ILLUSTRATOR: David McPhail
HC: Little Brown
THEMES: reading; imagination; courage; fathers and sons; mothers and sons; parents; adventure

A wonderful ode to reading and the power of the imagination. Edward's story-induced adventures are epic in scope and full of bravery and cleverness, but the fact that his parents are a large part of the story makes this a must for family reading time. One of McPhail's best, and a sequel to *Santa's Book of Names.*

Fair!   PICTURE BOOK

AUTHOR/ILLUSTRATOR: Ted Lewin

HC: Lothrop

THEMES: fairs; family; animals, farm; U.S.A. traditions

As in his *Market!*, Lewin shows us the ins and outs of a particular place and culture, this time the county fair. His usual luminous artwork combines with writing that makes you see, hear, and taste the delights of this quintessentially American experience.

Fin M'Coul, the Giant of Knockmany Hill   PICTURE BOOK

AUTHOR/ILLUSTRATOR: Tomie dePaola

HC/PB: Holiday House

THEMES: folklore; giants; strong women; resourcefulness; bullies; Ireland; comeuppance

The clever Oonagh saves the day and helps Fin to outwit the meanest giant in all of Ireland. An excellent retelling of this classic tale. For another bit of Irish folklore, look for dePaola's *Patrick, Patron Saint of Ireland*.

Gathering the Sun: An Alphabet in
Spanish and English   PICTURE BOOK NONFICTION

AUTHOR: Alma Flor Ada • ILLUSTRATOR: Simon Silva

HC: Lothrop

THEMES: Spanish language; bi-lingual; Mexican American; migrant farmworkers; alphabet

Poems and paintings come together to create an alphabetical treasure, celebrating the lives, experiences, and culture of the Spanish-speaking people who work the farmland of the American West.

★ Heckedy Peg   PICTURE BOOK

AUTHOR: Audrey Wood • ILLUSTRATOR: Don Wood

HC: Harcourt Brace • PB: Voyager

THEMES: mothers; witches; magic; food; strangers; disobeying; courage; rescue

If this tale doesn't convince children to listen to their mothers, we don't know what will. Seven children, each named for a day of the week, are warned about strangers. But when Heckedy Peg hobbles to their window—"I'm Heckedy Peg. I've lost my leg. Let me in!"—they let her in. The witch is so witchy it's hard to read this aloud without a croak in your voice. She casts a spell that only a mother can break. The Woods too have cast a spell. The result: a book rich in art and story that proves it's not smart to mess with someone's mother! Who modeled for the witch? It wasn't Audrey. And it wasn't the Woods' son, Bruce. . . .

I love to perform this book, and I carry it with me wherever I go, as it works when no other tale will. When I watch the faces of the audience, it is usually the mothers who show fear, not the children. I often see moms lift their little ones onto their laps during the scary parts, but the children handle their fears much better than their parents do.

I'm one of those moms. Although some very young ones love it, I saved it for my five year olds.

★ I Like the Music
PICTURE BOOK

AUTHOR: Leah Komaiko • ILLUSTRATOR: Barbara Westman
HC/PB: HarperCollins
THEMES: music; orchestras; cities; grandmothers and granddaughters; concerts; rhythm

". . . and I rapa-tapa-tapa on the hot concrete." The rhythm takes over and bounces within me for hours. I want to chant it and celebrate it. The musical prose is so clever, so rich that you should hear it. "I like the beat Of my feet When my shoes hit the street And I rapa-tapa-tapa On the hot concrete." Komaiko's chant moves from the beat of the street to the rhythm of the orchestra and back again. Read it through a couple of times to fully appreciate this masterpiece.

I Saw Esau
POETRY COLLECTION

AUTHORS: Iona and Peter Opie •
ILLUSTRATOR: Maurice Sendak
HC: Candlewick
THEMES: rhyme; childhood; chants

Why is it that adults often try to make us believe that childhood is nice? It certainly isn't a lot of the time, and the Opies know it. This classic collec-

> "To me all words are like music. They have a sound and a rhythm and a beat. They move and breathe like the people and places they describe. They are not just flat sticks on a page. If it weren't for the rhythm in the words, I don't think I would have learned how to read. Or, as someone put it better, 'It don't mean a thing if it ain't got that swing.' "
> —Leah Komaiko, author of *Annie Bananie*

STORYTELLING ADVICE FROM THE MOUTH OF THE GIANT

I call myself a storyteller, although I use books in my performances. I don't make a big distinction between the reader's art and the teller's, especially the way I do it. I do everything traditional storytellers do, and still hold up the book because I want the listener to make the connection with the source.

The way I see it, we are all storytellers, whether we think of ourselves as such or not. I get asked all the time if there are any rules to storytelling, any simple principles to remember. For me, there are three:

- *You must make the story personal.* Find the connection between yourself and the tale you tell, or find a different one. Allow yourself to express the emotions the story creates in you. If a story doesn't make us feel something, what good is it?

- *You must make the story interesting.* The teller has a responsibility to his listeners to consider what will hold and enthrall them. There is nothing worse than being on the receiving end of a boring story.

- Lastly, *you must hold nothing back* as you tell, especially to children. They spend so much of their lives being told their actions are inappropriate ("Sit still! Put that down! Remember your manners! Don't pick at that!"). When they encounter an adult with the chutzpah to throw caution to the wind while telling a story, not caring how foolish it may look, they sit up and pay attention. Now, I am not expecting people to tell stories the same way I do, but I do want them to be as uninhibited as they can be, within the bounds of their personalities. A little less reserve and a little more foolishness can go a long way toward getting a listener involved in a story.

My grandmother Mayes was one of the greatest natural storytellers I ever knew and a major influence on my life. She was refined, gracious, extremely well-read and the only person I have ever known who could do several things at once and do them all well. (Today we call it multi-tasking, but Gramma just liked to keep busy.) She did not, however, suffer fools gladly. When I would launch into one of my long, seven-year-old's recitation about my day, the playground, and what injustices my brother had visited upon me, she would let me go on only so long, digressing within digressions, before she would stop me by saying, "Dear, just because it happened to you does not necessarily make it interesting." And she was right. "A tale should not get lost in the telling," she used to say. I try to live by those words today.

A RESPONSE TO THE GIANT'S ADVICE

I love it when a storyteller looks into my eyes for just a moment, leans forward in his place and lures me into his spell as though I am one of the chosen few to be let in on the tale. "Not holding back" isn't about noise, but about the sincerity of the teller, regardless of style.

---

tion of chants and rhymes will take you back to your school days. The Opies made a life's work of chronicling the language, poetry, and song of childhood, and the taunts and teases are in here along with the riddles, counting songs, and those playground hits from long ago. Much has changed in the specific words and rhymes, but you can take this book to any school and try it out on kids, and they'll respond with many of their own variations. Sendak's illustrations are as irreverent as the rhymes, and add the perfect touch to the collection.

I Spy Mystery: A Book of Picture Riddles   PICTURE BOOK
AUTHOR: Jean Marzollo • ILLUSTRATOR: Walter Wick (photographs)
HC: Scholastic
THEMES: rhyme; riddles; photographs; searching game; puzzles

> "I spy a hammer, a rabbit, a pail,
> A whistle, a button, a horse on its tail;
> A pencil, a penguin, a car that is blue—
> What else should you find? The blocks give a clue . . ."

Each colorful page is jammed-packed with interesting items to find: Photographed sets of hundreds of fascinating antique and contemporary toys, jewelry, plants and other props that appeal to all ages. When you've finally gotten through your search, Extra Credit Riddles and More Mysteries send you back again. New titles appear regularly.

Incredible Ned   PICTURE BOOK
AUTHOR: Bill Maynard • ILLUSTRATOR: Frank Remkiewicz
HC: Putnam
THEMES: imagination; art; creativity; problem solving

An ode to creativity! Ned's ability to make real whatever he imagines proves to be a burdensome gift, until his art teacher realizes that the

solution is to encourage him to draw what he sees. The humorous illustrations and light verse can distract from the important message of the
book. Individuals like Ned need to be encouraged, not stifled. This is
sure to captivate as a read aloud and give a boost of confidence at the
same time.

January Rides the Wind: A Book of Months   POETRY COLLECTION
AUTHOR: Charlotte F. Otten • ILLUSTRATOR: Todd L. W. Doney
HC: Lothrop
THEMES: seasons; change; months; nature

Lovely poems and outstanding art combine to create a look at the seasons for young readers.

Lifetimes: The Beautiful Way to Explain
Death to Children   PICTURE BOOK NONFICTION
AUTHOR: Bryan Mellonie and Robert Ingpen
ILLUSTRATOR: Photographs
PB: Bantam
THEMES: death; loss; life cycle; love; change; healing

Eloquent and simple, this is a book for healing the pain of loss. Using
photographs of the cycle of nature, it illustrates that all things have a
birth, a life, and a death. It is never sappy, never preachy, but a gentle way to help children understand. It is so good that we recommend
it be read to children as a matter of course and not just in the event of
a loss.

Little Red Riding Hood   PICTURE BOOK
AUTHOR/ILLUSTRATOR: Trina Schart Hyman
HC/PB: Holiday House
THEMES: folklore; strong girls; grandmothers; wolves; forests; conse-
quences; disobeying

Trina Schart Hyman can illustrate anything she wants, and we will
probably find it compelling. In fact, we love her art so much that we
forget she is often a skilled reteller of the tales she chooses to illustrate.
This version of the Grimm Brothers' tale has not been cleaned up—the
wolf eats Red Riding Hood and the huntsman has to cut him open to
save her. It is once again a reminder of the price to pay for straying
from the path. We think it is good to see folktales with a clear eye and

encourage discussion of the ways that stories are used to influence and manipulate.

Make Way for Ducklings   PICTURE BOOK

AUTHOR/ILLUSTRATOR: Robert McCloskey
HC: Viking • PB: Puffin
THEMES: Boston; mothers; ducks; safety; home

A book so beloved that there are 9 statues of the ducks in Boston's Public Garden. The story of a mother duck who stops traffic to move her ducklings is a true delight, and McCloskey's drawings are splendid. Want to know the secret to remembering the names of all the ducklings? They all end in "ack" and start with the letters J-Q, going in order: Jack, Kack, Lack, Mack, Nack, Oack, Pack, and Quack!

Market!   PICTURE BOOK

AUTHOR/ILLUSTRATOR: Ted Lewin
HC: Lothrop
THEMES: shopping; markets; cultural diversity; jobs; food

Go to the marketplaces of Ecuador, Nepal, Ireland, Uganda, New York City, and Morocco with Ted Lewin, and see how goods are bought and sold. Colorful paintings and eye for detail make him a first-rate tour guide.

★ Monster Mama   PICTURE BOOK

AUTHOR: Liz Rosenberg • ILLUSTRATOR: Stephen Gammell
HC: Putnam • PB: Paperstar
THEMES: mothers and sons; family; monsters; courage; single parent; point of view; bullies

A book that can be read two ways: one as a fantasy tale of a boy with a bonafide monster for a mother, and the other as a healing story about living with a dysfunctional but loving parent. This mom is right up there with the mom from Heckedy Peg as one of the all-time great mothers in children's books. A brilliant, funny, powerful book useful for those times in all parents' lives when we see ourselves reflected back as a monster in our children's eyes.

My Painted House, My Friendly Chicken, & Me

PICTURE BOOK NONFICTION

AUTHOR: Maya Angelou • ILLUSTRATOR: Margaret Courtney Clarke
HC/PB: Clarkson Potter
THEMES: South Africa; creativity; community; chickens; art

Maya Angelou joins photographer Margaret Courtney Clarke in introducing Thandi, a girl who lives in a painted village in South Africa. Her people do not call anything beautiful. They say that the best thing is good. This is a beautiful, we mean—very good—way to introduce young readers to a new culture.

Mysterious Thelonious

PICTURE BOOK

AUTHOR/ILLUSTRATOR: Chris Raschka
HC: Orchard
THEMES: music; creativity; jazz; color; African American; songs

Many people will not appreciate this book, but with a little effort on the reader's part, it reveals itself to be more than just about creativity and music. Ingeniously using color to represent musical tones, Raschka has created a book that sings, and a brilliant tribute from one genius to another.

Night Sounds, Morning Colors

PICTURE BOOK

AUTHOR: **Rosemary Wells** • ILLUSTRATOR: David McPhail
HC: Dial
THEMES: night; sound; senses; sight; daytime; color

Wells' evocative language and McPhail's lovely paintings combine to give us a feast for the senses. One of our favorite examples of how collaborators bring out the best in each other.

Oh, No, Toto!

PICTURE BOOK

AUTHOR: Katrin Hyman Tchana • ILLUSTRATOR: Colin Bootman
HC: Scholastic
THEMES: Africa; grandmothers; food; markets; mischief; disobeying

A baby goes to the market in Cameroon with his grandmother and gets into all sorts of mischief, all with the running refrain of "Oh, No, Toto!" Vibrant art and fun to read aloud.

★ Oh, the Places You'll Go!   PICTURE BOOK

AUTHOR/ILLUSTRATOR: Dr. Seuss

HC: Random House

THEMES: self-respect; rhyme; journeys; future; individuality; change

"You have brains in your head.
You have feet in your shoes.
You can steer yourself any direction you choose.
You're on your own. And you know what you know.
And YOU are the guy who'll decide where to go."

This ode to the future packs the kind of forward surge found in the best marching bands. It's a cheer for individuality, a push up and over the mountain of success. There are warnings and advice:

"You'll get mixed up, of course, as you already know.
You'll get mixed up with many strange birds as you go.
. . . Just never forget to be dexterous and deft.
And never mix up your right foot with your left."

When my children were growing up, reading aloud to them was a very special part of our time together. Little did I suspect that as adults my son and daughter would recall these reading sessions to teach their mother a valuable lesson.

One day I was feeling discouraged and daunted in the face of an obstacle. My kids sat me down and handed me the Dr. Seuss book, *Oh, The Places You'll Go!*, the same children's book I had read to them years ago. My son told me to read it aloud and listen to the story's message.

The book describes the wonders of life and the ups and downs that are possible. It tells of the "high Heights" as well as the disappointments that happen to even the best of us. Through this wise little book, my children reminded me that as long as you try your best you are always a winner.

—California Senator Barbara Boxer

For a newborn, nursery school grad, or CEO, read it aloud with the promise that she too will succeed "98 and 3/4 percent guaranteed."

On the Day You Were Born   PICTURE BOOK

AUTHOR/ILLUSTRATOR: Debra Frasier

HC: Harcourt Brace

THEMES: birth; nature; planets; the Earth; music; birthdays; the environment

"On the eve of your birth, word of your coming passed from animal to animal . . . and the marvelous news migrated worldwide." This is a book to celebrate a new birth, becoming a parent or grandparent, birthdays, graduation and most events that honor life's changes and celebrate our arrival on earth. Frasier blends natural facts, rhythms, and vivid collage cut-outs to show how the natural world welcomes each new human member.

The Paper Bag Princess

PICTURE BOOK

AUTHOR: Robert Munsch • ILLUSTRATOR: Michael Martchenko
PB: Annick Press
THEMES: princesses; strong girls; dragons; gender roles

"Well, a princess! I love to eat princesses, but I have already eaten a whole castle today. I am a very busy dragon. Come back tomorrow." Princesses who have had their castle burnt up, left with only a paper bag to wear, who have trudged along the whole day trying to save the poor prince, well, they just don't take no for an answer. Our princess Elizabeth tricks the dragon, saves the prince, and will more than likely live very happily ever after. And when you reach the ending of this turn-the-tables-tale, you'll feel quite happy yourself!

The Paper Dragon

PICTURE BOOK

AUTHOR: Marguerite W. Davol •
ILLUSTRATOR: Robert Sabuda
HC: Atheneum
THEMES: China; folklore; dragons; artists; courage; creativity; triumph; wisdom; cleverness; community; art

An astonishing piece of art and engineering, coupled with a well-told tale of creativity triumphing over evil, make this a joy to have on the shelf. A retelling based on a Chinese legend, this book features intricate Chinese-style art in fold-out pages that do much to enhance this magical story. The gatefolds do make it hard to hold up and read aloud, but not impossible.

IF THE BOOK FITS, SHARE IT

Not all books are best utilized as stand-up read alouds; some are too unwieldy and need to lie flat; some are really lap books, best experienced one on one; some are so interactive that they need to be where the child can put his hands on them. Most books will benefit from a caring adult's reading them aloud, but think twice before performing for a large group a book with fold-out pages, tabs, or intricate illustrations that need to be seen to make the story work. Know your audience. Know your material. Know yourself and your strengths, and choose books that bring all of those into best light.

A Pinky Is a Baby Mouse and Other Baby Animal Names

PICTURE BOOK NONFICTION

AUTHOR: Pam Munoz Ryan • ILLUSTRATOR: Diane deGroat
HC: Hyperion
THEMES: nature; animal babies

I am a sucker for books that have cute baby animals and interesting facts. This book is a terrific collaboration and one of my favorites. See if you know all the names of the babies; I sure didn't.

Poems Go Clang!: A Collection Of Noisy Verse   POETRY COLLECTION

AUTHOR/ILLUSTRATOR: Debi Gliori
HC: Candlewick
THEMES: rhyme; sound; noise; onomatapoeia

Sounds of all sorts are featured in this rowdy collection of rollicking rhymes. Shout'em, wail'em, scream'em, blare'em; this will appeal to the noisy child in all of us.

★ The Polar Express

PICTURE BOOK

AUTHOR/ILLUSTRATOR: Chris Van Allsburg
HC: Houghton Mifflin
THEMES: trains; journeys; Christmas; Santa Claus; faith; childhood; gifts

If you are looking for the antidote to a saccharine, over-merchandised holiday season, this is it. For me and my family, this exquisitely bittersweet tale has become our holiday classic. Judging by the millions of copies it has sold since its 1984 publication, we are not alone. I have read this aloud every Christmas Eve since my son was born, and its poignancy brings a lump to my throat every time.

Every Christmas needs one good read-aloud story to pull at the heart strings. Yes, you could watch It's a Wonderful Life (we do), but we're talking about having a house full of family and friends that serves as the perfect captive audience for reading aloud. In addition to The Polar Express (Chris Van Allsburg), try these: A Christmas Memory (Truman Capote), Star Mother's Youngest Child (Louise Moeri), A Child's Christmas in Wales (Dylan Thomas), A Christmas Carol (Charles Dickens), The Christmas Miracle of Jonathan Toomey (Susan Wojciechowski), Santa Calls (William Joyce).

A Puzzling Day at Castle MacPelican   PICTURE BOOK

AUTHOR/ILLUSTRATOR: Scoular Anderson

HC: Candlewick

THEMES: puzzles; mystery; counting; Scotland; castles; searching game

Good for hours of entertainment. Anderson has given readers and observers a treasure hunt, several mysteries, multiple spot-and-count assignments, and puzzles galore as they journey along with Esmerelda and Thomas through the rooms and grounds of Castle MacPelican. For children with a strong sense of the visual, regardless of their reading level. We bet they solve the puzzles before you do!

Smudge   PICTURE BOOK

AUTHOR/ILLUSTRATOR: John A. Rowe

HC: North-South

THEMES: mice; belonging; home; babies; dogs; fish; rabbits; birds; squirrels

Smudge is a mouse who has lived an extraordinary life—he really got around! Though old now, he relates the tale of his many lives with families of birds, fishes, rabbits, and squirrels. Great fun, especially if you and your child have read *Stellaluna* by Janell Cannon.

Star Mother's Youngest Child   PICTURE BOOK

AUTHOR: Louise Moeri • ILLUSTRATOR: Trina Schart Hyman

PB: Houghton Mifflin

THEMES: Christmas; loneliness; celebrations; elderly and children; gifts; pets; dogs

In a hut at the edge of a forest a grumpy, lonely, old woman shouted, "Just once! I'd like to celebrate a Christmas! Is that too much to ask?" While up in the sky the Star Mother's Youngest Child complained, ". . . just once I want to celebrate Christmas like they do down there!" And so on Christmas day a grumbling, cranky old woman and an ugly, raggedy child find themselves together, making memories. Read this out loud on Christmas Eve and make some memories of your own.

Tar Beach   PICTURE BOOK

AUTHOR/ILLUSTRATOR: Faith Ringgold

HC: Crown • PB: Dragonfly

THEMES: African American; family; fantasy; flying; picnics; bridges; skyscrapers; New York; imagination

Ringgold's story quilts are adapted into book form in this loving reminiscence of hot summer nights, family dinners on the roof, and the longing to fly.

This Land Is My Land   PICTURE BOOK NONFICTION
AUTHOR/ILLUSTRATOR: George Littlechild
HC: Children's Book Press
THEMES: Native American; family history

A perfect family book to celebrate, understand, and learn from the lives of the first Americans. Littlechild's family represents all American families.

The Three Little Wolves & the Big Bad Pig   PICTURE BOOK
AUTHOR: Eugene Trivizas • ILLUSTRATOR: Helen Oxenbury
HC: Macmillan • PB: Aladdin
THEMES: folktale variations; wolves; pigs; triumph; violence; conflict and resolution

Who'd a thought that there was another twist in this tale? Well, this is more than clever, and is a welcome and funny addition to the canon of retold tales. Helen Oxenbury's illustrations add the perfect touch of hilarity. But there is another aspect to the book that makes it doubly valuable; as the wolves build stronger houses (bricks, concrete and then armor plates and iron bars) the pig destroys them with more violence— from a sledgehammer, to a pneumatic drill and then dynamite! This is funny on the surface but causes furrowed brows on the faces of parents and educators who would like children to practice peaceful conflict resolution. Then, when the last house gets built from flowers and the pig has a completely unexpected and silly response, the cycle of violence is undercut and the children get a fun example that never preaches. Watch the faces of some four and five year olds as they listen to the story, and you'll see some remarkable transformations.

Tom Thumb   PICTURE BOOK
AUTHOR/ILLUSTRATOR: Richard Jesse Watson
HC/PB: Harcourt Brace
THEMES: folklore; courage; knights; little folk

A gloriously illustrated version of the tale of a boy no bigger than a thumb. Tom's exploits are the stuff that dreams are made of, and Watson's retelling is full of adventure and daring. Read this aloud to your five-year-old and watch his eyes light up!

The Twelve Days of Christmas   PICTURE BOOK

AUTHOR/ILLUSTRATOR: Jan Brett

HC: Dodd, Mead & Co. • PB: Paperstar

THEMES: Christmas; repetition; songs; Christmas Carols; music; numbers; counting

As with many of Jan Brett's colorfully illustrated books, you don't want to miss the details in the margins. You'll find "Merry Christmas" in eleven languages, a love story, a family preparing for Christmas, and a forest filled with animals. And for those of you who would like to play and sing along to this classic carol, Brett has included the music.

The Whale's Song   PICTURE BOOK

AUTHOR: Dyan Sheldon • ILLUSTRATOR: Gary Blythe

HC: Dial • PB: Puffin

THEMES: whales; storytelling; gifts; grandmothers

Young Lily listens to her grandmother's stories of the gifts she gave to the whales long ago. Despite her uncle's warnings against listening to such rubbish, Lily gives a gift to the whales and gets a marvelous surprise. The art is exquisite and adds much richness to this story.

When Hunger Calls   PICTURE BOOK

AUTHOR/ILLUSTRATOR: Bert Kitchen

PB: Candlewick

THEMES: food chain; animals; hunger; predators

Artistic, accurate paintings of birds, mammals and insects catching and devouring their food will fascinate young readers. "A spitting spider glues its food to the ground before it takes a bite. Some frogs eat lizards, birds and mice." The curious will use this as a step into further research about these critters. See also *And So They Build*.

Wings: A Tale of Two Chickens   PICTURE BOOK

AUTHOR/ILLUSTRATOR: James Marshall

HC: Viking • PB: Puffin

THEMES: chickens; foxes; reading; disguises; adventure

In Wings, James Marshall creates a character that makes his beloved *Stupids* look smart by comparison. Winnie the chicken is so clueless, she gives new meaning to the term "dumb cluck." It is only through the efforts of her smarter sister Harriet—smart because she reads!!!!!!—that Winnie is saved from the clutches of a dastardly fox. Told in a melodramatic style that reads aloud wonderfully.

Winter White   PICTURE BOOK

AUTHOR: Joanne Ryder • ILLUSTRATOR: Carol Lacey
HC: Morrow
THEMES: trickster tales; Arctic; snow; sun; wisdom; strangers; lemmings; foxes; polar bears

An original tale, set in the Arctic, full of magic and wisdom. Fox and lemming strike a deal with a polar bear that seems to their advantage, but it soon turns out that they have bargained away all the sun's warmth. This is a cautionary trickster tale and a good look at Arctic life by a gifted storyteller.

These books, often longer and with more involved language than in those written for early readers, are chosen as examples of books to read to your older children while still engaging your younger ones—a trick that we feel is important to maintain family reading time into the teenage years.

Animalia

PICTURE BOOK

AUTHOR/ILLUSTRATOR: Graeme Base
HC: Abrams • PB: Puffin
THEMES: animals; alphabet; fantasy; searching game; alliteration; wordplay; vocabulary

YOU DO JUDGE A BOOK BY ITS COVER

After all, covers are the first thing consumers look at when choosing a book. If the cover gets your attention you are likely to pick up the book. If you pick it up, you are more likely to buy it. We've all made wrong choices by letting the cover sell us.

It's an understandable mistake: There was a time when art in children's books was limited to cute, pretty, or functional. But no longer. Picture books are now a showplace for art in our country. Style, not only in subject matter but also in media, is all over the board. Collages, paintings, drawings, photographs, paper cut-outs and combinations are found in under- and oversized books, paperbacks, board books and hardbacks. Zany, wacky and stunningly beautiful have been added to cute and pretty along with designed pop-ups. Functional has moved from careful renderings to include intricately detailed line drawings, computer enhanced graphics and state of the art photography. Stunning black-and-white art continues to captivate youngsters—from the powerful *Silver Pony* by Lynd Ward (1940's) to Chris Van Allsburg's *The Z Was Zapped* and *The Mysteries of Harris Burdick.*

Children—and those who choose books for them—have a better chance than ever to see a wide range in picture book art. But don't be fooled by stunning illustrations. We've learned in our combined forty years of pushing books that good illustrations go far in selling the newest titles. But to maintain popularity from year to year, a book depends on the worth of its text. Without a good story, well-written poem, or carefully worded text, a book will not hold its own.

That still leaves you standing before a sea of illustrated books for children. Elsewhere in this book we make light of the "absolute" rules that some people apply to books. We don't mean to imply that there isn't a set of standards that you can use. Here are some of ours:

• *For babies, try bold colors and contrasts* including photographs. *Keep it simple.* As they get older they love pointing out and naming each character.

• *Toddlers* benefit from *busy pictures with lots of things to find on* each page. They'll also want to carry around a loved story to read over and over.

• As the school years approach, *broaden their horizons with a variety of styles.* This is a good way to help them become more confident about their own preference.

• When choosing a picture book, assuming you are doing so for reasons other than "I like the art" (which is a good enough reason), *test a page or two by reading* it to yourself. See what connections are made between the words and the pictures. Does the art help you SEE more? Does it tell you things the words do not? Does it add a mood or a feeling to the way words work in your mind OR does the art distract you from the story? Do the details not match or is there a lack of feeling or personality that makes you feel that the words might be better off by themselves?

Can you tell that we really don't want to say what is good and bad where pictures are concerned? Everyone's taste is different. Valerie loves some artists' work that I cannot abide and vice versa, I'm sure. When I am forced to come up with a definition of what makes a good picture book I say that a good picture book is one where the words tell the story without needing pictures and the pictures tell a story without needing words—yet when the two are combined, you cannot imagine them existing apart.

When you select a book and bring it to your child to share, you are telling her something about what you value in a book—helping to shape her tastes and making her familiar with yours. But if the only books she sees are ones you like, her tastes will be limited. We advocate buying the books you love and going to the library for a wider selection. Ultimately your child's tastes will become clear.

"An Armored Armadillo Avoiding An Angry Alligator" "Ingenious Igua-
nas Improvising an Intricate Impromptu on Impossibly Impractical
Instruments." Base has created not a typical ABC book, nor simply a
play with alliterations, but a family volume to read together with enthusiastic shouts, or to be taken off alone for hours of perusal. Each stunning page is filled top to bottom with animals exotic and familiar, and
hidden on each page is the artist himself. Identify each figure beginning
with the appropriate letter, but don't try to complete this task in one sitting—even with the help of the whole family!

The Beauty of the Beast   POETRY ANTHOLOGY
EDITOR: Jack Prelutsky • ILLUSTRATOR: Meilo So
HC: Knopf
THEMES: animals; nature

The entire animal kingdom is represented in poems: insects, water creatures, reptiles and amphibians, birds and mammals. Prelutsky has chosen more than 200 poems from more than 100 poets of the twentieth
century. So's lively watercolors with Prelutsky's inspired choices make
this a long-term addition to your library. Prelutsky's strength as a poet
is well known, but this collection shows his genius as an anthologizer.
Other Prelutsky anthologies to look for are *For Laughing Out Loud* and
For Laughing Out Louder, and *Read-Aloud Rhymes for the Very Young*.

The Big Book for Our Planet   ANTHOLOGY
EDITOR: Ann Durell • ILLUSTRATOR: Various
HC: Dutton
THEMES: earth; environment; peace

More than forty of the best-loved authors and illustrators of children's
books pooled their talents to honor the planet Earth. Rhymes, tales, photographs, and essays present the belief that humans must live in harmony with the environment.

The Blue Fairy Book   FOLKLORE COLLECTION
AUTHOR: Andrew Lang • ILLUSTRATOR: H. J. Ford
PB: Dover
THEMES: folklore; fairytales

There was a time when the sun never set on the British Empire. Keep that
in mind as you read Andrew Lang's introductions to his collections of
tales from around the world. His imperialistic tone is shockingly out of

place in today's society, and so it is worthwhile to remember him as a man of his time when reading his books. His work in assimilating these anthologies is astonishing. These low-priced paperbacks are a must for any serious collector of folklore and will serve as an interesting take on different versions of the stories and tales. Also: *The Brown Fairy Book, The Crimson Fairy Book, The Green Fairy Book, The Grey Fairy Book, The Lilac Fairy Book, The Olive Fairy Book, the Orange Fairy Book, The Pink Fairy Book, The Red Fairy Book, The Violet Fairy Book, The Yellow Fairy Book.*

The Book of Little Folk: Faery Stories and Poems From Around the World
FOLKLORE COLLECTION

AUTHOR/ILLUSTRATOR: Lauren Mills
HC: Dial
THEMES: folklore; fairies; leprechauns; little folk

More delicate both in selection and art than Paul Robert Walker's book on the same subject (see: *Little Folk: Stories From Around the World*), Mills' work is also more comprehensive. The two books together make a very interesting look at world folklore, and this book is a perfect one-volume introduction to the world of faeries.

Celebrate America in Poetry and Art
POETRY ANTHOLOGY

EDITOR: Nora Panzer • ILLUSTRATOR: Various
HC: Hyperion
THEMES: art; poetry; U.S.A.; museums; photographs; sculpture; drawings; paintings; U.S. history

Paintings, sculpture, drawings, and photographs from the National Museum of American Art combine with poetry to create a vivid image of America, yesterday and today.

Celebrating America: A Collection of Poems and Images of the American Spirit
POETRY ANTHOLOGY

EDITOR: Laura Whipple • ILLUSTRATOR: Various
HC: Philomel
THEMES: poetry; art; paintings; U.S. history; U.S.A.

Through words chosen by anthologist Laura Whipple and art from the Art Institute of Chicago, readers get a glimpse of the aesthetic side of our country's history.

★ Children Just Like Me: A Unique Celebration of Children Around the World
NONFICTION

AUTHOR: Barnabas Kindersley • ILLUSTRATOR: Anabel Kindersley (photographs)

HC: DK

THEMES: children; cultural diversity; nations; home; family; school; United Nations; comparisons

In celebration of UNICEF'S 50th anniversary, this photo essay spans the globe in search of what makes us different and the same. The richness and diversity of children's daily lives—where they live, what they do and where they go to school—is celebrated. For a similar look at celebrations, holidays, and festivals around the world, find *Children Just Like Me—Celebrations!*

Classic Poems to Read Aloud
POETRY ANTHOLOGY

EDITOR: James Berry • ILLUSTRATOR: Various

HC/PB: Kingfisher

THEMES: poetry; seasons; nature; magic; conflict and resolution; celebrations; humor

A terrific selection of poems—old and new, classic and buried treasures—that work best when read aloud. The wide variety of styles make this a collection that will grow with your child, offering a poem for almost any age.

The Creation
PICTURE BOOK

AUTHOR: James Weldon Johnson •
ILLUSTRATOR: James Ransome
HC/PB: Holiday House
THEMES: religion; God; creation; African American; Bible stories; speeches

"And God stepped out on space,—And He looked around and said, 'I'm lonely—I'll make me a world.' Johnson first wrote *The Creation* in 1919, but it later appeared in *God's Trombones: Seven Negro Sermons In Verse* in 1927. Read-aloud rhythm and a touch of Southern imagery make this telling of the creation story accessible to all ages. In his Illustrator's Note, Ransome explains he has "tried to remain faithful to the spirit of Mr. Johnson's text by interspersing creation scenes with images of a southern country storyteller." He does it beautifully.

> ### CHOOSING TO CHOOSE
>
> Why do some people think choosing books is hard? Is it because they rarely had good experiences with choosing as a child? Does walking into the bookstore or library bring up all kinds of unresolved feelings of being not smart or not fitting in? If this is true for you, we encourage you to give yourself permission to let go of all that. Learn to choose as you would sample new foods; taste a little at a time until you become comfortable with one or two, then fill your plate with that kind and devour it!

D Is For Doufu: An Alphabet Book of Chinese Culture

PICTURE BOOK NONFICTION

AUTHOR: Maywan Shen Krach • ILLUSTRATOR: Hongbin Zhang
HC: Shen's Books
THEMES: China; language; alphabet

An invaluable introduction to Chinese language and culture! Beautifully produced, with notes of interest to any age child, this handsome book is illustrated with folk art and carefully rendered Chinese characters.

De Colores and Other Latin-American Folksongs for Children

SONGBOOK

TRANSLATOR: Jose-Luis Orozco • ILLUSTRATOR: Elisa Kleven
HC: Dutton
THEMES: music; bilingual; Mexico; Spanish; folksongs

Beaming with color and music, this bilingual book includes twenty-seven songs, chants and rhymes. Orozco has added games and special performance suggestions along with musical arrangements for piano, voice and guitar. A sequel *Diez Deditos,* is also available.

Dear World: How Children Around the World Feel About Our Environment

PICTURE BOOK

EDITOR: Lannis Temple • ILLUSTRATOR: Children From Around The World
HC: Random House
THEMES: mail; communication; nations; cultural diversity; environment; children's art; children's writing; United Nations

Through letters and illustrations, Unicef children from all over the world talk about their lands, and the world's environment. Each page tells where the child writer is from.

★ From Sea to Shining Sea

ANTHOLOGY

EDITOR: Amy Cohn • ILLUSTRATOR: Various
HC: Scholastic
THEMES: songs; music; poetry; folklore; U.S. History; artists; cultural diversity

More than 140 folk songs, tales, poems and stories tell the history of America and reflect its multicultural society. Art from fifteen Caldecott Award and Honor winners add their art for illustrations.

Gonna Sing My Head Off!:
American Folk Songs for Children   SONGBOOK

EDITOR: Kathleen Krull • ILLUSTRATOR: Allen Garns
HC: Knopf
THEMES: music; songs; folksongs; U.S.A.

Every library needs one solid compilation of American folk songs. For our money, this is one of the best. This collection gives the background to the songs, letting the reader learn the history as well as the words and the tune.

The Greatest Table   ANTHOLOGY

AUTHOR: Michael Rosen • ILLUSTRATOR: Various
HC: Harcourt Brace
THEMES: food; hunger; family; feasts; artists

"The greatest table isn't set inside a single home—oh no, it spans the continents, and no one eats alone." Compiled by Michael Rosen, with artwork by sixteen popular artists who donated these pieces to hunger relief. The team includes Chris Van Allsburg, Floyd Cooper, Anita Lobel and Patricia Polacco. This fascinating book becomes a frieze that can be displayed along a 12-foot wall.

I Have a Dream   PICTURE BOOK NONFICTION

AUTHOR: Dr. Martin Luther King, Jr. • ILLUSTRATOR: Various
HC: Scholastic
THEMES: Civil Rights; African American; U.S. History, the 60's; prejudice; artists; speeches

"I am happy to join with you today in what will go down in history as the greatest demonstration for freedom in the history of our nation." And so begins one of the greatest speeches in our nation's history. Thirteen artists, all winners of the Coretta Scott King Award or Honor for African American illustrators offer their own beautiful interpretations.

I Want to Be   PICTURE BOOK

AUTHOR: Thylias Moss • ILLUSTRATOR: Jerry Pinkney
HC: Dial
THEMES: milestones; imagination; self-respect

Poet Thylias Moss answers the question, "what do you want to be?" in metaphors that touch the senses. "I want to be still but not so still that I turn into a mannequin or get mistaken for a tree." This lovely book, illustrated by Caldecott Honor artist Jerry Pinkney, encourages children to stretch their imaginations. "I want to be a language, a way to share thoughts." Don't limit this to the very young. It's a perfect gift for mile-stones: birthdays, graduations, new jobs.

In Daddy's Arms I Am Tall: African Americans Celebrating Their Fathers
POETRY ANTHOLOGY

AUTHOR: various • ILLUSTRATOR: Javaka Steptoe
HC: Lee & Low
THEMES: African American; fathers; family; jobs

Twelve African American poets write about fathers and sons in this affecting and beautiful collaboration. Steptoe's rich and varied art holds this book together, using a wide range of styles to bring the right touch to each poem, like the one by Folami Abiade in which these words appear: ". . . when daddy spins me round & round & the whole world is crazy upside down I am big and strong & proud like him in daddy's arms my daddy." Read this aloud! Give it to fathers to cherish for generations.

★ It's Perfectly Normal
NONFICTION

AUTHOR: Robie Harris • ILLUSTRATOR: Michael Emberley
HC/PB: Candlewick
THEMES: sex; human body; health; change; growing; love; sexuality; diversity

One of the best books we have ever seen for introducing children to the topic of their bodies and their sexuality. A brilliant balance is struck between the "eww, gross!" parts and the stuff that holds us all in total fas-cination, all through the use of a bird and a bee who comment on the information from the sidelines, allowing the child reader to have an ally for his own feelings. This is the book you need to buy when your kids are five, and keep on hand where they can find it throughout their child-hood and adolescence, and refer to when the topics of sex and bodies come up. Our friend Nicky Salan says that you put this book in the bath-room and leave it there—it will get read (you can count on it) and they'll get correct information without having to embarrass themselves or you.

Jazz: My Music, My People

PICTURE BOOK BIOGRAPHY

AUTHOR/ILLUSTRATOR: Morgan Monceaux
HC: Knopf
THEMES: music; jazz; African American; musicians

In the foreword to this collection of the lives of jazz musicians, Wynton Marsalis says, "The music was so old that it was new. Everytime you heard it, it went so far back that time just looped around to today." From Buddy Balden in the 1900s to contemporary stars like Dizzy Gillespie and Lena Horne, *Jazz* includes 40 African-American musicians, plus an index and a glossary of terms.

Jump! The Adventures of Brer Rabbit

FOLKLORE COLLECTION

AUTHOR: Joel Harris (adapted by Van Dyke Parks and Malcolm Jones)
ILLUSTRATOR: Barry Moser
HC/PB: Harcourt Brace
THEMES: folklore; trickster tales; USA, the South; animals; rabbits; foxes; bears

Terrific retellings by Van Dyke Parks and Malcolm Jones that preserve the spirit of Harris' original tales. Moser's art makes the characters come vividly to life, introducing one of the cleverest tricksters in all of folklore: Brer Rabbit. More collections include: *Jump On Over! The Adventures of Brer Rabbit* and *Jump Again! More Adventures of Brer Rabbit*.

King Arthur's Camelot: A Popup Castle and Four Storybooks

POP-UP

AUTHOR: Lisa Rojany
ILLUSTRATOR: Laszlo Batki
HC: Dutton
THEMES: castles; knights; folklore; King Arthur; England

POP, SPIN, PEEK AND READ: NOVELTY BOOKS

How can you decide which of these book/toy combinations are worthwhile? First of all, there is a lot of junk out there. But the rules here are the same as for any book. Cost does not a good book make. If it's a pop-up check to see if it's sturdy and easy to manipulate. If it's shrink wrapped, ask for a sample. Otherwise take your chances; these are not usually available in libraries. Good bookstores can advise you as to which they have had the most success with. We find Klutz Press to be trustworthy in design and execution. As a matter of fact, look up *Klutz's Kids' Back Seat Survival Guide*. It's a perfect example of how a novelty mix of game and book can work.

I really like the way this book is put together, not to mention the design and the way it held the interest of my son at 4—he couldn't wait to get his hands on it. A big, fold-out castle, with four mini-books attached, this is more book than game, but the game element is crucial to capturing the reluctant reader.

The Macmillan Dictionary for Children   REFERENCE

AUTHOR: Robert B. Costello, Editor in Chief • ILLUSTRATOR: photographs
HC: Simon & Schuster
THEMES: words; language; spelling; vocabulary

The concept of a dictionary for children was completely lost on me as a child. We had an old Webster's Unabridged and as soon as I started asking "What's that mean?" I was told to go look it up. That dictionary was, and still is, a friend to me. When, for my seventh birthday, I received a copy of a *children's* dictionary from a well-meaning adult, I was highly insulted and my response was not kind, resulting in a lecture from my mother about gracious behavior. As an adult, I realize that there are many fine uses for a children's dictionary and that many children may be daunted by the task of finding the right word in the big, adult book, so I have happily recommended the Macmillan version for as long as I can remember. It has everything that I ask for of a dictionary, just a little bit less....

So, Walter, let's get to what it is about this dictionary we like: 1) Each word is followed by a simple, straightforward definition; other uses follow, with examples of its proper use in a sentence. 2) Word history and origin notations, science terms and language use are offered as points of interest. 3) Larger type and carefully chosen words (over 35,000) make this a volume at once accessible and useful to children.

Mangaboom   PICTURE BOOK

AUTHOR: Charlotte Pomerantz • ILLUSTRATOR: Anita Lobel
HC: Greenwillow
THEMES: strong women; giants; friendship

Terrific language abounds in this delicious tale about a boy and a giantess. Mangaboom is a fanciful, strong heroine, and a role model for all of us who are looking for tales of independent women. This will enchant readers and listeners far beyond the traditional picture book age.

Mufaro's Beautiful Daughters
PICTURE BOOK

AUTHOR/ILLUSTRATOR: John Steptoe
HC: Lothrop
PB: Mulberry
THEMES: African culture; folklore; fairy tales; kings; family; journeys; marriage; cruelty; folktale variations; greed; choices; judging; Africa

The king is searching for "the most worthy and beautiful daughter in the land" to be his wife. Mufaro has two. Nyasha is beautiful and kind. Her sister, Manyara, while physically attractive, is mean spirited. With breathtaking paintings, rich in texture and light, Steptoe weaves a magical tale to be read aloud, but not to a crowd, unless each listener can clearly see the art.

The Night Before Christmas
PICTURE BOOK

AUTHOR: Clement C. Moore • ILLUSTRATOR: Cheryl Harness
PB: Random House
THEMES: Christmas; Santa Claus; family; poem; reindeer; gifts; winter; fantasy

Moore's holiday poem is actually titled *A Visit From Saint Nicholas,* but the world knows it better by the first line of the poem. A lovely edition of this classic.

The Nutcracker
PICTURE BOOK

AUTHOR: E.T.A. Hoffman • ILLUSTRATOR: Roberto Innocenti
HC: Creative Editions
THEMES: Christmas; toys; fantasy; soldiers; castles; dance; music

If we were judging books by weight, this would have an edge. But it's not size that has our attention, it's the beauty in the choice of paper and font, the glint of gold, and Innocenti's magnificent art. Most important, Hoffman's classic is a delight to read aloud. This is the kind of volume passed down through generations, a tradition taken out once a year and enjoyed by the entire family.

One Wintry Night
PICTURE BOOK

AUTHOR: Ruth Bell Graham • ILLUSTRATOR: Richard Jesse Watson

HC: Baker Books

THEMES: Christianity; Christmas; Bible Stories; winter; God

This retelling of several key stories from the Christian tradition, leading up to the life of Christ, is complemented by the breathtaking illustrations. A good look at the basics of Christianity, beautifully written and illustrated.

Pass It On: African American Poetry for Children
POETRY ANTHOLOGY

AUTHOR: Wade Hudson • ILLUSTRATOR: Floyd Cooper

HC: Scholastic

THEMES: poetry; African American

An inspiring collection for children by African American poets with the added richness of Cooper's art.

Paul Revere's Ride
PICTURE BOOK

AUTHOR: Henry Wadsworth Longfellow • ILLUSTRATOR: Ted Rand

HC: Dutton • PB: Puffin

THEMES: Paul Revere; U.S. History, the American Revolution; horses; Massachusetts; poem

If you can have but one copy of this incredible historical poem, make this the one. Rand's dramatic lighting and vivid panoramas perfectly portray Revere's famous ride.

People
PICTURE BOOK

AUTHOR/ILLUSTRATOR: Peter Spier

HC/PB: Doubleday

THEMES: cultural diversity; diversity; characteristics; comparisons

The best book we have found that compares in detail the similarities and differences between people. Spier's hilarious pictures feature everything from noses (54 drawings), and hair ("People are funny: Some with straight hair want theirs to be wavy, and others with little curls want theirs straight.") to people's likes and dislikes (". . . not everybody's idea of a good time is alike."). Each page deserves hours of investigation, so leave it out where your child can peruse it on his own.

The Rainbow Fairy Book   FOLKLORE COLLECTION
AUTHOR: Andrew Lang • ILLUSTRATOR: Michael Hague
HC: Morrow
THEMES: folklore; fairytales

A one-volume compilation of Hague's favorite stories from all 12 volumes of the Lang fairy tale collections. For the complete collection, see *The Blue Fairy Book*.

Sacred Places   POETRY COLLECTION
AUTHOR: **Jane Yolen** • ILLUSTRATOR: David Shannon
HC: Harcourt Brace
THEMES: religion; geography; cultural diversity; rituals; traditions

"Hush, this is a holy place, a sacred place, where the visions dwell, where the dreaming of a race began . . ." And this incredible collection of twelve poems, describing twelve holy places, illustrated with twelve beautiful paintings, will enrich anyone's library whatever their faith.

★ Sing a Song of Popcorn: Every Child's Book of Poems   POETRY ANTHOLOGY
EDITOR: Beatrice Schenk deRegniers • ILLUSTRATOR: various
HC: Scholastic
THEMES: weather; animals; rhyme; scary poems and stories; artists

Author Spotlight on JANE YOLEN

We are often stunned by the work of Jane Yolen. Not for her sheer output, though she can rival any writer today with the number of books she has written and edited (more than 200 and counting) but by the wide range of her writing style and her ability to achieve excellence in practically any field she chooses. Author of picture books, folktales (both original and retellings), poetry, and novels for readers from beginners to adults, she skillfully employs fantasy as well as realism to give depth to a body of work that is superb in its use of language. As an editor, anthologizer, and compiler of collections of poetry, short stories, and songs, her ability to bring to light the talents of authors has given numerous writers entry into the world of children's books.

Here are some of our favorite Jane Yolen books, arranged by category, though many titles could easily reside in several:

PICTURE BOOKS
All Those Secrets of the World
Ballad of the Pirate Queens
Dove Isabeau
Eeny, Meeny, Miney Mole
Encounter
Good Griselle
Letting Swift River Go
Miz Berlin Walks
Owl Moon
Piggins

FOLK AND FAIRY TALES
The Emperor and the Kite
Sleeping Ugly
The Girl Who Cried Flowers
  and Other Tales

FANTASY
The Pit Dragon Trilogy
The Young Merlin Trilogy

POETRY
How Beastly! A Menagerie of
  Nonsense Poems
Sleep Rhymes Around the World
Sacred Places

NOVELS FOR ALL AGES
Commander Toad series
The Devil's Arithmetic
The Gift of Sarah Barker

COLLECTIONS AND ANTHOLOGIES
Baby Bear's Bedtime Book
The Three Bears Holiday Rhyme
  Book
The Haunted House: A Collection
  of Original Stories (ed. with Martin
  Greenberg)
Jane Yolen's Old MacDonald
  Songbook

And there are many more. It is not an overstatement to say that no matter what the stage of a reader's life, Jane Yolen has probably provided a book just right for it. The bounty of her talent enriches us all.

If you are looking for a wide selection of poetry for your permanent collection, this is it. If you find it handy to have them placed in sections—"Mostly Animals, Spooky Poems, Mostly People, Mostly Nonsense . . ." and so forth, you'll find those, illustrated by nine Caldecott Medal artists. One of our favorite anthologies.

Stories by Firelight
COLLECTION

AUTHOR/ILLUSTRATOR: Shirley Hughes

HC: Lothrop

THEMES: winter; wordless; Christmas; poetry; storytelling

A marvelous collection of poems and stories to celebrate winter, all accompanied by Hughes' warm illustrations. There is even a wordless story. Perfect for family sharing over several nights in December.

★ Thirteen
PICTURE BOOK

AUTHOR/ILLUSTRATOR: Remy Charlip and Jerry Joyner

HC: Simon & Schuster

PB: Aladdin

THEMES: creativity; magic; wordless; change; connections; point of view

Thirteen simultaneous stories. But don't expect to follow quickly through this masterpiece to "read" each one. Start at the beginning. Choose an image and follow it from page to page to the end. Then start over with another image. This is NOT a read aloud. It's an explore at your own pace book. Enjoy the pleasure of your own company. For another dose of originality read Charlip's *Arm in Arm* (Tricycle Press).

Those Amazing Ants
PICTURE BOOK NONFICTION

AUTHOR: Patricia Brennan Demuth • ILLUSTRATOR: S.D. Schindler

HC: Macmillan

THEMES: ants; science; nature; habitats

Ants are so common we don't give them much thought. But did you know that when ants care for their queen, they rub her back? They even bathe her. These kinds of details will make readers stoop down for a close look.

Until I Saw the Sea: A Collection of Seashore Poems

POETRY ANTHOLOGY

EDITOR/ILLUSTRATOR: Alison Shaw (photographs)

HC/PB: Henry Holt

THEMES: sea; seashore; beaches

"Until I saw the sea I did not know that wind could wrinkle water so." Lillian Moore, Myra Cohn Livingston, Robert Louis Stevenson and e.e. cummings add to this collection of seashore poems.

★ The Way Things Work

NONFICTION

AUTHOR/ILLUSTRATOR: David Macaulay

HC: Houghton Mifflin

THEMES: way things work; inventions; science; mammoths

CHOOSING THE "RIGHT" BOOK

Over the years we've seen parents concerned about the grade, reading, developmental and interest levels of books. Choosing the "right" one can get complicated. Walk into a bookstore and find hundreds of choices . . . picture books, novels, fiction, nonfiction, board books, bathtub books, award winners, books and toys, and books and tapes. There are books for everyone. But how does one choose a single book for someone in particular?

I had a customer once ask me to recommend a book for a "ten-year-old boy reading at second grade reading level interested in motorcycles." There was a book for him.

Most people don't know where to start. No wonder they reach for a doll or a truck. It is what it is. After all, you can't judge a book by its cover, but you sure can a toy.

Trust your instincts: When you reach for a children's book, you are most likely attracted by its cover—the title, the illustration. You take it home because it somehow appeals to you. It may be the writing style, the subject, the art style. Whatever the reason it's what makes you different from the next person, and that in itself invites your child to know more about you. So what if you or your child ends up not liking your choice? It's just a book. Bring home a stack of books for which you've both separately chosen some titles from the library and take turns reading them. You'll be spending time talking about what appeals to you and getting to know each other's tastes. And when you are excited about a book yourself, it comes across in body language and feelings as well as words. And remember, there is no such thing as one "right" book. Have fun!

From a simple zipper to computer microchips, if it works, this book tells how. Interesting information such as, "The high-speed drill that a dentist uses to cut into your teeth is a miniature descendant of the first windmill . . ." keeps the pages turning. We guarantee that even the least mechanically minded reader will want to follow the entertaining adventures of the woolly mammoth as he demonstrates principles found throughout the book. A section at the end on TECHNICAL TERMS is fascinating as well as helpful.

Woodlore   PICTURE BOOK

AUTHOR/ILLUSTRATOR: Cameron Miller & Dominique Falla
HC: Ticknor & Fields
THEMES: woodworking; vocabulary; crafts; wood

Here's proof that a good book can bring life to what could be a dull subject: woodlore. Poetry, paintings, and woodcarving show what a woodworker does, who uses what kind of wood and how.

"Bodgers made the Windsor chair
From beechwood, turned and left to air."

Words like bowyer, wheelwright, and bodger add a vocabulary challenge. Each illustration is framed so realistically you'll want to touch the grain. Notes in the back describe 13 different kinds of wood with historical information. Fascinating.

WHAT IF YOU MAKE A MISTAKE?

There is nothing in the world that can stop a child from wrinkling up his nose at a book for which you've just plopped down $18.00. That's why we suggest learning about what you like as a family at the library, where there is no risk.

"Free, free, free. Libraries are free!" I'm going to keep saying this until you all promise you'll go to the library once a week.

Mistakes do happen. If you bought a book exclusively for one child and that child rejects your choice, save it for the next birthday party you attend (books make excellent gifts). Or donate it to your child's school, a family shelter, or to your neighborhood library.

Sometimes your child isn't ready for a book. Save it.

If all else fails, most bookstores will allow books to be exchanged or returned as long as they are in excellent condition. (That means no bent pages, no scuffed covers, and no cracked spines.)

PART TWO

Books for Very Young Children

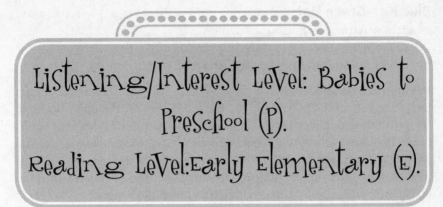

This section features books for babies, toddlers, and preschoolers that can be read to them by an early reader. Often these will be the kinds of books a very young child will sit and "read" to himself.

Barnyard Dance!   BOARD BOOK

AUTHOR/ILLUSTRATOR: Sandra Boynton
HC: Workman
THEMES: animals, farm; farms; barns; birthdays; monsters; numbers; counting

One of four hysterical board books that show off Boynton at her funniest. Great to read aloud, and the slightly larger format makes good use of the bold colors in the illustrations. The other titles are: *Birthday Monsters, Oh My Oh My Oh Dinosaurs!*, and *One, Two, Three.*

The Blanket   PICTURE BOOK

AUTHOR/ILLUSTRATOR: JOHN BURNINGHAM
PB: Candlewick
THEMES: babies; blankets; change; comfort

Simple illustrations of babies and things of concern to them. Delightful, though we liked these better when they were available as board books. Other titles include: *The Friend, The Baby,* and *The Dog.*

Blue Hat, Green Hat   BOARD BOOK

AUTHOR/ILLUSTRATOR: Sandra Boynton
HC: Little Simon
THEMES: color; humor; mistakes; dressing

Boynton's running refrain of a turkey making silly mistakes will delight
the youngest child. He will ask you to read it over for the opportunity to
"Oops" with you. Great fun! Also read the other titles in this marvelous
board book series: *A to Z* (alphabet), *But Not The Hippopotamus* (feeling
left out), *The Going To Bed Book* (bedtime; night), *Doggies: A Counting
And Barking Book* (dogs; counting). *Horns, Toes, and In-Between* (human
body), *Moo, Baa, La La La* (singing), and *Opposites* (opposites).

Charlie the Chicken   POP-UP

AUTHOR/ILLUSTRATOR: Nick Denchfield
HC: Harcourt Brace
THEMES: surprises; chickens

An irresistible, sturdy pop-up! Bright colors and simple text tell the story of a
chicken that youngsters will clamor for you to read again.

Read to them every day you have them. Read to them until they flat-
out refuse to stay in the same room with you, and then chase them from
room to room with the book in your hand, reading aloud.

Chatting   PICTURE BOOK

AUTHOR/ILLUSTRATOR: Shirley Hughes
HC/PB: Candlewick
THEMES: talking; communication

In one of her several picture books on concepts of interest to very young
children, Hughes' art and simple text perfectly capture the faces and
expressions of childhood. This charming series also includes *Bouncing,
Hiding,* and *Giving.*

Dressing

AUTHOR/ILLUSTRATOR: Helen Oxenbury
HC: Little Simon
THEMES: clothes; babies; dressing

Simple line drawings of basic activities in a baby's day. This is an example of a board book series that works well. Other titles include: *Family, Friends, Playing,* and *Working.*

BOARD BOOKS

Designed to be an indestructible, safe first book, board books are more popular now than ever. Reinforced pages, rounded corners, and vivid artwork are the hallmarks of the genre. However, creative authors and artists have broadened the definition to include more than the standard one-image-and-one-phrase-to-a-page style. This gives you a wide selection of types and styles from which to choose.

Publishers have taken successful picture books and reduced them to board book size, and many of them are delightful: *Goodnight Moon, The Very Hungry Caterpillar,* and *Time for Bed,* for example. What drives us nuts is the mania to put nearly any book that sells for a toddler audience into this format just because it will sell. Shrinking art that was meant to be full size, cutting the text, reducing a book that is too wordy, in short making a lovely reading experience into a marketing ploy offends us.

As with any other kind of book, we feel there is no magic involved in choosing a board book. Find a book that works for you and your child.

Fuzzy Yellow Ducklings

AUTHOR/ILLUSTRATOR: Matthew Van Fleet
HC: Dial
THEMES: animals; concepts; touch; senses

No lie, this is the CUTEST book of this type since that touch-and-feel classic, *Pat the Bunny.*

Textures, shapes, colors, and animals intermingle on the pages, culminating in a three-foot-long fold-out free-for-all at the end.

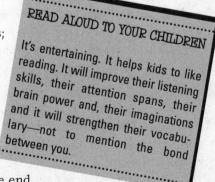

READ ALOUD TO YOUR CHILDREN

It's entertaining. It helps kids to like reading. It will improve their listening skills, their attention spans, their brain power and, their imaginations and it will strengthen their vocabulary—not to mention the bond between you.

I Can

AUTHOR/ILLUSTRATOR: Helen Oxenbury
HC: Candlewick
THEMES: babies; concepts; independence

One of four little books, just right for pre-toddlers ready to take on the world. Oxenbury's light touch makes these early concept books inviting, and they stand up to countless readings. Other titles are: *I Hear, I See,* and *I Touch.*

In the Driver's Seat

AUTHOR/ILLUSTRATOR: Max Haynes
HC: Doubleday
THEMES: cars; driving; adventure; humor

Look out! This picture book puts the reader at the wheel of the car with predictably silly results. Laugh-out-loud funny and illustrated in a zany style that has lots of kid appeal.

Jesse Bear, What Will You Wear?

AUTHOR: Nancy White Carlstrom • ILLUSTRATOR: Bruce Degen
HC: Simon & Schuster • PB: Aladdin
THEMES: dressing; rhyme; language

A great book to have on hand when it's time to let your toddler dress himself. Jesse is a bear children will love and identify with. His understanding and loving parents give the right mix of support and guidance in this story as well as other titles, which include: *Better Not Get Wet, Jesse Bear; How Do You Say It Today, Jesse Bear; It's About Time, Jesse Bear; Happy Birthday, Jesse Bear; Lets Count It Out, Jesse Bear.* Also available in a board book format.

K Is for Kiss Good Night: A Bedtime Alphabet

AUTHOR: Jill Sardegna • ILLUSTRATOR: Michael Hays
HC: Doubleday • PB: Dell
THEMES: bedtime; alphabet; rituals; family; diversity; cultural diversity

From "All ready for bed" to "Zzzz," a soft bedtime look at goodnight rituals with a multiethnic cast of characters.

Maisy Goes Swimming

AUTHOR/ILLUSTRATOR: Lucy Cousins
HC: Little Brown
THEMES: swimming; dressing; clothes

Lucy Cousins' cheerful mouse has worked her way into the hearts of preschoolers. Her popular stories with their brilliant colors have Maisy doing regular kid things, like getting ready for bed or changing her clothes for a swim. Sturdy with bright primary colors, this series offers preschoolers a chance to lift flaps, and play peek-a-boo, while Maisy Mouse goes about her daily routine. Titles include: *Maisy Goes to the Playground, Maisy's ABC, Maisy Goes to School, Maisy Goes to Bed* and the *Maisy Lift the Flap Activity Books* (Candlewick).

Mrs. Mustard's Baby Faces

BOARD BOOK

AUTHOR/ILLUSTRATOR: Jane Wattenberg
HC: Chronicle
THEMES: babies; faces; humor; emotions

Great photographs of baby faces in an accordion format—one side happy, one side sad. Adults will howl with laughter at some of the photos, but baby will stare with fascination.

FEED THEM, LOVE THEM, READ TO THEM

From birth to four years old is the time in life when most children get read to most. It is crucial to the healthy development of the brain that books and stories be read to and made available to even the youngest child. So enjoy this period of being your children's first teacher, knowing that giving them a story every day is one of the greatest contributions you can make as a parent. Also know, however—and we say this several times through out this book—you are not off the hook when they become readers at age five, six, or seven. Reading together needs to be a constant in your children's lives, a promise that you would not break any sooner than you would break your promise to feed them, love them, or make them wear a coat in winter.

The New Baby

PICTURE BOOK NONFICTION

AUTHOR: Fred Rogers • ILLUSTRATOR: Jim Judkis (photographs)
HC: Putnam • PB: Paperstar
THEMES: siblings; babies; jealousy; new baby

"You were once a new baby. You had a special place in your family then—and you still have a special place in your family now . . ." Warm, direct, and reassuring, Mr. Rogers talks to toddlers about their feelings concerning the new baby in their homes. A sampling of other books found in his *First Experience Books* for toddlers: *Going to the Dentist, Going to the Hospital, Going to the Potty, Making Friends,* and *Going to Daycare.*

Of Colors and Things
PICTURE BOOK

AUTHOR/ILLUSTRATOR: Tana Hoban
HC: Morrow • PB: Mulberry
THEMES: color; concepts; toys; food; guessing

Each colorful page shows four close-up photographs of food, toys, and other common objects grouped in squares according to color. Hoban cleverly reserves one of the squares as a simple guessing game for the young child learning to identify colors. Hoban's genius is also evident in her board books, especially her black-and-white ones. See: *White on Black*.

Pat the Bunny
NOVELTY

AUTHOR/ILLUSTRATOR: Dorothy
Kunhardt
HC: Golden
THEMES: touch; peek-a-boo; senses

We don't know why it works, but it does. First published in 1940, this pat, smell, look, feel book continues to be one of the most popular choices for baby's first books. Fond memories of the buyer's own childhood reading may be the reason, or perhaps it's simplicity. Line drawings encourage a child to play peek-a-boo, see her own reflection, scratch daddy's beard, and experience five other activities. There are numerous competitors who never quite match up to this classic.

> My books are about awareness. We are constantly exposed to things that desensitize us. I would like to think my books will help young people to observe and discover things that we take for granted in our daily lives . . . and might easily overlook. By sharing what I see with my readers. I hope to sharpen their powers of observation and perception.
> —Tana Hoban, author/illustrator of *White on Black*

Piggies
PICTURE BOOK

AUTHOR: Don & Audrey Wood • ILLUSTRATOR: Don Wood
HC/PB: Harcourt Brace
THEMES: fingerplay; counting; fingers; rhyme

A delightful riff on the old finger counting games popular with toddlers. This imaginative romp with wonderful art will hold the average two-year-old captive then leave him giggling when you're finished.

Rhymes for Annie Rose

POETRY COLLECTION

AUTHOR/ILLUSTRATOR: Shirley Hughes

HC: Lothrop

THEMES: rhyme; sisters; brothers

A lovely collection of poems about the toddler years, with Hughes's usual perfect illustrations. It made me wish my son was 2 all over again...Almost!

YOU CAN'T JUDGE A BOOK BY ITS LOW PRICE

When choosing a book for a child the only wrong choice is not to choose. People ask us what we think about Golden Books and others that can be picked up at grocery counters and drugstores. If a grandmother picks one up at the drugstore and takes it home to read to her grandson, we think they are great. If a child is excited by the new book added to the grocery basket, we think they are great. It's a step toward reading and a step closer to the library and the opportunity for a child to broaden his reading horizons.

Coloring books and sticker books and Little Golden books and low-priced paperbacks can't be treated as a lesser form of experience, because to the beginning reader they can be important books. Price and format can never be trusted as guarantees of the value a book may have to a child.

Time for Bed

PICTURE BOOK

AUTHOR: Mem Fox • ILLUSTRATOR: Jane Dyer

HC: Gulliver

THEMES: animals; rhyme; bedtime; comfort; animal babies

As darkness falls, parents and their young prepare for bed. Mice, horses, fish, sheep, birds, bees and other critters add a comforting thought to each page until the last child's "good night." Add this to your baby's library shelf along with the other necessities, *Good Night Moon, Pat the Bunny,* and *The Napping House.* It's meant to be read quietly, slowly, with emphasis—to let the reader or listener stop and ponder each illustration. A perfect bedtime book! Also available in a board book format.

Tom and Pippo Books

PICTURE BOOK

AUTHOR/ILLUSTRATOR: Helen Oxenbury

HC: Simon & Schuster

THEMES: toddlers; stuffed animals; family

In these sweet and simple stories, the daily life of a toddler and his stuffed monkey is lovingly chronicled. Real life, real situations, and real concerns will resonate deeply within the heart of every two year old and the parents who love him enough to share them with him. There are many titles, all beginning with *Tom and Pippo*, but our favorites are: . . . *And the Washing Machine*, . . . *Read a Story*, and . . . *See the Moon*. Some titles are available in a board book format.

These were favorites in our house, Anthony having the complete set that endured countless readings. They lived on the shelf by his bed but many nights found their way under the covers with him.

Too Many Rabbits & Other Fingerplays   NONFICTION

AUTHOR: Kay Cooper • ILLUSTRATOR: Judith Moffatt
HC: Scholastic
THEMES: fingerplay; science; nature

More than just fingerplay fun! When you and your preschooler are ready, take advantage of the scientific concepts about rain, stars, and nature in this outstanding book with excellent art.

Tumble Bumble   PICTURE BOOK

AUTHOR/ILLUSTRATOR: Felicia Bond
HC: Front Street
THEMES: friendship; animals; bugs

Sweet and bouncy, this tale in rhyme of a bug going for a walk is full of surprises. Along the way, he is joined by ten new friends, among them a bee, a bear, and a pig. Perfect read aloud for two and three year olds.

Very Scary   PICTURE BOOK

AUTHOR: Tony Johnston •
ILLUSTRATOR: Douglas Florian
HC: Harcourt Brace
THEMES: courage; Halloween; family; trick-or-treat

A good first Halloween book. Read it to your three-year-old

LET THE CHILD CHOOSE

It is wonderful when a child has parents who value books enough to buy them and create an at-home library. But we also believe children should have library experience so they can learn to make good choices for themselves. At the library, price is not an issue, money is no object. Your child may choose a book because it looks familiar. Or because the cover is weird. Or he may grab it because it's on top. It doesn't matter. If he changes his mind when he gets home, he can return them to the library—no questions asked.

before going trick-or-treating, and you will probably have fewer scares along the way.

What Am I? Looking Through Shapes at Apples and Grapes

PICTURE BOOK

AUTHOR: N.N. Charles • ILLUSTRATOR: Leo & Diane Dillon

HC: Blue Sky Press

THEMES: guessing; color; fruit; shapes; concepts

What am I? invites readers to peer through die-cut shapes to guess which fruit grows behind each page. Bold, delicious art.

Books like this make me feel stupid. I hated that feeling as a child (and still do today). I just don't get it.

HONESTY

Be honest about your feelings toward a book: if you don't like it, say so. If you just can't stand reading the same book over and over, it is OK to tell the child, but choose another book instead. Don't put down anyone else's choice of reading material, just be up front about your own response to something.

I know that sprinkles of "doesn't like it" or "thinks it's great" dust float around when you are reading. You are not going to fool anyone by pretending you are enjoying the process if you aren't—and you could send the unintended message that reading, itself, is no fun.

When the Goblins Came Knocking

PICTURE BOOK

AUTHOR/ILLUSTRATOR: Anna Grossnickle Hines

HC: Greenwillow

THEMES: Halloween; costumes

For younger readers who aren't quite sure that Halloween is as fun as their older siblings keep telling them it is. Read this *before* first dress-up Halloween adventure.

Where Does It Go?

PICTURE BOOK

AUTHOR/ILLUSTRATOR: Margaret Miller

HC: Greenwillow

THEMES: guessing; clothes; toys; prepositions; concepts; vocabulary

I used to have fun giving my preschoolers wrong responses to simple tasks. "Here are your shoes, let's put them on your ears where they belong." "No, they go on my feet!" they'd sing out. Margaret Miller must have played the same game. Her color photographs and stimulating questions inspire laugh-filled participation. "Where does Justin put his toothbrush? Through the apple? On the teddy bear? Among the colored pencils? In the spaghetti? In his mouth!"

White On Black

BOARD BOOK

AUTHOR/ILLUSTRATOR: Tana Hoban
HC: Greenwillow
THEMES: babies; comparisons; shapes

One of a set of board books with sharp, high-contrast, black-and-white illustrations. Perfect for birth to nine months, when a baby's ability to see color is limited. Your child will gravitate toward these if you put them near her, as the bold images are attractive and easy to see. The companion title, *Black on White* offers the same delights.

Who Said Boo?

PICTURE BOOK

AUTHOR: Nancy White Carlstrom • ILLUSTRATOR: R. W. Alley
HC: Simon & Schuster
THEMES: trick-or-treat; costumes; Halloween; rhyme

Cute poetry coupled with adorable illustrations. Perfect for that first Halloween.

A WARM FIRE, A COMFY CHAIR AND A GOOD BOOK . . .

The classic picture of family life. Our world and our families have changed throughout history, but nothing has taken the place of a good story. It calms, excites, consoles, inspires, motivates, and delights. There is no other single family activity that offers more in just about twenty minutes a day. It takes very little planning or energy. It provides an opportunity for families to learn how each member thinks and responds. It creates a quiet connection between family members. It puts joy into quality time. And children whose families include reading for pleasure as part of their daily routine are more likely to have children who choose to read.

Prepare your home for reading! Setting up a reading household has more to do with conviction than it does anything else. Once you decide that books will play an important role in the daily life of your family, finding time will be as routine as eating breakfast and brushing your teeth.

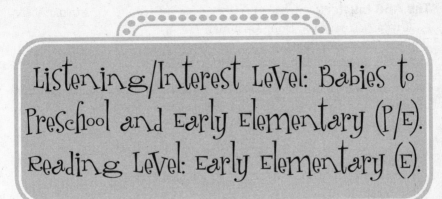

Listening/Interest Level: Babies to Preschool and Early Elementary (P/E). Reading Level: Early Elementary (E).

This listening level works for older preschoolers as well as for kindergarten through third graders, who also may be able to read these books aloud.

1 Is One   PICTURE BOOK

AUTHOR/ILLUSTRATOR: Tasha Tudor
PB: Aladdin
THEMES: rhyme; numbers; counting

Tudor's charming verse, along with illustrations of numbers from 1 through 20 make counting a pleasure with this award-winning picture book. Another Tudor book we enjoy is: *A Time to Keep: The Tasha Tudor Book of Holidays.*

12 Ways to Get to 11   PICTURE BOOK

AUTHOR: Eve Merriam • ILLUSTRATOR: Bernie Karlin
HC: Simon & Schuster • PB: Aladdin
THEMES: math; numbers; counting

Twelve simple combinations show various ways to arrive at the number eleven. There is no story line, but bold illustrations make beginning math more fun.

26 Letters and 99 Cents   PICTURE BOOK

AUTHOR/ILLUSTRATOR: Tana Hoban
HC: Greenwillow • PB: Mulberry
THEMES: alphabet; math; counting; money

A clever introduction to money, counting, and the alphabet, illustrated with Hoban's stunning photographs.

The ABC Mystery   PICTURE BOOK
AUTHOR/ILLUSTRATOR: Doug Cushman
HC/PB: HarperCollins
THEMES: mystery; alphabet; paintings; theft

Badger is a star sleuth who solves the puzzle of a stolen painting in this delightful first mystery for the youngest set. See *Aunt Eater Loves a Mystery,* for another mystery by Cushman.

★ Abiyoyo   PICTURE BOOK
AUTHOR: Pete Seeger • ILLUSTRATOR: Michael Hays
HC: Macmillan
THEMES: cultural diversity; giants; music; songs; magicians; South Africa; magic; fathers and sons

One of my all time favorite read (or sing) alouds. I first heard this story on a Pete Seeger album. Then I told it so often over the years, it became mine. When I discovered a book was being published I was afraid it would never match my vision. I was wrong. It even includes the song and music. This giant tale should be in every library!

Absolutely, Positively Alexander   PICTURE BOOK COLLECTION
AUTHOR: Judith Viorst • ILLUSTRATOR: Ray Cruz
HC: Simon & Schuster
THEMES: self-respect; change; bad days; money; siblings; brothers; allowance; moving

Alexander first appeared in 1972 in *Alexander and the Terrible, Horrible, No Good, Very Bad Day,* a tale beloved by children who laugh hysterically at poor Alexander, all the while identifying with him. "I went to sleep with gum in my mouth and now there's gum in my hair and when I got out of bed this morning I tripped on the skateboard and by mistake I dropped my sweater in the sink while the water was running and I could tell it was going to be a terrible, horrible, no good, very bad day." Next came *Alexander, Who Used to be Rich Last Sunday,* a delightful lesson in money and how quickly it disappears. *Alexander Who's Not (Do You Hear Me? I Mean It!) Going to Move,* is the third and shows feisty Alexander putting his foot down this time. All three Alexander books are in this one volume. Each story is also available individually.

Abuela
PICTURE BOOK

AUTHOR: Arthur Dorros • ILLUSTRATOR: Elisa Kleven
HC: Dutton • PB: Puffin
THEMES: grandmothers; flying; imagination; Spanish; bi-lingual

Rosalba wonders what it would be like to fly and finds herself soaring into the sky, her *abuela* by her side. This imaginative story of a girl and her grandmother is interspersed with Spanish words much like in any conversation with someone whose primary language is not the one spoken. Cheery art and a glossary at the back.

Albert's Play
PICTURE BOOK

AUTHOR/ILLUSTRATOR: Leslie Tryon
HC: Atheneum
THEMES: plays; cooperation; performing

Featuring Albert the duck and the other residents of Pleasant Valley, here is the story of a group of animals putting on a production of Edward Lear's *The Owl and the Pussycat*. Albert keeps a level head as usual, despite others losing theirs, and the play is a success. The entire story is told in rhyme with the same meter as the Lear poem. Albert's other adventures are chronicled in the books *Albert's Ballgame*, *Albert's Alphabet*, *Albert's Thanksgiving*, and *Albert's Field Trip*, among others.

Alejandro's Gift
PICTURE BOOK

AUTHOR: Richard Albert • ILLUSTRATOR: Sylvia Long
HC: Chronicle
THEMES: desert; loneliness; nature; environment

Alejandro felt lonely living in his adobe house by himself, until he took the time to learn about the animals that shared the desert with him. Try this for a dose of nature appreciation.

All About Alfie
PICTURE BOOK COLLECTION

AUTHOR/ILLUSTRATOR: Shirley Hughes
HC: Lothrop
THEMES: gentle boys; sisters; baby-sitters; community; courage; cleverness; shoes; birthday parties

Alfie is a young lad of about three years of age whose adventures are chronicled in a lovely series of books by Hughes, one of the cheeriest illustrators around. This hardcover collection contains the four basic books, *An Evening at Alfie's*, *Alfie Gives a Hand*, *Alfie's Feet*, and *Alfie Gets in First.* Warmly told tales of real-life situations, these will delight the child as well as the parent who gets to read them aloud. Also available in a miniature gift edition from Tupelo. Other titles to look for include *Rhymes for Annie Rose, The Big Alfie and Annie Rose Storybook,* and *The Big Alfie Out of Doors Storybook.*

AMERICANIZATION

Sometimes people are wary of imported books that have English, not American, spellings. Think of these as a gift, an opportunity to extend your child's horizons. Children won't be confused for long by the difference in spelling. It's easy to explain that in other English speaking countries "color" is spelled "colour." And if there are words that aren't clear, each time they ask or ponder they are learning that the U.S. is not the only place where English is spoken.

Once I had a teenager come to stay from Australia. The first time dear Chloe came to this country I asked her what she would like to experience here. "I'd like an Oreo cookie and a Hershey bar," she said. That's when I discovered she'd been raised with Beverly Cleary's "Ramona" books. So often books we import from English speaking countries are Americanized to remove any real trace of that country's language. What a lost opportunity for learning for our children.

Amelia Bedelia

EARLY READER

AUTHOR: Peggy Parish • ILLUSTRATOR: Fritz Siebel
PB: HarperCollins
THEMES: wordplay; humor; jobs; communication; misunderstanding; mistakes

Irrepressible Amelia is the star of this wonderful series that delights beginning readers! Every six year old can identify with Amelia's mistakes—better still, they can be smarter than she is and see the error first. Because she takes every instruction literally (when asked to "dress the chicken" for cooking, she makes a little outfit for it to wear), her mishaps are wildly comical, and throughout these books she often inadvertently saves the day, her good intentions and her wonderful fresh-baked cookies always getting her out of trouble. There is an Amelia Bedelia book for most any occasion, so pick one and enjoy! Some include: *Amelia Bedelia and the Baby* (paperback—Avon), *Amelia Bedelia*

Goes Camping (paperback—Avon), *Come Back, Amelia Bedelia* (paperback—HarperCollins), *Play Ball, Amelia Bedelia* (paperback—Harper-
Collins), and *Thank You, Amelia Bedelia* (paperback—HarperCollins).

★ Anansi and the Moss-Covered Rock   PICTURE BOOK
AUTHOR: Eric A. Kimmel • ILLUSTRATOR: Janet Stevens
HC/PB: Holiday House
THEMES: trickster tales; rocks; folklore; magic; repetition

This is one of those prizes where the ridiculous story and the hysterical
art are perfectly matched. Anansi, the famous trickster, discovers a moss-
covered rock that has the power to knock anything flat on its back. All he
has to do is say, "Isn't this a strange moss-covered rock?" Stevens' two-
page spread of four jungle animals passed-out is worth the price of the
book. Need a play for kids to act out, sheets for curtains? Try this one.
Also by Kimmel and Stevens: *Anasi Goes Fishing* and *Anansi and the
Talking Melon.*

*I've had success reading this—where one event clearly happens
after another—aloud to a group of schoolchildren. I then hold up
signs with the animal names asking a child to participate for each
animal. Then I let them line themselves up in the order they remember the events taking place. It's a great jumble of fun where the
whole class chimes in.*

And to Think That I Saw It On Mulberry Street   PICTURE BOOK
AUTHOR/ILLUSTRATOR: Dr. Seuss
HC: Random House
THEMES: imagination; rhyme; exaggeration

Dr. Seuss' first book, published in 1937 is a delightful tale that pushes
imagination into high gear. When told by his father to "see what you can
see," Marco decides to make his story more interesting. "That can't be
my story. That's only a start. I'll say that a ZEBRA was pulling that cart!"
Dr. Seuss allows Marco the pleasure of keeping his soaring imagination
to himself. Seuss has written more books than we can review here.
These are some of our favorites: *Horton Hatches the Egg, Horton Hears a
Who!, The Lorax, The Butter Battle Book,* and *The 500 Hats of Bartholomew
Cubbins,* and his classic holiday tale, *How the Grinch Stole Christmas.*

Angus and the Cat
PICTURE BOOK

AUTHOR/ILLUSTRATOR: Marjorie Flack
PB: Farrar Straus & Giroux
THEMES: dogs; curiosity; cats; getting along

This delightful trilogy of books about a VERY curious Scottie dog has delighted children and adults for years. We are happy to see them available once more. The other titles are: *Angus and the Ducks* and *Angus Lost*.

Animal Dads
PICTURE BOOK NONFICTION

AUTHOR: Sneed B. Collard III • ILLUSTRATOR: Steve Jenkins
HC: Houghton Mifflin
THEMES: fathers; childcare; animals; science; babies

Animal dads do lots of things human dads do. In this fascinating look at fish, beavers, gorillas, prairie voles, birds, even isopods, young readers see how the males of different species care for their young.

Appelemando's Dream
PICTURE BOOK

AUTHOR/ILLUSTRATOR: Patricia Polacco
HC: Philomel • PB: Paperstar
THEMES: dreams; imagination; community; art; friendship; magic; creativity

For Appelemando ". . . dreams were magic chariots pulled through his mind by galloping hues of color. For him, dreaming was a way of life." Not only for young dreamers whose imaginations take flight, it's also for the one who is ready to uncork his creativity and step for a time onto a palette of fantasy.

Apple Pie Tree
PICTURE BOOK

AUTHOR: Zoe Hall • ILLUSTRATOR: Shari Halpern
HC: Blue Sky Press
THEMES: apples; trees; seasons; recipes; birds; bees

From leaves to flower to fruit to dessert, children follow each season till they've tasted their pie. A recipe is included! For a different way to look at what goes into the making of a pie, see *How to Make an Apple Pie and See the World* by Marjorie Priceman.

Archibald Frisby
PICTURE BOOK

AUTHOR/ILLUSTRATOR: Michael D. Chesworth
HC: Farrar Straus & Giroux
THEMES: science; individuality; gifted children

Archibald Frisby is as crazy for science as a kid can be. A text of simple rhyme introduces a character focused on how and why things work. It's perfect to read before nonfiction science selections.

Are You My Mother?

EARLY READER

AUTHOR/ILLUSTRATOR: P.D. Eastman
HC: Random House
THEMES: mothers; lost; searches

A classic easy-to-read book about the search for a mother. Not by Seuss, as many think, but almost as good. See also: *Go, Dog, Go!*

CLIP THE STRINGS ATTACHED TO READING

For some reason, we parents feel that our child's reading is our own personal accomplishment. Pregnant women come into Hicklebee's requesting books that will prepare their baby to read. I always recommend something nontoxic. It is practical, and it makes far more sense for an infant to chew on the corners than to try reading the book.

When people offer a child a teddy bear, they do it with love, often holding Teddy to themselves before handing it over. No strings . . . just something to love. But with books this invisible thing happens. Those strings are there, and they whisper, "This is the one that will teach him . . ." I wish we could treat a book like a teddy bear. Love it. Hand it over after clutching it fondly to your chest because it is such a prize. That probably would raise reading achievement across the board!

I believe the Nancy Drew and Hardy Boys books continue to be popular because they are often introduced by someone who knows the characters by heart. The fondness for the series comes across with a sincere, "I've got a book I know you're going to love!" sentiment.

Understand, I've been there, showing words to my toddler thinking this was different, after all, wasn't she a bit brighter than most kids? We're only human, but should not take this early reader business too seriously. If you love reading, and you let your children know it through your example and enthusiasm—for your books, for theirs, for the library and the bookstore—you'll grow a reader, almost effortlessly.

Arrow to the Sun   PICTURE BOOK

AUTHOR/ILLUSTRATOR: Gerald McDermott

HC: Viking

THEMES: Native American; pueblo; sun; teasing; folklore

McDermott's bold graphics reveal the power of the Pueblo sun in this myth of how an unhappy boy brought the Lord of the Sun to the world of men.

Arthur's Camp-Out   EARLY READER

AUTHOR/ILLUSTRATOR: Lillian Hoban

HC/PB: HarperCollins

THEMES: camping; fear; bats; snakes; humor

While his sister goes camping with friends, Arthur goes into the woods alone. But there are scary creatures and sounds in the woods, and Arthur soon learns that venturing out alone is not much fun, even for a chimp! This is one of many Arthur stories in the second level of the "I Can Read Book" series. Level 2 stories are longer and have more sophisticated language and plots than Level 1. A sampling of others in the series are: *Arthur's Loose Tooth* (teeth; sisters; courage), *Arthur's Pen Pal* (penpals; friendship; writing; karate; drums; gender roles), *Arthur's Honey Bear* (growing up), *Arthur's Christmas Cookies* (Christmas; baking; gifts).

As the Crow Flies: A First Book of Maps   PICTURE BOOK

AUTHOR: Gail Hartman • ILLUSTRATOR: Harvey Stevenson

HC: Bradbury Press • PB: Aladdin

THEMES: geography; animals; point of view; maps; imagination; journeys

"As the rabbit hops . . . A path winds around a farmhouse, past a shed, to a garden where the sweet greens grow." The Rabbit's Map, along with ones from the perspectives of an eagle, crow, horse, and seagull allow youngsters to follow simple journeys and to see how handy a map can be.

Aunt Eater Loves a Mystery   EARLY READER

AUTHOR/ILLUSTRATOR: Doug Cushman

HC/PB: HarperCollins

THEMES: mystery; mistakes

A funny, easy-to-read series of mysteries featuring intrepid Aunt Eater who sees trouble and clues in almost everything. Though she makes mistakes, she is usually proven correct at the end of the story, and the child reader has the satisfaction of being smarter than Aunt Eater is. Other titles in the series: *Aunt Eater's Mystery Christmas* and *Aunt Eater's Mystery Vacation*.

A Baby Sister for Frances
PICTURE BOOK

AUTHOR: Russell Hoban • ILLUSTRATOR: Lillian Hoban
HC/PB: HarperCollins
THEMES: new baby; sisters; siblings; sibling rivalry; family; celebrations; friendship

A new baby has arrived and Frances jumps from jealousy to happiness and back again. Hoban is right on target when it comes to showing how children can feel. Other Frances books include: *A Birthday for Frances* (jealousy; sisters; siblings; birthdays; gifts), *A Bargain for Frances* (friendship; playing tricks; tea parties), *Bedtime for Frances* (bedtime; family), *Best Friends for Frances* (friendship; family; neighbors), and *Bread and Jam for Frances* (food; eating).

The Baker's Dozen: A Saint Nicholas Tale
PICTURE BOOK

AUTHOR: Aaron Shepard • ILLUSTRATOR: Wendy Edelson
HC: Atheneum
THEMES: U.S. History, Colonial America; bakers; magic; traditions; generosity; food; folklore; baking; Christmas; Dutch; New York

Van Amsterdam, the baker, gave his customers exactly what they requested, not more, not less. One Saint Nicholas Day an old woman asked for a dozen cookies. When the baker counted out twelve, she demanded thirteen. When he refused to give her more, she cast a spell that led the baker to poverty. Saint Nicholas and his gift of generosity set things right and brought us the origin of The Baker's Dozen. Enchanting, detailed art along with Shepard's well-told tale make this a perfect addition to the winter holiday library.

Bamboo Hats and a Rice Cake: A Tale Adapted from Japanese Folklore
PICTURE BOOK

AUTHOR: Ann Tompert • ILLUSTRATOR: Demi
HC: Crown
THEMES: Japan; alphabet; rebus; New Year

Right away the reader finds something unique. Illustrator Demi has incorporated characters from the Japanese alphabet into the text, much like a rebus. This story tells of a poor man who tries to trade his wife's valued kimono for rice cakes to insure good fortune in the New Year.

The Banging Book   PICTURE BOOK
AUTHOR: Bill Grossman • ILLUSTRATOR: Robert Zimmerman
HC: HarperCollins
THEMES: noise; onomatapoeia; comparisons; destruction; mending

"Banging, banging, girls and boys, Banging, banging, on their toys. Banging just to hear the noise. Banging, bopping, smashing, clanging . . ." And that's just the beginning. The rhythm builds up and down. Each section has a perfect place for children to chime in. Keep quiet books close at hand for reading after. But the best thing about this book is the way the children have to take responsibility for their destructive actions—the book comes full circle as the energy and noise they put into their play is channeled into constructive areas. This makes it a terrific way to get toddlers to understand having to pick up after themselves.

Barn Dance!   PICTURE BOOK
AUTHOR: Bill Martin, Jr. and John Archambault • ILLUSTRATOR: Ted Rand
HC/PB: Henry Holt
THEMES: barns; music; dance; rhyme; scarecrows; animals, farm; country life

The full moon's shining and a skinny kid sneaks out to the barn in time for a raucous dance led by the fiddle-playing Scarecrow. "Out came the skinny kid, a-tickin' an' a-tockin' An' a hummin' an' a-yeein' an' a-rockin' an' a-sockin'. An' he danced his little toe through a hole in his stockin'!" Rand's full-page watercolors and the rhythmic writing team have created a perfect blend for the eyes and ears, barnyard style!

Before I Go to Sleep   PICTURE BOOK
AUTHOR: Thomas Hood • ILLUSTRATOR: Maryjane Begin-Callanan
HC: Putnam • PB: Sandcastle
THEMES: bedtime; rhyme; animals; imagination

Hood's old poem is given rousing new life in the hands of a gifted illustrator. Through the unifying theme of a dog and a pair of pajamas, the bedtime musings of a small boy are made into mini-journeys through the animal kingdom. Full of whimsy and imagination, this is one great bedtime book!

Benny's Pennies   PICTURE BOOK

AUTHOR: Pat Brisson • ILLUSTRATOR: Bob Barner
HC: Doubleday • PB: Dell
THEMES: math; counting; sharing; family; money; numbers

"Benny McBride had five new pennies. 'What should I buy?' he asked."
In a simple tale that also provides an introduction to addition and sub-
traction, Benny's journey is complemented by Bob Barner's beautiful
cut-paper art.

Big Al   PICTURE BOOK

AUTHOR: Andrew Clements • ILLUSTRATOR: Yoshi
PB: Aladdin
THEMES: friendship; diversity; fish; fitting in; prejudice; fear; sea; dis-
guises; loneliness

Poor lonely Big Al is large and scary-looking, and the other fish swim
away from him. Even with disguises he can't get them to stay around.
One day when they are caught in a fisherman's net, Big Al comes to
their rescue, and they learn a thing or two about friendship. Yoshi's vivid
art perfectly blends with Clement's universal story of friendship.

The Big Red Barn   PICTURE BOOK

AUTHOR: Margaret Wise Brown • ILLUSTRATOR: Felicia Bond
HC/PB: HarperCollins
THEMES: barns; farm; animals; rhyme; daytime; night; counting

"By the big red barn in the great green field, there was a pink pig who
was learning to squeal." There were also horses and cows and hens and
other animals of the farm doing what they do during the day. Simple in
rhyme and art, after the first or second reading, it's what a young child
will choose to "read" to you! Also available in a board book format.

Bit by Bit   PICTURE BOOK

AUTHOR: Steve Sanfield • ILLUSTRATOR: Susan Gaber
HC: Philomel
THEMES: clothes; tailors; sewing; problem solving; folklore; Russian;
repetition; Yiddish; cumulative story

Sanfield tells his story in the rich tradition of a true storyteller, letting
the reader/listener in on a personal tale. Gaber's rich folk style full-color
art is the perfect blend to this cumulative story about Zundel the tailor,
who makes the most of his old, worn winter coat.

IT'S ALL IN THE TELLING

Some stories, like Bit by Bit *by Steve Sanfield, make me want to gather youngsters under a tree and tell them the story as if I'm sharing something from my own personal memory. In my children's preschool days, I did just that. Sometimes I'd simply pluck a tired leaf off a tree, look closely at it as if I were reading a secret message, then announce, "It looks like it's time for a story!" I like telling better than reading because I can connect with listeners as though in a conversation. When illustrations in a book are as important as the ones in* Bit by Bit, *I would take the book out afterward with excitement and say, "Look, pictures that go with this story!" I am certain Steve Sanfield wouldn't mind my introducing his story to a clutch of preschoolers in this fashion. After all, that's how most stories get passed down. Besides, when the children begin reading on their own, what delight they'll find in rediscovering Steve Sanfield's stories!*

Bootsie Barker Bites

PICTURE BOOK

AUTHOR: Barbara Bottner • ILLUSTRATOR: Peggy Rathmann
HC: Putnam • PB: Paperstar
THEMES: courage; strong girls; conflict; bullies; comeuppance

What a comfort this book can be! Any young child who is terrorized by a playmate but cannot get an adult to understand will identify with this tale of how horrible, biting Bootsie gets her comeuppance. The little girl in the story endures Bootsie's torments for as long as she can, but when faced with the prospect of Bootsie coming over to spend the night, she has to be resourceful and learns that big problems require big solutions. Hilarious to read aloud.

A Boy, a Dog, and a Frog

PICTURE BOOK

AUTHOR/ILLUSTRATOR: Mercer Mayer
HC/PB: Dial
THEMES: wordless; dogs; frogs; friendship

A boy and his dog run into wet trouble when they try to catch a frog. But when at last they give up, the frog follows them home. This cheery wordless series will have young ones telling the tale without missing a word. Also: *A Boy, a Dog, a Frog and a Friend* and *Frog on His Own*.

Brave Irene   PICTURE BOOK

AUTHOR/ILLUSTRATOR: William Steig

HC/PB: Farrar Straus & Giroux

THEMES: courage; strong girls; snow; storms; determination; illness; good deeds; perseverance

There is a raging snowstorm outside and Irene's mother can't deliver the dress she has sewn for the duchess to wear to the ball, so Irene offers to take it to her. The wind warns her to "GO HO—WO—WOME . . . or else," but Irene perseveres. Steig's art shows the strength of the storm as well as the full force of one determined, duty-bound young girl.

Bread Is for Eating   PICTURE BOOK

AUTHOR/ILLUSTRATOR: David Gershator

HC: Henry Holt

THEMES: food; jobs; Spanish; songs; music; bread; bi-lingual

In honor of bread and all the steps that bring it to our plate, a young boy and his mother thank the seed, earth, sun, and rain for the grain, and sing a celebration refrain in Spanish. Words and melody are found in the back of the book.

Bringing the Rain to Kapiti Plain   PICTURE BOOK

AUTHOR: Verna Aardema • ILLUSTRATOR: Beatriz Vidal

PB: Puffin

THEMES: Africa; Kenya; cumulative story; rain; weather; animals, land; drought

". . . These are the cows, all hungry and dry, Who mooed for the rain to fall from the sky . . ." And this is Kapiti Plain, in serious need of water, where Ki-pat, in charge of the herd, finds a way to bring down the rain. Appealing folk-art illustrations and catchy "This Is The House That Jack Built" rhythm make this a popular read aloud.

Brown Bear, Brown Bear, What Do You See?   PICTURE BOOK

AUTHOR: Bill Martin, Jr. • ILLUSTRATOR: Eric Carle

HC: Henry Holt

THEMES: cumulative story; repetition; color; animals

Make a place for *Brown Bear* in your toddler's library. First published in 1967, this colorful classic with its bold art and soothing, repetitive rhyme will have your child anticipating each page. Also available in a board book edition.

Bunny Money   PICTURE BOOK

AUTHOR/ILLUSTRATOR: **Rosemary Wells**
HC: Dial
THEMES: rabbits; money; math; shopping; grandmothers; siblings; humor

Max and Ruby are favorites of ours, and *Bunny Money* is hilarious! First of all, notice the money on the inside cover of the book. Now look at the back. These are the people Wells thinks should be on our money. Now, compose yourself and start reading this aloud to a young child. Not a word is wasted, and children who appreciate a loving grandmother will want to hear it again and again. Also featuring Ruby and Max: *Bunny Cakes* (cooking, writing, cake, food).

Busy Buzzing Bumblebees and Other
Tongue Twisters   EARLY READER

AUTHOR: Alvin Schwartz • ILLUSTRATOR: Paul Meisel
HC/PB: HarperCollins
THEMES: tongue twisters; humor; word play; alliteration

Kids love tongue twisters. This "I Can Read" book offers early readers the chance to try tripping across these.

By the Light of the Halloween Moon   PICTURE BOOK

AUTHOR: Caroline Stutson • ILLUSTRATOR: Kevin Hawkes
PB: Puffin
THEMES: Halloween; spooky stories; cumulative story; rhyme

"A witch! A watchful witch with streaming hair, Who snatches the cat, When he springs through the air to catch the toe that taps a tune . . ." And behind the witch lurk goblins, ghosts and more. Lots of fun with vibrant, magical illustrations. Use this to help tame the Halloween willies.

Cadillac   PICTURE BOOK

AUTHOR: Charles Temple • ILLUSTRATOR: Lynne Lockhart
HC: Putnam
THEMES: cars; grandmothers; humor; rhyme; driving

"BOOM SHACKA-LACKA-LACKA, BOOM SHACKA-LACK!" is the running refrain that punctuates this very funny book about a granny with questionable driving skills. Grown-ups hear this story and immediately want to get a copy for someone they know who drives just as poorly. Kids like the rhythm and the chance to chant along.

Can't You Sleep, Little Bear?   PICTURE BOOK

AUTHOR: Martin Waddell • ILLUSTRATOR: Barbara Firth
HC: Candlewick
THEMES: fear of dark; bedtime; fathers and sons; comfort; moon

Comfort. Reassurance. That's what you'll find here. Little Bear is afraid of the dark. "I don't like the dark," said Little Bear. "What dark?" said Big Bear. "The dark all around us," said Little Bear. Big Bear tries to show him that dark is nothing to be afraid of, but Little Bear isn't convinced. And then Big Bear remembers the bright moon and twinkly stars. This is the story night-shy youngsters will want to read over and over.

Caps for Sale: A Tale of a Peddler, Some Monkeys, and Their Monkey Business   PICTURE BOOK

AUTHOR/ILLUSTRATOR: Esphyr Slobodkina
HC/PB: HarperCollins
THEMES: hats; monkeys; peddlers; mischief; folklore; teasing

Published more than fifty years ago, here's proof that a good tale has lasting power. Children still laugh when the peddler loses his hats to a treeful of teasing monkeys!

STOPPING AT THE PEAK

There are those times in reading aloud when one moment you've got your children mesmerized, and the next they are bouncing all over the place. Wonder what happens? We are firm believers in stopping at the peak, in direct proportion to age. As children get older they can listen longer. We imagine a graph with an arch going gradually up, getting to a high point and then plummeting down the other side. It happens when children have had enough. If you can train yourself to stop just before they plummet—not to pick up just one more book while you've got their attention, or read one more chapter—they will be eager for your next read-aloud time. You can extend their listening time by adding a page or two at each session, but remember to leave them wanting more.

The Carrot Seed
PICTURE BOOK

AUTHOR: Ruth Krauss • ILLUSTRATOR: Crockett Johnson

HC/PB: HarperCollins

THEMES: carrots; gardening; perseverance; patience; self-respect; gardeners; individuality

One naysayer after the other warns a young gardener ". . . It won't come up!" But his patience and perseverance prove that belief in one's own possibilities can be worth the wait.

Casey at the Bat
PICTURE BOOK

AUTHOR: Ernest Lawrence Thayer • ILLUSTRATOR: Patricia Polacco

HC: Philomel • PB: Paperstar

THEMES: baseball; determination; strong girls; rhyme

Casey's been around since the 1800's; here's a chance to try this classic ballad with a dose of Patricia Polacco's spunky illustration. The setting isn't a classic, old-time baseball park, but a little league game. And Casey? Could be a girl's name or a boy's name. The reader gets the surprise at the end.

Chicka Chicka Boom Boom
PICTURE BOOK

AUTHOR: Bill Martin Jr. and John Archambault • ILLUSTRATOR: Lois Ehlert

HC: Simon & Schuster

THEMES: alphabet; chants; rhyme; trees; rhythm

Chants can be contagious, so be prepared for this one to bounce around your brain awhile. "Chicka chicka boom boom! Will there be enough room? Here comes H up the coconut tree . . ." And what better way to learn the ABCs than with a lively rhyme that sends youngsters up one side of the alphabet and down the other? This popular book is also available in a board book and a sticker book format, though to get the entire text, you need to buy the real thing.

Read aloud alert! This is a tricky one if you have not practiced it beforehand. The first two pages set a tempo that can easily get away from you, so don't go too fast or you will really be sorry right around the letter "J."

Chicken Man
PICTURE BOOK

AUTHOR/ILLUSTRATOR: Michelle Edwards

HC: Lothrop

THEMES: chickens; Israel; Jews; family; jobs; kibbutz; eggs; singing; optimism

Chicken Man made the most of his work. In fact, his job in the coop looked like such fun everyone in the kibbutz wanted a turn at it. When the new work list was posted, someone else got a turn with the chickens and Chicken Man was sent to the laundry. It wasn't long before folks thought that laundry work must be the most fun. And so it went! Chicken Man moved from job to job until finally the chickens rebeled. This delightful tale celebrates the art of positive thinking.

Clap Your Hands   PICTURE BOOK

AUTHOR/ILLUSTRATOR: Lorinda Bryan Cauley
PB: Paperstar
THEMES: rhyme; animals; clapping

Clap, jump, wriggle, spin along with children and animals in an action-packed rhyme. Don't save this one for bedtime!

Cleversticks   PICTURE BOOK

AUTHOR: Bernard Ashley • ILLUSTRATOR: Derek Brazell
HC: Crown • PB: Dragonfly
THEMES: chopsticks; self-respect; school; cultural diversity; readiness; comparisons; Chinese

Lin Sung was ready to give up on school. He couldn't tie his shoes, write his name or button his coat like other kids in class. Then he discovered what he could teach them—eating with chopsticks.

Cloudland   PICTURE BOOK

AUTHOR/ILLUSTRATOR: John Burningham
HC: Crown
THEMES: clouds; sky; fantasy; adventure; homesickness

This book clearly shows that Burningham remembers his child side. Albert trips and falls off a cliff and is (fortunately) caught by the cloud children whispering their magic words. He has a fine time until he misses his parents and is escorted back home. A fun fantasy with extraordinary art.

Colors Around Us: A Lift-the-Flap Surprise Book   NOVELTY

AUTHOR: Shelley Rotner and Anne Woodbull • ILLUSTRATOR: Shelley Rotner
HC: Little Simon
THEMES: color; riddles; guessing; alliteration; concepts

An irresistible color guessing game shows photographs featuring shades and hues of a different color on each page. Two flaps, one hiding the color's name and the other a riddle, keep young children involved through all the colors of the rainbow.

Colors Everywhere   PICTURE BOOK
AUTHOR/ILLUSTRATOR: Tana Hoban
HC: Greenwillow
THEMES: color; wordless; concepts; comparisons

Tana Hoban has snatched up everyday colors to create a visual matching game. There isn't a word of text. There's no need. The columns of color on each page will have children shouting out their own color words as they match—color for color—each brilliant photograph.

Communication   PICTURE BOOK NONFICTION
AUTHOR/ILLUSTRATOR: Aliki
HC: Greenwillow
THEMES: communication; talking; symbols; signs; sign language; writing; mail; listening; diaries; reading; pen pals

From the end papers picturing the upper and lower case English alphabet, the sign language alphabet, and the braille alphabet, to pages of simple conversations showing feelings, Aliki offers young readers a complete picture of communication.

Corn Is Maize: The Gift of the Indians   PICTURE BOOK NONFICTION
AUTHOR/ILLUSTRATOR: Aliki
HC/PB: HarperCollins
THEMES: corn; food; Native American; science; U.S. history, pre-Columbus; ancient man; farmers; Columbus; farming

"Corn cannot grow without the help of man. Then where did corn come from? How did it start?" With simple illustrations and words, Aliki tells about the history of corn; how it was used 5,000 years ago, what Columbus called it, and how it is milled today. A perfect book for start-up science buffs, and any curious child who will soon discover that his adults have a thing or two to learn as well!

Some of Aliki's other fascinating books in the *Let's Read And Find Out* science series include: *Ant Cities, Digging Up Dinosaurs, Dinosaurs Are Different, Fossils Tell of Long Ago, Milk From Cow to Carton, My Five Senses.*

Counting Crocodiles

PICTURE BOOK

AUTHOR: Judy Sierra • ILLUSTRATOR: Will Hillenbrand
HC: Harcourt Brace
THEMES: counting; math; monkeys; crocodiles; cleverness

A rhythmic, read-aloud text and wonderful illustrations make this a counting book that will hold up to the dozens of readings your children will surely request. They will love to watch the clever monkey use her counting skill to outwit the crocodiles and get the delicious bananas from the faraway island. Great for early math education.

The Country Bunny and the Little Gold Shoes

PICTURE BOOK

AUTHOR: Du Bose Heyward • ILLUSTRATOR: Marjorie Flack
PB: Sandpiper
THEMES: mothers; Easter; Easter Bunny; strong women; single parents; kindness; jobs; wisdom; yearnings

An Eastertime classic, this bunny makes all mothers proud. She is smart, organized, tidy, loving, thoughtful, and quick on her feet. For her bravery, Grandfather Bunny honors her with the title, "Gold Shoe Easter Bunny." Bring this out in springtime to show that there is no telling what good can happen to a child who learns to be "wise, and kind, and swift."

The Cow That Went Oink

PICTURE BOOK

AUTHOR/ILLUSTRATOR: Bernard Most
HC: Harcourt Brace
THEMES: farms; animals, farm; diversity; language; problem solving; bilingual; communication; teasing; friendship; individuality

Children who are teased at school, have difficulty with the language, or simply see themselves as not fitting in are bound to find relief in this tale about a cow who oinks and a pig who moos.

Crash! Bang! Boom!

BOARD BOOK

AUTHOR/ILLUSTRATOR: Peter Spier
HC: Doubleday
THEMES: noise; sound; concepts

From cars and trucks to marching bands, from daytime to nighttime, the pictures and the sound combinations in this "catalog of noises" offer an irresistible treat to "read" aloud. This book works very well with two year olds, but can also work with kindergartners. The other books in this format are: *Fast, Slow, High, Low* (concepts and comparisons) and *Gobble, Growl, Grunt* (animals, noises, sounds).

Curious George
AUTHOR/ILLUSTRATOR: H.A. Rey
HC/PB: Houghton Mifflin
THEMES: curiosity; monkeys; adventure

The original six stories about the most famous monkey of all are classics, made so by the fact that people simply love George. We do not wish to be curmudgeonly, but we need to say that much of George's appeal is lost on us as adults. Oh, we read them as children and later to our own children, and we acknowledge the fact that they delight. But we are at a loss to explain why they are popular. Is it just that George embodies curiosity so well that it dovetails perfectly with the developmental stage when youngsters find out the consequences of their own curiosity? Is it a nostalgia for simpler times, times, perhaps, when a man in a big yellow hat taking a monkey from the jungle could be looked upon fondly and not as a poacher? Or is it that George is simply beloved, period, and we just don't get it? Whatever the reason for our hesitation to wholeheartedly recommend these titles, do not let us stop you from making up your own mind as there is certainly plenty of George to go around. His tales are available in a variety of formats, including a big hardcover volume called *The Complete Adventures of Curious George.*

Dance, Tanya
AUTHOR: Patricia Lee Gauch • ILLUSTRATOR: Satomi Ichikawa
HC: Philomel • PB: Paperstar
THEMES: dance; siblings; ballet; strong girls

Tanya is too young to go with her sister to ballet class, so she copies the moves her sister learns. One day she puts on a special recital and shows she's ready to pack her slippers and go for a lesson of her own. Younger siblings will like Tanya's spunk, and whether they are interested in dance or marbles, they will learn a thing or two about determination. Other Tanya books are: *Bravo, Tanya* and *Tanya and Emily in a Dance for Two.*

Dancing Feet
AUTHOR/ILLUSTRATOR: Charlotte Agell
HC: Gulliver
THEMES: feet; rhythm; diversity; dance; comparisons

Dancing Feet uses the similarities in our bodies along with our differences in a rhythmic celebration of diversity. "Feet feet, walking down the street, dancing on the earth, skipping to the beat."

The Day of Ahmed's Secret   PICTURE BOOK

AUTHOR: Florence Parry Heide • ILLUSTRATOR: Ted Lewin
HC: Lothrop • PB: Mulberry
THEMES: reading; Egypt; jobs; secrets; coming of age; writing; literacy

The sights and sounds of Cairo, Ahmed's city, fill the day as he rides his donkey cart up streets, past buildings a thousand years old. He is eager for his work to be done so that he can go home and tell his secret to his family. His secret? He has learned to write his name!

Dear Mr. Blueberry   PICTURE BOOK

AUTHOR/ILLUSTRATOR: Simon James
HC: McElderry • PB: Aladdin
THEMES: whales; science; writing; mail; humor

This book of letters between a child who finds a whale swimming in her pond and her teacher, Mr. Blueberry, is fact-filled and funny.

Did You See What I Saw?:
Poems About School   POETRY COLLECTION

AUTHOR: Kay Winters • ILLUSTRATOR: Martha Weston
HC: Viking
THEMES: school; new experiences; playing; friendship; cooperation

Schoolchildren stand in line, get the chicken pox, swing, and slide in these poems about new experiences. Weston's illustrations add just the right touch.

Do You See a Mouse?   PICTURE BOOK

AUTHOR/ILLUSTRATOR: Bernard Waber
HC/PB: Houghton Mifflin
THEMES: mice; hotels; hiding; searching game

Everyone at the posh Park Snoot Hotel insists, "No, no, no, there is no mouse here." But the reader can find one hiding on each page. Great fun for the young detective.

Don't Count Your Chicks

PICTURE BOOK

AUTHOR/ILLUSTRATOR: Ingri and Edgar Parin D'aulaire

PB: Dell

THEMES: counting; math; chickens; Scandinavia; folklore; daydreams

An old woman goes off to town to sell her basket full of eggs. She imagines how much she will get for them. This Scandinavian folktale illustrates a Scandinavian saying: "Remember the Woman With the Eggs." It's another way to say, "Don't count your chickens before they're hatched."

Don't Laugh, Joe

PICTURE BOOK

AUTHOR/ILLUSTRATOR: Keiko Kasza

HC: Putnam

THEMES: opossums; humor; mothers and sons; bears; laughing

Mother Possum worries that her son Joe will never learn to play dead properly. He can't stop laughing. Children know what it's like to get the giggles, and this story makes them contagious.

Donna O'Neeshuck Was Chased by Some Cows

PICTURE BOOK

AUTHOR: Bill Grossman • ILLUSTRATOR: Sue Truesdell

HC/PB: HarperCollins

THEMES: cows; chases; farms; humor; rhyme

A herd of hilarious animals chases Donna O'Neeshuck. What do they want? Young children love guessing, so pause for a moment before this raucous rhyme is over.

Each Peach Pear Plum

PICTURE BOOK

AUTHOR/ILLUSTRATOR: Janet and Allan Ahlberg

PB: Puffin

THEMES: rhyme; searching game; folktale variations

"Each Peach Pear Plum I spy Tom Thumb." Nursery book characters hide on the pages, waiting to be found by "I Spy" squealing children. One of the best of its kind.

Earl's Too Cool for Me

PICTURE BOOK

AUTHOR: Leah Komaiko • ILLUSTRATOR: Laura Cornell

HC/PB: HarperCollins

THEMES: self-respect; comparisons; rhyme; friendship; humor; envy; judging

"Earl's got a bicycle made of hay. He takes rides on the Milky Way. Earl's too cool for me." Kids understand this story about wishing to be more like someone else. Komaiko's rhyme and Cornell's art warm the reader with the notion that when it comes to true friends, cool doesn't count.

Easter Egg Artists   PICTURE BOOK

AUTHOR/ILLUSTRATOR: Adrienne Adams
HC: Scribner • PB: Aladdin
THEMES: rabbits; artists; Easter; eggs; color; travel; decorating

It seems that just about anything can use a bit of decoration, and the Easter egg artists prove it's true. All it takes is paint and positive reinforcement. Read this bunny tale before decorating eggs.

Eating the Alphabet: Fruits & Vegetables From A to Z   PICTURE BOOK

AUTHOR/ILLUSTRATOR: Lois Ehlert
HC: Harcourt Brace
THEMES: alphabet; fruit; vegetables; vocabulary

Bananas, beans, beets, blueberries, broccoli and brussels sprouts blossom in brilliant color on the B page. Each letter of the alphabet introduces youngsters to a variety of fruits and vegetables. A glossary at the end offers additional information. Have you ever eaten a xigua?

★ Eeny, Meeny, Miney Mole   PICTURE BOOK

AUTHOR: **Jane Yolen** • ILLUSTRATOR: Kathryn Brown
HC/PB: Harcourt Brace
THEMES: spring; moles; sisters; curiosity; trailblazing; seasons; independence; individuality

This is one of our all-time favorite books about spring. At the bottom of a deep, dark hole where ". . . dark was light, day was night, and summer and winter seemed the same," lived three sisters. One had heard that "Up Above" things were both dark and light, so she set out to see for herself. Brown's hilarious creatures combined with Yolen's rich language, humor, and repetition make this feel-good find a delight to read aloud.

An Egg Is an Egg

PICTURE BOOK

AUTHOR/ILLUSTRATOR: Nicki Weiss

HC: Putnam • PB: Paperstar

THEMES: change; mothers and sons; comparisons; connections

There's a running refrain in this short, simple book: "Everything can change. Nothing stays the same." We see an egg become a chick, water become tea, and day become night, all accompanied by the soothing rhythm of the verse. But what makes this book so special is its end, when the mother tells her son that, though he is growing up, he can always be her baby. Ending with, "Some things stay the same. Some things never change," this book succeeds where many other books fail at expressing the eternal quality of a mother's love in a way that children can appreciate.

Farmer Duck

PICTURE BOOK

AUTHOR: Martin Waddell • ILLUSTRATOR: Helen Oxenbury

HC/PB: Candlewick

THEMES: animals, farm; community; farms; jobs; laziness; friendship

Poor Duck! He has to do all the work while the lazy farmer stays in bed all day. It's up to the other animals to right the situation, and in a satisfying conclusion they drive the farmer away and save the day. Though the story can be viewed as a socialist parable about the need for revolution and the good of the collective versus the evil of the despotic, capitalistic tyrant, children will most likely see it only as a great story.

> "Reading opens children up to a whole new world—that of other people's lives, thoughts and experience. Picture books are a stepping stone to learning to read and the pleasure that this embraces."
> —Helen Oxenbury, author/illustrator of the Tom and Pippo books

Feelings

PICTURE BOOK NONFICTION

AUTHOR/ILLUSTRATOR: Aliki

HC: Greenwillow • PB: Mulberry

THEMES: friendship; communication; jealousy; sadness; fear; anger; joy; love; emotions

Stories, pictures, poems and illustrated vignettes show a full gamut of emotions. A perfect book to encourage talking about feelings. See also: *Communication*.

First Flight

AUTHOR/ILLUSTRATOR: David McPhail
HC/PB: Little Brown
THEMES: airplanes; flying; teddy bears; fear of flying

Read this to a child before her first flight! She'll learn what to expect and will laugh along the way. McPhail's drawings will tickle the funnybone of any flyer—fearful and not—as she watches the antics of the unnamed bear who accompanies our hero on his trip. This device is used in several other books by McPhail, including *Lost!*, *The Bear's Toothache*, and *The Bear's Bicycle* (this last illustrated by McPhail but written by Emilie Warren McLeod).

The First Grade Takes a Test

AUTHOR: Miriam Cohen • ILLUSTRATOR: Lillian Hoban
HC: Greenwillow • PB: Dell
THEMES: first grade; tests; new experiences; friendship; individuality; school

Join Anna Maria, Jim, Alex, Danny and their other friends in this series of books about the experiences of a class of first graders. In each book we share their triumphs and tragedies—tests, getting lost on a field trip, losing a pet, and most of the real life things that the first grader in your life will identify with. Other titles include: *Bee My Valentine* (Valentine's Day), *Liar Liar Pants on Fire* (lying, truth), *Jim's Dog Muffins* (dogs, pets, death, loss, grief), *No Good in Art* (drawing; art), *When Will I Read?* (reading; anticipation), *Lost in the Museum* (lost; museums), *The Real-Skin Rubbermonster Mask* (costumes; fear), and *Starring First Grade* (acting).

First Things First

AUTHOR/ILLUSTRATOR: Betty Fraser
HC/PB: HarperCollins
THEMES: proverbs; language; wordplay

What to say when you are the first: "The early bird catches the worm. First come, first served." This colorful collection of proverbs for youngsters both teaches and entertains. What to say when it's all done: "All good things must come to an end."

Fish Faces

PICTURE BOOK NONFICTION

AUTHOR: Norbert Wu • ILLUSTRATOR: photographs
HC: Henry Holt
THEMES: fish; faces

Get nose to nose with a fish! Using outstanding underwater photography, we are treated to a vision of sea life up close and personal. This terrific book is a lot of fun to share with kids.

Five Minutes Peace

PICTURE BOOK

AUTHOR/ILLUSTRATOR: Jill Murphy
HC: Putnam
THEMES: mothers; baths; family; quiet; noise; solitude; meals

Follow the adventures of the Large family (elephants, of course) as the mother tries desperately to get some solitude and is thwarted by all three of her children. Funny and true to life, this will have little ones identifying with the plight of parents who need just a tiny break from the routine, and that is not a bad thing at all!

Family reading is for pleasure. Don't feel the need to teach.

Flora McDonnell's ABC

PICTURE BOOK

AUTHOR/ILLUSTRATOR: Flora McDonnell
HC: Candlewick
THEMES: animals; alphabet

Grand-scale paintings fill the pages with ants on alligators, bears and butterflies, cats in convertibles—from A to Z. We particularly like the fact that each letter is illustrated twice—once as a capital and once as a lowercase letter. Colorful, bright. If your preschool must limit its number of alphabet books, be sure to include this one! Kindergartners and first graders who are practicing their letters will find this helpful as well.

Frederick

PICTURE BOOK

AUTHOR/ILLUSTRATOR: Leo Lionni
HC/PB: Knopf
THEMES: mice; dreams; color; imagination; storytelling; poets

While the other mice collected and stored food to prepare for winter, Frederick sat and gathered warmth, colors, and words, preparing in his own way. And when the food ran out, Frederick's imaginative gatherings eased the difficult times. This is a tale of the value of different personalities and the power of words. There is also a sequel, *Frederick's Fables*, containing author Lionni's favorite stories. Lionni's distinctive watercolor style can be found in many other books, most notably *The Alphabet Tree, The Biggest House in the World, Matthew's Dream, Swimmy, A Color of His Own,* and *Inch by Inch.*

Freight Train   PICTURE BOOK

AUTHOR/ILLUSTRATOR: Donald Crews

PB: Mulberry

THEMES: trains; railroad; color; vocabulary; transportation

Gondola, trestles, hopper car, red, orange, yellow: few words, bright colors, and a train moving through tunnels and cities blend in this delightful, simple story about a train that comes, then goes. Also available in a board book format.

Friends   PICTURE BOOK

AUTHOR/ILLUSTRATOR: Helme Heine

HC: McElderry • PB: Aladdin

THEMES: friendship; dreams; diversity

Charlie Rooster, Fat Percy the pig, and Johnny Mouse are the best of friends and constant companions. Of course they have to learn that friends cannot do *everything* together, and so the book ends with them dreaming in their separate beds of more adventures. A perfectly delightful book about friendship, rendered in Heine's droll style, this one will hold up under the dozens of readings your children will request. When you need another visit, read *Friends Go Adventuring*.

Frog and Toad Are Friends   EARLY READER

AUTHOR/ILLUSTRATOR: Arnold Lobel

HC/PB: HarperCollins

THEMES: friendship; buttons; swimming; mail

Arnold Lobel knew how to create lovable, lasting characters in an early reader series. Frog and Toad are timeless, and they are no-fail. Linked short stories about these two give new readers the sense of a first chapter book with the humor and warmth that will move them on with enthusiasm to their next reading level. Sit back and listen while your child reads them to you. Others in the series: *Frog and Toad Together*,

Days with Frog and Toad (birthdays; kites), *Frog and Toad All Year* (seasons; Christmas).

Frog in Love
PICTURE BOOK

AUTHOR/ILLUSTRATOR: Max Velthuijs

HC: Farrar Straus & Giroux • PB: Sunburst

THEMES: love; friendship; relationships; diversity

Frog and Duck may seem an unlikely duo, but their love knows no bounds. Bright, colorful art and a sweet friendship blend in this romantic fable for the younger set.

Froggy Gets Dressed
PICTURE BOOK

AUTHOR: Jonathan London • ILLUSTRATOR: Frank Remkiewicz

HC: Viking • PB: Puffin

THEMES: snow; dressing; mothers and sons; humor; lessons; repetition

A terrific hit with preschoolers, but Froggy's popularity stretches to second and third grade. Perfectly paced and just repetitive enough, it has a payoff that sends kids into wild gales of laughter. It's silly, and that's the point! Froggy has more adventures in his other books: *Let's Go Froggy, Froggy Learns to Swim, Froggy Goes to School* and *Froggy's First Kiss.*

Performing *Froggy* can be a real highlight for me, regardless of the age of the audience. The book has become popular with the kindergarten set, so many kids already know it and are eager to shout out parts with me. Any book with the word "underwear" in it is bound to be a hit!

From Head to Toe
PICTURE BOOK

AUTHOR/ILLUSTRATOR: Eric Carle

HC: HarperCollins

THEMES: exercise; animals; imitation; pretending

With questions, answers, and oversized colored collages, Carle encourages youngsters to exercise by imitating the movements of a cat, penguin, giraffe, buffalo, seal, and other animals.

Galimoto
PICTURE BOOK

AUTHOR: Karen Lynn Williams • ILLUSTRATOR: Catherine Stock

HC: Lothrop • PB: Mulberry

THEMES: Africa; toys; cars; crafts; determination; collecting

Kondi is only seven years old, but he wants to make a *galimoto* (toy) out of wire. Set in an African village, this story shows the value of persistence and the pride in creating something of your very own.

The Ghost-Eye Tree
PICTURE BOOK

AUTHOR: Bill Martin, Jr. and John Archambault • ILLUSTRATOR: Ted Rand
HC/PB: Henry Holt
THEMES: fear of the dark; ghosts; siblings; trees; spooky stories

It's a full moon night and a boy and his sister must pass the ghost-eye tree on their way to town to fetch a pail of milk. Read this tale aloud, especially if you like playing with voices and sounds. The authors originally wrote it to be performed as theater.

Ginger
PICTURE BOOK

AUTHOR/ILLUSTRATOR: Charlotte Voake
HC: Candlewick
THEMES: cats; babies; sharing; curiosity; siblings

Ginger the cat fits fine in his snuggly wicker basket. Life for him is just about purrfect—and then "they" bring home a kitten. Cat lovers will recognize what happens when a cat not used to sharing deals with a curious kitten who is here to stay. Read this aloud to young children who have a new baby living in the house.

The Gingerbread Boy
PICTURE BOOK

AUTHOR/ILLUSTRATOR: Richard Egielski
HC: HarperCollins
THEMES: folklore; teasing; baking; chases; cities

Hysterical paintings show a flat, overconfident gingerbread boy teasing his way through big city streets. Pursued by his creators, a rat, some construction workers, street musicians, and a policeman, he meets his final demise in the mouth of a fox. Here's a new telling of an old tale with lots of humorous downtown detail.

The Girl Who Loved Caterpillars: A Twelfth Century Tale, From Japan
PICTURE BOOK

AUTHOR: Jean Merrill • ILLUSTRATOR: Floyd Cooper
PB: Paperstar
THEMES: caterpillars; Japan; determination; strong girls; gifted child; native; folklore; gender roles; individuality; children; nature

Izumi isn't interested in the pastimes of the ladies in the Emperor's court. She prefers spending her time with creatures of nature, like toads, worms and caterpillars. Cooper's radiant art illuminates the individuality of this determined twelfth-century Japanese girl.

★ Go Away, Big Green Monster!   NOVELTY
AUTHOR/ILLUSTRATOR: Ed Emberley
HC: Little Brown
THEMES: monsters; change

Irresistible graphics! Children follow along as with each turn of the page this monster grows and gets smaller right before their eyes. They'll have it memorized by the second time through. For another look at anticipation and a surprisingly small monster, see Tony Ross' *I'm Coming to Get You.*

Go, Dog. Go!   EARLY READER
AUTHOR/ILLUSTRATOR: P.D. Eastman
HC: Random House
THEMES: dogs; cars; parties; comparisons

"Do you like my hat?" "No, I do not like your hat." "Goodbye." "Goodbye." This exchange recurs throughout this amazing easy reader, between just two of the many dogs you'll meet. Dogs on the go and occasionally resting, dogs of all shapes and colors, dogs at work and play, all add to a book that will make a child say, as one dog says in the book: "Go around again!"

Goldilocks and the Three Bears   PICTURE BOOK
AUTHOR/ILLUSTRATOR: Jan Brett
HC: Putnam • PB: Paperstar
THEMES: lost; bears; concepts; folklore; comparisons

Some of our favorite Jan Brett art can be found in this classic nursery tale. A mouse family keeps busy in its own story tucked in the borders, but it's the detailed Scandinavian costumes and the close-up staring bears that give the reader a clear understanding of why Goldilocks jumped out the window never to return. Scary? Not really. The bears seem more baffled by the trespasser than ready to eat her.

Good Morning Pond   PICTURE BOOK
AUTHOR: Alyssa Satin Capucilli • ILLUSTRATOR: Cynthia Jabar
HC: Hyperion
THEMES: ponds; science; morning; rhyme; waking up

Follow the creatures of a pond with croaks, ribbits, and honks as they welcome in a new day. Young children will relish the chance to add their own chirps to the morning music!

Good Night, Gorilla   PICTURE BOOK

AUTHOR/ILLUSTRATOR: Peggy Rathmann

HC: Putnam

THEMES: mischief; repetition; surprises; zoos; escape; night; playing tricks

Gleefully funny, and a guaranteed delight to read aloud at bedtime or anytime. Follow the path of the zookeeper as he says goodnight to the animals. Follow also the path of the gorilla who comes right behind him with the purloined key, letting all the animals out of their cages, only to follow the sleepy zookeeper home and crawl unnoticed into his bedroom to sleep. It takes his wife to set things right, but the gorilla has the last laugh, which he shares with you and your child, who will most likely clamor to have it read again. Good thing it's so funny. Also available in a board book format.

★ Goodnight Moon   PICTURE BOOK

AUTHOR: Margaret Wise Brown • ILLUSTRATOR: Clement Hurd

HC/PB: HarperCollins

THEMES: bedtime; night; balloons

This is the classic first book for babies. It was published in 1947 and is the stand-out best-seller for babies still. We didn't trust its powerful magic until we had children of our own. It works. Ask any child . . . Also available in a board book format.

Grandfather Twilight   PICTURE BOOK

AUTHOR/ILLUSTRATOR: Barbara Berger

HC: Putnam • PB: Paperstar

THEMES: comfort; twilight; night; forests

"When day is done, he closes his book, combs his beard, and puts on his jacket." Then Grandfather Twilight begins his daily journey through the forest to bring night into the world. Soft, luminous art and text blend with imagination and possibilities in this gentle goodnight story.

Grandpa's Face
PICTURE BOOK

AUTHOR: Eloise Greenfield • ILLUSTRATOR: Floyd Cooper
HC: Philomel • PB: Paperstar
THEMES: grandfathers and granddaughters; actors; theater; fear; love; emotions

The simple heart of this story—a small part of a child's day—makes it all the more moving. Tamika and her grandfather are very close, and she can tell by his face how he is feeling. But one day she watches him rehearse for a play and sees an expression she has never seen before. It is a mean face that could never love, and it frightens her. Cooper's rich, earthy art and Greenfield's sensitive text are worth sharing with any child who will feel comfort in talking about feelings.

Green Eggs and Ham
EARLY READER

AUTHOR/ILLUSTRATOR: Dr. Seuss
HC: Random House
THEMES: eggs; ham; food; preferences; comparisons; new experiences

"I do not like green eggs and ham. I do not like them, Sam-I-am." What young child does not want to sing a chorus of "I do not like . . ."? Seuss hit the nail on the head when it came to kids. He took simple, child-familiar experiences and stretched them to imaginary extremes. And young readers delight in them. Other favorite Seuss "Beginner Books" are: *The Cat in the Hat, One Fish Two Fish Red Fish Blue Fish,* and *Hop on Pop.*

Growing Colors
PICTURE BOOK

AUTHOR/ILLUSTRATOR: Bruce McMillan
HC: Lothrop
THEMES: gardens; vegetables; fruit; color

Often the only encounter a child has with a fruit or vegetable is in the grocery story or on the table. Oranges piled in bins along with tomatoes, carrots, squash and other garden treats offer no clue as to how and where they grow. McMillan uses vibrant color photographs close-up and at a distance—of the entire plant—to solve the mystery.

Guess How Much I Love You
PICTURE BOOK

AUTHOR: Sam McBratney • ILLUSTRATOR: Anita Jeram
HC: Candlewick
THEMES: fathers and sons; love; family; comparisons

It's hard to measure feelings, and every time Little Nutbrown Hare tries to show how much he loves Big Nutbrown Hare, Big Nutbrown Hare shows that he can love him even more. " 'I love you as high as I can reach.' That is very high, thought Little Nutbrown Hare. I wish I had arms like that." In this cozy tale, Big Hare can represent dad, a brother, or an older friend. Also available in a board book format.

Gus and Grandpa   EARLY READER

AUTHOR: Claudia Mills • ILLUSTRATOR: Catherine Stock
HC: Farrar Straus & Giroux
THEMES: friendship; grandfathers
and grandsons

An utterly charming book for beginning readers, and the first of several books in this series. Destined
to take its place beside the *Mr. Putter and Tabby* and *Frog and Toad*
series as perfect transitional readers.

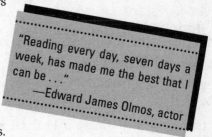

"Reading every day, seven days a week, has made me the best that I can be . . ."
—Edward James Olmos, actor

Hands   NOVELTY

AUTHOR/ILLUSTRATOR: Lois Ehlert
HC: Harcourt Brace
THEMES: art; mothers and daughters; fathers and daughters; carpentry;
sewing; comparisons; crafts; creativity

Shaped like a glove, this book compares the hand work of a child's mother and father. Ehlert's brightly colored mix of photography and collage cut-outs celebrates working with our hands, large and small.

Hannah and Jack   PICTURE BOOK

AUTHOR: Mary Nethery • ILLUSTRATOR: Mary Morgan
HC: Atheneum
THEMES: cats; pets; friendship; writing; mail; problem solving; separa-
tion; grandmothers

Hannah and her cat, Jack, do everything together. But when she takes a family trip to Grandma's, Jack can't come. Children who worry about separation see one child's solution and discover that being apart is only temporary.

Hansel and Gretel
PICTURE BOOK

AUTHOR/ILLUSTRATOR: James Marshall

HC: Dial

THEMES: Grimm's fairy tales; poverty; witches; folklore; abandonment; cleverness; courage; survival

James Marshall makes the forest huge and dark, the mother well-fed and mean, and the witch horrid and overdressed. Hansel and Gretel are very sweet and this tale will have you laughing at his pictures, moved by the story and cheering at the happy ending. Caution: if you think too much about the abusive parents, it takes the fun out of the whole tale.

Happy Birth Day
PICTURE BOOK

AUTHOR: H. Robie Harris • ILLUSTRATOR: Michael Emberley

HC: Candlewick

THEMES: babies; birth; hospitals; new baby

If you're a sucker for babies, this book, with its oversized close-up illustrations, will warm your heart. It reminds us of our newborns, just as loved and certainly as gorgeous as the infant here. Read this delightful story about one baby's first day of life to young children and give it to new parents to cherish.

Harold and the Purple Crayon
PICTURE BOOK

AUTHOR/ILLUSTRATOR: Crockett Johnson

HC/PB: HarperCollins

THEMES: drawing; imagination; art; crayons; creativity

Harold doesn't require a full spectrum of color to hold his interest, and neither will young readers. Crockett's character draws simple pictures with his crayon and then steps magically into the drawing, becoming a part of his own creation. Offer this one up with crayon and paper and let imaginations soar! Preschoolers looking for simple stories and children in early stages of reading will enjoy this.

Harvey Slumfenburger's Christmas Present
PICTURE BOOK

AUTHOR/ILLUSTRATOR: John Burningham

HC/PB: Candlewick

THEMES: Christmas; determination; jobs; Santa Claus; promises; repetition

After a long night of delivering presents to the boys and girls of the world, and after putting the reindeer to bed, Santa Claus discovers he has forgotten to deliver Harvey Slumfenburger's present. The epic journey that ensues will warm the heart of any adult and assure even the most skeptical child of the faithfulness of Santa. Never sickly-sweet, and told in a repetitive style that encourages children to join in the telling, this one is a modern masterpiece by one of our favorite authors.

Hattie & the Fox
PICTURE BOOK

AUTHOR: Mem Fox • ILLUSTRATOR: Patricia Mullins
HC: Bradbury
THEMES: courage; animals, farm; repetition; cumulative story; farms; communication; survival; triumph

If it's written by Mem Fox, you can count on a catchy rhythm and a repeatable tale. In this cumulative story, Hattie the hen spots danger but the other farmyard animals don't seem to care. Young children will ask you to read about Hattie outsmarting Fox over and over.

Hazel's Amazing Mother
PICTURE BOOK

AUTHOR/ILLUSTRATOR: **Rosemary Wells**
HC: Dial • PB: Puffin
THEMES: bullies; mothers; dolls; lost; rescue

Hazel makes a wrong turn and gets lost. That's when the three older kids begin to tease her. Hazel is too small to handle this herself. Bullies beware! There's no power like that of a mother whose child is being picked on. Down comes Hazel's amazing mother, righting wrongs and reminding young readers that you can always count on mom.

Henny Penny
PICTURE BOOK

AUTHOR/ILLUSTRATOR: Paul Galdone
HC/PB: Clarion
THEMES: folklore; farms; cumulative story; animals

"Goodness gracious me!" said Henny Penny. "The sky is falling! I must go and tell the King." And so begins this famous tale of a hen who along with Cocky Locky, Ducky Lucky, Goosey Loosey, and Turkey Lurkey goes off to warn the king. Ah, but foolish, quickly made observations prove to be the downfall of this well-meaning quintet. Fat Foxy Loxy and Mrs. Foxy Loxy and their seven little foxes can attest to that! If you are looking for a classic nursery tale, look for Paul Galdone. His simple, expressive illustrations and to-the-point tellings do the job every time. A sampling of his titles: *The Little Red Hen, The Teeny-Tiny Woman, The*

Elves and the Shoemaker, The Three Little Kittens, The Gingerbread Boy,
and *The Three Billy Goats Gruff.*

Henry and Mudge   EARLY READER
AUTHOR: **Cynthia Rylant** • ILLUSTRATOR: Sucie Stevenson
HC: Bradbury • PB: Aladdin
THEMES: friendship; dogs

Writing at a beginning reading level, Rylant perfectly captures the
friendship of a boy and his very large dog in a delightful series! Rylant's
writing proves that early readers do not have to suffer through boring
text just because the vocabulary is limited. Here's an example, from
Henry and Mudge and the Happy Cat: "Sitting on the steps was the shab-
biest cat Henry had ever seen. It had a saggy belly, skinny legs, and fur
that looked like mashed prunes." Rylant's writing is vivid. Her humor
makes us laugh. Try any of the books in this series—the titles all begin
Henry and Mudge. . . .When you run out of *Henry and Mudge* books, do
not despair. Rylant's charming style is also to be found in another early
reader series, *Mr. Putter and Tabby.*

Here Comes Henny   PICTURE BOOK
AUTHOR: Charlotte Pomerantz • ILLUSTRATOR: Nancy Winslow Parker
HC: Greenwillow
THEMES: cooperation; wordplay; mothers; picnics; manners

Irresistible because of its catchy, silly language, this is one kids will
want to learn by heart. Adults will appreciate the message—it's not wise
to be too picky!

Hey! Get Off Our Train   PICTURE BOOK
AUTHOR/ILLUSTRATOR: John Burningham
HC: Crown • PB: Dragonfly
THEMES: environment; fables; trains; dreams; animals, endangered;
humor

It may be a dream, but when a boy and his railroad engineer dog speed
along the tracks picking up endangered animals, the message is wide-
awake clear. Without a lecture, Burningham uses his signature humor to
create an entertaining story with a conscience.

"Hi, Pizza Man!" PICTURE BOOK
AUTHOR: Virginia Walter • ILLUSTRATOR: Ponder Goembel
HC: Orchard
THEMES: animals; imagination; wordplay; food; anticipation

Waiting isn't easy especially when you're hungry, but this hilarious morsel shows that imaginations at work can make waiting the best time of all. Vivian wonders, "Where, oh where, is that pizza man?" Mama asks what she'll say when he arrives. "Hi, Pizza Man!" Vivian says. But what if he were a dinosaur? What would you say then? This greeting game doesn't have to limit itself to pizza. Have fun with the pictures and all the possibilities.

Hilary Knight's The Twelve Days of Christmas PICTURE BOOK
AUTHOR/ILLUSTRATOR: Hilary Knight
HC: Simon & Schuster • PB: Aladdin
THEMES: songs; Christmas carols; repetition; humor; Christmas

For twelve days Benjamin Bear brings Bedelia his gifts. Cheery art designed for the younger set. See *The Twelve Days of Christmas* (Jan Brett).

Hog-Eye PICTURE BOOK
AUTHOR/ILLUSTRATOR: Susan Meddaugh
HC/PB: Houghton Mifflin
THEMES: books; reading; wolves; pigs; storytelling

Meddaugh's tale of a clever pig who knows the power of a good imagination will have you in stitches. Whether it's the storytelling pig who gets you laughing, or the asides from her family, read this one aloud. Humor can be as contagious as Green Threeleaf poison ivy.

A Hole Is to Dig: A First Book of First Definitions PICTURE BOOK
AUTHOR: Ruth Krauss • ILLUSTRATOR: Maurice Sendak
HC/PB: HarperCollins
THEMES: vocabulary; definitions; humor

Arms are for hugging and ears are for wiggling and these "first definitions" will delight young children who will practice new words as they wiggle and giggle at Sendak's characters.

Home Sweet Home   PICTURE BOOK

AUTHOR: Jean Marzollo • ILLUSTRATOR: Ashley Woolf
HC/PB: HarperCollins
THEMES: nature; animals; prayer; quiet

Looking for a book for the quiet times—one with a gentle message and
beautiful art? This simple prayer for the planet and its inhabitants, with
lovely art by Ashley Woolf, is just the thing.

Hooray, a Piñata!   PICTURE BOOK

AUTHOR/ILLUSTRATOR: Elisa Kleven
HC: Dutton
THEMES: birthdays; celebrations; piñatas; Mexico; parties; pets; friend-
ship; traditions

Piñatas add a festive touch to parties. They're decorative and create a
focus children look forward to. That is, unless that child is Clara, the
birthday girl, who has gotten attached to her piñata and doesn't want it
broken. Colorful, lively pictures add to the festivities in this story of
friendship, family, and finding a perfect solution to a sensitive situation.

Hooray for Me   PICTURE BOOK

AUTHOR: Remy Charlip • ILLUSTRATOR: Vera Williams
HC: Tricycle
THEMES: self-respect; family; neighbors; pets; relatives

Third cousin, great-uncle, stepbrother, nephew. There are lots of
responses to "What kind of me are you?" Charlip's cheery shouts of pride
show how we relate to our family, friends, and even pets. Williams adds
the color to this feel-good book.

A House for a Hermit Crab   PICTURE BOOK

AUTHOR/ILLUSTRATOR: Eric Carle
HC: Simon & Schuster
THEMES: crabs; science; nature; moving; animals, sea; fear of new
things; friendship; neighbors; change

Hermit Crab is frightened when he becomes too big for his first shell
house and must find a new one. When he moves into his empty, dull
new shell, neighbors come along to help him decorate. Children often
worry about change, and Carle's brilliant collages and Hermit's undersea community show that change can be the perfect move.

★ A House Is a House for Me   PICTURE BOOK

AUTHOR: Mary Ann Hoberman • ILLUSTRATOR: Betty Fraser
HC: Viking • PB: Puffin
THEMES: houses; rhyme; repetition; habitats; animals; architecture; dwellings; Native American; diversity; comparisons; imagination

"A hill is a house for an ant, an ant. A hive is a house for a bee. A hole is a house for a mole or a mouse. And a house is a house for me." So begins this incredible rhyme about dwellings. But don't think Hoberman has limited the subjects to animals. Young readers will delight in learning about houses for airplanes, teabags, cookies, jackets, and many more.

How Many Bugs in a Box?   POP-UP

AUTHOR/ILLUSTRATOR: David A. Carter
HC: Simon & Schuster
THEMES: bugs; counting; numbers

Kids who relish the thought of peeking, sneaking, comical bugs will find them popping out, in, over, and under colorful boxes in a sturdy pop-up form.

How My Parents Learned to Eat   PICTURE BOOK

AUTHOR: Ina R. Friedman • ILLUSTRATOR: Allen Say
HC/PB: Houghton Mifflin
THEMES: traditions; Japan; U.S.A.; England; eating; chopsticks; manners; cultural diversity

A young girl explains that in her house "some days we eat with chopsticks and some days we eat with knives and forks." Each of her parents had to learn when they met and fell in love in Japan. Eating styles of these two plus a third country are served up here, with a taste of humor and a touch of insight into how we are different and how we are all the same.

How to Be a Nature Detective   PICTURE BOOK NONFICTION

AUTHOR: Millicent E. Selsam • ILLUSTRATOR: Marlene Hill Donnelly
HC/PB: HarperCollins
THEMES: nature; animals; animal tracks; clues; habitats

A first look at tracks and other clues animals leave behind highlight this nature guide for young children. Part of the *Let's Read and Find Out* science series.

How to Lose All Your Friends   PICTURE BOOK
AUTHOR/ILLUSTRATOR: Nancy Carlson
HC: Viking • PB: Puffin
THEMES: friendship; problem solving; getting along; bullies

Never smile, never share, and when you don't get your way, be sure to
whine. While poking fun at bullies, tattletales, grouches, and other kids
who have a hard time keeping friends, these playful vignettes invite
readers to discuss positive behavior that bonds friendships.

Hunting the White Cow   PICTURE BOOK
AUTHOR: Tres Seymour • ILLUSTRATOR: Wendy Anderson Halperin
HC/PB: Orchard
THEMES: farms; cows; animals, farm; family; cooperation; problem solving

A young girl tells this tale about folks working together. Everyone's trying to figure out a way to catch the white cow. She is "one tough dude"
and manages to elude all attempts. From the farmhouse to the general
store to the meadows beyond, the full-page pencil-and-watercolor art
delightfully depicts the relaxed life on this farm.

Hush Little Baby   PICTURE BOOK
AUTHOR/ILLUSTRATOR: Aliki • PB: Aladdin
THEMES: songs; lullabies; folksongs; babies; mothers

If you'd like pictures to go along with this popular song, this is the book
for you. For a variation, see *Hush Little Baby* (Sylvia Long).

Hush Little Baby   PICTURE BOOK
AUTHOR/ILLUSTRATOR: Sylvia Long
HC: Chronicle
THEMES: lullabies; folksongs; nature; songs; babies; mothers

"Hush little baby, don't say a word, Mama's going to show you a hummingbird. If that hummingbird should fly, Mama's going to show you
the evening sky." Long has rewritten the original version, trading the
mother's "buying" (mockingbird, diamond ring . . .) for the comfort of
nature. For the original version, see *Hush Little Baby* (Aliki).

I Don't Care, Said the Bear   PICTURE BOOK
AUTHOR/ILLUSTRATOR: Colin West
HC/PB: Candlewick
THEMES: bears; mice; fear; rhyme; animals

Children chime in, "I don't care, said the bear, with his nose in the air," before the first reading is finished. A big brown bear is not afraid of a bad-tempered goose, a pig who is big or a snake from a lake. But a teeny-weeny mouse? That's a different story. And children love it!

I Like Books   PICTURE BOOK

AUTHOR/ILLUSTRATOR: Anthony Browne
PB: Dragonfly
THEMES: books; monkeys; reading; imagination

A lovesong to books, rendered in the imaginative style of Anthony Browne, where you have to look twice to see all that is happening on every page. Lots of fun to have your child point out the things she notices.

I Love You as Much . . .   PICTURE BOOK

AUTHOR: Laura Krauss Melmed • ILLUSTRATOR: Henri Sorensen
HC: Lothrop
THEMES: mothers; love; rhyme; lullabies; animal babies

Said the mother goat to her child, "I love you as much as the mountain is steep." Said the mother whale to her child, "I love you as much as the ocean is deep." This tender gathering of mother animals and their babies is a perfect sleep send-off.

I Went to the Zoo   PICTURE BOOK

AUTHOR: Rita Gelman • ILLUSTRATOR: Maryann Kovalski
HC/PB: Scholastic
THEMES: cumulative story; animals; zoos; rhyme

This tongue teaser is a fun read aloud! "Hippos soaking; bullfrogs croaking; monkeys swinging; koalas clinging."

I Went Walking   PICTURE BOOK

AUTHOR: Sue Williams • ILLUSTRATOR: Julie Vivas
HC/PB: Gulliver
THEMES: animals; cumulative story; repetition; walking; color

Just as *Brown Bear, Brown Bear, What Do You See?* asks questions and answers with cheery, oversized animals, so does this, but there's room on our shelves for both. On every page a hint of an animal appears at the next turn, allowing the child to guess what's coming. Vivas' fanciful paintings add a lively touch of humor.

★ I Wish I Were a Butterfly   PICTURE BOOK

AUTHOR: James Howe • ILLUSTRATOR: Ed Young

HC/PB: Harcourt Brace

THEMES: self-respect; crickets; spiders; gardens; ponds; friendship; insects

The littlest cricket in Swampswallow Pond wouldn't come out to sing with the others. He wanted to be a butterfly, not an ugly cricket. But with the help of a wise spider he learns—along with young listeners—to appreciate himself. The ending is perfect (we won't ruin it). If you are looking for a lesson in self-acceptance, or simply a warm and reassuring story, this is for you.

I'll Fix Anthony   PICTURE BOOK

AUTHOR: Judith Viorst • ILLUSTRATOR: Arnold Lobel

PB: Aladdin

THEMES: brothers; siblings; dreams; revenge

It is tough being Anthony's little brother. Here is a catalog of all the things Anthony's younger brother will do when he is six, and bigger at last than Anthony, gleefully told with spite and malice. This is a sibling book where the sibs never get along—Anthony is as mean to his brother at the end as he is at the beginning. Fantasizing along with the narrator about ways to "fix" Anthony may provide some comfort for put-upon youngsters who have to stay the youngest.

I'll See You When the Moon Is Full   PICTURE BOOK

AUTHOR: Susi Gregg Fowler • ILLUSTRATOR: Jim Fowler

HC: Greenwillow

THEMES: time; fathers; moon; fear of separation; math; science

A boy whose father is leaving on a business trip is confused when he is told, "I'll see you when the moon is full." Using a simple science lesson, along with a touch of sensitivity, Fowler solves the problem of a child's concern about the passing of time. Here's a chance for young children to keep track of time by using the moon, and all they'll need is a crayon and a piece of paper!

If You Give a Mouse a Cookie   PICTURE BOOK

AUTHOR: Laura Numeroff • ILLUSTRATOR: Felicia Bond

HC/PB: HarperCollins

THEMES: mice; cookies; cumulative story; predictable

The kind of book that children want to hear again and again, this cumulative tale goes full circle from the introduction of a young boy and a mouse and the gift of a cookie. Bond's clever details add much to the story, making it a delight to read aloud with a child on your lap, noticing the visual elements and how well they complement the words.

If You Were Born a Kitten   PICTURE BOOK NONFICTION

AUTHOR: Marion Dane Bauer
ILLUSTRATOR: JoEllen McAllister Stammen
HC: Simon & Schuster
THEMES: animal babies; birth; babies; comparisons; nature

"If you were a newborn opossum, you'd fit into a teaspoon . . . Your mother would lick you a path so you could climb to her pouch." Welcome twelve animal babies, popping, pecking, nudging and poking their way into the world. The finale? A human baby. Extraordinary, full-page illustrations fill each enchanting page. Read this when you and your child could use a snuggly, feel-good, learn-a-bit moment in your lives.

In Enzo's Splendid Gardens   PICTURE BOOK

AUTHOR/ILLUSTRATOR: Patricia Polacco
HC: Philomel
THEMES: restaurants; rhyme; cumulative story; bees; mishaps

"This is the bee that stopped on a tree in Enzo's splendid gardens . . ." And that's how the pandemonium begins. A boy drops his book to look at the bee and the waiter trips on the book and tips his tray.

Enzo's Restaurant really exists in Oakland, California. And the ladies, ". . . foo-foo and shee-shee, who lost their balance and spilled their tea, bumped by the matron, all dressed in pink" are real too. I know that, because one of them is me.

In the Desert   PICTURE BOOK NONFICTION

AUTHOR: David M. Schwartz • ILLUSTRATOR: Dwight Kuhn
PB: Creative Teaching Press
THEMES: desert; animals; cactus; nature

"Is this leg hairy enough for you? If not, there are seven more hairy legs where this one came from." The *Look Once, Look Again* science series by David Schwartz gives young children a close-up look at part of an animal with just enough words to hint what it might be. A turn of the page shows the answer with a brief explanation: "Tarantulas are the world's biggest spiders. Some are so large that they can eat lizards, small birds, and mice . . ." Dwight Kuhn's photo images get close enough to keep the pages turning on this guessing game. Others in the series include: *At the Pond, In the Forest, At the Seashore, Among the Flowers,* and *In a Tree.*

In the Night Kitchen

PICTURE BOOK

AUTHOR/ILLUSTRATOR: Maurice Sendak
HC/PB: HarperCollins
THEMES: dreams; kitchens; bakers; baking; milk; cake

Do not attempt to analyze or make sense of this wonderful, dreamlike romp—it would spoil the fun. Mickey discovers the secret behind the cake that gets baked in time for breakfast every morning and even helps out the three identical bakers, who look just like Oliver Hardy! Magical illustrations and a fun read-aloud rhythm make this a great toddler book, but it's been known to enthrall older children and adults as well.

HOW TO JUDGE A BOOK BY ITS COVER

Book covers are written by marketing people, not by authors. After you've looked at the cover, and taken in the image (studies tell us the average consumer gives each book a glance of less than a second), if your interest is piqued, there are words on the front, back, and inside flaps of the cover that can further guide you. If you're looking for literary quality, paperbacks will usually put quotes from reviews, awards and endorsements on the book. Hardcovers rarely offer such help, leaving you to read the inside cover flaps, which will usually offer a brief synopsis written by someone who writes advertising copy for a living.

If those words intrigue you, open the book to any two or three pages. Sample the writing. Don't assume that the "flap copy," as publishers call it, is representative of the author's work.

In the Tall, Tall Grass

PICTURE BOOK

AUTHOR/ILLUSTRATOR: Denise Fleming
HC/PB: Henry Holt
THEMES: grass; caterpillars; fireflies; rhyme; nature; animals; bees; sound

From the warmth of a sunny sky "crunch, munch, caterpillars lunch" to the cool shades of night "stop, go, fireflies glow," critters do what they do from a toddler's view in bright, bold, award-winning color collages. Also: *In the Small, Small Pond* (ponds, frogs)

In the Woods: Who's Been Here?   PICTURE BOOK NONFICTION

AUTHOR/ILLUSTRATOR: Lindsay Barrett George

HC: Greenwillow

THEMES: nature; forests; animals; animal tracks; habitats

This book concentrates on clues rather than facts. Two children take a walk in the woods and guess what critter has been there before them. Every other page has a remarkable close-up painting giving them the answer. Some books are backdrops for conversation and this is one. Children will want to know more about the animals and their habits. Also: *In the Snow: Who's Been Here?* (winter; snow)

Is This a House for Hermit Crab?   PICTURE BOOK

AUTHOR: Megan McDonald • ILLUSTRATOR: S.D. Schindler

HC/PB: Orchard

THEMES: nature; sea; science; crabs; home; change; moving; habitats

Hermit Crab tries a variety of places in his search for a new home. Not until a wave carries him far out to sea does he find the perfect place, a discarded snail's shell. A delightful story matched by Schindler's sandy, speckled pictures provides an entertaining balance between science and fiction.

Is Your Mama a Llama?   PICTURE BOOK

AUTHOR: Deborah Guarino • ILLUSTRATOR: Steven Kellogg

HC/PB: Scholastic

THEMES: llamas; predictable; rhyme; guessing; bats; swans; seals; kangaroos; cows

With whimsy and rhyme animals give hints to a llama who asks them, "Is your mama a llama?" Readers guess what everyone's mama really is and discover the answer with the turn of the page. Read this to one child or a group. We guarantee you'll get enthusiastic participation! Also available in a board book edition.

Jelly Beans for Sale   PICTURE BOOK NONFICTION

AUTHOR/ILLUSTRATOR: Bruce McMillan

HC: Scholastic

THEMES: money; math; counting; jelly beans

With very few words, McMillan uses colorful close-up photos to show how different combinations of pennies, nickels, dimes, and quarters can buy various amounts of jelly beans. And there is a bonus—a description of how jelly beans are made and information on ordering is listed in the back!

June Is a Tune That Jumps on a Stair   POETRY COLLECTION
AUTHOR/ILLUSTRATOR: Sarah Wilson
HC: Simon & Schuster
THEMES: imagination; seasons; months

". . . June is a bumble of one small bee. June is a hug from the sunshine to me." Playful and imaginative, Wilson's poems are a perfect start for a young child's poetry collection.

Just Like My Dad   PICTURE BOOK
AUTHOR: Tricia Gardella • ILLUSTRATOR: Margot Apple
HC/PB: HarperCollins
THEMES: fathers and sons; horses; ranches; cowboys

There is something heartwarming about a son following in the footsteps of his father. Dad's a ranch hand, and his son accompanies him as we watch them go through their daily routine. Margot Apple's warm illustrations portray the details of this rugged life alongside Gardella's simple and perfect story.

Just Me and My Dad   PICTURE BOOK
AUTHOR/ILLUSTRATOR: Mercer Mayer
PB: Golden
THEMES: fathers and sons; camping; fishing; confidence; mischief

Little Critter is a typical four year old full of mischief, confidence, and the inability to admit he can't do everything. In this book, as in its companion, *Just Me and My Mom*, Little Critter spends some time alone with one very patient parent. A good, inexpensive series which maintains its popularity well into elementary school.

Just Rewards   PICTURE BOOK
AUTHOR: Steve Sanfield • ILLUSTRATOR: Emily Lisker
HC: Orchard
THEMES: folklore; moon; greed; wealth; envy; comeuppance; rewards

A good neighbor finds an injured sparrow and cares for it till it's well.

Wanting him to receive a just reward, the bird drops a tiny, magical seed in the man's hand. Lucky good man. When his greedy neighbor gets wind of the good guy's riches, he injures a bird so he can get a reward of his own. He does—his just reward. Sanfield is a superb storyteller.

The Kids of the Polk Street School Series   EARLY READER
AUTHOR: Patricia Reilly Giff • ILLUSTRATOR: Blanche Sims
PB: Dell
THEMES: school; friendship; reading; holidays; teachers;

It is a fair bet that no writer has had a bigger impact on beginning readers than Patricia Reilly Giff. Her series of books about Richard, Emily, and the rest of the kids in Ms. Rooney's class have set the standard for fiction that is both readable and relevant to first and second graders. Every book in this series is full of characters and events that will be familiar to children and parents alike as they live through a year full of home and school adventures. When children work their way through this series, they start off doubting they can read anything so long and then finish with complete confidence in their reading ability. There are too many titles to include here, but some of our favorites are: *The Beast in Ms. Rooney's Room* (the first title in the series, and where we meet Richard "the beast" Best and Emily Arrow—additional categories include fitting in; new experiences; feeling special), *In the Dinosaur's Paw* (winter; snow; luck), *Look Out Washington DC!* (travel; Washington, DC; government; U.S. history), *Showtime at the Polk Street School* (plays; theater; acting), *Watch Out Man-Eating Snake* (siblings; new experiences), and *Count Your Money With the Polk Street School* (money; counting).

BYE-BYE DICK AND JANE: BEGINNING-TO-READ SERIES

Parents encounter a lot of confusion when choosing books within the category variously named "Easy to Read," "Beginning to Read," "Early Chapter Books," etc. Many publishers have specific lines of books aimed at the child just venturing into solo reading. These will range from titles with no more than six words on a page to books with full pages of text and pictures every third page or so.

How are you to make sense of the labels, color codes, levels and recommendations that shout at you from the covers? Many families find a series that works for them and stick with it. The most popular ones are the *I Can Read* (HarperCollins) series and *Step into Reading* (Random House). These series have well thought out and easy to understand guidelines for parental use. Each one divides its list of titles into levels designed to take a child from the letter recognition stage all the way to chapter books.

Whatever books or series you choose, we recommend that the child, the parent, and the child's teacher work together to select titles that will teach both the skill and the joy of reading. And remember this as you choose: a book that has fewer and simpler words does not have to be boring nor is it excused from telling a good story.

Here are some easy readers that many beginners enjoy:
Start to Read series (School Zone)
Let Me Read series (Addison Wesley)
Frog and Toad books, Arnold Lobel
Little Bear books, Else Holmelund Minarik
Little Critter books, Mercer Mayer
Hop on Pop, Dr. Seuss
Go, Dog. Go!, P.D. Eastman
Green Eggs and Ham, Dr. Seuss
Ready . . . Set . . . Read, Joanna Cole
Get Ready, Get Set, Read! series (Barrons)
Danny and the Dinosaur, Syd Hoff
Harry the Dirty Dog, Gene Zion

For more assured beginners we recommend:
Yearling First Choice Chapter Books (Dell)
The Bravest Dog Ever: The True Story of Balto by Natalie Standiford
Junie B. Jones series, Barbara Park
Magic Tree House series, Mary Pope Osborne
Nate the Great series, Marjorie Sharmat
New Kids at the Polk Street School series, Patricia Reilly Giff
Finding Providence, Avi
Dust for Dinner, Turner
Amelia Bedelia books, Peggy Parish
The Kids of the Polk Street School series, Patricia Reilly Giff
The Pee Wee Scouts series, Judy Delton
Adventures of the Bailey School Kids by Debbie Dadey & Marcia T. Jones

Many books, regardless of size, series, or format, will fit the bill when you are looking for enchanting first reads. Do not limit yourself to a publisher's preselected list, a library or bookstore's beginning reader section, or even our advice. Sit down with your child and a selection of books—both picture books and others that interest you. Many families have given birth to readers without the help of a beginning reader program.

★ King Bidgood's in the Bathtub   PICTURE BOOK

AUTHOR: Audrey Wood • ILLUSTRATOR: Don Wood
HC: Harcourt Brace
THEMES: kings; baths; queens; cleverness; repetition; resourcefulness

A bathtime story? Why not! King Bidgood's having too much fun in his bath to get out. So he invites all the members of his court to join him. This one is a winner. Its imploring refrain—"King Bidgood's in the bathtub, and he won't get out! Oh, who knows what to do?"—causes children to demand a repeat performance. You might mention that the queen is the spitting image of Audrey Wood. And the page? Their son Bruce is much older now, but that is definitely him!

Ladybird Favorite Tales Series   EARLY READER

AUTHOR: Various • ILLUSTRATOR: Various
HC: Ladybird
THEMES: folklore; fairy tales

Nicely made and just perfect for smaller hands, here is a series of retellings of classic fairy tales expressly made for the new reader. Children will want to read and collect these brief, affordable hardcovers including: *The Three Billy Goats Gruff, Jack & the Beanstalk, Thumbelina, Chicken Licken,* and *Goldilocks & the Three Bears.*

UNREADY

Sometimes kids are just not ready to try something new, like an overnight at a friend's, learning to swim, or starting school. Rosemary Wells has written a threesome that reminds children and their parents that things take longer for some than for others: *Edward Unready for a Sleep Over, Edward Unready for Swimming,* and *Edward Unready for School.*

Being unready is not limited to the preschool set, nor is it confined to the reluctant child. Judith Viorst's *Earrings!* shows the frustrations a child can feel when she thinks she is ready (to have her ears pierced) and her parents don't. Viorst is just plain funny. And these are times when a laugh is good medicine!

Leo the Late Bloomer   PICTURE BOOK

AUTHOR: Robert Kraus • ILLUSTRATOR: Jose Aruego
HC/PB: HarperCollins
THEMES: self-respect; mothers and sons; fathers and sons; readiness

We've all met Leo. He's not reading yet. He's having trouble writing. Leo is not ready. This reassuring tale shows late bloomers that, in time, they too will take off. See the "Unready" sidebar for more books on this subject.

Let's Be Enemies   PICTURE BOOK

AUTHOR: Janice May Udry • ILLUSTRATOR: Maurice Sendak
HC/PB: HarperCollins
THEMES: friendship; disagreements; sharing

Sometimes friends don't get along, but it doesn't have to be the end of the world. John has had it with James. A friend shouldn't always want to be the boss, or throw sand, or take all the crayons. But friends work things out, and Udry and Sendak know how to get this across without being too sweet.

Let's Talk About It: Adoption   PICTURE BOOK NONFICTION

AUTHOR: Fred Rogers • ILLUSTRATOR: Jim Judkis (photographs)
HC: Putnam • PB: Paperstar
THEMES: adoption; family; diversity

In spare text accompanied by color photographs, *Let's Talk About It* books offer Mr. Rogers' characteristic straightforward, reassuring responses to questions children have about various issues: "Being in a family means belonging . . . belonging because you are loved and cared for—and because you give love and give care, too." By simply turning pages, parents can bring up issues that may be on their child's mind. Others in the series: *Let's Talk About It: Divorce, Let's Talk About It: Stepfamilies.*

Lili Backstage   PICTURE BOOK

AUTHOR/ILLUSTRATOR: Rachel Isadora
HC: Putnam
THEMES: ballet; dance; theater; grandfathers; dancers; costumes

Take a peek at what goes on behind the scenes in the prop room, makeup room, canteen, costume room, orchestra pit and more—as dancers prepare for a ballet performance. Isadora's paintings and informative asides make this a perfect addition to the libraries of young dancers and admirers of art. Isadora's other Lili books include: *Lili on Stage* and *Lili at Ballet.*

A Lion Named Shirley Williamson
PICTURE BOOK

AUTHOR/ILLUSTRATOR: Bernard Waber
HC: Houghton Mifflin
THEMES: lions; zoos; names; animals; jealousy

Lions Goobah, Poobah and Aroobah are not happy with Shirley Williamson, the newest lion at the zoo. After all, she gets special treatment. ". . . Seymour, the zookeeper, served Shirley her meals on a tray. 'But what am I to do?' said Seymour, 'I just couldn't shove food at her— not at someone named Shirley Williamson.' " Waber, who also wrote and illustrated the tales of Lyle the Crocodile, is his typically silly self in this delightful tale where a worrisome situation ends with a happy solution.

Little Bear
EARLY READER

AUTHOR: Else Holmelund Minarik • ILLUSTRATOR: Maurice Sendak
HC/PB: HarperCollins
THEMES: family; bears

Hicklebee's doors first opened in 1979. Little Bear was on the shelf. The simple, tender stories with Sendak's art continue to be a popular classic for beginning readers. Other Little Bear stories: A Kiss for Little Bear: *When Grandma decides to send a kiss to Little Bear, she enlists the help of several other animals.* Little Bear's Friend: *Little Bear meets Emily, a human.* Father Bear Comes Home: *Father Bear goes fishing and Little Bear and his friends anticipate his homecoming.* Little Bear's Visit: *Little Bear is excited to visit his grandparents.*

Little Blue and Little Yellow
PICTURE BOOK

AUTHOR/ILLUSTRATOR: Leo Lionni
PB: Mulberry
THEMES: color; concepts; friendship; family; change; diversity; belonging

When a little blue spot and a little yellow spot give each other a big hug, they turn green. An imaginative primer for the earliest stages of mixing color. See *Mouse Paint, Who Said Red,* and Ruth Heller's *Color* for other excellent books on the subject.

The Little House
PICTURE BOOK

AUTHOR/ILLUSTRATOR: Virginia Lee Burton
HC/PB: Houghton Mifflin
THEMES: change; cities; country life; houses; home; environment

Delightfully old-fashioned, yet no other book on this topic has gotten it so right. A house in the country is, over time, gradually surrounded by the city. The child reading this book gets a sense of the passage of the years and the changes wrought on once pristine land. A classic.

The Little Mouse, the Red Ripe Strawberry, and the Big Hungry Bear   PICTURE BOOK

    AUTHOR: Don and Audrey Wood • ILLUSTRATOR: Don Wood
    HC/PB: Child's Play Ltd.
    THEMES: bears; mice; strawberries; fear; cleverness

Wood's oversized illustrations draw the reader nose to nose with the character. The story begins with a voice asking a little mouse what he is doing. And then the voice says, "But, little Mouse, haven't you heard about the big, hungry Bear?" This isn't scary. It's funny and exciting and will capture your preschooler's attention. But be prepared, he'll want you to read it again, and may even want a strawberry to go with it.

Little Toot   PICTURE BOOK

    AUTHOR/ILLUSTRATOR: Hardie Gramatky
    HC: Putnam • PB: Paperstar
    THEMES: boats; courage; fear; determination

Little Toot is terrified of stormy seas, but he musters up his courage when an ocean liner is in trouble. The story of this now famous tugboat was first published in 1939, and continues to entertain children encouraged by the little guy who saves the day. Look at *The Little Red Ant and the Great Big Crumb* for another take on someone who is ready despite thinking he's not.

Livingstone Mouse   PICTURE BOOK

    AUTHOR: Pamela Duncan Edwards • ILLUSTRATOR: Henry Cole
    HC: HarperCollins
    THEMES: mice; geography; habitats; humor; wordplay

Livingstone mouse is searching for China. He can't find it in a cupboard, a sneaker, a picnic basket, or a lamppost. Young readers will like recognizing Livingstone's silly mistakes, but may need some help with the play-on-words ending.

Louella Mae, She's Run Away!   PICTURE BOOK

AUTHOR: Karen Beaumont Alarcon • ILLUSTRATOR: Rosanne Litzinger
HC: Henry Holt
THEMES: lost; searching game; pigs; family; rhyme; predictable

A rollicking chase around the farmyard gears up young listeners to wonder where Louella Mae has gone. "Round up the horses! Hitch up the team! Hop in the buckboard and look by the . . ." They'll shout out their guesses but will have to wait till you turn the page for an answer.

Madeline   PICTURE BOOK

AUTHOR/ILLUSTRATOR: Ludwig Bemelmans
HC: Viking
PB: Puffin
THEMES: Paris; rhyme; school; strong girls; travel; orphans; illness; gifts; hospitals; jealousy; mischief

"In an old house in Paris that was covered with vines lived twelve little girls in two straight lines." And one of them was spunky Madeline who woke one night with an attack of appendicitis and was rushed to the hospital. Empathy and jealousy come lightly into play here, but they take a back seat to a fun sense of mischief and togetherness. Madeline's adventures have delighted young children since this classic was first published in 1939. Other adventures about this small, spirited heroine are: *Madeline and the Bad Hat, Madeline and the Gypsies, Madeline's Rescue, Madeline's Christmas,* and *Madeline in London.*

The Maestro Plays   PICTURE BOOK

AUTHOR: Bill Martin, Jr. • ILLUSTRATOR: Vladimir Radunsky
HC: Henry Holt • PB: Voyager
THEMES: music; orchestras; vocabulary; adverbs

Carefully chosen words match the tempo, upbeat colors ignite the illustrations, and stretching the vocabulary is a bonus with each exaggerated read-aloud word. Throw your whole dramatic self into the reading of this one.

The Maggie B.   PICTURE BOOK

AUTHOR/ILLUSTRATOR: Irene Haas
HC: McElderry • PB: Aladdin
THEMES: sailing; boats; wishes; siblings; sea; strong girl; brothers; sisters; yearnings

We've wished on our share of stars, but when Margaret Barnstable did, she woke to find herself in the cabin of her very own ship, the Maggie B., and with her for company was her dear baby brother, James. Luscious watercolor paintings show Maggie's ship filled with flowers, chickens, a goat, a toucan, and just about anything else a self-reliant sailor needs.

The Magic Fan

PICTURE BOOK

AUTHOR/ILLUSTRATOR: Keith Baker
HC: Harcourt Brace • PB: Voyager
THEMES: Japan; self-respect; magic; folklore; creativity

Yoshi was a boy who loved to build things: wagons, fences, houses, stairs, tables and walls—everything that was needed in his village by the sea. But one day, with the help of a magic fan, he built something that had never been built before and used it to save the people in his village. Baker's brilliant paintings have their own magic in the shape of fan cut-outs that allow the reader to discover answers to Yoshi's difficult questions.

Mama Don't Allow

PICTURE BOOK

AUTHOR/ILLUSTRATOR: Thacher Hurd
HC/PB: HarperCollins
THEMES: music; swamps; bands; family; cleverness; triumph

Miles plays his saxophone a little too loudly for people's taste, and his bandmates are the only ones in town who appreciate his talents, so they go down to the swamp to play. Of course, the alligators in the swamp just love their music and invite the swamp band to play for them, and then be their dinner! This charming story has rhythm, cleverness, and a lot of heart. You will love reading—or even singing—this aloud to your family.

Math Start Series

PICTURE BOOK

AUTHOR: Stuart J. Murphy • ILLUSTRATOR: Various
HC/PB: HarperCollins
THEMES: math; counting; numbers; comparisons; time; problem solving

Stuart Murphy might have liked math when he was a kid if only it had been explained differently. He thinks people understand things best when they can see them, so he has come up with a series of his own math story books illustrated by Lois Ehlert, G. Brian Karas, Nadine Bernard Westcott, Frank Remkiewicz and other fabulous artists. They are divided into three levels: 1: Counting, ordering, patterning, and comparing sizes, ages 3 and up. 2: Adding, subtracting, time lines, estimating and fractions, ages 6 and up. 3: Multiplying, dividing, equations, problem solving, ages 7 and up. Here is just a sampling of the titles: Level 1: *The Best Bug Parade* (Holly Keller), *A Pair of Socks* (Lois Ehlert), *Just Enough Carrots* (Frank Remkiewicz) Level 2: *Elevator Magic* (G. Brian Karas), *Get Up and Go!* (Diane Greenseid), *The Best Vacation Ever* (Nadine Bernard Westcott) Level 3: *Betcha!* (S.D. Schindler), *What Color Is Camouflage?* (Megan Lloyd), *Too Many Kangaroo Things to Do!* (Kevin O'Malley).

Max
PICTURE BOOK

AUTHOR/ILLUSTRATOR: Rachel Isadora
HC: Simon & Schuster • PB: Aladdin
THEMES: dance; baseball; ballet; humor; gender roles; gentle boys

Max discovers that his sister's ballet class is a perfect place for him to improve his baseball skills. An enlightening story for young male athletes.

Max and Ruby's First Greek Myth: Pandora's Box PICTURE BOOK

AUTHOR/ILLUSTRATOR: **Rosemary Wells**
HC: Dial • PB: Puffin
THEMES: storytelling; myths; Greek mythology; folklore; curiosity

Max's sister Ruby has a jewelry box that Max finds irresistible, so she decides to read him a story about snooping. And what would be a more perfect choice than *Pandora's Box*? Wells has fun with this first introduction to Greek myths. Your kindergartner will too.

Problem! The retelling of the myth in this book plays a little too loose for me. I am all for encouraging storytellers, but the fact of the matter is that *Pandora's Box* doesn't go the way Ruby tells it. It is very Ruby-like to bend a myth to suit her purpose, but there is nothing in the book to indicate that the original story has been changed.

AUTHOR SPOTLIGHT ON ROSEMARY WELLS

Rosemary Wells gets it. There is no better writer today who can hone in on the emotional, sometimes funny, sometimes not, concerns of very young children. *Noisy Nora* arrived with a "monumental crash!" showing that Wells understands about being a middle child. There are not always advantages to being the youngest either, so Wells provided Morris and his "disappearing bag" (*Morris' Disappearing Bag*).

No matter where they fit in a family, children are sometimes just not ready, so Edward was created to comfort children who need a bit more time (*Edward in Deep Water, Edward Unready for School, Edward's Overwhelming Overnight*). And then there are Max and Ruby; Max knows exactly what he wants, but so does his older sister, Ruby.

Although Wells' work frequently combines her talents as author and illustrator, she does not always illustrate her own books. David McPhail's paintings in *Night Sounds, Morning Colors* are a perfect fit for Wells' poetic text. She teamed with artist Susan Jeffers in several outstanding ventures, including a retelling of Eric Knight's *Lassie Come Home; Forest of Dreams,* a poem that celebrates nature; and McDuff (*McDuff and the Baby, McDuff Comes Home, McDuff Moves In*), an irresistible dog who looks a good deal like the pets of both Jeffers and Wells.

Wells' range is astonishing. She has stretched the picture-book format to include families touched by war in *Waiting for the Evening Star* and *The Language of Doves.* She has also written *The Man in the Woods, When No One Was Looking,* and *Through the Hidden Door,* mysteries for young adults.

Two of Wells' works deserve special mention: Her illustrations for Iona Opie's *My Very First Mother Goose* showcase her talents as an artist at their most endearing and perfectly match Opie's selections of rhymes; and Wells surely deserves a place in heaven for the three-book collection, *Voyage to the Bunny Planet.* Through work that is poignant, humorous, and understanding, Rosemary Wells is a child's best friend. She shares children's concerns and lovingly brings them to their parents' attention.

Wells knows that board books do not have to be boring, so she uses them as a hilarious stage for Max and Ruby: *Max's Bath, Max's Bedtime, Max's Birthday, Max's Ride.*

Just a few more we can't resist mentioning: *Hazel's Amazing Mother, Bunny Cakes, Fritz and the Mess Fairy, Max's Dragon Shirt, Silent Night.*

And we know there's more wonder to come, so don't stop where this list does, by any means!

Max's Dragon Shirt   PICTURE BOOK

AUTHOR/ILLUSTRATOR: **Rosemary Wells**

HC: Dial • PB: Puffin

THEMES: siblings; shopping; lost; brothers; sisters; yearnings

"Dragon shirt, please!" says Max as he and older sister Ruby shop for clothing. Ruby reminds him that his pants are "disgusting," and there's only enough money to buy new pants, but by the book's end, Max has his shirt. Max and Ruby's predicaments bring smiles of recognition to young brothers and sisters who understand this pair.

May I Bring a Friend?   PICTURE BOOK

AUTHOR: Beatrice Schenk deRegniers • ILLUSTRATOR: Beni Montresor

HC: Simon & Schuster • PB: Aladdin

THEMES: manners; humor; kings; queens; comparisons; tea parties; friendship; diversity

When one has a daily invitation for tea from the king and queen, it makes sense to bring a friend. This fun Caldecott Medal winner shows how unusual friends can be.

Mean Soup   PICTURE BOOK

AUTHOR/ILLUSTRATOR: Betsy Everitt

HC: Harcourt Brace • PB: Voyager

THEMES: problem solving; bad days; emotions; mothers and sons

Get ready to throw your whole body into this read aloud. Sometimes when you feel crabby, you don't want to talk about it. Horace feels so mean at the end of a bad day that his mother helps him vent by making Mean Soup! This is not only fun on the good days, but perfect for letting out the mean stuff on bad ones.

The Midnight Farm   PICTURE BOOK

AUTHOR: Reeve Lindberg • ILLUSTRATOR: Susan Jeffers

HC: Dial • PB: Puffin

THEMES: bedtime; numbers; farms; animals, farm; fear of dark

"Here is the dark in the barn at night, where six cows stand, all black and white." It's easy not to notice that this is a counting book. Jeffers' enchanting art veils the farm's images in a film of darkness and combines with Lindbergh's soothing text to create a bedtime story that comforts on even the darkest nights.

Millions of Cats

PICTURE BOOK

AUTHOR/ILLUSTRATOR: Wanda Gag

HC: Putnam • PB: Paperstar

THEMES: cats; loneliness; pets; repetition; fighting

"Hundreds of cats, Thousands of cats, Millions and billions and trillions of cats" is what the old man brought home when his wife sent him off to find one pet to keep them company. That was far too many to feed, so the cats had to choose which one would stay. Gag's classic tale, first published in 1928, has the rhythm and repetition you find in a tune and it bounces around in your mind. Prepare for your child to request this one repeatedly.

Minerva Louise at School

PICTURE BOOK

AUTHOR/ILLUSTRATOR: Janet Morgan Stoeke

HC: Dutton

THEMES: school; chickens; wordplay; misunderstanding; humor; curiosity

We enjoy finding books where the child gets the joke before the character in the story does. Minerva Louise is one of those characters. This feather-brained hen who mistakes a school for a barn and cubbies for nesting boxes will keep young readers in stitches. Other titles include: *Minerva Louise* and *A Hat for Minerva Louise*.

The Miracle of the Potato Latkes

PICTURE BOOK

AUTHOR: Malka Penn • ILLUSTRATOR: Giora Carmi

HC/PB: Holiday House

THEMES: Judaism; Russia; Hanukkah; Jews; potatoes; faith; cooking; miracles; good deeds; recipes; neighbors

Tante Golda was a generous lady. Every year at Hanukkah time she "would reach into her wooden barrel and pick out eight of the biggest potatoes she could find . . . and fry them into the most delicious potato latkes in all of Russia." Each Hanukkah her friends and neighbors would crowd into her kitchen to taste her scrumptious latkes. But one year a poor harvest left her with no potatoes, and Tante Golda had to depend on a miracle. This story's joyful ending is made even happier with the inclusion of her "famous" latke recipe. Enjoy.

Mirette on the High Wire PICTURE BOOK

AUTHOR/ILLUSTRATOR: Emily Arnold McCully
HC: Putnam • PB: Paperstar
THEMES: friendship; teachers; talent; strong girls; courage

When Mirette sees one of her mother's boarders walking on the clothes-line, she is enchanted. Young readers, too, will be captivated by Bellini's skill as well as by the lessons learned by a teacher and his young student.

Miss Bindergarten Gets Ready for Kindergarten PICTURE BOOK

AUTHOR: Joseph Slate • ILLUSTRATOR: Ashley Wolff
HC: Dutton
THEMES: school; kindergarten; teachers; diversity; new experiences; rhyme; alphabet

A perfect starter for any child about to begin kindergarten or preschool. Every other two-page spread shows students at home: "Adam Krupp wakes up. Brenda Heath brushes her teeth," and their teacher "Miss Bindergarten gets ready for kindergarten." They'll recognize familiar activities as students prepare for school, and will be intrigued and perhaps comforted to see some of what their teacher does when she's not with them.

The Monster at the End of This Book PICTURE BOOK

AUTHOR: Jon Stone • ILLUSTRATOR: Mike Smollin
PB: Golden
THEMES: anticipation; surprises; monsters; humor; embarrassment; frustration

Lovable, furry old Grover stars in this Little Golden Book based on the character from Sesame Street. Warning the reader that scares lie ahead, Grover tries in vain to convince the reader not to turn the page, as it will bring her closer to "the monster at the end of this book." As your giggling child reader turns the pages anyway, Grover becomes more and more frustrated, trying more elaborate methods to stop the inevitable. With a desperate plea, he makes a final stand on the next to last page, only to have it revealed that HE is the monster. This is an example of how you cannot judge a book by format or price—good stories can be found anywhere.

The Monster Bed   PICTURE BOOK
AUTHOR: Jeanne Willis • ILLUSTRATOR: Susan Varley
HC: Lothrop
THEMES: fear of monsters; fear of the dark; bedtime; humor; comfort

Dennis is a monster afraid to sleep in his bed because there may be a human hiding underneath. Read this to the wary and to the ones who remember worrying about nighttime monsters. Fun, with a surprise ending, that will be a favorite.

Mordant's Wish   PICTURE BOOK
AUTHOR/ILLUSTRATOR: Valerie Coursen
HC: Henry Holt
THEMES: moles; wishes; turtles; connections

Mordant Mole wishes his cloud were a real turtle and that it was his friend. From a wish to a dandelion puff to a bike rider to a snow cone drip, a chain of events ultimately makes two wishes come true.

Writing with children? Try this. Read Mordant's Wish *out loud. Then, starting with a group (up to six), have each child write the name of an animal [peacock] on the top of the page and a made-up name [Prudence]. Next, they write a sentence beginning "I wish . . ." and ending with "said X" ["I wish I had a boysenberry pie" said Prudence]." Then the fun begins. Each child passes his sentence to the person on his left who adds a sentence. Once it's gotten back to its original place, that author ties the last sentence to the first. What a jumble! What fun to read each aloud!*

⋆ More, More, More, Said the Baby:
3 Love Stories   PICTURE BOOK
AUTHOR/ILLUSTRATOR: Vera Williams
HC: Greenwillow • PB: Mulberry
THEMES: babies; fathers; grandmothers; mothers; love; affection; cultural diversity

Here's a baby love story in three parts. Daddy, grandma and mama show their affection with hugs, chases, tosses, swings, tastes of toes, and a tuck into bed. Williams' cheery paintings capture the warmth of these babies imploring "More, More, More!" in a perfect bedtime book. Also available in a board book format.

Mouse Mess   PICTURE BOOK

AUTHOR/ILLUSTRATOR: Linnea Riley

HC: Scholastic

THEMES: mice; food; rhyme; messiness; kitchens

If you have to get rid of a mouse around your house, don't read this to your child. He'll want it for a pet. In the story, Mouse waits for the family to tiptoe upstairs to bed so he can get busy in their kitchen. "Crunch crunch he wants a cracker. Munch-munch, a cookie snacker." Brilliantly colored cut-paper collages provide the visuals, silly rhyme makes up the text, and the ending words are guessed before the last page is turned by delighted listeners.

Mouse Paint   PICTURE BOOK

AUTHOR/ILLUSTRATOR: Ellen Walsh

HC/PB: Harcourt Brace

THEMES: color; mice; art; paint; concepts; change

Three white mice find three jars of paint; red, yellow and blue. They think it's mouse paint and climb right in. Now there are three colored mice who puddle and mix and come up with other colors. Cheery, bold collages mix with humor to make this a fine choice for young ones experimenting with their own colors.

Mr. Rabbit and the Lovely Present   PICTURE BOOK

AUTHOR: Charlotte Zolotow • ILLUSTRATOR: Maurice Sendak

HC/PB: HarperCollins

THEMES: gifts; mothers and daughters; birthdays; color; imagination

A matter-of-fact conversation between a rabbit and a young girl searching for the perfect birthday gift for her mother makes up this long-loved tale.

Mr. Willowby's Christmas Tree   PICTURE BOOK

AUTHOR/ILLUSTRATOR: Robert Barry

PB: Dell

THEMES: Christmas; recycling; rhyme; trees; sharing; connections

The ultimate book on recycling the Christmas tree! Mr. Willowby's tree is too tall for the space intended, so the top gets lopped off. What to do? As the tree top shrinks, it gets passed on to another person, then another, finally winding up in the home of a mouse family. An endearing family read aloud that holds up year after year.

My Dog Never Says Please   PICTURE BOOK
AUTHOR: Suzanne Williams • ILLUSTRATOR: Tedd Arnold
HC: Dial
THEMES: manners; dogs; family; pets; misbehaving

Ginny Mae is tired of human habits like worrying about manners, cleaning her room and wearing shoes. Her complaint, "I want to be a dog,"
results in her joining the family's pet in the doghouse. Fun and spunky,
this character will delight children who struggle with their own parents'
unrelenting requests for good behavior.

My House Has Stars   PICTURE BOOK
AUTHOR: Megan McDonald • ILLUSTRATOR: Peter Catalanotto
HC: Orchard
THEMES: houses; cultural diversity; stars; geography; dwellings; nature

As night falls, children all over the world describe their houses and their
stars. "My house rocks me to sleep at night. I hear the water lapping the
sides of our boat, lapping the sides, lapping the sides." ". . . the sky looks
like a blue bowl filled with popcorn." A map is included on the last page
for geography buffs, but the point here is the children: the differences
in where they live, the similarities in the warmth of their families.

★ My Very First Mother Goose   PICTURE BOOK
EDITOR: Iona Opie • ILLUSTRATOR: **Rosemary Wells**
HC: Candlewick
THEMES: rhyme; Mother Goose

Destined to be a classic: more than sixty nursery rhymes chosen by Iona
Opie, illustrated in oversized full color art by Rosemary Wells. Nothing
scary here, these are rhymes to comfort. Pay attention to Wells' pictures,
she sneaks in an occasional surprise, as on page 14. We all know the
story of Humpty Dumpty, but look closely: Ah, now we know why he
fell in the first place! Some of these rhymes are also available in individual board books.

My Visit to the Aquarium   PICTURE BOOK NONFICTION
AUTHOR/ILLUSTRATOR: Aliki
HC/PB: HarperCollins
THEMES: aquariums; fish; animals, sea; rain forest; tide pools; rivers

Did you know that sharks don't have bones? Aliki provides all sorts of
curious facts about life in the water as she strolls the reader through a

tropical coral reef, a steamy rain forest, deep seas, tidepools, and rivers. By the way, see if you can find the child wearing a "Hicklebee's" tee-shirt!

Nana Upstairs & Nana Downstairs   PICTURE BOOK
AUTHOR/ILLUSTRATOR: Tomie dePaola
HC: Putnam • PB: Puffin
THEMES: family; death; grandmothers; loss; comparisons

Tommy loves his Sunday visits with his grandmother who lives downstairs, and his great-grandmother who lives upstairs. When 94-year-old Grandmother Upstairs dies, Tommy's family helps him adjust to her death and to understand that life's natural process is to start out young, grow old, perhaps very old, then die. For a warm, comforting story that shows young children that it is possible to cope with loss from death, this one is among the best.

Nanta's Lion: A Search-and-Find Adventure   PICTURE BOOK
AUTHOR/ILLUSTRATOR: Suse MacDonald
HC: Morrow Junior Books
THEMES: lions; strong girls; hunting; Africa; point of view

A fun book with clever pages cut into shapes that slowly reveal the lion that Nanta is hunting. Great fun to read to preschoolers.

★ The Napping House   PICTURE BOOK
AUTHOR: Audrey Wood • ILLUSTRATOR: Don Wood
HC: Harcourt Brace
THEMES: rhyme; cumulative story; bedtime; grandmothers; pets; naps

It's nap time, and in this house you'll find a cozy bed with a snoring granny, a dreaming child, a dozing dog . . . a pile of sleepy pets and people snuggled for a nap—until a tiny wakeful flea comes into the picture. Notice how Wood's paintings go from sleepy blues to wake-up yellows.

When people ask what three books are necessary for starting a baby's library, I always say, "Goodnight Moon, Pat the Bunny, and The Napping House."

Nate the Great   EARLY READER
AUTHOR: Marjorie Weinman Sharmat • ILLUSTRATOR: Marc Simont
PB: Dell
THEMES: mystery; dogs; gifted child; community; cleverness

A must for the reader just beginning to read chapter books. This outstanding series features the exploits of the smartest detective around, Nate the Great, and his dog, Sludge, as they uncover and solve mysteries in their neighborhood. Other titles include: *Nate the Great and the Stolen Base, Nate the Great and the Tardy Tortoise,* and *Nate the Great and the Pillowcase.* If you'd like another series on the same reading and interest level that will further delight your mystery lover, look for the *Cam Jansen* books, by David Adler.

Nell Nuggett and the Cow Caper   PICTURE BOOK
AUTHOR: Judith Enderle and Stephanie Gordon Tessler • ILLUSTRATOR: Paul Yalowitz
HC: Simon & Schuster
THEMES: strong girls; cows; horses; U.S. history, the Old West; triumph

With a text that will please many a preschooler at read-aloud time, here is the story of how Nell gets her best cow, Goldie, back from the baddest man anywhere, Nasty Galoot. A sly sense of humor in the illustrations and an ear for repetitive rhythm make this a true foot-stomper!

Night Becomes Day   PICTURE BOOK
AUTHOR/ILLUSTRATOR: Richard McGuire
HC: Viking
THEMES: predictable; wordplay; zany; connections

Each page evolves into the next with subtle associations: "Night becomes day, And day becomes bright, Bright becomes sun, And sun becomes . . . shine." It's great fun to have young listeners guess what word is coming next. There are no wrong answers for the youngest ones, just great opportunities to talk about words. Older children can go further with the words, to try and guess which one the author chose in the sequence.

Nine-In-One Grr! Grr!: A Folktale from the Hmong People of Laos   PICTURE BOOK
AUTHOR: Blia Xiong • ILLUSTRATOR: Nancy Hom
HC/PB: Children's Book Press
THEMES: Hmong; tigers; birds; trickster tales; Laos; folklore

It takes a smart bird to trick a tiger. And this colorful book, which shows off the Hmong folk art tradition of appliquéd story cloths, offers up a trick clever enough to limit the tiger population to one every nine years.

No Fighting, No Biting!   PICTURE BOOK

AUTHOR: Else Holmelund Minarik • ILLUSTRATOR: Maurice Sendak
HC/PB: HarperCollins
THEMES: siblings; fighting; disagreements

Simple to read and a must to have ready for those times when the children's quarreling gets out of hand. You can read it to them or they can read it to you. Either way there is sure to be peace and quiet, at least while reading the book.

★ Noisy Nora   PICTURE BOOK

AUTHOR/ILLUSTRATOR: **Rosemary Wells**
HC: Dial
THEMES: new baby; jealousy; frustration; family; rhyme; siblings

Nora's a middle child. Her older sister gets to do all the fun things and her baby brother needs constant attention, so Nora has to wait. "First she banged the window, then she slammed the door, Then she dropped her sister's marbles on the kitchen floor."

This was a favorite in our house, and I didn't even have a middle child .

(Although I suppose the fact that you are the fourth of five children has no bearing on your liking this...)

Nuts to You   PICTURE BOOK

AUTHOR/ILLUSTRATOR: Lois Ehlert
HC: Harcourt Brace
THEMES: squirrels; birds; insects; plants

Artist Lois Ehlert loves watching squirrels from her window, and on the day one worked his way inside, this story came to life. On each page Ehlert identifies plants, birds, and insects, and she includes a glossary of details.

★ Nutshell Library   PICTURE BOOK BOXED SET

AUTHOR/ILLUSTRATOR: Maurice Sendak
HC: HarperCollins
THEMES: alphabet; alligators; seasons; soup; months; counting; misbehaving; mischief

Sheer perfection! Contained in one little box are four tiny hardcover books: *Chicken Soup with Rice* is a guide to the months and seasons, each one a better occasion than the last for eating that wholesome comfort food, chicken soup with rice; *Pierre* is a cautionary tale in which a boy who says only "I don't care!" gets eaten by a lion and learns to care; *Alligators All Around* is an alphabet book; and *One Was Johnny* is a counting book of considerable mischief. Sendak's illustrations match the subject matter perfectly, and the tiny size is just right for young hands. Individual paperback editions are available of the four titles.

Oink   PICTURE BOOK
AUTHOR/ILLUSTRATOR: Arthur Geisert
HC/PB: Houghton Mifflin
THEMES: pigs; mothers; farms; humor; discipline

Almost wordless, but there is nothing about this book that's quiet. When mother pig falls asleep, her babies sneak off and get in trouble over their heads. Point the sound words out to young listeners and they too will be shouting, "Oink!"

The Old Ladies Who Liked Cats   PICTURE BOOK
AUTHOR: Carol Greene • ILLUSTRATOR: Loretta Krupinski
HC/PB: HarperCollins
THEMES: cats; science; Darwin; connections; nature

A town's mayor demands that all cats be locked up at night, thereby disturbing the balance of nature. Based on a story Charles Darwin told about cats and clover, this tale teaches an important lesson about how we depend on other creatures.

The Old Man & His Door   PICTURE BOOK
AUTHOR: Gary Soto • ILLUSTRATOR: Joe Cepeda
HC: Putnam
THEMES: misunderstanding; Spanish; humor; wordplay; Mexico

"La puerta. El puerco. There's no difference to el Viejo!" The door. The pig. There's no difference to the old man! Soto's tale of an old man who is very good at working in his garden but not so good at listening to his wife offers the same kind of silly situations found in Jewish tales of Chelm. Have fun with these, and learn some Spanish words while you're at it. A glossary is included.

Old Mother Hubbard and Her Wonderful Dog PICTURE BOOK

AUTHOR/ILLUSTRATOR: James Marshall
HC/PB: Farrar Straus & Giroux
THEMES: dogs; friendship; humor; rhyme; community; folktale variations

James Marshall could be very funny, and this twist to an old nursery rhyme is hilarious. From the dog's shocked expression in finding the cupboard bare, and his feigned death—"Dear Mother H, I simply cannot live without me bones, Love, Your Dog"—to the final curtsy, there's a chuckle a page.

On Market Street PICTURE BOOK

AUTHOR: Arnold Lobel • ILLUSTRATOR: Anita Lobel
HC: Greenwillow • PB: Mulberry
THEMES: alphabet; shopping; rhyme; markets; food; imagination

". . . Such wonder there on Market Street
So much to catch my eye!
I strolled the length of Market Street
To see what I might buy.
and I bought . . ."

Inspired by 17th-century French trade engravings, Lobel's fascinating paintings are of the shopkeepers patterned entirely of his or her wares. With word and painting to a page, the first few pages are comprised of these words: apples, books, clocks, doughnuts. The Lobels claim that "A" representing "apple" and "B" for "books" was intentional, "One is nourishment for the body, the other is nourishment for the mind." This treat is nourishment for the imagination.

On Mother's Lap PICTURE BOOK

AUTHOR: Ann Herbert Scott • ILLUSTRATOR: Glo Coalson
HC/PB: Clarion
THEMES: new baby; jealousy; Inuit; sisters; siblings

Michael learns there is plenty of room on mother's lap for his new baby sister, his boat, dolly, puppy, reindeer blanket and himself.

Once There Was a Bull . . . (Frog)   PICTURE BOOK
AUTHOR: Rick Walton • ILLUSTRATOR: Greg Hally
HC: Gibbs Smith
THEMES: wordplay; animals; guessing; humor; connections

What a thrill it was to discover this gem! From the three year old who will get a kick out of the pictures to the second grader who can't wait to outsmart grown-ups, this play on words—and pictures—will delight anyone who likes active participation in stories. Frog has lost his hop. He looks for it under a toad . . . (stool), behind a dog . . . (house) and under a hedge . . . (hog). Make this into a guessing game, and prepare yourself for a surprise at each turn of a page!

1 Gaping Wide-Mouthed Hopping Frog   PICTURE BOOK
AUTHOR/ILLUSTRATOR: Leslie Tryon
HC: Atheneum
THEMES: frogs; mail carrier; numbers; counting; repetition; cumulative story; math

Frog is the mail carrier who takes us through a busy village, hopping forward through numbers and back again. This lively approach to counting, with its cumulative rhyme, has the kind of text children like to repeat.

Onstage & Backstage at the Night Owl Theater   PICTURE BOOK
AUTHOR: Ann Hayes • ILLUSTRATOR: Karmen Thompson
HC: Harcourt Brace
THEMES: theater; acting; vocabulary; folktale variation

"Cinderella" will be opening in four weeks. "Actors must be chosen, lines must be learned, costumes must be sewn, and sets must be built." From choosing the players to the final curtain call, a complete cast of animal characters shows how it all gets done. A glossary of "Theater Words" is included.

Our Granny   PICTURE BOOK
AUTHOR: Margaret Wild • ILLUSTRATOR: Julie Vivas
HC/PB: Houghton Mifflin
THEMES: grandmothers; comparisons; humor; diversity

Wild's words and Vivas' hilarious art add up to a very funny comparison of today's grannies.

Owl Babies   PICTURE BOOK
AUTHOR: Martin Waddell • ILLUSTRATOR: Patrick Benson
HC: Candlewick
THEMES: owls; mothers; animal babies; fear of separation

"What's all the fuss?" Owl Mother asked. "You knew I'd come back."
These comforting words are just what owl babies need. And this reassuring story is the perfect antidote for youngsters who worry when their
parents leave. Also available in a board book format.

Ox-Cart Man   PICTURE BOOK
AUTHOR: Donald Hall • ILLUSTRATOR: Barbara Cooney
HC: Viking • PB: Puffin
THEMES: oxen; jobs; U.S.A., New England; social studies; U.S. history,
19th century; seasons; markets; family

A family makes mittens, a shawl, birch brooms, candles and shingles.
They gather goose feathers, honey, and wool. They grow turnips and
cabbages, potatoes and apples. One working-together family creates
enough to sell at Portsmouth Market to buy what they need to begin the
cycle again. Look back at life in 19th century New England with a simple turn of each beautifully illustrated page.

Papa, Please Get the Moon for Me   PICTURE BOOK
AUTHOR/ILLUSTRATOR: Eric Carle
HC: Simon & Schuster
THEMES: moon; fathers and daughters; gifts; science; humor

Monica wants to play with the moon and her father tries hard to get it
for her. Pages open up and out for tall, wide, humor-filled looks at the
sky and the phases of the moon. Supplement your reading of this book
with Seymour Simon's *Star Walk* or *Our Solar System*.

Papa!   PICTURE BOOK
AUTHOR/ILLUSTRATOR: Philippe Corentin
HC: Chronicle
THEMES: fear of monsters; bedtime; parents; fathers; monsters

Stories about monster children afraid of humans have been done before,
but in this treasure both boys—human and monster—will make you
laugh. It's a great bedtime book if you like serving up a few giggles with
good night.

Pass the Fritters, Critters   PICTURE BOOK

AUTHOR: Cheryl Chapman • ILLUSTRATOR: Susan Roth
HC: Macmillan
THEMES: manners; communication; meals

Here's a tasty lesson in manners that shows how to act at the dining table: polite.

Peck, Slither, and Slide   PICTURE BOOK

AUTHOR/ILLUSTRATOR: Suse MacDonald
HC: Harcourt Brace
THEMES: vocabulary; verbs; guessing; animals; puzzles

A vocabulary stretching guessing game for the very young . . . on the first page a bold verb, on the second the animal it describes!

Pee Wee Scouts series   EARLY READER

AUTHOR: Judy Delton • ILLUSTRATOR: Alan Tiegreen
PB: Dell
THEMES: friendship; school; clubs; belonging

The *Pee Wee Scouts* series is written for children ready for early chapter books, dead center of our "E" category. They are entertaining and deal with subjects of keen interest to that age range. *Camp Ghost Away* for example, deals with the excitement of going camping with friends and the reality of how moods can change in the middle of the night when strange noises take over. These are great choices for reading aloud first chapters, or trading chapters, with beginning readers. Because they deal with a variety of subjects, you can begin by choosing titles with specific interest for you or your child. Representative titles in the series include: *Camp Ghost Away* (homesickness; camping; summer; fear of the dark), *Teeny Weeny Zucchinis* (gardening; harvest; celebrations; money), *Pee Wee Pool Party* (swimming; summer; courage), *All Dads on Deck* (boats; gentle boys; fathers; fishing; self-respect; diversity), *Piles of Pets* (animals; pets; problem solving), *Lights, Action, Land-Ho!* (theater; acting; teamwork; Columbus; selfishness), *Moans and Groans and Dinosaur Bones* (dinosaurs; travel; cooperation; trains; museums), and *Bookworm Buddies* (reading; responsibility; competition; libraries).

Peter Spier's Rain
PICTURE BOOK

AUTHOR/ILLUSTRATOR: Peter Spier
HC: Doubleday • PB: Dell
THEMES: wordless; comparisons; rain; weather; storms; play; siblings; mud; family

Dark clouds gather above as a brother and sister play in their backyard. At the onset of rain, they dash inside to the coziness of a warm home and family. In the morning the storm is over, and into their galoshes they step, put on their slickers and venture outside to the magic of puddles, mud and reflections. Not a single word is found here, but with each turn of the page you'll find images of the joy of nature or the comfort of home. For another look at how rain affects us, see *The Rain,* by Michael Laser.

Peter's Chair
PICTURE BOOK

AUTHOR/ILLUSTRATOR: Ezra Jack Keats
PB: HarperCollins
THEMES: siblings; new baby; brothers; sisters; jealousy; African American

Life isn't easy for Peter with that new baby sister, but he comes around. Keats' collages combine with a common theme to keep this classic popular. For another book on the same topic, but with a girl protagonist, see: *Julius, The Baby of the World.*

The Philharmonic Gets Dressed
PICTURE BOOK

AUTHOR: Karla Kuskin • ILLUSTRATOR: Marc Simont
PB: HarperCollins
THEMES: orchestras; music; dressing; diversity; cities; musical instruments; readiness

They clean themselves, put on their clothes, and travel to the concert, all 105 members of the orchestra. How Kuskin thought to find fascination in the different ways people get ready, we don't know, but it's there. It's fun, and it allows a child a glimpse into what goes on behind the scenes. Like Komaiko's *I Like the Music,* and Hayes' *Meet the Orchestra,* this is a terrific book to read before a first concert.

Pigs in the Mud in the Middle of the Rud
PICTURE BOOK

AUTHOR: Lynn Plourde • ILLUSTRATOR: John Schoenherr
HC: Blue Sky Press
THEMES: animals, farm; repetition; grandmothers; family; problem solving; mud

Some stories are raucous. This is one. If you are planning on a book to read before bedtime, we don't recommend it at all. If you don't like raising your voice in exuberance don't pick this one up. It is fun, hilarious. There are a feisty grandmother in a Model-T Ford, pigs that won't budge, hens that won't scatter, sheep that won't shuffle, and bulls that won't charge. Lots of repetition and anticipation. This picture book works perfectly.

The Piñata Maker/El Piñatero   PICTURE BOOK NONFICTION
AUTHOR/ILLUSTRATOR: George Ancona (photographs)
HC/PB: Harcourt Brace
THEMES: Mexico; piñatas; celebrations; bilingual

Here's a bilingual, photographic glimpse of life in a Mexican village. From the initial gathering of paper to the final breaking at the end, we're given a complete tour of the art of making a piñata.

The Popcorn Book   PICTURE BOOK NONFICTION
AUTHOR/ILLUSTRATOR: Tomie dePaola
HC/PB: Holiday House
THEMES: popcorn; cooking; recipes; science; ancient history

DePaola's typical fun pictures add humor to interesting facts about popcorn. He also includes two recipes for popcorn enthusiasts.

Possum Magic   PICTURE BOOK
AUTHOR: Mem Fox • ILLUSTRATOR: Julie Vivas
HC: Gulliver • PB: Voyager
THEMES: magic; Australia; grandmothers; food; snakes; opussum

Mem Fox takes some of her own storytelling magic and gives it to Hush's grandmother, who could make "wombats blue and kooka burras pink. She made dingoes smile and emus shrink. But the best magic of all was the magic that made Hush invisible." But when Grandma Poss forgets the magic that makes her visible again, she and Hush set out across Australia to find the needed blending of food. Magic, new foods, and a glossary of Australian words are just the right mix.

Pretend You're a Cat   PICTURE BOOK
AUTHOR: Jean Marzollo • ILLUSTRATOR: Jerry Pinkney
HC: Dial • PB: Puffin
THEMES: rhyme; pretending; acting; animals

"Can you climb? Can you leap? Can you stretch? Can you sleep? Can you hiss? Can you scat? Can you purr like a cat?" What else can you do? Snort. Run. Dig. Leap. Make room, this picture book will get your youngster moving.

Quick as a Cricket   PICTURE BOOK
AUTHOR: Audrey Wood • ILLUSTRATOR: Don Wood
HC: Child's Play
THEMES: comparisons; self-respect; wordplay; similes

"I'm as tough as a rhino, I'm as gentle as a lamb. I'm as brave as a tiger, I'm as shy as a shrimp . . ." A celebration of "all I can be," this cheery, colorful collection of comparisons continues to be a hit.

The Quilt Story   PICTURE BOOK
AUTHOR: Tony Johnston • ILLUSTRATOR: Tomie dePaola
HC: Putnam • PB: Paperstar
THEMES: quilts; moving; art; social studies; pioneers; mothers and daughters; crafts

A pioneer mother stitched a quilt to keep her daughter warm. Many years later, a young girl discovers the quilt and makes it her own. DePaola's folk-art style and Johnston's warm telling make this a cozy, wrap-up-in-a-quilt-and-listen story.

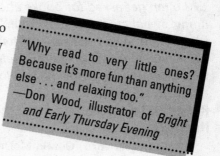

"Why read to very little ones? Because it's more fun than anything else . . . and relaxing too."
—Don Wood, illustrator of Bright and Early Thursday Evening

Rain Talk   PICTURE BOOK
AUTHOR: Mary Serfozo • ILLUSTRATOR: Keiko Narahashi
HC: Atheneum • PB: Aladdin
THEMES: rain; sound; onomatopoeia

A lovely read aloud, combining the sounds of rain and watercolor illustrations to give the feeling of being in a rainstorm.

The Rainbabies   PICTURE BOOK
AUTHOR: Laura Krauss Melmed • ILLUSTRATOR: Jim LaMarche
HC: Lothrop
THEMES: parents; magic; moon; wishes; adoption; little folk

Kids love the idea of having tiny people of their own to play with. Rainbabies offers up a whole handful, twelve to be exact. This fantasy with its touch of moon magic shows that loyal, loving caretakers can have their own dreams come true. If you see the cover of this book you will be compelled by the luminous art to open it!

Not me! I thought books like this were creepy when I was a kid. Don't even get me started on *Stuart Little!*

Rat and the Tiger　　　　　　　　　PICTURE BOOK
AUTHOR/ILLUSTRATOR: Keiko Kasza • PB: Paperstar
THEMES: bullies; friendship; triumph; sharing; humor; playing

Rat decides that even though he is just a tiny little rat, he will not be bullied by his best friend, Tiger. Great fun and perfect for the child who has Tigers in his life.

I often get asked for books about sharing and about bullies. This funny, sweet story includes both. The bully reminds me of someone I know, and when the rat—"What could I say? I'm just a tiny little rat"—finally stands up for himself, I want to cheer. Read this aloud to your youngster. You'll have a lot to talk about.

Raven: A Trickster Tale from the Pacific Northwest　　　　　　　　　PICTURE BOOK
AUTHOR/ILLUSTRATOR: Gerald McDermott
HC: Harcourt Brace
THEMES: ravens; birds; Native American; trickster tales; sun; U.S.A., the Pacific Northwest

Raven feels sorry for those who have to live in a dark world, and when he discovers it's the Sky Chief who has hoarded all the light, he moves into action. McDermott's award-winning illustrations—brilliant colors with bold graphic characters—prove that some of our finest art is found on the pages of children's books.

Read-Aloud Rhymes for the Very Young　　　　POETRY ANTHOLOGY
EDITOR: Jack Prelutsky • ILLUSTRATOR: Marc Brown
HC: Knopf
THEMES: celebrations; rhymes

200 poems, chosen with care by poet Prelutsky, celebrate all a young child encounters from morning to night. Add this to your permanent collection.

Richard Scarry's Best Word Book Ever   REFERENCE
AUTHOR/ILLUSTRATOR: Richard Scarry
HC: Golden
THEMES: words; vocabulary

You have seen Richard Scarry's books everywhere from bookstores to supermarkets to gas station gift shops. His popularity comes from his ability to combine detail with cute in a way that kids love and parents can stand. His busy picture books are ideal for the ages of 2 to 5, and this word book is one of our favorites. Of the seemingly millions of his other titles, the others we strongly admire are: *Richard Scarry's Busy Town* (towns; cities; home; jobs; community), *Richard Scarry's Cars and Trucks and Things That Go* (cars; trucks; airplanes; trains; buses; transportation; motorcycles), and *Richard Scarry's What Do People Do All Day* (jobs; careers).

Rosalie   PICTURE BOOK
AUTHOR: Joan Hewitt • ILLUSTRATOR: Donald Carrick
HC: Lothrop
THEMES: dogs; aging; pets; veterinarians; family

Pets grow old and lose their spunk. Rosalie is an old dog who can't hear, and can't hike, but she is loved. And don't worry, she does not die.

Ruby the Copycat   PICTURE BOOK
AUTHOR/ILLUSTRATOR: Peggy Rathmann
HC/PB: Scholastic
THEMES: friendship; teachers; school; self-respect; envy; copycats

Ruby is a new student in Miss Hart's class. Angela is the girl with the pretty red bow in her hair. Soon Ruby wears a pretty red bow and copies Angela until Miss Hart helps her to see that she has talents of her own. Rathmann makes kids laugh, and hits typical school-age insecurites right on the mark.

The Runaway Bunny   PICTURE BOOK

AUTHOR: Margaret Wise Brown • ILLUSTRATOR: Clement Hurd
HC/PB: HarperCollins
THEMES: mothers; love; patience; trust; imagination; connections; comfort; running away

Children can't help but be comforted by this mother, steadfast in showing her son that she will be there for him, regardless of how far his imagination takes him. First published in 1942, generations of readers have been reassured by its loving message. Also available in a board book format.

The Salamander Room   PICTURE BOOK

AUTHOR: Anne Mazer • ILLUSTRATOR: Steve Johnson
HC: Knopf • PB: Dragonfly
THEMES: salamanders; pets; nature; environment; gentle boy

Kids want to take in critters, which might be all right for the child but not so good for the critter. This is the book to help explain to a child that every living thing has its proper place. Told in a gentle, cumulative style, the message of the story is accompanied by astounding art that brings you right inside the book.

Sam and the Tigers   PICTURE BOOK

AUTHOR: Julius Lester • ILLUSTRATOR: Jerry Pinkney
HC: Dial
THEMES: tigers; cleverness; folktale variations; triumph

"There was a little boy in Sam-sam-sa-mara named Sam. Sam's mama was also named Sam. So was Sam's daddy. In fact, all the people in Sam-sam-sa-mara were named Sam. But nobody ever got confused about which Sam was which, and that's why nobody was named Joleen or Natisha or Willie." Julius Lester knows how to come up with a straight-talk, curious, wonder-what's-coming tale. And this retelling of the *Story of Little Black Sambo* is just that. The conversations between Sam and the tigers who want to eat him are hysterical. Pinkney's paintings wrap around the pages, beautiful and action-packed. For a very different retelling, see *The Story of Little Babaji.*

Santa's Favorite Story   PICTURE BOOK

AUTHOR: Aoki Hisako and Ivan Gantschev • ILLUSTRATOR: Ivan Gantschev

HC: Simon & Schuster • PB: Aladdin

THEMES: Christmas; animals; Santa Claus; Nativity; storytelling; Christianity

The forest animals are concerned that Christmas can't happen without Santa. He assures them that it will come with or without him by telling them the story of the first Christmas. Watercolors provide a cozy background to this blending of a popular holiday character with the true meaning of Christmas.

Santa's Short Suit Shrunk and Other
Christmas Tongue Twisters   EARLY READER

AUTHOR: Nola Buck • ILLUSTRATOR: Sue Truesdell

HC/PB: HarperCollins

THEMES: Christmas; tongue twisters; humor

Great fun for early readers, these silly sentences will have them giggling as they learn to read. Don't forget the Halloween version: *Creepy Crawly Critters!*

Scared Silly   PICTURE BOOK

AUTHOR/ILLUSTRATOR: Marc Brown

HC/PB: Little Brown

THEMES: humor; monsters; courage

It may be "a book for the brave," but with Brown's silly illustrations it's clear that the theme in this collection of poems and stories is not to frighten children, but to help them replace fear with humor.

Scary, Scary Halloween   PICTURE BOOK

AUTHOR: **Eve Bunting** • ILLUSTRATOR: Jan Brett

HC/PB: Clarion

THEMES: Halloween; fear of dark; monsters; ghosts; witches; pumpkins; fear of monsters; cats; rhyme

Scary, yes, but only as scary as you want it to be. Brett's monsters have enough dance in their steps to cancel terror. Bunting's rhyme can be read as scary as your child desires. A Halloween book you can have fun with, from preschoolers to second graders dressing up for the holiday.

Seven Blind Mice   PICTURE BOOK

AUTHOR/ILLUSTRATOR: Ed Young
HC: Philomel
THEMES: India; elephants; folklore; blindness; rhyme; mice; color;
senses; point of view

"Knowing in part may make a fine tale, but wisdom comes from seeing
the whole." Ed Young's moral comes at the end of his version of the old
story, "The Blind Men and the Elephant." Each extraordinary page again
shows that some of our country's most striking art is found in picture
books.

She'll Be Comin' Round the Mountain   PICTURE BOOK

AUTHOR: Tom and Debbie Birdseye • ILLUSTRATOR: Andrew Glass
HC/PB: Holiday House
THEMES: music; family; songs; imagination

The Birdseyes have put a twist on this familiar song where the whole
family gets involved making up verses. Children will have fun singing
this one—and adding rhythms and refrains of their own!

Sheep in a Jeep   PICTURE BOOK

AUTHOR: Nancy Shaw • ILLUSTRATOR: Margot Apple
HC/PB: Houghton Mifflin
THEMES: jeeps; rhyme; mishaps; sheep

An irresistible series of picture books featuring a hapless group of sheep,
all told in a few carefully chosen rhyming words. Not only side-split-
tingly funny, but a great example of how to get the most story out of the
fewest words, especially if there's a clever illustrator like Margot Apple
to assist. Other adventures include *Sheep in a Shop, Sheep on a Ship,
Sheep Out to Eat, Sheep Take a Hike,* and *Sheep Trick or Treat.*

Shy Charles   PICTURE BOOK

AUTHOR/ILLUSTRATOR: **Rosemary Wells**
HC: Dial • PB: Puffin
THEMES: self-respect; shyness; babysitters; gentle boys; courage; par-
ents

Charles is painfully shy, but when a situation requires him to move into
action, he performs like a hero. Wells portrays parents and friends who
possess the sensitivity and understanding we wish all shy children could
find.

Sitting on the Farm
PICTURE BOOK

AUTHOR: Bob King • ILLUSTRATOR: Bill Slavin

HC: Orchard

THEMES: rhyme; farms; animals, farm; cumulative story; food; songs; meals; repetition

Much like a campfire chant, this cumulative verse builds with repetition that stays in your mind all day. Youngsters love it. "Sitting on the farm, happy as can be, I had a little bug on my knee. I said, 'Hey, Bug, get off my knee.' Well, that old bug said, 'No siree!' So I picked up the telephone . . ." Cheery illustrations from a variety of perspectives add to the humor of this tale of a young girl who invites bigger animals to help her get rid of smaller ones. We guarantee you'll have youngsters shouting out "Munch! munch! munch!" the first time through. Music is at the back.

Six Creepy Sheep
PICTURE BOOK

AUTHOR: Judith R. Enderle and Stephanie G. Tessler • ILLUSTRATOR: John O'Brien

HC: Boyds Mills • PB: Puffin

THEMES: Halloween; spooky stories; rhyme; sheep

A cute read aloud, perfect for Halloween or any other lightly scary occasion. Sequels include *Six Snowy Sheep, Six Sleepy Sheep,* and *Six Sandy Sheep.*

Six Sick Sheep
PICTURE BOOK

AUTHOR: **Joanna Cole** • ILLUSTRATOR: Alan Tiegreen

HC: Morrow

THEMES: tongue twisters; vocabulary

If you like word play, this is the book for you. There are more than 100 short, long, wide, thin, vocabulary-stretching, tongue-tangling twisters!

Skip Across the Ocean: Nursery Rhymes
From Around the World
POETRY ANTHOLOGY

AUTHOR: Floella Benjamin • ILLUSTRATOR: Sheila Moxley

HC/PB: Orchard

THEMES: rhyme; lullabies; cultural diversity; nature; geography; social studies

Organized by Lullabies, Action Rhymes, Nature and Grab Bag, gaming, galloping, singing rhymes come from all over the world to make up this multicultural collection. Some are in their own language as well as English. Some come with instructions: "Bounce baby slowly for the first verse, then faster and faster as you 'gee up.'" All are brightly illustrated and show the richness of rhyme across the globe.

Small Green Snake   PICTURE BOOK
AUTHOR: Libba Moore Gray • ILLUSTRATOR: Holly Meade
HC/PB: Orchard
THEMES: snakes; lessons; mothers; mischief; wordplay; misbehaving

"With a zip and a zag, and a wiggle and a wag, Small Green Snake slid down a moss green stone and startled his mother, who was stretched out in the grass like a lush lime ribbon." The language is great fun, and as a bonus, this brightly colored picture book offers an important lesson in listening to your elders!

The Snail's Spell   PICTURE BOOK
AUTHOR: Joanne Ryder • ILLUSTRATOR: Lynne Cherry
HC: Viking • PB: Puffin
THEMES: snails; gardens; nature; science; point of view; imagination

In a garden rich with wildlife, a young boy shrinks in size and experiences life as a snail might. In colorful details and few words, this quiet gem offers a child new perspective and frees his imagination to curl up and find a place under a petal of its own.

The Snowy Day   PICTURE BOOK
AUTHOR/ILLUSTRATOR: Ezra Jack Keats
HC: Viking • PB: Puffin
THEMES: snow; African American; weather; play

Keats' bold, Caldecott Medal-winning art shows a young boy enveloped in the quiet magic of the first snowfall. Also available in a board book edition.

Somebody Loves You, Mr. Hatch   PICTURE BOOK
AUTHOR: Eileen Spinelli • ILLUSTRATOR: Paul Yalowitz
HC: Simon & Schuster • PB: Aladdin
THEMES: friendship; love; mail carrier; mail; self-respect; Valentine's Day; celebrations; neighbors; community; change

"Mr. Hatch was tall and thin and he did not smile." That is, until he got an anonymous valentine with a message that read "Somebody loves you." It's amazing how a person changes when he feels loved. It can change the whole neighborhood, which is exactly what happens in this story. A warm Valentine for the entire year.

Something From Nothing   PICTURE BOOK

AUTHOR/ILLUSTRATOR: Phoebe Gilman
HC: Scholastic
THEMES: folklore; Judaism; comfort; change

When Joseph's baby blanket becomes tattered and worn, his mother suggests, "It is time to throw it out." But Joseph's grandpa saves the day. With a snip! snip! the blanket becomes a jacket. And when the jacket is too small, it becomes a vest. At each stage grandpa performs miracles with his snipping and stitching until nothing is left, except a final treat from Joseph. Another version of this tale can be found in *Bit by Bit*.

Splash!   PICTURE BOOK

AUTHOR/ILLUSTRATOR: Ann Jonas
HC: Greenwillow
THEMES: math; concepts; ponds; animals; comparisons

Bright colors dazzle the young reader who soon finds out that keeping track of the critters hopping in and out of the pond is the trick.

A Squash and a Squeeze   PICTURE BOOK

AUTHOR: Julia Donaldson • ILLUSTRATOR: Axel Scheffler
HC: McElderry
THEMES: humor; animals; lessons; rhyme; change

"A little old lady lived all by herself, with a table and chairs and a jug on the shelf. A wise old man heard her grumble and grouse, 'There's not enough room in my house.' " With rollicking rhyme and fun illustrations, the old man helps and gives this lady a lesson in appreciating what she has.

Stone Soup   PICTURE BOOK

AUTHOR/ILLUSTRATOR: Marcia Brown
PB: Aladdin
THEMES: soldiers; trickster tales; soup; food; hunger; change; cleverness; fear of strangers; community

"Such men don't grow on every bush" is the moral in this classic tale. Three tired, hungry soldiers arrive in a village seeking food and a place to sleep. The villagers claim they have neither, for they fear strangers. But the clever soldiers create a feast for all from stones and a few offerings from the folks in the village. This is great fun for children who like "getting it" when the characters in the story don't.

The Story About Ping
PICTURE BOOK

AUTHOR: Marjorie Flack • ILLUSTRATOR: Kurt Wiese
HC: Viking • PB: Puffin
THEMES: ducks; adventure; family; rivers; boats; danger; China; independence

Ping does not want to get the spank always given the last duck to board Master's boat. So he hides, and far from the safety of his family his adventures begin. First published in 1933, and set against the background of China's Yangtze River, this tale of a duckling who thinks for himself is also a reminder not to stray too far away from the security of family.

The Story of Ferdinand
PICTURE BOOK

AUTHOR: Munro Leaf • ILLUSTRATOR: Robert Lawson
HC: Viking • PB: Puffin
THEMES: bulls; peace; individuality; gentle boys; bullies; teasing

Ferdinand, whose story was first published in 1936, is known worldwide as the bull who would just as soon smell the flowers as fight. This is not just for bullies and children on the receiving end, it's also for any child who chooses to be different.

The Story of Little Babaji
PICTURE BOOK

AUTHOR: Helen Bannerman • ILLUSTRATOR: Fred Marcellino
HC: HarperCollins
THEMES: tigers; India; triumph; cleverness; change

Helen Bannerman wrote and illustrated the original "Little Black Sambo" in 1899 after living in India for many years. This new edition of her classic tale takes place in India where the boy and his parents have authentic Indian names: Babaji, Mamaji, and Papaji. Marcellino's pictures show that tigers can be grand, perplexed, enraged and buttery, and that a clever Indian boy can be quite satisfied with one hundred and sixty-nine pancakes. For another version of this tale, see *Sam and The Tigers*.

Strega Nona   PICTURE BOOK

AUTHOR/ILLUSTRATOR: Tomie dePaola

HC: Simon & Schuster • PB: Aladdin

THEMES: Italy; folklore; history, medieval times; witches; competition; magic

Strega Nona was a witch with a magic touch. She could cure illness, help young ladies find husbands and get rid of warts! Why, she could even get a pasta pot to cook on its own. Big Anthony helped Strega Nona around the house until the day he misused a tiny taste of magic and learned a lesson: It's not nice to fool with Strega Nona. A fun tale with a touch of Italy. More titles about Strega Nona include: *Strega Nona Meets Her Match, Big Anthony and the Magic Ring,* and *Strega Nona: Her Story.*

A String of Beads   PICTURE BOOK

AUTHOR: Margarette S. Reid • ILLUSTRATOR: Ashley Wolff

HC: Dutton

THEMES: beads; cultural diversity; diversity; vocabulary; math; Native American; concepts; comparisons; vegetables; minerals; jewelry; crafts

Grandma agrees that its the hole that makes a bead a bead. But it's not just beads that makes this book worthwhile. Comparing sizes, shapes, textures, colors and a touch of history a young girl and her grandmother explore beads and where they come from. It would be great fun to make beads from Wolff's dazzling art, but we suggest you simply follow instructions at the back for making some of your own.

Suddenly!   PICTURE BOOK

AUTHOR/ILLUSTRATOR: Colin McNaughton

HC: Harcourt Brace

THEMES: wolves; pigs; chases; humor; surprises

Preston the pig is completely unaware that a toothy, mean-looking wolf is stalking him. But each time the wolf starts to pounce, Preston changes direction—outsmarting him. Children can't help laughing in relief as danger lurks at the turn of every page. A close look at the pictures is required, so limit your reading aloud to smallish groups.

Sun Song   PICTURE BOOK

AUTHOR: Jean Marzollo • ILLUSTRATOR: Laura Regan

HC/PB: HarperCollins

THEMES: Sun; time; comparisons; change

Gentle lyrics and soft paintings show how life reacts to sunshine during the course of a day.

★ Sylvester and the Magic Pebble   PICTURE BOOK
AUTHOR/ILLUSTRATOR: William Steig
HC: Simon & Schuster • PB: Aladdin
THEMES: magic; wishes; fear; rocks; problem solving; family; change; loneliness

It's one thing when you've been frightened by a lion to find a magic pebble and wish yourself into a rock. It's another thing altogether to have to figure out how to get hold of that much needed magic pebble when you're stuck as a rock. This isn't simply a lesson in planning ahead, it's a much loved tale perfect for reading aloud.

Tacky the Penguin   PICTURE BOOK
AUTHOR: Helen Lester • ILLUSTRATOR: Lynn Munsinger
HC/PB: Houghton Mifflin
THEMES: individuality; penguins; community; friendship; triumph

Tacky was an odd bird. His companions were graceful, he wasn't. They ". . . greeted each other quietly and politely, but Tacky greeted them with a hearty slap on the back and a loud 'What's happening?' " But when hunters came around looking for pretty penguins, it was Tacky's individuality that saved the day. Choose this tale for the child (or adult) who moves to the beat of his own drum: There's a sequel called *Three Cheers for Tacky* that is also great fun.

The Tale of Peter Rabbit   PICTURE BOOK
AUTHOR/ILLUSTRATOR: Beatrix Potter
HC/PB: Warner
THEMES: rabbits; vegetables; farmers; farms; family; disobeying; consequences; adventure

The story of Peter Rabbit and his close escape from Mr. McGregor was first published in 1902. Poor Peter is a curious, naughty little rabbit who does not follow his mother's instructions. That can lead to real trouble, which Peter quickly discovers. Children quickly discover they love Peter and his escapades, along with the other delightful creatures (rodents, felines, waterfowl and more) created by Potter. Along with *The Tale of Peter Rabbit,* the following make up the first ten of the original 23 Peter Rabbit Books: *The Tale of Squirrel Nutkin, The Tailor of Gloucester, The Tale of Benjamin Bunny, The Tale of Two Bad Mice, The Tale of Mrs. Tiggy-Winkle, The Tale of Tom Kitten, The Tale of Mr. Jeremy Fisher, The Tale of Jemima Puddle-Duck,* and *The Tale of the Flopsy Bunnies.*

The Teddy Bears Picnic   PICTURE BOOK
AUTHOR: Jerry Garcia and David Grisman • ILLUSTRATOR: Bruce What-ley
HC: HarperCollins
THEMES: songs; animals; teddy bears; food; picnics; music

Here's an upbeat rendition of this popular song with a bluegrass touch by Jerry Garcia and David Grisman. A cassette is included.

Tell Me Again About the Night I Was Born   PICTURE BOOK
AUTHOR: Jamie Lee Curtis • ILLUSTRATOR: Laura Cornell
HC: HarperCollins
THEMES: babies; adoption; birth; family; love; humor

A young girl asks her mother and father to re-tell the tale of her birth-night. "Tell me again how the phone rang in the middle of the night and they told you I was born. Tell me again how you screamed." Not just for adopted children, this love story will please any youngster, who will ask then about the day he was born. Curtis and Cornell are an apt match of sweetness and humor.

The Tenth Good Thing About Barney   PICTURE BOOK
AUTHOR: Judith Viorst • ILLUSTRATOR: Erik Blegvad
HC: Atheneum • PB: Aladdin
THEMES: death; cats; loss; pets; grief

A child whose cat has just died wonders about death. This sensitive story from a child's perspective confronts the questions and feelings of loss that come with the death of a loved one.

There's a Nightmare in My Closet   PICTURE BOOK
AUTHOR/ILLUSTRATOR: Mercer Mayer
HC: Dial • PB: Puffin
THEMES: fear of monsters; nightmares; monsters; self-respect; fear of the dark; problem solving

If children begin to see monsters in their closets and require lights on at night, bring out this gem in the light of day. Monsters are in the closet, but they are terrified—just like the boy who takes things into his own hands and finally gets some sleep.

This Is the Hat: A Story in Rhyme   PICTURE BOOK
AUTHOR: Nancy Van Laan • ILLUSTRATOR: Holly Meade
HC/PB: Little Brown
THEMES: rhythm; rhyme; hats; cumulative story; animals

Like a catchy tune, this rhyming tale will have you tapping to the rhythm in no time. "This is the hat, This is the man who wore the hat, He wore the hat when he walked in the rain, TAP-A-TAP-TAP! with his old wooden cane."

The Three Bears Holiday Rhyme Book   POETRY COLLECTION
AUTHOR: **Jane Yolen** • ILLUSTRATOR: Jane Dyer
HC/PB: Harcourt Brace
THEMES: seasons; holidays; rhyme; celebrations

Jane Yolen even includes May Day in this collection of fifteen poems for special occasions.

The Three Blind Mice Mystery   EARLY READER
AUTHOR: Stephen Krensky • ILLUSTRATOR: Lynn Munsinger
PB: Dell
THEMES: mystery; wolves; pigs; mice; folktale variations

Cleverly connecting several fairy tales, this is an engaging mystery that will enchant as well as encourage a beginning reader.

Three in a Balloon   PICTURE BOOK
AUTHOR/ILLUSTRATOR: Sarah Wilson
HC/PB: Scholastic
THEMES: balloons; rhyme; sheep; roosters; ducks; farms; flying

Over France they flew in a Montgolfier hot air balloon in 1783, a sheep, duck, and a rooster, the world's first air passengers. Based on a true story, Wilson's colorful telling, often from the animal's point of view, captures the magic of this eight-minute voyage.

Through Moon and Stars and Night Skies   PICTURE BOOK
AUTHOR: Ann Turner • ILLUSTRATOR: James Graham Hale
HC/PB: HarperCollins
THEMES: adoption; Asia; love; travel; airplanes; memory; cultural diversity

A young boy remembers his flight across the world to his new family in America. This tender tale will pull the heartstrings of adults who have adopted and offer loving reassurance to youngsters who are learning about adoption.

Tight Times   PICTURE BOOK

AUTHOR: Barbara Shook Hazen • ILLUSTRATOR: Trina Schart Hyman
HC: Viking • PB: Puffin
THEMES: family; jobs; city life; cats; hardship; pets; change; choices

A family is going through some financial hardship—"tight times" the parents call it—and the young narrator is having trouble understanding why this will prevent them from getting a dog. Told with honesty and love, this story will resonate with many families who have experienced similar problems. Hyman's black-and-white art skillfully evokes the emotion on the character's faces.

Time to Sleep   PICTURE BOOK

AUTHOR/ILLUSTRATOR: Denise Fleming
HC/PB: Henry Holt
THEMES: winter; animals; hibernation; bears; snails; ladybugs; skunks; turtles; connections; woodchucks

Things come full circle in this chain of events that starts with a sniffy bear who smells winter in the air. Off he goes to tell Snail who must tell Skunk, who must tell Turtle. Each animal puts off sleep till the Ladybug wakes up Bear to tell him the news. Cozy, grand, colorful pictures and animal friends make a just-right bedtime story.

To Market, to Market   PICTURE BOOK

AUTHOR: Anne Miranda • ILLUSTRATOR: Janet Stevens
HC: Harcourt Brace
THEMES: rhyme; humor; animals; vegetables; shopping; food; soup

Vegetarians one and all, here's a book full of laughs for you! Starting with the rhyme, "To market, to market, to buy a fat Pig," the narrator tries over and over again to bring animals home from the store—the pig, a hen, goose, trout, lamb, cow, duck and goat. But this unruly bunch interferes with the cooking of lunch until there is a change in the menu. Stevens's black-and-white photos combined with brilliant, zany paintings will make you howl, especially if you know legendary storyteller Coleen Salley, whose image shines throughout.

Today Is Monday   PICTURE BOOK
AUTHOR/ILLUSTRATOR: Eric Carle
PB: Paperstar
THEMES: cumulative story; food; meals; days of the week; animals; rhythm

"Today is Monday, Monday stringbeans, Tuesday spaghetti, Wednesday zoooop . . ." A snazzy cumulative song with colorful collages. Young children will call out in response as they memorize the tasty treat of each previous page.

The Tortilla Factory   PICTURE BOOK
AUTHOR: **Gary Paulsen** • ILLUSTRATOR: Ruth Wright Paulsen
HC: Harcourt Brace
THEMES: food; tortillas; cultural diversity; farming; jobs; Mexico

Simple, poetic language and expressive paintings show respect for the worker as well as an appreciation for each step—from seed to store—to create a tortilla.

Tough Boris   PICTURE BOOK
AUTHOR: Mem Fox • ILLUSTRATOR: Kathryn Brown
HC: Harcourt
THEMES: pirates; death; loss; grief

Tough Boris has the elements of Fox's other successes: language best read aloud, suspense, invitations for child participation and a lesson. Boris Von der Borch is a tough pirate, but even tough guys cry when they lose someone they love!

The Train to Grandma's   PICTURE BOOK
AUTHOR/ILLUSTRATOR: Ivan Ghantschev
HC: Simon & Schuster
THEMES: trains; grandmothers; travel

A speedy steam train picks up Marina and Jeff for a ride to grandma's. Over bridges, through tunnels, past farms and towns, the train races on in a format where pages change with the landscape.

The Tree in the Wood: An Old Nursery Song   PICTURE BOOK
ADAPTOR/ILLUSTRATOR: Christopher Manson
HC: North-South
THEMES: cumulative story; folksongs; rhyme; trees; nature

"All in a wood there grew a fine tree, the finest tree you ever did see, and the green grass grew all around, all around, and the green grass grew all around." Manson's colorful hand-painted woodcuts walk us through this familiar folk song.

A Tree Is Nice   PICTURE BOOK

AUTHOR: Janice May Udry • ILLUSTRATOR: Marc Simont
HC/PB: HarperCollins
THEMES: trees; nature

"Trees are very nice. They fill up the sky. They go beside the river and down the valleys. They live up on the hills." Udry lists the reasons trees are so nice, and children will want to come up with a few of their own.

Tree of Cranes   PICTURE BOOK

AUTHOR/ILLUSTRATOR: Allen Say
HC/PB: Houghton Mifflin
THEMES: Japan; Christmas; mothers and sons; cultural diversity; traditions; origami

The spirit of Christmas comes through in this tender story of a young Japanese boy whose mother tells him how she celebrated Christmas in America. "You give and receive, child. It is a day of love and peace. Strangers smile at one another. Enemies stop fighting. We need more days like it." Poignant. Simple. Say knows how to touch a reader's heart, with affecting words and radiant art.

Verdi   PICTURE BOOK

AUTHOR/ILLUSTRATOR: Janell Cannon
HC/PB: Harcourt Brace
THEMES: snakes; change; self-respect; aging; time; comparisons

For a snake, *Verdi* is downright huggable. He doesn't want to grow old and green. Old snakes seem boring. And just as wrinkles creep up on humans, Verdi can't avoid the green tones covering his yellow youth. Cannon's characters—including *Stellaluna,* the eponymous cuddly bat— are sweeeeet, and this is no exception.

The Very Busy Spider   PICTURE BOOK

AUTHOR/ILLUSTRATOR: Eric Carle

HC: Philomel

THEMES: spiders; farms; animals, farm; touch; concentration; repetition; jobs

It takes a lot of concentation to focus on your work when all the animals on the farm come, one-by-one, to divert your attention. But Spider dutifully spins. Carle has added a tactile touch to this repetitive tale: the web can be felt as well as seen.

★ The Very Hungry Caterpillar   PICTURE BOOK

AUTHOR/ILLUSTRATOR: Eric Carle

HC: Putnam

THEMES: caterpillars; cocoons; hunger; butterflies; change; concepts; eating

Here is one famous caterpillar. Millions of copies of this modern classic have been sold, and, Carle's tale has been translated into over a dozen languages. It begins with a hungry caterpillar who pops out of a tiny egg. As he searches for food, young readers learn the days of the week, and numbers one to ten, and by peeking through die cut pages they see the caterpillar's metamorphisis into a brightly colored butterfly. Also available as a board book.

The Very Quiet Cricket   PICTURE BOOK

AUTHOR/ILLUSTRATOR: Eric Carle

HC: Philomel

THEMES: crickets; insects; sound; repetition

Bugs of all kinds chirp, whiz, bubble, screech and hum their greetings, but as much as he tries, Cricket cannot make a sound. There is comfort in the message that when we are ready, we can do amazing things. But what children enjoy most is the repetition, followed by a glorious final chirp!

We Are a Rainbow   PICTURE BOOK

AUTHOR/ILLUSTRATOR: Nancy Maria Grande Tabor

PB: Charlesbridge

THEMES: comparisons; cultural diversity; moving; friendship; prejudice; Spanish

"You say sol. I say sun. But no matter how we say it, it is the same one." Simple paper cut-outs and comparisons celebrate personal similarities while showing that even with our differences we are "so much the same."

Welcome Little Baby PICTURE BOOK

AUTHOR/ILLUSTRATOR: Aliki
HC: Greenwillow
THEMES: babies; mothers; new baby; greetings

Aliki's sweet welcome for a new baby is just the one for an older sibling—beginning to read—to share with the newest member of the family.

Welcoming Babies PICTURE BOOK

AUTHOR: Margy Burns Knight • ILLUSTRATOR: Anne Sibley O'Brien
HC/PB: Tilbury House
THEMES: babies; greetings; songs; new baby; celebrations; affection; gifts; traditions; ritual

Every day babies are born all over the world. This salute to life and diversity shows that there are many ways to celebrate their arrivals. The text is simple and straightforward. "We Sing" tells about the women near Afam's house who sing, at the sound of his first cry, "Beautiful one, beautiful one, welcome!" For the curious, an informative glossary can be found at the end of the book.

What a Wonderful Day to Be a Cow PICTURE BOOK

AUTHOR: Carolyn Lesser • ILLUSTRATOR: Melissa Bay Mathis
HC: Knopf
THEMES: country life; self-respect; animals, farm; farms; vocabulary

Lovely lyrics and rich paintings glimpse into rural life with the message, "What a wonderful day to be!"

What's What? A Guessing Game PICTURE BOOK

AUTHOR: Mary Serfozo • ILLUSTRATOR: Keiko Narahashi
HC: Simon & Schuster
THEMES: dogs; concepts; rhyme; comparisons; guessing

Questions about familiar concepts—what is hard or soft, dark or light and others—are answered in rhyme and illustrated in cheerful watercolor paintings.

The Wheels on the Bus
NOVELTY

AUTHOR/ILLUSTRATOR: Paul Zelinsky
HC: Dutton
THEMES: buses; songs; repetition; music; transportation

The wheels actually go round, the wipers go swish and Zelinsky's humorously detailed pictures will keep the pop-up, sing-along pages turning for this familiar song.

When Bluebell Sang
PICTURE BOOK

AUTHOR/ILLUSTRATOR: Lisa Campbell Ernst
HC: Simon & Schuster • PB: Aladdin
THEMES: cows; farmers; farms; singing; songs; fame

When Farmer Swenson discovers how well his cow Bluebell can sing, he takes her to town for a taste of show business. It doesn't take long for crafty Big Eddie, a talent agent with dollar bills on his mind, to sign her up. Fortunately, he underestimates the clever duo who outsmart him and end up right back home where they belong.

When I Was Little: A Four-Year-Old's Memoir of Her Youth
PICTURE BOOK

AUTHOR: Jamie Lee Curtis • ILLUSTRATOR: Laura Cornell
HC/PB: HarperCollins
THEMES: growing up; babies; memories; comparisons; childhood

"When I was little, I kissed my mom and dad good night every night. I still do, but only after they each read me a book and we play tickle torture." A spunky four year old compares being a baby with now. Read this to a child who's got a new baby in the house, or when you both can use a good laugh. Curtis is a movie star who knows how to write stories for children and illustrator Cornell's hilarious watercolors perfectly match her words. Be sure to check for details in everything from shoes to toothpaste tubes.

When I'm Sleepy
PICTURE BOOK

AUTHOR: Jane Howard • ILLUSTRATOR: Lynne Cherry
HC: Dutton
THEMES: bedtime; animals; sleep; habitats; imagination

Guaranteed to induce pleasant drowsiness. A young girl imagines sleeping with all sorts of animals in their habitats. Cherry's art adds splendid detail that makes this a book for learning as well as for bedtime. Also available in a board book format.

When the Big Dog Barks
PICTURE BOOK

AUTHOR: Munzee Curtis • ILLUSTRATOR: Susan Avashai
HC: Greenwillow
THEMES: fear of strangers; comfort; dogs; parents; fear of new things

Strangers, new situations, big dogs: things that scare little children are dealt with here in a straightforward and reassuring way. Children learn that it is OK to be afraid sometimes, and that parents are here to protect them.

When We Married Gary
PICTURE BOOK

AUTHOR/ILLUSTRATOR: Anna Grossnickle Hines
HC: Greenwillow
THEMES: family; step families; weddings; stepparents

A simple and lovely story about stepfathers and children, based on Hines' own family. The endpapers have pictures of the different stages of the family's life—a nice touch.

When Zaydeh Danced on Eldridge Street
PICTURE BOOK

AUTHOR: Elsa Okan Rael • ILLUSTRATOR: Marjorie Priceman
HC: Simon & Schuster
THEMES: Jews; grandfathers and granddaughters; celebrations; New York; dance; Judaism; curiosity

Zeesie's grandfather Zaydeh is stern and scary, and she's not looking forward to staying with him and Bubbeh. And when he asks her to go alone with him to the synagogue to celebrate Simchas Torah, she is worried. But on this magical night she earns a kiss and a dance from Zaydeh and learns a thing or two about curiosity.

Where's My Teddy?
PICTURE BOOK

AUTHOR/ILLUSTRATOR: Jez Alborough
HC/PB: Candlewick
THEMES: teddy bears; bears; rhyme; fear; forests

A boy named Eddie has lost his teddy and goes searching for it in the woods. A gigantic bear with a similar problem meets him face to face. Just scary enough to be requested again and again. Have fun with your voice while reading this one.

Where's Spot?
NOVELTY

AUTHOR/ILLUSTRATOR: Eric Hill

HC: Putnam • PB: Puffin

THEMES: dogs; hiding; animals; guessing

Children love to peek and hide, and Spot is the perfect pup to play with. Each page shows a dog searching for Spot, the hiding puppy. "Is he behind the door?" "No" responds a honey-slurping bear who can be seen when the door flap is opened. "Is he in the closet?", "No" responds a lounging lion. Fortunately, many books in this popular series are available in paper, because your child will want to "read" Spot, again and again.

Who Is the Beast?
PICTURE BOOK

AUTHOR/ILLUSTRATOR: Keith Baker

HC/PB: Harcourt Brace

THEMES: tigers; self-respect; fear; jungle

Poor tiger. He is confused to find that he is the beast the other animals fear. Beautiful in art and message, this tender tale encourages a look at the whole picture before being quick to judge.

Who cares if you are a great reader? Just be the connection to story by keeping books in your child's life.

Who Said Red?
PICTURE BOOK

AUTHOR: Mary Serfozo • ILLUSTRATOR: Keiko Narahashi

HC: McElderry • PB: Aladdin

THEMES: color; rhyme; change

With simple concepts and easy to read text, this one is perfect to use when talking about colors with young readers. Other wonderful color books include: *Mouse Paint, Color* by Ruth Heller, *Hailstones and Halibut Bones,* and *The Gift of Driscoll Lipscomb.*

The Wide-Mouthed Frog: A Pop-Up Book
POP-UP

AUTHOR: Keith Faulkner • ILLUSTRATOR: Jonathan Lambert

HC: Dial

THEMES: frogs; humor; animals; alligators

We used to tell this story as a joke. It was entertaining then, and it's no less so in this pop-up form, which is sturdy, with amazing engineering (wait'll you see the alligator!). Enjoy the book and then try telling the story without using your hands.

William's Doll   PICTURE BOOK
AUTHOR: Charlotte Zolotow • ILLUSTRATOR: William Pene Du Bois
HC/PB: HarperCollins
THEMES: gentle boys; fathers; brothers; gender roles; self-respect; toys; grandmothers and grandsons; dolls

William wants a doll to hold, to tuck in, to feed and to kiss goodnight. His father gives him a basketball. He gets good at playing ball, but William still wants a doll. His father gives him an electric train. He enjoys playing with it, but William still wants a doll. His grandmother buys a doll for William and explains that now he can practice being a father. In the story the boy next door chants, "Sissy, sissy," but there is nothing "sissy" about this gentle message.

Wind Says Good Night   PICTURE BOOK
AUTHOR: Katy Rydell • ILLUSTRATOR: David Jorgensen
HC/PB: Houghton Mifflin
THEMES: cumulative story; animals; night; insects; bedtime

Animals, insects, and even the night sky cooperate to help a restless child fall asleep. With soft expressive pencil drawings, it's a bedtime charm!

Witch Way to the Country?   EARLY READER
AUTHOR: Barbara Mariconda • ILLUSTRATOR: Jon McIntosh
PB: Dell
THEMES: witches; wordplay; comparisons; humor; city life; country life

A laugh-out-loud funny book for beginning readers, featuring a pair of witches with decidedly unusual ways of doing things. Clever wordplay and funny line art make this a winner for the first or second grader who likes to laugh while she reads.

Wombat Divine   PICTURE BOOK
AUTHOR: Mem Fox • ILLUSTRATOR: Kerry Argent
HC: Harcourt Brace
THEMES: wombats; Christmas; animals; celebrations; fitting in; Australia

Wombat wants to be in the Nativity play, but he has trouble finding the right part—he seems to be wrong for every role. But when he is assigned the role of the baby Jesus, he fits the part perfectly. A sweet holiday read aloud.

The World Is Full of Babies!: How All Sorts of Babies Grow and Develop
PICTURE BOOK NONFICTION

AUTHOR: Mick Manning • ILLUSTRATOR: Brita Granstorm
HC: Doubleday
THEMES: babies; birth; comparisons; animals; new baby

"If you had a cuckoo for a mom, the first thing you would do after you hatched is push all the other eggs out of the nest." Humorous pictures and facts combine in this book of baby comparisons. Read this to curious youngsters to give them a treat—and for a perfect excuse to start your own conversation about how babies come about.

Would You Rather . . . ?
PICTURE BOOK

AUTHOR/ILLUSTRATOR: John Burningham
HC: HarperCollins
THEMES: imagination; questions; journeys; possibilities

Not a story, but a series of questions posed to the young listener: "Would you rather an elephant drank your bath water, an eagle stole your dinner, a pig tried on your clothes, or a hippo slept in your bed?" Burningham's simple, clever illustrations show the possible result of each choice the child could make. As the book progresses, the child comes to realize there is no right answer, only the results of what she chooses. The possibilities take young listeners far from their day to day world but never outside the realm of their own imaginations. Some questions are scary, some are silly, but the child is always the one in control, doing the choosing. And, at the end, after a wide range of experiences, the reader is gently brought back home and put into her own bed, safe and sound. This valuable book can be used in a variety of situations, from long car trips to getting to know each other sessions at preschools.

The Year at Maple Hill Farm
PICTURE BOOK

AUTHOR/ILLUSTRATOR: Alice and Martin Provensen
PB: Aladdin
THEMES: farms; animals, farm; seasons; weather

The activities on Maple Hill farm change from season to season in this beautifully illustrated picture book. *Our Animal Friends at Maple Hill Farm* (Random House) shares this story's setting.

You Be Good and I'll Be Night   POETRY COLLECTION

AUTHOR: Eve Merriam • ILLUSTRATOR: Karen Lee Schmidt

HC: Morrow • PB: Mulberry

THEMES: rhyme

Many poets have tried to catch the spirit of classic nursery rhymes, but none has captured it so well as Eve Merriam. This marvelous collection of what she calls "Jump on the Bed Poems" is a delight to read aloud and share with young children.

Za-Za's Baby Brother   PICTURE BOOK

AUTHOR/ILLUSTRATOR: Lucy Cousins

HC/PB: Candlewick

THEMES: babies; siblings; new baby; family

Irresistible. Bold, bright, full-page illustrations and simple, straightforward text combine to show how busy it can get with a new baby in the house.

Zoom! Zoom! Zoom! I'm Off to the Moon   PICTURE BOOK

AUTHOR/ILLUSTRATOR: Dan Yaccarino

HC: Scholastic

THEMES: outer space; adventure; rhyme; astronauts; moon

A romp for the imagination, taking the child reader on a journey to the moon and back in a rhythmic and brightly colored adventure. The irregular rhyme makes this a bit of a challenge to read aloud, but take it slow and you'll soon get the hang of it.

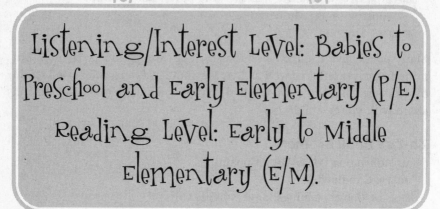

Beginning readers may be challenged by the vocabulary and the size of the print in some of these books, but good, strong early readers will be able to read them to their younger siblings.

A Is for Africa

PICTURE BOOK NONFICTION

AUTHOR/ILLUSTRATOR: Ifeoma Onyefulu
HC: Cobblehill • PB: Puffin
THEMES: Africa; alphabet; family; traditions; folk art

Onyefulu uses stunning photographs taken in Nigeria to illustrate her favorite images of the Africa she knows. Each letter represents warm family ties and life in a traditional village.

The Acorn Tree & Other Folktales

COLLECTION

AUTHOR/ILLUSTRATOR: Anne Rockwell
HC: Greenwillow
THEMES: cultural diversity; folklore

A good first look at the world's folklore. Ten stories from ten different countries.

The Adventures of Taxi Dog

PICTURE BOOK

AUTHOR: Debra and Sal Barracca • ILLUSTRATOR: Mark Buehner
HC: Dial
THEMES: dogs; taxicabs; New York; rhyme; friendship

Maxi the dog and his owner, Jim, are best friends. They go everywhere and do everything together, and meet all sorts of interesting people, mostly in the streets of New York in Jim's taxi. Kids love reading about their adventures, so we are lucky that there are more of them, including: *Taxi Dog Christmas*.

All About Alligators   PICTURE BOOK NONFICTION
AUTHOR/ILLUSTRATOR: Jim Arnosky
HC/PB: Scholastic
THEMES: alligators; crocodiles; science; comparisons; habitats; nature

In watercolor paintings and straightforward language Arnosky explains where alligators live, what they eat, how they are different from crocodiles.

All I See   PICTURE BOOK
AUTHOR: **Cynthia Rylant** • ILLUSTRATOR: Peter Catalanotto
HC/PB: Orchard
THEMES: art; communication; Beethoven; point of view; music; artists; painting

Rylant does a fine job of showing two points of view: that of an artist who whistles Beethoven's Fifth as he paints, and that of a boy who watches from a distance. This is also a story about communication and a great way to introduce Beethoven!

All the Places to Love   PICTURE BOOK
AUTHOR: Patricia MacLachlan • ILLUSTRATOR: Mike Wimmer
HC/PB: HarperCollins
THEMES: farms; family; diversity; individuality; comparisons

Everyone in Eli's family has his or her own favorite place, as different as their personalities and ages might be. Gentle text and lovely paintings show the simple pleasures of life on a farm.

Angelina Ballerina   PICTURE BOOK
AUTHOR: Katharine Holabird • ILLUSTRATOR: Helen Craig
HC: Crown
THEMES: dance; ballet; school; determination; friendship; humor

A dream-come-true story of a tutu-clad, slippered, light-as-a-feather mouse who can't seem to stop dancing. Angelina tales will delight young dancers as well as those preoccupied with music, art, sports or hobbies. Other stories in the Angelina series include. *Angelina's Birthday Surprise, Angelina and the Princess,* and *Angelina on Stage.*

Aunt Nancy and Old Man Trouble   PICTURE BOOK
AUTHOR: Phyllis Root • ILLUSTRATOR: David Parkins
HC: Candlewick
THEMES: cleverness; trickster tales; humor; magic; strong women;
optimism

When Old Man Trouble comes calling the spring dries up, the fire goes
out, the glass breaks and all sorts of problems pop up. But Aunt Nancy
is too clever for this trickster and before long has him heading down the
road. A great read aloud!

Babushka Baba Yaga   PICTURE BOOK
AUTHOR/ILLUSTRATOR: Patricia Polacco
HC: Philomel
THEMES: witches; grandmothers; loneliness; Russia; disguises

In this telling of the legendary Baba Yaga, Babushka Baba feels lonely
and disguises herself as an old woman so that she too can know the joys
of being a grandmother.

★ Badger's Parting Gifts   PICTURE BOOK
AUTHOR/ILLUSTRATOR: Susan Varley
HC: Lothrop • PB: Mulberry
THEMES: death; animals; community; loss; grief; friendship; memo-
ries; gifts; wisdom

Mole, Frog, Fox and Rabbit are stunned by their loss when old Badger
dies. He had been their friend, helpmate and advisor. But when they
begin to remember the different things he taught them, memories ease
their mourning. There are numerous books on the subject of death, but
when it comes to expressing feelings of loss, this is our favorite for
young children.

A Beautiful Feast for a Big King Cat   PICTURE BOOK
AUTHOR: John Archambault and Bill Martin Jr. • ILLUSTRATOR: Bruce
Degen
HC/PB: HarperCollins
THEMES: teasing; mothers; cats; mice; rhyme; lessons

With a tone reminiscent of the teasing *Gingerbread Man* this book features a main character in the form of a tiny mouse who mercilessly
taunts a cat. "Big cat, big cat, catch me if you can! The mouse teased the

cat and ran, ran, ran." Children will wait anxiously to see what happens when this fool-hardy mouse goes too far!

Big Bad Bruce

PICTURE BOOK

AUTHOR/ILLUSTRATOR: Bill Peet
HC/PB: Houghton Mifflin
THEMES: bullies; lessons; fantasy; witches

Bill Peet has created a menagerie of delightful animal characters who find themselves in all sorts of human situations. One of them is Bruce. Children who have been bullied love to read about Bruce, the big bad bear bully. He never picks on anyone his own size till he gets a taste of his own medicine from a small but clever witch. Some of Peet's other books and characters are: *Chester the Worldly Pig*, who would like to join the circus; *Cock-A-Doodle Dudley*, a rooster who thinks he causes the sun to rise every morning; *Cowardly Clyde*, a horse who wishes he were braver; *Eli*, a feeble lion who learns a lesson about friendship. *Encore for Eleanor*, about an artistic elephant who has retired from the circus and has begun a new career as the resident artist in the city zoo, and *Fly, Homer, Fly*, about a farm pigeon who learns that life in the city is not all it's made out to be.

Big Bear's Treasury: A Children's Anthology

ANTHOLOGY

AUTHOR/ILLUSTRATOR: various
HC: Candlewick
THEMES: variety; rhyme

When you're looking for a collection of stories and poems to read aloud to the younger set, we recommend this one. Included in the mix of popular authors and illustrators are Helen Oxenbury, Dick King-Smith, Martin Waddell, Russell Hoban, Shirley Hughes and more. A second and third volume are available.

Big David, Little David

PICTURE BOOK

AUTHOR: S. E. Hinton • ILLUSTRATOR: Alan Daniel
HC: Doubleday • PB: Dell
THEMES: fathers and sons; kindergarten; jokes; playing tricks; comeuppance; competition; imagination

Very funny. A father and son, both jokers, try to outwit each other in a game of make-believe identity. When the boy triumphs, Father gets his comeuppance, and the parents are left to wonder what kind of little trickster they have on their hands. The plot may need explaining to the littlest listeners, but if you have a kid who is a practical joker, you need this book!

Bugs
PICTURE BOOK NONFICTION

AUTHOR/ILLUSTRATOR: Nancy Winslow Parker and Joan R. Wright

HC: Greenwillow • PB: Mulberry

THEMES: science; bugs; insects; slugs; spiders; dragonflies; centipedes

Humor, plus a perfect blending of facts, equals this Bug encyclopedia. There's just enough creepy crawly to pique attention and information to make a young child want a closer look at insects. *Frogs, Toads, Lizards, and Salamanders* offers Parker and Wright's look at the world of slimy reptiles and amphibians.

Castle Builder
PICTURE BOOK

AUTHOR/ILLUSTRATOR: Dennis Nolan

HC: Macmillan • PB: Aladdin

THEMES: imagination; beaches; knights; dragons; castles; history: medieval times; choices

A small boy builds a sand castle and goes inside it, conquering dragons and knights in his imagination. But when he is confronted by the crashing waves of the ocean, he learns that there are some things that can't be beaten. Creates an excellent opportunity to discuss the value of stopping a battle you cannot win, thereby enabling you to fight another day.

There is something primal about this book that I didn't appreciate until I watched my son play by himself in his sandbox. It speaks to the need to control inside us all.

The Cat's Purr
PICTURE BOOK

AUTHOR/ILLUSTRATOR: Ashley Bryan

HC: Atheneum

THEMES: cats; rats; friendship; Caribbean; folklore; playing tricks; sharing; jealousy

Cat didn't always purr; this West Indian folktale will tell you about when Cat and Rat were friends. "Uh Huh!" It'll tell you that when cat got a drum and rat didn't have one, he played a trick on Cat that made them not friends. And it'll tell you about how the cat got his purr, "purrum, purrum." The best way for it to be read is out loud. "Uh Huh!"

Cherries and Cherry Pits   PICTURE BOOK

AUTHOR/ILLUSTRATOR: Vera B. Williams

HC: Greenwillow • PB: Mulberry

THEMES: art; imagination; fruit; drawing; creativity

Bidemmi loves to draw, and when she does, her imagination soars.

Chester's Way   PICTURE BOOK

AUTHOR/ILLUSTRATOR: **Kevin Henkes**

HC: Greenwillow • PB: Mulberry

THEMES: friendship; comparisons; family; strong girl; humor; diversity

On its own, a wonderful book about friendship, but notable for presenting the first appearance of Henkes' irresistible Lilly, later to star in her own books.

The Cow Buzzed   PICTURE BOOK

AUTHOR: Andrew and David Zimmerman • ILLUSTRATOR: Clemesha Meisel

HC/PB: HarperCollins

THEMES: germs; farms; animals, farm; health; connections

Start with a sneeze, add farm animals, and young children get involved—actively—waiting for the next one to imitate! This hilarious tale offers advice from a rabbit who says, "Keep your coughs and sneezes to yourselves!"

Coyote: A Trickster Tale From the American Southwest   PICTURE BOOK

AUTHOR/ILLUSTRATOR: Gerald McDermott

HC/PB: Harcourt Brace

THEMES: trickster tales; coyotes; Native American; folklore; U.S.A., the Southwest

Coyote stories are the most often told trickster tales of Native American tradition. In this Zuni folktale from the American Southwest, Coyote wants to sing, dance, and fly like the crows, so he begs them to teach him. The crows agree until they tire of his boasting and decide to teach him a lesson instead.

The Cozy Book   PICTURE BOOK

AUTHOR: Mary Ann Hoberman • ILLUSTRATOR: Betty Fraser

HC: Harcourt Brace

THEMES: rhyme; senses; friendship; comfort

If it's cozy, it's in this book. Cozy people, cozy beds, cozy smells, cozy sounds, and cozy rhymes that remind young children about life's comforts.

…and if you say the word "cozy" one more time, I'll scream. This pushes my limit for cute and quiet. Maybe for others, but not for me!

Day of the Dead
PICTURE BOOK

AUTHOR: Tony Johnston • ILLUSTRATOR: Jeanette Winter
HC: Harcourt Brace
THEMES: Day of the Dead; Mexico; celebrations; dance; singing; memories; traditions; rituals

Black borders frame brilliantly colored scenes of a family preparing for the Day of the Dead. This undersized book is perfect for the little hands of a child who will learn a few Mexican words along with how family and community work together, then dance, sing, and share memories of their loved ones in celebration of this annual holiday.

Dear Dr. Sillybear
PICTURE BOOK

AUTHOR: Dian Curtis Regan • ILLUSTRATOR: Randy Cecil
HC: Henry Holt
THEMES: doctors; nurses; wordplay; humor; problem solving

Clever wordplay that begs to be read aloud, and bold, lighthearted illustrations make this a gem. Dr. Sillybear is appropriately named, and what he would do without Nurse Rabbit we can't imagine! If your children love *The Stupids* and *Amelia Bedelia,* then this will be a big hit.

Did You Hear Wind Sing Your Name?: An Oneida Song of Spring
PICTURE BOOK

AUTHOR: Sandra De Coteau Orie • ILLUSTRATOR: Christopher Canyon
HC/PB: Walker
THEMES: Native American; nature; seasons; spring

Lovely and lyrical, this is an English translation of a joyous ode to Spring, sung by the Oneida people. The art is breathtaking, and it serves to show how strongly this tribe is connected to the seasons.

Dinosaurs Divorce   PICTURE BOOK

AUTHOR: Marc Brown and Laurie Krasny Brown • ILLUSTRATOR: Marc Brown
HC/PB: Little Brown
THEMES: divorce; family; emotions; change

A useful guide to the breakup of a marriage, as seen from the point of view of a family of dinosaurs. The distancing that the dinosaurs provide offers the child reader some room to sort out his own feelings. Helpful without overstepping the bounds into preachiness, this is as good a book as any to help a young child deal with one of life's biggest disappointments. The Browns and their family of dinosaurs take on issues of health and safety in *Dinosaurs Alive and Well!*, and *Dinosaurs, Beware!*

Do Not Open   PICTURE BOOK

AUTHOR/ILLUSTRATOR: Brinton Turkle
PB: Puffin
THEMES: strong women; monsters; courage; cleverness; storms

Miss Moody has weathered some pretty strong storms, safe in the knowledge that her sturdy house was built to last and that storms bring treasures to the beach in their aftermath. But when one of those treasures releases a horrid being capable of causing terrible things, she and her cat, Capt. Kidd, work together to defeat it in a tale that has a wonderfully satisfying ending.

Dragonfly   PICTURE BOOK NONFICTION

AUTHOR/ILLUSTRATOR: Durga Bernhard
HC/PB: Holiday House
THEMES: dragonflies; insects; folklore; science; nature

Dragonflies soared through the air one hundred million years before dinosaurs walked the earth. The Bernhards present interesting scientific and historical facts, as well as myths, folklore, and superstitions about this intriguing insect.

The Eyes of Gray Wolf   PICTURE BOOK

AUTHOR: Jonathan London • ILLUSTRATOR: Jon Van Zyle
HC/PB: Chronicle
THEMES: wolves; nature; animal, endangered

London describes the grace and dignity of wolves and Van Zyle enhances the description with spectacular art. Detailed facts and a list of organizations dedicated to preserving wolves can be found in the back of the book.

The Fabulous Firework Family   PICTURE BOOK
AUTHOR/ILLUSTRATOR: James Flora
HC: McElderry
THEMES: Mexico; celebrations; Spanish; bilingual; traditions

Anyone who has attended a major Mexican fiesta has more than likely
seen it end with a glorious fireworks display. This book introduces children to this spectacular tradition. Spanish words found throughout provide a language lesson.

The Fire Children: A West African Creation Tale   PICTURE BOOK
AUTHOR: Eric Maddern • ILLUSTRATOR: Frane Lessac
HC: Dial
THEMES: creation; folklore; Africa; geography; cultural diversity; clay

Nyame, the great sky god, sneezes and the fire children fly down to
earth. So begins a tale explaining why the world is filled with people of
many different colors. Add to the fun by introducing clay, or take advantage of the opportunity for a simple geography lesson.

Fire Race: A Karuk Coyote Tale About
How Fire Came to the People   PICTURE BOOK
AUTHOR: Jonathan London • ILLUSTRATOR: Sylvia Long
HC/PB: Chronicle
THEMES: Native American; coyotes; cooperation; wasps; fire; animals;
folklore; trickster tales

Inspired by an ancient Native American legend of the Karuk people, this
California tale explains how fire came to the people. Coyote, a trickster
in many Native American stories, comes up with a plan that will work
only with help from his friends. The focus is cooperation, and there's a
bonus . . . learn how the yellowjacket got its stripes.

Five Live Bongos   PICTURE BOOK
AUTHOR: George Ella Lyon • ILLUSTRATOR: Jacqueline Rogers
HC: Scholastic
THEMES: music; rhythm; family; bands; creativity

Take out the pots and pans! This upbeat combo of language, music and
art is a natural invitation to start a neighborhood or classroom rhythm
band.

The Gingerbread Doll
PICTURE BOOK

AUTHOR/ILLUSTRATOR: Susan Tews

HC: Houghton Mifflin

THEMES: Christmas; family; poverty; resourcefulness; U.S. history, the Depression

Nostalgic and warm-hearted, this tale of growing up in poverty has a perfect ending. Never cloying or sickly-sweet, a family tale that deserves to live for generations.

Grandad Bill's Song
PICTURE BOOK

AUTHOR: **Jane Yolen** • ILLUSTRATOR: Melissa Bay Mathis

HC: Putnam

THEMES: death; grandfathers; memories; emotions

When someone dies, people show their feelings in different ways. A young boy asks those around him what they did when Grandad died. He gets a variety of responses—and memories—and then talks about his own feelings.

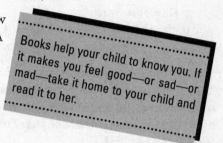

Books help your child to know you. If it makes you feel good—or sad—or mad—take it home to your child and read it to her.

Grandmother's Nursery Rhymes/Las Nanas De Abuelita
POETRY COLLECTION

AUTHOR: Nelly Jaramillo • ILLUSTRATOR: Elivia Savadier

HC/PB: Henry Holt

THEMES: bilingual; Spanish; grandmothers; rhyme; riddles; rhythm

Sounds, rhythm and riddles are wonderful ways to introduce language to young children. This bilingual collection works in both English and Spanish.

Have You Seen Trees?
PICTURE BOOK

AUTHOR: Joanne Oppenheim • ILLUSTRATOR: Jean and Mou-Sien Tseng

HC/PB: Scholastic

THEMES: trees; nature; rhyme

This tree language is so much fun it's hard not to chant it aloud. "High trees, wide trees, reaching-to-the-sky trees. Did you ever hide behind a wide high tree?" "Wrinkled bark, rough bark, twisted, corky, cracked bark. White bark, smooth bark, slick-without-a-groove bark." Four pages of tree facts can be found in the back of the book.

Here Is the Tropical Rain Forest   PICTURE BOOK NONFICTION

AUTHOR: Madeleine Dunphy • ILLUSTRATOR: Michael Rothman
HC/PB: Hyperion
THEMES: rain forest; plants; animals; environment; rain

The plants and animals of the rain forest are celebrated with a familiar rhythm. "Here is the eagle who hunts the sloth that hangs from the tree, which holds the bromeliad that shelters the frog who bathes in the rain . . ." The last page shows line drawings of rain forest animals and includes the address of the National Wildlife Federation for the child who wants to learn more about protecting the rain forests.

The House That Drac Built   PICTURE BOOK

AUTHOR: Judy Sierra • ILLUSTRATOR: Will Hillenbrand
HC: Harcourt Brace
THEMES: rhyme; haunted houses; Halloween; spooky stories; cumulative story; monsters; bats; vocabulary; repetition

"This is the cat that bit the bat that lived in the house that Drac built." This is a tale with a familiar rhythm, spooky at first until the children come and set things straight for the monsters, werewolves, fiends and more who inhabit the house that Drac built. Just what they'll want for Halloween reading.

I Hate English   PICTURE BOOK

AUTHOR: Ellen Levine • ILLUSTRATOR: Steve Bjorkman
HC/PB: Scholastic
THEMES: immigration; Chinese; self-respect; school; frustration; teachers; language, learning

Sometimes it is easier to remain silent than to chance making a fool of yourself while learning a new language. A Chinese girl refuses to speak English until a sympathetic teacher helps her out, and the result is something many newcomers to English will recognize.

I Never Did That Before   POETRY COLLECTION

AUTHOR: Lilian Moore • ILLUSTRATOR: Lillian Hoban
HC: Atheneum
THEMES: milestones; new experiences; playing; friendship

First experiences and new adventures, told in rhyme for the younger set. Poems about hanging upside down from the monkey bars and such are treated as the milestones they are. Very nice combination of words and pictures.

It's a Spoon, Not a Shovel   PICTURE BOOK

AUTHOR: Caralyn Buehner • ILLUSTRATOR: Mark Buehner
HC: Dial
THEMES: manners; family; friendship; humor

Children laugh out loud as they choose the right answers to multiple choice politeness quizzes that test one's consideration of others.

It's Pumpkin Time!   PICTURE BOOK

AUTHOR: Zoe Hall • ILLUSTRATOR: Shari Halpern
HC: Blue Sky Press
THEMES: pumpkins; gardening; Halloween; seasons; harvest

Pumpkin season starts with summer and children planting a pumpkin patch and ends with a Halloween celebration! A colorful chart shows stages of growth from seed to Jack O'Lantern!

It's So Nice to Have a Wolf Around the House   PICTURE BOOK

AUTHOR: Harry Allard • ILLUSTRATOR: James Marshall
HC: Doubleday • PB: Dell
THEMES: wolves; elderly; friendship; change; conscience

Cuthbert Q. Devine, a wolf with "a charming personality," becomes a companion to an old man and his aged pets. A sweet and funny collaboration from the people who gave us *The Stupids*.

Jack's Garden   PICTURE BOOK NONFICTION

AUTHOR/ILLUSTRATOR: Henry Cole
HC: Greenwillow • PB: Mulberry
THEMES: gardening; flowers; bugs; insects; connections; cumulative story; plants; gardens

"This is the garden that Jack planted. These are the seeds that fell on the soil that made up the garden that Jack planted . . ." Against the rhythm of the familiar cumulative verse, readers can watch a garden grow from seed to bloom. Cole's realistic pictures include birds, bugs, and butterflies familiar to gardners.

John Henry
PICTURE BOOK

AUTHOR: Julius Lester • ILLUSTRATOR: Jerry Pinkney
HC: Dial
THEMES: folklore; tall tales; storytelling; heroes; railroad; jobs; change; determination

On the day he was born, John Henry "grew until his head and shoulders busted through the roof which was over the porch. John Henry thought that was the funniest thing in the world. He laughed so loud, the sun got scared." Lester writes for reading aloud. Jerry Pinkney's watercolors burst with John Henry's energy.

Jojo's Flying Side Kick
PICTURE BOOK

AUTHOR/ILLUSTRATOR: Brian Pinkney
HC: Simon & Schuster
THEMES: African American; martial arts; strong girls; grandfathers; courage

It's surprising how much braver Jojo is after her Tae Kwon Do class; not even the big tree in the front yard scares her any more.

The Jolly Postman, or Other People's Letters
NOVELTY

AUTHOR: Janet and Allan Ahlberg • ILLUSTRATOR: Allan Ahlberg
HC: Little Brown
THEMES: communication; fairy tales; mail; rhyme; folktale variations; mail carrier

The Jolly Postman delivers mail to fairy tale characters. It's great fun to imagine what Goldilocks has sent to the Three Bears, or who the wedding announcement is from. Each envelope actually opens and tiny, readable letters, invitations, and even junk mail are found inside.

King Snake
PICTURE BOOK

AUTHOR: Wendy Slotboom • ILLUSTRATOR: John Manders
HC: Houghton Mifflin
THEMES: snakes; mice; survival; cleverness; storytelling

Stories that show little guys outsmarting big ones are very appealing to small children. They'll have fun with Tinkerton and Henry, two mice who use their heads when trapped by a very talkative snake.

Let's Eat
PICTURE BOOK

AUTHOR: Ana Zamorano • ILLUSTRATOR: Julie Vivas
HC/PB: Scholastic
THEMES: meals; family; new baby; manners; food

A warm book about a Spanish family and mealtime. Each evening a different member of the family misses the dinner Mama has worked hard to prepare because of something else they have to do. When Mama is the one absent, it is to deliver her new baby, who joins the entire family at the next meal. Terrific art by Julie Vivas. This book makes us hungry.

Sorry, but more than hungry, it makes me frustrated because when someone fixes you dinner, you don't ignore mealtime because it's inconvenient. And if you can't be there you don't just not show up!

Well, sure, you grew up in a family where they put tongue on the table and you had to eat it. I think you're projecting a little bit here, sort of, "If I had to stay at the table, no way am I gonna be happy about anyone else getting away!"

The Library   PICTURE BOOK
AUTHOR: Sarah Stewart • ILLUSTRATOR: David Small
HC: Farrar Straus & Giroux
THEMES: books; reading; humor; strong girls; rhyme; obsession

Is there a book nut in your life? This story in rhyme of the life of Elizabeth Brown makes a perfect gift for any reading fanatic: "Books were piled on top of chairs, And spread across the floor. Her shelves began to fall apart, As she read more and more."

★ Lilly's Purple Plastic Purse   PICTURE BOOK
AUTHOR/ILLUSTRATOR: **Kevin Henkes**
HC: Greenwillow • PB: Mulberry
THEMES: school; teachers; anger; strong girls; regret; consequences; conscience; taking action

Kevin Henkes' characters usually make us laugh. Lilly makes us howl. She represents our fears, our hopes, our frustrations, and our guilt. When her favorite teacher, Mr. Slinger, takes away her purple plastic purse for the day, Lilly's stomach lurches. Then she becomes sad. And then angry. And when she's angry she takes action against Mr. Slinger. Youngsters and the adults fortunate enough to read this aloud will find themselves or someone they know in this funny, strong-willed, vulnerable character.

AUTHOR SPOTLIGHT ON KEVIN HENKES

ONE of our most insightful observers of childhood, Kevin Henkes writes and illustrates picture books that celebrate the painful and joyful transitions of early school-age children. His charming mouse community has served to remind us just how seriously children take issues like names, blankets, little brothers, belonging to a group, and being special in books such as *Chester's Way; Chrysanthemum; Julius, The Baby of the World; Lilly's Purple Plastic Purse;* and *Owen.* Lilly has become his superstar: a strong-willed little mouse who is not afraid to speak her mind, she has moved completely to center stage after being introduced in *Chester's Way,* and her exploits serve to remind us of the fragile feelings that lie at the heart of even the strongest of our children.

Henkes does not always illustrate his own work, sometimes collaborating instead with artists including Nancy Tafuri (*Biggest Boy*), Marisabina Russo (*Good-Bye Curtis*), and Victoria Chess (*Once Around the Block*) on picture books that have their own delights, even if Lilly isn't in them.

He is also an accomplished novelist, and among his works for middle readers are *Sun and Spoon, Protecting Marie,* and *Words of Stone,* books of grace and wonder that deal with older children's concerns and are written with his customary sensitivity, though they lack the side-splitting quality he brings to his picture books. These make excellent bridges from middle-grade fiction to young adult novels.

In his young career, Kevin Henkes has done much to remind us of how much care our children's souls require, sometimes with humor, sometimes with sadness and always with lyrical writing and an eye for truth. We look forward to new insights he will share in works to come.

Listen to the Desert (Oye El Desierto)   PICTURE BOOK
AUTHOR: Pat Mora • ILLUSTRATOR: Francisco X. Mora
HC: Clarion
THEMES: desert; bilingual; Spanish; animals; sound

Sounds of the desert are described in this simple poem in two languages. It invites children to participate in both Spanish and English, and offers a chance for them to pipe in with sounds of their own.

The Little Red Ant and the Great Big
Crumb—A Mexican Fable   PICTURE BOOK
AUTHOR: Shirley Climo • ILLUSTRATOR: Francisco X. Mora
HC/PB: Clarion
THEMES: Mexico; ants; folklore; Spanish language; animals; self-respect

A small red ant finds a piece of cake in a Mexican cornfield. It's all she'd need to feed herself through the winter, but she doesn't feel strong enough to move it on her own. She asks other animals to help her, but has no luck until she learns, "You can do it if you think you can." Climo adds some Spanish words to the mix. A glossary is included.

Little Red Cowboy Hat   PICTURE BOOK
AUTHOR: Susan Lowell • ILLUSTRATOR: Randy Cecil
HC/PB: Henry Holt
THEMES: U.S.A., the Southwest; grandmothers and granddaughters; folktale variations

A twist on an old tale. This Little Red Riding Hood rides her pony, Buck, to Grandma's ranch to deliver a jar of cactus jelly.

Mama, Do You Love Me?   PICTURE BOOK
AUTHOR: Barbara M. Joosse • ILLUSTRATOR: Barbara Lavallee
HC: Chronicle
THEMES: love; mothers; Arctic; whales; wolves; puffins; comfort

A little girl asks, "Mama, do you love me?" "Yes I do, Dear One." "How much?" And Mother responds by comparing her love to the animals of the Arctic. "I'll love you until the umiak flies into the darkness, till the stars turn to fish in the sky, and the puffin howls at the moon." Beautifully illustrated, this warm, reassuring story goes perfectly with a hug during quiet time.

Margaret and Margarita   PICTURE BOOK
AUTHOR/ILLUSTRATOR: Lynn Reiser
HC: Greenwillow
THEMES: comparisons; bilingual; Spanish language; communication

Reiser writes: "Words can be a bridge, or a barrier. In this bilingual book the adults immediately respond to differences. Their words make a barrier. The children recognize similarities." Her visuals show body language, her words a delightful merging of languages and a great way to teach basic words, including colors!

Meet the Marching Smithereens   PICTURE BOOK
AUTHOR: Ann Hayes • ILLUSTRATOR: Karmen Thompson
HC: Gulliver
THEMES: music; bands; musical instruments; animals; rhythm; musicians

As a jaunty crew of animals marches along playing their favorite tunes, we learn facts about brass, percussion, and woodwind instruments. "The largest horns have the lowest voices. The sousaphone, the bullfrog of the band, was invented by John Philip Sousa, a famous composer of band music. It has the widest throat and the biggest bell of all the brass, grumping and groaning with a deep umm-pa, ummpa, umm-pa-pa." This is the perfect companion to Hayes' *Meet the Orchestra!*

Meet the Orchestra   PICTURE BOOK
AUTHOR: Ann Hayes • ILLUSTRATOR: Karmen Thompson
HC/PB: Harcourt Brace
THEMES: musical instruments; music; orchestras; musicians; animals

Animal musicians gather for their evening performance. All of their instruments have an important role in the orchestra and young readers are introduced to each with a rollicking rhythm and lively watercolor close-ups. For a romp with a marching band, try Hayes' *Meet the Marching Smithereens.*

The Mitten   PICTURE BOOK
AUTHOR/ILLUSTRATOR: Jan Brett
HC: Putnam
THEMES: folklore; Ukraine; mittens; animals; lost

It's difficult to see a white mitten in the snow, so the boy doesn't even know it's missing. But it's soon discovered by a mole, rabbit, badger and other animals. Pay attention to Brett's details. She often creates an entire story in her borders, and this book is no exception.

"I remember the quiet times when, as a child, I felt I could enter my beautiful children's books. One of the joys of reading is that you can pause whenever you wish, to think, imagine, dream, and then return with the turn of a page."
—Jan Brett, author of *The Mitten*

More Than Anything Else   PICTURE BOOK

AUTHOR: Marie Bradby • ILLUSTRATOR: Chris K. Soentpiet
HC/PB: Orchard
THEMES: biography; African American; reading; writing; literacy

On the last page you find out that this is the story of Booker T. Washington, but you do not need to know that to enjoy the story. A testament to the power of reading and the need for books in all children's lives.

Mouse and Mole and the Year-Round Garden   PICTURE BOOK NONFICTION

AUTHOR/ILLUSTRATOR: Doug Cushman
HC: W. H. Freeman
THEMES: gardening; friendship; cooperation; science

Mole shows mouse how to plant a garden. Through all stages of growing and harvesting, these friends share work and play each season till it comes time to plant again. Informational boxes on the bottom of each page offer simple scientific tips.

Mud Pies and Other Recipes: A Cookbook for Dolls   NONFICTION

AUTHOR: Marjorie Winslow • ILLUSTRATOR: Erik Blegvad
PB: Walker
THEMES: cooking; dolls; mud; fantasy; playing; recipes; tea parties

Absolutely straightforward without a hint of condescension, this book is just as the title claims; a collection of recipes for that doll tea party in the backyard.

Remember boys make mudpies, too! Though I didn't feed them all gen-teel-like to dolls. I tried to cram them down my stuffed elephant's throat. I can see uses for this book with both sexes and am putting in my plea not to leave the boys out of the fun.

My Life With the Wave
PICTURE BOOK

AUTHOR: Catherine Cowan adapted from a story by Octavio Paz •
ILLUSTRATOR: Mark Buehner
HC: Lothrop
THEMES: sea; friendship; fantasy; searching game; family

Parents ought to feel safe sending their son off to the ocean. After all, what could he bring home? A shell? Sand? In this wacky story he brings home neither. Instead he arrives with a wave—a sweet, shimmering, whispering, howling, sighing, wailing, moody wave. And until her chill-ing departure the family living in the house nearly goes crazy. This stretch-the-imagination story is based on one written by Nobel Prize lau-reate Octavio Paz. Buehner's extraordinary pictures hide a cat, dog, mouse, whale, and sea horse in almost every illustration.

My Little Sister Ate One Hare
PICTURE BOOK

AUTHOR: Bill Grossman • ILLUSTRATOR: Kevin Hawkes
HC: Crown
THEMES: cumulative story; hunger; counting; humor, gross; connec-tions; repetition; eating

This is a story we knew at first glance would cause children to howl in hysterics. It does. It is absurd, silly and repeats "We thought she'd throw up then and there" on almost every page. Try it before lunch or after school. We do not recommend it for bedtime. It is not calming.

My Mama Says There Aren't Any Zombies, Ghosts, Vampires, Creatures, Demons, Monsters, Fiends, Goblins, or Things
PICTURE BOOK

AUTHOR: Judith Viorst • ILLUSTRATOR: Kay Chorao
HC: Atheneum • PB: Aladdin
THEMES: monsters; fear of monsters; humor; imagination; mothers

Judith Viorst is very funny. Here she manages to keep up the hilarity as young Nick worries about whether his mom is right when she says that monsters do not exist. She often makes mistakes, and those monsters look mighty real. Fears of what could be lurking in the closet or behind a door are very real, too, but have fun with this one.

My Place in Space   PICTURE BOOK
AUTHOR: Robin and Sally Hirst • ILLUSTRATOR: Roland Harvey and Joe Levine
HC/PB: Orchard
THEMES: outer space; connections; comeuppance; home

When a bus driver asks Henry Wilson and his sister if they know where they live, Henry answers him by telling him exactly—from their house address to their place in the universe. This funny blend of fact and fiction is guaranteed to astound children who will be fascinated by the concept of their own place in space.

My Visit to the Zoo   PICTURE BOOK NONFICTION
AUTHOR/ILLUSTRATOR: Aliki
HC/PB: HarperCollins
THEMES: animals, endangered; birds; zoos; habitats; nature; geography; insects; comparisons

Based on several real zoos, Aliki's journey takes young readers through a rambling parklike enclosure designed to preserve its inhabitants. Interesting information fills each page. "You can tell where a monkey comes from by its nose." ". . . the thick-skinned rhinoceros, (has been) hunted to near extinction for its long horns . . ." A map at the end shows where endangered and vulnerable animals exist in the world.

I find zoos to be among the more depressing places on earth. Anthony Browne knows what I mean—find his book *Zoo* and get the animals' point of view. Aliki addresses this issue well, making this a zoo book even for people who don't like zoos.

Number One Number Fun   PICTURE BOOK
AUTHOR/ILLUSTRATOR: Kay Chorao
HC: Holiday House
THEMES: math; numbers; animals; farms; vocabulary

Children are encouraged to figure out the answers in this adding and subtracting animal circus. "How many pigs are piled in fun? Add four plus three plus two plus one." "Two drop off . . . the others wobble, how many chickens . . . are left to squabble?"

Okino and the Whales   PICTURE BOOK

AUTHOR: Arnica Esterl • ILLUSTRATOR: Marek Zawadzki
HC/PB: Harcourt Brace
THEMES: environment; Japan; taking action; nature; whales

The watercolor depictions of the undersea world are reason enough to own this haunting tale of Japan. The strong ecological message is a bonus.

Old Black Fly   PICTURE BOOK

AUTHOR: Jim Aylesworth • ILLUSTRATOR: Stephen Gammell
HC/PB: Henry Holt
THEMES: alphabet; family; humor; flies

Funny enough to make you laugh at the flies during hot, buggy, summer days. When a fly pesters each member of the family in this unorthodox ABC book, Baby decides she's had enough. Ayelsworth's catchy refrain encourages kids to chant along.

Old Devil Wind   PICTURE BOOK

AUTHOR: Bill Martin Jr. • ILLUSTRATOR: Barry Root
HC: Harcourt Brace
THEMES: Halloween; cumulative story; spooky stories

Martin is a master of rhythm, and this spooky tale offers language that builds suspense and inspires exaggeration in sound and the imagination. This is just what many children want at Halloween time. Root's dark and stormy illustrations add to the fun!

Oliver's Vegetables   PICTURE BOOK

AUTHOR: Vivian French • ILLUSTRATOR: Alison Bartlett
HC: Orchard
THEMES: vegetables; gardens; grandfathers; new experiences

A clever introduction to the idea of eating new foods. Oliver's grandfather tends a large garden, full of things Oliver says he won't eat. By involving the child in the whole process of gardening, from planting to eating, Oliver's grandfather wears down his reluctance, and a vegetable eater is born.

On Sally Perry's Farm   PICTURE BOOK

AUTHOR: Leah Komaiko • ILLUSTRATOR: Cat Bowman Smith
HC: Simon & Schuster
THEMES: farms; imagination; crafts; rhyme; rhythm; teamwork; city life; gardening; gardens

Komaiko's rhythm takes a few times through before you get it, but what fun you'll have when you do! Sally Perry's farm is smack dab in the middle of the city. She grows fruit and vegetables and with a little help from crafty neighborhood kids, pigs and horses show up too.

The Ornery Morning   PICTURE BOOK
AUTHOR: Patricia B. Demuth • ILLUSTRATOR: Craig McFarland Brown
HC: Dutton
THEMES: cooperation; jobs; farms; farmers; consequences; animals, farm; fathers and daughters; problem solving; stubbornness; misbehaving

When Rooster decides not to crow one morning because he doesn't feel like it, his negative attitude infects the whole farmyard. But when the farmer appears to "catch" the lack of cooperation, the animals rally as quick as a cock-a-doodle-doo. Farmer's clever daughter understands the importance of working together and saves the day in this funny, repetitive read aloud.

This is one of my favorites to recommend to the person who wants a no-fail read aloud for a preschooler to first grader. The problem is they come back wanting another just like it, and I'm often hard pressed to find it.

★ Owen   PICTURE BOOK
AUTHOR/ILLUSTRATOR: **Kevin Henkes**
HC: Greenwillow
THEMES: growing up; comfort; family; busybodies; problem solving; neighbors

Owen is not ready to give up his fuzzy yellow blanket. "Fuzzy goes where I go," says Owen. He loves it with all his heart. After all, he's had it since he was a baby. This is for the youngest school child who understands the difficulties of growing up, and for the parents who could use a good laugh when faced with their side of the struggle.

The Painter   PICTURE BOOK
AUTHOR/ILLUSTRATOR: Peter Catalanotto
HC: Orchard
THEMES: family; home; artists; fathers and daughters; jobs; paintings

When your office is in your home, it is frequently frustrating to loved ones that you are so near and yet so unavailable. Catalanotto's clever, touching story about a father who paints and a daughter who is inspired by him offers a solution for the increasing number of families dealing with this arrangement.

★ Possum Come A-Knockin'   PICTURE BOOK

AUTHOR: Nancy Van Laan • ILLUSTRATOR: George Booth
HC: Knopf • PB: Dragonfly
THEMES: opossums; humor; rhyme; rhythm; family; playing tricks

Caution! This book will skip a rap tune through your mind all day. Raucous and wild, it begs to be read aloud. "Brother was untanglin' all the twiny line for fishin' while Sis was tossin' Baby and Pappy was a-whittlin' and Pa was busy fixin' and Ma was busy cookin' and Granny was a-knittin' when a possum come a-knockin' at the door." Pay attention to the possum. He has an entire routine going on all by himself.

This is the book that taught me there is no "right" way to tell a story. I heard banjos picking in my head the first time I read it, and I perform it at a fast clip, but I have seen it read sing-songy slow, and it works just fine!

Rattlebone Rock   PICTURE BOOK

AUTHOR: Sylvia Andrews • ILLUSTRATOR: Jennifer Plecas
HC: HarperCollins
THEMES: Halloween; rhyme; community; graveyards; ghosts

Jumping, jouncing, jangly poetry that gets little feet tapping and big feet moving. We like to have non-scary titles for reading aloud at Halloween time—this is a favorite.

Shepherd Boy   PICTURE BOOK

AUTHOR: Kristine L. Franklin • ILLUSTRATOR: Jill Kostner
HC: Atheneum
THEMES: Native American; shepherds; Navajo; U.S.A., the Southwest; sheep; courage

In Navajo country, Ben sets out to rescue one of his family's sheep that has been left behind. "Across the mesa they run with hearts that beat like drums until at last they come to the canyon where the Old Ones lived and painted pictures on smooth stone walls." The words and art are calming and beautiful.

Soap! Soap! Don't Forget The Soap!:
An Appalachian Folktale

PICTURE BOOK

AUTHOR: Tom Birdseye • ILLUSTRATOR: Andrew Glass
HC/PB: Holiday House
THEMES: humor; memory; U.S.A., Appalachia; folklore

The people of Sassafras Hallow know about Plug Honeycut. Why, he has "such a poor memory some say he'd forget his own name." This Appalachian folktale, packed with humor in both language and art, is great for reading aloud. Be sure each listener can see the pictures.

Stellaluna

PICTURE BOOK

AUTHOR/ILLUSTRATOR: Janell Cannon
HC: Harcourt Brace
THEMES: courage; new experiences; bats; mothers; solitude; change; birds; adoption; comparisons

Bats are not always a popular subject, not often thought of as cute or soft. Stellaluna has changed all that. Cannon tells this bat story with incredible detail, down to the furry face of her bat heroine, down to the moment she finds her mother. A fantasy, beautifully painted, filled with feeling. Each page will delight you.

Swamp Angel

PICTURE BOOK

AUTHOR: Anne Isaacs • ILLUSTRATOR: Paul O. Zelinsky
HC: Dutton
THEMES: tall tales; strong women; bears; folklore

When she "took her first gulp of air on this earth, there was nothing about the baby to suggest that she would become the greatest woodswoman in Tennessee. The newborn was scarcely taller than her mother and couldn't climb a tree without help. But feisty Angelica Longrider could hold her own against any varmint including Thundering Tarnation, the "low down pile of pelts" bear that was making everybody miserable. Read this original tall tale aloud, and be sure to share the incredible pictures. Caldecott honor artist Zelinsky's oil-on-wood paintings offer up a fun, folk art view of the tall-tale characters in the Tennessee wilderness.

The Tale of Rabbit and Coyote   PICTURE BOOK

AUTHOR: Tony Johnston • ILLUSTRATOR: Tomie dePaola
HC: Putnam
THEMES: trickster tale; folklore; Mexico; Spanish words; coyotes; rabbits

Johnston and dePaola look to the folklore of Oaxaca, Mexico, for this trickster tale. Rabbit outsmarts coyote and readers discover why coyotes howl at the moon. A glossary of Spanish expressions is included.

Talking Like the Rain: A First Book of Poems   POETRY ANTHOLOGY

EDITOR: X.J. and Dorothy Kennedy • ILLUSTRATOR: Jane Dyer
HC/PB: Little Brown
THEMES: family; magic; time; animals; rhyme; songs; weather

There is something for every young child in this collection of more than 100 poems by popular poets Robert Louis Stevenson, Edward Lear, Nikki Giovanni, Jack Prelutsky and others. Arranged in categories from play and fun to day and night (with families and animals in between) Dyer's cheery watercolor paintings fill the oversized pages.

The Three Billy Goats Gruff   PICTURE BOOK

AUTHOR/ILLUSTRATOR: Janet Stevens
HC/PB: Harcourt Brace
THEMES: bullies; trolls; goats; folklore; bridges

We all have a pretty good notion about what the mean, ugly troll looks like, but what about the billy goats? That big one has got to be tough: after all he can out Trip Trap anyone. And Stevens has him perfectly drawn, black leather jacket and all. It's modern, bridge-wise, and hilarious.

A Tooth Fairy's Tale   PICTURE BOOK

AUTHOR/ILLUSTRATOR: David Christiana
HC: Farrar Straus & Giroux
THEMES: fairy tales; tooth fairy; imagination; fantasy

"Once upon a time all the fairies in the world lived in a sand castle. However, they were turned into stones by a giant's evil eye, until only one remained. She was a tooth fairy and she lived in the castle with her father, the Sandman." An oversized visual delight, with the tiniest details carefully rendered, full of characters that children will love to believe in.

Tops and Bottoms   PICTURE BOOK

AUTHOR/ILLUSTRATOR: Janet Stevens
HC: Harcourt Brace
THEMES: gardening; trickster tales; cleverness; vegetables; triumph

Hare offers to do all the labor on Bear's land, if Bear will split the crop
in half and share it with him. All Bear has to do is to choose the half he
wants—tops or bottoms. Readers learn that some vegetables grow above
the ground and others below. The lazy Bear discovers that even with all
his land and money, he doesn't stand a chance against a clever hare
with nothing but a hungry family! The book opens top to bottom to show
off brilliant paintings that fill each page.

The Tortoise and the Hare   PICTURE BOOK

AUTHOR/ILLUSTRATOR: Janet Stevens
HC/PB: Holiday House
THEMES: fables; competition; triumph; determination; folklore; racing;
tortoises; hares; bullies; teasing

"Tortoise crossed the line just before the tornado of dust and fur that was
Hare flew by," and thank goodness for that. After all, Tortoise's shy,
want-to-please self makes young readers root for him, while Hare's
boasting, bullying character makes him the kind of guy you want to
come in last. And since this is a classic retelling of this well loved tale,
that is exactly what happens. Stevens' portrayal of the long-eared hare
and somewhat stricken old tortoise add a perfect blend of humor.

Town Mouse Country Mouse   PICTURE BOOK

AUTHOR/ILLUSTRATOR: Jan Brett
HC: Putnam
THEMES: individuality; home; mice; cats; owls; diversity; lessons; city
life; country life; comparisons

Brett's rendition of this classic tale includes two mice couples who agree
to swap homes and a cat and owl who stalk them. Lush country scenes
and an elegant Victorian townhouse are the backdrop of an adventure
that reminds us things are not always greener on the other side.

We're Back!: A Dinosaur's Story   PICTURE BOOK

AUTHOR/ILLUSTRATOR: Hudson Talbott
HC/PB: Crown
THEMES: time travel; humor; New York; museums; dinosaurs; com-
parisons; fitting in

Young dinosaur enthusiasts are bound to request this time travel tale. Straight from the Tyrannosaurus' mouth it starts, "One day as I was beginning a little afternoon snack, I noticed a small but tasty-looking creature approaching me . . ." And that little creature posts a pack of pre-historic pals into the twentieth century, straight toward the Museum of Natural History. Steven Spielberg's son liked this book so much his dad made it into a movie!

Why Mosquitoes Buzz in People's Ears   PICTURE BOOK
AUTHOR: Verna Aardema • ILLUSTRATOR: Leo & Diane Dillon
HC: Dial • PB: Puffin
THEMES: Africa; mosquitoes; folklore; sound

Why do mosquitoes buzz in people's ears? You'll get the answer here, along with award-winning graphics, a menagerie of tattle-tales, and a story teeming with personalities and sound effects to match!

★ The World of Christopher Robin: The Complete When We Were Very Young and Now We Are Six   POETRY COLLECTION
AUTHOR: A. A. Milne • ILLUSTRATOR: Ernest H. Shepard
HC: Dutton
THEMES: rhyme; family; friendship; fantasy; animals

If you were to make me choose one can't-do-without title; one book that can be read again and again and be worth its weight in gold, this is the one. I read it for myself. I read it for my children. When I cautioned them against straying too far from the house they repeated James James Morrison Morrison Weatherby George Dupree's verse, "You must never go down to the end of the town, if you don't go down with me." We loved Jonathan Jo who had ". . . a mouth like an 'O' And a wheelbarrow full of surprises. If you ask for a bat, or for something like that, he has got it, whatever the size is." When they caught cold, we'd wonder along with Christopher Robin ". . . If wheezles could turn into measles, if sneezles would turn into mumps; ". . . and we'd laugh at the prospect of visiting the zoo where ". . . There are biffalo-buffalo-bisons, and a great big bear with wings, There's a sort of a tiny potamus, and a tiny nosserus too . . . ." It's all here. And how can you get your small child inter-ested in a novel-sized book with small black and white illustrations and mostly words? Easy. Start her young. Share your delight in the words. Memorize your favorites. The complete texts of When We

Were Very Young *and* Now We Are Six *are found in this remarkable volume. You can also find them separately.*

The World of Pooh: The Complete Winnie the Pooh and The House at Pooh Corner   COLLECTION

AUTHOR: A. A. Milne • ILLUSTRATOR: Ernest H. Shepard
HC: Dutton
THEMES: bears; honey; bees; animals; childhood; imagination; friendship; community

"Here is Edward Bear, coming downstairs now, bump, bump, bump, on the back of his head, behind Christopher Robin. It is, as far as he knows, the only way of coming downstairs, but sometimes he feels that there really is another way, if only he could stop bumping for a moment and think of it." This is how Winnie the Pooh is first introduced to readers, pulled down the stairs by Christopher Robin who has hold of his arm. Milne is a master storyteller. But Pooh has been sold as a book for babies, Disneyfied, turned into coloring books and pop-ups and flaps and every possible sales tie-in. The writing has been left somewhere on a back shelf to be accidentally discovered. Discover it! Open it to any page and delight in its images. Read it to a five or six year old. Laugh with it. Don't for a minute think that the Disney or spin-off books are Milne's Pooh. They are a completely different breed of bear! The complete texts of *Winnie the Pooh* and *The House at Pooh Corner* are in this wonderful volume. You can also find them in separate volumes.

Zin! Zin! Zin! A Violin   PICTURE BOOK

AUTHOR: Lloyd Moss • ILLUSTRATOR: Marjorie Priceman
HC: Simon & Schuster
THEMES: music; musical instruments; vocabulary; counting; math

A trombone is playing alone. Soon a trumpet makes a duet, a french horn a trio, and the music continues until a full orchestra "soars, implores, with notes galore that causes the audience to shout, Encore!" Moss' rhythmic verse not only introduces the orchestra, but stretches vocabulary, too!

Listening/Interest Level: Babies to Preschool, Early and Middle Elementary (P/E/M). Reading Level: Early Elementary (E).

Family reading works best when all members feel involved. When your children begin to read is a good time to invite them to read aloud to the family. Some children will be eager to try; others may want to wait and build confidence. When your child is ready, these books offer variety—with a wide range of subject matter and a reading level that early readers can try.

Art Dog
PICTURE BOOK

AUTHOR/ILLUSTRATOR: Thacher Hurd

HC/PB: HarperCollins

THEMES: art; dogs; heroes; creativity; humor; puns; jobs; taking action; artists; theft; museums

Using the complete range of colors in his palette, Hurd tells the story of the mysterious hero, Art Dog, and his rescue of priceless masterpieces stolen from the Dogopolis Museum of Art. Funny, loaded with puns and inspiring to future artists; a fun book to read before visiting an art museum for the first time.

Ben's Trumpet
PICTURE BOOK

AUTHOR/ILLUSTRATOR: Rachel Isadora

PB: Mulberry

THEMES: music; cities; musical instruments; community; jazz; musicians; yearning

Ben yearns to play a real trumpet, not just the pretend one that nobody else can see. It's the early 1920's and his dream comes true with the help of a trumpeter from the neighborhood jazz club. Black-and-white Caldecott Honor illustrations are breathtaking, and this sweet story of a talented young boy is captivating.

Bumps in the Night   EARLY READER
AUTHOR: Harry Allard • ILLUSTRATOR: James Marshall
PB: Dell
THEMES: spooky stories; misunderstanding; humor

A funny, easy-to-read tale that makes a good read aloud for those who can only handle a lightly spooky story. The creators of *The Stupids* are in fine form here.

The Cat in the Hat   EARLY READER
AUTHOR/ILLUSTRATOR: Dr. Seuss
HC: Random House
THEMES: mischief; boredom; adventure; rhyme

The book that made Dr. Seuss a superstar and launched millions of children on the road to reading all by themselves. Also see: *Green Eggs and Ham.*

Chickens Aren't the Only Ones   PICTURE BOOK NONFICTION
AUTHOR/ILLUSTRATOR: Ruth Heller
PB: Sandcastle
THEMES: science; chickens; eggs; birds; snakes; dinosaurs; amphibians; fish; spiders; nature

"Chickens aren't the only ones, most snakes lay eggs and lizards, too, and crocodiles and turtles do, and dinosaurs who are extinct, but they were reptiles, too." Heller's brilliant illustrations and simple text pique the interest of young scientists as well as any child interested in how things come to be. Others in this series where each page reveals the magic of nature are: *Plants That Never Ever Bloom* and *The Reason for a Flower.*

Clown   PICTURE BOOK
AUTHOR/ILLUSTRATOR: Quentin Blake
HC: Henry Holt
THEMES: adventure; wordless; homelessness; toys; poverty; friendship; home; clowns; problem solving

A clown begins this tale in a garbage can, and ends it with a happy-ever-after family. In between, adventures keep the pages turning—and all without a word. Hooray for Blake! His action-filled plot with its heart tugging moments makes this book a worthwhile addition to anyone's library.

Commander Toad in Space   EARLY READER
AUTHOR: **Jane Yolen** • ILLUSTRATOR: Bruce Degen
PB: Paperstar
THEMES: science fiction; adventure; toads; outer space

Great fun for the youngest fans of science fiction, written in an easy to read format. Five other titles include *Commander Toad . . . . and the Big Black Hole, ... and the Intergalactic Spy, ... and the Planet of the Grapes; . . . and the Dis-Asteroid, . . . and the Space Pirates.*

Delphine   PICTURE BOOKS
AUTHOR/ILLUSTRATOR: Molly Bang
HC: Morrow Junior Books
THEMES: giants; strong girls; courage; new experiences; fear of new things; worry; gifts; bicycles

Delphine is a giant who lives atop a hill with wild animals for pets. She climbs mountains, crosses dangerous ravines on a tightrope, braves thunder and lightning, and seems to be an all-around fearless sort. Then why is she so worried about the present her grandmother sent her? It turns out she has never ridden a bike before, and her nervousness shows us that there is a first time for everything and everyone gets afraid sometimes. Delphine's ethnicity is never defined, allowing a wide range of children to imagine themselves as brave as she. For a different look at a remarkable female giant, see *Mangaboom* by Charlotte Pomeranz.

Doctor De Soto   PICTURE BOOK
AUTHOR/ILLUSTRATOR: William Steig
HC: Farrar Straus & Giroux
PB: Sunburst
THEMES: dentists; mice; foxes; humor; teeth

Doctor De Soto is a mouse dentist who makes his practice available to just about anyone who isn't a danger to mice. But then one day Fox comes crying in agony with a terrible toothache. What's a good dentist to do? If it's like pulling teeth to get your child to sit down for a story, try this witty one. For more adventures, see *Doctor De Soto Goes to Africa.*

Elbert's Bad Word   PICTURE BOOK

   AUTHOR: Audrey Wood • ILLUSTRATOR: Audrey & Don Wood
   HC/PB: Harcourt Brace
   THEMES: humor; magic; wizards; misbehaving; fantasy; problem solving; gardeners; words

Elbert was at an elegant dinner party with his family when he heard a word he hadn't heard before. "The word floated by like a small storm cloud. It was ugly and covered with dark, bristly hairs. With a swift flick of his wrist, Elbert snatched the word from the air and stuffed it into his back pocket." When the word found its way to Elbert's mouth, the dinner guests were shocked. This original story with its comical illustrations (the bad word is a very prickly monster) allows children, like Elbert, to enjoy thinking up fun, acceptable substitutes for inappropriate language.

The Empty Pot   PICTURE BOOK

   AUTHOR/ILLUSTRATOR: Demi
   HC/PB: Henry Holt
   THEMES: truth; gardening; folklore; China; flowers

An elderly emperor proclaims to the children in his land that his successor would be "whoever can show me their best in a year's time." He then gives special flower seeds to each. Young Ping was especially happy: after all, he had always been a successful gardener. But, as hard as he tried, nothing grew. At the end of the year, he was the only child with an empty pot. We don't want to ruin this story for you, but we can tell you that the ending is a happy one that comes with a lesson in honesty. Demi's beautiful art is in a style unique to her. Demi has created many other books with detailed illustrations and well told stories—fiction and non. Some include: *Demi's Secret Garden,* and *Demi's Dragons and Fantastic Creatures.*

★ Fables   PICTURE BOOK

   AUTHOR/ILLUSTRATOR: Arnold Lobel
   HC/PB: HarperCollins
   THEMES: animals; fables; advice; folklore; lessons

Published in 1980, *Fables* has already become a classic. Lobel's twenty original stories each fit on a single page with a facing award-winning full-color illustration. The tales are a delight to read aloud, and the morals at the end of each add value on their own. "It is the high and mighty who have the longest distance to fall. Without a doubt, there is such a thing as too much order. When the need is strong, there are those who will believe anything." This is the book to take to children's appointments. Open to any page for a complete story, a chuckle, and a perfect way to pass waiting-room time.

Farm Morning   PICTURE BOOK

AUTHOR/ILLUSTRATOR: David McPhail
HC: Harcourt Brace
THEMES: farms; animals, farm; morning; fathers and daughters; rituals

A perfect father/daughter book, *Farm Morning* details the daily rituals of a farm morning with lovely, gentle words and watercolors. Other books by McPhail that reflect this mood are *Ed & Me* and *Night Sounds, Morning Colors,* by Rosemary Wells, which he illustrated.

Felix's Hat   PICTURE BOOK

AUTHOR: Catherine Bancroft • ILLUSTRATOR: Hannah Gruenberg
HC: Macmillan
THEMES: hats; family; comfort; siblings; humor; loss; bad days

One way of showing love is through understanding in a crisis. When Felix's favorite orange baseball cap is lost, his family rises to the occasion. Gruenberg's funny illustrations show the personalities of this five-frog family: Frank, Philomena, Felix, Freda, and Phoebe. Humor and family support are the prescription for helping Felix through his bumpy time.

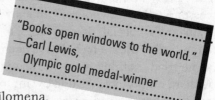

"Books open windows to the world."
—Carl Lewis,
Olympic gold medal-winner

Fortunately   PICTURE BOOK

AUTHOR/ILLUSTRATOR: Remy Charlip
PB: Aladdin
THEMES: self-respect; repetition; luck; travel; mail; comparisons

"Fortunately one day, Ned got a letter that said, 'Please Come to a Surprise Party': But unfortunately the party was in Florida and he was in New York." First published in 1964, *Fortunately* continues to delight youngsters who repeat an enthusiastic, "fortunately" followed by an exasperated, "unfortunately" for weeks following this story. And why not? They have experienced Charlip who, fortunately, is an artist whose wit, talent and understanding of children has created books that continue to delight over the span of ages, no unfortunately about it.

Frogs in Clogs   PICTURE BOOK

AUTHOR/ILLUSTRATOR: Sheila White Samton
HC: Crown
THEMES: vocabulary; language; frogs; rhyme; wordplay; rhythm; shoes

Language is what this book is all about! "Frogs. Bog. Frogs in the bog. Boggy frogs. Soggy frogs. Frogs in clogs." Rhymes, along with the pairing of silly characters and words make this an inspiration for young writers who want to try their own. A study in fanciful wordplay and vocabulary expander in one!

A Fruit and Vegetable Man   PICTURE BOOK

AUTHOR: Roni Schotter • ILLUSTRATOR: Jeanette Winter
HC/PB: Little Brown
THEMES: jobs; responsibility; aging; pride; cultural diversity; fruit; vegetables; community; change; family store

Ruby Rubenstein is a fruit and vegetable man who works hard and is loved by the people in his New York neighborhood. Young Sun Ho visits Ruby every day and learns the business himself. This simple story is loaded with conversation-starting text. It's about pride in one's work, growing old, making changes, and learning a trade.

★ The Gardener   PICTURE BOOK

AUTHOR: Sarah Stewart • ILLUSTRATOR: David Small
HC: Farrar Straus & Giroux
THEMES: gardening; mail; family; separation; generosity; U.S. history, the Depression; uncles; nieces; baking; bakers; optimism; resourcefulness; emotions; compassion; neighbors; gardens; country life; diversity; city life; gardeners

Lydia Grace's uncle doesn't smile. That's what she discovers when she is sent to live with him during her family's difficult times. But his crabby expression is no match for Lydia's cheery disposition. In no time, with her green thumb at work, she brightens up the world around her uncle's bakery and learns that people show love in various ways. Small's full-page art stretches the bigs to enormous, the littles to minute, and flowers to joy. This sweet story, told through art and letters home, will touch your heart.

Good Dog, Carl   PICTURE BOOK
AUTHOR/ILLUSTRATOR: Alexandra Day
HC: Green Tiger • PB: Aladdin
THEMES: wordless; dogs; babysitters; babies

When Carl the dog is told "Look after the baby, Carl, I'll be back shortly,"
the text ends and the action begins. Carl works like a dog—keeping the
baby safe as it ventures from one room to the other. This is the first and
our favorite of several Carl books.

Grandmother's Pigeon   PICTURE BOOK
AUTHOR: Louise Erdrich • ILLUSTRATOR: Jim LaMarche
HC/PB: Hyperion
THEMES: grandmothers; fantasy; magic; birds; family

Grandmother hitched a ride to Greenland on a passing porpoise and
hasn't been heard of for a year. It makes sense for the family to check
her bedroom which has been sealed closed the entire time. You can
imagine their surprise when they find rare pigeons hatching in a nest.
Where could they have come from? La Marche's breathtaking paintings
and Erdrich's intriguing story are just the right blend for this mysterious
tale.

The Grey Lady and the Strawberry Snatcher   PICTURE BOOK
AUTHOR/ILLUSTRATOR: Molly Bang
PB: Aladdin
THEMES: wordless; strawberries; adventure; theft; chases; blackberries;
monsters

The strawberry snatcher is in hot pursuit of the Grey Lady's strawberries, until he discovers blackberries. A full-color, action-packed wordless
treasure.

Here Come the Aliens   PICTURE BOOK
AUTHOR/ILLUSTRATOR: Colin McNaughton
HC: Candlewick
THEMES: outer space; humor; imagination

A funny tale of impending conquest by the slimiest, weirdest bunch of
extraterrestrials you've ever seen. Children love the surprise ending!

Lunch   PICTURE BOOK

AUTHOR/ILLUSTRATOR: Denise Fleming

HC/PB: Henry Holt

THEMES: concepts; vegetables; fantasy; color; food; mice; fruit; vocabulary

A spunky mouse eats his way through a feast of oversized, brightly colored fruits and vegetables. This is a great color concept book, but it's one we'd use with older readers to stretch the vocabulary. Fleming uses two words to describe each vegetable or fruit: crisp white turnip; tasty orange carrots. Have third or fourth graders (or older) rewrite her story replacing the adjectives with others that fit.

Marvin's Best Christmas Present Ever   EARLY READER

AUTHOR: Katherine Paterson • ILLUSTRATOR: Jane Clark Brown

HC: HarperCollins

THEMES: cleverness; Christmas; family; gifts

Wanting to make this a truly memorable holiday, Marvin searches for a way to make a present better than the ones his sister makes. This terrific, easy-to-read story is about a boy's loving, lasting gift to his family.

My Map Book   PICTURE BOOK NONFICTION

AUTHOR/ILLUSTRATOR: Sara Fanelli

HC: HarperCollins

THEMES: maps; point of view; drawing; self-respect; human body; community

Maps of "my room" and "my neighborhood" we've seen before, but a map of "my stomach" and "my heart"? The concept is clever, but the art seemed weird to us at first. Now we're convinced that it's just what young children need to encourage them to use maps to help them explore their own worlds.

★ Officer Buckle and Gloria   PICTURE BOOK

AUTHOR/ILLUSTRATOR: Peggy Rathmann

HC: Putnam

THEMES: safety; friendship; police; dogs; school; humor; mishaps; teamwork

An example of how to do everything right in creating a picture book. Here's a story that is kid-friendly (Officer Buckle's boring safety assemblies get livened up by the addition of Gloria, a dog of more than a few tricks), a message everyone can agree on (safety is important, but friendship is the most important thing), and a humorous illustration style that is so tightly woven into the narrative, you cannot imagine the book existing any other way. We have read this book countless times and are still noticing the cleverness of Rathmann's eye for detail—check out Officer Buckle's pajamas. This is one funny book!

Old Pig   PICTURE BOOK

AUTHOR: Margaret Wild • ILLUSTRATOR: Ron Brooks
HC: Dial
THEMES: grandmothers; pigs; death; grief; loss

Old Pig is ready to die. When she feels strong enough she takes her granddaughter on a slow walk around the town to feast her eyes on the trees, the flowers, the sky—on everything!" Sad and sweet, this book shows youngsters the tender relationship between two loved ones and how although loss is inevitable, the gift of sharing time and memories will live on.

Don't be fooled by the illustrations into limiting this book to the youngest child. A fourth grader whose grandparent is ill will discover that he can help with a song, story or simple walk. Parents, read it first and prepare to talk about the ending.

Once There Were Giants   PICTURE BOOK

AUTHOR: Martin Waddell • ILLUSTRATOR: Penny Dale
HC/PB: Candlewick
THEMES: family; growing up; strong girls

A sweet and affecting read aloud, perfect for children and parents to read together. Told in rhyme, this story details a girl's growing up, stopping in to visit her at various stages of her childhood and observing the changes in her life and those around her. At the end it comes full circle, as she joins the giants of her youth and welcomes her new baby into the family. This will bring a lump to your throat.

The Paperboy   PICTURE BOOK

AUTHOR/ILLUSTRATOR: Dav Pilkey
HC: Orchard
THEMES: morning; jobs; pets

THE ABCs OF FEELINGS

Sometimes the cure for easing a difficult time is to discover you are not alone, that someone understands how you feel. Books can be the ointment that lessens the pain during these times. Other occasions may be zany, mischievous, happy ones, a perfect time for a wacky tale.

This list is only a starting point. Books don't have to be *about a* specific feeling to do the job. Here you'll find stories with characters who display feelings in situations children will recognize. There are tons of titles that can help you discuss feelings and concerns with your child. The important thing is to choose books you will enjoy sharing, that will communicate the feelings kids have in common.

Anxious: *Can't You Sleep Little Bear?* (Waddell)

Bashful: *Shy Charles* (Wells)

Competitive: *Don't Fidget A Feather* (Silverman)

Disagreeable: *Contrary Mary* (Jeram)

Embarrassed: *Airmail to The Moon.* (Birdseye)

Frustrated: *To Market to Market* (Miranda)

Gutsy: *Liza Lou and the Yeller Belly Swamp* (Mayer)

Humiliated: *Moog-Moog Space Barber* (Teague)

Insecure: *I Wish I Were A Butterfly* (Howe)

Jealous: *Julius The Baby of the World* (Henkes)

Kind: *Brave Irene* (Steig)

Loving: *Guess How Much I Love You* (McBratney)

Mean: *Mean Soup* (Everitt)

Nervous: *Harriet's Recital* (Carlson)

Ornery: *The Ornery Morning* (Demuth)

Powerful: *Bootsie Barker Bites* (Bottner)

Quarrelsome: *Rat and the Tiger* (Keiko)

Regretful: *Lilly's Purple Plastic Purse* (Henkes)

Self-conscious: *Weird Parents* (Wood)

Scared: *Papa!* (Corentine)

Smug: *Some Smug Slug* (Edwards)

Teased: *The Cow That Went Oink* (Most)

Uncool: *Earl's Too Cool for Me* (Komaiko)

Vulnerable: *Frosted Glass* (Cazet)

Wishful: *Mordant's Wish* (Coursen)

Xenophobic: *The Araboolies Of Liberty Street* (Swope)

Yearning: *Earrings!* (Viorst)

Zany: *A Day with Wilbur Robinson* (Joyce)

A quiet ode to a paperboy's early morning routine. The quality of writing is matched by the shadowy paintings, making this a lovely book to share in quiet moments. Hush, or you'll break the magic of its spell. . . .

Some Smug Slug   PICTURE BOOK

AUTHOR: Pamela Duncan Edwards • ILLUSTRATOR: Henry Cole
HC: HarperCollins
THEMES: slugs; confidence; vocabulary; animals; alliteration

"Slowly the slug started up the steep surface, stringing behind it scribble sparkling like silk." Read-out-loud language that leaves images may be the best part of this incredible book, although some might argue it's the full-page illustrations that offer a bug's-eye-view. Whatever it is, the ending will surprise the reader as much as it does one overconfident slug. If there is a moral here, it's "take your mind off of yourself long enough to open your eyes and your ears."

Stephanie's Ponytail   PICTURE BOOK

AUTHOR: Robert Munsch • ILLUSTRATOR: Michael Martchenko
PB: Annick
THEMES: hair; strong girls; copy cats; fads; cleverness; school

From storyteller Munsch, here is a tale of the ridiculousness of fads told in a way that will make kids howl with laughter. No matter how differently Stephanie decides to wear her hair, it seems everyone at school copies her. When she has finally had enough, she announces that "tomorrow I am going to shave my head!" When she shows up the next day with a full head of hair, the shocked looks on the faces of an entire school of baldies is worth the price of the book.

What Do You Do When Something
Wants to Eat You?   PICTURE BOOK NONFICTION

AUTHOR/ILLUSTRATOR: Steve Jenkins
HC: Houghton Mifflin
THEMES: animals; predators; animal defenses; food chain

Jenkins' fascinating nature books have delighted us with their mix of ingenious juxtapositions of facts and terrific, cut-paper art. This book is no exception. Looking at the relationship between the hunter and the hunted provides a great introduction to the ways animals have developed defenses and strategies to protect themselves from being devoured. Other terrific titles by Jenkins include: *Big and Little, Looking Down*, and *Biggest, Fastest, Strongest.*

Willy the Wimp   PICTURE BOOK

AUTHOR/ILLUSTRATOR: Anthony Browne
HC: Knopf • PB: Dragonfly
THEMES: apes; bullies; gentle boys; clumsiness; shyness

Willy is a chimp who could use a big dose of self-esteem. Slight, bespectacled, and shy, he is the very picture of a spineless wimp. Browne's paintings and story bring Willy vividly to life, endearing him to readers who may be a little unsure of themselves as well. Willy's adventures continue in *Willy and Hugh, Willy the Champ, Willy the Wizard,* and *Willy the Dreamer*.

A Year on My Street   POETRY COLLECTION

AUTHOR: Mary Quattlebaum • ILLUSTRATOR: Cat Bowman Smith
PB: Dell
THEMES: seasons; friendship; neighbors; city life; community

Poems about life in an urban neighborhood, all written in an easy to read style. Each season is chronicled from a child's point of view, and each short poem offers a familiar event or person—the mail carrier, the first snow, jumping rope, etc.—continuing to look at a child's world.

A fascinating mix—fiction and nonfiction—makes up this next section. The wide-ranging listening level may include several members of the family, and although these books may challenge readers, older siblings readily can participate in these family read alouds.

Amazing Grace   PICTURE BOOK

AUTHOR: Mary Hoffman • ILLUSTRATOR: Caroline Binch
HC: Dial
THEMES: strong girl; family; grandmothers; storytelling; imagination; prejudice; self-respect; determination; African American; plays; gender roles; pretending

In this beautifully illustrated picture book, we are introduced to story-loving Grace, an only child with a rich imagination and the ability to put it to good use. Stories are so integral a part of her life that acting them out is a daily ritual. When the play of "Peter Pan" is being put on at school, her classmates tell her that she cannot be Peter because she is a) a girl, and b) Black. With the help of her wise grandmother she reaffirms what she already knows: She can be anything she wants, if she puts her mind to it. A life-affirming book made special by Hoffman's stirring message and Binch's extraordinary paintings. A sequel, *Boundless Grace*, picks up the story a few years later and is for slightly older children.

Away From Home   PICTURE BOOK

AUTHOR/ILLUSTRATOR: Anita Lobel
HC: Greenwillow
THEMES: alliteration:; guessing; cultural diversity; travel; theater; costumes; alphabet; geography

An alliteration of friends from A to Z travel the world in 25 scenes. "Isaac idled in Innsbruck. John juggled in Jerusalem." Readers have fun with words while they play a geographical guessing game. Match the cities to the countries. Notice the costumes in each scene. Lobel has paid attention to detail, from A to Z. The last page describes specific locations pictured in this journey.

Be Good to Eddie Lee   PICTURE BOOK

AUTHOR: Virginia Fleming • ILLUSTRATOR: Floyd Cooper
HC: Putnam • PB: Paperstar
THEMES: handicaps; friendship; Down's syndrome

Eddie Lee's friends discover he has something of value to offer. This beautifully illustrated story about a boy with Down's syndrome never becomes condescending.

Beaver at Long Pond   PICTURE BOOK NONFICTION

AUTHOR: William T. and Lindsay Barrett George • ILLUSTRATOR: Lindsay Barrett George
HC: Greenwillow
THEMES: beavers; nature; habitats; ponds

A four-book look at the inhabitants of a northeastern watery habitat, *Beaver at Long Pond* and its companions are a trip to the country in book form. Solid nature writing and vivid paintings are the hallmark's of this outstanding nature series, whose other titles are *Box Turtle at Long Pond, Fishing at Long Pond,* and *Christmas at Long Pond.*

Caves and Caverns   PICTURE BOOK NONFICTION

AUTHOR/ILLUSTRATOR: Gail Gibbons
HC/PB: Harcourt
THEMES: caves; adventure; geology

Children are fascinated by underground hideaways. Here they can journey through sea caves, lava caves, and ice caves, and get basic information on where to go, what to bring and how to have a safe adventure. A great lesson in geology. For a great lesson in a variety of topics, turn to

Gail Gibbons. Her subjects range from books about holidays (Halloween and Easter) to dinosaurs and beyond.

A Child's Garden of Verses   POETRY COLLECTION
AUTHOR: Robert Louis Stevenson • ILLUSTRATOR: Tasha Tudor
HC: Simon & Schuster
THEMES: rhyme; variety

Full-color Tasha Tudor art and 66 of Stevenson's poems for children. Also see *A Child's Garden Of Verses* illustrated by Jessie Willcox Smith, below.

A Child's Garden Of Verses   POETRY COLLECTION
AUTHOR: Robert Louis Stevenson • ILLUSTRATOR: Jessie Willcox Smith
HC: Atheneum
THEMES: rhyme; variety

The work of Jessie Willcox Smith first appeared on the covers of *Good Housekeeping* in 1905. If you are looking for the familiar, old-fashioned illustrations of Stevenson's classic poems for children, this is the one. See *A Child's Garden of Verses* illustrated by Tasha Tudor, above.

Clay Boy   PICTURE BOOK
AUTHOR: Mirra Ginsburg • ILLUSTRATOR: Joseph A. Smith
HC: Greenwillow
THEMES: folklore; Russia; greed; bullies; clay; storytelling; eating; gluttony; triumph

A fabulous retelling of an old Russian folktale, with great art! The greedy clay boy grows larger and larger, eating everything and everyone in the small village, until he is thwarted by a brave young goat.

★ Come a Tide   PICTURE BOOK
AUTHOR: George Ella Lyon • ILLUSTRATOR: Stephen Gammell
HC/PB: Orchard
THEMES: floods; family; courage; disaster; U.S.A., Appalachia

This warmly told tale, full of funny characterizations and humorous details about a rural family experiencing a flood, enchanted us both from the start. But it wasn't until we had the opportunity to read it in communities where disaster had recently occurred that we began to realize its greater value. No matter what the natural disaster, at some point in the picking-up-and-putting-it-all-back together stage, children will likely want to know why they have to live in a place where such things happen—"Why don't we move to where disaster can't harm us?" This book is very helpful in explaining that the love of home and family are strong in many of us—so strong that we often choose to stay and rebuild. Gammell's artwork is a plus for any book, but his depiction of the water coming down, rising and receeding is simply superb.

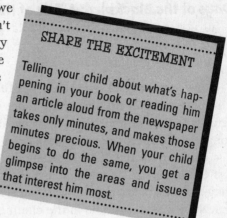

SHARE THE EXCITEMENT

Telling your child about what's happening in your book or reading him an article aloud from the newspaper takes only minutes, and makes those minutes precious. When your child begins to do the same, you get a glimpse into the areas and issues that interest him most.

Coyote in Love   PICTURE BOOK

AUTHOR/ILLUSTRATOR: Mindy Dwyer
HC: Alaska Northwest
THEMES: folklore; stars; Native American; coyotes; love

A retelling of a Northwest coyote legend, "an old tale about love and the way things came to be." Headstrong coyote, in love with a beautiful blue star, goes to the top of the highest mountain and grabs hold of her, but she will have none of him. She takes him way up high and drops him, forming Crater Lake in the process. After reading this one, whenever you hear coyote howling on a starry night, you'll be reminded of his song of love.

Dancing With the Wind   PICTURE BOOK

AUTHOR: Sheldon Orser • ILLUSTRATOR: James Bernardin
HC: Rising Moon
THEMES: wind; teamwork; comfort; weather; storytelling; folklore

An original folktale about how the wind became invisible, told as a comforting story to a fearful young child. The animals of the forest realize that none of them is strong, brave, or smart enough to release the wind from her human captor, so they band together in a marvelous example of teamwork. Once freed, the wind decrees, "Never again will you know where and when I will dance. You will feel only the tease of my gusts and breezes to remind you of what you once knew."

Days of the Blackbird: A Tale of Northern Italy   PICTURE BOOK
AUTHOR/ILLUSTRATOR: Tomie dePaola
HC: Putnam
THEMES: Italy; birds; illness; fathers and daughters; kindness

Gemma's father is ill, and the songs of birds filling his courtyard give him pleasure. But no bird offers more comfort than La Colomba, who refuses to fly south for the winter because she knows he will miss her songs. In the author's note, dePaola explains that the idea for this tender tale comes from Italy's Le Giornate della Merla, "which takes place the last three days of January. It is called Days of the Blackbird because they are the coldest days of the year. The story goes that it gets so cold that the white doves hide in the chimney tops to stay warm. And when they come out, they are black from the soot." DePaola has added exquisite paintings, Italian fresco style, to this moving story.

★ Dem Bones   PICTURE BOOK NONFICTION
AUTHOR/ILLUSTRATOR: Bob Barner
HC: Chronicle
THEMES: science; songs; music; bones; human body

"Toe bone connected to da foot bone. . . . Foot bone connected to da ankle bone. . . ." Children have been singing the popular tune for ages. Barner's lively, colorful illustrations of skeletons dance, horns blaring, through the pages of this anatomy book for youngsters. "The foot bones are the basement of your skeleton. The twenty-two bones in your foot support the entire weight of your body." As the song bounces through the pages Barner also relates about different bones in the human body.

Have fun with this one. It's a sing-along book. It's a science book. I like to go from page to page, singing and pointing out the clever scientific facts as though they were coming from my brain. Why not? You won't get caught unless you share this with a reader.

Dogs   PICTURE BOOK NONFICTION
AUTHOR/ILLUSTRATOR: Gail Gibbons
HC/PB: Holiday House
THEMES: communication; dogs; pets

Gail Gibbons writes straightforward, fact-filled books about familiar subjects four year olds will understand and eight-year-olds will find fascinating. Brightly illustrated, the series that includes *Dogs* is one of the best nonfiction series for our youngest children. Look for her list of other titles including: *Wolves* and *The Puffins are Back.*

A Fish in His Pocket   PICTURE BOOK

AUTHOR/ILLUSTRATOR: Denys Cazet
HC: Orchard
THEMES: guilt; school; worry; death; responsibility

Sometimes you do something you can't take back. It's too late. All that's left is guilt and worry. That's what happens to Russell who stops to look into a pond on his way to school. Accidentally his notebook slips into the water, and he has to retrieve it. That's when he discovers a small dead fish inside. He puts it into his pocket and goes to school where he spends the day worrying about what to do. Cazet handles the subject with sensitivity. A good choice for discussing feelings with your young child. Another Cazet gem that deals straight on with feelings is *Frosted Glass.* Find it in your library; it's worth the search.

Frogs   PICTURE BOOK NONFICTION

AUTHOR/ILLUSTRATOR: Gail Gibbons
HC/PB: Holiday House
THEMES: frogs; toads; comparisons

Did you know there are more than 38,000 kinds of frogs? Here you'll learn just about everything you ever wanted to know about them—from how their bodies change as they grow to how frogs are different from toads. Some others in this popular series are *Sharks, Whales, Sea Turtles, Spiders* and *Monarch Butterflies.*

From Seed to Plant   PICTURE BOOK NONFICTION

AUTHOR/ILLUSTRATOR: Gail Gibbons
HC/PB: Holiday House
THEMES: spring; plants; gardening; vegetables

Simple and straightforward, it's a book that will come in handy for those springtime plant-a-bean projects. Gibbons writes about nature in an accessible style, good for that first nonfiction experience. Another book we like is *Honeymakers,* about bees.

Gila Monsters Meet You at the Airport   PICTURE BOOK

AUTHOR: Marjorie Weinman Sharmat • ILLUSTRATOR: Byron Barton
PB: Puffin
THEMES: New York; comparisons;
moving; U.S.A., the West; change;
fear of new things

A boy moving west from New York
City is full of apprehension—he's
heard it's really strange out west!
He meets a boy at the airport
who is moving to New York with
similar fears. A fun look at the
misinformation we sometimes
let rule our choices.

> **BOOKS TALK**
>
> From siblings to classmates, from worrying about fitting in to celebrating holidays, books present situations familiar to children. Choose books that relate to your child's current interests while providing a natural link to discussion.

Goody O'Grumpity   PICTURE BOOK

AUTHOR: Carol Ryrie Brink • ILLUSTRATOR: Ashley Wolff
HC: North South Books
THEMES: cake; baking; poem; recipes; Pilgrims; U.S. history, Colonial
America

"When Goody O' Grumpity baked a cake . . . the pigs came nuzzling out
of their pens, the dogs ran sniffing and so did the hens, and the children
flocked by the dozens and tens . . ." Wolff's hand-colored linoleum prints
add a taste of Early America to this poem so rich with spices you can
almost smell cake cooking. For those who think that's a good idea, a
spice cake recipe is included.

The House on East 88th Street   PICTURE BOOK

AUTHOR/ILLUSTRATOR: Bernard Waber
HC/PB: Houghton Mifflin
THEMES: family; New York; crocodiles; friendship; fitting in; city life

Welcome to the world of lovable Lyle, the urban crocodile. These charming tales (including *Lyle, Lyle Crocodile*, and *Lyle at the Office*) won't tell
you much about how real crocodiles behave, but watching Lyle interact
with people in the city will give you plenty of chuckles.

Hush! A Thai Lullaby   PICTURE BOOK
AUTHOR: Minfong Ho • ILLUSTRATOR: Holly Meade
HC: Orchard
THEMES: lullabies; comfort; Thailand; animals; insects; rhyme; mischief; babies; mothers; predictable; bedtime

From a teeny mosquito to an enormous elephant, creatures surrounding the thatch-roofed house where the baby sleeps are hushed by the child's mother. At the end, everyone, even mother, is asleep—except for the baby who has come out of the hammock to play. Fun and beautifully illustrated, this makes a delightful before sleep story.

I Got a Family   PICTURE BOOK
AUTHOR: Melrose Cooper • ILLUSTRATOR: Dale Gottlieb
HC: Henry Holt
THEMES: family; community; love

Sure, it's not grammatically correct, but it has real heart. A warm, inclusive book for all families.

I'll Always Love You   PICTURE BOOK
AUTHOR/ILLUSTRATOR: Hans Wilhelm
HC: Crown
THEMES: dogs, death; loss; love; grief

A poignant reminder of how our loved ones live on with us after we die. This is a good book to use in the event of a pet's death, as its comforting message and warm illustrations will help to soothe as well as give strength.

Imogene's Antlers   PICTURE BOOK
AUTHOR/ILLUSTRATOR: David Small
HC: Crown • PB: Dragonfly
THEMES: change; strong girls; humor; fantasy

Taking an absurd notion and treating it as if it were possible is one of the trademarks of David Small's picture books. Here, Imogene wakes up one morning with quite an impressive rack, and though she takes it in stride, the rest of the world has trouble coping. Hilarious!

DEALING WITH DEATH

What do you offer a child who has experienced the death of a family member, neighbor, school chum—or even a cherished pet? There are excellent books available, but we suggest you read them aloud before they are needed. Even with the best intentions, family members who want to ease the sorrow and answer difficult questions are often upset themselves. While even the best book can only begin to help ease the grief, if a story and its ideas are already familiar, it will be more of a comfort. And even a child fortunate enough to never have to go through one of these experiences may need help understanding a friend's situation.

We strongly recommend *Badger's Parting Gifts* and *Lifetimes.* Each has a different approach and works as a starting point for discussion. Badger is told in story format and deals primarily with feelings about loss. *Lifetimes* is nonfiction, a straightforward account of living and dying.

For the middle-school child who may want something more substantial to read on his own, try *Death Is Hard to Live With*, by Janet Bode. Reading this no-nonsense collection of firsthand accounts of teenagers who have experienced loss, is like sitting in a room full of peers who offer the promise, "you will survive this."

Other titles you may wish to consider: *You Hold Me and I'll Hold You, The Tenth Good Thing About Barney, Waiting for the Whales, Grandad Bill's Song, Fireflies, Peach Pies and Lullabies, The Dead Bird, The Bridge to Terabitha, Everett Anderson's Goodbye, Missing May, I'll Always Love You, Annie and the Old One, Nana Upstairs, Nana Downstairs, Mick Harte Was Here,* and *On My Honor.*

Jeremy Kooloo
                                                                    PICTURE BOOK
AUTHOR/ILLUSTRATOR: Tim Mahurin

HC: Dutton

THEMES: wordplay; cats; connections; alphabet

Jeremy Kooloo is an irresistible cat whose story is told in ABC order with one word from each letter of the alphabet. "Indeed, Jeremy Kooloo Loves Milk. Nonfat." This is a lot more difficult than it looks. Try it. Or better yet, make it into a family project or get (older) children to come up with their own stories.

★ The Keeping Quilt
                                                                    PICTURE BOOK
AUTHOR/ILLUSTRATOR: Patricia Polacco

HC: Simon & Schuster

THEMES: Russia; quilts; family; weddings; celebrations; Jews; immigration; symbols

For four generations, a quilt made from Anna's babushka, Uncle Vladimir's shirt, Aunt Havelah's nightdress and scraps from a basket of other old clothes, is passed from mother to daughter, from celebration to celebration. Moving and rich in family tradition, Polacco's story of her own Russian family gives young readers an understanding of the value of tradition.

Children may not recognize their own family traditions. Here's a perfect chance to point them out. Mine included Hawaiian leis and hot bread pudding at Christmas time.

The Legend of the Poinsettia   PICTURE BOOK
AUTHOR/ILLUSTRATOR: Tomie dePaola
HC: Putnam
THEMES: Christmas; flowers; poinsettias; gifts; miracles; folklore; Mexico; Spanish

DePaola tells the Mexican legend of how, with a miracle and a little girl's gift, poinsettias have become part of the Christmas celebration. Two other legends are retold in dePaola's *Legend of the Bluebonnet* and *Legend of the Indian Paintbrush*.

The Library Dragon   PICTURE BOOK
AUTHOR: Carmen Agra Deedy • ILLUSTRATOR: Michael P. White
HC: Peachtree
THEMES: dragons; librarians; libraries; school; books; reading; change

A fun read aloud about a library with an actual dragon for a librarian! Miss Lotta Scales is more concerned with keeping her library in order— DO NOT TOUCH THE BOOKS, the sign reads—than with the children who come there, and her fiery personality has scared everyone away. When a nearsighted child dares to read aloud in the library, a remarkable transformation occurs. Every librarian in America needs a copy of this for story hour.

Lon Po Po: A Red-Riding Hood Story From China   PICTURE BOOK
AUTHOR/ILLUSTRATOR: Ed Young
HC: Philomel • PB: Paperstar
THEMES: China; fairy tales; sisters; wolves; strong girls; folklore

Young's dramatic use of watercolors and pastels will get your attention in this powerful book. Look for a moment at his first haunting image of

AUTHOR SPOTLIGHT ON JOANNA COLE

IF Joanna Cole had contributed nothing to the world of children's books other than her *Magic School Bus* books, her popularity would still be assured. That phenomenon has brought science into the homes of countless children and made many a schoolteacher wish that she were as gifted as the fictional Miss Frizzle. But there is so much more that Joanna Cole has to offer children.

Science is clearly her love, and the series of younger books that look at the bodies of animals (*A Bird's Body, A Cat's Body, A Dog's Body*) belong in every library in the country. Featuring clear and precise text accompanied by black-and-white photos, these are perfect nature books for the young and curious.

Her concern for the trials and tribulations of childhood is evident in her books about children's rites of passage: *Asking About Sex and Growing Up, How I Was Adopted, Your New Potty,* and *The New Baby at Your House.*

As a collaborator with gifted artists like illustrator Bruce Degen and photographer Jerome Wexler, she is expert at blending the visual and the word. As a co-writer with Stephanie Calmenson, Cole has created a series of books that archive the folklore of childhood, *Anna Banana: 101 Jump-Rope Rhymes; Give a Dog a Bone: Stories, Poems, Jokes, and Riddles About Dogs, Pin the Tail on the Donkey and Other Party Games* and *Pat-A-Cake and Other Play Rhymes.*

As if all this weren't enough, she has compiled some of the best anthologies for family reading in her books *Ready . . . Set . . . Read!: The Beginning Reader's Treasury, Ready . . . Set . . . Read—And Laugh: A Funny Treasury For Beginning Readers,* and *The Read-Aloud Treasury.* Each volume presents delightful excerpts and complete renditions of books that are (or ought to be) childhood favorites. Through these reasonably priced anthologies, families are offered a look at a wide range of stories and appealing illustrations, and through her exemplary work, Joanna Cole has helped to introduce thousands of families to the joys of reading and the windows reading opens to many of life's other joys.

a wolf. Then go on to enjoy every word of this ancient Red Riding Hood tale from China.

Mac and Marie and the Train Toss Surprise   PICTURE BOOK
AUTHOR: Elizabeth Howard • ILLUSTRATOR: Gail Carter
HC: Four Winds
THEMES: family; uncles; guessing; surprises; trains; African American

Two siblings eagerly await a surprise their uncle from faraway Florida promises to toss from the train. What's in the package? Close that page and let your child guess. (By the way, it's a giant seashell with echoes of their uncle's home.)

The Magic School Bus in the Time of the Dinosaurs   PICTURE BOOK NONFICTION
AUTHOR: **Joanna Cole** • ILLUSTRATOR: Bruce Degen
HC/PB: Scholastic
THEMES: dinosaurs; science; adventure; nature; animals, prehistoric

Fasten your seat belts and get ready for a tour of the Triasic, Jurassic, and Cretaceous periods with one of the country's favorite teachers— Miss Frizzle! This time her magic School Bus goes to *The Time of the Dinosaurs*. Author Cole and illustrator Degen have fun with this one— from the fact-filled pages to their author photos where they emerge as Joannasaurus Rex and Bruceratops! In addition to dinosaurs this remarkable series seems able to take on any science topic of interest to kids and deliver with a touch of comic book style that draws readers in to the words. A ton of information gets conveyed in these books, and there are gobs of outstanding titles to check out, including Magic School Bus adventures . . . *Lost in the Solar System*, . . . *Inside a Beehive*, . . . *Inside the Body*, and . . . *At the Waterworks*.

The Minstrel and the Dragon Pup   PICTURE BOOK
AUTHOR: Rosemary Sutcliff • ILLUSTRATOR: Emma Chichester Clark
HC/PB: Candlewick
THEMES: dragons; fantasy; pets

There is nothing like the impact of good writing, and Sutcliff is an expert. "It had green goose-pimply skin and a long tail, and two little flapping things rather like small damp kid gloves that were the promise of wings on its back, and a round pink stomach that, as it dried off in the sunshine, began to be fuzzy with a kind of green swan's down." Imaginations will soar as young readers, or listeners, meet this dragon pup and its person.

My Father's Dragon   FICTION
AUTHOR/ILLUSTRATOR: Ruth Stiles Gannett
PB: Knopf
THEMES: fantasy; dragons; family

A fantasy that will hold the interest of a child just becoming comfortable with chapter books. It has all the elements of fantasy writing and can be read aloud in one long sitting by an adult. The sequels, written in the same charming style, are *The Dragons of Blueland* and *Elmer and the Dragons*.

My Hen Is Dancing   PICTURE BOOK NONFICTION
AUTHOR: Karen Wallace • ILLUSTRATOR: Anita Jeram
HC/PB: Candlewick
THEMES: science; nature; farms; chickens

Hens preen themselves every day with oil they get from where their tale feathers grow. They use their beaks to clean up and they scratch their ears with their toenails. Interesting hen facts and fun illustrations will pique the interest of curious young readers. Other titles in this series by various authors and illustrators include *A Piece of String Is a Wonderful Thing, I Love Guinea Pigs, All Pigs Are Beautiful, Caterpillar, Caterpillar, Spider Watching, Think of an Eel,* and *Think of a Beaver*.

My Song Is Beautiful: Poems and Pictures
in Many Voices   POETRY ANTHOLOGY
EDITOR: Mary Ann Hoberman • ILLUSTRATOR: Various
HC: Little Brown
THEMES: cultural diversity; comparisons; friendship

"Daddy says the world is a drum tight and hard and I told him
I'm gonna beat out my own rhythm"—Nikki Giovanni

Fourteen poems show the similarities and differences that make up our friendships and who we are.

★ Piggie Pie   PICTURE BOOK
AUTHOR: Margie Palatini • ILLUSTRATOR: Howard Fine
HC/PB: Clarion
THEMES: wordplay; humor; folktale variation; witches; disguises; farms; hunger; animals, farm; cooking; triumph

Hilarious! One of the funniest books we know. Very strong visuals make this a small-group book, but you will love reading it to your own child. Gritch the witch is on a search for piggies to put into her pie, but the pigs outsmart her at every turn. When she meets up with a wolf, also the victim of the pigs' cleverness, the two very hungry nasties go off arm in arm to an imagined conclusion that is fitting and funny.

The Planets
PICTURE BOOK NONFICTION

AUTHOR/ILLUSTRATOR: Gail Gibbons
HC/PB: Holiday House
THEMES: planets; Solar System; outerspace

Basic information on the planets in our solar system, including how they orbit and rotate. Gibbons' take on astronomy can be found in *Star Gazers*.

Puff . . . Flash . . . Bang! A Book About Signals
PICTURE BOOK NONFICTION

AUTHOR/ILLUSTRATOR: Gail Gibbons
HC: Morrow
THEMES: communication; signs and signals

Gibbons uses vivid art as a form of teaching the history of signals and how they are used today. See how many a child recognizes. When you want good, solid information for young readers on a variety of subjects, turn to Gibbons. Other titles include *Pirates, Recycle, Beacons of Light* (lighthouses), and *Catch the Wind* (kites) are all good.

Puffins Climb, Penguins Rhyme
PICTURE BOOK NONFICTION

AUTHOR/ILLUSTRATOR: Bruce McMillan (photographs)
HC: Gulliver
THEMES: puffins; penguins; Iceland; Antarctica; wordplay; vocabulary; verbs; comparisons

While puffins live at the top of the world in Iceland and penguins at the bottom in Antarctica, readers can observe them through photographs. Each two-page spread is made up of simple, four-word rhymes. "Puffins land. Puffins stand." "Penguins glare. Penguins share." Cover up the last word on each second page and ask your child to guess which word is hidden. Some will come up with the same word and others will find new words that work just as well. It's a fun way to boost verb vocabulary.

Robin Hood & Little John   PICTURE BOOK

AUTHOR: Barbara Cohen • ILLUSTRATOR: David Ray
HC: Philomel
THEMES: folklore; England; Robin Hood

For beginning readers and for reading aloud, this is an excellent introduction to the legend of Robin Hood.

Rumpelstiltskin   PICTURE BOOK

AUTHOR/ILLUSTRATOR: Paul O. Zelinsky
HC: Dutton • PB: Puffin
THEMES: fairy tales; folklore; Germany; history, medieval times; resourcefulness; guessing; playing tricks; little folk

Zelinsky's extraordinary oil paintings set in medieval times make this our choice for Grimm's popular tale.

Seven Candles for Kwanzaa   PICTURE BOOK NONFICTION

AUTHOR: Andrea Davis Pinkney • ILLUSTRATOR: Brian Pinkney
HC: Dial
THEMES: Kwanzaa; African American; celebrations; traditions

Kwanzaa, which is Swahili for "first fruits of the harvest," is an African American holiday celebrated by millions every year between December 27 and January 1. The Pinkney team's book about Kwanzaa is both beautiful and informative.

Sing Sophie!   PICTURE BOOK

AUTHOR: Daylè Ann Dodds •
ILLUSTRATOR: Roseanne Utzinger
HC/PB: Candlewick
THEMES: thunder; creativity; strong girl; songs; music; imagination; singing; rhyme

Make up your own tune to this cowgirl song fest. Sophie Adams will give you the words. "My dog ran off, my cat has fleas, my fish won't swim, and I hate peas. But I'm a cowgirl through and through yipee-ky-yee! yippee-ky-yuu!" We

RAISING A READER . . .

is easier said than done. We want our children to become independent and able to make their own decisions. Learning the consequences of their choices is the goal, but sometimes the temptation to protect and soften the blow gets in the way. Standing between a child and her choices can cause her to leave you out of the process. Better to be involved, reading what she reads and available to answer questions or discuss the hard issues with her. Nourish her questioning mind and guide her. Stifle it and she may back away from reading altogether.

like her words, but her family would just as soon she go off somewhere else to sing. They change their tune when one of her songs saves the day. Be prepared for a rousing singing response to this rollicking read aloud.

Tales of Trotter Street   COLLECTION

AUTHOR/ILLUSTRATOR: Shirley Hughes
HC: Candlewick
THEMES: family; friendship; trucks; houses; community; neighbors; new baby; Christmas; school; elderly and children

Four storybooks in one volume, each a glimpse at life in an urban neighborhood in England. In *The Snow Lady, The Big Concrete Lorry, Wheels,* and *Angel Mae,* Hughes shows us the events and people of Trotter Street in her customary warm style. Longer than her books aimed at younger children, but still picture books, these are excellent introductions to English way of life. The vocabulary hasn't been Americanized, so Mom is Mum and a truck is a lorry and pajamas are spelled "pyjamas." Except for these few touches, these stories could be set in any number of places, so universal are Hughes's themes and characters.

Ten Sly Piranhas: A Counting Story in Reverse
(A Tale of Wickedness—and Worse!)   PICTURE BOOK

AUTHOR: William Wise • ILLUSTRATOR: Victoria Chess
HC: Dial
THEMES: rhythm; humor; math; counting; fish

A school of ten sly piranhas gradually dwindles as they waylay and eat each other. There's read-aloud rhythm in numbers from ten to one, and Chess's chunky pictures are bound to make you laugh.

The Three-Legged Cat   PICTURE BOOK

AUTHOR: Margaret Mahy • ILLUSTRATOR: Jonathan Allen
HC: Viking
THEMES: hats; humor; cats; travel; mistaken identity

This is one of those surefire read alouds that is silly enough to capture the most passive listener! Cyril the swagman accidently carries off his sister's three-legged cat, mistaking it for his furry hat. The cat is thrilled to travel and his sister enjoys the hat! "I've never had a better cat. it's true that it moults, but we all have our faults. It's cheap to keep and is always asleep."

LIBRARY 911

I was asked to observe a library to offer my opinion as to why children were not checking out books. When I walked through the doors, I was confronted with shelves of drab, spine-out volumes set in orderly rows in the stale library air. "Color!" I thought. "This place needs color!" But when I heard the librarian caution a class of second graders, "Do not touch a book unless you can read it," I recognized the true problem. This librarian didn't understand children. She didn't realize that part of the fun is in the choosing, not just reading. Whether their choices are based on the favorite of a friend, the picture on the front, or the subject matter, children need to go through the process of making a choice. Only when they've had the freedom to do that will they learn to make the right choices for themselves.

The Toll-Bridge Troll   PICTURE BOOK

AUTHOR: Patricia Rae Wolff • ILLUSTRATOR: Kimberly Bulcken Root
HC: Browndeer
THEMES: trolls; school; riddles; cleverness; playing tricks; lessons

Every day on his way to school, Trigg comes upon a young troll who demands a penny to cross his bridge. Trigg knows that over time a penny a day could become expensive, so each day he comes up with a riddle to outsmart the troll. The ultimate lesson here is that to become smart, it's a good idea to go to school!

Tony's Bread   PICTURE BOOK

AUTHOR/ILLUSTRATOR: Tomie dePaola
HC: Putnam • PB: Paperstar
THEMES: folklore; fathers and daughters; bakers; bread; Italy; creativity

A baker with big dreams, his beautiful daughter, a wealthy nobleman who wants to marry her, and three gossipy sisters are the cast of characters in this wonderful retelling of the Italian legend of the origin of *panettone*, or Tony's Bread.

Turtle in July

POETRY COLLECTION

AUTHOR: Marilyn Singer • ILLUSTRATOR: Jerry Pinkney
HC: Atheneum • PB: Aladdin
THEMES: turtles; animals; seasons; mice; owls; insects; nature; snakes; point of view

From the voices of mice, owls, snakes and bugs come poems set in different times of the year. Rich reading for any season.

Twilight Comes Twice

PICTURE BOOK NONFICTION

AUTHOR: Ralph Fletcher • ILLUSTRATOR: Kate Kiesler
HC: Clarion
THEMES: time; night; daytime; twilight; dusk; dawn

Evocative poetry combines with luminous artwork to create a picture book that helps define twilight, dawn and dusk. The use of language is splendid, and the images remain long after the book is closed.

When Africa Was Home

PICTURE BOOK

AUTHOR: Karen Lynn Williams • ILLUSTRATOR: Floyd Cooper
HC/PB: Orchard
THEMES: friendship; Africa; homesickness; cultural diversity; change; family; community

There are many books about missing home. This is one of the finest, not just for the unusual perspective of a white boy missing his African homeland, but for the brilliant paintings of Floyd Cooper and the text of Karen Lynn Williams, who knows how to take a story about a specific longing and make it universal.

Windsongs and Rainbows

PICTURE BOOK

AUTHOR: Albert Burton • ILLUSTRATOR: Susan Stillman
HC: Simon & Schuster
THEMES: weather; rain; wind; sun; storms; senses; vocabulary; rainbows

Alert your senses to the feel of the weather. See, hear and feel the wind, the rain, the sun, the storm. "See the rain pock the soil and freckle the walk. Pluck the roses and pearl the web. Huddle the ducks, puddle the paths, and color the sky with rainbows." This kind of language is a delight to read out loud while it challenges your child's vocabulary skills.

The Wing Shop   PICTURE BOOK
AUTHOR: Elvira Woodruff • ILLUSTRATOR: Stephen Gammell
HC/PB: Holiday House
THEMES: homesickness; home; wings; flying; fantasy

Matthew hates his new neighborhood and wants to go back to his old house. On his journey, he stumbles upon Featherman's Wing Shop, where the wings are "guaranteed to get you somewhere or your money back." The adventures he has when he tries on several pairs of wings convince him to give his new home a try.

You Hold Me and I'll Hold You   PICTURE BOOK
AUTHOR: Jo Carson • ILLUSTRATOR: Annie Cannon
HC/PB: Orchard
THEMES: comfort; death; family; funerals; loss; grief

A useful book on grief. A young girl whose aunt has just died observes the preparations for the funeral. With commentary on the way adults handle loss that is honest and simple, the book is never maudlin. The comforting solution is found in the story's title.

> We get so frustrated when we hear parents in bookstores or libraries overriding their children's book selections in an arbitrary fashion. We have to bite our tongues when we hear them saying a book is too old, too young, or not good enough. If a child chooses a book that is too long for him to read, let him discover for himself how difficult a choice he has made. If you feel it might be too scary, how else will he find the limit of his imagination unless he gets good and scared?

Zeke Pippin   PICTURE BOOK
AUTHOR/ILLUSTRATOR: William Steig
HC/PB: HarperCollins
THEMES: music; magic; family; problem solving; running away; bullies; adventure

While moseying down his street one morning, Zeke Pippin picked up a harmonica that fell out of a garbage wagon. Zeke proved to be quite a good musician, but the magic in that piece of fallen garbage worked like a sleeping pill—which children soon discover has its bad points and its good. Steig is an expert at painting pictures with words and at illustrating his words with pictures. For a look at a similar theme for younger readers try *Mama Don't Allow* by Thacher Hurd.

Although they boast a wide range in listening level, these books include some dialect, words in other languages, or a format that add challenge to the reading level. Read these aloud or offer them up to your M reader to share with the rest of the family.

Alice Nizzy Nazzy: The Witch of Santa Fe   PICTURE BOOK

AUTHOR: Tony Johnston • ILLUSTRATOR: Tomie dePaola

HC: Putnam

THEMES: Spanish words; witches; triumph; folklore; U.S.A., the Southwest; folktale variations

Writer Tony Johnston says, "There's nothing like a good witch to stir the imagination. But the witch I love best, Russia's Baba Yaga, has a story told countless times." So she moves Baba to Santa Fe, gives her a horned lizard for a pet, an old adobe hut with road runner legs and calls her Alice Nizzy Nazzy.

"If you know how and love to read, you can find out ANYTHING about EVERYTHING and EVERYTHING about ANYTHING."
—Tomie dePaola, author/illustrator of Clown of God

A fun read aloud with three voices: a Spanish speaking lizard, a young girl who can't find her sheep, and Alice Nizzy Nazzy. Blend repetition, good-over-evil, and the charm of the Southwest, then add Tomie dePaola's wild illustrations, and you have a character that will cause children to cackle!

All of You Was Singing

PICTURE BOOK

AUTHOR: Richard Lewis • ILLUSTRATOR: Ed Young

HC: Macmillan • PB: Aladdin

THEMES: Aztec; music; folklore; creation

From the ancient Aztec tale of how music came to the world. Rich and musical language with pictures to match.

Arroz Con Leche: Popular Songs and Rhymes From Latin America

SONGBOOK

AUTHOR/ILLUSTRATOR: Lulu Delacre

HC/PB: Scholastic

THEMES: rhyme; Latin America; songs; music; Spanish language; bilingual

Help yourself to a bilingual festival of twelve traditional Latin-American songs with the music to match. Delacre has even included a recipe for Arroz Con Leche!

Ashanti to Zulu: African Traditions

PICTURE BOOK

AUTHOR: Margaret Musgrove • ILLUSTRATOR: Leo & Diane Dillon

PB: Puffin

THEMES: alphabet; Africa; traditions

Award-winning art and informative text have kept this stunning ABC primer of African Culture in print for over twenty years.

Badger's Bring Something Party

PICTURE BOOK

AUTHOR: Hiawyn Oram • ILLUSTRATOR: Susan Varley

HC: Lothrop

THEMES: fitting in; friendship; self-respect; parties; gifts; emotions; embarrassment

Everyone brought something to *Badger's Bring Something Party*. Everybody but mole, that is. He goes to the party ". . . without anything, just himself. His muddy, unwashed, unslicked-down self, not at all neat or dressed up." He feels self-conscious and embarrassed until he is reminded about his "interesting" self who has been forgotten. Children sometimes find themselves feeling like mole, and will certainly have something to say about how different characters behave in this tale. It may even lead to a discussion about their own "friends." This same community is lovingly portrayed in *Badger's Bad Mood* and *Badger's Parting Gifts*.

The Bee Tree   PICTURE BOOK

AUTHOR/ILLUSTRATOR: Patricia Polacco

HC: Philomel

THEMES: disability; books; reading; family; school; traditions; bees; literacy; honey; handicaps

If you treasure the love of reading, then this book will bring a lump to your throat. Based on an actual tradition in Polacco's family.

Bein' With You This Way   PICTURE BOOK

AUTHOR: W. Nikola-Lisa • ILLUSTRATOR: Michael Bryant

HC/PB: Lee & Low

THEMES: neighbors; rhythm; cultural diversity; friendship; community

This neighborhood rap has a finger-snapping rhythm so catchy that young readers will memorize it. Author Nikola-Lisa and illustrator Bryant have created a canvas that points out our differences and chants our similarities!

Birdsong   PICTURE BOOK

AUTHOR: Audrey Wood • ILLUSTRATOR: Robert Florczak

HC: Harcourt Brace

THEMES: birds; habitats; U.S.A., the states; flowers

The calls and songs of 18 North American birds are featured in this beautifully illustrated book. If you have a child who is interested in birds, this is a great first encounter with bird watching.

★ Bo Rabbit Smart for True: Tall Tales
From the Gullah   PICTURE BOOK

AUTHOR: Priscilla Jaquith • ILLUSTRATOR: Ed Young

HC: Philomel

THEMES: folklore; African American; U.S.A., the Southeast; Gullah; trickster tales; tall tales

It's great fun to tell stories that end with a clear lesson. You'll find those here. "No matter how little you are, if you're smart for true, you can best the biggest crittuh in the sea and the biggest crittuh on earth. It stands so." We feast on tales that offer sound effects, "But hard as Elephant pull, hrup, hrup, hrup, he can't pull Whale out of the sea." Clear, picture-producing prose helps to stretch the imagination. ". . . Crane is forever hungry. His stomach stands so far from his mouth that when the victual travels down his throat, before he's swallowed it good, his stomach rings the bell to tell his mouth dinner time has come again." All of the above and more are found in a delightful, read-from-the-top-to-the-bottom package of Southern Gullah tales storytellers can't resist.

California, Here We Come!   PICTURE BOOK NONFICTION

AUTHOR: Pam Munoz Ryan • ILLUSTRATOR: Kay Salem
HC/PB: Charlesbridge
THEMES: California; U.S. history; rhyme

Solid information about the most populated state in the nation, delivered in a fun, rhyming style that will fill children's heads with facts as it entertains them. Have this in the car on your next California vacation.

★ Chato's Kitchen   PICTURE BOOK

AUTHOR: Gary Soto • ILLUSTRATOR: Susan Guevara
HC: Putnam • PB: Paperstar
THEMES: Spanish words; survival; Hispanic; cats; mice; Los Angeles; triumph, cleverness; humor; meals

Soto's words and Guevara's hilarious paintings turn this read aloud into a "tell it again" repeater! Chato is the coolest low-riding cat in East L.A. and has just discovered that his new next door neighbors are the plumpest, juiciest, tastiest-looking family of mice to move into the barrio in a long time! There is great language here, in English and Spanish. A glossary of Spanish words is included.

A Child's First Bible   COLLECTION

AUTHOR: Sandol Stoddard • ILLUS-
TRATOR: Tony Chen
HC: Dial
THEMES: religion; Christianity

Forty bible stories from the old and new testaments are adapted for children and perfectly complemented by Chen's extraordinary watercolors. Another fine collection is Tomie dePaola's *Bible Stories*.

> ### LINKING BOOKS TO LIFE
>
> Plan some of your family activities around book themes or vice versa. It can be as simple as playing "freeze in place" after reading *Don't Fidget a Feather* by Erica Silverman, or writing a letter to the Amazonia Foundation following *Amazon Diary, The Jungle Adventures Of Alex Winters*, by Hudson Talbott. Your children will notice a direct connection between reading and how it positively affects their lives and you'll all have fun in the process!

★ Don't Fidget a Feather

AUTHOR: Erica Silverman • ILLUSTRATOR: S.D. Schindler
HC: Simon & Schuster
THEMES: competition; friendship; geese; ducks; foxes

This one captured us immediately! Duck and Gander have a freeze-in-place contest to decide who is the champion of champions. Bees, bunnies, crows, not even the wind can get them to move . . . not even Fox, who stuffs them into a bag and takes them home for dinner. We've tested this tale on various elementary ages. Stop reading just after Fox lifts Gander high over the soup pot and says, "In we go." Children's pleas of "go on!" and "don't stop now!" add to the fun!

Down by the River: Afro-Caribbean Rhymes, Games, and Songs for Children

ANTHOLOGY

AUTHOR: Grace Hallworth • ILLUSTRATOR: Caroline Binch
HC: Scholastic
THEMES: rhyme; songs; games; jumping rope; folklore; Caribbean

A good source for anyone looking to expand their repertoire of games and songs, made especially fine by Binch's illustrations.

The Dragons Are Singing Tonight

POETRY COLLECTION

AUTHOR: Jack Prelutsky • ILLUSTRATOR: Peter Sis
HC: Greenwillow
THEMES: dragons; vocabulary

"I am counting off the seconds till my dragon first appears, Poking through the shell to freedom with a horn, I can't wait to see its winglets, tiny muzzle, tail and ears, When my brand new baby dragon's finally born." Jack Prelutsky's poems often stretch a child's vocabulary, and these are no exception. Another fine collaboration between Prelutsky and gifted illustrator Peter Sis is *Monday's Troll*.

Finster Frets

PICTURE BOOK

AUTHOR: Kent Baker • ILLUSTRATOR: H. Werner Zimmermann
PB: Stoddart
THEMES: humor; hats; birds; problem solving; worry

Old Finster awakens one morning with a bird-nest in his hair. "What's this?", he says. "Has someone strawed my topside? Has someone broomed my brain?" He then goes to his wife for help. "Holly Berry, my faithful, my fortress, my white-haired puppy love, look what I have on my head!"

Their attempts to get rid of the hatlike intruders not only makes a funny read aloud, but also leaves a place at the end for guessing.

The Great Ball Game: A Muskogee Story　　PICTURE BOOK

AUTHOR: Joseph Bruchac • ILLUS-
TRATOR: Susan L. Roth
HC: Dial
THEMES: Native American; competition; diversity; cooperation;
bats; solitude; comparisons;
games; folklore

Bruchac's retelling of a Muskogee Indian story shows how the bat came to be accepted as an animal instead of a bird, and why it is that birds fly south each winter. This legend will pique curiosity about bats.

> BATS . . .
> are not blind. In fact, they can see very well! There are close to a thousand different kinds of bats in the world. Baby bats are called pups, and mother bats carry them when they search for food. *Bats: Nightfliers* by Betsy Maestro reveals fascinating facts about these highly unusual, intelligent animals. *Stellaluna* by Jannell Cannon will also lead readers into seeking more information about bats. Other "bat" titles include *Zipping Zapping Zooming Bats, Shadows of the Night, Outside Inside Book of Bats,* and *The Great Ball Game, a Muskogee Story.*

Harvey Potter's Balloon Farm　　PICTURE BOOK

AUTHOR: Jerdine Nolen • ILLUSTRATOR: Mark Buehner
HC: Lothrop
THEMES: balloons; farms; farmers; individuality; magic; fantasy

"Harvey Potter was a very strange fellow indeed. He was a farmer, but he didn't farm like my daddy did. He farmed a genuine, U.S. Government Inspected Balloon farm. No one knew exactly how he did it. Some folks say that it wasn't real, that it was magic. But I know what I saw, and those were real, actual balloons growing out of the plain ole ground!" Buehner's vivid, colorful paintings bring the reader right into the pages. A fantastic read aloud!

Kratts' Creatures:
Our Favorite Creatures　　PICTURE BOOK NONFICTION

AUTHOR: Martin and Chris Kratt • ILLUSTRATOR: various (photographs)
PB: Scholastic
THEMES: nature; animals

A series of engaging nature books, based on the hit PBS show, featuring wild photos and anecdotes of the Kratt Brothers' escapades as America's favorite animal kingdom authorities. Other titles include: *Going Baboony*, *In Search of the Real Tasmanian Devil*, and *Off to Elephant School*.

ACCESS DENIED

When libraries shelve books according to age and interest levels, it serves two purposes that may contradict each other—one purpose is to help the reader find, books they would be interested in, and the other is to limit access to books outside of their designated abilities. Many adults lose sight of the fact that the child reader can usually determine her level all by herself. Saying that because she is seven she must only select from books approved and designated for six to eight year olds can be damaging to a reader bound to find the right book for herself—it sends a message of exclusion about reading that the child can interpret as denial of her interests, and could result in her deciding that reading just isn't for her—too many restrictions. Better for you and your child to use what the book is about as a guide, rather than what level or age it is written for. Some organization is needed, of course, but let that organization serve as a starting point in making choices, not as law.

The Mouse and the Motorcycle

FICTION

AUTHOR: Beverly Cleary • ILLUSTRATOR: Louis Darling
HC: Morrow • PB: Avon
THEMES: mice; adventure; motorcycles; friendship; secrets; humor

The first of three novels that tell the tale of a motorcyle-mad mouse named Ralph, befriended by a boy named Keith, who keeps the secret of their adventures despite Ralph's impetuous nature. Ralph is the hero of this fun and involving read that will delight young readers embarking on long chapter books for the first time. Subsequent books are: *Runaway Ralph* and *Ralph S. Mouse*.

Never Take a Pig To Lunch: And Other Poems About the Fun of Eating

POETRY ANTHOLOGY

EDITOR/ILLUSTRATOR: Nadine Bernard Westcott
HC: Orchard
THEMES: food; humor, eating; rhyme

A tasty collection of more than 60 poems for young readers to laugh at—all about eating—by Jack Prelutsky, Ogden Nash, Eve Merriam, and others.

Nursery Tales Around the World   FOLKLORE COLLECTION
AUTHOR: Judy Sierra • ILLUSTRATOR: Stefano Vitale
HC: Clarion
THEMES: folklore; cultural diversity; storytelling

Eighteen tales, divided into six themes: Runaway Cookies, Incredible
Appetites, The Victory of the Smallest, Chain Tales, Slowpokes and
Speedsters, and Fooling the Big Bad Wolf. Sierra's energetic tales are perfect for reading aloud. Have fun with the comparisons. In this country
we sing along with the Gingerbread Man, "Run run, as fast as you can,
You can't catch me I'm the Gingerbread Man!" In Russia's "The Bun" the
tune is a bit different: "I'm a bun! I'm a bun! I was scraped from the
bin, . . . I ran away from Grandma. And I'll run away from you!" Notes
for the storyteller are included along with a bibliography.

The People Who Hugged Trees:
An Environmental Folk Tale   PICTURE BOOK
AUTHOR: Deborah Lee Rose • ILLUSTRATOR: Birgitta Saflund
HC/PB: Roberts Rinehart
THEMES: trees; forests; environment; strong girls; India; conflict and
resolution; courage; taking action; folklore

This is an example of a book with a strong message that never preaches
or sacrifices the story to get the moral across. Amrita Devi refuses to
allow the forest near her village to be cut down and with her determination helps to convince others to become Chipko, the people who hug
the trees. This classic Indian folktale is a great way to let kids know how
one person can make a difference.

The Random House Book of Poetry
for Children   POETRY ANTHOLOGY
EDITOR: Jack Prelutsky • ILLUSTRATOR: Arnold Lobel
HC: Random House
THEMES: poets; variety; rhyme

Even if your poetry shelf is packed, add this one. The upbeat match of
Lobel's illustrations with Prelutsky's selections offers a choice collection
for any child.

A Regular Flood of Mishap   PICTURE BOOK

AUTHOR: Tom Birdseye • ILLUSTRATOR: Megan Lloyd
HC/PB: Holiday House
THEMES: mishaps; mistakes; family; country life

Those who enjoyed "Airmail to the Moon" with its spunky heroine and
rustic dialogue will find Ima Bean from Mossyrock Creek an unforgettable character. She means well, but every time she tries to help out, she
goofs, resulting in a chain of events that spin wildly and hilariously out
of control. Fun to read aloud.

Rootabaga Stories, Part One   COLLECTION

AUTHOR: Carl Sandburg • ILLUSTRATOR: Michael Hague
HC/PB: Harcourt Brace
THEMES: fantasy; humor; imagination

Who marched in the procession when the Rag Doll married the Broom Handle? "Well, first came the Spoon Lickers. Every one of them had a tea spoon,
or a soup spoon, though most of them had a big table spoon. On the spoons,
what did they have? Oh, some had butter scotch, some had gravy, some had
marshmallow fudge . . ." Carl Sandburg's collection of stories is a fantasy
feast for every child's imagination with titles like, "The Story of Jason Squiff
and Why He Had a Popcorn Hat, Popcorn Mittens and Popcorn Shoes; How
Bimbo the Snip's Thumb Stuck to His Nose When the Wind Changed; Never
Kick a Slipper at the Moon; Two Stories About Corn Fairies, Blue Foxes,
Flongboos and Happenings that Happened in the United States and
Canada." Forty-nine wacky, wild stories will animate a child's daily routine
and send imaginations soaring. While the current editions include art by
Michael Hague and Paul Zelinsky (*More Rootabagas*), we also recommend look-
ing for the older editions with the original art by Maud and Miska Petersham
for a nostalgic treat. Also: *Rootabaga Stories, Part Two* and *More Rootabagas*.

Say Hola to Spanish   PICTURE BOOK

AUTHOR: Susan Middleton Elya • ILLUSTRATOR: Loretta Lopez
HC/PB: Lee & Low
THEMES: communication; rhyme; Spanish words; vocabulary

"Your hair is your pelo, your nose is nariz. Your grandmother's pelo is
probably gris." These ridiculous rhymes using everyday words will
tickle and teach at the same time. It won't be long before your young
reader is reciting all seventy Spanish words. You'll find a glossary in the
back.

Somewhere in the World Right Now   PICTURE BOOK

AUTHOR/ILLUSTRATOR: Stacey Schuett
HC/PB: Knopf
THEMES: geography; time; comparisons

Tour around the world via lushly painted maps and lyrical writing, and learn about the concept of time zones. It's practical, and you don't even have to pack!

South and North, East and West:
The Oxfam Book of Children's Stories   COLLECTION

EDITED BY: Michael Rosen • ILLUSTRATOR: various
HC: Candlewick
THEMES: cultural diversity; folklore; geography

Well-told tales from all over the world to read aloud. An excellent collection.

That Kookoory!   PICTURE BOOK

AUTHOR: Margaret Walden Froehlich • ILLUSTRATOR: Marla Frazee
HC: Browndeer
THEMES: farms; roosters; weasel; fairs; triumph

Kookoory is a rooster who is so excited about going to the fair that he thinks the moon is the rising sun, and he goes off to awaken his friends. The villain, a lurking weasel, is surprised to find his prey flapping along the path toward a farmyard cottage. "Like a checker piece, weasel sneaked from shadow smudge to shadow smudge." Once in a while we come across a read aloud where the clever gathering of words sets up perfect images. This is one.

What About Ladybugs?   PICTURE BOOK

AUTHOR/ILLUSTRATOR: Celia Godkin
HC: Sierra Club
THEMES: gardening; nature; ladybugs; insects

Interfering with the balance of nature can cause disastrous results. When a well-meaning gardener decides to get rid of the "bad" insects, he almost ruins his beautiful garden. A ladybug saves the day and children see how each insect has a job. Vibrant close-up illustrations add color to this important lesson.

SERIES FICTION

Every five to ten years, a new group of parents has their turn to get upset over some series their children are reading. Whether it is *Nancy Drew, Sweet Valley High,* or *Goosebumps,* series fiction has a tremendous value to the young reader—but gets condemned as "junk" by parents, teachers, and librarians. We think this is a lot of bother about nothing.

OK, so these books aren't great literature. We can all agree on that. But most of us went through a similar phase in our own development as readers. And besides, we don't all read only great literature as adults—some of us like a little "junk" once in a while ourselves. But we understand the concerns of adults who see children reading series at the exclusion of all else. To them we say, it will pass. Reading series books almost always leads to reading other books, and if a series gets them started identifying themselves as readers, it is an identity they will have for a lifetime.

Parents tell us all the time about the reading habits and tastes of their children. Here's one anecdote that perfectly illustrates the role of "junk" in the development of a lifetime reading habit:

"My son got as far as fifth grade without ever having finished a complete book. Reading intimidated him. In fifth grade, he discovered *Goosebumps*. He read one and finished it. Then he started reading them all, from #1 to #34, and he always looked forward to getting the next one in the series. But after #34, when I offered to take him to the bookstore for #35, he said he wasn't interested. They were getting boring and they really weren't that scary. We went to the bookstore anyway and picked out some John Bellairs books. At first, he was reluctant to try them because he didn't know what he was getting, but they were the closest thing he could find to a *Goosebumps* book, so he bought them. A week or two later, I asked him if he liked the books. His reply was "*Goosebumps* are junk, aren't they, Mom?' So, not only did *Goosebumps* get my son to read, they taught him the difference between reading a book, reading a better book, and reading a good book. My son is in eighth grade now and reads voraciously. Sometimes he reads junk, sometimes he doesn't. But if it weren't for *Goosebumps,* I don't think he'd be reading at all."

PART THREE

Books for Children of Reading Age

Not to say that the books in earlier sections aren't for readers also, but here begins the list of titles that we like to use best with children of reading age. Either because of subject matter or complexity of the story, these books work better with children five and up, and can serve as excellent choices for you to read together.

Angel Child, Dragon Child
PICTURE BOOK

AUTHOR: Michele Maria Surat • ILLUSTRATOR: Vo-Dinh Mai

PB: Scholastic

THEMES: daughters; school; problem solving; Vietnam; family; separation; bullies; communication; mothers and daughters; friendship; immigration

Ut has just come to the United States from Vietnam, and she is miserable. At school children laugh when she speaks, and she misses her mother who had to stay behind. This tender story reminds children to take time to understand differences. The happy-ever-after ending shows that with caring and creativity, sad situations can change.

Go Away, Dog
EARLY READER

AUTHOR: Joan L. Nodset • ILLUSTRATOR: Paul Meisel

PB: HarperCollins

THEMES: dogs; pets; friendship; change

"Go away, you bad old dog. Go away from me" . . . The fact that the story begins with those words from a small boy is guaranteed to make beginning reader or interested adult turn the page for more. First written over 30 years ago, updated illustrations give a new life to this old favorite. Part of the *I Can Read Series* from HarperCollins.

GREAT OPENINGS: BOOKS THAT WILL GRAB THEM IN SECONDS

Try one of these when you need a story where the first line or paragraph is so compelling they'll want to know what is next.

"The night Max wore his wolf suit and made mischief of one kind and another his mother called him wild thing . . ."
Where the Wild Things Are

"Seventeen kings on 42 elephants going on a journey through a wild wet night . . ."
Seventeen Kings and 42 Elephants

"Patrick Edward was a wonderful boy, but his mother was a monster."
Monster Mama

"Go away, you bad old dog. Go away from me."
Go Away Dog

"My name is Ora Mae Cotton of Crabapple Orchard and last night somebody stole my tooth."
Airmail to the Moon

"Down the dusty roads and far away, a poor mother once lived with her seven children named Monday, Tuesday, Wednesday, Thursday, Friday, Saturday and Sunday."
Heckedy Peg

"Old black fly's been buzzin' around, buzzin' around, buzzing around. Old black fly's been buzzin' around, and he's had a very busy bad day."
Old Black Fly

"My little sister ate one hare. We thought she'd throw up then and there."
My Little Sister Ate One Hare

"Before Julius was born, Lilly was the best big sister in the world."
Julius, the Baby of the World

"Swallow a slug by its tale or its snout. Feel it slide down. Feel it climb out."
Slugs

"My dad and I live in an airport."
Fly Away Home

"On August 1, 1815, when Angelica Longrider took her first gulp of air on this earth, there was nothing about the baby to suggest that she would become the greatest woodswoman in Tennessee. The newborn was scarcely taller than her mother and couldn't climb a tree without help."
Swamp Angel

"On Monday in math class, Mrs. Fibonacci says, 'You know, you can think of almost everything as a math problem.' On Tuesday I start having problems."
Math Curse

"Everybody in my class knows my name. It's Fran Ellen Smith. I'm nearly ten. I suck my thumb, and everybody says I smell bad."
The Bears' House

"Take this guy. See how grumpy he is? He's been grumpy since he got out of bed, stepped on his little boy's beach ball, slid halfway across the house, and flew out the window into the rosebush."
A Barrel of Laughs, a Vale of Tears

"Dawn was indeed well up the sky, but over the Greek camp there was little light, for Zeus had spread a churning mass of black cloud across the sky above them: though where the Trojans gathered on the higher ground the sky was clear and the light strong. And soon, from the menacing cloud roof rain began to fall: rain that was as red as blood."
Black Ships Before Troy

"My dad left when I still had a month to go in the darkroom, and historically when people have tried to figure me out (as in, 'What went wrong?'), they usually conclude that Mom spoiled me; gave me everything I wanted because I had no pappy."
Staying Fat for Sarah Byrnes

"They say Maniac Magee was born in a dump. They say his stomach was a cereal box and his heart a sofa spring. They say he kept an eight-inch cockroach on a leash and that rats stood guard over him while he slept."
Maniac Magee

"Manny Bustos awakened when the sun cooked the cardboard over his head and heated the box he was sleeping in until even a lizard could not have taken it, and he knew, suddenly, that it was time. This was the day."
The Crossing

"Eleven-year-old Muhammad Bilal flinched. The sore on his ankle rubbed against the iron shackle that held him, sending shivers of pain up his thin leg. He pushed his foot closer to the wooden board to which he was fastened and tried to shift his body."
The Glory Field

"12th Day of September—
I am commanded to write an account of my days: I am bit by fleas and plagued by family. That is all there is to say."
Catherine, Called Birdy

"The first time Teresa saw Brother was the way she would think of him ever after. It was love at first sight in a wild beating of her heart that took her breath. But it was a dark Friday three weeks later when it rained, hard and wicked, before she knew Brother Rush was a ghost.
Sweet Whispers, Brother Rush

Hill of Fire   EARLY READER

AUTHOR: Thomas P. Lewis • ILLUSTRATOR: Joan Sandin
HC/PB: HarperCollins
THEMES: volcanos; Mexico; farmers; disasters

Fire and smoke bursts from the ground, sending a farmer and his son running in this tale based on the actual eruption of the volcano Paricutin in Mexico. Level Three of the *An I Can Read Book* series adds historical fiction, nonfiction and chapters to the early reader mix. A sampling of other titles at this level: *Egg to Chick* by Selsam, *Dolphin* by Morris, *The Josefina Story Quilt* by Coerr, *Weather Poems for All Seasons* by Hopkins.

How Many, How Many, How Many   PICTURE BOOK

AUTHOR: Rick Walton • ILLUSTRATOR: Cynthia Jabar
HC/PB: Candlewick
THEMES: rhyme; numbers; riddles

These number riddles are filled with rollicking verse and depend on a child's familiarity with nursery rhymes. "Spiders like to steal her seat, How many things does Muffett eat?" Two (curds and whey).

Learning to Swim in Swaziland: A Child's Eye-View of a Southern African Country   PICTURE BOOK NONFICTION

AUTHOR/ILLUSTRATOR: Nila Leigh
HC: Scholastic
THEMES: children's writing; science; social studies; geography; Africa

Nila Leigh wrote this when she was eight, during the year she lived in Swaziland with her parents. Here are a few facts about Swaziland: "It is smaller than New Jersey but sort of round. It is ruled by a king. There are no lions." Young Nila shares her observations of geography, science, history and social studies. Here's a perfect model for a school project.

My Great-Aunt Arizona   PICTURE BOOK

AUTHOR: Gloria Houston • ILLUSTRATOR: Susan Condie Lamb
HC/PB: HarperCollins
THEMES: U.S.A., Appalachia; teachers; aunts; family

A heartwarming tribute to teaching. Read about this lively, dedicated lady from Appalachia, and then give the book away to a teacher or your favorite aunt. It will be a perfect gift.

Noel the First
PICTURE BOOK

AUTHOR/ILLUSTRATOR: Jim McMullan
HC/PB: HarperCollins
THEMES: dance; self-respect; competition; jealousy; Christmas; ballet

Noel was proud to take her place at the barre as leader. "Noel the First," she thought. "That's me!" But when the new girl "twirled like a twister," and "leaped like a leopard," Noel concentrated on competing rather than on the joy of ballet. Don't limit this book to dancers; share it with any child who finds pleasure in a particular skill. More dancing adventures can be found in *Nutcracker Noel*.

Oliver Button Is a Sissy
PICTURE BOOK

AUTHOR/ILLUSTRATOR: Tomie dePaola
PB: Harcourt Brace
THEMES: self-respect; teasing; individuality; dance; gentle boys

Oliver Button has to put up with teasing. He is not like the sports-playing boys; he likes to read books, paint pictures, and tap dance. This story's for young teasers as well as for individuals who feel out of synch.

One Hundred Hungry Ants
PICTURE BOOK

AUTHOR: Elinor Pinczes • ILLUSTRATOR: Bonnie Mackain
HC: Houghton Mifflin
THEMES: numbers; math; ants; picnics; rhyme

One hundred hungry ants hurry to their picnic, but marching single file seems too slow for 100 empty tummies. The youngest ant suggests they travel in two rows of 50, four rows of 25 . . . and the division begins. This will tickle the funnybone as children learn basic principles of division in rhyme.

Poppleton
EARLY READER

AUTHOR: **Cynthia Rylant** • ILLUSTRATOR: Mark Teague
HC: Blue Sky Press
THEMES: friendship; truth; reading; libraries; books

Our favorite thing about Poppleton the pig is his love of reading. If there were only one adventure—"The Library"—it would be enough to make this early reader worthwhile, but you get three!

The Red Racer

AUTHOR/ILLUSTRATOR: Audrey Wood

HC: Simon & Schuster

THEMES: bicycles; humor; teasing; neighbors; embarrassment

"Clunker, clunker, clunker . . . Nona's got a junker!" teased the neighborhood kids. Nona would do anything to be able to have the Deluxe Red Racer bike on display in the hardware store window. "You already have a bicycle," says her father, and her mother agrees. But Nona can't stop thinking about that Red Racer, until her wicked thoughts take over. She decides to roll her bike off a cliff, then into a pond and under a train. But nothing she does can make that bike go away, until. . . . We won't ruin the end, but we will tell you that if you'd like a story that shows that new isn't always best, this is a perfect choice!

MAKING THE CASE FOR READING

Of course reading is good. It's important. You've heard it all your life. We've all heard the lecture about books and reading. It ranks right up there with "take your vitamins" and "look both ways before crossing the street." However, one of the reasons children lose interest in books and reading is because of the emphasis put on how "good" it is for them rather than on how exciting it can be. We advocate fewer lectures and more setting an example. Be a reader, both for them and yourself. They'll get the message.

Three Stories You Can Read to Your Dog

AUTHOR: Sara Swan Miller • ILLUSTRATOR: True Kelley

HC/PB: Houghton Mifflin

THEMES: humor; dogs; reading

Miller offers this advice in her introduction: "When you feel bored, you can read a book. But dogs can't read. Here's a good way to make your dog happy. You can read these stories out loud. Your dog will like them. They are about the things that dogs understand best."

Burglars, bones and running free—all from

BEGINNING TO READ

The transition into reading often requires a sensitivity on the part of adults to a child's ability to handle change. Becoming a reader is a big deal. Some children respond by grabbing their favorite storybook from preschool and reading it over and over again. Others charge ahead to chapter books.

a dog's point of view! This hits the spot for an easy chuckle, and offers a child the chance to read aloud to an audience that won't intimidate him as many adults would. The companion book *Three Stories You Can Read to Your Cat* is equally fun.

While this section interests children in their early elementary years, the books challenge beginning readers and are best read by more confident ones.

The Ancestor Tree   PICTURE BOOK

AUTHOR: Obinkaram Echewa • ILLUSTRATOR: Christy Hale

HC: Lodestar

THEMES: change; traditions; Africa; storytelling; trees; elderly and children

In the African village of Amapu there lived an old man—the oldest in the village. Every morning when the children woke up they ran to hear his stories. When it is time for him to die, the children decide to plant a tree for him in the forest of The Ancestors, even though it is against the custom. Echewa dedicates his original folktale to "Children everywhere, who sometimes may feel an urge to better a tradition they have received."

Everybody Cooks Rice   PICTURE BOOK

AUTHOR: Norah Dooley • ILLUSTRATOR: Peter Thornton

HC/PB: Lerner

THEMES: neighbors; rice; cultural diversity; food; cooking; meals; community; eating; recipes

At dinnertime a child goes to several neighbors' homes in search for his younger brother. He learns about various cultures by seeing the different ways rice is prepared for each family. Recipes are included.

100 PAGES

Many teachers require that any book a child reads for a book report be at least 100 pages long. Never mind the fact that because of the way books are made there is no such thing as a 100-page book: the message this arbitrary rule sends is plain wrong. Good books come in all lengths, and we can think of no reason that a book like *Nightjohn* by Gary Paulsen, *Sarah, Plain and Tall* by Patricia MacLachlan, or *Seedfolks* by Paul Fleischman would be unsuitable for reading and writing about, and they are each less than 100 pages in length.

If the teacher is concerned that all students read a minimum number of pages, we think a solution would be to have them read two short books to equal the requirement, not to turn away great books because they don't fit the page criteria.

Finding Providence: The Story of Roger Williams   EARLY READER
AUTHOR: Avi • ILLUSTRATOR: James Watling
HC/PB: HarperCollins
THEMES: Rhode Island; U.S. history, Colonial America; biography

An excellent, easy-to-read biography, perfect for introducing younger readers to Colonial America or for a reluctant reader who needs to do a book report but is not able to do one on a book 100 pages in length.

Inside the Amazing Amazon   PICTURE BOOK NONFICTION
AUTHOR: Don Lessem • ILLUSTRATOR: Michael Rothman
HC: Crown
THEMES: science; habitats; Amazon; rainforest; jungles; nature; animals

The most detailed look at an environment you'll ever see, short of actually going there. The information and the paintings are truly wondrous.

The Lotus Seed   PICTURE BOOK
AUTHOR: Sherry Garland • ILLUSTRATOR: Tatsuro Kiuchi
HC/PB: Harcourt Brace
THEMES: Vietnam; war; hope; grandmothers; family; immigration; plants; refugees

Grandmother Ba has come all the way from Vietnam with only one momento from home, a lotus seed. This poignant story of war, loss of homeland, and life in a new country ends with a ray of hope.

THE ELEVEN MOST IMPORTANT RULES
ABOUT READING AND CHILDREN: <u>NOT!</u>

1. Always choose a book to fit the age of the child . . .
2. Children's books should enrich as well as inform . . .
3. Never skip pages . . .
4. Some children are simply too old for picture books . . .
5. Make sure what you read to your child is appropriate . . .
6. Comic books are a lesser form of reading . . .
7. Certain books for children really aren't very well written and you should avoid these titles . . .
8. The best time to read to children is just before bedtime . . .
9. Children should be encouraged to read a certain number of pages a day . . .
10. Girls will always read books about boys. Boys will never read books about girls . . .
11. Growing up is difficult enough, children don't need books that show unpleasant situations . . .

THE ELEVEN MOST IMPORTANT RULES
ABOUT READING AND CHILDREN: <u>NOT!</u>

We say:

1. There is no such thing as a "nine year old" book. Age can be used as a guide, not the determining factor in choosing a book.

2. Lighten up! Children need first of all to read for pleasure. Enrichment and information is a bonus. Once they develop a love of reading, a lifetime of learning will follow.

3. Anyone who has read to a two year old knows the value of page skipping. When children get antsy it's a perfect time to move more quickly through the pages. Of course, once your child has memorized the story, you'll never get away with it! One of the things about reading is that you can do it your own way. If you get bogged down in a story, skipping pages or some of the text is a good way to get through it.

4. We live in a society where children are rewarded for reading by having the art taken away. Some children need visuals to help them through a story. Others simply enjoy the pleasure of a good picture book—much like the ones found on their parents' coffee tables.

5. What is suitable for one child or for another can be very different. Worry less about what is appropriate. Instead, offer up a sampling of all kinds of writing on a variety of subjects. They'll learn to make the choices best for them.

6. Some of the best writing today can be found in comics, though often the subject matter requires a mature reader. A comic book reader can experience a world of masterful storytelling, sophisticated vocabulary and complex imagery. The reader will choose his favorites. Comics are not for everyone, and, like books, they range in quality, but they can be a vital and creative form of reading for those who choose them.

7. How are we going to teach them the difference between good writing and bad writing if we don't let them sample the latter?

8. Bedtime is a terrific opportunity for reading in a lot of households. But it isn't the only time. Look for moments in your day where stories will fit. It's more important that you do it every day than at a particular time.

9. Children should be encouraged to read at their own pace, not at somebody else's.

10. We don't think so.

11. You have to make a lot of hard decisions as a parent. We have never found that soft pedaling an issue has worked with our kids, and we have been grateful for books that were available to help us explain some of life's difficulties.

Martha Speaks

PICTURE BOOK

AUTHOR/ILLUSTRATOR: Susan Meddaugh
HC/PB: Houghton Mifflin
THEMES: dogs; language; humor; soup; alphabet; family; pets

The whole idea of a dog learning to speak English because of its diet of alphabet soup is silly enough. Add Meddaugh's pictures with the ballooned dog comments, and this threesome is a runaway hit. Other Martha books: *Martha Calling, Martha Blah Blah.*

Mendel's Ladder

PICTURE BOOK

AUTHOR: Mark Karlins • ILLUSTRATOR: Elaine Greenstein
HC: Simon & Schuster
THEMES: weather; problem solving; taking action; folklore; rain

One summer after sixty-one days without rain, seven-year-old Mendel Moscowitz builds a ladder to the sky. When his shocked parents discover him climbing, they hurry up the ladder after him. At the top they find the Rainmaker sitting on a cloud. He is not interested in helping. After all, why should he? People no longer appreciate rain. "They used to make prayers, gracious thank-you's, offerings—Now not a single 'please,' not a single 'thank you,' not a single 'my, what a good job you've done.' " Use this tale to introduce others about weather.

The Peppermint Race,

EARLY READER

AUTHOR: Dian Curtis Regan • ILLUSTRATOR: Anna Dewdney
HC/PB: Henry Holt
THEMES: competition; single parents; generosity; libraries; reading; music; musical instruments; elderly; authors; candy

To fill their new library with books, Tony and the rest of the fourth graders sell peppermints, with prizes for the ones who sell the most. Tony is determined to win, and his adventures along the way will ring true for children everywhere. A story about competition and generosity, with a subplot about reading and favorite authors.

This section boasts a wide selection of picture books, evenly distributed between fiction and nonfiction that will interest E and M level listeners.

Ali, Child of the Desert

PICTURE BOOK

AUTHOR: Jonathan London • ILLUSTRATOR: Ted Lewin

HC: Lothrop

THEMES: camels; storms; desert; courage; fathers and sons; adventure; friendship; lost

Ali and his father were headed for the Moroccan town of Rissani when suddenly "the wind came howling like a pack of wild dogs. Ali heard his father's voice calling, 'Ali! Come here! Stay close behind me!' Then he heard nothing but the whirling sand. It swallowed the sun, and the herd—and his father." Friendship and courage give strength to a lost boy, and readers a glimpse of desert life through London's words and Lewin's magnificent paintings.

Allison

PICTURE BOOK

AUTHOR/ILLUSTRATOR: Allen Say

HC: Houghton Mifflin

THEMES: adoption; dolls; Japan; anger; frustration; family; cats; cultural diversity; fitting in; comparisons; solitude; problem solving

When Allison realizes she looks more like her Japanese doll than her parents, she becomes confused and angry. While there are several good books that deal with adoption—with being loved and being part of a family—few confront the feelings a child may have with physical differences in an interracial family. Say captures heart-tugging expressions with his watercolors and the need for belonging with words.

Annie and the Old One
PICTURE BOOK

AUTHOR: Miles Miska • ILLUSTRATOR: Peter Pamall

HC/PB: Little Brown

THEMES: death; Native American; nature; grandmothers and grand-daughters

"The sun comes up from the edge of earth in the morning. It returns to the edge of earth in the evening. Earth, from which good things come for the living creatures on it. Earth, to which all creatures finally go." Annie cannot control the passage of time, even if it means that her grandmother will soon ". . . go to mother earth." A sensitive story, where a young girl, through the voice of her Navajo grandmother learns the concept of death.

Anno's Math Games, Volumes I, II, And III
PICTURE BOOK NONFICTION

AUTHOR/ILLUSTRATOR: Mitsumasa Anno

HC: Philomel • PB: Paperstar

THEMES: math; games; puzzles

Anno's ability to convey information in a highly visual style is well known to fans of his wordless picture books (see *Anno's Journey*). Here, he takes math into a realm we haven't before visited. Yes, they are games, but what a creative way to challenge math-oriented children while still inviting participation from those who find math a chore. Also look for *Anno's Mysterious Multiplying Jar*.

At the Beach
PICTURE BOOK

AUTHOR/ILLUSTRATOR: Huy Voun Lee

HC/PB: Henry Holt

THEMES: Chinese language; Chinese characters; drawing

Young children are introduced to the beauty and logic of one of the oldest picture-languages in the world. With simple words and illustrations, here is a chance to learn and draw Chinese characters. A pronunciation guide from the Mandarin dialect is included.

At the Crossroads
PICTURE BOOK

AUTHOR/ILLUSTRATOR: Rachel Isadora

HC: Greenwillow

THEMES: South Africa; fathers; mines; jobs; patience; yearning; anticipation; miners

Zola, Sipho and Nomsa play their
rhythm instruments and sing "Our
fathers are coming home! Our
fathers are coming home!" Today is
the day the fathers return from
their months of work at the
mines. Mr. Sisulu closes his store
and people from the town come
to wait. They wait and they wait.
Soon it gets dark and folks go
home to sleep, except for children who won't go home till their
fathers arrive. This sweet South African tale makes you
want to weep with tired delight when finally the children are able to
play and sing, "Our fathers are home! Our fathers are home!"

> **DON'T GUESS**
>
> We are fooling ourselves if we think
> "I don't like the book, nor do I under-
> stand its appeal, but maybe the kids
> will." If you are unsure, don't guess.
> Choose what you like or ask the
> child.

Barefoot: Escape on the Underground Railroad   PICTURE BOOK
AUTHOR: Pamela Duncan Edwards • ILLUSTRATOR: Henry Cole
HC/PB: HarperCollins
THEMES: courage; animals; African American; feet; Underground Rail-
road; escape; U.S. history, pre-Civil War; slavery; adventure; chases

Dark, close-up images, with slight suggestions of light creep through the
forest, all from the perspective of eyes close to the ground. An escaped
slave searches for safety while Heavy Boots close in. The animals watch
and ease the way to his shelter. Historical fiction and a touch of fantasy
merge in this stunning picture book suggesting nature's role on the
pathways leading from one "safe house" to another as slaves escaped
northward to freedom.

Barn   PICTURE BOOK
AUTHOR/ILLUSTRATOR: Debby Atwell
HC/PB: Houghton Mifflin
THEMES: U.S. history; barns; change

Two hundred years of history is told from the perspective of a barn. A
barn? Yes, and it works. From the late eighteenth century to the present
day the barn stands as its owners fight for their living in a changing
world.

A Chocolate Moose for Dinner   PICTURE BOOK

AUTHOR/ILLUSTRATOR: Fred Gwynne
PB: Aladdin
THEMES: language; wordplay; homonyms; humor

A young girl visualizes the things her parents talk about. "At the ocean Daddy says watch out for the under toe," and "Daddy say lions pray on other animals." Gwynne has experience with this type of humorous wordplay. Others in his series are *The King Who Rained, A Little Pigeon Toad,* and *The Sixteen Hand Horse.* Here's a perfect way to laugh at our crazy language. Have fun thinking up other homonyms.

Company's Coming   PICTURE BOOK

AUTHOR: Arthur Yorinks • ILLUSTRATOR: David Small
HC/PB: Crown
THEMES: aliens; diversity; judging; flying saucers; humor; gifts; anticipation

A ridiculous story that turns the reader into a real ham, *Company's Coming* is one of our favorites. "On the day Shirley had invited all of her relatives to dinner and Moe, her husband, was pleasantly tinkering in the yard, a flying saucer quietly landed next to their toolshed." Try a monotone voice for the aliens. It's perfect (and it's easy).

For writing and lively reactions, I read this aloud up to the moment when Shirley is about to open her gift. "It's a. . . . it's a . . ." Close the book and ask, "What do you think it is?" You'll get great responses.

Dragonfly's Tale   PICTURE BOOK

AUTHOR/ILLUSTRATOR: Kristina Rodanas
HC/PB: Clarion
THEMES: Native American; folklore; U.S.A., the Southwest; corn; dragonflies; nature; kindness; crafts; siblings

In this Zuni legend, a brother's kindness to his younger sister starts the process that brings life back to their starving village. Young readers discover where dragonflies come from and why they hum about the cornfield. Full-color art shows off the rich and vast landscape of the American Southwest.

The Drinking Gourd: A Story of the Underground Railroad
EARLY READER

AUTHOR: F.N. Monjo • ILLUSTRATOR: Fred Brenner
PB: HarperCollins
THEMES: slavery; U.S. history, pre-Civil War; Underground Railroad; prejudice; courage; stars; navigation; escape

Through the Underground Railroad, a boy and his father help slaves escape to Canada. A fine match of words and reading readiness, this story works for a new reader learning about these difficult times.

Ed Emberley's Big Purple Drawing Book
PICTURE BOOK NONFICTION

AUTHOR/ILLUSTRATOR: Ed Emberley
HC/PB: Little Brown
THEMES: art; drawing

Ed Emberley's drawing books allow anyone to draw. From grapes to pirate ships and centipedes to swamp creatures, simple shapes result in subjects you can actually identify. Emberley offers a drawing alphabet: shapes that form pictures like letters form words. Easy and accessible, a perfect solution for quiet times.

His other titles include: *Ed Emberley's Drawing Book of Animals, Ed Emberley's Drawing Book: Make A World, Ed Emberley's Big Orange Drawing Book, Ed Emberley's Halloween Drawing Book, Ed Emberley's Big Green Drawing Book, Ed Emberley's Thumbprint Drawing Book, Ed Emberley's Drawing Box, Ed Emberley's Three Science Flip Books.*

Emma's Rug
PICTURE BOOK

AUTHOR/ILLUSTRATOR: Allen Say
HC: Houghton Mifflin
THEMES: art; talent; school; teachers; magic; self-respect; comfort; confidence; creativity

Who knows where an artist gets her creativity? Emma's may come from the small, shaggy rug someone gave her when she was a baby. Or maybe it's all in her mind. Allen Say takes on a new topic for children's books: artistic inspiration. And while the reader is left to some interpretation of her own, there is no question that Say himself is artistically inspired. Look at Emma's quiet pride on page 13 and recoil at her anguish on page 23.

The Fantastic Drawings of Danielle   PICTURE BOOK

AUTHOR/ILLUSTRATOR: Barbara McClintock
HC/PB: Houghton Mifflin
THEMES: fathers and daughters; painting; mentors; photographers; artists; individuality; Paris; imagination; art; comparisons; drawing

A photographer who shoots exactly what he sees, and his daughter who can draw only what she imagines, prove that real art shows itself in many forms. Offer this story to confident young artists as well as those who don't fit the mold.

The Flying Tortoise: An Igbo Tale   PICTURE BOOK

AUTHOR: Tololwa Mollel • ILLUSTRATOR: Barbara Spuril
HC/PB: Clarion
THEMES: trickster tales; tortoises; lessons; birds; flying; folklore; Africa

When the birds are invited to a feast in Skyland, Mbeku wants to go too, but tortoises can't fly. He seeks help from the birds but then repays them with a trick. In this traditional Igbo tale from Nigeria, it's the tortoise who gets the last lesson.

Grandfather Tang's Story   PICTURE BOOK

AUTHOR: Ann Tompert • ILLUSTRATOR: Robert Andrew Parker
HC: Crown • PB: Dragonfly
THEMES: tangrams; origami; storytelling; art; folklore; shapes; math; puzzles; China

By arranging tangram pieces, Grandfather Tang tells Little Soo a story. Foxes, fairies, rabbits, dogs, squirrels, hawks, turtles and other tangram creatures appear to help with the tale. A tangram and description of the puzzle game are included along with instructions on paper folding and shadow art.

Homeplace   PICTURE BOOK

AUTHOR: Anne Shelby • ILLUSTRATOR: Wendy Anderson Halperin
HC/PB: Orchard
THEMES: social studies; U.S. history; farms; family; relatives; genealogy; family history; change; grandparents

From the time her great-great-great-great-grandpa built the house where the family still lives, a child traces almost two hundred years of family history. Over one hundred fifty softly rendered pictures detail generations of change. Don't try to see it all in one reading. Read the story aloud once, then set it aside for perusal.

I Am the Dog, I Am the Cat
PICTURE BOOK

AUTHOR: Donald Hall • ILLUSTRATOR: Barry Moser
HC: Dial
THEMES: dogs; cats; comparisons; point of view

When conducting writing workshops for children, we look for books with interesting points of view. This one shows a distinct difference in personalities between a Rottweiler and a cat. Not only are the voices fun here, but the possibilities in stretching the imagination are endless! Try this with *Three Stories You Can Read to Your Dog/Cat.*

Komodo
PICTURE BOOK

AUTHOR/ILLUSTRATOR: Peter Sis
HC: Greenwillow
THEMES: dragons; maps; Indonesia; Komodo dragon; lizards

When you read a Peter Sis book, take time for the illustrated details. *Komodo* has few words on each page—"It is always easy to find me in school pictures because of my dragon T-shirt"—but it may take you ten minutes to find this dragon-loving boy who sets off with his parents to Indonesia in search of a real monitor lizard—the last living dragon. Facts mix with imagination in this simple tale.

Maples in the Mist: Children's Poems From the Tang Dynasty
POETRY ANTHOLOGY

AUTHOR: Minfong Ho • ILLUSTRATOR: Jean & Mou-sien Tseng
HC: Lothrop
THEMES: China; ancient history

Written more than a thousand years ago during the Tang Dynasty, these poems were traditionally taught to children. The words apply just as much today.

> "My little pine tree is just a few feet tall.
> It doesn't even have a trunk yet.
> I keep measuring myself against it
> But the more I watch it, the slower it grows."
> —Wang Jian.

Marvin Redpost: Alone in His Teacher's House   EARLY READER

AUTHOR: Louis Sachar • ILLUSTRATOR: Barbara Sullivan
HC/PB: Random House
THEMES: teachers; dogs; pets; school; friendship; responsibility; humor

Marvin is excited when his teacher asks him to dog-sit Waldo while she
is away for a week. But things don't go well for Marvin, or for Waldo.
Sachar can find a kid's funny bone as readily as he can identify what
worries kids most, and combine them with ease. Others in this popular
series of chapter books are: *Marvin Redpost: Kidnapped at Birth* with line
drawings by Neal Hughes; *Marvin Redpost: Why Pick on Me?* (Barbara Sullivan illustrations); and *Marvin Redpost: Is He a Girl?* (Barbara Sullivan
illustrations).

Masai and I   PICTURE BOOK

AUTHOR: Virginia Kroll • ILLUSTRATOR: Nancy Carpenter
HC: Four Winds
THEMES: social studies; cultural diversity; comparisons; Africa; African
American; imagination

Linda is a city girl who learns about the Masai people in school and wonders what life would be like for her if she were Masai. As she prepares
for her grandmother's party, she bathes in scented soap and dries her
skin with a thick towel. "If I were Masai preparing for a celebration, I'd
rub my skin with cows' fat mixed with red clay so that my skin would
shine. I'd want to smell nice if I were Masai, just like I do now, so I'd
crush sweet-smelling leaves to rub along my shiny skin." As Linda goes
through her day's routine she compares her simple tasks with those of
the Masai. A fascinating way to learn about another culture.

New Hope   PICTURE BOOK

AUTHOR/ILLUSTRATOR: Henri Sorensen
HC: Lothrop
THEMES: towns; U.S. history; immigration; ancestors; trailblazing; ori-
gins; family history

How does a town get started? When Jimmy asks about *New Hope*, his
Grandpa tells him how his great-great-great-great-grandfather started the
town because his axle broke. Sorensen's story traces a town from its
beginning.

The Patchwork Quilt   PICTURE BOOK
AUTHOR: Valerie Flournoy • ILLUSTRATOR: Jerry Pinkney
HC: Dial
THEMES: quilts; grandmothers; illness; family; storytelling; memories; family history; African American

Each piece grandmother stitches on her quilt comes with a memory, and Tanya loves hearing the stories. When Grandma becomes ill, Tanya takes on the job of finishing the magnificent heirloom. When read aloud, this heartwarming story of a close intergenerational family makes a perfect segue into sharing your own family stories.

Pink Paper Swans   PICTURE BOOK
AUTHOR: Virginia Kroll • ILLUSTRATOR: Nancy Clouse
HC: Eerdmans
THEMES: listening; cultural diversity; Japanese American; neighbors; elderly and children; community; origami; crafts; friendships; problem solving

When she discovers her elderly neighbor can no longer fold her origami figures, young Janetta comes up with a solution that keeps them both working: "Janetta is the fingers and Mrs. Tsujimoto the mind." This story of two people, young and old, who learn from each other ties in neatly to a paper folding project. Instructions are in the back of the book.

Sewing Quilts   PICTURE BOOK
AUTHOR: Ann Turner • ILLUSTRATOR: Thomas B. Allen
HC: Macmillan
THEMES: pioneers; U.S. history, frontier life; U.S.A., the prairie; U.S. history, Westward movement; family; quilts; fear

Glimpse into family life on the prairie in this cozy story full of the comfort of quilting and the fears of growing up on the frontier.

A Snake Is Totally Tail   PICTURE BOOK
AUTHOR: Judi Barrett • ILLUSTRATOR: Lonni Sue Johnson
HC: Atheneum • PB: Aladdin
THEMES: characteristics; animals; humor; wordplay; nature

From bees to giraffes, simple sentences and comical pictures show the main characteristics of a variety of creatures. Teachers, challenge your fourth and fifth graders to come up with their own.

Some Swell Pup, or Are You Sure You
Want a Dog?   PICTURE BOOK

AUTHOR: Maurice and Matthew Margolis Sendak • ILLUSTRATOR: Maurice Sendak

HC: Farrar Straus & Giroux

THEMES: dogs; pets; pet care

A perfect training manual for any youngster in charge of a new puppy. Sendak's love for dogs is clear in the cartoon panels that are not only funny but teach anyone a thing or two about raising pups.

Thunder Cake   PICTURE BOOK

AUTHOR/ILLUSTRATOR: Patricia Polacco

HC: Philomel • PB: Paperstar

THEMES: grandmothers and granddaughters; fear of storms; thunder; storms; baking; recipes

Clever Babushka drives away her granddaughter's fear of storms by showing her how to make a Thunder Cake. Polacco's warm tale includes the very same recipe her own grandmother baked for her.

Tiger Flowers   PICTURE BOOK

AUTHOR: Patricia Quinlan • ILLUSTRATOR: Janet Wilson

HC: Dial

THEMES: death; AIDS; grief; illness; uncles; family; loss

In this moving story of a young boy who has lost his favorite uncle to AIDS, the family consoles each other as they deal with their grief.

Toad or Frog, Swamp or Bog?: A Big Book
of Nature's Confusables   PICTURE BOOK NONFICTION

AUTHOR: Lynda Graham-Barber • ILLUSTRATOR: Alec Gillman

HC: Macmillan

THEMES: nature; animals; comparisons; mistaken identity

A book of nature's confusables. One page offers a simple question comparing closely related creatures or other confusions of nature, while the next gives the answers as well as other supporting facts.

BRIDGING GAPS

Books can be used to bridge gaps.

There are times when as adults we'd like to have the words for something, to apologize, to offer comfort, to guide someone . . . and we don't. One of the solutions for these times is a story.

Your three year old comes home from preschool and has had a wretched day . . . *Mean Soup* works well. It shows that you understand. You don't have to make a big deal about it.

When your six year old comes home from kindergarten with a similar problem, you can read her *Voyage to the Bunny Planet*. This child will get the message.

When you get unusually angry at your child and then would give anything to erase the last 30 seconds of your life, when you've seen that look on his face that says "you are a monster," you may not be able to say the right thing. But after a cooling down period, you can read *Monster Mama* to him. The story can start the healing process. The words of the story can help you and your child find your own words for each other.

Spinky Sulks can be used to explain that everybody has felt as put out as Spinky, and will serve as an outlet for a child who has backed himself into a corner with an emotional tantrum he is too proud or stubborn to quit.

Prideful situations come up a lot. A child who has gone to her room and refuses to come out could benefit from having *Now Everybody Really Hates Me* slid under the door with a note that says "We are ready when you are." It gives you the means to demonstrate both that you care and that it isn't as big a deal as she may think.

Wilfred Gordon MacDonald Partridge bridges the gap between the very young and very old so brilliantly that it catches adults off guard with its gentle power. For a more difficult situation between an older child and a grandparent, try *The War With Grampa,* or *Sun and Spoon.*

Nearly any situation that comes up in a child's life has had a book written about it; if you or your child is in need of assistance, turn to the subject listings at the back of this book. Look for your issue or problem, then flip to a title and see if it sounds like something that will help. If what you need isn't listed here, go to your bookstore or library and ask for assistance. Families have so many things to deal with that it would be a shame if something so accessible as a story were overlooked as a starting point on the way to a solution.

Today I'm Going Fishing With My Dad   PICTURE BOOK

AUTHOR: N. L. Sharp • ILLUSTRATOR: Chris Demarest

HC/PB: Boyds Mills

THEMES: comparisons; gentle boys; fishing; fathers and sons; preferences

A young boy does not like fishing . . . or the buzzing mosquitoes, or the wiggly worms, or the smelly fish or eating them. But he loves spending time with his dad. A fine book for discussing. We don't have to feel the same way about things that others do—we can still participate at our own level.

The Wagon   PICTURE BOOK

AUTHOR: Tony Johnston • ILLUSTRATOR: James E. Ransome

HC: Tambourine

THEMES: African American; freedom; slavery; family; U.S. history, Civil War

A young boy tells his story of slavery, from birth to when—after twelve plantings had come and gone—he was finally freed.

Working Cotton   PICTURE BOOK

AUTHOR: Sherley Anne Williams • ILLUSTRATOR: Carole Byard

HC/PB: Harcourt Brace

THEMES: migrant farm workers; African American; jobs; California

They get to the fields early, before it's even light. The bus comes for them again when it's almost dark. In between, the migrant families pick cotton in central California. Shelan describes her day in that field. "It be cold, cold, cold. The field fire send up a gray trail to the hazy sky. Everyone speak in smoky whispers." She's too young to carry her own sack so she piles cotton in the middle of the row for her mamma to collect. Byard's luminous paintings earned her a Caldecott Honor.

Listening/Interest Level: Early and Middle Elementary (E/M). Reading Level: Early to Middle Elementary (E/M).

The listening level in this section stretches from E to M; an early reader can share them aloud or read them on his own.

A My Name Is Alice

PICTURE BOOK

AUTHOR: Jane Bayer • ILLUSTRATOR: Steven Kellogg
PB: Puffin
THEMES: rhyme; animals; jumping rope; alliteration; alphabet

"A my name is Alice and my husband's name is Alex. We come from Alaska and we sell ants" (Alice is an APE. Alex is an ANTEATER). Twenty-six verses of this jump rope rhyme take the reader through the alphabet. The natural next step is for children to make up their own verses. Take time to enjoy the details in Kellogg's very funny drawings.

The Adventures of Captain Underpants

FICTION

AUTHOR/ILLUSTRATOR: Dav Pilkey
HC: Blue Sky Press • PB: Scholastic
THEMES: adventure; humor, adolescent; friendship; playing tricks

An outstanding piece of juvenalia by one of the most warped minds in the children's book world—and we mean that in the nicest possible way. This rollicking adventure features two best friends who hypnotize their principal into believing he is that great, nearly unclothed super hero, Captain Underpants! Written squarely on a third-grade humor level, this one is going to delight every boy from 7 to 70 with its silly antics and outrageous situations.

When my son was eight he thought this was the funniest book he ever read.

The Always Prayer Shawl   PICTURE BOOK

AUTHOR: Sheldon Oberman • ILLUSTRATOR: Ted Lewin
HC: Boyds Mills • PB: Puffin
THEMES: traditions; Jews; Russia; Judaism; grandfathers and grandsons; immigration; war; change; faith

"Some things change. And some things don't," said Adam's grandfather. He then gave Adam the Prayer Shawl he had received from *his* grandfather. When Adam had to leave Russia for America he knew that there was one thing he could count on: "I am always Adam and this is my Always Prayer Shawl. That won't change." Ted Lewin's paintings, from black and white to full color, illuminate this tender tale of family tradition. Compare this to Patricia Polacco's *The Keeping Quilt* and use it to discuss the traditions in your own family.

Amber Brown Is Not a Crayon   FICTION

AUTHOR: Paula Danziger • ILLUSTRATOR: Tony Ross
HC: Putnam • PB: Scholastic
THEMES: strong girls; humor; family; school; friendship

A delightful series of books about an irrepressible young girl and her adventures. For all those kids who love *Pippi Longstocking* and *Ramona the Pest,* the Amber books are written on a reading level that will encourage readers who are not yet ready for long chapter books. Other titles include *You Can't Eat Your Chicken Pox, Amber Brown, Amber Brown Goes Fourth,* and *Amber Brown Wants Extra Credit.*

Amber on the Mountain   PICTURE BOOK

AUTHOR: Tony Johnston • ILLUSTRATOR: Robert Duncan
HC: Dial
THEMES: friendship; reading; books; strong girls; comparisons; literacy; mountains; country life

Isolated on the mountain where she lives, Amber meets a girl from the city who gives her the determination to read and write. A good book about friendship and the power of the written word.

Amigo
PICTURE BOOK

AUTHOR: Byrd Baylor • ILLUSTRATOR: Garth Williams
PB: Aladdin
THEMES: prairie dogs; rhyme; pets; desert; loneliness; yearning

Francisco is lonely and longs for a pet, a friend to keep him company in the desert. Amigo is a prairie dog who finds a boy. And this heartwarming story shows how wishes can come true.

An Angel for Solomon Singer
PICTURE BOOK

AUTHOR: **Cynthia Rylant** • ILLUSTRATOR: Peter Catalanotto
HC/PB: Orchard
THEMES: loneliness; New York; friendship; restaurants; cats; solitude; yearning

Solomon Singer is a wanderer. He ". . . was lonely and had no one to love and not even a place to love, and this was hard for him." But a smiling-eyed waiter in a small restaurant notices and makes all the difference in the world. This quiet gem is beautiful in illustration and prose, and may remind young readers of someone in their neighborhood who could use a smile.

Author: A True Story
PICTURE BOOK BIOGRAPHY

AUTHOR/ILLUSTRATOR: Helen Lester
HC: Houghton Mifflin
THEMES: writing; frustration; authors; autobiography; handicaps; perseverance; triumph

Helen Lester is known for writing Tacky The Penguin and other popular books. But writing wasn't always easy for her. She writes with humor of her own rejections and successess. She even adds a few tips for the young author, like "practice helps" and "keep a Fizzle Box."

Author's Day
PICTURE BOOK

AUTHOR/ILLUSTRATOR: Daniel Pinkwater
PB: Aladdin
THEMES: authors; school; humor; mistaken identity

A funny account by one of America's greatest humorists of an author's visit to a school that goes all wrong. We suspect that Pinkwater is writing from experience . . .

Baba Yaga and Vasilisa the Brave   PICTURE BOOK

AUTHOR: Marianna Mayer • ILLUSTRATOR: Kinuko Craft
HC: Morrow
THEMES: witches; folklore; fairy tales; Russia; stepfamilies; folktale
variations

The popularity of this fairy tale is not limited to the very young and
will capture the reader with its suspenseful text and extraordinary art.
The frightening witch, Baba Yaga, adds a twist to this Russian tale about
gentle, beautiful Vasilisa who lives with her jealous stepmother and
stepsisters. You will recognize familiar themes from old tales woven
here.

Baseball Saved Us   PICTURE BOOK

AUTHOR: Ken Mochizuki • ILLUSTRATOR: Dom Lee
HC/PB: Lee & Low
THEMES: suspicion; U.S. history, World War II; prejudice; baseball;
Japanese American; self-respect; captivity; family

Shorty and his family had to leave their home and move to a Japanese
internment camp during World War II. It was hard living, but when his
dad built a baseball field, Shorty started to gain the confidence he would
need when he left the heat, dust, and staring eyes of the guards at the
camp. Young readers may ask questions about this time in our history.
An Author's Note has some of the answers.

Bats About Baseball   PICTURE BOOK

AUTHOR: Jean Little and Claire MacKay • ILLUSTRATOR: Kim LaFave
HC: Viking
THEMES: baseball; jobs; communication; humor; wordplay; grand-
mothers and grandsons

Bats About Baseball isn't just about the sport; it's about careers, wit, and
about a child who wonders whether grown-ups listen at all! When Ryder
asks his grandmother, "Nana, do you think I should be an ornithologist
when I grow up?" she responds, "The Jays play the Orioles today." When
he says, "I could be a mathematician when I grow up," Nana yells "Three
and two, full count. This guy's 0 for 19. Strike three!" Little and MacKay's
game of wits is a great jumping off place for wordplay.

The Big Bazoohley

AUTHOR: Peter Carey • ILLUSTRATOR: Abira Ali
HC: Henry Holt • PB: Paperstar
THEMES: contests; money; problem solving; humor; truth; triumph; taking action

lt's one thing for Sam to have a dad who isn't much good with money, but when he gets the chance to win the big bazoohley, he does what any smart child abducted by a money hungry, starstruck stage mom might do. Good wins over evil here, and humor saves the day!

This book reminded me of Roald Dahl at his meanest. That is not to say this is a book that children won't enjoy, but I have lost my taste for books (like this and many of Dahl's) that feature such cruelty, especially to children.

Now, I'm not a lover of violence. This is NOT violent. But I do think good villains are fun to get mad at. And when the child character outsmarts the villain, young readers have a chance to cheer. I do like that!

Big Cats

AUTHOR: Seymour Simon • ILLUSTRATOR: Photographs
HC/PB: HarperCollins
THEMES: nature; animals, land; lions; tigers

Seymour Simon makes science and nature interesting. His flowing writing style is accompanied by stunning photography, making him one of the best writers of nonfiction for younger readers. Anything by him is a safe bet, but our favorites are his books about outer space (*Our Solar System, Jupiter, Comets, Meteors & Asteroids*), and his books about the earth and its natural forces (*Earthquakes, Volcanoes, Icebergs & Glaciers*). He is so prolific and writes about so many science topics of interest that it is hard to return from a trip to the library without a Seymour Simon book!

Biggest, Strongest, Fastest

AUTHOR/ILLUSTRATOR: Steve Jenkins
HC/PB: Houghton Mifflin
THEMES: comparisons; animals; characteristics

Did you know that the biggest snake, the anaconda, can swallow a goat whole? Or that a tiny flea can jump 130 times its own height? You'll find fascinating detail and comparisons on each page of this introduction to the world records held by fourteen members of the animal kingdom.

A Bird's Body   PICTURE BOOK NONFICTION
AUTHOR: **Joanna Cole** • ILLUSTRATOR: Jerome Wexler
HC: Morrow
THEMES: birds; nature

One of a series of straightforward books on the bodies of various animals. Interesting and good to have on hand when children are learning about bodies and asking questions. Other titles include: *A Cat's Body*, *A Horse's Body*, and *A Snake's Body*.

The Black Snowman   PICTURE BOOK
AUTHOR: Phil Mendez • ILLUSTRATOR: Carole Byard
HC/PB: Scholastic
THEMES: African American; snow; self-respect; storytelling; folklore; slavery; poverty; African culture; anger; pride

Jacob hates being poor and he hates being black. He doesn't want to build a snowman out of the watery, black snow people have trampled on. But he does, and when the snowman comes to life he helps Jacob discover the beauty of his African heritage and pride in himself.

The Blue Hill Meadows   FICTION
AUTHOR: **Cynthia Rylant** • ILLUSTRATOR: Ellen Beier
HC/PB: Harcourt Brace
THEMES: country life; family; pets; love; Virginia

Each story—sweet, simple and strangely familiar—shows how tender times between family members become our own stories. This poignant foursome can be read aloud or offered to a young reader ready to be enveloped in a gentle world where simple acts of caring are the rule.

The Bracelet   PICTURE BOOK
AUTHOR: Yoshiko Uchida • ILLUSTRATOR: Joanna Yardley
HC: Philomel • PB: Paperstar
THEMES: captivity; friendship; U.S. history, World War II; memory; prejudice; Japanese American

Emi, a Japanese American in the second grade, is sent with her family to an internment camp during World War II. Her best friend gives her a bracelet as a farewell gift. When Emi loses her precious gift, she learns that she does not need a physical reminder of friendship.

The Brocaded Slipper and
Other Vietnamese Tales
FOLKLORE COLLECTION

AUTHOR: Lynette Vuong • ILLUSTRATOR: Vo-Dinh Mai
HC/PB: HarperCollins
THEMES: Vietnam; folklore; fairytales; folktale variations

"Cinderella," "Thumbelina," and "'The Frog Prince" are part of this collection of Vietnamese fairy tales. Here's a fine way to show that folklore is universal and that while we think of many of these old stories as ours, they belong to children across the world.

Bugs!
PICTURE BOOK

AUTHOR: David Greenberg • ILLUSTRATOR: Lynn Munsinger
HC: Little Brown
THEMES: bugs; rhyme; humor, gross

The author of one of our favorite squirmy stories (see: *Slugs*) strikes again, delivering a subversive read aloud that will have listeners squiggling and squealing.

Burnt Toast on Davenport Street
PICTURE BOOK

AUTHOR/ILLUSTRATOR: Tim Egan
HC: Houghton Mifflin
THEMES: wishes; magic; marriage; fantasy

Egan's trademark whimsy (see: *Chestnut Cove*) and social commentary (see: *Metropolitan Cow*) are dosed with a bit of magic, courtesy of a fly that grants three wishes to Arthur Crandall, a dog with a life that is already pretty good. Though the fly gets the wishes fouled up, the outcome serves to illustrate one of the finest, most time-honored traditions in all of children's literature: there's no place quite like your own home. Sly, humorous touches abound in this unique tale.

Calling the Doves/El Canto
De Las Palomas
PICTURE BOOK BIOGRAPHY

AUTHOR: Juan Felipe Herrera • ILLUSTRATOR: Elly Simmons
HC/PB: Children's Book Press
THEMES: bilingual; Spanish language; Mexico; rhyme; poets; farms; migrant farmworkers; family; biography; storytelling; California; Mexican

Herrera tells of his migrant farmworker childhood in the fields of California: his father's stories; his mother's poems, their different homes, their meals together. Love for the land and for each other set the foundation for young Herrera's future, ". . . I knew one day I would follow my own road. I would let my voice fly the way my mother recited poems, the way my father called the doves." We are all richer for it.

Captain Abdul's Pirate School   PICTURE BOOK

AUTHOR/ILLUSTRATOR: Colin McNaughton
HC/PB: Candlewick
THEMES: pirates; strong girls; humor; school; mail

A rollicking account of the only school where the children get good grades by defying their teachers. The school is run by bona fide pirates, which leads to some hilarious adventures, not the least of which is a mutiny where the students take charge. The surprise ending where the ringleader turns out to be a girl will catch a few readers off guard.

Chanukkah in Chelm   PICTURE BOOK

AUTHOR: David Adler • ILLUSTRATOR: Kevin O'Malley
HC: Lothrop
THEMES: Chelm; Hanukkah; Jews; folklore; fools; humor

There's nothing like a tale of the ridiculous to make kids aware of the right way to solve a problem. And this story about the good-hearted, foolish folks of Chelm is about as ridiculous as it gets. Adler's silly asides— "Is that herring I'm hearing, or smelt I smell?"—may be lost on the youngest listeners, but interspersed with the story they offer additional chuckles for the comprehending. This read aloud does not have to be limited to the Hanukkah season.

The Cherokees   PICTURE BOOK NONFICTION

AUTHOR: Virginia Driving Hawk Sneve • ILLUSTRATOR: Ronald Himler
HC/PB: Holiday House
THEMES: Native American; creation; rituals; U.S. history; maps; folklore; celebrations; traditions

Beginning with a creation story, Sneve explains the history and migration of each tribe in the series. If you are looking for a straightforward introduction to the first Americans, this it it. Interesting facts combined with Himler's beautifully detailed paintings make this series a must for children interested in Native American life. Others in *The First Ameri-*

cans series include: *The Cheyennes, The Hopis, The Iroquois, The Navajos, The Nez Perce, The Seminoles,* and *The Sioux.*

Chestnut Cove
PICTURE BOOK

AUTHOR/ILLUSTRATOR: Tim Egan
HC/PB: Houghton Mifflin
THEMES: cooperation; friendship; competition; contests

The peaceful village of Chestnut Cove is changed for the worse by a contest to grow the biggest watermelon. Usually cooperative neighbors (all hippos, by the way) become secretive and competitive. It takes a small disaster to bring them all together and get their priorities in order. Funny and the social commentary never gets in the way of the good story.

Cinderella's Rat
PICTURE BOOK

AUTHOR/ILLUSTRATOR: Susan Meddaugh
HC/PB: Houghton Mifflin
THEMES: magic; siblings; surprises; rats; change; secrets; folktale variation

"I was born a rat. I expected to be a rat all my days. But life is full of surprises." From the unique perspective of one of the rats turned into a coachman by Cinderella's fairy godmother, a new twist to this old tale. Meddaugh's animated art and wild imagination ensure laughs, so sit down with your child and read it aloud for a spell.

Cloudy With a Chance of Meatballs
PICTURE BOOK

AUTHOR: Judi Barrett • ILLUSTRATOR: Ron Barrett
HC: Atheneum • PB: Aladdin
THEMES: wordplay; food; weather; storytelling; change; fantasy

Grandpa tells the story of a town called Chewandswallow where there were no food stores. "They didn't need any. The sky supplied all the food they could possibly want . . . Whatever the weather served, that was what they ate." It rained soup and juice. It snowed mashed potatoes and a big storm could blow in hamburgers. Tweak imaginations with this tall tale and watch the children come up with their own food fantasies.

Coming Home
PICTURE BOOK BIOGRAPHY

AUTHOR/ILLUSTRATOR: Floyd Cooper
HC: Philomel
THEMES: biography; African American; Harlem; grandmothers; Langston Hughes; poets; authors

Langston Hughes was young when he lived with his storytelling grandma. She told him about men like Booker T. Washington and about his uncles who were buffalo soldiers. He loved her stories, but Langston longed to live in a normal home with a mom and a dad. Cooper's picture biography tells about Hughes when he was a young boy and about Harlem, where he stayed the longest.

Courtney
PICTURE BOOK

AUTHOR/ILLUSTRATOR: John Burningham
HC: Crown
THEMES: dogs; judging; pets; fantasy; talent

Children have been instructed to go to the Dog's Home to find a proper dog—one with a pedigree. But they choose an old mongrel nobody else wants. Courtney, a dog of unusual talents, epitomizes why a dog is man's best friend and reminds readers not to judge by appearances! We assure you, the ending will have you talking.

The Culpepper Adventures
FICTION

AUTHOR: **Gary Paulsen**
PB: Dell
THEMES: friendship; adventure; humor, adolescent

A perfect series for the kid who says he won't read. Paulsen knows a thing or two about enticing readers, and he has succeeded in making these adventurous in a way that apes TV but delivers a terrific reading experience! Some of our favorite titles include: *The Case of the Dirty Bird, Dunc's Undercover Christmas, Amos Goes Banana, Dunc's Halloween,* and *Amos and the Vampire.*

Dakota Dugout
PICTURE BOOK

AUTHOR: Ann Turner • ILLUSTRATOR: Ronald Himler
PB: Aladdin
THEMES: pioneers; dwellings; home; U.S. history, frontier life; U.S.A., the prairie; U.S. history, Westward movement; family

Beautifully rendered black and white drawings with little text describe prairie life in a sod house from the voice of a woman who remembers.

The Day Jimmy's Boa Ate the Wash   PICTURE BOOK

AUTHOR: Trina Hakes Noble • ILLUSTRATOR: Steven Kellogg
HC: Dial
THEMES: farms; snakes; humor; field trips

This cleverly constructed tale is told in flashback by a young girl who is relating what happened on a field trip. Using the usual blasé style that kids have of telling about their day to contrast with the highly outrageous goings on at the farm, Noble creates a story whose pages we can't wait to turn, and she is ably assisted by Kellogg's outstandingly detailed illustrations.

A Day With Wilbur Robinson   PICTURE BOOK

AUTHOR/ILLUSTRATOR: William Joyce
HC/PB: HarperCollins
THEMES: humor; family; grandfathers; friendship; fantasy; zany

Wilbur Robinson must be the envy of every young reader. He lives in an enormous house with a wacky family, unusual pets and wild servants. Each time we open this book, we find something we'd missed—even grandfather's teeth, which had been the subject of an all day search. If you don't like zany, don't read this. Save it for a kid who does.

A Day's Work   PICTURE BOOK

AUTHOR: **Eve Bunting** • ILLUSTRATOR: Ronald Himler
HC/PB: Clarion
THEMES: truth; jobs; Spanish words; conscience; problem solving; Mexican; grandfathers and grandsons; responsibility; cooperation

This tale begins in a parking lot with men lined up hoping a truck or car will appear with a driver looking for workers. Francisco is there with his grandfather, who doesn't speak English. Francisco knows they need the work, so he lies about their experience with gardening—which results in a lot more work than he'd planned on and a lesson in honesty.

AUTHOR SPOTLIGHT ON: EVE BUNTING

Eve Bunting is a writer of wide range, both in the types of books she writes (folktale retellings, picture books, and novels for all ages of reader) and in the range of topics she covers. Her interests are seemingly boundless and each year brings at least one new picture book examining an aspect of the human condition in her characteristically caring and strongly felt style. Bunting's desire to shed light on some of the more disturbing aspects of life often results in books that stir up our feelings, many of them uncomfortable, about the issues at hand.

Issues like homelessness (*Fly Away Home*), urban riots (the Caldecott-winning *Smoky Night*), illiteracy (*The Wednesday Surprise*), and the Vietnam War (*The Wall*) are explored with compassion in picture book format. Bunting's books often make the perfect introduction to discussions of these hard topics. This author does not always offer solutions, but allows a means to discuss these issues with our children so that they can grow up to find the solutions that have eluded us.

But Eve Bunting is not only a writer of issue-oriented books. Our delight in her work stems chiefly from the way she can move between genres, from a funny, contemporary look at a sixth-grade class learning the burdens of parenthood (*Our Sixth Grade Sugar Babies*) to a stunning look at ancient Egypt through the eyes of one of its residents (*I Am the Mummy Heb-Nefert*), from holiday-oriented books aimed at younger readers (*St. Patrick's Day in the Morning, The Valentine Bears,* and *A Turkey for Thanksgiving*) to picture books illuminating the injustice embedded in the American way of life (*Cheyenne Again* and *Train to Somewhere*).

Bunting is at heart an Irish storyteller, a Shanachie, who, in more than 100 books spanning 40 years of creative fertility has transcended her roots to become one of America's best-loved and most thoughtful writers for children. Her concern for the lives of children shines on the pages of every story she tells.

Dear Willie Rudd   PICTURE BOOK
AUTHOR: Libba Moore Gray • ILLUSTRATOR: Peter Fiore
HC: Simon & Schuster
THEMES: African American; U.S.A., the South; memories; civil rights;
taking action; prejudice; regret; mail; writing

Many of us have had an adult in our life we later wish we had told how
much we loved. With a child's longing and an adult's regret, Miss Elizabeth sits on the porch of her house one afternoon, remembering Willie
Rudd, the "colored" woman who took care of her when she was a child.
Wishing more than anything that she could go back and right the wrongs
of the past, she comes up with a remarkably simple and healing solution. Though it deals with a specific relationship, the story's theme is
universal and is told with a great deal of love.

Dinner at Alberta's   FICTION
AUTHOR: Russell Hoban • ILLUSTRATOR: James Marshall
PB: HarperCollins
THEMES: manners; family; meals; crushes; siblings

Every evening at the dinner table, Arthur chews with his mouth open,
plays with the saltshaker, and generally exhibits the table manners of a
beast. He is a crocodile, after all, but his family is nevertheless at a loss
as to how to deal with him. It is only when he meets Alberta and wishes
to impress her that he shows any interest in proper dinnertime deco-
rum. This is a terrific book about table manners—it shows rather than
preaches and is very funny. Have this on hand when your own beasts
get out of control; it may help bring about a remarkable change!

Dogteam   PICTURE BOOK
AUTHOR: **Gary Paulsen** • ILLUSTRATOR: Ruth Paulsen
HC: Delacorte • PB: Dell
THEMES: dogs; winter; snow; racing; night; forests

The first picture book by the three-time Newbery Honor author, with
beautiful art by his wife, Ruth. A prose poem about going out into the
cold and running a team of dogs, by a man who has been there and done
it. Lyrical writing.

Don Quixote

PICTURE BOOK

AUTHOR/ILLUSTRATOR: Marcia Williams
HC/PB: Candlewick
THEMES: humor; love; knights; adventure; comic book style; magic

Cervantes' classic tale is told in comic strip format. We guarantee it will get the attention of the child who likes detail as well as the one who roars with laughter at slapstick silliness. Other titles that receive the same treatment include: *Greek Myths, Sinbad the Sailor, The Iliad and The Odyssey,* and *King Arthur and the Knights of the Round Table.*

The Dragon's Robe

PICTURE BOOK

AUTHOR/ILLUSTRATOR: Deborah Nourse Lattimore
HC: HarperCollins
THEMES: China; ancient history; drought; weaving; greed; strong girl; dragons

Kwan Yin is an orphan who has only a small loom, but when her village is threatened, it is her weaving that saves the day. Lattimore's paintings of ancient Chinese landscapes offer more than rich illustration. Look carefully: you'll find dragon tracings circling mountains on several pages of her original tale.

The Dragonling

FICTION-FANTASY

AUTHOR: Jackie French Koller • ILLUSTRATOR: Judith Mitchell
HC: Little Brown • PB: Pocket
THEMES: adventure; community; courage; rituals; traditions; family; friendship; dragons; fantasy; prejudice

The first in a series of books that provide a terrific stepping stone from early readers to longer chapter books. Set in a world where people and dragons are enemies, this series tells the story of a boy who befriends a dragon pup and raises him, despite the fears and prejudices of his community and family. What raises this book above the pack is author Koller's ability to wrestle with big moral issues in a way that is both appropriate and understandable to a seven-year-old, without losing sight of the fact that the story needs to come first. Later titles include *A Dragon in the Family, Dragon Quest,* and *The Dragons of Krad* and they live up to the standard set by this first installment.

TELEVISION, SCREENS, AND READING

Some say we are reading less, that our screen-filled lives have dampened our passion for the word. Whether or not this is true, children need to spend less time hypnotized by screens, and more time losing themselves in pages. Television delivers a story in a highly visual manner, rarely allowing time for interpretation. Canned laughter and ominous music tell us how we are supposed to feel. Rapid-fire graphics of computer games do much the same thing, at an even faster pace. It isn't that "screens" are bad, but too often their images are delivered without giving us time to think or reflect before having to deal with the next one. One of the great things about reading is how it engages the imagination on so many levels at once yet allows the reader to absorb at her own pace.

Earrings!   PICTURE BOOK

AUTHOR: Judith Viorst • ILLUSTRATOR: Nola Langner Malone
HC: Atheneum
THEMES: yearning; family; jewelry; comparisons

She wants to have her ears pierced. Her parents want her to wait a couple of years. She tells them "I'm the only girl in my class, in my school, in the world, in the solar system whose mom and dad won't let her have pierced ears." This is for every child who knows she or he is the only one who can't have "it" or do "it." It's also for the rotten parents.

Eight Hands Round:
A Patchwork Alphabet   PICTURE BOOK

AUTHOR: Ann Whitford Paul • ILLUSTRATOR: Jeanette Winter
HC/PB: HarperCollins
THEMES: quilts; crafts; alphabet; folk art; symbols; U.S. history

An ABC of patchwork quilts, in which each letter introduces a pattern and its history, starting with A for Anvil. The page shows an anvil design and explains that "Two hundred years ago most towns had a blacksmith. An anvil always sat on a flat stump in his shop . . ." B is for Buggy Wheel, C is for Churn Dash, and patterns proceed through the alphabet to "Zigzag," the symbol for lightning. A fascinating way to learn history and respect for the folk art tradition.

El Chino
PICTURE BOOK BIOGRAPHY

AUTHOR/ILLUSTRATOR: Allen Say

HC/PB: Houghton Mifflin

THEMES: jobs; yearning; cultural diversity; Chinese American; Spain; bullfighting; biography; determination

Billy Wong wants to learn the art of bullfighting. He is a Chinese American in Spain and his chances are slim. He studies hard, practices and one day finds faith in himself: "And as I stared in the mirror, a strange feeling came over me. I felt powerful. I felt that I could do anything I wished—even become a matador!" Say's watercolor paintings make this book a treasure to hold and his account of the true story of Billy Wong will encourage young readers who have dreams of their own.

Eleanor
PICTURE BOOK BIOGRAPHY

AUTHOR/ILLUSTRATOR: Barbara Cooney

HC: Viking

THEMES: first ladies; biography; U.S. history, late 19th century; orphans; journeys; abandonment; solitude

A glimpse into the childhood of Eleanor Roosevelt—wealthy, privileged and orphaned at nine.

★ Elijah's Angel: A Story for Chanukah and Christmas
PICTURE BOOK

AUTHOR: Michael J. Rosen • ILLUSTRATOR: Aminah Brenda Lynn Robinson

HC/PB: Harcourt Brace

THEMES: religion; friendship; cultural diversity; Christmas; Judaism; Chanukah; artists; symbols; comparisons; elderly and children

A story for Chanukah and Christmas. Michael worries about how his parents will feel if he brings home the beautiful Christmas Angel his friend Elijah has carved for him. After all, it is a forbidden graven image. Rosen sensitively handles the problems that can occur during holiday times when religions and personal beliefs differ.

Encyclopedia Brown Series
FICTION-MYSTERY

AUTHOR: Donald Sobol

PB: Bantam

THEMES: detectives; clues; mystery

Leroy Brown is the son of the chief of police in Idaville. No one except his parents and an occasional teacher calls him Leroy. He is known far and wide as Encyclopedia Brown, the smartest and most observant young sleuth in the world. This wonderful series is perfect for enticing beginning readers to become more confident. Have your kids read all the Nate the Greats and Cam Jansens? Then it's time to introduce them to these. Each book contains multiple short mysteries and encourages sleuthing on the part of the reader. The clues are all there, allowing the reader to match wits with "the Sherlock Holmes in sneakers." There are many titles in this series, and they all begin with *Encyclopedia Brown*.

Everybody Needs a Rock   PICTURE BOOK
AUTHOR: Byrd Baylor • ILLUSTRATOR: Peter Parnall
PB: Aladdin
THEMES: rocks; choices; diversity; individuality; comparisons

I collected rocks as a child. I liked the way they felt in my hand. Some were good for rubbing. Their value depended on the differences between them. Sparkle meant magic and color meant jewels. From Byrd's Rule Number 8 on finding the perfect rock: ". . . if your rock is going to be special it should look good by itself in the bathtub." That's just one. A perfect book for any collector—child or adult.

Family Reunion   POETRY COLLECTION
AUTHOR: Marilyn Singer • ILLUSTRATOR: R. W. Alley
HC: Macmillan
THEMES: family; picnics; diversity; relatives; reunion

A poetry-packed picnic of personalities that celebrates the individual differences found in all families.

Fanny's Dream   PICTURE BOOK
AUTHOR: Caralyn Buehner • ILLUSTRATOR: Mark Buehner
HC: Dial
THEMES: change; marriage; family; strong women; folktale variations; yearning

Sometimes you give up your dreams and learn to make the best of what you have. And sometimes your prince is right there under your nose. Taking a page from the Cinderella story and setting it in the pioneer days, this funny and bittersweet tale is a terrific way to introduce children to the concept of lifelong commitment between a couple that is based on reality, not fantasy.

Fireflies, Peach Pies & Lullabies   PICTURE BOOK
AUTHOR: Virginia Kroll • ILLUSTRATOR: Nancy Cote
HC: Simon & Schuster
THEMES: death; change; loss; grief; funerals; memories; elderly and children

A lovely story, though we wish the art were more inviting. This is a useful and moving book about dealing with death and loss and coping with Alzheimer's. It also serves as a guide to properly remembering someone after she dies.

Flight   PICTURE BOOK BIOGRAPHY
AUTHOR: Robert Burleigh • ILLUSTRATOR: Mike Wimmer
PB: Paperstar
THEMES: flying; Charles Lindbergh; U.S. history, early 20th century; airplanes; navigation; trailblazing; heroes; biography

"It is 1927, and his name is Charles Lindbergh. Later they will call him the Lone Eagle. Later they will call him Lucky Lindy. But not now. Now it is May 20, 1927. And he is standing in the still-dark dawn." The reader gazes between Lindbergh's boots at the *Spirit of St. Louis* parked in the distance. Wimmer's incredible close-up perspectives fuse with Burleigh's text to create an outstanding account of Lindbergh's famous flight.

The Fortune-Tellers   PICTURE BOOK
AUTHOR: Lloyd Alexander • ILLUSTRATOR: Trina Schart Hyman
HC: Dutton
THEMES: prophecy; humor; playing tricks; Africa; wordplay; folklore

When the fortune-teller comes into town, a young carpenter seeks advice. "You shall wed your true love," said the fortune-teller, "if you find her and she agrees. And you shall be happy as any in the world if you can avoid being miserable." Colorful, richly textured illustrations and the think-twice-about-it foretelling will hold the attention of a wide span of ages. Read this one aloud to fully appreciate the wordplay.

NONFICTION COMES ALIVE!

Nonfiction is not just for book reports! Children often turn to it for their pleasure reading when a subject interests them, and the books that serve that group of children are distinguished by the same things found in good fiction—an identifiable point of view on the part of the writer, a strong narrative drive that balances the who and what with enough texture and style to make the plot—the events chronicled in the work—come to life.

Good nonfiction for children has the pull of world-building fiction. It transcends the distribution of facts, takes the reader to a place he has never before been and makes the trip worthwhile, whether it's written about fish, the space program, polar ice caps, woman's suffrage, or the colonization of Africa. Like good fantasy, good nonfiction begins with an introduction to the people, the land, the rules and the traditions of this new place, equipping the reader with the lay of the land and the tools to follow her to the desired destination.

There has been much change in the world of nonfiction writing since the late 1980s. It has become more dependent upon visual elements, especially graphics, with charts, color photographs, sidebars, and graphic-design techniques that break up the text into easily digestible bites.

DK Publishing, originally from England, is largely credited with initiating this trend with their *Eyewitness Books.* Eye-popping visuals and an organizational style that flows from page to page distinguish this remarkable line of books, making them favorites with children and teachers alike. DK soon adapted this successful style across its publishing program, and while the books look much the same, there is plenty of room in the format for growth and change. Other publishers have copied their highly successful style, adding their own refinements.

In many cases nonfiction writing has followed the visual trend by getting tighter, shorter, more to the point. Writers like **Kathleen Krull** (*Lives of the Writers*) and **Diane Stanley** (picture book biographies of Charles Dickens, William Shakespeare, and Queen Elizabeth I) have done much to dispel the notion that biography writing has to be long and brimming with facts to be good. Sometimes a taste of the life of a famous person is all a young reader requires. If the taste proves intriguing, then the reader can seek out longer, more detailed biographies, of which there are many well-written examples.

The best nonfiction writers have distinctive styles of writing. **Dorothy Hinshaw Patent, Aliki, Russell Freedman, Seymour Simon, Caroline Arnold, Sandra Markle, Laurence Pringle, Gail Gibbons** and **Cheryl Harness** have distinguished themselves by their consistently high level of excellence in their books: always informative and compulsively readable, they deliver the facts to children ages 7 to 14 on a variety of topics in a variety of ways. Each is possessed of a writer's "voice," and they use that gift to make what was once thought of as dry and boring ("Ewwww! Nonfiction!") into something children will read and reread.

Frank and Ernest
PICTURE BOOK

AUTHOR/ILLUSTRATOR: Alexandra Day
HC/PB: Scholastic
THEMES: slang; restaurants; jobs; definitions; vocabulary; language

Frank and Ernest learn "diner language" to prepare for their new job. ". . . burn one, take it through the garden, and pin a rose on it." A vocabulary stretcher and guessing game in one, this is for the child who delights in wordplay.

For a writing challenge, have youngsters (fourth grade and up) create their own diner lingo. Then have them guess each other's menu. It's harder than it looks, but illustrates how fun language can be.

Friends and Amigos Series
EARLY READERS

AUTHOR: Patricia Reilly Giff • ILLUSTRATOR: Dyanne DiSalvo-Ryan
PB: Dell
THEMES: friendship; Spanish words; cultural diversity; school

A series about friendships between Spanish speaking and English speaking kids. There is enough rudimentary Spanish in each book to give a taste of a new language to young readers just becoming confident in reading their own. Titles include: *Say Hola, Sarah!*, *Good Dog, Bonita*, and *Ho, Ho Benjamin, Feliz Navidad!*

Fun! No Fun!
PICTURE BOOK

AUTHOR/ILLUSTRATOR: James Stevenson
HC: Greenwillow
THEMES: games; comparisons; friendship; memories; childhood

A perfect lead-in to a "Fun-No Fun" game. Stevenson recalls events of his childhood and divides them into two different categories. "Fun was being a Cub Scout. No fun was going to a Cub Scout meeting if you had to walk past tough kids to get there. Fun Baseball hat. No Fun Cap with flaps." Part of his seven-book picture book reminiscence. See: *When I Was Nine*.

Gather Up, Gather In: A Book of Seasons
PICTURE BOOK

AUTHOR: M. C. Helldorfer • ILLUSTRATOR: Judy Pedersen
HC: Viking
THEMES: seasons; senses; weather; change

This gem is so rich in language and image, we recommend you read it aloud for a treat for your senses.

Geography From A To Z: A Picture Glossary
PICTURE BOOK NONFICTION

AUTHOR: Jack Knowlton • ILLUSTRATOR: Harriett Barton
HC: HarperCollins
THEMES: geography; glossary

From "archipelago" to "zone," this colorful glossary of geographic terms is a perfect resource for young geographers!

★ The Gift of Driscoll Lipscomb
PICTURE BOOK

AUTHOR: Sara Yamaka • ILLUSTRATOR: Joung Un Kim
HC: Simon & Schuster
THEMES: mentors; color; friendship; artists; patience

It's rare in our busy world for a story to honor the gift of time. This quiet gem is about friendship, the art of seeing and about taking time to appreciate the wonders of our world. Each year on Molly's birthday, Driscoll Lipscomb gives her a brush and a pot of paint, and for one year she paints with only that color. "When I turned seven, Driscoll gave me a brush and a pot of green paint. And for one year I painted leaves and limes and shiny green beetles alongside Driscoll Lipscomb. My grass seemed to ripple across the canvas." *The Gift of Driscoll Lipscomb* is a gift for any artist.

The Gifts of Wali Dad: A Tale of India and Pakistan
PICTURE BOOK

AUTHOR: Aaron Shepard • ILLUSTRATOR: Daniel San Souci
HC: Atheneum
THEMES: India; gifts; generosity; folklore; magic; wealth

Wali Dad, a simple grass-cutter living in India, comes home from market each day with a few coins, some to spend and some to save. Before long he finds he has saved more than he thought. Needing nothing more than he has, he decides to give it away. That's when the confusion begins! An exchange of gifts, each more extravagant than the one before, teaches Wali Dad that gifts can be a mixed blessing.

Golem   PICTURE BOOK

AUTHOR/ILLUSTRATOR: David Wisniewski

HC: Clarion

THEMES: folklore; Jews; Prague;
monsters; creation; magic;
Judaism; fathers and sons;
clay

Four hundred years ago, the
story goes, a Rabbi plunged his
hands into an enormous lump
of clay, shaped it into a giant
man, and brought him to life
to watch over the Jews. The
cut-paper illustrations left us
thinking about Wisniewski,
an artist who must have
incredible patience to work
his craft with such preci-
sion. To see more of his
amazing visual style, get
a copy of *Rain Player*.

> **READING AS A SOUL ACTIVITY**
>
> Most meaningful reading is done
> because the reader wants to, not
> because he has to. Yes, it can be
> handy to read if you want to know
> how to build a deck or bake a seven-
> layer cake or find the capital of Alba-
> nia. But it is your soul that feeds on
> the adventures of Tom Sawyer and
> Huck Finn, that grows as a result of
> Jess's devastating loss in *The Bridge
> to Terabithia*, that leaps up in glad-
> ness at the inspiring words of poets
> like Nikki Grimes and tellers like
> Joseph Bruchac. Without that soul
> stirring, we die, plain and simple. We
> can always live without that new
> deck.

★ Grandfather's Journey   PICTURE BOOK

AUTHOR/ILLUSTRATOR: Allen Say

HC: Houghton Mifflin

THEMES: Japan; immigration; grandfathers and grandsons; journeys;
Japanese American; cultural diversity; war; comparisons; memories

Master craftsman Say offers a poignant look at how it feels to be raised
in two cultures. Beautifully rendered, with a perfect combination of art
and text, this masterpiece illuminates the joys and conflicting emotions
many bi-cultural people feel. As the narrator says: "The funny thing is,
the moment I am in one country, I am homesick for the other." There
is a piece of the author's heart on every page.

Grass Sandals: The Travels of Basho   PICTURE BOOK BIOGRAPHY

AUTHOR: Dawnine Spivak • ILLUSTRATOR: Demi

HC: Atheneum

THEMES: Japan; poets; biography; writing; journeys

Rich, descriptive writing brings the famed Japanese poet Basho to life . . . and Demi's art adds the perfect touch. Basho's adventures will be a great motivator to young writers.

The Great White Man-Eating Shark: A Cautionary Tale
PICTURE BOOK

AUTHOR: Margaret Mahy • ILLUSTRATOR: Jonathan Allen
HC: Dial • PB: Puffin
THEMES: lessons; disguises; sharks; swimming; dreaming; playing tricks

Hilarious! In the tradition of Victorian cautionary tales, here is the story of Norvin, who looks like a shark and uses this fact to wreak havoc in the peaceful waters of Caramel Cove. Pretending to be a shark in order to frighten the other swimmers away gives him great satisfaction and results in his having the waters all to himself. He learns his lesson when a real shark mistakes him for a potential mate. A stitch to read aloud!

The Green Truck Garden Giveaway: A Neighborhood Story and Almanac
PICTURE BOOK

AUTHOR: Jacqueline Briggs Martin • ILLUSTRATOR: Alec Gillman
HC: Simon & Schuster
THEMES: gardening; community; sharing; taking action; neighbors

A good story and art combination that will enchant even the most reluctant gardener. This tale celebrates community and social conscience. Have it on hand when spring planting comes around.

Gulliver's Adventures in Lilliput
PICTURE BOOK

AUTHOR: Jonathan Swift, Retold by Ann Keay Beneduce • ILLUSTRATOR: Gennady Spirin
HC: Philomel
THEMES: fantasy; little folk; boats; storms; war; friendship; adventure

Before you open this book, Gennady's Spirin's cover art will get your attention. And when you turn the pages, hoping for more full-page paintings reminiscent of European masters, you will not be disappointed. The story takes place in 1699 when Lemuel Gulliver's ship sinks in a storm in the South Pacific, and Gulliver finds himself in the land of Lilliput, where the people are no taller than his finger. Swift's tale, first published in 1726, has been condensed for younger readers as a read-aloud, or to enjoy on their own savoring each magnificent page.

Halloween ABC   PICTURE BOOK
AUTHOR: Eve Merriam • ILLUSTRATOR: Lane Smith
PB: Aladdin
THEMES: spooky stories; alphabet; rhyme; Halloween

Mayhem-filled rhyme coupled with eerie illustrations make this a perfect read aloud for older children at Halloween time:

"Icicle
An icy stabbing so swiftly done,
the victim scarcely felt it.
The police are baffled: 'Where's the weapon?'
The sun shines down to melt it."

Happy New Year! Kung-Hsi Fa-Ts'ai!   PICTURE BOOK NONFICTION
AUTHOR/ILLUSTRATOR: Demi
HC: Crown
THEMES: Chinese New Year; Chinese culture; traditions; food; celebrations; social studies; dragons

Demi's cheery, colorful paintings and straightforward text present the Chinese New Year. Children learn about the animal zodiac, parades, dances, dragons and how families prepare for the holiday. A perfect book for sharing in January or February when the celebration takes place.

★ Hawk, I'm Your Brother   PICTURE BOOK
AUTHOR: Byrd Baylor • ILLUSTRATOR: Peter Parnall
PB: Aladdin
THEMES: hawks; flying; Native American; nature; desert

Rudy Soto wants to soar across the sky like a hawk, so he captures one in the hopes that their friendship will bring him closer to flying. Baylor's poetry and Parnall's black-and-white drawings resonate with the power of freedom and a young boy's lesson learned.

Higgins Bend Song and Dance   PICTURE BOOK
AUTHOR: Jacqueline Briggs Martin • ILLUSTRATOR: Brad Sneed
HC: Houghton Mifflin
THEMES: fishing; fish; humor; tall tales

The story of fisherman Simon Henry, his friend Potato Kelly, and the wiliest catfish ever, Oscar. Try as he might, Simon Henry just cannot outwit that old bait-stealer. At least, not until he uses an unorthodox kind of bait that results in a tumultuous adventure. Full of fabulous language and Sneed's customary, slightly "off" perspectives, this is a whopper of a story that is slightly outrageous—just the way a fishing tale ought to be.

The Hired Hand,
An African-American Folktale   PICTURE BOOK

AUTHOR: Robert D. San Souci • ILLUSTRATOR: Jerry Pinkney
HC: Dial
THEMES: African American; laziness; magic; folklore; U.S. history, Colonial America; comeuppance

A kind heart mixed with a dose of magic can go far in creating good. But a lazy, promise-breaking man looking for a shortcut to gold can get himself into a lot of trouble. You'll find both in this tale, along with stunning artwork and a lesson in attitude.

The Hobyahs   PICTURE BOOK

AUTHOR: Robert San Souci • ILLUSTRATOR: Alexi Natchev
HC: Doubleday • PB: Dell
THEMES: folklore; good vs. evil; loyalty; orphans; triumph; fools; dogs; monsters; spooky stories

The evil Hobyahs, catlike creatures who live in the forest, want to eat the residents of a little house—an old man and woman and a little orphan girl—at the edge of the woods. Only the faithful dogs (Tippy, Topie, Turpie, Tarry, and Teeny) keep them away, but their barking disturbs the sleep of the old man and old woman. In spite of the pleas of the little orphan girl, the foolish old couple whip and drive away the dogs one by one. With no dogs to protect them, they are easy prey for the Hobyahs who, with the approach of night, surround the house . . . Sounds mighty bleak, eh? But San Souci's retelling has a wonderful happy ending, full of just deserts, that will gratify all except the most faint of heart.

How Big Is a Foot?   EARLY READER

AUTHOR/ILLUSTRATOR: Rolf Myller
PB: Dell
THEMES: math; measurement; kings; queens; gifts; beds

A simple, fun tale with lots of math application. A king wants to build a bed for his queen, but first he has to figure out how big it is to be. How big IS a foot, he wonders, and his journey of discovery, with the aid of almost everyone in the kingdom, will delight children just coming to terms with the 12 inches in a foot and the three feet in a yard.

How to Eat Fried Worms   FICTION
AUTHOR: Thomas Rockwell • ILLUSTRATOR: Emily Arnold McCully
HC: Franklin Watts • PB: Dell
THEMES: worms; dares; wagers; humor, gross

Short, funny chapters and one of the best titles ever make this one of a handful of books we suggest confidently for boys who say they don't like reading. Billy's bet that he could eat fifteen worms gets him into all kinds of squirmy, gross, disgusting situations. Those fifteen worms get eaten. And the reader is there for every one of them.

How to Make an Apple Pie and See the World   PICTURE BOOK
AUTHOR/ILLUSTRATOR: Marjorie Priceman
HC: Knopf • PB: Dragonfly
THEMES: geography; baking; travel; recipes; pies

A young baker leads the reader around the world gathering ingredients for making an apple pie. Sound interesting to you? Probably not. So how come this is one of our picks? Priceman's sense of humor prevails on every page, delivering facts and fun along the way. Maps are found on the end papers, as well as the recipe for the pie. Yum!

In Coal Country   PICTURE BOOK
AUTHOR: Judith Hendershot • ILLUSTRATOR: Thomas B. Allen
HC: Knopf
THEMES: coal; miners; jobs; family; Ohio; U.S. history, the Depression

"Papa dug coal from deep in the earth to earn a living. He dressed for work when everyone else went to bed." Through the voice of a young girl, readers glimpse into the life of a mining family in the 1930s. This is a book you'll read aloud in hushed tones as you marvel at the coal-washed illustrations.

In Flight With David McPhail: A Creative Autobiography   BIOGRAPHY

AUTHOR/ILLUSTRATOR: David McPhail

HC: Heinemann

THEMES: authors; illustrators; writing; books; autobiography

Photos, drawings, paintings and words make up this visual treasure filled with interesting information about writing, illustrating, and publishing. A delightful autobiography of the creator of dozens of books for children, including *Emma's Pet, Farm Morning, Santa's Book of Names,* and *Pigs Aplenty, Pigs Galore.*

Into the Sea   PICTURE BOOK NONFICTION

AUTHOR: Brenda Z. Guiberson • ILLUSTRATOR: Alix Berenzy

HC: Henry Holt

THEMES: animal; life cycles; turtles; sea; science; nature

From the "tap, tap, scritch" of the tiny hatchling to the "thump, scrape, whoosh, wheeze" of the hardworking turtle returned to lay her eggs, young readers learn the life cycle of the sea turtle. The pictures are rich and colorful and the words read like a story. A perfect blend of fiction and nonfiction.

It's Hard to Read a Map With a Beagle on Your Lap   POETRY COLLECTION

AUTHOR: Marilyn Singer • ILLUSTRATOR: Clement Oubrerie

HC/PB: Henry Holt

THEMES: rhyme; dogs

In this collection of playful poems, have fun with phrasing like, "floppy, sloppy, standing high, springy, wingy, butterfly . . ." The rhyming is infectious and may even cause an epidemic of poetry chanting in your home.

John Patrick Norman McHennessy: The Boy Who Was Always Late   PICTURE BOOK

AUTHOR/ILLUSTRATOR: John Burningham

HC: Crown

THEMES: tardiness; imagination; school; teachers; discipline; truth; bullies; triumph; comeuppance

"John Patrick Norman McHennessy set off along the road to learn," but a crocodile makes him late for school. His teacher doesn't like his explantation and makes him write 300 times before he can go home, "I must not tell lies . . ." We both roared with laughter at this one. Poor John's excuses for being late, followed up by his teacher's disciplinary actions and the twisted ending will delight "misunderstood" youngsters.

I think it is sooo important for children to have fictional opportunities to triumph over nasty people who are bigger than they, whether they are teachers, parents or anyone else who abuses power. Face it, they're bullies, and when John Patrick Norman McHennessy puts it to his teacher, I find it to be as satisfying a moment as any in children's books. We don't get that kind of chance very often in real life.

★ Julius, the Baby of the World   PICTURE BOOK

AUTHOR/ILLUSTRATOR: **Kevin Henkes**

HC: Greenwillow

THEMES: jealousy; new baby; humor; brothers; family; change; strong girl

The definitive book on sibling jealousy, told in a side-splitting manner. Lilly will win you over in spite of her outrageous behavior, and if you can't get enough of her, she returns in *Lilly's Purple Plastic Purse*.

The King's Equal   PICTURE BOOK

AUTHOR: Katherine Paterson • ILLUSTRATOR: Vladimir Vagin

HC/PB: HarperCollins

THEMES: fairytales; strong girls; princes; princesses; self-respect; comeuppance

A hardworking, kindhearted farmer's daughter shows Prince Raphael a thing or two about real princesslike behavior. Patterson's modern-day fairytale will delight young readers who like a little self-respect with their happily ever after.

The Korean Cinderella   PICTURE BOOK

AUTHOR: Shirley Climo • ILLUSTRATOR: Ruth Heller

HC: HarperCollins

THEMES: Korea; fairy tale; folklore; folktale variation

With the help of animal magic, Pear Blossom finds her way to the village festival in spite of her wicked stepmother. Careful research in art (the paintings are stunning) and words make this Cinderella tale a feast for the eyes and mind.

The Last Dragon PICTURE BOOK

AUTHOR: Susan Nunes • ILLUSTRATOR: Chris Soentpiet
HC: Clarion
THEMES: dragons; community; aunts; neighbors; Chinese-American; Chinese culture

Peter did not want to spend the summer with his great aunt in a small apartment above a noodle factory—until he saw a dragon in the window of the Lung Fung Trading Company. The unique culture of Chinatown is celebrated in this story where neighbors rally to restore a dragon for a young boy who learns a thing or two about community.

The Lion's Whiskers: An Ethiopian Folktale PICTURE BOOK

AUTHOR: Nancy Raines Day • ILLUSTRATOR: Ann Grifalconi
PB: Scholastic
THEMES: Africa; courage; love; folklore; determination; stepparents

Fanaye lives high in Ehiopia's mountains. One day she goes to a medicine man known far and wide for his wisdom. "Please," she begs him, "make a magic potion that will cause my stepson to love me as much as I love him." "First," the wise man tells her, "I need three whiskers from the chin of the fierce, old lion." Ann Grifalconi adds extraordinary collages to illustrate this tale about a determined, caring woman.

★ Liza Lou and the Yeller Belly Swamp PICTURE BOOK

AUTHOR/ILLUSTRATOR: Mercer Mayer
PB: Aladdin
THEMES: monsters; swamps; opossums; witches; strong girls; folktale variations; witches; cleverness; triumph

It was a read-aloud hit for my daughters' kindergarten, first- and second-grade classrooms—and years later is still a guaranteed no fail. Clever Liza Lou has the spunk kids like. Her story has swamp haunts, witches, devils, gobblygooks, repeatable poems, "how's she gonna get out of this mess" intrigue, and a possum who has a page to page wordless story all of his own. Liza Lou is a must read!

Hey folks, if there are those among you who like a real storytelling workout, this is a good one to try! There are ten different voices to use and a mess of southern /swamp dialects to try out. Have fun!

Lizard in the Sun: A Just for the Day Book   PICTURE BOOK NONFICTION
AUTHOR: Joanne Ryder • ILLUSTRATOR: Michael Rothman
HC: Morrow
THEMES: nature; imagination; habitats; lizards

Ryder has created a series of books where children can visualize what it might be like to be an animal for a day. Other titles in this series, called *Just for a Day* books, include: *Jaguar in the Rain Forest, Winter Whale,* and *Shark in the Sea.* Ryder creates another celebration of nature in *Chipmunk Song,* with illustrations by Lynne Cherry.

Look to the North: A Wolf Pup Diary   PICTURE BOOK NONFICTION
AUTHOR: Jean Craighead George • ILLUSTRATOR: Lucia Washburn
HC: HarperCollins
THEMES: wolves; animal, life cycle; nature; seasons; growing up

"1 Day Old: When you see dandelions turning silver, look to the north. Wolf pups are being born." Brief diary entries mark the passing of the seasons and the growth of three wolf pups. Breathtaking paintings show close-ups of their development from one day to ten and a half months old. George's warmth and respect for these animals is clear throughout, but is best portrayed in her introduction: "In these nursing, tumbling, fighting, and growing children of the wild I see all children. And they are wonderful."

The Loup Garou   FICTION
AUTHOR/ILLUSTRATOR: Berthe Amoss
HC: Pelican
THEMES: Canada; Louisiana; wolves; folklore; werewolves; courage; escape

This piece of historical fiction tells of how the French settlers were forced out of Nova Scotia by the British, many settling in Lousiana. The Loup Garou is a werewolf, in this story used not to frighten but to show how our stories travel with us as we move: this one came originally from France, then to the Canadian settlement of Acadia and is still prevalent in the storytelling of the Cajun people of Louisiana.

Luka's Quilt   PICTURE BOOK
AUTHOR/ILLUSTRATOR: Georgia Guback
HC: Greenwillow
THEMES: Hawaii; traditions; grandmothers and granddaughters; compromise; disagreements; quilts; feelings, hurt

Luka's grandmother makes a traditional two-colored Hawaiian quilt for her, but Luka thinks it should have lots of colors, like the flowers in her garden. Each has a strong opinion of her own, and hurts the other's feelings. This is a story of compromise, and of putting aside differences.

I didn't like Luka's response. I thought she should have been thrilled that her grandmother made her a quilt at all and eternally grateful she had a grandmother!

Mama Is a Miner
PICTURE BOOK

AUTHOR: George Ella Lyon • ILLUSTRATOR: Peter Catalanotto
HC: Orchard
THEMES: miners; coal; jobs; worry; family; strong women; gender roles; mothers and daughters; mines

Though this is a book about a specific situation—a mother who works as a coal miner—this can be used with any child whose parent works in a potentially dangerous job. Telling the story of Mama's daily routine, the young narrator offers bits of information she has heard about the mines, miner rhymes and songs, her concerns, and, finally, her artwork as the story moves back and forth between the family evening routine and Mama's day. We feel this girl's love for her mother and her worry for her safety and we see, through Catalanotto's always remarkable illustrations, that this family is no different from any loving family: They offer the girl support and reassurance while still allowing her to work through her fears her own way. This delicate partnership between author and illustrator is a hallmark of much of Catalanotto's work. Look at *The Rolling Store* by Angela Johnson to see more of his unique style.

A Man Called Raven
PICTURE BOOK

AUTHOR: Richard Van Camp • ILLUSTRATOR: George Littlechild
HC: Children's Book Press
THEMES: Canada; ravens; folklore; Native American; nature; environment

Two brothers who had been trying to hurt and corner a raven are approached by an elderly stranger who tells them his story of the raven. Littlechild's brilliant colors and style show the mystery surrounding the raven man, who gives a lesson in respecting nature. Van Camp's story is taken from the legends told to him by his Dogrib elders.

Meet Danitra Brown   <small>POETRY COLLECTION</small>

AUTHOR: Nikki Grimes • ILLUSTRATOR: Floyd Cooper
HC: Lothrop • PB: Mulberry
THEMES: friendship; strong girls; African American; bullies; self-respect

In thirteen lively poems, Zuri tells us about Danitra, her best friend. Warm, sweet and spunky—read this to a friend.

Metropolitan Cow   <small>PICTURE BOOK</small>

AUTHOR/ILLUSTRATOR: Tim Egan
HC/PB: Houghton Mifflin
THEMES: prejudice; friendship; diversity; city life

A terrific piece of social commentary that never forgets how to tell a good story, *Metropolitan Cow* tells of a city where there are upper-class cows and working-class pigs. When cow Bennett Gibbons expresses a desire to jump in the mud and play with the pigs, his parents make their disapproval quite clear: "Don't be ridiculous. You know cows don't go in the mud. We're far too dignified for such nonsense." But after he is befriended by Webster Anderson, the pig next door, the temptation proves too great for Bennett. How Webster and Bennett's families come together as friends is the heart of this charming and whimsical tale of defeating class prejudice.

Moonstruck: The True Story of the Cow Who Jumped Over the Moon   <small>PICTURE BOOK</small>

AUTHOR: Gennifer Choldenko • ILLUSTRATOR: Paul Yalowitz
HC: Hyperion
THEMES: point of view; Mother Goose; determination; folktale variation; fantasy

Here's the answer to that oft-asked question, "What the heck was a cow doing jumping over the moon?" A little forced in the telling, but too fun to be denied. Yet another in a long line of descendants of *The True Story of the Three Little Pigs*—a retelling from a different point of view of a well-known childhood rhyme or story.

The Muffin Fiend   <small>FICTION</small>

AUTHOR/ILLUSTRATOR: Daniel Pinkwater
HC: Lothrop
THEMES: Mozart; muffins; mystery; music

An easy-to-read mystery in which young Wolfgang Amadeus Mozart figures out what happened to the stolen muffins. Quirky fun with a dose of history.

My Family Tree: A Bird's Eye View   NOVELTY
AUTHOR/ILLUSTRATOR: Nina Laden
HC: Chronicle Books
THEMES: family; relatives; genealogy; connections

"Maybe your grandparents came from another country, your uncle has five stepbrothers, or your second cousins once-removed are identical twins." Whatever the mix, this book includes a family-tree poster to fill out, as well as an illustrated explanation of who is who. It makes room for a variety of family connections—including step families—in a fun, easy to understand style.

One Grain of Rice: A Mathematical Folktale   PICTURE BOOK
AUTHOR/ILLUSTRATOR: Demi
HC: Scholastic
THEMES: math; India; cleverness; folklore; wealth; rice

In a time of famine, as a reward for a good deed, young Rani asks the greedy raja for just one grain of rice doubled every day for thirty days. In a month she collects more than one billion grains of rice, enough to save the hungry people of her village and to teach the raja a thing or two about wisdom. Demi's traditional Indian art includes fold-out pages and a mathematical table that shows how quickly one grain of rice doubles into so many more. We have always liked this story (a chapter book version can be found in *A Grain of Rice* by Helena Claire Pittman), but in Demi's hands it becomes a favorite. Watch kids' eyes light up as they catch on to the trick. Brilliant graphics make this a must for hands-on use in the classroom.

One Small Blue Bead   PICTURE BOOK
AUTHOR: Byrd Baylor • ILLUSTRATOR: Ronald Himler
HC: Atheneum
THEMES: U.S. history, pre-Columbus; Native American; desert; beads; U.S.A., the Southwest

A small blue bead hidden in the grass takes the reader back ten thousand years to those who once inhabited the desert. Baylor's gentle prose is skillfully matched by Himler's dramatic paintings.

★ Owl Eyes

AUTHOR/ILLUSTRATOR: Frieda Gates
HC: Lothrop
THEMES: owls; creation; Native American; manners; folklore; clay; characteristics

In Mohawk legend, Raweno is the master of all spirits and the every-thing-maker. He creates the creatures of the Woodland and gives each a chance to choose its own form and colors. As Raweno works, Owl gives his own nonstop and opposing opinion about each creature. Finally it's Owl's turn. When he is finished, Raweno explains: ". . . your ears are open enough to hear when you are told what you are not to do. Your

---

READING REPELLANTS: THINGS TO AVOID DOING
(COMMON OCCURRENCES THAT SHRINK ENTHUSIASM FOR BOOKS)

What happens in some schools . . .
Arbitrary rules: Accepting reports only on books of 100 pages or more sends the message that length is a determining factor of a book's worth.

Examination: Using trade books for testing, checking spelling, psychoanalyzing the author, underlining adjectives and forgetting that reading is also for joy.

Judging: Responding to a student's book choice with, "Johnny, why don't you choose something 'sensible,' or 'well-written?' "

Oral Reports: Expecting a daily update. Kids will concentrate on responses rather than the pleasure of the story.

What happens in some homes . . .
Disapproving: "Why are you reading that junk?"

Comparing: "Your sister Elizabeth read that when she was in the second grade!"

Disciplining: "Clean your room or you will not be allowed to read for a week!"

Missing the point: "What are you doing reading inside on a sunny day like this?"

Overzealous enthusiasm (curiosity kills the story): An overenthusiastic parent can remove the privacy factor (We can't win, can we?). Reading is a solitary act and too much intrusion robs the child of that rich sense of doing something by himself.

eyes are big enough to see in the dark, and your feathers are dull, for you will seldom be seen. And because I work only by day, you will be awake only at night!" This funny, imaginative tale will get children thinking about other creatures and how they came to be.

Peppe the Lamplighter   PICTURE BOOK
AUTHOR: Alisa Bartone • ILLUSTRATOR: Ted Lewin
HC: Lothrop
THEMES: jobs; immigration; family; courage; taking action

Ted Lewin's paintings illuminate this story about a young boy who insists on taking a job when his immigrant father becomes ill. The lesson here is to take pride in your work, regardless of the job.

Picture Book Biography Series   PICTURE BOOK NONFICTION
AUTHOR: David Adler • ILLUSTRATOR: John and Alexandra Wallner
HC: Holiday House
THEMES: biography; U.S. history, general

A thorough and readable style of recounting lives and facts delivered in a picture book format makes these excellent choices for that first biography. Subjects in the series include: Benjamin Franklin, Davy Crockett, Anne Frank, Paul Revere, Thomas Jefferson and Rosa Parks.

A Pioneer Sampler: The Daily Life
of a Pioneer Family in 1840   PICTURE BOOK NONFICTION
AUTHOR: Barbara Greenwood • ILLUSTRATOR: Heather Collins
HC/PB: Houghton Mifflin
THEMES: pioneers; family; bees; U.S. history, frontier life; recipes

Facts blend with fiction in these stories about the Robertson family, who live on a farm in the mid-1800s. One story that tells about the family's search for a bee tree is followed by several pages of interesting facts about bees, including why it was important to pioneer families to go to the trouble to find them. Readers also learn what it was like to attend school, shear sheep, spin wool and make cheese. Maps, recipes, crafts, a glossary and index are included in this fascinating introduction to life on the frontier.

Polar the Titanic Bear   PICTURE BOOK NONFICTION

AUTHOR: Daisy Spedden • ILLUSTRATOR: Laurie McGaw

HC: Little Brown

THEMES: survival; disaster; teddy bears; mail; memories; photographs; boats; *Titanic;* mothers and sons; writing

Eighty years ago Daisy Spedden, a survivor of the sinking of the *Titanic,* wrote a story for her young son Douglas. Through the voice of a teddy bear she gives a true, eyewitness account of her experience. Family photographs and postcards add historical reality to the watercolor illustrations.

Pole Dog   PICTURE BOOK

AUTHOR: Tres Seymour • ILLUSTRATOR: David Soman

HC: Orchard

THEMES: animal rights; abandonment; animal shelter; dogs; taking action

An old dog is dropped off near a telephone pole and waits and waits for someone to care. Fortunately, in this story, somebody does. The author advises people to call the animal shelter. After you read this book with a youngster, you might want to add your own two cents in discussing the treatment of animals.

A Rainy Day   PICTURE BOOK NONFICTION

AUTHOR: Sandra Markle • ILLUSTRATOR: Cathy Johnson

HC: Orchard

THEMES: weather; rain; storms; worms

"Earthworms need to be wet to breathe because air seeps in through their skin only when it's damp . . ." This book is saturated with basic weather concepts and simple facts anyone can use in case of a storm.

Rechenka's Eggs   PICTURE BOOK

AUTHOR/ILLUSTRATOR: Patricia Polacco

HC: Philomel

THEMES: Easter; eggs; festivals; Ukraine; folk art; miracles; artists; geese; creativity

Each year Old Babushka spent the long cold winter painting eggs. People everywhere knew about their beauty and looked forward to seeing them at the annual festival. So you can imagine what a shock it was for her when Rechenka, the goose whose life she saved, tipped over her basket of eggs and caused them to fall shattering in pieces on the floor. Poor old

Babushka. Thank goodness for miracles. This story of talent, and compassion is filled with miracles, and makes a perfect springtime read aloud.

Rikki-Tikki-Tavi
PICTURE BOOK

AUTHOR: Rudyard Kipling • ILLUSTRATOR: Jerry Pinkney
HC: Morrow
THEMES: mongooses; cobras; India; cleverness; triumph

Rikki, a brave young mongoose, is the hero. Two cobras, Nag and Nagaina, are the villains, and Jerry Pinkney is the artist who adds his stunning full-page watercolors to Kipling's classic tale. Read this aloud. It will bring out voice inflection you didn't even know you had!

Riptide
PICTURE BOOK

AUTHOR: Frances Ward Weller • ILLUSTRATOR: Robert Blake
HC: Philomel • PB: Paperstar
THEMES: dogs; beaches; survival; swimming

A dog in jeopardy book where the dog does not die! Great art helps tug at your heart. The ending makes the whole thing tense, but finally OK.

Ruby Mae Has Something to Say
PICTURE BOOK

AUTHOR/ILLUSTRATOR: David Small
HC: Crown
THEMES: United Nations; peace; determination; taking action; self-respect; speeches; communication

Ruby Mae Foote wants to deliver a message of universal peace and understanding at the United Nations. The problem is, she's tongue-tied. Her nephew Billy Bob comes up with a solution. The lesson here is that it's not how you say it, but what you have to say that's important.

Sadako
PICTURE BOOK

AUTHOR: Eleanor Coerr • ILLUSTRATOR: Ed Young
HC: Putnam
THEMES: Japan; courage; illness; death; family; peace; friendship; origami; war

You'd think a picture book version of *Sadako and the Thousand Paper Cranes* might lose some of its potency, but the story of a young girl's courageous death in postwar Japan is just as affecting in this format. Ed Young's powerful art makes a strong impression and we recommend that you read it first before deciding to share it with a child under seven.

Sally Arnold

PICTURE BOOK

AUTHOR: Cheryl Ryan • ILLUSTRATOR: Bill Farnsworth
HC: Cobblehill
THEMES: U.S.A., Appalachia; elderly and children; music; crafts; friendship; diversity; collecting

Sally Arnold is old, dresses strangely, talks to herself, and is always walking around town collecting things that nobody wants. Jenny is sure she's a witch. But after making music in her grandfather's country store with Sally, Jenny decides to find out more about her. A mountain woman with folk wisdom and the good sense to see use in things others throw away, Sally becomes Jenny's friend, teaching her crafts and secrets. Farnsworth's paintings capture the feel of an Appalachian spring, and the reader is reminded not to judge people by their appearances. See *Captain Snap and the Children of Vinegar Lane* for another take on this subject.

Saving Sweetness

PICTURE BOOK

AUTHOR: Diane Stanley • ILLUSTRATOR: G. Brian Karas
HC: Putnam
THEMES: strong girls; orphans; U.S.A., the West; humor; running away; adoption; cleverness

Mrs. Sump is awfully mean for someone who runs an orphanage, so Sweetness, the littlest orphan—with more than her share of spunk—decides to run away to find a better life. That's when she comes across the sheriff, outsmarts him, and finds a firm foundation for herself and the others in the orphange. Read this aloud for fun and a taste of the wild west.

Secret Places

POETRY ANTHOLOGY

Editor: Charlotte Huck • ILLUSTRATOR: Lindsay Barrett George
HC: Greenwillow
THEMES: solitude; quiet

This beautifully illustrated anthology of ways to find your own quiet place includes works by Rachel Field, A.A. Milne, Myra Cohn Livingston and more.

Smoky Night

PICTURE BOOK

AUTHOR: **Eve Bunting** • ILLUSTRATOR: David Diaz
HC: Harcourt Brace
THEMES: prejudice; getting along; Los Angeles; Korean American; African American; violence; cultural diversity; cats

A night of rioting brings neighbors together along with the lesson that getting along is worth the effort regardless of one's background or nationality. See Author Spotlight on Eve Bunting.

Sod Houses on the Great Plains   PICTURE BOOK NONFICTION
AUTHOR/ILLUSTRATOR: Glen Rounds
HC: Holiday House
THEMES: home; U.S.A., the prairie; U.S. history, frontier life; dwellings

The only building material for pioneers who moved onto the Great Plains was sod, taken from the prairie itself. Writer/illustrator Glen Rounds was born in a sod house so he is in the ideal place to show the clever and not-so-clever techniques used in building these shelters. Here you'll find a perfect mix of humor and information that will stick . . . like sod.

Something Big Has Been Here   POETRY COLLECTION
AUTHOR: Jack Prelutsky • ILLUSTRATOR: James Stevenson
HC: Greenwillow
THEMES: humor; variety; rhyme

Prelutsky poems produce kid howls. Here are three first lines. Your child will find the others. "I wave goodbye when butter flies"; "My brother's bug was green and plump"; "Who pulled the plug in my ant farm?" Other Prelutsky collections that you will enjoy include: *New Kid on the Block, Read Aloud Rhymes for the Very Young, A Pizza the Size of the Sun, Ride a Purple Pelican,* and *Beneath a Blue Umbrella.*

The Spice Alphabet Book: Herbs, Spices, and Other Natural Flavors   PICTURE BOOK NONFICTION
AUTHOR: Jerry Pallotta • ILLUSTRATOR: Leslie Evans
PB: Charlesbridge
THEMES: alphabet; spices; cooking; diversity; plants

Add some spice to your child's life with this colorful alphabet of herbs, flavors and spices. Pallotta's *Nature Alphabet* series includes a wide variety of subjects. Some of them are: *The Icky Bug Alphabet Book, The Desert Alphabet Book,* and *The Yucky Reptile Alphabet Book.*

Spinky Sulks   PICTURE BOOK
AUTHOR/ILLUSTRATOR: William Steig
HC/PB: Farrar Straus & Giroux
THEMES: family; feelings; hurt; sulking; problem solving; anger

No matter how hard they try or what they offer him, Spinky refuses to forgive his family for their awful behavior. So he sulks. A lot. Until neither he nor anyone else is sure what exactly got him so mad in the first place, but by then he's almost too deep into it to find a graceful way out. But he does. This is a book for any child who has backed himself into an emotional corner, not sure what's supposed to happen next. And it's funny!

Star Walk   POETRY ANTHOLOGY

EDITOR: Seymour Simon • ILLUSTRATOR: photographs
HC: Morrow
THEMES: planets; constellations; science; astronomy; outer space

In this collection, poems—as varied as their writers—accompany photographs of space. A brief description of each picture is included, adding a touch of science to the remarkable words of poets like Walt Whitman and Diane Ackerman.

★ The Stinky Cheese Man and Other
Fairly Stupid Tales   PICTURE BOOK

AUTHOR: Jon Scieszka • ILLUSTRATOR: Lane Smith
HC: Viking
THEMES: humor; fairy tales; folktale variations; zany

Scieszka's introduction pretty well sums it up: "The stories in this book are Fairly Stupid Tales. I mean, what else would you call a story like Goldilocks and the Three Elephants?" When Scieszka and Smith get together, there is sure to be riotous laughter, pathetic puns, ridiculous rewrites, and off-the-wall art that shatters every convention of traditional illustration. We get the results in zany tales like "Little Red Running Shorts" with nags from the Little Red Hen. ("Over fifty pages of nonsense and I'm only in three of them.") It will be over the heads of younger children, but this is the humor that infects third graders and fifth graders too!

The Story of Babar the Little Elephant   PICTURE BOOK

AUTHOR/ILLUSTRATOR: Jean deBrunhoff
HC/PB: Random House
THEMES: elephants; hunters; cities; friendship; family; cousins; kings; orphans

Little Babar runs away to the city after a hunter kills his mother. There he meets an old lady who fits him in fine clothes and gives him a place to live. In this classic tale (published in 1933) Babar becomes a proper gentleman, finds a wife, and returns to the forest to be king of the elephants. Children love Babar. What a relief that such impossibly good things can happen to an orphaned elephant who has had his share of bad luck! Other titles we are fond of are *Babar and His Children, Travels of Babar* and *Babar the King*.

The Summer of Stanley   PICTURE BOOK

AUTHOR: Natalie Kinsey-Warnock • ILLUSTRATOR: Donald Gates
HC: Cobblehill
THEMES: U.S. history, World War II; siblings; goats; gardens; rescue

Victory gardens, the end of the World War II, sibling rivalry, and a goat named Stanley combine to make for an engaging, nostalgic read. Although Stanley's a pest, and will eat anything, Molly and her family learn to love him, especially after he saves her little brother from drowning. Lovely illustrations.

Supergrandpa   PICTURE BOOK BIOGRAPHY

AUTHOR: David M. Schwartz • ILLUSTRATOR: Bert Dodson
HC: Lothrop
THEMES: grandfathers; bicycles; Sweden; racing; community; determination; judging; aging

"Gustaf Hakansson was sixty-six years old. His hair was snow white. His beard was a white bush. His face rippled with wrinkles whenever he smiled." And when he was told he was too old to join Sweden's 1,000-mile bicycle race, he rode anyway . . . unofficially. To the delight of his countrymen, who greeted him at every turn, "Supergrandpa" was the first to cross the finish line. Based on a true story that took place in Sweden in 1951, "Supergrandpa" defies old-age stereotypes and offers a lesson or two in perseverance.

The Talking Eggs   PICTURE BOOK

AUTHOR: Robert D. San Souci • ILLUSTRATOR: Jerry Pinkney
HC: Dial
THEMES: witches; magic; kindness; mystery; folktale variations; folklore

Kind, gentle Blanche must do all the work for her lazy mother and sister, until one day an old woman comes along and changes everything. Stunning watercolors and a touch of magic make this Creole version of Cinderella one of our favorites.

Teammates
PICTURE BOOK BIOGRAPHY

AUTHOR: Peter Golenbock • ILLUSTRATOR: Paul Bacon
HC/PB: Harcourt Brace
THEMES: baseball; prejudice; self-respect; athletes; taking action; friendship; cultural diversity; biography

When black players were not allowed in the major leagues, Jackie Robinson had to break down barriers to play ball. With the help of teammate Pee Wee Reese, he led the way for players who followed. This is the story of Reese and Robinson's friendship, illustrated in black and white photographs and full-color art.

A Three Hat Day
PICTURE BOOK

AUTHOR: Laura Geringer • ILLUSTRATOR: Arnold Lobel
HC/PB: HarperCollins
THEMES: hats; loneliness; love; obsession; friendship; individuality

An engaging story about eccentric R. R. Pottle the Third, who loves hats, and his search for happiness. Without preaching or being overly sweet, the message gets across—there is someone for everyone in this world.

Thunder at Gettysburg
FICTION

AUTHOR: Patricia Lee Gauch • ILLUSTRATOR: Stephen Gammell
HC: Putnam • PB: Dell
THEMES: U.S. history, Civil War; war; coming of age; change; community.

Tillie thinks it will be fun to watch the Union soldiers beat the pants off the Rebels, and she plans to spend all day watching them from the attic window of her Gettysburg home. She is irrevocably changed as she finds herself right in the middle of the events of July 1-3, 1863, and a better introduction to the horrors of war we can't imagine. Gammell's stark black-and-white illustrations match Gauch's spare prose, making this a book not just for younger readers, but for anyone interested in the Civil War.

Too Many Pumpkins
PICTURE BOOK

AUTHOR: Linda White • ILLUSTRATOR: Megan Lloyd
HC/PB: Holiday House
THEMES: pumpkins; gardening; cooking; baking; stubbornness; problem solving

Rebecca Estelle hates pumpkins. Stubborn and set in her ways, she refuses to acknowledge the pumpkin patch that is growing by accident in her front yard. When she can ignore it no longer, she is motivated to do some major baking, enough for the whole town to share. This fun read aloud is great for fall and harvest time.

Too Many Tamales   PICTURE BOOK
AUTHOR: Gary Soto • ILLUSTRATOR: Ed Martinez
HC: Putnam • PB: Paperstar
THEMES: Christmas; hispanic; family; cooking; Mexican culture; cousins; conscience; consequences

Maria loses her mother's diamond ring in the masa when helping to make the Christmas tamales, so she makes her cousins eat the entire batch in search of it. Of course the ring isn't in them, but on her mother's finger. This is a charming read aloud at holiday time, full of humor and warmth.

SEEING OURSELVES

If your interest is in giving your child an understanding of cultural diversity through books, it's important to choose titles showing children from different races and religions in situations the reader can identify with. Children need to find themselves in books. Using just one example, a Chinese-American child who only has access to books about Chinese legends may find this limiting version of his heritage unfamiliar. If he has access to books featuring Chinese-American kids in contemporary life he will see himself reflected back from the page. If his culture is not Chinese, it's helpful for him to see Chinese Americans in realistic, contemporary situations, where he can see people who look like him living their daily lives in ways similar and dissimilar to his own. This will enable him to draw his own conclusions about who he is, who "they" are, and ultimately develop some cultural empathy. Yes, history is important and so are myths and legends, but here we're talking about learning to respect and getting to know the diverse backgrounds of those who live around us.

The Uninvited Guest & Other
Jewish Holiday Tales   FOLKLORE COLLECTION
AUTHOR: Nina Jaffe • ILLUSTRATOR: Elivia Savadier
HC: Scholastic
THEMES: Judaism; folklore; holidays; Hanukkah; Passover

For children of all religions, this collection of tales that describe the major Jewish holidays will be welcomed at Hanukkah and other special times through the year.

Velcome!   PICTURE BOOK

AUTHOR/ILLUSTRATOR: Kevin O'Malley
HC: Walker
THEMES: humor, adolescent; jokes; puns; spooky stories; Halloween

The goofiest Halloween book ever! Full of silliness, outrageous puns and a wacky sense of humor, this will delight many of the same kids who find *The Adventures of Captain Underpants* funny. O'Malley has outdone himself with this combination of horror and humor.

Visiting the Art Museum   PICTURE BOOK NONFICTION

AUTHOR: Laurie Krasny and Marc Brown • ILLUSTRATOR: Marc Brown
HC: Dutton
THEMES: art; museums; paintings; family

Read this together before that first trip to a museum. The kids act like real kids, the paintings are presented in a way that will encourage discussion, and the experience is made to be something a child would be interested in. Useful and entertaining.

"The apple doesn't fall far from the tree. If you are an avid reader, your child will undoubtedly follow your lead. Make a child's own place for books as important as a place for toys. Find a cozy spot that's special for reading times. Make it a daily ritual. But above all, have fun reading to your child. Select books you can truly enjoy together."
—Marc Brown, author of the *Arthur* books

The Way West: Journal of a
Pioneer Woman   PICTURE BOOK BIOGRAPHY

AUTHOR: Amelia Stewart Knight • ILLUSTRATOR: Michael McCurdy
HC: Simon & Schuster
THEMES: pioneers; journeys; U.S. history, frontier life; Native American; Oregon; diaries; strong women; determination; survival; U.S. history, Westward movement; hardship; storms

"Saturday, April 9, 1853. Started from home about eleven o'clock and traveled eight miles and camped in an old house; night cold and frosty." The story of Amelia Stewart Knight's journey in 1853, from Iowa to Oregon, begins with these words. Filled with fascinating details—Mrs. Knight cooked with "buffalo chips" over fires and rolled her pie dough on the wagon seat—this authentic journal gives young readers a glimpse at the hardship and determination of one family of nine as they struggle West to a better life.

Whaling Days
PICTURE BOOK NONFICTION

AUTHOR: Carol Carrick • ILLUSTRATOR: David Frampton
HC: Clarion
THEMES: whales; U.S. history, Colonial America; environment; animals, endangered

We were not looking forward to reading a book that details the harpooning of a whale, but we have to admit there is an incredible history here and fascinating details. "A sperm whale head would be cut off and hauled onto the deck. Climbing into the case, a cavity in the upper part of the head, a man with a bucket bailed out the oil." Stunning woodcuts show the beauty and power of the whale. This history of whaling in America from Colonial times to the present includes a glossary of whaling terms, an index and bibliography.

When I Was Nine
PICTURE BOOK

AUTHOR/ILLUSTRATOR: James Stevenson
HC: Greenwillow
THEMES: memory; childhood; U.S. history, the Depression

Watercolor paintings with details left to the imagination and a hauntingly beautiful text are the hallmarks of this and six other books of reminiscence by Stevenson. Capturing both the universal experience of childhood and the specific time and place of the author's youth, each book is a treasure, full of warmth. Titles include: *Fun/No Fun, Higher on the Door, July, Don't You Know There's a War On?, I Meant to Tell You,* and *I Had a Lot of Wishes.*

When Jo Louis Won the Title
PICTURE BOOK

AUTHOR: Belinda Rochelle • ILLUSTRATOR: Larry Johnson
HC/PB: Houghton Mifflin
THEMES: family; names; boxing; embarrassment; grandfathers and granddaughters; pride; African American

The first day at a new school is hard enough, but imagine being a young girl whose name is Jo Louis. John Henry, Jo's grandfather, helps her feel better when he tells her why she is named for the heavyweight boxing champion. This warm story about given names that can be difficult to bear is also about pride.

When the Monkeys Came Back   PICTURE BOOK

AUTHOR: Kristine Franklin • ILLUSTRATOR: Robert Roth
HC: Macmillan
THEMES: environment; taking action; Costa Rica; monkeys; rain forest;
trees; habitats; Central America; strong women; change

When Dona Marta was a little girl, she lived in a tree covered valley in
Costa Rica. Howler monkeys hooted and barked and howled to each
other every morning and evening. But one day men from the city cut
down the trees and all the monkeys disappeared. Marta planted trees on
a new piece of land, cared for them, and waited until the monkeys
returned. This book shows how one person's action can make a positive
difference in our world where it is easy to feel helpless in the face of
huge environmental concerns.

Wilma Unlimited: How Wilma Rudolph Became the World's
Fastest Woman   PICTURE BOOK BIOGRAPHY

AUTHOR: Kathleen Krull • ILLUSTRATOR: David Diaz
HC: Harcourt Brace
THEMES: sports; biography; African American; triumph; illness; polio;
Olympics; athletes; track and field; strong women

Against all odds, Wilma Rudolph stopped wearing the leg brace she
needed as a child and went on to become the first woman ever to win
three gold medals in track in a single Olympics. This is her story, illustrated with a striking combination of paintings and photos by David
Diaz.

Zilla Sasparilla and the Mud Baby   PICTURE BOOK

AUTHOR: Judith Gorog • ILLUSTRATOR: Amanda Harvey
HC: Candlewick
THEMES: mothers and sons; fear; wisdom; mud; rivers; single parents

All parents worry about the fate of their children, whether they will be
safe when out of sight. But Zilla Sasparilla's child is a mud baby, pulled
from the golden mud at the banks of the river, and she worries that the
river might want him back. A lovely, warm tale about motherly protec-
tiveness and the wisdom of children, sprinkled with soothing insight
delivered by Granny Vi, a mountain woman who counsels Zilla and
soothes her fears.

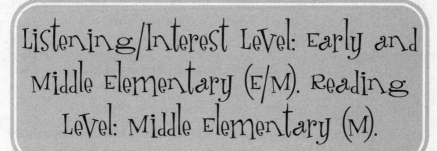

Listening/Interest Level: Early and Middle Elementary (E/M). Reading Level: Middle Elementary (M).

These titles feature a vocabulary that matches the ability of M readers but offers a range of listening experiences that they and their younger siblings can enjoy together.

Adopted by the Eagles: A Plains Story of Friendship and Treachery
PICTURE BOOK

AUTHOR/ILLUSTRATOR: Paul Goble
HC: Simon & Schuster
THEMES: friendship; betrayal; Native American; hunters; birds

This Plains Indian story about friendship tells of treachery between two hunters when they are far from home, and birds who rescue them.

The Adventures of High John the Conqueror
FICTION

AUTHOR: Steve Sanfield
PB: August House
THEMES: African American; folklore; slavery; jobs; cleverness; U.S. history, pre-Civil War; trickster tales

Sixteen folktales show how John can out-trick just about anyone, particularly his white master. Another in a long line of folklore collections from August House, a publisher who is doing more to preserve America's storytelling heritage than any other.

★ Airmail to the Moon
PICTURE BOOK

AUTHOR: Tom Birdseye • ILLUSTRATOR: Stephen Gammell
HC/PB: Holiday House
THEMES: family; strong girls; teeth; U.S.A., Appalachia; tooth fairy; humor

Ore Mae Cotton of Crabapple Orchard loses her first tooth and hunts down the no good varmint who stole it out from underneath her pillow. She hears a lot of conflicting information about the tooth fairy, but can't seem to find out who stole her tooth. So funny it hurts!

Alvin Ailey   PICTURE BOOK BIOGRAPHY
AUTHOR: Andrea Davis Pinkney • ILLUSTRATOR: Brian Pinkney
HC: Hyperion
THEMES: dance; biography; African American; trailblazing; dancers

Swirling scratchboard drawings illustrate this lively biography of dancer and choreographer Alvin Ailey, who created his own modern dance company.

All the Lights In the Night   PICTURE BOOK
AUTHOR: Arthur A. Levine • ILLUSTRATOR: James E. Ransome
HC: Tambourine Books • PB: Mulberry
THEMES: Hanukkah; escape; Israel; Jews; brothers; immigration; courage; faith; separation; journeys

Life has become intolerable for Russian Jews, so when brothers Moses and David have a chance to go to Palestine, their mother helps them escape. To stave off fear during their dangerous journey, they tell each other the ancient story of Hanukkah. Lustrous oil paintings dominated by blues and greens provide the backdrop for this moving story of faith and courage.

Amelia's Road   PICTURE BOOK
AUTHOR: Linda Jacobs Altman • ILLUSTRATOR: Enrique O. Sanchez
HC/PB: Lee & Low
THEMES: Mexican; change; moving; home; migrant farm workers; problem solving

A strong portrayal of the migrant farm worker life, and how a young girl comes to develop a sense of "home" despite all odds. Leaving behind mementos of her life and family ensure Amelia of something familiar upon her return to one of her many homes. A useful book on problem solving.

The American Girl Series   FICTION
AUTHOR: Various
PB: Pleasant Company
THEMES: U.S. history; strong girls; cultural diversity

The American Girl series has helped to make historical fiction accessible and popular, offering a glimpse of the past that will liven up any history lesson. Each girl in this popular series represents a different time in history and receives her own set of stories: *Addy*: 1864—The Civil War, *Josefina*: 1824—Hispanic girl in New Mexico during the movement west, *Felicity*: 1774—Colonial times, *Kirsten*: 1854—Pioneer life, *Samantha*: 1904—raised by her Victorian grandmother, *Molly*: 1944—World War II.

Anastasia Krupnik   FICTION

AUTHOR: Lois Lowry
HC: Houghton Mifflin
PB: Dell
THEMES: family; gifted child; strong girls; siblings

Irrepressible and too bright for her own good, Anastasia Krupnik is the star of a delightful series of books that will bring readers from the age of chapter books almost up to the age of the young adult novel. Full of fun and warm details about a charming and often hilarious family, these books are perfect family read alouds when you are looking for a dose of contemporary as opposed to historical or fantasy fiction. Anastasia has gotten too old to be the star of this series and still fit the mold of middle-grade novels, so thank goodness for her younger brother, Sam, who moved to center stage in the books *All About Sam, Attaboy, Sam!,* and *See You Around, Sam.* All the Anastasia books start with her name, so they are easy to find in the library or bookstore. Look for: *Anastasia Again, Anastasia at Your Service, Anastasia Has the Answers, Anastasia on Her Own,* and *Anastasia's Chosen Career.* Enjoy!

Arabian Nights: Three Tales   FOLKLORE COLLECTION

AUTHOR/ILLUSTRATOR: Deborah Nourse Lattimore
HC: HarperCollins
THEMES: desert; China; fairy tales; folklore; camels; Middle East

In the Author's Note Lattimore describes her choices in retelling the Arabian Nights. "*Aladdin,* because the story shows that even if a person has a slow start in life, he or she can triumph one day; *The Queen of the Serpents,* because of the Queen's compassion and knowledge and the passing of wisdom from generation to the next; and *Ubar, The Lost City of Brass,* because Uba. . . . makes me wonder: Maybe those old, old stories aren't just make-believe after all!" And our reasons for choosing Lattimore's retelling? See above. Then add her lavish illustrations of glittering jewels, sultans, and serpents and feel the magic. This ought to pique your child's interest for a reading of the original volumes when he's ready.

★ The Araboolies of Liberty Street   PICTURE BOOK
AUTHOR: Sam Swope • ILLUSTRATOR: Barry Root
HC: Crown • PB: Dragonfly
THEMES: taking action; bullies; cultural diversity; neighbors; prejudice; community; comeuppance

Such a wonderful tale! General Pinch and his wife have their entire street completely under their thumb, forcing their tastes upon everyone with threats to call in the army shouted through a bullhorn. But when the non-English-speaking, multicolored, glow-in-the-dark Araboolies move in right next door, with their huge family, large menagerie of animals, and unusual decorating ideas, the inspiration for a little rebellion is born in one of the neighborhood kids. Reading how the kids turn the tables on the bullying, bigoted Pinches makes for a terrific lesson in civil disobedience. And the art is great, too!

Aster Aardvark's Alphabet Adventures   PICTURE BOOK
AUTHOR/ILLUSTRATOR: Steven Kellogg
HC: Morrow Junior Books • PB: Mulberry
THEMES: rhyme; alliteration; alphabet; tongue twisters

"Aster Aardvark had an aversion to the alphabet. Appalled by Aster's attitude, Acorn Acres Academy alerted her and Agnes, who arranged for an airplane to aid Aster's academic advancement. . . ." Kellogg's alphabet will twist tongues and challenge minds of anyone predisposed to inventing alliterative phrases of his own.

This is part of my permanent "writing" collection. Read a few of these aloud, then give young writers (4th grade+) dictionaries and have them come up with their own sentences. You can count on raucous vocabulary-bending results!

Babe, the Gallant Pig   FICTION
AUTHOR: Dick King-Smith • ILLUSTRATOR: Mary Raynor
HC: Crown • PB: Knopf
THEMES: animals, farm; pigs; sheep; farmers; farms; courage; competition; talent; triumph

There are few writers who can make animals come alive as well as Dick King-Smith, and his best loved book is *Babe*. The story of the pig who becomes a sheepherder has been made into a successful movie and has created interest in other works by this remarkable author. These include: *Harry's Mad, Ace: The Very Important Pig,* and *The School Mouse.*

Bard of Avon: The Story of William Shakespeare

PICTURE BOOK BIOGRAPHY

AUTHOR: Diane Stanley and Peter Vennema • ILLUSTRATOR: Diane Stanley
HC: Morrow
THEMES: biography; Shakespeare; theater; England; poets; playwrights; actors and acting

Stanley and Vennema have figured out that it's more fun to learn about history through story than through a listing of facts. Some parts of Shakespeare's life remain a mystery (like exactly when he was born), but by looking at the times in which he lived, gathering information left by his fellow writers and friends, and adding paintings, these authors have created a fascinating picture book account of his life.

> Families who read together get more in the bargain than just well-read kids.
>
> There is plenty of statistical proof that children who have books in their lives have better opportunities and more choices than children who don't.

A Bear Called Paddington

FICTION

AUTHOR: Michael Bond • ILLUSTRATOR: Peggy Fortnum
PB: Dell
THEMES: bears; trains; theater; shopping; beaches

"Please look after this bear. Thank you," is the sign hanging around the poor bear's neck. From Darkest Peru, he finds himself sitting in Paddington Railway Station in London. It's lucky for him that Mr. and Mrs. Brown come along to care for him, even though their lives will never be quite the same. Read this aloud. It's great fun and if you enjoy exaggerated voices, you can try them here. There are at least ten other Paddington chapter books in this series. If you enjoy this one, try another.

The Bear That Heard Crying   PICTURE BOOK
AUTHOR: Natalie Kinsey-Warnock and Helen Kinsey • ILLUSTRATOR: Ted Rand
HC: Dutton • PB: Puffin
THEMES: U.S. history, Colonial America; bears; lost

A true story, certain to raise questions from children who will be inclined to disbelieve it. A young girl is lost in the woods in Colonial times, only to be found days later, telling the story of the "large brown dog" that protected her in his cave.

Big Blue Whale   PICTURE BOOK NONFICTION
AUTHOR: Nicola Davies • ILLUSTRATOR: Nick Maland
HC: Candlewick
THEMES: whales; nature

Beautiful blue, watery illustrations and well-presented information about the biggest animal ever! A must for whale lovers.

Big Men, Big Country: A Collection of American Tall Tales   FOLKLORE COLLECTION
AUTHOR: Paul Robert Walker • ILLUSTRATOR: James Bernardin
HC: Harcourt Brace
THEMES: tall tales; pioneers; folklore; U.S. history, frontier life

This outstanding collection of nine American Tall Tales, from Davy Crockett to Pecos Bill, is terrific for introducing read alouds with fewer pictures! Each story can be read in one sitting, and there is one full-color painting and one pencil drawing per story—just enough to provide a visual element for five and six year olds. You'll find historical notes at the end of each story that will help make this a book you will turn to again and again, whenever the topic of American folklore comes up.

Bone Poems   POETRY COLLECTION
AUTHOR: Jeff Moss • ILLUSTRATOR: Tom Leigh
HC: Workman
THEMES: dinosaurs; museums; extinction; prehistoric animals; science; nature

One of our favorite poets turns his attention to the world of dinosaurs in this collection of verse guaranteed to teach while it entertains. As in his first book, The Butterfly Jar, Moss's poetry here ranges from lighthearted to thought-provoking. Readers will learn about a variety of creatures, where they lived, what they ate, and how they became extinct. Accompanied by Tom Leigh's whimsical illustrations, these poems will find a home in the library as well as the science lab.

The Boy and the Cloth of Dreams   PICTURE BOOK
AUTHOR: Jenny Koralek • ILLUSTRATOR: James Mayhew
HC/PB: Candlewick
THEMES: grandmothers and grandsons; dreams; nightmares; courage

A finely crafted, elegant tale of a boy who faces his fears with the help of his wise grandmother. Powerful and just a tad scary, in a way that youngsters troubled by nightmares will completely understand. The art is key to the impact of this story.

The Boy Who Dreamed of an Acorn   PICTURE BOOK
AUTHOR: Leigh Casler • ILLUSTRATOR: Shonto Begay
HC: Philomel
THEMES: Native American; individuality; coming of age; gentle boy; dreams

A Chinook boy dreams of an acorn while his companions dream of mountain lions and black bears—"They will become strong"—and of the white-headed eagle—"They will become great hunters." But what becomes of a boy who dreams of acorns? A wise man advises, "Be happy with your own gift, and be at peace with your own dream. For in the smallest of acorns there is a thing that is mighty, and the seasons will show you the wonders it holds." Author Casler includes a list of Chinook words, along with their spelling and pronunciation in this gentle story of individuality.

Bunnicula   FICTION-MYSTERY
AUTHOR: Deborah and James Howe • ILLUSTRATOR: Alan Daniel
HC: Atheneum • PB: Aladdin
THEMES: rabbits; dogs; cats; vampires; mystery; family; vegetables; pets; humor

A very funny book about a vampire bunny! Narrated by Harold, the well-meaning and slightly put-upon dog of the Monroe family, it recounts the introduction of a new member to the household—the mysterious white rabbit named Bunnicula. Chester the cat, who reads a lot and knows almost everything, is absolutely certain that this is no ordinary bunny, and when white vegetables are found in the kitchen, Chester concludes that Bunnicula must be a vampire. Of course, the humans in the house fail to sense any trouble and things keep going awry, so that Chester and Harold get blamed for everything. This is one of those perfect books for the age when a sense of humor and the ability to read longer books both emerge, hungry for a great adventure! A series of sequels follows, guaranteeing that your child will have plenty more adventures with Bunnicula and the gang after the last chapter of this book, which they no doubt will clamor for! Don't say we didn't warn you. Other titles include: *The Celery Stalks at Midnight, Nighty-Nightmare, Howliday Inn,* and *Return to Howliday Inn.*

Burnt Stick
PICTURE BOOK

AUTHOR: Anthony Hill • ILLUSTRATOR: Mark Sofilas
HC: Houghton Mifflin
THEMES: aborigines; Australia; mothers and sons; courage

Set in Australia among the Aborigine during the early 1900s, when the government would take any child of partial white blood away from his mother to be raised as white, this is a devastating tale of man's cruelty and one mother's cleverness. The mother is able to conceal her son by covering him from head to toe with ashes, but this trick is ultimately discovered and the child is taken away in a heartbreaking scene. Powerful and useful in the way it raises questions about how people can treat each other so cruelly. For a look at a similar episode in American history, see Eve Bunting's *Cherokee Summer.*

The Castle in the Attic
FICTION-FANTASY

AUTHOR: Elizabeth Winthrop
HC: Holiday House • PB: Dell
THEMES: castles; magic; knights; England; mystery

A magical adventure story, where a lonely boy learns the secret of the mysterious model of a castle. Filled with toys come to life, knights, and wizards, this castle transports the reader along with William on a fantastic quest of daring-do. Sequel: *The Battle for the Castle.*

Catwings
FICTION-FANTASY

AUTHOR: Ursula LeGuin • ILLUSTRATOR: S. D. Schindler
HC: Orchard • PB: Scholastic
THEMES: fantasy; cats; flying

An imaginitive piece of writing that is sure to appeal to cat lovers as well as those who are ready to begin reading fantasy. Short in length but rich in character and detail, this is an excellent book to use as a first longer chapter book. It also reads aloud beautifully. The sequels are *Catwings Return* and *Wonderful Alexander and the Catwings*.

The Chalk Doll
PICTURE BOOK

AUTHOR: Charlotte Pomerantz • ILLUSTRATOR: Frane Lessac
HC/PB: HarperCollins
THEMES: Jamaica; mothers; memories; childhood; change

Simple language is used to relate everyday events that Rose's mom remembers from her Jamaican childhood.

Charlie and the Chocolate Factory
FICTION-FANTASY

AUTHOR: Roald Dahl • ILLUSTRATOR: Joseph Schindelman
HC: Knopf • PB: Puffin
THEMES: fantasy; contests; food; grandfathers and grandsons; candy; chocolate; comeuppance; misbehaving

Charlie Bucket and his grandfather take the journey of their lifetimes through the gates of Willy Wonka's famous chocolate factory. Four other children—a glutton for anything he can put in his stomach, a television fanatic, a spoiled brat, and a gum-loving girl who chews herself blueberry blue—join them. They travel along rivers of chocolate to a world where anything sweet is possible, unless you are not so sweet and end up as a bad nut or with Everlasting Gobstoppers or Fizzy Lifting Drinks. In typical Dahl fashion, young readers can rejoice in the rotten eggs getting their comeuppance while honest, brave, kind, good eggs like Charlie have the time of their lives. The sequel, *Charlie and the Great Glass Elevator,* picks up right where this leaves off and is almost as good.

Chocolate Fever
FICTION

AUTHOR: Robert Kimmel Smith • ILLUSTRATOR: Gioia Fiammenghi
PB: Dell
THEMES: chocolate; obsession; adventure; change; family; illness; doctors

Henry Green loves chocolate. Nothing gets past his mouth without some form of chocolate on it or in it. When his obsession with his favorite food causes him to break out in little brown spots, he is diagnosed with Chocolate Fever! A funny look at what happens when we get too much of a good thing.

The Chocolate Touch   FICTION

AUTHOR: Patrick Skene Catling • ILLUSTRATOR: Margot Apple
HC: Morrow • PB: Beechtree
THEMES: chocolate; greed; mothers; folktale variations

". . . he didn't see the change right away. Then his lips began to feel
sticky. He opened his eyes. His mother had turned into a lifeless statue
of chocolate!" John Midas loves chocolate. He also loves his mother. Due
to his greed and his unfortunate misuse of a strange old coin, everything
he touches becomes the thing he most desires.

The Christmas House   POETRY COLLECTION

AUTHOR: Ann Turner • ILLUSTRATOR: Nancy Edwards Calder
HC: HarperCollins
THEMES: Christmas; family; point of view; writing; rhyme

Poet Ann Turner shows a variety of feelings about what Christmas
means—ranging from those of the children to the dog, and even the dining room table! These perspectives are just the thing to get a young
writer's imagination working.

Cinder Edna   PICTURE BOOK

AUTHOR: Ellen Jackson • ILLUSTRATOR: Kevin O'Malley
HC: Lothrop
THEMES: fairy tales; individuality; jobs; folktale variation; strong girls;
step families

Cinder Edna is Cinderella's next door neighbor. Each one has a wicked
stepmother and wicked stepsisters. But while Cinderella sits among the
cinders thinking about all her troubles, Cinder Edna is learning a thing
or two from doing all that housework—such as how to get spots off
everything from rugs to ladybugs. On the night of the ball, Cinder Edna
puts on a practical dress and penny loafers and hops on a bus. At the ball
she meets the prince's brother who "runs the recycling plant and a
home for orphaned kittens." It's a fun contrast and the young reader is
left with no doubt as to who lives happily ever after.

Close Your Eyes So You Can See: Stories of Children in the Life of Jesus COLLECTION

AUTHOR: Michael Card • ILLUSTRATOR: Stephen Marchesi
HC: Harvest House
THEMES: Christianity; Jesus; biography; storytelling

Because we are not fans of any books that preach at the expense of story, we are highly selective when choosing books with religion as a theme. When we find one that works as an example of fine storytelling, it is a pleasure to recommend it. This is such a book. Written in short "you are there" style chapters with some questions to ponder after the story, these tales tell of encounters that children had with Jesus in the New Testament. This is a delightful reminder of the true meaning of Jesus' life and words, and would be a useful book to help children learn of the power of goodness. Beautiful paintings enhance the storytelling and make this an excellent gift.

Color PICTURE BOOK NONFICTION

AUTHOR/ILLUSTRATOR: Ruth Heller
HC: Grosset & Dunlap
THEMES: color; art; vocabulary; change

Art terms like "achromatic" and "secondary hue" are introduced when Ruth Heller demonstrates how color gets reproduced from the artist's pictures to the printed page. Vibrant hues and clear plastic overlays show the endless combinations of color that can be found on the printer's palette.

Come Look With Me: Enjoying Art With Children PICTURE BOOK NONFICTION

AUTHOR: Gladys Blizzard • ILLUSTRATOR: Various paintings
HC: Thomasson-Grant
THEMES: art; paintings; museums

The first of a terrific series of books that adults can use to help bring an appreciation of art to young children. Mixing open-to-interpretation questions with just enough facts, these books focus on seeing as opposed to knowing, and offer a welcoming entry into museums. Other titles in the *Come Look With Me* series include: *Animals in Art, World of Play,* and *Exploring Landscape Art With Children.*

★ Cut From the Same Cloth   FOLKLORE COLLECTION

AUTHOR: Robert San Souci • ILLUSTRATOR: Jerry Pinkney
HC: Philomel
THEMES: folklore; strong women; tall tales; U.S. history; heroes

Ask anyone to list some Tall Tales characters and see what names come up. All men, right? Well, as Jane Yolen wrote in her introduction to this collection of legends and tales about American women, "They have been here all along, these American women of wonder, women of power . . . They have shot game and given birth, cut logs for the fire, sewn the shrouds for their neighbors, hoed and hewed and harvested. But silently." San Souci's collection of stories from every region in the country brings back those voices.

Dance of the Sacred Circle   PICTURE BOOK

AUTHOR/ILLUSTRATOR: Kristina Rodanas
HC: Little Brown
THEMES: Native American; horses; creation; folklore

In this Blackfoot legend, a young boy goes looking for the Great Chief of the Sky in hopes of finding help for his starving tribe. The Chief, moved by the boy's daring, gives him a gift formed from mud, trees, birds and animals . . . the first horse!

Dear Rebecca, Winter Is Here   PICTURE BOOK

AUTHOR: Jean Craighead George • ILLUSTRATOR: Loretta Krupinski
HC: HarperCollins
THEMES: solstice; mail; grandmothers; writing; winter

A grandmother writes to her granddaughter Rebecca on December 21, our shortest day of the year. " 'Winter is here,' we say. It is here, but you can't touch it or serve it snacks. You can't read it a book or make it do anything. But it makes us do all sorts of things. I turn on my lights. You put on your mittens. The birds fly to the sunny underside of the Earth." George has captured the Winter Solstice, and in her notes she describes the four seasons in relation to the rotation of the earth around the sun.

Don't Read This Book, Whatever You Do   POETRY COLLECTION

AUTHOR: Kalli Dakos • ILLUSTRATOR: G. Brian Karas
HC: Simon & Schuster
THEMES: school; teachers; friendship; variety

"Caution! warning, alarm . . . I am your teacher and I'm begging you, don't read this book, whatever you do!" More poems about school from Dakos, the same writer who brought us *If You're Not Here, Please Raise Your Hand.*

Dove Isabeau   PICTURE BOOK

AUTHOR: **Jane Yolen** • ILLUSTRATOR: Dennis Nolan
HC/PB: Harcourt Brace
THEMES: folklore; love; dragons; magic; fantasy

A tale of magic, dragons, and the redemptive power of love by the unbeatable combination of Jane Yolen and Dennis Nolan.

Earth, Fire, Water, Air   FOLKLORE COLLECTION

AUTHOR: Mary Hoffman • ILLUSTRATOR: Jane Ray
HC: Dutton
THEMES: folklore; science; nature; cultural diversity

A unique look at the old world and its beliefs, told through stories and legends. Drawn from a wide range of cultures, these stories explore the four elements of the ancient world in considerable depth. A real treasure trove!

Earth, Sky and Beyond: A Journey
Through Space   PICTURE BOOK NONFICTION

AUTHOR: Jean-Pierre Verdet • ILLUSTRATOR: Pierre Bon
HC: Lodestar
THEMES: solar system; science; earth; sky; astronomy

Up, up, up you'll go, from earth, past birds, clouds, and planes, into orbit, with stunning realistic art and scientific facts in this cleverly designed book. The first part is designed to be held vertically, allowing you to move upward from earth to the moon and beyond. When you reach the sun, the book is turned horizontally to go across the solar system till you reach the outer universe.

The Easter Egg Farm   PICTURE BOOK

AUTHOR/ILLUSTRATOR: Mary Jane Auch
HC/PB: Holiday House
THEMES: Easter; eggs; art; creativity; farm; chickens

Auch's pictures of her hilarious hens make you laugh before you read their stories. Here a hen lays wildly patterned eggs, ready to add to the fanciest Easter basket. Read this before egg decorating, for inspiration and a good laugh. Auch's other talented hens are found in: *Peeping Beauty, Hen Lake* and *Eggs Mark the Spot.*

Everglades   PICTURE BOOK NONFICTION
AUTHOR: Jean Craighead George • ILLUSTRATOR: Wendell Minor
HC: HarperCollins
THEMES: Everglades; environment; Native American; storytelling

George begins with a storyteller poling children into a sunny water glade as he explains, "My story will be different from any you have heard, because this river is like no other river on Earth. There is only one Everglades." Wendell Minor's beautiful paintings add rich color to this tale of the environment, which, incidently, ends with a hopeful note.

Everyday Mysteries   PICTURE BOOK NONFICTION
AUTHOR/ILLUSTRATOR: Jerome Wexler
HC: Dutton
THEMES: guessing; photographs; point of view

Stunning full-color photographs of everyday objects, but from a perspective you've never looked at until now. Guessing games will abound at home and in the classroom.

Faith and the Electric Dog   FICTION-FANTASY
AUTHOR: Patrick Jennings
HC/PB: Scholastic
THEMES: Mexico; moving; flying; dogs; fantasy

Faith is a young girl unhappy with her new life in Mexico. This is her story, told by a multilingual Mexican dog. If you can't have fun with fantasy, this one may drive you crazy!

The First Strawberries: A Cherokee Story   PICTURE BOOK
AUTHOR: Joseph Bruchac • ILLUSTRATOR: Anna Vojtech
HC: Dial
THEMES: Native American; disagreement; anger; strawberries; problem solving; sun

A quarrel between a man and his wife is resolved with the knowledge that "friendship and respect are as sweet as the taste of ripe, red berries." This Cherokee story shows that even after people argue they can still find peace and love with each other. There's a bonus: discover how strawberries first came into this world.

Follow the Dream   PICTURE BOOK

AUTHOR/ILLUSTRATOR: Peter Sis
HC: Knopf
THEMES: Columbus; history: Age of Exploration; Native American; trailblazing; imagination

It's not possible to look quickly through a Peter Sis book, there's too much to discover. And this 15th-century voyage with Christopher Columbus is no exception. Illustrations show details of the explorer's life as well as the imaginative speculations people had on what he would find when he ventured outside of their world. The story on its own is fascinating. Words and art combined, Sis has created an historical treasure.

The Forgotten Door   FICTION-SCIENCE FICTION

AUTHOR: Alexander Key
PB: Scholastic
THEMES: science fiction; communication; gifted child; home; fitting in

One of the most memorable books from my childhood. I spent sixty-five cents of my own money and ordered this from the school book club because the description sounded so good. It more than lived up to my expectations, and I reread it many times over the next few years. Still in print, this novel about a boy from another world trying to get home while coping with life on Earth can be a doorway to science fiction for the young reader.

Fox Song   PICTURE BOOK

AUTHOR: Joseph Bruchac • ILLUSTRATOR: Paul Morin
PB: Paperstar
THEMES: grandmothers and granddaughters; Native American; nature; crafts; weaving; ancestors; wisdom

A young girl remembers many things her great grandmother shared with her in her natural surroundings—from making baskets to appreciating nature to recognizing the wisdom passed from generation to generation. Bruchac uses stories from his own Abenaki family, with careful descriptions of Native American ways.

The Ghost Dance

PICTURE BOOK

AUTHOR: Alice McLerran • ILLUSTRATOR: Paul Morin
HC: Clarion
THEMES: peace; Native American; war; dance; courage

Astounding art, fusing collage and paintings, and spare, evocative writing make this an important addition to the bookshelf. The hopeful message will give inspiration to those involved in the endless dance for peace.

Giants! Stories From Around the World

FOLKLORE COLLECTION

AUTHOR: Paul Robert Walker • ILLUSTRATOR: James Bernardin
HC: Harcourt Brace
THEMES: tall tales; giants; folklore; cultural diversity

Featuring lesser-known as well as the obvious tales, this book is a treat for those who like to read aloud. Walker is a teller as well as a writer, and the stories find a perfect balance between the demands of the two disciplines. Notes follow each story, giving background to the tale and helping the reader find more information on a particular giant.

The Girl Who Loved Wild Horses

PICTURE BOOK

AUTHOR/ILLUSTRATOR: Paul Goble
HC: Simon & Schuster • PB: Aladdin
THEMES: horses; Native American; flowers; insects; animals; birds

Goble's story tells of a young Indian girl who so loves the wild horses that graze near her village, she eventually becomes one. Caldecott Award illustrations boast full, double-page spreads of Goble's signature stylized art that reveal his respect for Native American culture. Other Goble books in the same tradition include: *Buffalo Woman* and *Star Boy*.

Girls to the Rescue

ANTHOLOGY

EDITOR: Bruce Lansky
PB: Meadowbrook
THEMES: strong girls; folklore; gender roles; folktale variations; comparisons

A collection we can all use—fairy tales, all original, in which the girls do all the saving and demonstrate terrific moments of gallantry usually denied them in classic fairy tales. Want more? Look for Volumes 2, 3 and 4.

Grandma Essie's Covered Wagon   PICTURE BOOK BIOGRAPHY

AUTHOR: David Williams • ILLUSTRATOR: Wiktor Sadowski

HC/PB: Knopf

THEMES: grandmothers; pioneers; biography; storytelling; family history

As far back as he can remember, David Williams listened to Grandma Essie's stories. Her grandma's father had once known Jesse James and she knew Wyatt Earp's cousin. Grandma was 87 years old when she visited him in the Fall of 1988 and that is when they began to write. She remembered sleeping under the stars, experiencing tornados and droughts, burying her sister with a song, and seeing papa sawing pieces for the covered wagon. In capturing his grandmother's stories on paper, Williams has preserved his family history and provides readers with inspiration to do the same.

STORIES

Once upon a time all our stories were spoken. Before TV, books, or even the written word, people sat in their dwellings in the darkness telling stories to keep their fears at bay. Throughout the ages, stories have been proclaimed in town squares, sung at festivals by troubadours, and woven around campfires.

The first writers of stories borrowed freely from the oral traditions of the tellers and created their own versions, tailored for the page. Theater, movies, radio, and television rely on writers who can tell a good tale. Today, even with all the ways stories come to us, the primary method remains simple telling. You may not think of them as stories, but unless you live the life of a hermit, you can't get through a day without telling one.

Teachers tell stories to explain lessons, parents come home from work and talk about their day, teenagers gossip on the telephone. Practically every job you can name indulges in some element of storytelling. Like the stories our ancestors told, these stories tell us who our heroes are, who is good, who is evil—and where, how, and why we belong. They are our past, present, and future.

Whether they've been told to us, read to us, made up from our own imaginations, or delivered electronically, stories are still stories. Unfortunately, the more we come to depend upon screens for our stories, the less human contact is involved. People need to read and share stories together, in person, in order to learn to communicate, empathize, and understand each other far better than any other method can teach or provide.

Gray Wolf, Red Wolf   PICTURE BOOK NONFICTION

AUTHOR: Dorothy Hinshaw Patent • ILLUSTRATOR: William Munoz (photos)

HC/PB: Clarion

THEMES: wolves; nature; animals, life cycle; habitats

Writing in a style that makes every subject come vividly to life, Dorothy Patent has made a career of giving young readers outstanding non-fiction. This book, a look at the lives and behavior of two species of North American wolves, is one of her best. Her writing is accompanied by outstanding photographs by William Munoz. Other nature titles in this series include: *Buffalo, The Way of the Grizzly, Where Bald Eagles Gather,* and *Where the Wild Horses Roam.*

The Great Kapok Tree   PICTURE BOOK

AUTHOR/ILLUSTRATOR: Lynne Cherry

HC: Harcourt Brace

THEMES: rain forest; Brazil; animals, endangered; environment; con-science; taking action

Brilliantly colored paintings ini-tially draw readers to this book, but it's the ecological message that maintains its popularity. Many creatures of the Brazilian rain forest try to persuade an ax-wielding man not to cut down their home. End papers include a map of the tropical rain forests of the world.

PICTURE BOOKS ARE FOR ALL AGES

Regardless of your child's reading skill, no child is too old to enjoy illus-trations. Some of the best readers request picture books.

The Great Pirate Activity Book   PICTURE BOOK NONFICTION

AUTHOR: Deri Robins • ILLUSTRATOR: George Buchanan

PB: Kingfisher

THEMES: pirates; folklore; history, world; games; puzzles

A low-priced, fun collection of activities and lore, perfect for that bud-ding Jolly Roger. A lot of kids go through their pirate phase, and this one will provide them and you with hours of entertainment!

Henry Huggins   FICTION

AUTHOR: Beverly Cleary
HC: Morrow • PB: Avon
THEMES: friendship; dogs; family; neighbors; humor

The cycle of books featuring Henry, his dog Ribsy, his sometime friend/
sometime nemesis Beezus, and her little sister, Ramona, begins with
this book. All the adventures of the children who live on Klikitat Street
have stood the test of time and prove that Cleary is a writer who understands universal truths. As long as there is a thing called childhood,
these books will remain popular for boys and girls who like a good
laugh, a gentle reminder that we are all human and can make mistakes,
and characters that seem like your best friends. Henry and the gang's
adventures continue in *Henry and Beezus, Henry and Ribsy, Henry and
the Clubhouse, Henry and the Paper Route,* and *Ribsy.* Ramona takes off on
her own in other titles. See: *Ramona the Pest.*

Here Comes the Storyteller   FOLKLORE COLLECTION

AUTHOR: Joe Hayes • ILLUSTRATOR: Richard Baron (photographs)
PB: Cinco Puntos Press
THEMES: storytelling; U.S.A., the Southwest; Spanish words

A collection of eight stories, each illustrated with photos of the storyteller at work and full of hints on how to tell. Based in the southwest,
Hayes is a master teller, drawing his tales from the people and culture
of New Mexico and his own experiences. This is a terrific book for those
interested in the art of storytelling.

Homer Price   FICTION

AUTHOR/ILLUSTRATOR: Robert McCloskey
HC: Viking • PB: Puffin
THEMES: towns; humor; community; neighbors; relatives; restaurants;
U.S.A., the Midwest; contests; heroes

Life in a midwestern small town never sounded as good as when
McCloskey describes it in this book and the sequel, *Centerburg Tales.*
Homer is a good-old, all-around American boy, and you come to know
him, his family and the whole town of Centerburg mighty fine in these
six stories about doughnuts, missing jewelry, progress, small town politics, the Pied Piper, history pageants, and more doughnuts.

I Spy Two Eyes: Numbers in Art   PICTURE BOOK NONFICTION
AUTHOR: Lucy Micklethwait • ILLUSTRATOR: various
HC: Greenwillow
THEMES: counting; numbers; art; artists; paintings

A counting book featuring twenty works of art, ranging from the 15th century to the present. Each page challenges a child to find the correct number of images by becoming familiar with the famous paintings. Also in this series: *I Spy Two Eyes, I Spy: An Alphabet in Art.*

I Want to Be a Veterinarian   PICTURE BOOK NONFICTION
AUTHOR: Stephanie Maze and Catherine O'Neil Grace • ILLUSTRATOR: photographs
HC: Harcourt Brace
THEMES: jobs; veterinarians; animals

There are private practices, house calls, farm calls, zoo calls and jungle calls. This overview of what it takes to be a veterinarian doesn't simply whet young appetites, it lists sources of information and suggests that if you have the qualities it takes to be a vet, "go for it." Others in the series: *I Want to Be an Astronaut, I Want to Be a Dancer,* and *I Want to Be an Engineer.*

I, Houdini   FICTION
AUTHOR: Lynne Reid Banks
HC: Doubleday • PB: Avon
THEMES: hamsters; escape; family; self-respect; confidence

"I am Houdini. No, no, no. Not that one—of course not. He's dead long ago. Besides, he was a human being and I am a hamster. But let me assure you, that as my namesake was no ordinary man, I am no ordinary animal." That is the voice of Houdini, a boastful hamster who tells his story. Anyone who has had a hamster will understand that they come with escape claws that allow them to dig in and out of most anywhere. Young readers will want to dig into this story for a glimpse of what goes on in their furry little minds.

If You're Not From the Prairie   PICTURE BOOK
AUTHOR: David Bouchard • ILLUSTRATOR: Henry Ripplinger
HC: Atheneum
THEMES: U.S.A., the prairie; writing; rhythm; repetition

Through poetry, the sun, the wind, the sky, the flatness of the plain are remembered in this visually stunning book about contemporary life on the prairie. The rhythm and repetition of the language invites young writers to reflect similarly on their own memory of a familiar place.

If You're Not Here, Please Raise Your Hand   POETRY COLLECTION

AUTHOR: Kalli Dakos • ILLUSTRATOR: G. Brian Karas
HC: Four Winds • PB: Aladdin
THEMES: school; self-respect; friendship; teachers; point of view

Funny and thought-provoking, Dakos writes with sensitivity about what students and teachers experience and feel.

> **LIBRARY "SHOPPING" #1**
>
> When Beverly Corbett was 8 years old she moved to Pine Hill, a small town south of Eureka, California. She was thrilled to be in the city. Every week she could ride her bike to the Carnegie library all by herself (about 30 blocks). The children's section consisted of a wall of shelves surrounding a window. She would sit in a sun puddle for hours reading all she could. Bev grew up to become a mother of five. Every Monday morning she took all five kids to the Carnegie library. Each got to choose five books that suited them. You could tell who chose what just by looking at the empty spaces in the stacks. If they got home and after looking through a couple of pages didn't think they'd like something, it was fine. They'd put it down and get a different one next Monday.

If Your Name Was Changed at Ellis Island

PICTURE BOOK NONFICTION

AUTHOR: Ellen Levine • ILLUSTRATOR: Wayne Parmenter
HC/PB: Scholastic
THEMES: immigration; Ellis Island; courage; change; names

If you and your child are discussing immigrants, take a look at this. It answers questions children might ask about people arriving on Ellis Island. What happened if you were sick?" "Where would you sleep?"

In the Beginning . . .   REFERENCE

AUTHOR: Richard Platt • ILLUSTRATOR: Brian Delf
HC: DK
THEMES: history; origins; trailblazing; science

An amazing one-volume illustrated reference that details the history of almost everything! Clear and logically organized, this will be the definitive book of its type for many years to come.

James and the Giant Peach   FICTION-FANTASY

AUTHOR: Roald Dahl

HC: Knopf • PB: Puffin

THEMES: fantasy; peaches; aunts; family; grasshoppers; worms; spiders; ladybugs; centipedes; New York; courage; survival

When James Henry Trotter was about four years old, his ". . . mother and father went to London to do some shopping, and there a terrible thing happened. Both of them suddenly got eaten up (in full daylight, mind you, and on a crowded street) by an enormous angry rhinoceros which had escaped from the London Zoo." Poor James has to go live with his horrible Aunts Sponge and Spiker. It wasn't till the little man with the glowing bag came and the peach grew and James found that a centipede, earthworm, spider, ladybug, grasshopper and glowworm could become his family that life took a turn for the best.

The Kid in the Red Jacket   FICTION

AUTHOR: Barbara Park

HC/PB: Knopf

THEMES: moving; self-respect; friendship; humor; school; change; neighbors; community

Howard thinks moving from Arizona to Massachusetts is rotten. When he gets there all the kids in his new town act as though he's invisible—except for a six-year-old neighbor girl who he can tell right away is weird. For anyone who's felt out of place, here's a big dose of humor with some understanding mixed in.

Kidding Around Washington, D.C.   NONFICTION

AUTHOR: Debbie Levy

PB: John Muir Publications

THEMES: travel; Washington, D.C.

This series is so cool we can't think why someone didn't think of it earlier. Aimed at eight to twelve year olds, but useful when read to their younger siblings, these travel guides address their interests and needs and make the prospect of family travel inclusive. Most guidebooks give lip service to kid concerns, but these speak directly to them. Buy one for your kids before going on a trip—they'll thank you! Cities include Atlanta, Boston, New York, Paris, Santa Fe and San Francisco, among others.

The Kingfisher Book of the Ancient World REFERENCE

AUTHOR: Hazel Mary Martell
HC: Kingfisher
THEMES: history, ancient history; ancient Egypt; ancient Greece; ancient Rome

The best book of its kind for kids, full of maps, charts, interesting text and all the information you could ever want about every region of the world and the cultures that existed there long ago.

Eric Knight's Lassie Come Home PICTURE BOOK

AUTHOR: **Rosemary Wells** • ILLUSTRATOR: Susan Jeffers
HC: Holt
THEMES: dogs; pets; friendship; journeys; England; Scotland; hardship

Jeffers's incredible art is a perfect match for Wells's retelling of this classic tale. No Hollywood here. Taken from Knight's original novel (published in 1940), the version from this gifted duo has brought the story of a dog and his long journey home to his boy to a new age of readers.

The Last Princess: The Story of Princess Ka'iulani of Hawai'i PICTURE BOOK BIOGRAPHY

AUTHOR: Fay Stanley • ILLUSTRATOR: Diane Stanley
HC: Simon & Schuster
THEMES: Hawaii; princesses; biography; islands; cultural diversity; courage; taking action

Diane Stanley's vibrant paintings are a perfect match for her mother Fay's biography of Hawaii's Princess Ka'iulani.

Leagues Apart: The Men and Times of the Negro Baseball Leagues PICTURE BOOK NONFICTION

AUTHOR: Lawrence Ritter • ILLUSTRATOR: Richard Merkin
HC: Morrow
THEMES: baseball; African American; prejudice; determination

Before the 1950s, racist rules prevented black athletes from playing in the major leagues, regardless of their skills. In this story of the Negro Leagues, where players like Hank Aaron and Willie Mays got their starts, Lawrence Ritter blends history with brief biographies, and reminds his readers not to glamorize the Negro league experience. "These talented men were not in the Negro Leagues by choice. They were there because of high walls erected in the name of segregation and maintained by racism."

The Life and Times of the Apple   PICTURE BOOK NONFICTION

AUTHOR/ILLUSTRATOR: Charles Micucci
HC/PB: Orchard
THEMES: apples; history; nature; farming; science

Who says nonfiction isn't interesting? Certainly not a reader of Charles Micucci. How an apple is harvested, grafted, cross bred, used—just about anything a young reader wonders about an apple is in here.

The Life and Times of the Honeybee   PICTURE BOOK NONFICTION

AUTHOR/ILLUSTRATOR: Charles Micucci
HC: Houghton Mifflin
THEMES: bees; nature; honey; gardening; science

If you want to know about bees, this book will hook you. It's packed with interesting facts like "To make one pound of honey, a colony of bees collects nectar from over a million flowers" and "A honeybee has two pairs of wings that can beat 250 times a second." There are growth charts and cross-sections, a honey flower menu, even a calendar showing what bees do each month of the year.

The Life and Times of the Peanut   PICTURE BOOK NONFICTION

AUTHOR/ILLUSTRATOR: Charles Micucci
HC: Houghton Mifflin
THEMES: peanuts; history; farming; geography

"Each year, Americans eat more than 800 million pounds of peanut butter." If you'd like to know how it's been used from 900 B.C. until now, where it's grown, what the plant looks like, or how your cat uses it, this is the book for you.

Linnea In Monet's Garden   PICTURE BOOK NONFICTION

AUTHOR: Christina Bjork • ILLUSTRATOR: Lena Anderson
HC: R & S books
THEMES: Monet; art; Paris; plants; flowers; travel; artists; painting; gardens

Begin with Anderson's watercolor illustrations of a young traveler curious about Monet's waterlilies. Add photographs of his garden along with reproductions of his paintings, and you have the story of Linnea, a delightful character who offers a colorful lesson in art history.

The Little Painter of Sabana Grande   PICTURE BOOK
AUTHOR: Patricia Markun • ILLUSTRATOR: Robert Casilla
HC: Bradbury
THEMES: artists; paint; creativity; community; painting

An artistic child solves his own problem when he realizes he has nothing to paint on. Based on a true story from Panama about a young boy who painted pictures and brightened his community.

Ma Dear's Aprons   PICTURE BOOK
AUTHOR: Patricia McKissack • ILLUSTRATOR: Floyd Cooper
HC: Atheneum
THEMES: mothers and sons; African American; jobs; family; love; single parents; U.S. history, Reconstruction; strong women

A collaboration between a master storyteller and an illustrator, who are both at the height of their powers. Ma Dear has an apron for each day of the week, signaling that day's particular chore—taking in wash, cleaning the house, baking pies. Told by her young son, this picture of life in the South during Reconstruction is so loving you can feel Ma Dear's hugs.

Make a Wish Molly   FICTION
AUTHOR: Barbara Cohen • ILLUSTRATOR: Jan Naimo Jones
HC: Doubleday • PB: Dell
THEMES: traditions; celebrations; Passover; cultural diversity; immigration; friendship; Jews; birthdays; birthday parties

Molly, a recent immigrant, has to find a balance between her own background and the traditions of her new friends. Birthday celebrations, Passover, religious tolerance and the meaning of friendship are all touched on here. Companion to Cohen's "Molly's Pilgrim."

Matilda   FICTION-FANTASY
AUTHOR: Roald Dahl • ILLUSTRATOR: Quentin Blake
HC: Viking • PB: Puffin
THEMES: school; self-respect; teachers; family; strong girls; gifted children; playing tricks; comeuppance; cruelty

"It is bad enough when parents treat ordinary children as though they were scabs and bunions, but it becomes somehow a lot worse when the child in question is extraordinary, and by that I mean sensitive and brilliant." Children are bound to be drawn to this hysterically funny novel about a girl with special powers who gets back at her parents for treating her like a blockhead. And when the mean headmistress, Miss Trunchbull, picks on Matilda's favorite teacher, she gets her back in major proportions. As usual Dahl offers up a treat for young readers who wish they could be Matilda—if only for one day experiencing their own get-backs through practical jokes and concentrated energy.

Mean Margaret   FICTION-FANTASY

AUTHOR: Tor Seidler • ILLUSTRATOR: Jon Agee
HC: HarperCollins
THEMES: humor; babies; woodchucks; squirrels; snakes; skunks; bats; siblings; cruelty; bullies; abandonment; adoption

It is ridiculous to even imagine a couple of newly wedded woodchucks taking in a bad-mannered human baby. Especially when one of the woodchucks can't stand messes in his burrow. But it's all here, silly and waiting to be read.

The Mennyms   FICTION-FANTASY

AUTHOR: Sylvia Waugh
HC: Greenwillow • PB: Avon
THEMES: fantasy; family; pretending; dolls; England

The Mennyms are a family living together at Number 5 Brocklehurst Grove. But they are no normal family. "They were not human, you see—at least not in the normal sense of the word. They were not made of flesh and blood. They were just a whole, lovely family of life-size rag dolls." The "almost ordinary" situations they find themselves in offer a delightful stretch for the imagination. Their adventures continue in *The Mennyms in the Wilderness, The Mennyms Under Seige, The Mennyms Alone,* and *The Mennyms Alive.*

Mermaid Tales From Around the World   FOLKLORE COLLECTION

AUTHOR: Mary Pope Osborne • ILLUSTRATOR: Troy Howell
HC: Scholastic
THEMES: mermaids; cultural diversity; folklore

African, European, Asian, and Native American cultures are represented in this collection of twelve tales about mermaids.

BOOK BONDS

In the village of Moelfre on the Welsh Island of Anglesey, I met Evan Owen. He is a link to my father's family. He is a born storyteller and his descriptions of each member of the family were colorful and entertaining. When I asked why one fellow had been left off the family tree, he simply said, "Well, he was a bit lightly baked. He hadn't been at the far end of the oven long enough."

When Evan saw my interest piqued by his tale of one uncle's long years at the helm of a rescue boat on the dangerous shores of Anglesey, he proudly handed over a book, The Golden Wreck, by Alexander McKee, about the wreck of the Royal Charter—a disaster the locals talk about still. And while the old man lives in a faraway place, there is a book on my shelf that replays the pounding of the Welsh surf and ties my past to now.

Minty: A Story of Young
Harriet Tubman
PICTURE BOOK BIOGRAPHY

AUTHOR: Alan Schroeder • ILLUSTRATOR: Jerry Pinkney

HC: Dial

THEMES: Harriet Tubman; biography; slavery; Underground Railroad; African American; courage; escape

When Harriet Tubman was a child, her father taught her how to find the North Star to mark her way and how to read trees. She learned how to skin a squirrel, to fish with only a string and a nail, to do birdcalls, and to run barefoot through the woods without making a sound. This is the story of a strong-willed child who escaped from slavery and someday would help hundreds of others to do the same.

Misoso: Once Upon a Time
Tales From Africa
FOLKLORE COLLECTION

AUTHOR: Verna Aardema • ILLUSTRATOR: Reynold Ruffins

HC/PB: Knopf

THEMES: Africa; fables; folklore; traditions; history; African culture

These African fables are great fun to read on your own or aloud to someone who can use a good story. Glossaries and interesting notes about African history and traditions are included with each tale.

Molly's Pilgrim   FICTION
AUTHOR: Barbara Cohen • ILLUSTRATOR: Michael J. Deraney
PB: Dell
THEMES: immigration; Russia; traditions; cultural diversity; teasing; fitting in; Thanksgiving; celebrations; school; Pilgrims; Jews

Molly wants to go back home to Russia where she fit in, or even to New York, where there were other Jewish kids. In Winter Hill she looks and sounds different from everyone else in her third-grade class. This tender tale of a modern day Pilgrim confronts the feelings of children who are teased by their classmates because of their differences. For more about Molly, see *Make a Wish Molly*.

Monster Motel   POETRY COLLECTION
AUTHOR/ILLUSTRATOR: Douglas Florian
HC/PB: Harcourt Brace
THEMES: monsters; spooky stories; imagination; fantasy

Each poem describes an original monster. Great fun for young readers, artists, and writers who like to invent monsters of their own.

Mrs. Piggle-Wiggle   FICTION
AUTHOR: Betty MacDonald • ILLUSTRATOR: Hilary Knight
HC/PB: HarperCollins
THEMES: humor; manners; problem solving

Mrs. Piggle-Wiggle's wisdom knows no bounds—every single child with a problem has been sent to her by parents at their wit's end and she has cured them all of their ailments, be they lying, stealing, not taking a bath or being a crybaby. These clever books, four in all, are a bit dated, but their heart is still intact—children love Mrs. Piggle-Wiggle, then and now!

Neve Shalom Wahat Al-Salam:
Oasis of Peace   PICTURE BOOK NONFICTION
AUTHOR: Laurie and Ben Dolphin • ILLUSTRATOR: Ben Dolphin
(photographs)
HC: Scholastic
THEMES: Jews; Arabs; cooperation; peace; cultural diversity

Cooperation? This is a perfect look at it in action. A unique Jewish/Arab community school in Israel has been nominated four times for the Nobel Peace Prize. This is a true story of two boys with different customs and languages, both wanting to live at peace in their homeland.

One Night: A Story From the Desert   PICTURE BOOK
AUTHOR: Cristina Kessler • ILLUSTRATOR: Ian Schoenherr
HC: Philomel
THEMES: desert; Africa; Arabs; grandmothers; courage; goats; nature; wisdom; pride; survival

Courage, the resilience of North Africa's Tuareg people, their traditions, and pride combine in this story of one young boy who remembers the advice of his grandmother during a night he is forced to spend alone in the desert.

Outside and Inside Snakes   PICTURE BOOK NONFICTION
AUTHOR: Sandra Markle • ILLUSTRATOR: photos
HC: Bradbury
THEMES: snakes; science; nature

Vivid, action-filled photographs show close-ups of the outsides of snakes—stretching, hunting, hatching, shedding—and the insides—bones, teeth, heart, muscles. Interesting information like why a snake flicks its tongue and why it doesn't blink can be found throughout. Markle's splendid series of accessible *Outside & Inside* science books include volumes on birds, spiders, sharks, trees, and you!

> **LIBRARY "SHOPPING" #2**
>
> Trust your child's instincts: Children gravitate toward things that give them what they need. Let your child make his own choices. It should be fun. A good thing about going to the library is that if a child makes a poor choice for himself, he can turn it in for another one. Allow him to check out several books at a time.

Pablo Remembers:
The Fiesta of the Day of the Dead   PICTURE BOOK NONFICTION
AUTHOR/ILLUSTRATOR: George Ancona
HC: Lothrop
THEMES: Day of the Dead; Mexico; ancestors; family; community; rituals; traditions

On October 30, Mexican people everywhere prepare for The Day of the Dead. Ancona describes the elaborate preparations through the eyes of a young Mexican boy and his family. Colorful photographs capture details of this celebration honoring the spirits of the dead. Here is a book that presents with care a holiday observed by many Mexican-American families. Ancona's other photo essays about native American and Mexican life include: *The Pinata Maker*, *Fiesta USA* and *Pow Wow*.

Paddle-to-the-Sea   PICTURE BOOK

AUTHOR/ILLUSTRATOR: Holling Clancy Holling
HC: Houghton Mifflin • PB: Sandpiper
THEMES: sea; boats; maps; journeys; adventure; geography; Canada; Native American

In Canada an Indian boy carves a foot-long canoe. "I made you, Paddle Person, because I had a dream. . . . You will go with the water and you will have adventures that I would like to have. But I cannot go with you, because I have to help my father with the traps." First published in 1941, this mapped adventure continues to enthrall readers who float, dive, and wash along on a canoe journey from Lake Superior all the way to the Atlantic Ocean.

The Phantom Hitchhiker   FOLKLORE COLLECTION

AUTHOR: Daniel Cohen • ILLUSTRATOR: Elsie Lennox
PB: Kingfisher
THEMES: scary stories; folklore

Low priced and fun to read, this one will work for reluctant readers, as well as those hooked on scary stories and mysteries. A collection of supposedly true stories, this is a good opportunity to learn about the concept of "urban legends."

A Piece of String Is a Wonderful Thing   PICTURE BOOK NONFICTION

AUTHOR: Judy Hindley • ILLUSTRATOR: Margaret Chamberlain
HC/PB: Candlewick
THEMES: string; ancient history; inventions; rhyme; history, general

Did you know a single thread of wool is as strong as a thread of gold? What do a spider's web and a yo-yo have in common? A single thread of string pulls us through page after page of history presented with rhyme and detailed drawings. Lots of facts and plenty of teaching spinoffs.

The Pirate's Handbook: How to Become a Rogue of the High Seas   PICTURE BOOK NONFICTION

AUTHOR: Margarette Lincoln

HC: Cobblehill

THEMES: pirates; history; sailing; boats; adventure; folklore

If your child loves pirates, this book will take him beyond the basics and fill him full of facts and lore about the deadliest men ever to sail the seven seas. In addition, the suggested activities make this a book of multiple uses, perfect for expanding the pirate experience beyond the last page.

Punga, the Goddess of Ugly   PICTURE BOOK

AUTHOR/ILLUSTRATOR: Deborah Nourse Lattimore

HC: Harcourt Brace

THEMES: Maori; point of view; New Zealand; folklore

Imagine sticking out your tongue to look more beautiful. This Maori folktale is about two sisters who learn to do just that.

Ramona the Pest   FICTION

AUTHOR: Beverly Cleary • ILLUSTRATOR: Louis Darling

HC: Morrow • PB: Avon

THEMES: sisters; humor; family; neighbors; school; friendship; mistakes

Ramona, who started off as a supporting character in Beverly Cleary's *Henry Huggins* books, quickly asserted her irrepressible self and became the subject of a bunch of novels of her own. A child nearly everyone can identify with, Ramona is one of the most beloved characters in children's books—her mistakes, her schemes and ideas, and most of all, her hilarious adventures have endeared her to millions of children. All her books read aloud well, and we suggest starting off with this title and working your way through the others, which include: *Ramona the Brave, Beezus and Ramona, Ramona and Her Father,* and *Ramona and Her Mother.*

The Real McCoy: The Life of an African-American Inventor   PICTURE BOOK BIOGRAPHY

AUTHOR: Wendy Towle • ILLUSTRATOR: Wil Clay

HC/PB: Scholastic

THEMES: biography; African American; trains; jobs; inventions; prejudice; courage; determination

Read about Elijah McCoy, honored in this biography for his inventions, including a lubricating cup that made his job on the railroad more efficient. Others tried to copy his designs, but engineers asked for *The Real McCoy*.

Red Hot Hightops   FICTION

AUTHOR: Matt Christopher
PB: Little Brown
THEMES: sports

The premier writer of sports fiction for children, Christopher has been there for kids when they go through the phase of reading only books with games in them. His comforting style, stressing character and the rules of the game, will attract reluctant readers of a wide range of ages. Though he wrote mostly of baseball in his earlier novels, his later work included a variety of sports that reflect the interests of today's children. Here are some of Walter's son Anthony's favorites: *Baseball Flyhawk*, *The Basket Counts*, *The Comeback Challenge*, *Ice Magic*, *The Year Mom Won the Pennant*, *The Hockey Machine*, and his biographies of Steve Young, Emmet Smith, and Ken Griffey, Jr.

Saint Francis   PICTURE BOOK BIOGRAPHY

AUTHOR/ILLUSTRATOR: Brian Wildsmith
HC: Eerdmans
THEMES: saints; peace; Catholicism; biography; animals; Italy; Christianity; religion

A gloriously illustrated and deeply religious account of the life of Saint Francis of Assisi, the founder of the Franciscan Order of friars.

Sato and the Elephants   PICTURE BOOK

AUTHOR: Juanita Havill • ILLUSTRATOR: Jean and Mou-sein Tseng
HC: Lothrop
THEMES: elephants; ivory; art; carvers; animals, endangered; Japan

Following in his father's footsteps, Sato works toward becoming a master carver. From morning to night he carves beautiful figures from creamy white pieces of ivory—until he discovers the source of his treasure: the slaughter of elephants. Inspired by the true story of a Japanese ivory carver, Sato's theme is human responsibility for the preservation of the natural world.

The Seasons and Someone   PICTURE BOOK
AUTHOR: Virginia Kroll • ILLUSTRATOR: Tatsuro Kiuchi
HC/PB: Harcourt Brace
THEMES: seasons; Alaska; survival; dwellings; Inuit; traditions

Luminous art and poetic descriptions tell about the Eskimo culture from Winter to Spring—what Eskimos eat, and how they survive when "Sun disappears leaving Moon in her daytime place—when blizards swallow the village and wind pounds at the igloo door."

The Secret Garden   FICTION
AUTHOR: Frances Hodgson Burnett • ILLUSTRATOR: Tasha Tudor
HC/PB: HarperCollins
THEMES: gardens; illness; secrets; magic; birds; orphans; uncles; England; strong girls; imagination; friendship; faith

First published in 1911, this classic novel continues to bolster home, school, library and bookstore shelves. It's got the right elements to tug on heartstrings: Mary Lennox, recently orphaned, bedridden Colin Craven, and Dickon, who can make anything grow and understands the language of nature. Rich with imagination, friendship and faith. Read it aloud or relish it quietly alone.

See You Around, Sam   FICTION
AUTHOR: Lois Lowry
HC: Houghton Mifflin • PB: Dell
THEMES: family; running away; Halloween; neighbors; community

A very funny book about running away from home. It's part of the *Anastasia Krupnik* series, but a standout that merits special mention.

Sideways Stories From Wayside School   FICTION
AUTHOR: Louis Sachar • ILLUSTRATOR: Julie Brinckloe
HC: Morrow • PB: Avon
THEMES: humor; school; friendship; teachers; zany

Laugh-out-loud funny tales about the craziest school in fiction. A novel-length collection of stories, it's one of the surest books to turn on a reluctant reader that we have found. More Wayside stories can be found in *Wayside School Is Falling Down* and *Wayside School Gets a Little Stranger*.

The Silk Route: 7000 Miles of History   PICTURE BOOK NONFICTION
AUTHOR: John Major • ILLUSTRATOR: Stephen Fieser
HC/PB: HarperCollins
THEMES: China; Mideast; history; silk; journeys; trade; maps; ancient history

Trace the early journey of the silk trade and learn some history about the stops on the way. Beginning in the capital city of China's Chang'an, this voyage takes readers 7,000 miles to the marketplace in Byzantium. A map of the route is included along with "A Closer Look," more details for the curious.

A Small Tall Tale From the Far Far North   PICTURE BOOK
AUTHOR/ILLUSTRATOR: Peter Sis
HC/PB: Knopf
THEMES: Arctic; journeys; folklore; maps; trailblazing; Inuit; tall tale

One hundred years ago folk hero Jan Welzi rode off in a horse-drawn cart, traded the cart for a sled pulled by reindeer, and was gone for thirty years. This is his story. Sis' detailed paintings include maps, storyboards, panoramas and even an Inuit myth told in pictographs. A perfect book for sharing, but each child will want time to quietly absorb these details.

Soon, Annala   PICTURE BOOK
AUTHOR: Riki Levinson • ILLUSTRATOR: Julie Downing
HC: Orchard
THEMES: immigration; sisters; patience; New York; cultural diversity; Polish American

Annala is a young Polish immigrant in New York who waits for what seems forever for her brothers to cross the sea to America.

★ Stone Fox   FICTION
AUTHOR: John Reynolds Gardiner • ILLUSTRATOR: Marcia Sewall
HC/PB: HarperCollins
THEMES: dogs; grandfathers; Native American; farms; courage; pets; competition; determination; kindness

Heart-tugging, inspiring, 81 pages long, Stone Fox takes the breath away. We recommend reading it aloud or as a jewel to be taken off for the pleasure of enjoying alone. Little Willy's struggle to save his family's farm from the tax collector and Stone Fox's need to buy back land for his

Shoshone people make them both determined to win prize money in a sled race. The ending will stay with you. It will warm your heart.

 Break your heart is more like it. Get that hankie ready!

Stories From Firefly Island   PICTURE BOOK

AUTHOR/ILLUSTRATOR: Benedick Blathwayt
HC: Greenwillow
THEMES: animals; imagination; tortoises

Tortoise is the oldest and wisest of all the animals, so he answers questions like, "Why do frogs croak at night?," "What is the moon?," "What are stories?" When he doesn't know the answers, he simply supposes them up. "Tortoise supposed the moon was a cluster of glow-worms and each star a bright firefly asleep on the blackness of the night: Surely this was how it was—and it would always be the same." The magic here is in imagination. "Supposing" is fun. Try it with your child and let your imaginations soar. Teachers, ask the class next door to offer some questions for your students to answer. Then switch. A great writing opportunity that gets everyone thinking!

Stringbean's Trip to the Shining Sea   PICTURE BOOK

AUTHOR: Vera B. Williams • ILLUSTRATOR: Vera B. & Jennifer Williams
HC: Greenwillow • PB: Scholastic
THEMES: mail; travel; U.S.A., the West; writing

Stringbean and his brother took a trip west one summer in a truck with a little house built on the back. They tell their story through postcards and snapshots sent home. "We went to see the oldest living things in the whole world. They are trees called Bristlecone Pine trees. They are much older than you, Grandpa. One of them might need 4900 candles." Young readers will laugh, learn about things on the way, and perhaps discover a new interest in writing.

Stuart Little   FICTION-FANTASY

AUTHOR: E.B. White • ILLUSTRATOR: Garth Williams
HC/PB: HarperCollins
THEMES: mice; adventure; birds; searches; family

Stuart Little is a properly dressed mouse who lives in New York City with his human family. He enjoys adventures. But when his best friend Margalo disappears from her nest, he sets out to find her and ends up having the biggest adventure of his life.

Sweet Clara and the Freedom Quilt   PICTURE BOOK

AUTHOR: Deborah Hopkinson • ILLUSTRATOR: James Ransome

HC/PB: Knopf

THEMES: slavery; courage; African American; quilts; gifted children; cleverness; maps; escape; freedom; navigation

A clever young slave creates a quilt with a map stitched into it to guide herself and others to freedom. A powerful blend of prose and art.

Sweetwater Run   PICTURE BOOK

AUTHOR/ILLUSTRATOR: Andrew Glass

HC: Doubleday • PB: Dell

THEMES: Pony Express; mail; U.S. history, pre-Civil War; biography; U.S. history, frontier life; horses; adventure

We reckon e-mailing, fax-sending youngsters might get a kick out of seeing what young Buffalo Bill Cody had to do to deliver mail. Words right out of thirteen-year-old Cody's mouth pack this tale with real history!

Talking Walls   PICTURE BOOK NONFICTION

AUTHOR: Margy Burns Knight • ILLUSTRATOR: Anne Sibley O'Brien

HC/PB: Tilbury House

THEMES: walls; cultural diversity; social studies; China; Australia; Egypt; Africa; Peru; New Mexico; Mexico; Quebec; Washington, D.C.; France; Jerusalem; religion; India; Germany

"Before I built a wall I'd ask to know What I was walling in or walling out . . ." Robert Frost

Differences and similarities of cultures throughout the world are viewed from the perspective of the walls they have built. From the Great Wall of China to the Berlin Wall, a fascinating tour. Also see *What Is a Wall After All?*, for another look at walls.

The Ten Mile Day and the Building of the Transcontinental Railroad   PICTURE BOOK NONFICTION

AUTHOR/ILLUSTRATOR: Mary Ann Fraser

HC: Henry Holt

THEMES: U.S. history, Westward movement; railroad; Chinese American; Irish American; Chinese culture; Irish culture; jobs; competition; change

One amazing day the East and West were linked for train travel in an event in which hundreds of Chinese and Irish workers raced to lay ten miles of track on the Transcontinental Railroad. This is their story.

They're Off!: The Story of the Pony Express

PICTURE BOOK NONFICTION

AUTHOR/ILLUSTRATOR: Cheryl Harness

HC: Simon & Schuster

THEMES: Pony Express; U.S. history, pre-Civil War; horses; mail; U.S.A., the West; courage; determination

Harness's account of the story of the Pony Express is a history lesson made interesting. Did you know that, even though mail delivery by pony had a tremendous impact on the development of the west, it ran for less than two years? The remarkable story of the men who delivered the mail—at all costs—comes vividly to life.

A Treasury of Mermaids: Mermaid Tales From Around the World

FOLKLORE COLLECTION

AUTHOR: Shirley Climo • ILLUSTRATOR: Jean and Mou-sien Tseng

HC: HarperCollins

THEMES: mermaids; folklore; cultural diversity

From Ireland's "Mrs. Fitzgerald the Merrow" to New Zealand's "Pania of the Reef," Climo tells eight enchanting stories. Fascinating historical facts are also here. Did you know that "most mermen are as ugly as mermaids are beautiful"? The Irish merman is "green toothed, red nosed, and squint eyed." Action-filled full-color paintings embellish each tale.

A Treasury of Princesses

FOLKLORE COLLECTION

AUTHOR: Shirley Climo • ILLUSTRATOR: Ruth Sanderson

HC: HarperCollins

THEMES: Princesses; fairy tales; folklore; cultural diversity

If your child likes princess tales, this is the book for you. Each story is preceded by a page telling of similar princesses from across the globe.

A Tree Is Growing

PICTURE BOOK NONFICTION

AUTHOR: Arthur Dorros • ILLUSTRATOR: S.D. Schindler

HC/PB: Scholastic

THEMES: nature; trees; life cycle

Maybe it's because I am now too big to climb them, but good tree books make me wistful, and this is a great one. All about the mighty oak, it has terrific art, and a layout full of sidebars and spot illustrations that conveys a lot of tree information in small, fascinating bites.

SPOTLIGHT ON LAURENCE YEP

Laurence Yep writes for the outsider in every child. Growing up as a non-Chinese speaking Chinese American in a black neighborhood in San Francisco, and attending school in Chinatown, Yep had a great deal of trouble fitting in. As a response to his feelings of alienation, he began to write science fiction and was first published while still in high school. In his own words "When I wrote . . . I could reach into the box of rags that was my soul and begin stitching them together . . ."

Laurence Yep knows what it feels like to try and fit in, and it shows in his novels. As he began to discover and claim his cultural identity through writing, setting his stories in and around Chinese as well as Chinese American locales, he explored themes of tolerance and the use of the imagination as a survival mechanism of childhood; the result has been insightful novels that transcend culture and speak to all children. Any child can identify with his sensitivity to growing up feeling out of synch, but it is the burgeoning adolescent who will find his works like *Child of the Owl*, *Dragonwings* (a Newbery Honor book), and *Dragon's Gate* (also a Newbery Honor book) most compelling.

Yep's retellings of myths and legends of old China show how stories hop continents and settle, grow, and change with each generation while maintaining their essential core. *The Rainbow People, Tongues of Jade,* and the picture book *The Man Who Tricked a Ghost* all demonstrate Yep's ability to capture a classic tale and make it new and fresh in the telling.

Yep's sequence of fantasy novels about the dragon princess Shimmer and her quest to regain her lost kingdom ranks as one of the best of the genre. *Dragon of the Lost Sea, Dragon Steel, Dragon Cauldron,* and *Dragon War* make up this quartet.

As an editor, Yep has overseen the publication of *American Dragon: Twenty-five Asian American Voices,* an outstanding anthology. In collaboration with artists Kam Mak and the team of Jean and Mou-Sien Tseng, he has created beautiful picture books, among them *The Dragon Prince, The City of Dragons,* and *The Boy Who Swallowed Snakes.* His fictional retelling of the events surrounding the dropping of the first atomic bomb makes for compelling reading in *Hiroshima: A Novella,* and his memoir *The Lost Garden* gives tremendous insight into the making of a writer.

Yep's prodigious output never diminishes the high quality of his work. Whatever he chooses to write about, he has established himself as a voice with which to be reckoned, and we count him among the authors whose work never ceases to thrill us.

Tree of Dreams: Ten Tales From the Garden of Night
FOLKLORE COLLECTION

AUTHOR: **Laurence Yep** • ILLUSTRATOR: Isadore Seltzer

HC: Bridgewater

THEMES: dreams; cultural diversity; folklore

Yep tells ten stories—from Brazil to China, India to Japan. Each one is connected to a dream. Perfect for an opportunity to show how dreams can be a springboard to storytelling.

★ The True Story of the Three Little Pigs
PICTURE BOOK

AUTHOR: Jon Scieszka • ILLUSTRATOR: Lane Smith

HC: Viking • PB: Puffin

THEMES: wolves; pigs; humor; folktale variations; zany

Jon Scieska and Lane Smith make us laugh. This twisted tale will get you laughing, too. If you think you know the story of the Three Little Pigs, A. Wolf will set you straight. ". . . I'll let you in on a little secret. Nobody knows the real story, because nobody has ever heard my side of the story." It's outrageous, and this author and illustrator's perfectly matched words and art result in a picture book third graders will love, if their older siblings are willing to share.

Tucker Pfeffercorn
PICTURE BOOK

AUTHOR/ILLUSTRATOR: Barry Moser

HC/PB: Little Brown

THEMES: folklore; U.S.A., the South; folktale variation; change; cruelty

When Jefferson Tadlock invents a tale about a woman who could spin cotton into gold, he doesn't expect to be overheard by the meanest man in the mountains. "Hezakiah Sweatt stared at Jefferson Tadlock. A drool of brown tobacco juice leached out of the corner of his mouth. '. . . you better be right, you slack-twisted sand-lapper. Go git her so's I can see for myself.'" For Rumpelstiltskin fans, here is a new telling. This one is set in the South with language begging to be read aloud.

Uncle Jed's Barbershop
PICTURE BOOK

AUTHOR: Margaree Mitchell • ILLUSTRATOR: James Ransome

HC: Simon & Schuster

THEMES: family; determination; African American; pride; jobs; community; self-respect; patience

Uncle Jed has a goal: to own his own barbershop. Even when times get hard, he never loses sight of his vision. This picture book tale is a testament to determination, pride, and a person's need to have something he can call his own.

Where Are You Going, Manyoni?   PICTURE BOOK

AUTHOR/ILLUSTRATOR: Catherine Stock
HC: Morrow
THEMES: Africa; school; animals; African words

Author's notes, a glossary of unfamiliar words, and a picture dictionary of African wildlife extend this picture book into a lively look at life in Zimbabwe, all seen through the eyes of a child who, like most of her friends, is accustomed to walking two hours to school every day.

Where's That Insect?   PICTURE BOOK NONFICTION

AUTHOR: Barbara Brenner • ILLUSTRATOR: Carol Schwartz
PB: Scholastic
THEMES: insects; science; searching game; comparisons

Each page is filled with colorful detail and interesting facts about insects. "Which is which? These are monarch butterflies; one is a male and one is a female. They are almost exactly alike so look very carefully. The male monarch has a black spot on each wing. Now look at the big picture. See if you can find two male monarchs on the butterfly tree." Schwartz fills the pages with insects peeking out from their hiding places, inviting you to try and find them.

White Dynamite & Curly Kidd   PICTURE BOOK

AUTHOR: Bill Martin, Jr. and John Archambault • ILLUSTRATOR: Ted Rand
HC/PB: Henry Holt
THEMES: cowboys; fathers and daughters; courage; yearnings; rhythm

The combination of Bill Martin, Jr. and John Archambault has produced some clever, complex read alouds, and this is one of their best. Young Lucky's dad is a bull rider, called Curly Kid. As they help prepare Curly for a ride on White Dynamite, Lucky keeps up a nervous one-sided conversation about the bull, other rodeo riders and Lucky's desire to be a bull rider someday, occasionally punctuated by a one-syllable response from Curly. Using rhythm and a sure knack for the spoken word, the authors have created a dialogue that reveals volumes about the characters and tells a compelling story, but still offers a surprise on the last page—Lucky is a girl. Another collaboration from this pair also featuring the luminous art of Ted Rand is *Knots on a Counting Rope*, which shares many of the pleasures and themes of *White Dynamite*—a dialogue between a child and an adult, a child yearning for something beyond expectations, and a surprise ending.

The Whittler's Tale   PICTURE BOOK

AUTHOR: Jennifer Armstrong • ILLUSTRATOR: Valerie Vasilieu
HC: Tambourine
THEMES: magic; woodworking; imagination; storytelling; animals

A stranger tells stories as he carves little animals out of wood—animals that magically come to life. Here's a tale that stretches the imagination. Is the magic in the whistler's pocket knife? Or is it in the wood he carves? Or is there a little magic in all of us?

Will You Sign Here, John Hancock?   PICTURE BOOK BIOGRAPHY

AUTHOR: Jean Fritz • ILLUSTRATOR: Trina Schart Hyman
PB: Paperstar
THEMES: biography; U.S. history, American Revolution; Declaration of Independence; John Hancock

Adept at making historical events come vividly to life, Jean Fritz is the best writer we know for biographies aimed at 2nd to 4th grades. She gets all the facts down and presents them in a way that feels like a story and not just history. As a bonus, all her books are marvelously illustrated. Others in the series include: *And Then What Happened, Paul Revere?*, *Shh! We're Writing the Constitution*, *You Want Women to Vote, Lizzie Stanton*, and *What's the Big Idea, Ben Franklin?*

Wish You Were Here: Emily's Guide
to the 50 States   PICTURE BOOK NONFICTION

AUTHOR: Kathleen Krull • ILLUSTRATOR: Amy Schwartz
HC: Doubleday
THEMES: travel; geography; family history; mail; grandmothers and granddaughters; U.S.A., the states; writing

Don't plan on just leafing through this one; you'll get pleasantly slowed down by the details. It is filled with drawings, maps and interesting facts about every one of the 50 states and Washington, D.C. ". . . more people buy dieting magazines in Spokane (Washington) than in any other American city." This is not your typical geography book. It's all from the perspective of a young girl traveling with her grandma, filled with the kinds of details children care about.

The Wonderful Wizard of Oz   FICTION-FANTASY

AUTHOR: L. Frank Baum • ILLUSTRATOR: W.W. Denslow

HC: Morrow

THEMES: home; magic; wizards; adventure; witches; friendship; courage; fantasy; self-respect; journeys; strong girl

One of the great American works of fiction. If you have only seen the movie, you don't know half of it! This lovingly produced facsimile of the original edition makes the perfect gift for any child. There are many subsequent books about Oz, Dorothy, and the gang, and they vary in quality. Many people go on to read as many of them as they can find. But don't let a child grow up without at least one trip to Oz!

Yeh-Shen: A Cinderella Story From China   PICTURE BOOK

RETOLD BY: Ai-Ling Louie • ILLUSTRATOR: Ed Young

HC: Philomel

THEMES: China; step families; kings; folktale variation; jobs; festivals

Most of us are familiar with the European fairy tale of Cinderella. As a matter of fact, we've even categorized "Yeh-Shen" as a "folktale variation." But, surprisingly, this version was found in one of the ancient Chinese manuscripts written during the T'ang dynasty. That would make it at least 1,000 years older than the earliest known Western version of the story. That's an interesting bit of information, but the reason to choose this is not its history, it's because of the beauty of Young's radiant pastel and watercolor paintings and because it's a story well told.

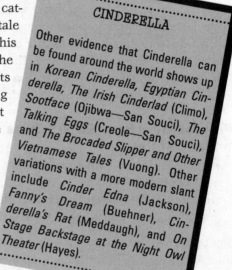

CINDERELLA

Other evidence that Cinderella can be found around the world shows up in Korean Cinderella, Egyptian Cinderella, The Irish Cinderlad (Climo), Sootface (Ojibwa—San Souci), The Talking Eggs (Creole—San Souci), and The Brocaded Slipper and Other Vietnamese Tales (Vuong). Other variations with a more modern slant include Cinder Edna (Jackson), Fanny's Dream (Buehner), Cinderella's Rat (Meddaugh), and On Stage Backstage at the Night Owl Theater (Hayes).

CLASSICS

Classics are books that have withstood the test of time and have been favorites of children for many years. We've listed some acknowledged classics here along with a few we believe will fit the category in time, for listeners and readers at various levels. Try some of these with your children. Some will become your favorites; others may not work for your child. Together you will learn how to choose your own classics.

Picture Books:
Make Way for Ducklings (McCloskey)
Goodnight Moon (Brown)
Mike Mulligan and His Steam Shovel (Burton)
Where the Wild Things Are (Sendak)
The Story of Ferdinand (Leaf)
The Very Hungry Caterpillar (Carle)
Angus and the Ducks (Flack)
The Little Engine That Could (Piper)
A Tree Is Nice (Udry)
Moja Means One (Feelings)
The Tale of Peter Rabbit (Potter)
Caps for Sale (Slobodkina)
The Napping House (Wood)
Time for Bed (Fox)
Chicka Chicka Boom Boom (Martin, Jr. and Archambault)

Novels to Read Aloud:
Charlotte's Web (White)
The Chronicles of Narnia (Lewis)
Ramona the Pest (Cleary)
Winnie the Pooh (Milne)
Alice's Adventures In Wonderland (Carroll)
The Wonderful Wizard of Oz (Baum)

The Little House in the Big Woods (Wilder)
Mr. Popper's Penguins (Atwater)
The Adventures of Pinnochio (Collodi)
Homer Price (McCloskey)
The Story of Doctor Doolittle (Lofting)

Folktales, Fairy Tales, Myths and Legends
Just So Stories (Kipling)
The Merry Adventures of Robin Hood (Pyle)
Rapunzel (Zelinsky)
Rootabaga Stories (Sandburg)
The Red Fairy Book (Lang)
Riki-Tiki-Tavi (Kipling)

Longer Novels to Read Aloud
Heidi (Spyri)
The Hobbit (Tolkien)
Peter Pan (Barrie)
The Secret Garden (Burnett)
Treasure Island (Stevenson)
The Wind in the Willows (Grahame)
The Jungle Book (Kipling)
Around the World in 80 Days (Verne)
Understood Betsy (Canfield)

Young Guinevere
PICTURE BOOK

AUTHOR: Robert San Souci • ILLUSTRATOR: Jamichael Henterly
HC: Doubleday • PB: Dell
THEMES: King Arthur; magic; history, medieval times; strong girl; fantasy

Beginning with her childhood, this is Guinevere's story. San Souci's retelling is masterly, allowing us to focus on the origins of the individual characters in this well-known saga. Henterly has provided beautiful, historically accurate paintings; even the tapestry style was taken from the eleventh century. Other Arthurian retellings by San Souci include *Young Merlin, Young Lancelot* and *Young Arthur.*

Young John Quincy   PICTURE BOOK BIOGRAPHY

AUTHOR/ILLUSTRATOR: Cheryl Harness
HC: Simon & Schuster
THEMES: government; biography; U.S. history, Colonial America; American Revolution; John Quincy Adams; John Adams; Declaration of Independence

Learning history works best when children can visualize what life may have been like "back then." This book offers that opportunity. It begins in the spring of 1775 when John is eight years old, and takes us to a year later when Ma reads a letter from Pa that contains the wording of the Declaration of Independence. Paintings and detailed maps give attention to the historical events leading up to the American Revolution. Through the scratching of quill pens, sunset glinting off pewter plates, and the chores in the family farmhouse, Harness shows what it must have been like to live in those times.

Zee   PICTURE BOOK

AUTHOR: Elizabeth Enright • ILLUSTRATOR: Susan Gaber
HC: Harcourt Brace
THEMES: fairies; solitude; magic; little folk; strong girl

"Zee was a bad fairy and proud of it. She lived alone and always had. She had no mother, father, sisters, brothers, uncles, aunts, or cousins and never had any. About a hundred years before this story begins, she had invented herself by magic . . ." This tiny live wire finds herself in lots of prickly situations children will not be able to resist!

We broaden the range for listeners in this section, offering picture books and fiction whose style, tone, subject matter, or presentation will hold most children, but can be read by the earliest readers.

Go Hang a Salami! I'm a Lasagna Hog!   PICTURE BOOK
AUTHOR/ILLUSTRATOR: Jon Agee
HC: Farrar Strauss & Giroux
THEMES: palindromes; wordplay; vocabulary; language; humor

Exercise your vocabulary. More than 60 palindromes—". . . a word, verse or sentence which reads the same backward and forward"—will give readers a workout. Wow! Another book in the same style is *So Many Dynamos!*

The Handmade Alphabet   PICTURE BOOK NONFICTION
AUTHOR/ILLUSTRATOR: Laura Rankin
HC: Dial • PB: Puffin
THEMES: alphabet; sign language; communication; wordless; cultural diversity; deafness

Realism and imagination merge as colored pencil drawings fill pages with hand shapes representing the twenty-six letters of the American Sign Language alphabet. Words are not needed as hands do all the talking; a gloved hand forms the letter "G," fingers dipping into a palette of paint form the letter "P," and an X-rayed hand offers up the "X." A perfect guide for the curious as well as the proficient.

I'll See You in My Dreams   PICTURE BOOK
AUTHOR: Mavis Jukes • ILLUSTRATOR: Stacey Schuett
HC: Knopf
THEMES: illness; daydreams; problem solving; flying; strong girls; uncles; loss; airplanes; hospitals

When painful and difficult situations come up—even death—good books help. Jukes's story is about a young girl traveling to visit her critically ill uncle. It's about the worry of saying good-bye, and the daydreams that accompany that fear.

Many Luscious Lollipops   PICTURE BOOK NONFICTION
AUTHOR/ILLUSTRATOR: Ruth Heller
HC: Putnam • PB: Sandcastle Books
THEMES: adjectives; language; rhyme

To have had this series when we were learning grammar would have been a stimulating experience. Alas, it wasn't available then. But children today can learn about adjectives with astonishing, colorful art and poetic descriptions. "An adjective's terrific when you want to be specific. It easily identifies by number, color, or by size. Twelve large, blue, gorgeous butterflies." Memorize them. Enjoy them again and again. The others in this extraordinary series include; *A Cache of Jewels and Other Collective Nouns; Up, Up and Away: A Book About Adverbs; Merry-Go-Round: A Book About Nouns; Kites Sail High: A Book About Verbs; Behind the Mask: A Book About Prepositions;* and *Mine, All Mine: A Book About Pronouns.*

Miss Nelson Is Missing!   PICTURE BOOK
AUTHOR: Harry Allard • ILLUSTRATOR: James Marshall
HC/PB: Houghton Mifflin
THEMES: school; teachers; mystery; substitute teachers; misbehaving; mischief

The creators of The Stupids deliver another hysterical creation in the person of Miss Viola Swamp, the meanest teacher in the whole world. The alter ego of the title character, though only the reader is allowed to know that, Viola Swamp whips a class of unruly and disruptive kids into shape in no time. We suspect that most teachers have a little of Miss Swamp in them, and that's why these books have become classroom favorites. The other titles are *Miss Nelson Is Back* and *Miss Nelson Has a Field Day.*

★ Silver Pony   PICTURE BOOK

AUTHOR/ILLUSTRATOR: Lynd Ward
PB: Houghton Mifflin
THEMES: wordless; horses; farms; fantasy; friendship; good deeds; geography; cultural diversity

Moving and suspenseful, this chapter book has no words. Pictures in shades of black and white tell the story of a farm boy's adventure with a powerful winged horse. Start at the front and don't skip pages. You will be mesmerized.

I like it as a read-by-yourself book, but was happy to have my children point out parts I'd missed, like clues given by weather vanes.

DON'T UNDERESTIMATE THE POWER OF A WORDLESS BOOK

Books aren't the bad guys. But reading them can create problems. Sometimes the frustrations of learning to read cause a child to "hate" books. Offer that child one that is wordless. If that seems "babyish," try Ward's *Silver Pony*—a chapter book without words—and watch them get pulled in. Or, show a child *Zoom,* by Banyai. Adults often request that one for themselves. Sometimes frustrated children need a break from words. But don't let them take it out on books.

Wordless books allow a child's imagination to soar. Without interruptions or intrusions, they come up with words of their own. It's impossible to read *Clown* by Blake without "hearing" the words. Children who follow detail will be engrossed by books like David Weisner's *Free Fall.*

When my daughter Kaela was five years old, she showed her frustration at not being able to read well by chirping noisily while her older sister Laura read aloud. Wordless books solved our problem. Kaela took her turn reading those books aloud—from the front to the back page, night after night, using the same words.

Here are some wordless and mostly wordless books we recommend.

Colors Everywhere (Hoban)	*Grey Lady and the Strawberry*
Zoom (Banyai)	*Snatcher* (Bang)
Will's Mammoth (Martin)	*Time Flies* (Rohmann)
Peter Spier's Rain (Spier)	*Silver Pony* (Ward)
A Boy, a Dog, a Frog, and a Friend (Mayer)	*Free Fall and Tuesday* (Wiesner)
Clown (Blake)	*Good Dog Carl* (Day)
On Christmas Eve (Collington)	*R.E.M.* (Banyai)
The Angel and the Soldier Boy (Collington)	*Re-Zoom* (Banyai)
Anno's Journey (Anno)	

The Stupids Step Out   PICTURE BOOK
AUTHOR: Harry Allard • ILLUSTRATOR: James Marshall
HC/PB: Houghton Mifflin
THEMES: humor; family; comparisons; opposites; point of view; fools

Meet the Stupids! In story after story, Allard and Marshall delight readers and listeners of all ages with the adventures of the dumbest family
in all of literature. Not only are they clueless, but they excel at doing
exactly the opposite of what the reader would do in any given situation,
frequently resulting in the comment, "Man, they are really stupid!"
. . . and that is the point. Look for these other titles: *The Stupids Have a
Ball*, *The Stupids Take Off*, and *The Stupids Die*.

Toby   PICTURE BOOK
AUTHOR: Margaret Wild • ILLUSTRATOR: Noela Young
HC: Ticknor and Fields
THEMES: change; grief; aging; dogs; pets

Sara is almost twelve years old. Her dog Toby is fourteen. He's going
blind and deaf and is often smelly. The family understands, but Sara
pushes him away when he goes to her for comfort. Her younger brothers don't understand how she can be so mean. Here is a picture book
that not only invites discussion of how different people react to grief,
but also touches on growing up and learning to adapt to change.

The Z Was Zapped: A Play in Twenty-Six Acts   PICTURE BOOK
AUTHOR/ILLUSTRATOR: Chris Van Allsburg
HC: Houghton Mifflin
THEMES: alphabet; plays; guessing; vocabulary

*That tingly moment again—opening up a gem that shines
beyond its concept. Van Allsburg presents the alphabet as a 26-act
play. Each letter is one act, one image:*
  "Act I: The A . . . was an Avalanche."
  "Act II: The B . . . was badly bitten."
*First you see the image and then you turn the page to read Van Alls-
burg's clever twist on each black-and-white letter. In front of a classroom of fourth graders, I discovered the creative potential in this
drama. Holding up the "D" page, I asked, "The D was . . . ?" Hands
went up and the children hollered, "Dipped!" "Dunked!"
"Drowned!" "Dead!" "Dripping!" "Destroyed!" "My," I thought,
". . . all this excitement over a 'D'—over a letter in the alphabet."*

As the reading level rises, the experiences offered in this selection of mostly picture books are more in-depth, offering some great opportunities for reading that will provoke reflection and discussion afterward.

The 500 Hats of Bartholomew Cubbins

PICTURE BOOK

AUTHOR/ILLUSTRATOR: Dr. Seuss

HC: Random House

THEMES: hats; courage; respect; kings; wisdom; counting

A wonderful, magical tale of the boy who could not take his hat off to show respect for the King, as there was always another, more elaborate one underneath it. Wise men and wizards are confounded and the King orders Bartholomew's execution, but the executioner cannot chop off his head unless he removes his hat. Longer, more storybook Seuss than his other books, and only in two colors, but how splendid he makes the hats look!

Boundless Grace

PICTURE BOOK

AUTHOR: Mary Hoffman • ILLUSTRATOR: Caroline Binch

HC: Dial

THEMES: strong girls; grandmothers; fathers and daughters; parents, absent; step families; Africa

A return visit with one of our favorite spunky heroines (see *Amazing Grace*). Grace has grown considerably and is very interested in finding

out more about her father, who lives in Africa. A lovely story of reunion
and extended family that is intended for an audience a few years older
than for the first book.

Brown Honey in Broomwheat Tea   POETRY COLLECTION

AUTHOR: Joyce Carol Thomas • ILLUSTRATOR: Floyd Cooper
HC/PB: HarperCollins
THEMES: African American; self-respect; family; individuality

This collection of poems by Joyce Carol Thomas, illustrated with Floyd
Cooper's glowing paintings, is about family, individuality and pride of
heritage. "I sprang up from mother earth. She clothed me in her own
colors. I was nourished by father sun. He glazed the pottery of my skin.
I am beautiful by design. The pattern of night in my hair. The pattern
of music in my rhythm. As you would cherish a thing of beauty. Cherish me." Another collection by this same team, *Gingerbread Days*, offers
a poem each month and is also a treasure.

The Buck Stops Here:
Presidents of the United States   PICTURE BOOK NONFICTION

AUTHOR/ILLUSTRATOR: Alice Provensen
HC: HarperCollins
THEMES: U.S. presidents; government; U.S. history; politics; rhyme

It's a rap, and children who learn it will remember a bit about each one
of our country's presidents. "Harding, Twenty-nine, no doubt should
have cleaned his Cabinet out." Illustrations including interesting details
of each president's tenure fill the oversized pages. Teachers: this book
begs to introduce a project. Have students research the rap details to
explain their meaning.

Buddha   PICTURE BOOK BIOGRAPHY

AUTHOR/ILLUSTRATOR: Demi
HC: Henry Holt
THEMES: biography; India; Buddhism; religion; coming of age

A picture book introduction to the life of Buddha. Also check out Demi's
retellings of ten key stories of the Buddha in her picture book *Buddha
Stories*.

The Bunyans   PICTURE BOOK

AUTHOR: Audrey Wood • ILLUSTRATOR: David Shannon
HC: Scholastic
THEMES: tall tales; humor; puns; geography; family

Wood and illustrator Shannon have great fun with geography, puns, and tall tales in this book. There has to be a certain amount of geographical literacy for the kids to get the joke. When they do, the laughs are plentiful.

The Butter Battle Book   PICTURE BOOK

AUTHOR/ILLUSTRATOR: Dr. Seuss
HC: Random House
THEMES: war; weapons; deadlocks; rhyme; comparisons

A parable for the nuclear age that had many up in arms upon its publication. "It's a portrait of hopelessness," cried some, "and children cannot live without hope." "It is a portrait of reality," cried others, "and we all must come to terms with reality, even the children." Both sides missed the point. We feel this is an opportunity for discussion, a chance to read a book that really leaves you hanging and almost forces you to decide what happens after the story is over. Whichever answer you and your child come to will be a "right" one.

Celebration!   PICTURE BOOK

AUTHOR: Jane Resh Thomas • ILLUSTRATOR: Raul Colon
HC: Hyperion
THEMES: African American; slavery; U.S. history, Civil War; family; pride; freedom; celebrations; holidays

Juneteenth, the recognition of the day slaves in Texas learned of their freedom, is being celebrated more and more, and not just in the South. This tale is perfect for extending African-American History beyond the designated month of February.

The Clown of God   PICTURE BOOK

AUTHOR/ILLUSTRATOR: Tomie dePaola
HC/PB: Harcourt Brace
THEMES: juggling; folklore; Italy; history, the Renaissance; gifts; aging; jobs; faith; religion

Sweetly told, with beautiful, Renaissance-style illustrations, dePaola's version of the story of the juggler and his gift to God is one of his best books. Giovanni starts out as a poverty-stricken youth, but through his juggling ability he becomes a famous entertainer. When times grow hard and he returns to his boyhood home, Giovanni gives one last performance before a statue of The Madonna and Child. Moving and unforgettable.

Dawn   PICTURE BOOK
AUTHOR/ILLUSTRATOR: Molly Bang
HC: Morrow
THEMES: folklore; strong girls; boats; geese; change; patience; artists; secrets

A powerful retelling of the Japanese folktale "The Crane Wife" set in New England. A poor shipbuilder saves a goose's life and meets a beautiful young woman, a sailmaker. They marry and have a daughter, and when he finishes making a boat for the three of them, she presents him with a set of sails "so light and fine and yet so strong they were that people called them Wings of Steel." When he pressures her into making another set of sails, she agrees, but when he breaks his promise not to enter the room while she is weaving, she is revealed to be a goose, making the sails from feathers she has plucked from her own breast. Told in flashback to their daughter, the title character, the book ends uncertainly with Dawn setting out to find her mother in the boat with the Wings of Steel. Bang's marvelous art, alternating between black-and-white and color, adds depth to the tale, offering clues to the observant as to the true nature of the sailmaker.

Demi's Dragons and Fantastic Creatures   PICTURE BOOK
AUTHOR/ILLUSTRATOR: Demi
HC: Henry Holt
THEMES: folklore; dragons; fantasy

Demi's stylish art brings vividly to life a bounty of imaginary creatures. Beautiful to look at and certain to enchant both young and old.

Dogzilla   PICTURE BOOK
AUTHOR/ILLUSTRATOR: Dav Pilkey
HC/PB: Harcourt Brace
THEMES: humor; dogs; monsters; parodies; puns

One of the funniest books we've encountered in years. This parody of the famous Japanese monster movie is illustrated in a photocollage style, with the author's dog playing the monster and his pet mice standing in for the terrified population of "Mouseopolis." Full of atrocious puns that will have adults groaning and kids rolling in the aisles, this is one of the best books for enticing an older boy into reading, especially if he thinks he is too cool to be bothered. For another outrageous adventure, be sure to get a copy of Pilkey's *Kat Kong*.

Festivals

POETRY COLLECTION

AUTHOR: Myra Cohn Livingston • ILLUSTRATOR: Leonard Everett Fisher
HC: Holiday House
THEMES: holidays; festivals; celebrations; cultural diversity

Organized chronologically, here are fourteen poems, each a look at important days around the world combining a balance of cultures and festivals. Livingston's style of poetry varies from page to page, matching the spirit of each festival.

Fly Away Home

PICTURE BOOK

AUTHOR: **Eve Bunting** • ILLUSTRATOR: Ronald Himler
HC: Clarion
THEMES: homelessness; airports; courage; fathers and sons; home; yearning; poverty; jobs; single parents

A boy and his dad live in an airport, striving to remain unnoticed. A devastating look at the effects of homelessness, rendered in Bunting's usual poignant style.

From Pictures to Words: A Book About Making a Book

PICTURE BOOK NONFICTION

AUTHOR/ILLUSTRATOR: Janet Stevens
HC: Holiday House
THEMES: authors; illustrators; writing; books; creativity

Stevens takes us on the journey an author takes to write and illustrate a book. Her characters intrude, comment, and generally get in the way, but the reader gets a solid understanding of the process. See *How a Book Is Made* by Aliki for another look at this topic.

⋆ Hershel and the Hanukkah Goblins   PICTURE BOOK

AUTHOR: Eric Kimmel • ILLUSTRATOR: Trina Schart Hyman
HC/PB: Holiday House
THEMES: Hanukkah; cleverness; courage; candles; monsters; spooky
stories; faith; folklore; Jews; traditions

Kimmel's retelling of the story of Hershel of Ostropol and how he
restores Hanukkah to a town where goblins reign supreme is outstanding. Match his words with Caldecott Honor winning illustrations by
Hyman and you have a treasure that stands up to countless readings
every holiday season. There is much humor here, as well as cleverness,
scares, and heartwarming faith.

Heroes   PICTURE BOOK

AUTHOR: Ken Mochizuki • ILLUSTRATOR: Dom Lee
HC/PB: Lee & Low
THEMES: war; heroes; playing; friendship; fitting in; teasing; fathers
and sons; uncles; taking action; Japanese American; soldiers; prejudice

It is hard not to acknowledge the power of this book and the lump it left
in our throats upon reading it, but we have decidedly mixed feelings
about its message. Young Donnie is taunted by his classmates as they act
out their own version of the Vietnam War—it is the 1960s—because he
"looks like the enemy." His friends cannot believe his claims that his
father fought for the U.S. in World War II—how could there have been
Japanese soldiers on our side, they demand? His father's reserved manner and simple reply that heroes don't brag frustrates Donnie, and it
takes firsthand evidence of the teasing he has endured to motivate both
his father and uncle to take action.

In a scene of quiet power and grace, they show up after school in full
uniform, both proving their point and silencing Donnie's tormentors.
Though it speaks volumes about the true nature of heroism, we felt that
somehow it glorified war more than we could feel comfortable about.
You will need to see this book for yourself and decide its message for
you and your children.

How Much Is a Million?   PICTURE BOOK NONFICTION

AUTHOR: David Schwartz • ILLUSTRATOR: Steven Kellogg
HC: Lothrop • PB: Mulberry
THEMES: math; numbers; counting; measurement; concepts; compar-
isons

An outstanding counting book that goes beyond 1-2-3 and gives concrete examples of the enormity of big numbers! Many children become obsessed with numbers, the bigger the better. In this book, Schwartz and Kellogg bring to life the concepts of million, billion, and beyond in ways that contribute greatly to children's understanding. For example: "If you sat down to count from one to one billion . . . you would be counting for 95 years." Great fun, with detailed explanations at the back of the book from the author, and clever touches throughout by the illustrator. Look also for their book on money, *If You Made a Million.*

I'm in Charge of Celebrations　　　　PICTURE BOOK
AUTHOR: Byrd Baylor • ILLUSTRATOR: Peter Parnall
HC: Atheneum • PB: Aladdin
THEMES: celebrations; nature; Native American; desert; U.S.A., the Southwest; rhyme

Byrd Baylor celebrates the extraordinary events of nature; meteors, rainbows, the quick movement of an animal.

Jack and the Beanstalk　　　　PICTURE BOOK
AUTHOR/ILLUSTRATOR: Steven Kellogg
HC: Morrow
THEMES: folklore; giants; magic; courage; triumph

When reading a book illustrated by Steven Kellogg, you have to start looking at the first illustrations you come to—the endpapers and title pages of his books often have important parts of the story in them! In fact, you have to look closely at all his pictures, as he is a master at adding touches in his illustrations that add depth and richness to every tale he tells. In this version of the classic tale, Jack finds not a giant at the top of the beanstalk, but a hideous ogre, and Kellogg does not hold back in his depiction. Another outstanding contribution to the world of retold tales from one of our favorite creators!

Jumanji　　　　PICTURE BOOK
AUTHOR/ILLUSTRATOR: Chris Van Allsburg
HC: Houghton Mifflin
THEMES: games; magic; mystery; jungles; animals; boredom; problem solving; consequences

We need to stress: FORGET THE MOVIE! This is a simple and terrifying tale of what happens to two children who play a board game without fully understanding the rules. Creepy black-and-white illustrations and a spare text make this a book that beckons the reader inside over and again.

The Lorax   PICTURE BOOK

AUTHOR/ILLUSTRATOR: Dr. Seuss

HC: Random House

THEMES: trees; environment; taking action; rhyme; nature

"I am the Lorax. I speak for the trees." . . . and someone sure has to. In this environmental fable, Seuss walks a perilous line between preaching and telling a good story, but such is his magic that he never crosses over into the realm where the message is the medium. Many people read Seuss' work and think they know something about how to make a children's book—he made it look too easy, especially with his topical subjects and easy rhyme. But what most people fail to realize is that he was a genius; a truly gifted master of the word and the minds of children. His timeless appeal cannot be copied, as it would require a talent and a heart like his, the likes of which we will never see again. Other longer Seuss titles we like are: *On Beyond Zebra, McElligott's Pool, Yertle the Turtle,* and *The Sneetches and Other Stories.*

WATCH THE TELEVISION

Books give children choices. Our concern is that while television dictates a response to a child—when to think something is funny, or scary, which characters are good or evil—the child is not learning to develop his own responses. Children need to cultivate their ability to make decisions on their own.

Mailing May   PICTURE BOOK

AUTHOR: Michael O. Tunnell •

ILLUSTRATOR: Ted Rand

HC: Greenwillow

THEMES: railroad; mail; Idaho; fathers and daughters; cleverness; mail carrier; promises; problem solving

Based on the true tale of how young Charlotte May's father

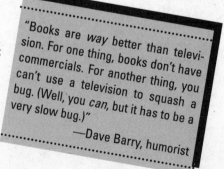

"Books are *way* better than television. For one thing, books don't have commercials. For another thing, you can't use a television to squash a bug. (Well, you *can,* but it has to be a very slow bug.)"

—Dave Barry, humorist

gets her delivered by the U.S. Postal Service to her grandma, 75 miles away. This is a charming and informative look at life in rural Idaho in 1914 and a tribute to the cleverness of a loving father.

The Man Who Could Call Down Owls   PICTURE BOOK

AUTHOR: **Eve Bunting** • ILLUSTRATOR: Charles Mikolaycak
HC: Macmillan • PB: Aladdin
THEMES: owls; folklore; revenge; comeuppance; secrets

Eerie and mysterious, with black-and-white illustrations that perfectly fit the mood, this cautionary tale is about the misuse of power. When a stranger steals the tools of the man who could call down the owls, the owls take their revenge on him, preferring instead the boy who has earned the right to their secret.

Math Curse   PICTURE BOOK

AUTHOR: Jon Scieszka • ILLUSTRATOR: Lane Smith
HC: Viking
THEMES: school; math; humor; problem solving; zany; point of view

A rollicking look at the effects of math education on all aspects of a bewildered child's life. Great fun for even the most math-phobic. Another successful collaboration from a team that delights in showing us new ways of looking at old subjects. See also: *The Stinky Cheese Man and Other Fairly Stupid Tales*.

Meanwhile . . .   PICTURE BOOK

AUTHOR/ILLUSTRATOR: Jules Feiffer
HC: HarperCollins
THEMES: imagination; comic book style; adventure; cleverness; fantasy

Told in comic book style, these fun adventures culminate in cliffhangers. Comic book obsessed Raymond has to get himself out of them, so he uses the time-honored device of changing the scene with a "Meanwhile . . ." It works, up to a point, and then he has to use his own ingenuity to get himself out of his final scrape. Great fun for the reluctant reader, but there is no reason why the rest should be deprived of the enjoyment. Feiffer's two novels, *A Barrel of Laughs, A Vale of Tears* and *The Man in the Ceiling* offer similar fun for older readers.

Meteor!   PICTURE BOOK

AUTHOR/ILLUSTRATOR: Patricia Polacco
PB: Paperstar
THEMES: family; community; miracles; magic; communication

A meteor lands in the yard of the Gaw family, bringing all sorts of miracles to the town of Union City, Michigan. Based on an incident in Polacco's childhood, her retelling captures the feel of the small town, the gossip, and the sense of magic this extraordinary event instills in everyone who touches the meteor.

Miro in the Kingdom of the Sun   PICTURE BOOK

AUTHOR: Jane Kurtz • ILLUSTRATOR: David Frampton
HC: Houghton Mifflin
THEMES: strong girls; folklore; Incas; courage; birds; listening; healing; illness

Miro is more clever than her brothers. When the prince falls ill, many men search for the cure, including her brothers, who fail and are imprisoned. Miro learns the language of the birds and uses this knowledge along with her courage to free her brothers from captivity. Kurtz's retelling of this Inca tale is also distinguished by the woodcuts of illustrator Frampton.

★ Miss Rumphius   PICTURE BOOK

AUTHOR/ILLUSTRATOR: Barbara Cooney
HC: Viking • PB: Puffin
THEMES: strong women; gardening; taking action; travel; independence; individuality; journeys; elderly and children; aging; self-respect; responsibility; friendship

This powerful recounting of the life of a woman who lives on her own terms and still remembers her responsibility to make the world more beautiful is one of our favorites. Its quiet strength and wisdom stay with the reader and listener long after the story has finished. We'd like our sons and daughters to think about Miss Rumphius when they make their own life decisions.

Moonstick: The Seasons of the Sioux   PICTURE BOOK

AUTHOR: **Eve Bunting** • ILLUSTRATOR: John Sandford
HC/PB: HarperCollins
THEMES: coming of age; seasons; time; calendar; nature; Native Americans

The Sioux kept track of time by counting the thirteen moons, and gave them names representing the natural world around them. One is called the "Moon of the Thunderstorms." "Thunder rolls with the voice of many drums. Light sweeps the cloudy sky. It is time to move to higher ground." Celebrate nature, the seasons, and a young boy's move toward manhood with each notch his father cuts into the moon-counting stick.

My First Book of Proverbs/Mi Primer Libro De Dichos

PICTURE BOOK NONFICTION

AUTHOR/ILLUSTRATOR: Ralfka and Ana Gonzalez
HC: Childrens Book Press
THEMES: proverbs; wordplay; Mexican American; Spanish language; bilingual; Mexico

"Pig out while you have the chance" and "Experience is the Mama of Science" are only a couple in this playful, bilingual collection of Mexican-American proverbs. Bright, colorful paintings capture Mexico's folk art style.

★ The Mysteries of Harris Burdick

PICTURE BOOK

AUTHOR/ILLUSTRATOR: Chris VanAllsburg
HC: Houghton Mifflin
THEMES: mystery; magic; writing; storytelling; imagination; guessing

In a sequence of unrelated pictures each accompanied by one tantalizing caption, Van Allsburg opens a world of possibilities to the reader. If you take him at his word, and we have no reason to disbelieve him, he has found these pictures unaccompanied by any writing except the sentences he includes, and is offering them without editorial comment in the hopes that they will inspire some storytelling creativity on the part of the reader. We guarantee that children will have lots to say.

When my daughter Kaela was in the fourth grade, she reminded me that Harris Burdick was a very scary book and that I should warn parents when they bought it. Yet she had poured over the pages for hours the year before, never mentioning her concerns. His images force a reader response, and to Kaela they were frightening. Oh, the power of Van Allsburg, whose art can linger in the backs of our minds! I've used this incredible book for years during writing workshops with fascinating results. It lives permanently in our library.

The Mysterious Tadpole

PICTURE BOOK

AUTHOR/ILLUSTRATOR: Steven Kellogg

HC: Dial • PB: Puffin

THEMES: friendship; pets; frogs; monsters; Scotland; cleverness; triumph

Louis' uncle sends him a birthday surprise from Scotland—a tadpole that turns out to be related to the Loch Ness Monster. How Louis and his family cope with the growth and appetite of Alphonse and how the day is ultimately saved by a combination of boyish ingenuity and a deep diving pet makes for a whopper of a tale. Kellogg's wonderful sense of humor is abundantly evident in all the details of the illustrations, from the names on the signs to the faces and clothes of the characters. A delight from beginning to surprising end!

Nathaniel Talking

POETRY COLLECTION

AUTHOR: Eloise Greenfield • ILLUSTRATOR: Jan Spivey Gilchrist

HC: Black Butterfly

THEMES: gentle boys; African American; rhyme; love; family; loss; music; grief; rhythm; lessons

"One day I was dumb enough to let somebody bet me into a fight and then I was mad with two stupid boys—the one who was hitting me and the one who was hitting him." Nathaniel B. Free is a spirited nine year old who tells his story through rap and rhyme. Funny, poignant, strong and sad, his poems will stay with you. Greenfield has included directions on how to write a twelve-bar blues poem at the back of the book.

The Other Way to Listen

PICTURE BOOK

AUTHOR: Byrd Baylor • ILLUSTRATOR: Peter Parnall

HC: Atheneum • PB: Aladdin

THEMES: nature; listening; Native American; elderly and children

Parents and teachers talk on about the merits of listening, and the chattering continues. This quiet gem uses few words in a conversation between an old man and a boy who talk about the virtues of taking the time to listen. Extraordinary line drawings by Parnall with just a touch of color.

Parents in the Pigpen, Pigs in the Tub   PICTURE BOOK

AUTHOR: Amy Ehrlich • ILLUSTRATOR: Steven Kellogg
HC: Dial
THEMES: farms; animals, farm; barns; family; comparisons; zany

Hysterical fun, as the farm animals move into the house and the family moves into the barn! Kellogg's usual outstanding art takes Ehrlich's already funny story and makes it a laugh riot.

Piggybook   PICTURE BOOK

AUTHOR/ILLUSTRATOR: Anthony Browne
HC: Random House • PB: Dragonfly
THEMES: gender roles; mothers; family; jobs; change; pigs; lessons

Mrs. Piggott has had quite enough of her horrid husband, her churlish children and their boorish behavior. They let her do all the housework and the cooking (in addition to her own job) and they lie around the house, taking her alarmingly for granted. Leaving a note saying only, "You are pigs." she leaves them in the lurch, and—Lo, and behold!—they turn into real pigs. With art that demands close inspection to catch all the story's hints and clues, Browne has created a funny and thought-provoking look at fairness in the home.

★ The Relatives Came   PICTURE BOOK

AUTHOR: **Cynthia Rylant** • ILLUSTRATOR: Stephen Gammell
HC: Macmillan • PB: Aladdin
THEMES: family; travel; relatives; reunions; visits

Rylant text and Gammell art, both at the top of their form, make this a warm and lovely picture book ode to visiting relatives, ripe summer fruit, and memories. Give this as a gift when you visit your relatives.

Rolling Harvey Down the Hill   POETRY COLLECTION

AUTHOR: Jack Prelutsky • ILLUSTRATOR: Victoria Chess
HC: Greenwillow • PB: Mulberry
THEMES: friendship; bullies; city life; competition

Gleefully told poems about the adventures of five boys, all friends, who endure the antics of bully Harvey up to a point, then finally roll him down the hill to teach him a lesson. A funny and irreverent portrait of urban boyhood.

AUTHOR SPOTLIGHT ON CYNTHIA RYLANT

The power of words has no greater friend than Cynthia Rylant. Whether writing poetry, short stories, novels for every age, or picture books, she continually astounds us with her insight and gentle wisdom. Children who read a book by Rylant receive the gifts of her understanding voice and her ability to get directly to the heart of the concerns of childhood.

Her picture books have been illustrated by such masters as Peter Catalanotto, Barry Moser, and Stephen Gammell and include gems like: *All I See*, *The Old Woman Who Named Things*, *When I Was Young in the Mountains*, *The Relatives Came*, and *An Angel for Solomon Singer*. She has even taken to illustrating her own books on occasion.

Her insight into the lives of young women growing up in Appalachia, where she grew up, is evident in her novels *A Blue-Eyed Daisy* and the Newbery-winning *Missing May*, as well as her poetry collections *Waiting to Waltz: A Childhood* and *Something Permanent*. But she is perhaps more astounding when she writes novels and poetry where she crawls inside the minds of boys, displaying a cross-gender empathy that few writers possess. These novels include the Newbery honor book *A Fine White Dust*, a novel of youthful religious fervor and heartbreaking betrayal, *I Had Seen Castles*, a devastating account of soldier life on the front lines of World War II that can stand with the best antiwar fiction, and the astonishing *Soda Jerk*, a novel in poems about the inner life of a teenaged boy in a small town that perfectly captures male adolescence on the brink of manhood. And some novels do not fit neatly into categories, such as her lovely ode to magic and believing in a small town, *The Van Gogh Cafe*.

The *Henry and Mudge* series as well as the *Mr. Putter and Tabby* books have set new standards of excellence for books aimed at beginning readers; her short story collections *Every Living Thing* and *A Couple of Kooks and Other Stories About Love* are excellent in breadth and style; and her picture autobiography *But I'll Be Back Again* is a charming and informative account of childhood in the 60's. In every area where she chooses to shine her talent, her brilliant illuminations open the world of great literature to young readers.

Rose Blanche

PICTURE BOOK

AUTHOR/ILLUSTRATOR: Roberto Innocenti
HC: Creative education • PB: Harcourt Brace
THEMES: war; peace; the Holocaust; strong girls; conscience; history, World War II; Germany; taking action; captivity; soldiers

Read this heart-wrenching picture book before sharing it with your child. The subject is tough, but so is war. And the point is compassion and an argument for peace. Innocenti's art details a small German town overtaken by German soldiers during World War II. Through joyless gray-brown tones comes young, caring Rose doing what she can to make a difference. Choose it when you have time; this book calls for discussion.

Roxaboxen

PICTURE BOOK

AUTHOR: Alice McLerran • ILLUSTRATOR: Barbara Cooney
HC: Lothrop
THEMES: childhood; memories; playing; imagination; community; desert; U.S. history, early 20th century

A wistful re-creation of a long-ago childhood and the imaginary town of Roxaboxen. This is an ode to children's fantasy play, where the rules of conduct and society mimic the adult world enough to be recognizable, but have a logic that is more fitting for childhood. "In Roxaboxen you can eat all the ice cream you want." Any child who has ever picked up a stick and pretended it was something else knows Roxaboxen. A lovely book.

Saint George and the Dragon

PICTURE BOOK

AUTHOR: Margaret Hodges • ILLUSTRATOR: Trina Schart Hyman
HC: Little Brown
THEMES: dragons; knights; courage; England; folklore; fighting

The greatest dragon battle in all fiction is herein rendered by a suitably powerful pair of storytellers—Hyman, with her deservedly Caldecott Medal-winning illustrations and Hodges, whose retelling of the epic fight exhausts and exhilarates.

Saint Patrick and the Peddler

PICTURE BOOK

AUTHOR: Margaret Hodges • ILLUSTRATOR: Paul Brett Johnson
HC/PB: Orchard
THEMES: Ireland; folklore; dreams; luck; journeys

A poor peddler dreams of Saint Patrick, who urges him to go to Dublin and stand on the bridge that crosses the River Liffey. The starving, poverty-stricken peddler makes the long journey and receives a tip that leads to riches beyond his imagining. Many versions of this story exist, from a variety of cultures, but Margaret Hodges' is the best to tell, and it reads aloud beautifully.

Sally Ann Thunder Ann Whirlwind Crockett   PICTURE BOOK

AUTHOR/ILLUSTRATOR: Steven Kellogg

HC: Morrow

THEMES: tall tales; strong girls; folklore; Davy Crockett

Kellogg's version of this tall tale features this wild lady right alongside (and out in front of) her more famous husband Davy. Part of his retellings of American Tall Tales, the other volumes of which include: *Mike Fink, Pecos Bill, Paul Bunyan,* and *I Was Born About 10,000 Years Ago.*

Seven Brave Women   PICTURE BOOK

AUTHOR: Betsy Hearne • ILLUSTRATOR: Bethanne Andersen

HC: Greenwillow

THEMES: courage; genealogy; strong women; U.S. history; peace; family history

"In the old days, history books marked time by the wars that men fought. The United States began with the Revolutionary War. Then there was the War of 1812, the Civil War, the Spanish-American War . . ." Betsy Hearne has looked to her own history and found seven brave women who fought their share of battles—but never in a war. They cared for the sick, worked on farms, started hospitals, studied in men's schools, built their homes, and told their stories. This incredible book shows how brave, devout, and determined women have left their tracks through time.

This book reminded me of my mother, who clipped photos from newspapers, tears in her eyes, to implant in us the faces of children in war. She also talked of women whose strength showed in their intellect and spirit. Use these stories to discuss the history makers in your child's past.

Slugs   PICTURE BOOK

AUTHOR: David Greenberg • ILLUSTRATOR: Victoria Chess

HC/PB: Little Brown

THEMES: slugs; rhyme; revenge; humor, gross

"Swallow a slug by its tail or its snout
Feel it slide down
Feel it climb out."

Gleefully gross, and sure to induce shivers and squeals, this is one of our favorite "no redeeming value" books. There is nothing in *Slugs* that will cause adults to shove it at a child saying, "Read this. It's good for you!" Sure, it has an ending that could be interpreted as "Be nice to animals or else," but the kids know that it's there to placate the grown-ups. Try this book on any age child who flat-out refuses to listen to you read aloud and see if this doesn't grab some attention.

Someday a Tree
PICTURE BOOK

AUTHOR: **Eve Bunting** • ILLUSTRATOR: Ronald Himler
HC: Clarion
THEMES: trees; environment; taking action; community

Inspired by a true incident, Bunting writes about a favorite oak tree that has been poisoned by toxic chemicals and can't be saved.

A Spoon for Every Bite
PICTURE BOOK

AUTHOR: Joe Hayes • ILLUSTRATOR: Rebecca Leer
HC: Orchard
THEMES: U.S.A., the Southwest; folklore; Mexico; wealth; spoons; neighbors; cleverness; comeuppance; obsession

A clever story with a twist young children don't see coming. A rich man is outwitted by a poor couple who claim to know of a man who uses a different spoon for every bite. Fun to read aloud.

The Three Little Javelinas
PICTURE BOOK

AUTHOR: Susan Lowell • ILLUSTRATOR: Jim Harris
HC/PB: Northland
THEMES: folktale variation; pigs; deserts; hispanic; cleverness; coyote; U.S.A., the Southwest

Javelinas are a piglike creature that roam the American desert southwest, and boy are they ugly! Using them as the main characters in this wild and funny retelling of *The Three Little Pigs* is a stroke of genius. You will love reading this aloud, and so will your kids.

Waiting for the Whales   PICTURE BOOK
AUTHOR: Sheryl McFarlane • ILLUSTRATOR: Ron Lightburn
HC: Putnam
THEMES: death; grandfathers and granddaughters; whales; aging; lone-
liness

An old man's life regains meaning with the birth of his granddaughter
and he passes on to her his love of the orcas who visit the shore once a
year. When the old man dies, a new whale joins the pod and a simple
story of connections to nature and family gets a message of hope and
rebirth. A great book to use in grief and loss situations.

The Wall   PICTURE BOOK
AUTHOR: **Eve Bunting** • ILLUSTRATOR: Ronald Himler
HC/PB: Clarion
THEMES: Vietnam Veterans Memorial; grandfathers; grief; fathers and
sons

A young boy's visit to the Vietnam Veteran's Memorial, rendered with
heartbreaking sensitivity.

The Wednesday Surprise   PICTURE BOOK
AUTHOR: **Eve Bunting** • ILLUSTRATOR: Donald Carrick
HC/PB: Clarion
THEMES: reading; literacy; grandmothers and granddaughters; gifts;
surprises; family; fathers and daughters

A young girl and her grandmother are preparing a surprise gift for dad's
homecoming. When the child reader discovers the gift is that Grandma
can now read, it presents a perfect opportunity to discuss issues of literacy.

What You Know First   PICTURE BOOK
AUTHOR: Patricia MacLachlan • ILLUSTRATOR: Barry Moser
HC: HarperCollins
THEMES: moving; change; U.S.A., the prairie; family

A stunning collaboration between a gifted writer and a master artist.
Leaving the prairie to move to the ocean, the young narrator tells us in
simple, affecting prose exactly how she feels about the prospect. Perfectly grasping the wrenching sadness of any childhood uprooting, as
well as the specifics of this individual child's life, MacLachlan explains
how we all are a part of where we've been, and how "What you know

first stays with you." If you know of a child who is moving away, this book can be his salvation.

When Clay Sings
PICTURE BOOK

AUTHOR: Byrd Baylor • ILLUSTRATOR: Tom Bahti
HC: Atheneum • PB: Aladdin
THEMES: Native American; clay; crafts; folk art; desert; U.S.A., the Southwest; U.S. history, pre-Columbus

Baylor steps back into history through ancient pots and shards found in the deserts of America's Southwest. She tells how some pieces were made and how others were used. As usual, Baylor's rich prose makes for fascinating reading. Bahti's award-winning drawings reflect the primitive figures found on the outsides of the pottery.

The Worry Stone
PICTURE BOOK

AUTHOR: Marianna Dengler • ILLUSTRATOR: Sybil Graber Gerig
HC: Northland
THEMES: loneliness; storytelling; friendship; elderly and children; folklore; Native American

Richly textured, with a story within a story within a story format, this tale of an old woman befriending a lonely boy in a park will comfort the most isolated among us. Beautiful illustrations that capture the faces of the characters help the tale to spring off the page.

Yonder
PICTURE BOOK

AUTHOR: Tony Johnston • ILLUSTRATOR: Lloyd Bloom
HC: Dial
THEMES: farms; family history; life cycle; seasons; change; country life

With poetic language and folk art–style paintings, Johnston and Bloom portray the story of a family farm, from the planting of the first tree to the burial of the now aged farmer. Along the way we are shown the cycle of seasons and lifetime and given a lovely reminder of the power of renewal.

Young Larry
PICTURE BOOK

AUTHOR: Daniel Pinkwater • ILLUSTRATOR: Jill Pinkwater
HC: Marshall Cavendish
THEMES: polar bears; brothers; mothers and sons; swimming; jobs; friendship; muffins

"The day finally came when Larry and Roy's mother called them to her, and hit each of them in the head. 'Get lost,' she said. 'Go and fend for yourselves.' " Before you get upset or wonder what kind of monster Larry and Roy's mother is, let us assure you that her behavior is perfectly normal, for a polar bear. Here is the story of how Larry, separated from his brother, finds a way to fit in a world of humans. Pinkwater's dry sense of humor lends a sense of the absurd to this tale, allowing readers of all ages to enjoy Larry's adventures as a lifeguard ("It has been brought to my attention that you are a polar bear," says the Chief Lifeguard.) and finally, companion to Mr. Frobisher, who will keep him supplied with the muffins he dearly loves, as long as he never acquires a taste for humans.

A mix of folklore, nonfiction, longer picture books, and fiction, this section offers a wide variety of subjects in titles that require real comfort with reading for the child who approaches them on his own.

The Adventures of Tintin   FICTION
AUTHOR/ILLUSTRATOR: Herge
HC/PB: Little Brown
THEMES: adventure; mystery; science fiction; comic-book style

This comic-book adventure series featuring the exploits of the world's greatest boy reporter, Tintin and his dog, Snowy has stood the test of time. Set in the first half of the 20th century and possessed of that era's world view, these are breathtakingly paced: Tintin goes around the world and has more adventures per book than the Hardy Boys and Nancy Drew combined. The comic-book style makes these books look deceptively easy to read. The vocabulary is not easy, but the reader has the visuals to fall back on. These find their way into lots of hands at various stages of reading development—third graders who like adventure will devour these, yet so will fifth and sixth graders for whom reading is a chore. Great fun. There are many titles, available in individual, oversized paperback editions, and lately their publisher has been collecting them into three-in-one hardcover collections.

All-of-a-Kind Family   FICTION

AUTHOR: Sydney Taylor • ILLUSTRATOR: Helen John
HC: Taylor • PB: Dell
THEMES: family; sisters; Judaism; New York; U.S. history, early 20th
century; growing up; new baby; traditions

Ella, Henny, Sarah, Charlotte, and Gertie are five sisters, each two years
older than the next, forming a human stairstep when they stand
together and earn themselves the name The All-of-a-Kind Family. As
they grow up in New York's lower east side at the turn of the century in
a loving Jewish family, we see them celebrating the festivals and holidays of their faith as well as universal experiences, such as going to the
library, family members' birthdays and the birth of a baby brother! A
warm family series, with four sequels: *More All-of-a-Kind Family*, *All-of-
a-Kind Family Uptown*, *All-of-a-Kind Family Downtown*, and *Ella of All-of-
a-Kind Family*.

★ Amazon Diary:
The Jungle Adventures of Alex Winters   PICTURE BOOK

AUTHOR/ILLUSTRATOR: Hudson Talbott and Mark Greenberg
HC: Putnam
THEMES: Amazon; Yanomami; adventure; courage; jungles

This is one cool book! Adventure lovers certainly get their fill at the
hands of writer/illustrator Talbott and writer/photographer Greenberg.
Alex's diary of his amazing experience is rendered here, complete with
his drawings, all in diary form, giving the reader a "you-are-there" experience! Along the way we learn a lot about the customs and cultures of
the Yanomami people. This is an example of how fiction and nonfiction
writing blend to create something daringly different that succeeds
tremendously. We cannot imagine this book failing to captivate an eight-
to eleven-year-old adventurer!

The Animal Family   FICTION

AUTHOR: Randall Jarrell • ILLUSTRATOR: Maurice Sendak
HC: HarperCollins
THEMES: family; mermaids; hunters; bears; lynx; adoption

A lovely and quiet tale of a lonely hunter who makes his own family.
This is a great read aloud, especially for the chance to truly savor some
of Jarrell's poetic writings by hearing them spoken. A meditation on
what makes a family, told with humor and wisdom.

The Arabian Nights   FOLKLORE COLLECTION
AUTHOR: Brian Alderson • ILLUSTRATOR: Michael Foreman
HC: Morrow
THEMES: folklore; storytelling; Arab culture; magic; Mideast

As good a retelling of these classic tales as one could ask for in a children's book. Foreman's art adds considerably to the package, making this our choice of the *Arabian Nights* to own.

Atalanta's Race: A Greek Myth   PICTURE BOOK
AUTHOR: Shirley Climo • ILLUSTRATOR: Alexander Koshkin
HC: Clarion
THEMES: Greek mythology; strong girls; folklore; competition; racing; track and field

This excellent introduction to longer myths showcases Climo's ability to retell tales. Great to have a picture book version of this story.

The Ballad of the Pirate Queens   PICTURE BOOK
AUTHOR: **Jane Yolen** • ILLUSTRATOR: David Shannon
HC: Harcourt Brace
THEMES: pirates; strong women; taking action; courage

Told in verse, this is the true story of two women who terrorized the sea as pirates. A fantastic collaboration.

Bay Shore Park: The Death and
Life of an Amusement Park   PICTURE BOOK NONFICTION
AUTHOR: Victoria Crenson • ILLUSTRATOR: Bryn Barnard
HC: W.H. Freeman
THEMES: nature; plants; animals; insects; environment; change

Do not judge this book by its cover!. The run-down remnants of an old amusement park held no interest for us. But the rich text and art showing how life returned to the land is fascinating. Big iron gates were locked to keep trespassers out when Bay Shore Park was closed in 1947. But gates could not keep nature out. Little by little life returned to the park. This is the story of how that happened. "They come on the Bay breeze, sailing in on downy parachutes. They hitch rides in the mud balls on ducks' feet. They arrive hooked on the feathers of gulls. Seeds. Zillions of seeds." And with them plants, insects and animals of all kinds. This extraordinary book gives fascinating facts without lecturing.

The BFG
FICTION-FANTASY

AUTHOR: Roald Dahl • ILLUSTRATOR: Quentin Blake
HC: Farrar Straus & Giroux • PB: Puffin
THEMES: giants; friendship; imagination; fantasy; adventure; good vs. evil; orphans; strong girls

It's a good thing it was The Big Friendly Giant who lifted Sophie (an orphan) from her bed and whisked her out the window. It would have been a different story if it had been Fleshlumpeater, Gizzardgulper, Bonecruncher or any one of the other giants. They are disgusting and enjoy swallomping nice little "childers" who Sophie and the BFG set out to save. Like many great writers, Dahl was never shy about inventing words when he needed them—his "giant language" of snozzcumbers, frobscottles and whizzpoppers will leave young readers howling.

Bill Peet: An Autobiography
PICTURE BOOK BIOGRAPHY

AUTHOR/ILLUSTRATOR: Bill E. Peet
HC/PB: Houghton Mifflin
THEMES: biography; artists; art; movies; cartoons; careers; authors; jobs; writing

The story of a man who had two great careers—one as a Disney animator on some of the greatest cartoons of all time, the other as the beloved author of dozens of books for children, including *Chester, the Worldly Pig, Big Bad Bruce,* and *Eli.* This is a great book to read if you want to know more about how artists create, or if you just like Peet's books.

Birdie's Lighthouse
PICTURE BOOK

AUTHOR: Deborah Hopkinson • ILLUSTRATOR: Kimberly Bulcken Root
HC: Atheneum
THEMES: lighthouses; diaries; strong girls; Maine; courage; sea; family; fathers and daughters

It is 1855 and Birdie and her family live on an island off the coast of Maine where her father works as the lighthouse keeper. Birdie wants very much to be her father's assistant and learns all there is to know about keeping the light lit and the surrounding sea safe for the ships navigating the treacherous, rock-strewn path to shore. When her father is taken ill and a brutal northeaster hits, it is up to brave Birdie to save the day. Through a diary format, we hear Birdie's words as she describes the joys and sorrows of her life and we experience her thrills and doubts right along with her. A wonderful portrait of a remarkable young girl.

The Body Atlas   REFERENCE
AUTHOR: Steve Parker • ILLUSTRATOR: Giuliano Fornari
HC: DK
THEMES: human body; science; nature; health

Do you know the correct name for your funny bone? Or why you yawn?
Here's a good-sized book that maps the human body inside and out.
Detailed illustrations examine the workings of every muscle and organ.

The Bone Man: A Native American Modoc Tale   PICTURE BOOK
AUTHOR: Laura Simms • ILLUSTRATOR: Michael McCurdy
HC: Hyperion
THEMES: Native American; courage; wisdom; coming of age; scary sto-
ries; grandmothers; fate; folklore

A chilling Modoc tale, made all the more eerie by Michael McCurdy's
stunning illustrations. The warnings of his grandmother have made
quite an impression on young Nulwee—that his fate is inexorably bound
to the monstrous skeleton known as the Bone Man. This is a book about
fate, courage and understanding that will give courage to any child who
has to face an obstacle that seems overwhelming.

The Book of North American Owls   PICTURE BOOK NONFICTION
AUTHOR: Helen Sattler • ILLUSTRATOR: Jean Day Zallinger
HC: Clarion
THEMES: owls; nature; maps

The ancient people who drew them on walls of caves eighteen thousand
years ago believed that owls were spirits with magic powers. Until
recently, people didn't really know much about them, but that's
changed. *The Book of North American Owls* is packed with up-to-date
information and includes a glossary of twenty full-color pages.

The Borrowers   FICTION-FANTASY
AUTHOR: Mary Norton • ILLUSTRATOR: Beth and Joe Krush
HC/PB: Harcourt Brace
THEMES: little folk; family; adventure; England; secrets; friendship; escape

The Clock family have lived quite happily for years, under the floor of
an old English country home, "borrowing" what few things they need
from the larger "human beans" who reside above. Everything is very
British and proper. Things get a bit knotty when young Arrietty
befriends a human boy and the Borrowers' secret existence is discov-

ered. If you have ever wanted an explanation for why things mysteriously disappear in your home, read this book (and its sequels: *The Borrowers Afield, The Borrowers Aloft, The Borrowers Afloat, Poor Stainless,* and *The Borrowers Avenged*).

Brother Eagle, Sister Sky: A Message From Chief Seattle

PICTURE BOOK

    AUTHOR: Chief Seattle • ILLUSTRATOR: Susan Jeffers
    HC: Dial
    THEMES: Native American; responsibility; nature; environment

"How can you buy the sky? How can you own the rain and the wind?" These words, attributed to Squamish Chief Seattle over one hundred years ago, express his respect for the earth. Jeffers has matched the beauty of words with stunning, luminous paintings and leaves readers with the final message, "Preserve the land and the air and the rivers for your children's children and love it as we have loved it." An extraordinary combination.

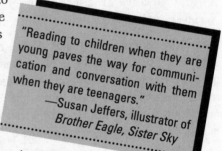

"Reading to children when they are young paves the way for communication and conversation with them when they are teenagers."
—Susan Jeffers, illustrator of *Brother Eagle, Sister Sky*

Brown Angels: An Album of Pictures and Verse

POETRY COLLECTION

    AUTHOR: **Walter Dean Myers** • ILLUSTRATOR: antique photographs
    HC: HarperCollins
    THEMES: African American; photographs; childhood

Myers has written poems to go with his collection of turn-of-the century photographs of children. These may inspire young poets to add their own poetry to cherished old family photos.

Celebrations

POETRY COLLECTION

    AUTHOR: Myra Cohn Livingston • ILLUSTRATOR: Leonard Everett Fisher
    HC/PB: Holiday House
    THEMES: celebrations; holidays; variety

Bold paintings fill the pages in this celebration of sixteen significant days. From New Year's Eve ". . . Old is dying. New is born . . ." and April Fool ". . . Is that a spider on your back? I ate the whole pie by myself" to

Labor Day and birthdays, Livingston's poems feature special times that highlight the year.

Charles Dickens: The Man Who Had
Great Expectations
PICTURE BOOK BIOGRAPHY

AUTHOR: Diane Stanley and Peter Vennema • ILLUSTRATOR: Diane Stanley

HC: Morrow

THEMES: biography; history, 19th century; England; authors

Diane Stanley and Peter Vennema have carefully researched London in the 19th century with its extremes of poverty and wealth, and brought Charles Dickens and his times vividly to life. Passages like the following show readers why we tend to imagine young Dickens' world as one of hungry children in shadowed alleys. "To pay the butcher or baker, the Dickens family was forced to sell things. Charles would be sent to the pawnshop from time to time with an armload of books. It made him sad to part with them, for reading was now his only escape from drudgery."

Charlie Drives the Stage
PICTURE BOOK

AUTHOR: Eric Kimmel • ILLUSTRATOR: Glen Rounds

HC/PB: Holiday House

THEMES: strong girls; determination; U.S. history, the Old West; stage-coaches; trains; surprises

Based on a true story. Charlie Drummond is the only stage driver crazy enough to face a rising river, stick-up men, and a host of other dangers in order to get a self-important senator on the train to Washington, D.C. Nothing can stop Charlie, who looks barely 14 and has more cunning and courage than most adults. Faced with obstacle after obstacle, Charlie refuses to turn back until the prestigious politician is safely on board the train. The senator, much impressed with Charlie's skill and daring, offers to tell the President about the brave young man who, on the last page, is revealed to be a girl. Absolutely wonderful! For in-depth looks at Charlie's life, read Pam Munoz Ryan's *Riding Freedom* and *One-Eyed Charley, the California Whip,* by Randall A. Reinstedt.

★ Charlotte's Web
FICTION

AUTHOR: E.B. White • ILLUSTRATOR: Garth Williams

HC/PB: HarperCollins

THEMES: spiders; death; farms; courage; love; friendship; miracles; family; animals; life cycle; wisdom; change; pigs; fairs; self-respect

We agree with read-aloud advocate Jim Trelease when he recommends this book to be read aloud for your child's first long chapter book. Wilbur, Fern, Templeton and the rest have been delighting children for generations, but it is Charlotte herself who provides the book with its soul. Many children first encounter the cycle of life through this story, and its depiction of birth, growth, change, death, loss, and renewal has the power to move children and adults alike. Charlotte's death is without question a monumentally sad event in the world of children's books, but such is the power of White's prose that it is how she lived that we remember. There may be no finer book on friendship ever written.

A CHAPTER A DAY

Children need to learn to listen and visualize. Reading a chapter a day is a wonderful way to make that happen. Start with *Charlotte's Web* (White). It's well written, with characters you care about from the second you meet them, and the chapters are not long. After that, we can make some suggestions, but ultimately you'll have to find your own way. All children are individuals with their own set of readiness and tastes. Remember just a chapter or two at a time, building up listening endurance. In addition to the standard *Charlotte's Web,* try these:

The Wonderful Wizard of Oz (Baum)   *The Cricket in Times Square* (Selden)
My Father's Dragon (Gannett)   *Misty of Chincoteague* (Henry)
Hugh Pine (de Wetering)   *Freddy the Detective* (Brooks)
The Borrowers (Norton)   *The Railway Children* (Nesbit)
Babe, the Gallant Pig (King Smith)   *A Bear Called Paddington* (Bond)
Mr. Popper's Penguins (Atwater)

Story collections give you an opportunity to sample a wide range of styles and types of stories. They offer a chance to learn about family tastes and naturally break up reading into manageable pieces. These are some of our favorites:

The People Could Fly (Hamilton)
Cut From the Same Cloth (San Souci)
From Sea to Shining Sea (Cohn, ed.)
Big Men Big Country (Walker)

Cheyenne Again
PICTURE BOOK

AUTHOR: **Eve Bunting** • ILLUSTRATOR: Irving Toddy

HC: Clarion

THEMES: U.S. history, frontier life; Native American; change; defeat

Taking historical fact and making a story picture book out of it is a particular strength of Bunting's, but this tale of the forced education of Cheyenne children into the ways of the white man is a potent reminder of the evils of indoctrination. Contrast this with *Burnt Stick* by Anthony Hill.

The Children's Book of Kwanzaa: A Guide to Celebrating the Holiday
PICTURE BOOK NONFICTION

AUTHOR/ILLUSTRATOR: Dolores Johnson

PB: Aladdin

THEMES: celebrations; Kwanzaa; African American; recipes; symbols; family history; biography; crafts

Kwanzaa begins each year on December 26. Johnson has created a guide to the celebration of Kwanzaa, its history and its purpose. She's included biographies of Africans and African Americans; principles and symbols of Kwanzaa; recipes, crafts and suggestions on how to participate.

The Christmas Miracle of Jonathan Toomey
PICTURE BOOK

AUTHOR: Susan Wojciechowski • ILLUSTRATOR: P.J. Lynch

HC: Candlewick

THEMES: redemption; solitude; Christmas; loss; family; artists; woodworking; grief; single parents; creativity; loneliness

They call him Mr. Gloomy. Woodcarver Jonathan Toomey is a sour, bitter man, living a life of solitude and still mourning the loss of his wife and child. How a widow and her son help him rejoin the human race is told in a heart-tugging style, with warm and beautiful illustrations, all combining to make a holiday classic.

The Christmas Menorahs: How a Town Fought Hate
PICTURE BOOK NONFICTION

AUTHOR: Janice Cohn • ILLUSTRATOR: Bill Farnsworth

HC/PB: Albert Whitman

THEMES: Hanukkah; bullies; courage; taking action; Montana; prejudice

When a brick is thrown through the window of his home because it has a menorah in it, the entire town rallies behind Issac Schnitzer's family and puts menorahs in their windows. Based on events that happened in Billings, Montana in 1993, this story is somewhat preachy but very useful in showing how bigotry and hate can be fought in a nonviolent fashion.

The Chronicles of Narnia   FICTION-FANTASY

AUTHOR: C.S. Lewis
HC/PB: HarperCollins
THEMES: courage; siblings; friendship; redemption; sacrifice; adventure; fantasy; good vs. evil

One of the most beloved children's series of all time, and an excellent introduction to more sophisticated fantasy storytelling. Start reading these aloud to your five or six year old and let the magic take effect. These are very well written, both in terms of the plotting and the characters—you believe in these children. You even believe in the talking lion, Aslan, as noble and majestic a character as ever written. There is a strong element of Christianity in the telling, and the whole thing can be viewed as an allegory, but it doesn't have to be—children usually don't see the parallels—and it is the power of Lewis's storytelling that compels, not the message.

In recent years there has been some controversy as to the proper order in which to read the books. Indeed, their publisher renumbered the series, driving Narnia purists to distraction. The reasoning behind this was to put the stories in order of Narnia chronology. Though this makes sense, we feel that *The Lion, the Witch & the Wardrobe* is such a perfect introduction to Lewis' world and the children that it should be read first, followed by *The Magician's Nephew, Prince Caspian, The Voyage of the Dawn Treader, The Silver Chair, The Horse and His Boy,* and *The Last Battle.*

Circling the Globe: A Young People's Guide to
Countries and Cultures of the World   REFERENCE

EDITOR: Sue Grabham
HC: Kingfisher
THEMES: geography; history, general; cultural diversity; maps

A one-volume tour through every country on Earth. An excellent reference and fun to read.

Cleopatra
PICTURE BOOK BIOGRAPHY

AUTHOR/ILLUSTRATOR: Diane Stanley
HC: Morrow
THEMES: ancient history; biography; ancient Egypt; maps; Cleopatra; strong women

Many people think of Cleopatra as one of the ancient queens of Egypt. Although she was born in 69 BC, the pyramids already had been there for about 2,500 years. She was a queen at eighteen years old and died when she was 39. In addition to fascinating information about her life, this picture biography includes notes of ancient sources, maps, a pronunciation guide and a bibliography.

Cowboy Country
PICTURE BOOK

AUTHOR: Ann Herbert Scott • ILLUSTRATOR: Ted Lewin
HC: Clarion
THEMES: cowboys; grandfathers; horses; ranches; camping; jobs; U.S.A., the West

A grandfather shows his grandson the ropes in this realistic portrayal of cowboy life. Perfect for horse, western and cowboy lovers.

The Cricket in Times Square
FICTION

AUTHOR: George Selden • ILLUSTRATOR: Garth Williams
HC: Farrar Straus & Giroux • PB: Dell
THEMES: cats; mice; crickets; New York; cities; family; friendship

A street-wise, motormouth mouse named Tucker, his sidekick, a cat named Harry, a kindly boy named Mario Bellini, and a country cricket named Chester make up an unlikely quartet of friends in this loving look at the city of New York in the late 1950's. Mario's parents run a newsstand, though not very successfully, and in between their jaunts uptown and down the four pals manage to find a way to finally bring Mama and Papa Bellini the success they have longed for. Selden's characters make subsequent appearances in *Harry Cat's Pet Puppy, Tucker's Countryside,* and *Harry Kitten and Tucker Mouse,* and several other books.

D'Aulaire's Book of Greek Myths
FOLKLORE COLLECTION

AUTHOR/ILLUSTRATOR: Ingri and Edgar Parin D'Aulaire
HC: Doubleday • PB: Dell
THEMES: Greek mythology; heroes; ancient history; folklore; ancient Greece

Arguably the best single-volume look at Greek mythology for kids. The D'Aulaires cover every major character and many of the minor ones in a readable and engaging style that has set the standard for mythology writing since the 1940s. If you only need one book on the subject, this is it.

The Day of the Dead:
A Mexican-American Celebration   PICTURE BOOK NONFICTION

AUTHOR: Diane Hoyt-Goldsmith • ILLUSTRATOR: Lawrence Migdale (photographs)

HC/PB: Holiday House

THEMES: Day of the Dead; celebrations; traditions; Mexican culture; Spanish words; death; remembrance

Twins Ximena and Azucena gather with their relatives to enjoy the traditional Day Of The Dead celebration. Hoyt-Goldsmith's description of this Mexican American holiday is accented with detailed photographs of decorations, foods, and the community celebrating at a nearby cemetery. This author/photographer duo has created a rich resource of books about a variety of subjects. Some of these are: *Apache Rodeo, Buffalo Days, Celebrating Hanukkah, Celebrating Kwanzaa,* and *Pueblo Storyteller.*

★ Dear Mr. Henshaw   FICTION

AUTHOR: Beverly Cleary • ILLUSTRATOR: Paul O. Zelinsky

HC: Morrow • PB: Avon

THEMES: writing; mail; authors; gentle boys; trucks; loneliness; single parents

Moving and gently written, this is the bittersweet story of Leigh Botts, a lonely boy who misses his absent father and reaches out through letters to a writer of children's books. Sensitively exploring Leigh's heartache, Cleary has created one of her most memorable characters in a departure from her Henry, Beezus, and Ramona books, and won the Newbery Award in the process.

Dinosaurs!: Strange and Wonderful   PICTURE BOOK

AUTHOR: Laurence Pringle • ILLUSTRATOR: Carol Heyer

HC: Boyd Mills • PB: Penguin

THEMES: dinosaurs; variety

A good, one-volume dinosaur reference book, full of colorful illustrations and paleontological facts, from an accomplished nonfiction writer.

Dippers   PICTURE BOOK

AUTHOR: Barbara Nichol • ILLUSTRATOR: Barry Moser
HC: Tundra
THEMES: Canada; illness; mystery; mothers and daughters; fantasy;
community

This is a strangely inviting tale, perfect for reading aloud. It tells of the
time, long ago, when the dippers came to town, large flying animals,
with leathery wings and big eyes, that resemble daschunds. No one
knows where they came from. Some people are bothered by them, and
others aren't. With an air of mystery and in a tone that serves hushed
remembrance, Nichol has crafted a tale that is remarkable as much for
what it leaves out as for what it contains. Moser's illustrations are so
good we can't imagine them done by another artist.

Draw 50 Series   ACTIVITY

AUTHOR/ILLUSTRATOR: Lee J.Ames
PB: Doubleday
THEMES: art; drawing

Everything the budding artist wants to draw is covered in one of these
books. Simple and straightforward, with tips to help the absolute begin-
ner as well as those more comfortable holding a pencil, titles include
*Draw 50 Cats, Draw 50 People, Draw 50 Athletes, Draw 50 Creepy Crawlies,
Draw 50 Famous Cartoons,* and *Draw 50 Dinosaurs and Other Prehistoric
Animals.*

A Drop of Water   PICTURE BOOK NONFICTION

AUTHOR/ILLUSTRATOR: Walter Wick (photographs)
HC: Scholastic
THEMES: water; photographs: magnification; vocabulary; science
experiments

Extraordinary photography magnifies water in its many states—steam,
frost, ice, dew, rainbow—each explained in simple text. Sit down with a
cool, awesome glass of water and enjoy each page.

The Eagle's Gift   PICTURE BOOK

AUTHOR: Rafe Martin • ILLUSTRATOR: Tatsuro Kiuchi
HC: Putnam
THEMES: Alaska; Inuit; folklore; joy; storytelling; journeys; coming of
age; dance; singing

A magical retelling of the Inuit people's legend of how joy was brought to them. Martin's gift for sensitive and powerful storytelling is complemented by Kiuchi's evocative illustrations. This reads aloud very well and belongs in all collections of Alaskan folklore.

East o' the Sun and West o' the Moon　　　FOLKLORE COLLECTION
TRANSLATED BY: George W. Dasent • ILLUSTRATOR: P.J. Lynch
HC/PB: Candlewick
THEMES: fantasy; magic; Norway; fairy tales; comparisons; mystery; adventure; love

Hags, heroes, spells and magic, they're here in breathtaking pictures and spellbinding words. Don't limit this to the younger set. This picture-book gem is perfect for any adventure-lover who enjoys an exciting story and the aesthetics of fine art.

Oftentimes when a child learns to read, we take away his art. After all, chapter books are a sign of advancement, and picture books? I'm afraid they are left for the younger set. Don't let that happen here.

The Elements Series　　　PICTURE BOOK NONFICTION
AUTHOR/ILLUSTRATOR: Ken Robbins (photographs)
HC: Henry Holt
THEMES: nature; fire; air; water; earth; environment

Earth, Air, Fire, and *Water* are all depicted in Robbins' hand-tinted, black and white photographs, making these books works of art as well as informative. With a strong ecological voice, Robbins serves as both guide and voice of reason in his tour of the planet and its four classic elements.

Eloise　　　PICTURE BOOK
AUTHOR: Kay Thompson • ILLUSTRATOR: Hilary Knight
HC: Simon & Schuster
THEMES: hotels; mischief; New York; strong girls; humor

The sensibilities and humor are decidedly adult, but two generations of children have grown up to the adventures of the little girl who lives at the Plaza Hotel, and the next will surely follow. What makes Eloise work is her sheer, rampant self-absorption—the world exists for her and her alone. This child-centered view is especially funny when taken to the extreme of having a little girl terrorize the staff and guests of New York's finest hotel. Thompson's language is affected and starchy and Knight's illustrations are old-fashioned and only in two colors, but these are part of the charm, so enjoy!

Emily
PICTURE BOOK

AUTHOR: Michael Bedard • ILLUSTRATOR: Barbara Cooney
HC: Doubleday
THEMES: individuality; shyness; writing; authors

Elegant writing combined with Cooney's usual fine paintings make this a treasure for anyone interested in the story of this reclusive writer. An imagined encounter between a young girl and poet Emily Dickinson is rendered with sensitivity and a feel for the period.

The Enormous Egg
FICTION

AUTHOR: Oliver Butterworth • ILLUSTRATOR: Louis Darling
HC/PB: Little Brown
THEMES: dinosaurs; farms; love; pets; responsibility; surprises; comparisons; science; scientists; eggs

A chicken lays an egg that hatches a triceratops and a young boy struggles to balance his pet's needs and the media circus that ensues. Young Nate does the best he can, but it isn't every day a real dinosaur makes the papers. With the help of a kindly scientist it all turns out OK in the end, but along the way this fantasy moves from rural New England to Washington, D.C., and the adventures that follow are the sort you might expect when an extinct species makes a sudden reappearance. Folksy and full of fun, and Louis Darling's illustrations are, well, darling.

Extra Innings: Baseball Poems
POETRY ANTHOLOGY

SELECTED BY: Lee Bennett Hopkins • ILLUSTRATOR: Scott Medlock
HC: Harcourt Brace
THEMES: baseball

For kids more into baseball than poetry, this collection just may get them reading.

Extremely Weird Animal Defenses
PICTURE BOOK

AUTHOR: Sarah Lovett • ILLUSTRATOR: Various (photographs)
PB: John Muir
THEMES: nature; animals

This series features close-up, color photographs of some of the most biz-zare members of the animal kingdom. Full of interesting facts presented in an entertaining style, these books work with nature buffs as well as kids who are only interested in the strange or gross. Other titles include: *Extremely Weird Animal Disguises*, *Extremely Weird Bats*, *Extremely Weird Endangered Species*, *Extremely Weird Frogs*, *Extremely Weird Insects*, *Extremely Weird Micro Monsters*, *Extremely Weird Reptiles*, and *Extremely Weird Spiders*.

The Faithful Friend
PICTURE BOOK

AUTHOR: Robert San Souci • ILLUSTRATOR: Brian Pinkney
HC: Simon & Schuster
THEMES: friendship; loyalty; Caribbean; folklore; zombies; magic; comeuppance

A folktale of loyalty, magic, and just deserts set on the island of Mar-tinique. San Souci's sparkling prose gives an immediacy to the tale, and as Hippolyte bravely sacrifices himself to save the life of his friend, you cannot help but be captivated. Pinkney's art has the vivid palate of the tropics and the warmth of friendship throughout. Folklorist San Souci has amassed a body of story retellings that set the standard for solid research (he always includes fascinating notes about where he found the stories and how he chose to adapt them), as well as spirited retellings that affect the flavor of the culture he is portraying. Whether it is the Blackfoot Indians of *The Legend of Scarface* (illustrated by his brother, Daniel San Souci), or in the American South his other collabo-rations with Brian Pinkney including *The Boy and the Ghost*, *Sukey and the Mermaid* and *The Hired Hand*, his authenticity is never in question. This is a writer who loves folklore and has given the gift of his love to children a hundred times over.

The Feather Merchants and Other Tales of the Fools of Chelm
FOLKLORE COLLECTION

AUTHOR: Steve Sanfield • ILLUSTRATOR: Mikhail Magaril
HC: Orchard
THEMES: folklore; Chelm; fools; humor

Storyteller Sanfield's first word to the reader is, "Enjoy!"—and you will. His voice is so clear that you can hear the telling as you read these thir-teen hilarious tales about the ridiculous folks of Chelm. Enjoy!

Fiesta   PICTURE BOOK NONFICTION

AUTHOR/ILLUSTRATOR: George Ancona (photographs)

HC: Lodestar

THEMES: celebrations; folklore; Mexican American; festivals; Mexican culture; holidays; Day of the Dead; San Francisco; New Mexico; Spanish words; New York

Ancona's vibrant photographs capture the spirit of four fiestas celebrated by Mexican Americans in the United States. Costumed marchers carry candles through the streets of San Francisco to celebrate The Day of The Dead. In Albuquerque, New Mexico, farolitas light the way for participants in Las Posadas. On New Years Day in Northern New Mexico strangely dressed figures are led by a masked man with a whip in his hand. And on January 7, folks in East Harlem celebrate Three King's Day. If this books catches your attention, look for *Powwow,* also by Ancona.

The Floating House   PICTURE BOOK

AUTHOR: Scott Russell Sanders • ILLUSTRATOR: Helen Cogancherry

HC: Macmillan

THEMES: Indiana; boats; pioneers; U.S. history, frontier life

It's 1815 and this pioneer family is heading west, not in a covered wagon, but on the Ohio River, along with keelboats, skiffs, canoes, barges and rafts. Here's a new look at how settlers traveled.

Folks Call Me Appleseed John   PICTURE BOOK

AUTHOR/ILLUSTRATOR: Andrew Glass

HC: Doubleday

THEMES: apples; folklore; tall tales; biography; journeys; brothers

Children start hearing tall tales when they're young, but they don't always know that many of these stories grow from seeds of truth. This one is based on stories that John Chapman, the real Johnny Appleseed liked to tell. Glass adds his own homespun humor along with biographical notes and a map of his travels.

The Fool of the World and the Flying Ship   PICTURE BOOK

AUTHOR/ILLUSTRATOR: Christopher Denise

HC: Philomel

THEMES: folklore; Russia; mice; cooperation; fools; flying boats

Overflowing with odd characters, this Russian folktale is about a mouse who is considered a fool by his family. He sets out on an impossible journey to win the hand of a princess. Read this aloud! Children will root for this zany bunch who prove that by sticking together they can accomplish even the toughest task.

Gary Paulsen's World of Adventure Series   FICTION
AUTHOR: **Gary Paulsen**
PB: Dell
THEMES: adventure; courage; friendship

Short, action-packed, featuring both boys and girls in leading roles, and about everything from exploring caves to video games—these are perfect for kids who won't read because they think it's boring.

The Gentleman and the Kitchen Maid   PICTURE BOOK
AUTHOR: Diane Stanley • ILLUSTRATOR: Dennis Nolan
HC: Dial • PB: Puffin
THEMES: art; paintings; artists; problem solving; cleverness; museums; love; strong girls

Great art comes to life in the enchanting fantasy of two paintings that fall in love with each other, and the young artist who brings them together.

Getting to Know the World's
Great Artists Series   PICTURE BOOK BIOGRAPHY
AUTHOR/ILLUSTRATOR: Mike Venezia
PB: Children's Press
THEMES: art; paintings; artists; sculpture

A nicely made, low priced introduction to some of the most famous painters, their lives and work. Artists include Paul Klee, Botticelli, Rembrandt, Mary Cassatt, Edward Hopper, Diego Rivera, and Monet.

Giants in the Land   PICTURE BOOK NONFICTION
AUTHOR: Diana Appelbaum • ILLUSTRATOR: Michael McCurdy
HC: Houghton Mifflin
THEMES: trees; environment; life cycle; U.S. history, Colonial America

Scratchboard pictures show the human skill and ingenuity that ultimately led to the end of giant trees chopped down during Colonial times to be sent across the ocean to England. The giant forests are gone. Nothing paints a clearer picture of the future than a good strong peek into the past.

The Glass Bottle Tree
PICTURE BOOK

AUTHOR: Evelyn Coleman • ILLUSTRATOR: Gail Gordon Carter
HC: Orchard
THEMES: grandmothers; family; ancestors; African American; magic

An unusual story about the African American practice of putting bottles on tree limbs to hold the spirits of ancestors. The relationship between the young girl and her grandmother is sensitively portrayed.

The Golden Carp and Other Tales From Vietnam
FOLKLORE COLLECTION

AUTHOR: Lynette Dyer Vuong • ILLUSTRATOR: Manabu Saito
HC: Lothrop
THEMES: Vietnam; history; folklore; traditions; Vietnamese culture; Vietnamese words

Tales of ancient Vietnam—through the jungle, along the coast, into a city and out to the countryside. For the history buffs, author's notes tell about the history and customs, and there's a pronunciation guide to Vietnamese names. Also see: *The Brocaded Slipper and Other Vietnamese Tales.*

Golem: A Giant Made of Mud
PICTURE BOOK

AUTHOR/ILLUSTRATOR: Mark Podwal
HC: Greenwillow
THEMES: folklore; monsters; Jews; clay; magic; Prague

A terrific version of the classic Jewish folktale. Full of mayhem, making this attractive to kids who might otherwise shun classic tales.

The Good, the Bad, and the Goofy
FICTION

AUTHOR: Jon Scieszka • ILLUSTRATOR: Lane Smith
HC: Viking • PB: Puffin
THEMES: time travel; adventure; humor

This is great to give to reluctant readers, as it is action packed and full of fun! A rollicking set of adventures through time and space, full of laughs. When your child finishes this one, there are several more, including *Your Mother Was a Neanderthal, Knights of the Kitchen Table, The Not-So-Jolly Roger*, and *2095*.

Grandmother Bryant's Pocket   PICTURE BOOK

AUTHOR: Jacqueline Briggs Martin • ILLUSTRATOR: Petra Mathers
HC: Houghton Mifflin
THEMES: loss; grandparents; herbs; wisdom; patience; courage; Colonial America; U.S.A., New England; yearning; healing

A small book that holds a lot of wisdom. During Colonial times, young Sarah is sent from her Maine home to get away from the memories of a barn fire, and goes to live with her grandparents. The remedies of herbs and time work their magic, ministered by Grandmother Bryant, Shoe Peg (her grandfather), and a one-eyed cat. A simple and lovely look at grief and healing.

The Graphic Alphabet   PICTURE BOOK

AUTHOR/ILLUSTRATOR: David Pelletier
HC: Orchard
THEMES: alphabet; language; point of view

Each letter takes on a graphic story of its own in this visual alphabet. The top of the A falls off in an avalanche. B bounces across the page. C circles in motion. D turns down to the devil. A turn of the page presents a separate work of art where vivid colors on black squares create an alphabet for those who know their letters. For another take on this concept, see: *The Z Was Zapped*.

The Great Piratical Rumbustification   FICTION

AUTHOR: Margaret Mahy • ILLUSTRATOR: Quentin Blake
HC: Godine • PB: Beech Tree
THEMES: pirates; parties; librarians; change; reading

This story and its companion, *The Librarian and the Robbers*, form a pair of reading delights in this slim volume, but be assured, there is plenty here to entrance the reader. Mahy's devil-may-care prose and vocabulary may challenge beginning readers, so we suggest these be read aloud. You will enjoy the tale of a pirate party to end all parties and then the story of a librarian who is kidnapped but winds up teaching her captors the love of reading.

Green Tales   FOLKLORE COLLECTION

AUTHOR/ILLUSTRATOR: Beatrice Tanaka
HC: 4 Walls & 8 Windows
THEMES: folklore; environment; cultural diversity

Eight tales from eight cultures all illustrate the need for man to be mindful of his connection to the Earth—often with warnings of dire consequences when that connection is ignored. Oral tradition tales that read and tell beautifully.

Hailstones and Halibut Bones   POETRY COLLECTION

AUTHOR: Mary O'Neill • ILLUSTRATOR: John Wallner
HC/PB: Doubleday
THEMES: poetry; color; similies

Vibrant poems about color that leap off the page. Used by schools for the blind to instruct their students about the world of colors, this is a masterpiece of descriptive writing and will encourage artists and writers to reach for new heights. We all need a lesson on seeing now and then, and boy, does this book offer one.

★ Half Magic   FICTION-FANTASY

AUTHOR: Edward Eager • ILLUSTRATOR: N.M. Bodecker
HC/PB: Harcourt Brace
THEMES: magic; family; reading; responsibility; fantasy; adventure; books; single parents

Jane, Mark, Katherine, and Martha have their lives turned upside down by a magic coin that grants exactly half of what its holder wishes. The first of seven marvelous adventures in the realm of magic by Eager, each featuring literate and clever children who must learn to tame the magic in their possession. Though they are old-fashioned—they were written in the 1950s but have the feel of classic children's fantasy—they hold up very well and make delightful read alouds. Eager connects the books in clever ways, with *Magic by the Lake* being a sequel to *Half Magic* and Jane and company making a guest appearance in *Seven Day Magic*. Katherine and Martha's children (Roger, Ann, Jack, and Eliza) take center stage in *The Knight's Castle* and its sequel, *The Time Garden*. Kip, Gordy, James, Laura, Lydia, and Deborah are introduced in *Magic or Not?* and their adventures continue in *The Well-Wishers*. It's a good thing there are this many, as reading one will just make you want to read more!

Harris and Me   FICTION

AUTHOR/ILLUSTRATOR: **Gary Paulsen**
HC: Harcourt Brace • PB: Dell
THEMES: friendship; adventure; humor, adolescent

One of the funniest books we have read! Great fun with the best pair of friends since Tom and Huck. If you aren't embarrassed by bodily function humor, this is a great read aloud to fifth graders—we guarantee they will listen!

Heartland   PICTURE BOOK
AUTHOR: Diane Siebert • ILLUSTRATOR: Wendell Minor
HC/PB: HarperCollins
THEMES: poem; U.S.A., the prairie

Glorious, epic, demands-to-be-read-aloud poetry highlights each of Siebert's books, three of them odes to distinctive geographic regions of the USA (*Heartland, Sierra* and *Mojave*—each with illustrations by Wendell Minor), and three of them songs of transportation (*Truck Song, Plane Song,* and *Train Song*). Her poetry, coupled with fine illustrations for each book, offers a beautiful introduction to both the grandeur of her subjects and the lyrical power of poetry.

Her Stories   FOLKLORE COLLECTION
AUTHOR: **Virginia Hamilton** • ILLUSTRATOR: Leo & Diane Dillon
HC: Blue Sky Press
THEMES: African American; strong girls; biography; folklore

Strong women abound in this collection of tales and biographies of inspiring African American women.

★ Hey World, Here I Am!   POETRY COLLECTION
AUTHOR: Jean Little • ILLUSTRATOR: Sue Truesdell
HC/PB: HarperCollins
THEMES: writing; family; friendship; self respect; school

When I get up in front of a large group of people, sometimes I reach into my "insurance" bag for quotable treasures from books to help me through the first few minutes of shaky quivers. Jean Little's Hey World, Here I Am! *is one of my all-time favorites. She gets to the heart of things with humor and candid insights of a girl named Kate Bloomfield. I can go to any page and find a poem, or a vignette that opens my audience to me with a shared experience. But I can't quote an example here. From* Today *and* About Notebooks *to* After English Class *and* Louisa Louisa, *I can't bear to quote just a part—the whole is required. So, find this gem, fall into a cozy chair and read all or part before handing it over to your child to savor.*

The High Rise Glorious Skittle Skat Roarious Sky Pie Angel Food Cake
PICTURE BOOK

AUTHOR: Nancy Willard • ILLUSTRATOR: Richard Jesse Watson
HC/PB: Harcourt Brace
THEMES: angels; mothers and daughters; cake; baking; family; secrets; magic; love

A young girl's wish to make a truly special present for her mother's birthday is heard by a trio of angels. Full of love, humor, and magic, this is a combination of the work of a master storyteller and a gifted artist that makes a great gift and a story that will become a family favorite.

Hip Cat
PICTURE BOOK

AUTHOR: Jonathan London • ILLUSTRATOR: Woodleigh Hubbard
HC: Chronicle
THEMES: jazz; rhythm; music; individuality

Jazzy and very cool, this is a fabulous read-aloud picture book. Caution: the complex rhythms mimic those of an improvisational jazz performance. Read it through a few times to get comfortable with them and, like the hip cat daddy-o title character, you'll be the toast of the town with this delightful ode to individuality and music.

Honey, I Love and Other Love Poems
POETRY COLLECTION

AUTHOR: Eloise Greenfield • ILLUSTRATOR: Leo and Diane Dillon
HC/PB: HarperCollins
THEMES: African American; love; children; family

Sixteen "love" poems from a child's perspective tell of family, friends, train rides and jumping rope. Open to any page and rejoice in the Dillons' art, then read one aloud to someone you love.

Hoover's Bride
PICTURE BOOK

AUTHOR/ILLUSTRATOR: David Small
HC: Crown
THEMES: zany; love; humor; fantasy

This absurdly twisted picture book tale told in rhyme of a man who falls in love with a vacuum cleaner will have kids rolling in the aisles. Adults may appreciate it as well, but we suspect for different reasons.

READING FOR PLEASURE

Create time in your child's life to read for pleasure. In the midst of our hurried lives, when we see our kids settling down with a book, it's hard not to say, "Isn't there something you should be doing?" "Don't you have homework?" Help them find time during the day to experience the excitement of reading a book of their choice. This should be part of every child's daily routine.

How a Book Is Made   PICTURE BOOK NONFICTION

AUTHOR/ILLUSTRATOR: Aliki
HC/PB: HarperCollins
THEMES: books; authors; illustrators; color; creativity; writing; patience; reading

With thoroughness, Aliki shows how the author gets the idea, the idea gets written down, the publisher decides to publish, and the book gets made as well as sold, allowing the reader to follow the process every step of the way. The information is conveyed in a two-level method, with the main story in larger type and the more detailed nuts and bolts in smaller type, but what nuts and bolts they are! You can learn all you want to know about the mechanics of publishing a book here, making this an excellent book to use with writers, young and old.

I Want to Be a Dancer   PICTURE BOOK NONFICTION

AUTHOR: Stephanie Maze • ILLUSTRATOR: various (photographs)
HC: Harcourt Brace
THEMES: careers; dance; jobs; dancers

Emphasizing all forms of dance, not just the usual ballet, here's a terrific photo essay about a career that intrigues a lot of girls at certain points in life. In depth and full of basic information, this is part of a series of books on careers, which include: *I Want to Be an Astronaut*, *I Want to Be an Engineer*, and *I Want to Be a Veterinarian*.

In a Messy, Messy Room &
Other Scary Stories   SHORT STORY COLLECTION

AUTHOR: Judith Gorog • ILLUSTRATOR: Kimberly Bulcken Root
HC: Philomel • PB: HarperCollins
THEMES: scary stories; mystery

Gorog tells stories that get under your skin. You can't forget her imagery, and kids especially are drawn to her style of writing—she draws them in, hooks them, leads them along her well-plotted path and then she yanks the rug out from under them in the last paragraph. Perfect to read aloud, this collection of her stories will work for third grade up through middle school, and they are easy enough to read that they can be used with older kids who shy away from everything else.

In the Beginning: Creation Stories
From Around the World   FOLKLORE COLLECTION
AUTHOR: **Virginia Hamilton** • ILLUSTRATOR: Barry Moser
HC/PB: Harcourt Brace
THEMES: folklore; creation; cultural diversity

All peoples have explanations for how the world got here. Hamilton gives us a fascinating look at many cultures and their stories.

In the Next Three Seconds   PICTURE BOOK NONFICTION
AUTHOR: Rowland Morgan • ILLUSTRATOR: Rod and Kira Josey
HC: Lodestar
THEMES: animals; guessing; weather; future; comparisons; math; trivia; environment; health

In the next three seconds amazing things will happen. If you like predictions, here you'll find them . . . "In the next three seconds Italians will drink a stack of cases of mineral water as high as the Statue of Liberty." "In the next three hours Americans will use paper that requires 375,000 trees to make." "In the next three thousand years . . . based on present trends, the icy North and South poles will have melted." Not only will you enjoy the author's forecasts, but by the time you've finished this over-sized book of illustrated trivia, you will have learned to make your own calculations and predictions! Fascinating and sometimes disturbing. You'll find yourself (and your kids) saying "Really?", a lot while reading this.

★ Josepha: A Prairie Boy's Story   PICTURE BOOK
AUTHOR: Jim McGugan • ILLUSTRATOR: Murray Kimber
HC: Chronicle
THEMES: gifts; farms; misunderstanding; literacy; language; immigration; great plains; Canada; farming; school; friendship; teachers

Josepha was needed on the farm and school was hard so he had to say good-bye to his teacher and friend. This powerful story not only shows a facet of pioneer life we have read little about, but it also gives a voice to the many children who feel isolated in school today.

Katya's Book of Mushrooms   PICTURE BOOK
AUTHOR: Katya Arnold • ILLUSTRATOR: Sam Swope and Katya Arnold
HC: Henry Holt
THEMES: mushrooms; folklore; healing; nature

A thoroughly entertaining look at a fascinating subject. Everything you want to know about mushrooms, their lore, uses and dangers is detailed in this compulsively readable book.

Keepers of the Earth: Native American Stories and Environmental Activities for Children   FOLKLORE COLLECTION
AUTHOR: M.Caduto and J. Bruchac • ILLUSTRATOR: J.K. Fadden and C. Wood
HC: Fulcrum
THEMES: Native American; environment; animals; plants; crafts; nature

Keepers of the Earth is the first of an incredible trilogy packed full of Native American stories, information, and projects to help children appreciate and conserve our natural world. Other titles include: *Keepers of the Animals* and *Keepers of Life:Discovering Plants Through Native American Stories and Earth Activities for Children*.

King of the Wind   FICTION
AUTHOR: Marguerite Henry • ILLUSTRATOR: Dennis Wesley
PB: Aladdin
THEMES: adventure; Mideast; racing; horses

If you have a horse lover on your hands, introduce her to this classic, Newbery Award-winning novel about a champion race horse, by the author of *Misty of Chincoteague*.

Kingfisher Science Encyclopedia   REFERENCE
AUTHOR/ILLUSTRATOR/EDITOR: Kingfisher
HC: Kingfisher
THEMES: science

A solid one-volume, all-purpose science reference. The organization and design are very appealing and we could find what we were looking for easily.

Kite Flier   PICTURE BOOK

AUTHOR: Dennis Haseley • ILLUSTRATOR: David Wiesner
HC: Four Winds • PB: Aladdin
THEMES: kites; fathers and sons; loss; coming of age; separation;
artists; single parents; crafts

A powerful (and not easy) picture book about fathers and sons, loss,
manhood and how we all have to find a means of expression that is true
to ourselves, especially when words fail us.

The Knight's Castle   FICTION-FANTASY

AUTHOR: Edward Eager • ILLUSTRATOR: N.M. Bodecker
HC/PB: Harcourt Brace
THEMES: magic; time travel; family; reading; books; responsibility;
medieval England; knights; adventure

Journey back in time to the days of Ivanhoe in this magical adventure
from the author of *Half Magic*.

Larger Than Life: The Adventures of
American Legendary Heroes   FOLKLORE COLLECTION

AUTHOR: Robert San Souci • ILLUSTRATOR: Andrew Glass
HC: Doubleday • PB: Dell
THEMES: folklore; tall tales; storytelling

A terrific collection of tall tales by a master reteller. Included are the stories of
Paul Bunyan, Sluefoot Sue, Old Stormalong, Strap Buckner, and John Henry.

The Librarian Who Measured
the Earth   PICTURE BOOK BIOGRAPHY

AUTHOR: **Kathryn Lasky** • ILLUSTRATOR: Kevin Hawkes
HC: Little Brown
THEMES: math; language; biography; ancient Greece; geography;
Eratosthenes; punctuation; librarians

Over 2,000 years ago a very smart baby was born . . . His name was
Eratosthenes. In his lifetime he asked a lot of questions, and he wrote
the first geography book. . . . invented punctuation and grammar . . .
made the first map of the world . . . used a grapefruit to measure the
earth (and was only about 200 miles off by today's standards). A fascinating picture biography!

AUTHOR SPOTLIGHT ON KATHRYN LASKY

Kathryn Lasky's ability to write fiction and nonfiction for all ages puts her in a very select group of authors, who continually amaze us. We're not talking about the kind of writers who are known primarily for one genre of book and then dabble in another—Lasky can and does write fiction, both contemporary and historical, with the same level of assurance and quality that she does nonfiction or picture books.

Because of her storytelling gift, Lasky writes nonfiction in a thoroughly engaging style, resulting in books that are informative and entertaining. She is one of the few writers to receive a Newbery Honor for a nonfiction work, for *Sugaring Time*, an account of the Vermont tradition of gathering maple sap to make maple syrup. A writer of a wide range of interests, Lasky happens to be married to gifted photographer Christopher G. Knight. They have collaborated on a variety of remarkable photo essays, including *Days of the Dead, Monarchs* (about butterflies), *The Most Beautiful Roof in the World* (the rain forest), and *Searching for Laura Ingalls: A Reader's Journey*, which we recommend as a supplement to any child's enjoyment of the *Little House on the Prairie* books.

Venturing into the realm of picture book biography, Lasky wrote *The Librarian Who Measured the Earth* (illustrated by Kevin Hawkes), which tells the story of Eratosthenes, an ancient Greek who, among other feats, accurately determined the circumference of the Earth thousands of years before modern science.

Her picture books are a diverse lot, ranging from her somber original Native American tale *Cloud Eyes* (illustrated by Barry Moser) to her inspiring account of a seventy-five-year-old woman's learning to swim, *Sea Swan* (illustrated by Catherine Stock). A marvelous sense of place and time enhances most of her work, none more so than *Marven of the Great North Woods* (illustrated by Kevin Hawkes), based on her father's childhood adventure in a logging camp. Her love of Boston flavors both the warmly engaging *I Have an Aunt on Marlborough Street* (illustrated by Susan Guevara) and the historically accurate and often absurdly humorous retelling of the founding of the Audubon Society, *She's Wearing a Dead Bird on Her Head!* (illustrated by David Catrow). For younger readers, her delightful story of the trials and tribulations of the cafeteria, *Lunch Bunnies* (illustrated by Marilyn Hafner), will give confidence and more than a few giggles.

In the area of fiction, Lasky has struck gold with her *Starbuck Family Adventures*, three exciting novels about two pairs of telepathic twins and the mysteries they solve. These are examples of the very best formula fiction; bridging the gap between science fiction and mystery, they are perfect books to give to adventure-hungry fourth and fifth graders. The individual titles are: *A Voice in the Wind, Double Trouble Squared,* and *Shadows in the Water.*

Lasky's novel *Memoirs of a Bookbat* is one of her most powerful, dealing with the issue of book banning and fundamentalism. Harper Jessup is a reader, the kind of kid who always has a book going. As she relates the story of her family's near collapse and then salvation through conversion to a fundamentalist faith she shares the titles of the books she is reading along the way. Through reading she has learned to have a open and inquiring mind, and when her family becomes instrumental in the banning of books in their community, she realizes that she is part of what her parents are against and not one of them, in this book of tough choices and coming of age. These characteristics are also found in Lasky's historical fiction, ranging from her first novel *Night Journey* (illustrated by Trina Schart Hyman), a gripping story of escape and emigration from Tsarist Russia, to her chronicles of American history *Beyond the Burning Time* (about the Salem Witch Trials), *True North: A Novel of the Underground Railroad,* and her superb account of a young Amish girl's westward trek, *Beyond the Divide.*

In all of her writing, Lasky's respect for the reader shines. She knows that if she can write about something she finds interesting and tell a good story, she has done her job. No matter what the subject or format, Lasky never lets the reader down—her name on a book is a sign of quality and a promise from a storyteller that a treasure lies waiting within.

Little Folk: Stories From Around the World   FOLKLORE COLLECTION

AUTHOR: Paul Robert Walker • ILLUSTRATOR: James Bernardin
HC: Harcourt Brace
THEMES: fairies; little folk; cultural diversity; magic; folklore; leprechauns

Walker and illustrator James Bernardin, who also created *Giants!*, take on the pixies, fairies, sprites, gnomes and leprechauns of world folklore. Terrific notes follow each tale.

The Little House on the Prairie   FICTION

AUTHOR: Laura Ingalls Wilder • ILLUSTRATOR: Garth Williams
HC/PB: HarperCollins
THEMES: commmunity; relatives; courage; change; U.S. history, frontier life; U.S. history, Westward movement; U.S.A., the prairie; family

TV promoted *The Little House on the Prairie,* making it the most familiar and most often requested of the books by Laura Ingalls Wilder. Published in 1932, *Little House in the Big Woods* was the first of nine books about Laura Ingalls and her family. Lest you think, however, that TV is the only reason these have stood the test of time, we want to assure you that there may be no finer depiction of American prairie life in all of fiction. Beginning in a log house in Wisconsin when Laura was a young girl, the series takes the family west by covered wagon and ends with grown-up Laura marrying, moving with her husband into their own homestead and giving birth to their daughter.

Others in the series: *Farmer Boy, On the Banks of Plum Creek, By the Shores of Silver Lake, The Long Winter, Little Town on the Prairie, These Happy Golden Years, The First Four Years.*

Little Ships: The Heroic Rescue at
Dunkirk in World War II   PICTURE BOOK

AUTHOR: Louise Borden • ILLUSTRATOR: Michael Foreman
HC: McElderry
THEMES: history, World War II; boats; strong girls; courage; community; England; rescue

Gripping stuff—the kind of storytelling that makes history come alive. The amazing story of the evacuation at Dunkirk is told through the eyes of a young girl, a passenger on her father's boat. Her narration makes this moment of epic bravery into a personal event, thereby reminding us that great moments in history happened to real people, not just names in a book.

Lives of the Athletes: Thrills, Spills (and What the Neighbors Thought)   BIOGRAPHY COLLECTION

AUTHOR: Kathleen Krull • ILLUSTRATOR: Kathryn Hewitt
HC: Harcourt Brace
THEMES: athletes; sports; biographies; cultural diversity; humor; trivia

Before a game Babe Ruth would say "I feel hitterish today." Of course that's not a surprise coming from a man who hit more than seven hundred home runs at a time when home runs were rare. This is the kind of information you can find about athletes—from Jim Thorpe to Flo Hyman, from football to volleyball—in this biographical collection of star athletes and their fears, habits and quirks.

★ Lives of the Musicians: Good Times, Bad Times (and What the Neighbors Thought)   BIOGRAPHY COLLECTION

AUTHOR: Kathleen Krull • ILLUSTRATOR: Kathryn Hewitt
HC: Harcourt Brace
THEMES: biography; music; humor; creativity; cultural diversity

Personal stories of twenty musicians from Vivaldi to Woody Guthrie. What a way to take children into the past! Give them details, individual quirks, the behind the scenes nitty gritty. Beethoven "couldn't be bothered with clean or stylish clothes. When his clothes became too dirty and disgusting, his friends took them away during the night and brought new ones. Beethoven never noticed." Describes the good times and bad times through the life stories of diverse musical figures from Vivaldi to Guthrie. Artists, athletes and writers get the same treatment in Krull and Hewitt's other books in this format.

Lives of the Writers: Comedies, Tragedies (and What the Neighbors Thought)   BIOGRAPHY COLLECTION

AUTHOR: Kathleen Krull • ILLUSTRATOR: Kathryn Hewitt
HC: Harcourt Brace
THEMES: biography; cultural diversity; humor; creativity; authors

Packed full of interesting tidbits about famous authors—like Mark Twain, who was always in some kind of trouble—for putting snakes in his aunt's serving basket, hiding bats in his pockets for his mother to find, or faking death to get out of going to school. Krull's ability to find humorous details in her research make learning about people's lives a delight for children!

Looking for Atlantis   PICTURE BOOK

AUTHOR/ILLUSTRATOR: Colin Thompson
HC: Knopf
THEMES: grandfathers; searching games; love; gifts; treasure; mentors

Organized chaos is the style of illustration that Colin Thompson seems to favor. His remarkable paintings have lots of boxes, corners, straight lines, and frames, all bursting to the max with wild assortments of objects, people, animals, writing and everything else you can imagine. He has clever running gags and recurring characters from book to book and a knack for visual and written puns that many will find addictive. You can spend days looking at his books and not see everything, and for us that is the best part, as we find his stories a bit preachy. *Looking for Atlantis* is a lovely tale of a grandfather's legacy to his grandson—the gift of learning how to truly see. Other titles, such as *The Paper Bag Prince, The Tower to the Sun,* and *How to Live Forever* deal with issues of environmentalism and spirituality, but we tend to ignore the text altogether and just stare in wonder at the art.

Max Makes a Million   PICTURE BOOK

AUTHOR/ILLUSTRATOR: Maira Kalman
HC: Viking
THEMES: jobs; family; yearnings; art; creativity; friendship; zany; writing; poets

Max the poet, the dreamer, the dog, makes his memorable debut. Full of zany characters, richly odd art, fabulous language, and jokes galore, this is at heart a story about growing up and leaving home. It's about the two things every child needs: roots and wings. You will cheer as you watch Max soar on his wings.

Mistakes That Worked   NONFICTION

AUTHOR: Charlotte Foltz Jones • ILLUSTRATOR: John O'Brien
HC/PB: Doubleday
THEMES: inventions; creativity; biography; mistakes; history

A treasure trove of interesting facts and behind-the-scenes information about lots of things we use every day, all of them created unintentionally. Clever line drawings add a touch of humor, enticing nonreaders as well as fact buffs. *Accidents May Happen* is a companion book.

Misty of Chincoteague   FICTION
AUTHOR: Marguerite Henry • ILLUSTRATOR: Wesley Dennis
PB: Aladdin
THEMES: horses; Virginia; captivity; family

For years, the best books about horses came from Marguerite Henry. Though based on real animals, her books are fiction, and her story-telling skills make these engaging reads that children have loved for generations. Misty tells the story of the wild ponies of Asateague Island, Virginia, and the annual pony roundup where the horses are driven across an inlet to captivity. Misty appears again in *Stormy, Misty's Foal.* Other terrific books by Henry include the Newbery-winning *King of the Wind, Brighty of the Grand Canyon,* and *Born to Trot.*

Miz Berlin Walks   PICTURE BOOK
AUTHOR: **Jane Yolen** • ILLUSTRATOR: Floyd Cooper
HC: Philomel
THEMES: storytelling; elderly and children; friendship;

A love song to the power of storytellers, made magical by Yolen's eloquent mastery of language and perfectly matched by the richness of Cooper's illustrations. This is a book to treasure.

Monarchs   PICTURE BOOK NONFICTION
AUTHOR: **Kathryn Lasky** • ILLUSTRATOR: Christopher Knight (photographs)
HC: Gulliver • PB: Harcourt Brace
THEMES: butterflies; migration; geography; life cycle

In a bay off the coast of Maine a single female Monarch butterfly lays four hundred eggs. A new butterfly hatches and then flies more than 2,000 miles in its migration south to California or Mexico. Lasky and her husband, photographer Christopher Knight, show the lives of these monarchs and the people who look forward to their annual migration.

Money, Money, Money: The Meaning of the Art and Symbols on United States Paper Money   PICTURE BOOK NONFICTION
AUTHOR/ILLUSTRATOR: Nancy Winslow Parker
HC: HarperCollins
THEMES: money; government; U.S. history; symbols

Loot. Greenbacks. Scratch. Clams. Moolah. Do you know which bills don't have pictures of presidents? How many $100,000 bills are in circulation? What techniques have been invented to stop counterfeiters? Entertaining and informative, this book provides everything you'll need to know about the history of United States paper money.

The Morgan's Dream   POETRY COLLECTION

AUTHOR: Marilyn Singer • ILLUSTRATOR: Gary Drake
HC: Henry Holt
THEMES: point of view; dreams; family

Exquisite poems revealing the inner lives and dreams of 13 members of the Morgan family. Singer's way of describing dreams is deeply personal and just right for each character. When the book ends, we have learned a great deal about everyone as individuals and as a family. Handy to use with children to help develop the vocabulary to discuss dreams.

Mr. Popper's Penguins   FICTION

AUTHOR: Richard and Florence Atwater
HC/PB: Little Brown
THEMES: penguins; skating; U.S. history, the 1920s; gifts; resourcefulness; problem solving

An unexpected gift of penguins from the explorer Admiral Peary results in a houseful of waddling, fish-eating pets. A classic that produces much hilarity in the scenes of a houseful of penguins and the poor, at wits'-end Popper family. Becoming entertainers seems to be the best solution, and a family of skating, trick-performing penguins is what they become. Delightful.

READ ALOUD TO CHILDREN WHO READ

It's easy to forget that reading aloud goes beyond the pages of a book. This is a powerful opportunity to share a common experience. When your children begin reading, don't desert them. Have them read to you. Take turns reading parts of the same book or alternate books. Remember, this is a natural time for sharing interests and responses, a time to build your quiet connections. Read books to them they wouldn't be inclined to be reading. It's also a good chance for you to catch up on all those classics you never read.

Navajo: Visions and Voices Across the Mesa   POETRY COLLECTION

AUTHOR/ILLUSTRATOR: Shonto Begay
HC: Scholastic
THEMES: Native American; comparison; change; art

Begay has combined twenty of his paintings with poetry and stories that describe the Navajo world—from ancient times to the present high-tech, contemporary white man's world that surrounds him.

Nicholas Pipe   PICTURE BOOK

AUTHOR: Robert San Souci • ILLUSTRATOR: David Shannon

HC: Dial

THEMES: love; sea; taking action; mermaids; strong girls; magic; adventure

A winning collaboration between master storyteller San Souci (here telling an original tale) and artist David Shannon. Seafaring, mermaids, forbidden love—it's all in here. Reads aloud very well.

Only Opal: The Diary of a Young Girl   PICTURE BOOK BIOGRAPHY

AUTHOR: Opal Whiteley & Jane Boulton • ILLUSTRATOR: Barbara Cooney

HC: Philomel • PB: Paperstar

THEMES: U.S. history, early 20th century; death; frontier life; solitude; nature; Oregon; pioneers; biography; diaries; U.S. history, frontier life

Opal Whiteley describes her love of nature and her life following her parents' death at the turn of the century. In this adaptation of her writings the language is rich, and the story brings the reader to a time where a child's day was filled with work, hope, and time to appreciate the quiet of the plants, animals, birds, and space. "When I feel sad inside I talk things over with my tree. I call him Michael Raphael. It is such a comfort to nestle up to Michael Raphael. He is a grand tree. He has an understanding soul." It is a good thing for children to be exposed to all kinds of writing and art. This gem provides fine examples of both.

> **LET YOUR CHILD SEE YOU READ**
>
> In this exhausting working, driving, sports activities, music lesson life we are lucky to read a few minutes before falling asleep at bedtime. If children don't see their parents reading for pleasure—newspapers, magazines or a good book—how will they develop the habit?

Owls in the Family   FICTION

AUTHOR: Farley Mowat • ILLUSTRATOR: Robert Frankenberg

PB: Bantam

THEMES: owls; family; pets; humor; Canada

A youthful reminiscence from one of North America's great nature writers. Billy, Bruce, and Mutt, the stars of Mowat's earlier book *The Dog Who Wouldn't Be*, return, adding Wol and Weeps, a pair of owls, to the family menagerie, driving Mutt crazy and creating several hilarious adventures. Our favorite is the scene where Wol interrupts family dinner by showing off his latest kill—a dead skunk!

Peacebound Trains   FICTION

AUTHOR: Haemi Balgassi • ILLUSTRATOR: Chris Soentpiet
HC: Clarion
THEMES: Korea; war; family; separation; hardship; immigration; trains; peace; memories

A look at the devasting effects war has on families. This war is the Korean conflict, and this family is author Balgassi's mother's. Told in a straightforward style and with luminous art by Soentpiet, this tale of wartime separation will linger in the memory and the heart.

★ The People Could Fly   FOLKLORE COLLECTION

AUTHOR: **Virginia Hamilton** • ILLUSTRATOR: Leo & Diane Dillon
HC/PB: Knopf
THEMES: folklore; African American; storytelling

An outstanding collection of African American folklore, with perfect illustrations by the Dillons. Hamilton's gift for adapting oral tradition stories into written form is unsurpassed.

Pulling the Lion's Tail   PICTURE BOOK

AUTHOR: Jane Kurtz • ILLUSTRATOR: Floyd Cooper
HC: Simon & Schuster
THEMES: Africa; dance; stepparents; lions; patience; wisdom

This retelling of an Ethiopian folktale is a beautiful story about a young girl's attempt to understand her stepmother. Learning about the patience needed to pluck a hair from the tail of a lion seems an unlikely connection to the problem, but Kurtz's retelling has the air of authority needed to pull it off—she lived in Ethiopia for many years. Cooper's art offers an able assist, making this a book of universal appeal that families of all kinds can share, read, and remember.

Puzzle Maps U.S.A

PICTURE BOOK NONFICTION

AUTHOR/ILLUSTRATOR: Nancy L. CIouse
HC: Henry Holt
THEMES: maps; U.S.A., the states; geography; puzzles; shapes

Clouse has taken the shapes of each state, cut them out and mixed them up so that each forms a piece of a puzzle. Some of the shapes are then put together in simple mosaics making up flowers, people and even horses. The trick is to figure out which states (shapes) make up each mosaic. It's a brilliant concept, and useful for the visual learner.

Oh, if only this had been there when I struggled through the memorization of each state and where it fit. Boring! Had this book been available, I would have spent hours of fun while getting geographically wiser. Classroom teachers: after reading this book, give kids a kit of colorful pieces representing each state to create their own "geography art." Classrooms could do exchanges and keep the puzzle going!

The Raggly Scraggly, No-Soap, No-Scrub Girl

PICTURE BOOK

AUTHOR: David F. Birchman • ILLUSTRATOR: Guy Porfirio
HC: Lothrop
THEMES: tall tale; family; baths; meals; visits; dance; strong women; strangers

Wild! A real performance piece for people who like to throw themselves into the telling of a story. An original folktale that, like many, doesn't make a lick o' sense if you think about it—so don't think about it! Just enjoy the terrific tale and the vivid art.

The Rainbow Bridge

PICTURE BOOK

AUTHOR: Audrey Wood • ILLUSTRATOR: Robert Florczak
HC: Harcourt Brace
THEMES: Native American; folklore; creation; California

A stunning collaboration! The creation myth of the Chumash people, who lived on the Channel Islands off the Santa Barbara coast, retold with extraordinary paintings.

★ Rapunzel

AUTHOR/ILLUSTRATOR: Paul O. Zelinsky

HC: Dutton

THEMES: folklore; captivity; love; magic; solitude; hair; separation; mothers and daughters; change; coming of age

A beautifully crafted retelling that features museum-quality art, all from the hands of one of our most gifted author/illustrators. His sensitive retelling stresses different aspects of the story than you may have grown up with, and his paintings give tremendous weight to his themes, each surpassing the previous in its beauty and depth of feeling. A stunning piece of work.

★ Rattlesnake Dance: True Tales, Mysteries, and Rattlesnake Ceremonies

AUTHOR/ILLUSTRATOR: Jennifer Owings Dewey

HC: Boyds Mills

THEMES: Native American; nature; snakes; biography; folklore

By the second sentence we were hooked. ". . . I felt the strike. There was stunning pain from the instant the twin fangs pierced the soft, fleshy side of my hand." Dewey is a pro at fusing interesting scientific facts with her own experiences. When she was nine she was bitten by a rattlesnake. A year later she observed Hopi snake dancers, and as an adult saw a "rattlesnake dance" between two male rattlers. Each account of her own experiences include detailed drawings and "fact boxes" featuring information about the snakes. Just about any curiosity you have about rattlers will be answered here, including where in the United states you can find them.

A Ring of Tricksters: Animal Tales From North America, the West Indies, and Africa

AUTHOR: **Virginia Hamilton** • ILLUSTRATOR: Barry Moser

HC: Blue Sky Press

THEMES: trickster tales; Caribbean; folklore; Africa; African American

Drawing from the African and African American traditions, Hamilton and Moser deliver once again with this fabulous collection of familiar and unfamiliar trickster tales. As always,

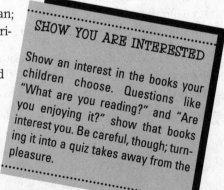

SHOW YOU ARE INTERESTED

Show an interest in the books your children choose. Questions like "What are you reading?" and "Are you enjoying it?" show that books interest you. Be careful, though; turning it into a quiz takes away from the pleasure.

Hamilton's exquisite ability to render character through dialogue shines throughout, complemented by Moser's outstanding illustrative portrayals.

The River That Went to the Sky: Twelve Tales by African Storytellers   FOLKLORE COLLECTION

EDITOR: Mary Medlicott • ILLUSTRATOR: Ademola Akintola
HC: Kingfisher
THEMES: Africa; folklore; storytelling; history; African culture

Spanning the continent and giving a fuller look at African cultures than most collections, it is the words that carry this book. Editor Medlicott has gotten down on paper the stories of some of the best African storytellers and we are all richer for their efforts.

Rome Antics   PICTURE BOOK

AUTHOR/ILLUSTRATOR: David Macaulay
HC: Houghton Mifflin
THEMES: Rome; Italy; birds; journeys; cities; architecture

A bird's-eye view takes on full meaning in this swooping, tumbling, soaring view of Rome's famous architectural wonders. The Coliseum, Pantheon, palazzos, and arches are seen from the perspective of a pigeon delivering a note. Future architects and travelers will find hours of details from the Arch of Constantine to the walls of the Palazzo Spada. And the pigeon's message? It will leave you smiling. Other highly recommended titles by Macaulay include: *Mill, Unbuilding, Castle, Underground, Pyramid, City, Cathedral,* and *Ship.*

Round Buildings, Square Buildings, & Buildings That Wiggle Like a Fish   PICTURE BOOK NONFICTION

AUTHOR/ILLUSTRATOR: Philip M. Isaacson
HC/PB: Knopf
THEMES: architecture; buildings; dwellings; way things work

From temples to shacks to airline terminals, readers get a close-up look at all kinds of structures. Full-color photographs and poetic text make the discussion of architectural materials and elements anything but boring. Don't limit this book to future architects. Choose it for anyone interested in design and how things work.

Sadako and the Thousand Paper Cranes   FICTION

AUTHOR: Eleanor Coerr • ILLUSTRATOR: Ronald Himler
PB: Dell
THEMES: Japan; courage; illness; death; family; peace; friendship;
origami; war

A heartbreaking tale that serves to remind us of the personal cost of war.
Stricken with leukemia as a result of the bombing of Hiroshima, brave
Sadako vows to fold one thousand paper cranes so that the gods will
make her well. When she dies, her classmates fold the remaining 356. A
statue of Sadako stands in Hiroshima Peace Park, a testament to her
courage and the wish for peace. A picture book version of this story is
available: *Sadako*, illustrated by Ed Young.

Santa Calls   PICTURE BOOK

AUTHOR/ILLUSTRATOR: William Joyce
HC: HarperCollins
THEMES: Christmas; brothers; Santa Claus; adventure; heroes; villains;
Arctic; good vs. evil; siblings; friendship; sisters

This is not your typical Christmas story: An epic journey to the North
Pole to assist Santa in battling the evil Ice Queen and her minions is raucous and filled with adventure. The unexpected ending, in the traditional spirit of Christmas, will touch even the hardest heart.

Scary Stories to Tell in the Dark: Collected From
American Folklore   FOLKLORE COLLECTION

AUTHOR: Alvin Schwartz • ILLUSTRATOR: Stephen Gammell
HC/PB: HarperCollins
THEMES: horror; scary stories; folklore

A terrific collection of read aloud, scream aloud and shriek aloud tales,
mostly short and creepy. Schwartz collected various versions of well-
known and obscure tales from all over the U.S. Accompanied by Gammell's eerie and disturbing line drawings, these make for some pretty
ghoulish reading. They work like a charm at campfires, sleepovers or
any time you want to put a little fright into the occasion. There are two
sequels, *More Scary Stories to Tell in the Dark* and *Scary Stories Three*.

Seven-Day Magic   FICTION-FANTASY

AUTHOR: Edward Eager • ILLUSTRATOR: N.M. Bodecker
HC/PB: Harcourt Brace
THEMES: magic; family; reading; books; responsibility; fantasy; adventure

A book from the library turns out to be magic in this delightful, literary adventure from the author of *Half Magic*.

Shaker Boy   PICTURE BOOK
AUTHOR: Mary Lyn Ray • ILLUSTRATOR: Jeanette Winter
HC: Harcourt Brace
THEMES: family; adoption; change; religion; Shakers; community

Caleb Whitcher came to live with the Shakers and suddenly found himself with 141 brothers and 138 sisters. He was six years old, and had never seen such a huge family, nor such an unusual house. Shaker rules and responsibilities and the pleasure of their music are shown in words and paintings.

Shortcut   PICTURE BOOK
AUTHOR/ILLUSTRATOR: David Macaulay
HC: Houghton Mifflin
THEMES: point of view; adventure; journeys; racing; consequences; guessing; comparisons

Actions sometimes have unpredictable consequences. Macaulay's amazing visual storytelling style leads us into a new way of looking at ordinary things. We like this even better than his Caldecott winning *Black & White*.

The Shrinking of Treehorn   FICTION
AUTHOR: Florence Parry Heide • ILLUSTRATOR: Edward Gorey
HC: Holiday House • PB: Dell
THEMES: family; humor; point of view; change

Dry and unsettling, this hilarious story introduces a small boy who is shrinking, and no one seems to notice except the reader and him. Heide and Gorey work in tandem to produce a look at how the adult world ignores children not found in other books—except the sequels, *Treehorn's Treasure* and *Treehorn's Wish*.

Sleeping Ugly   PICTURE BOOK
AUTHOR: **Jane Yolen** • ILLUSTRATOR: Diane Stanley
PB: Paperstar
THEMES: folktale variations; point of view; folklore; strong girls

One of the best examples of how to take a well-known story and twist it into something new and fresh. The title lets you know what to expect, but it is Yolen's skill as a writer that makes this concept into an original and entertaining tale.

Small Talk: A Book of Short Poems　　　POETRY ANTHOLOGY
EDITOR: Lee Bennett Hopkins • ILLUSTRATOR: Susan Gaber
HC: Harcourt Brace
THEMES: language; variety

Verses with few words deliver clear images in these gems collected by
Lee Bennett Hopkins.

Sootface: An Ojibwa Cinderella Story　　　PICTURE BOOK
AUTHOR: Robert San Souci • ILLUSTRATOR: Daniel San Souci
HC: Doubleday • PB: Dell
THEMES: Native American; folktale variations; sisters; cruelty; kind-
ness; magic; good vs. evil

In this Cinderella story the slippers are not glass, but appear as a pair of
moccasins worn by a mighty warrior who has the power to make himself
invisible. Sootface, named by her lazy, bad tempered sisters, is worked to
exhaustion. When flames from the cooking fire singed her hair or burned
her skin, her sisters laugh. And when she takes her turn to seek a husband,
they laughed again. But the last laugh comes from Sootface, who finds her
prince in a Warrior who knows the value of a "kind and honest heart."

Speak! Children's Book Illustrators
Brag About Their Dogs　　　ANTHOLOGY
EDITOR: Michael Rosen • ILLUSTRATOR: various
HC: Harcourt Brace
THEMES: dogs; illustrators

A gathering of dog-loving illustrators, each with a tale from his or her
own dog house. For a dog lover of any age. It's a perfect way to encourage young authors and illustrators to try a similar venture. Also check
out the cat version: *Purr!*

★ Starry Messenger: Galileo Galilei　　　PICTURE BOOK BIOGRAPHY
AUTHOR/ILLUSTRATOR: Peter Sis
HC: Farrar Straus & Giroux
THEMES: Galileo; astronomy; biography; math; Italy; scientists; sci-
ence; telescopes; stars

This view of the life of Galileo Galilei works at several levels. The first
time through you might consider turning the pages just for the purpose
of admiring each detail of art. Next, read the simple text at the bottom
of each page for the story of this extraordinary man. And then for a

grand finale, look for the handwritten details of history along with Galileo's own words, written more than 30 years ago. The whole family can find pleasure here, individually or as a group.

Stephen Biesty's Incredible
Cross-Sections   PICTURE BOOK NONFICTION
AUTHOR: Richard Platt • ILLUSTRATOR: Stephen Biesty
HC: Knopf
THEMES: architecture; castles; boats; trains; planes; buildings

If you were to take an ancient castle and cut out a cross section, you'd see quite a few fascinating details, like how toilets work and that the staircases always rose clockwise. The large-sized format with fold-out displays give readers detailed views of what happens inside a subway, jumbo jet, steam train, ocean liner and fourteen other structures. Biesty's careful attention to detail—even in the funnier parts—reveals hidden features that could take the curious hours to devour. Other titles to look at include: *Stephen Biesty's Cross Sections: Castle, Stephen Biesty's Cross Sections: Man of War, Stephen Biesty's Incredible Explosions*.

The Story of Money   PICTURE BOOK NONFICTION
AUTHOR: Betsy & Guillio Maestro • ILLUSTRATOR: Giulio Maestro
HC: Clarion
THEMES: money; history; ancient history

Here's the most thorough book we have seen on the subject of money. Beginning in prehistoric times, it traces the use of money through 5,000 years to now.

The Swan Stories   FOLKLORE COLLECTION
AUTHOR: Hans Christian Andersen • ILLUSTRATOR: Chris Riddell
HC: Candlewick
THEMES: storytelling; folklore; fairy tales; swans; magic; change

A beautifully produced volume of Andersen stories, selected for their connection to the theme of transformation in Andersen's life as well as his stories. Riddell's illustrations bring the stories vividly to life.

Sweet Corn: Poems   POETRY COLLECTION
AUTHOR/ILLUSTRATOR: James Stevenson
HC: Greenwillow
THEMES: poetry; rhymes

Short poems. Simple, affecting, and to the point. A treasure.

★ Sweet Words So Brave: The Story of
African American Literature
PICTURE BOOK NONFICTION

AUTHOR: Barbara K. Curry & James Michael Brodie • ILLUSTRATOR: Jerry Butler
HC: Zino
THEMES: African American; authors; U.S. history; grandfathers and granddaughters; writing; slavery

From Phillis Wheatley, the first published African American poet, to Toni Morrison, the first African American to win the Nobel Prize for literature, this compelling chronicle of black American writers is told by a man to his grandaughter. "Come sit by me, child, I have stories to tell about folks from places like Nigeria and Senegal. They were orators turned into writers, brave all in all." Pay attention to this powerful work with bold oil paintings and inspiring quotes, that tells the history of the storymakers whose words have created the rich work that make up African American literature.

The Tale of Ali Baba and the Forty Thieves
PICTURE BOOK

AUTHOR: Eric Kimmel • ILLUSTRATOR: Will Hillenbrand
HC: Holiday House
THEMES: folklore; greed; strong women; Mideast; comeuppance; treasure

Combine the masterful retelling by Kimmel with terrific paintings by Hillenbrand and you have the best version of Ali Baba available. The classic story from the Arabian Nights is here with none of the gory parts removed, lending an opportunity to discuss with your children how violence has been used in stories in appropriate and inappropriate ways.

GATEKEEPERS

Often those of us in the business of deciding and providing what children "should" read act like gatekeepers, as if we have forgotten that the wonderful world of literature we are guarding isn't ours in the first place. Children are not adults-in-training, but people in their own right, full of opinions and needs. If we are less than thrilled to have them reading certain books, better to be involved in their lives and grateful that they are reading than rail against their choices. It is not the selection of a particular book that is a problem, but the lack of a concerned and interested adult to help young readers understand their choices.

Tales Alive: Ten Multicultural Folktales with Activities
FOLKLORE COLLECTION

AUTHOR: Susan Milord • ILLUSTRATOR: Michael Ronato

HC/PB: Williamson

THEMES: folklore; crafts; art; cultural diversity; gardening; music; animals; constellations

This collection got our attention with the relevant, hands-on activities that support ten folktales from around the world. It works. A lot of books in this genre don't, because the stories are written to fit the activity as opposed to the other way around.

Tales of King Arthur Series
PICTURE BOOK

AUTHOR/ILLUSTRATOR: Hudson Talbott

HC: Morrow

THEMES: King Arthur; adventure; England; folklore; heroes; knights; love

If you are going to do a picture book of King Arthur, there should be bigger-than-life hear-the-horses-gallop scenes, and Talbott knows how to do them. He even adds an occasional see-the-dragon-breathe-fire scene. Exquisitely rendered paintings are guaranteed in a Talbott book, but it should be mentioned that his skill as a reteller makes these more than coffee table books. Read them aloud to your children when the time comes to introduce them to Camelot. Three in the series include: *King Arthur: The Sword and the Stone; King Arthur and the Round Table; Excalibur.*

The Tales of Uncle Remus
FOLKLORE COLLECTION

AUTHOR: Julius Lester

HC: Dutton

THEMES: folklore; African American; trickster tales; humor

Forty-eight hysterical tales of one wily rabbit who out tricks (or tries to) just about every big and little critter around, including Brer Bear and Mr. Man. Lester adds just enough dialect to stay in touch with the original stories and keeps the fun in these tales of Brer Rabbit and his friends—and enemies. For more of Lester's Uncle Remus try *More Tales of Uncle Remus.*

Tatterhood and the Hobgoblins:
A Norwegian Folktale   PICTURE BOOK

AUTHOR/ILLUSTRATOR: Lauren Mills

HC/PB: Little Brown

THEMES: courage; individuality; princes; queens; folklore; Norway; strong girls

A marvelous epic tale that features as strong and independent a heroine as you are likely to find in folklore. Tatterhood, so called because she dresses in rags, is one of a pair of twins born to a queen who makes an unfortunate bargain with the hobgoblins. As the story unfolds, Tatterhood is shown to be the only one in the kingdom with a lick of sense or the courage to battle the hobgoblins. When she meets a prince and, as always, the topic of marriage comes up, she makes it very clear that she will marry on her terms only. Lauren Mills' classic illustrations perfectly complement her exciting retelling.

Thirteen Moons on Turtle's Back: A Native American
Year of Moons   FOLKLORE COLLECTION

AUTHOR: Joseph Bruchac and Jonathan London • ILLUSTRATOR: Thomas Locker

HC: Philomel • PB: Paperstar

THEMES: folklore; turtles; Native American; seasons; moon

Moon stories from the Cherokee, Cree, Sioux, Pomo and others find their beginnings on the shell of a turtle's back. Each scale represents one of the thirteen moons in a year. Here young readers will find a legend for each moon, illustrated with brilliant oil paintings by Thomas Locker.

Tog the Ribber, or Granny's Tale   PICTURE BOOK

AUTHOR: Paul Coltman • ILLUSTRATOR: Gillian McClure

HC: Farrar Straus & Giroux

THEMES: spooky stories; grandmothers; ghosts; vocabulary; imagination; poem; storytelling

At first reading the words don't make sense, but McClure's frightening images will move the curious to read again. "I shuddud in the glavering goom as homing through the only wood I skibbed and teetered past Tog's tomb." In the tradition of Lewis Carroll's *Jabberwocky*, Coltman's poem spellbinds. Practice, then read this aloud.

Tomas and the Library Lady
PICTURE BOOK BIOGRAPHY

AUTHOR: Pat Mora • ILLUSTRATOR: Raul Colon
HC: Knopf
THEMES: reading; migrant farmworkers; grandfathers; Hispanic; story-telling; libraries; librarians

The best book we have seen about the wonderful way librarians can change lives. Tomas' grandfather is a storyteller, and no matter where they are in their yearly migration between Texas and Iowa, the family gathers around the fire each evening after their work in the fields is done and is treated to the gift of a story. Tomas knows them all by heart and hungers for more, so his grandfather tells him about the stories to be found in the library. Tomas' tenuous approach to this strange and wonderful place is perfectly met by a kind, patient and generous librarian who helps him find the world of stories he longs for. This would be a good enough tale, but the reader finds out that it really happened—Tomas grew up to become the first minority Chancellor of the University of California! This is a beautiful, inspiring testament to the power of story, both told and written, and a vision of the rewards of education that will reach across cultures.

True Lies: 18 Tales for You to Judge
FOLKLORE COLLECTION

AUTHOR: George Shannon • ILLUSTRATOR: John O'Brien
HC: Greenwillow
THEMES: lying; truth; folklore; point of view; cultural diversity

The truth is not always clear cut, and often depends on your point of view. Here are 18 stories from a variety of sources, perfect for reading and discussing.

The Tyger
PICTURE BOOK

AUTHOR: William Blake • ILLUSTRATOR: Neil Waldman
HC: Harcourt
THEMES: tigers; poem

Blake's famous poem was first published in 1794. Here it is in picture book form with bold, brilliant illustrations by Neil Waldman.

Until I Met Dudley: How Everyday Things Really Work
PICTURE BOOK NONFICTION

AUTHOR: Roger McGough • ILLUSTRATOR: Chris Riddell

HC: Walker

THEMES: imagination; science; comparisons; the way things work; humor

This book is packed with solid information about how common household items really work, but its real treasure is the imaginative explanations that the children concoct before being told the truth. This is a delightful combination of fact and fancy and will appeal to both realists and dreamers.

The Velveteen Rabbit
FICTION

AUTHOR: Margery Williams • ILLUSTRATOR: William Nicholson

HC: Doubleday • PB: Avon

THEMES: toys; rabbits; love; illness; magic; fairies; Christmas; change

One day the velveteen rabbit asked the skin horse, "What is real?" "When a child loves you for a long, long time, not just to play with, but REALLY loves you, then you become Real," said the skin horse. ". . . by the time you are Real, most of your hair has been loved off, and your eyes drop out and you get loose in the joints and very shabby. But these things don't matter at all, because once you are Real you can't be ugly, except to people who don't understand."

From its first waiting moment in the Christmas stocking, to its final release by the nursery magic Fairy, the velveteen rabbit's enchanting tale leaves young readers and listeners taking a new look at their own favorite toys.

Volcano: The Eruption & Healing of Mount St. Helens
NONFICTION

AUTHOR: Patricia Lauber • ILLUSTRATOR: (photographs)

HC: Simon & Schuster • PB: Aladdin

THEMES: nature; volcanoes; science

Lauber is an author who can be counted on to bring an interesting perspective to nonfiction. Always informative in an accessible style, she is a good author to turn to for book reports and research for 3rd to 7th graders. This is one of the best books about volcanoes we know. Be sure to check out her book *Hurricanes: Earth's Mightiest Storms*.

Waiting for the Evening Star   PICTURE BOOK
AUTHOR: **Rosemary Wells** • ILLUSTRATOR: Susan Jeffers
HC: Dial
THEMES: country life; brothers; trains; U.S. history, early 20th century; separation; war

It is not only the recapturing of a lost pace of life but the sense of foreboding that makes this picture book collaboration between Wells and Jeffers memorable long past the turning of the last page.

Walking the Bridge of Your Nose   POETRY ANTHOLOGY
EDITOR: Michael Rosen • ILLUSTRATOR: Chloe Cheese
HC: Kingfisher
THEMES: humor; tongue twisters; riddles; rhyme; puns; language; aphorisms; wordplay

Wordplay abounds in this collection, a veritable treasure trove of puns, rhymes, tongue twisters and other types of witty uses of language. A lot of fun!

The War With Grandpa   FICTION
AUTHOR: Robert Kimmel Smith
PB: Dell
THEMES: grandfathers and grandsons; home; solitude; sharing; conflict; problem solving; anger; war; lessons

War is serious stuff, not a game. Peter learns this when he decides to wage war on his grandfather to get his room back. A widower, Grandpa has moved into the house and takes Peter's room because it does not require climbing stairs to get to. Peter gets angry and Grandpa decides to teach him a lesson. This is a sensitive and thought-provoking novel. For other looks at grandparent-grandchild conflict, see *Sun and Spoon* by Kevin Henkes, and *Luka's Quilt* by Georgia Guback.

The Weaving of a Dream   PICTURE BOOK
AUTHOR/ILLUSTRATOR: Marilee Heyer
HC: Viking • PB: Puffin
THEMES: China; folklore; weaving; fantasy; magic; fairies; greed; envy; mothers and sons

A skillful retelling of a Chinese folktale, accompanied by breathtaking art. The story of a weaver whose tapestries come to life could find no better vessel than Heyer's vivid paintings.

Welcome to the Green House

PICTURE BOOK

AUTHOR: **Jane Yolen** • ILLUSTRATOR: Laura Regan
HC: Putnam • PB: Paperstar
THEMES: rain forest; environment; animals; plants

"Welcome to the hot house. Welcome to the land of the warm, wet days."
Choose this if you'd like enchanting text and remarkable full-page paintings that describe life in a tropical rain forest.

When the Whippoorwill Calls

PICTURE BOOK

AUTHOR: Candice F. Ransom • ILLUSTRATOR: Kimberly Bulcken Root
HC: Tambourine
THEMES: change; moving; country life; home

Set in the Blue Ridge Mountains and possessed of a strong sense of
place, this picture book portrays being relocated due to so-called
progress and having to give up the life you know for an uncertain future.

Where the Sidewalk Ends: Poems and Drawings

POETRY COLLECTION

AUTHOR/ILLUSTRATOR: Shel Silverstein
HC: HarperCollins
THEMES: variety; humor; rhyme

At his best, there is no one better than Silverstein at grasping the essential qualities of humor, irreverence, and subversion in childhood. He
understands how much of their lives children spend at the mercy of
adults who have simply forgotten what being a kid is all about, and he's
not afraid to reveal things that adults think should be kept secret. His
poems and drawings have become classics, and are mentioned as
favorites by children everywhere, even if they say they don't like
poetry. His later collections, *The Light in the Attic* and *Falling Up,* offer
more of the same, but for our money, this is the book we cannot live
without.

The Whipping Boy

FICTION

AUTHOR: Sid Fleischman • ILLUSTRATOR: Peter Sis
HC: Greenwillow • PB: Troll
THEMES: mischief; responsibility; literacy; adventure; kidnapping;
princes; comparisons; villains

Nasty Prince Brat gets away with all sorts of horrid behavior. Whenever
he is to be punished, he has his whipping boy brought in to be his sur-

rogate. When they switch places for real, each learns something about the life of the other. They reunite at story's end as friends, but not until after a whole lot of adventures. Fast paced and entertaining, this New-bery Medal winner is one of the most reader friendly books ever to win that award.

White Socks Only
PICTURE BOOK

AUTHOR: Evelyn Coleman • ILLUSTRATOR: Tyrone Geter
HC: Albert Whitman
THEMES: African American; prejudice; magic; bullies; misunderstanding; comeuppance; Civil rights

Grandma tells of when she was a little girl and wanted to see if it was really possible to fry an egg on the sidewalk on the hottest day of the year. But the sidewalk was in town, and one can get mighty thirsty watching an egg fry in the noon day sun. This was the South, years ago, when water fountains were labled "Whites Only." This uplifting story tells of how a young girl's honest mistake (she thought the word "whites" referred to her socks) inspired blacks to give bigotry its comeuppance, with the help of a little magic from the Chicken Man.

Who Belongs Here? An American Story
PICTURE BOOK NONFICTION

AUTHOR: Margy Burns Knight • ILLUSTRATOR: Anne Sibley O'Brien
HC/PB: Tilbury House
THEMES: comparisons; prejudice; refugees; Cambodia; cultural diversity; immigration

Knight and O'Brien have designed a book with three voices. The first belongs to a boy from Cambodia who is making his home in the United States. The second is the narrator's, who gives anecdotes relating experiences of other refugees and their contributions to American culture, and the third is the voice that asks questions like "What if everyone who lives in the U.S. but whose ancestors came from another country, was forced to return to his or her homeland?" "Who would be left?" This is a natural for encouraging children to talk about their feelings of intolerance.

The Wonderful Towers of Watts
PICTURE BOOK

AUTHOR: Patricia Zelver • ILLUSTRATOR: Frane Lessac
HC: Tambourine • PB: Mulberry
THEMES: collecting; creativity; monuments; artists; crafts; creativity; poverty; individuality; problem solving; diversity

People thought old Sam was crazy. He wore ragged overalls and an old hat and kept pretty much to himself. But Sam had a dream. He spent thirty years building a monument out of old junk he collected. His work is now known to the people of Los Angeles as the *Wonderful Towers of Watts*. Every year people come from all over the world to marvel at old Sam's dream. This is his story.

The Wreck of the Zanzibar   FICTION

AUTHOR: Michael Morpurgo • ILLUSTRATOR: Francois Place

HC: Viking

THEMES: bats; sea; strong girls; turtles; family; England; diaries; brothers; siblings

An exciting account of life on a British island at the turn of the century, told in diary form. Brave Laura writes of how her family almost had to leave the Isle of Bryher, how her beloved brother Billy ran off to be a cabin boy, how she and her grandmother rescue a sea turtle and, most thrillingly, of the wreck of the Zanzibar, a sailing ship that provides the island with renewed life and vigor. Terrific attention to detail and strong characters make this a compelling read.

Yikes! Your Body, Up Close   PICTURE BOOK NONFICTION

AUTHOR: Mike Janulewicz • ILLUSTRATOR: photos

HC: Simon & Schuster

THEMES: human body; photography, magnification; guessing; science; humor, gross

Full of highly magnified photographs that show the wonders of the human body in all its disgusting glory, this is a most aptly named book. Fold out pages enable the reader to use this as a guessing game, trying to figure out if that's a moon crater or the upclose, cavitied surface of your tooth! There's a companion book: *Yuck!: A Big Book of Little Horrors*.

Yo, Hungry Wolf!   PICTURE BOOK

AUTHOR: David Vozar • ILLUSTRATOR: Betsy Lewin

HC: Delacorte • PB: Dell

THEMES: wolves; folktale variations; rhyme; rhythm

A retelling of *The Three Little Pigs, The Boy Who Cried Wolf,* and *Little Red Riding Hood,* set to a rap beat, making for an infectious, toe-tapping read aloud!

PART FOUR

Books for Children in Middle Elementary Grades

Middle to upper elementary grades are most likely to find a match of their interests with their reading levels in this section.

Amelia's Notebook

PICTURE BOOK

AUTHOR/ILLUSTRATOR: Marissa Moss
HC: Tricycle
THEMES: school; friendship; moving; diaries; humor

Amelia's Notebook looks as if it's written on a regular composition book. It is filled with writings and drawings and thoughts and ideas—all belonging to nine-year-old Amelia, who has just moved to a new house. As Amelia adjusts to her new school she gripes about cafeteria food, misses her best friend, makes new ones, and experiences a lot of the feelings shared by other nine-year-olds who will read every detail. See the sequels: *Amelia Writes Again* and *My Notebook (With Help From Amelia)*.

Are You There God? It's Me, Margaret

FICTION

AUTHOR: Judy Blume
PB: Dell
THEMES: coming of age; humor; secrets; family

Funny, irreverent, and as pertinent to kids' lives as she was 20 years ago, Blume remains a powerful force in books for children. Her status as one of the most banned authors in America seems not to be fading, and it is her no-holds barred style that both delights children and irritates censors. Whether writing about families, school, friendship or secrets, Blume knows how kids of all ages feel and isn't afraid to let them know she is on their side. Our favorites of her books besides this one include: *Blubber, Here's to You Rachel Robinson, Otherwise Known as Sheila the Great, Tales of a Fourth Grade Nothing,* and *Superfudge.*

Around the World in a Hundred Years   PICTURE BOOK NONFICTION

AUTHOR: Jean Fritz • ILLUSTRATOR: Anthony Bacon Venti
HC: Putnam
THEMES: history, 16th century; geography; courage; trailblazing; maps; journeys

From Henry the Navigator to Magellan, Fritz follows the achievements of ten men who traveled to India, Africa, the Americas and eventually around the world. Each chapter begins with a map of an explorer's voyage. Straightforward text and humor make up the stories that bring these historical characters to life.

Ben and Me   FICTION

AUTHOR/ILLUSTRATOR: Robert Lawson
HC/PB: Little Brown
THEMES: U.S. history, American Revolution; mice; kites; U.S. history, Colonial times; electricity; friendship; lightning; storms; inventions; trailblazing

The classic story of Ben Franklin, as told by a mouse who was there for all the history. He now steps forward to let the world know of his important role in Ben's achievements. This is a whimsical look at history and a good way to interest kids in it. Also see: *Mr. Revere & I*

Beyond Amazing: Six Spectacular Science Pop-Ups   POP-UP

AUTHOR/ILLUSTRATOR: Jay Young
HC: HarperCollins
THEMES: science; science experiments

Another incredible piece of book-engineering combined with fascinating science experiments from the man who gave us *The Most Amazing Science Pop-Up Book.* Sturdy and full of hours of learning fun.

Cyber.Kdz Series   FICTION-MYSTERY

AUTHOR: Bruce Balan
PB: Avon
THEMES: computers; self-respect; cruelty; mystery; problem solving; friendship; school; writing; internet; cultural diversity; teasing; diversity

The Cyber.kdz chat line stretches from New York to Seattle, Brazil, and France. They chat about what goes on in their lives, and challenge each other with on-line projects. The Cyber.kdz put their international skills to work in solving the mysteries and computer savvy kids will enjoy their adventures. The first two titles are: *In Search of Scum* and *A Picture's Worth*.

Fire in the Forest: A Cycle of Growth and Renewal

PICTURE BOOK NONFICTION

AUTHOR: Laurence Pringle • ILLUSTRATOR: Bob Marshall
HC: Atheneum
THEMES: forests; destruction; lifecycle; animals; fire

Fascinating and beautiful. Sets the record straight about the important role fire plays in the cycles of nature. You'll never think of forest fires the same way after you read this.

Five Children and It

FICTION-FANTASY

AUTHOR: E. Nesbit
PB: Puffin
THEMES: magic; wishes; adventure; family; fairies; fantasy; siblings

A delightful and influential fantasy about the discovery of a Psammead, or sand fairy, by a quintet of siblings. Wishes abound, once the Psammead gets over having his sleep disturbed. The adventures of these very British children are a bit precious by today's standards, but every writer since who has written of children and magic owes a debt to Nesbit. Reading aloud will help smooth over some of the unfamiliar language and, after all, why should the children have all the fun?

The Four Story Mistake

FICTION

AUTHOR: Elizabeth Enright
PB: Puffin
THEMES: family; dance; siblings

A charming series that has been a favorite of children for generations. The Melendy family are the stuff of classic children's writing—solid characters you care about, humorous and believable adventures, and a family that you wish was your own. The other titles are: *The Saturdays, Then There Were Five,* and *Spiderweb for Two.*

Front Porch Stories at the One-Room School   PICTURE BOOK

AUTHOR: Eleanora Tate • ILLUSTRATOR: Eric Velasquez
PB: Dell
THEMES: storytelling; community; family; schools; African American

On a hot summer night in Missouri, twelve-year-old Margie Carson and her seven-year-old cousin sit on the steps of their one-room school-house to listen to her dad's stories. Read these aloud, or offer them up to fourth or fifth graders to enjoy on their own.

A Game of Catch   PICTURE BOOK

AUTHOR: Richard Wilbur • ILLUSTRATOR: Barry Moser
HC: Harcourt Brace
THEMES: conflict; fitting in; baseball; teasing

A thought-provoking story that is sure to create discussion. Two boys are playing ball; another wants to play but has no mitt. The boys reluctantly welcome him into the game, but slowly begin to exclude him. How he then taunts them is a classic example of misfit behavior, and it ends with unfortunate results. This is a book about the dynamics of boy relation-ships, and though it gives real pause to adults who want to for-get how nasty children can be to each other, no fourth grader will fail to recognize the truth of the story.

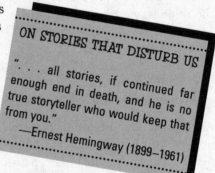

ON STORIES THAT DISTURB US

". . . all stories, if continued far enough end in death, and he is no true storyteller who would keep that from you."
—Ernest Hemingway (1899–1961)

Get on Board: The Story of the Underground Railroad   NONFICTION

AUTHOR: Jim Haskins
HC/PB: Scholastic
THEMES: slavery; escape; Underground Railroad; songs; courage

This gives details of some of the people who traveled the secret and risky route out of slavery. There's even a chapter of railroad songs that helped release emotions, as well as spread information.

The Giant   PICTURE BOOK
AUTHOR/ILLUSTRATOR: Mordicai Gerstein
HC: Hyperion
THEMES: giants; change; courage; coming of age

Not all picture books should be limited to young children. This coming
of age story, full of mystery, perfectly captures the sensibility of young
women on the brink of maturity. Read this aloud to your 4th and 5th
graders. An allegorical tale that you'll remember long after the last page.

Good Griselle   PICTURE BOOK
AUTHOR: **Jane Yolen** • ILLUSTRATOR: David Christiana
HC: Harcourt Brace
THEMES: patience; redemption; wagers; mothers; cathedrals; Paris;
gargoyles; adoption; angels

A lovely story about a wager between the gargoyles and the angels at the
cathedral of Notre Dame. Is there such a thing as a truly good person?
The gargoyles curse the lonely Griselle with a demonic child, confident
it is a surefire way to tempt her from goodness, but she rises to the challenge and loves her adopted son with all the patience of a saint. This is
a story about the redemptive power of a mother's love, and stands as a
testament to Yolen's magnificent power as a storyteller.

The Headless Haunt & Other African-American
Ghost Stories   FOLKLORE COLLECTION
AUTHOR: James Haskins • ILLUSTRATOR: Ben Otero
PB: HarperCollins
THEMES: horror; African American; storytelling; ghosts; scary stories

A mix of European and African folklore, here are 21 scary stories passed
down to us by generations of telling. Perfect for reading aloud.

How Now, Brown Cow?   POETRY COLLECTION
AUTHOR: Alice Schertle • ILLUSTRATOR: Amanda Schaffer
HC: Browndeer
THEMES: cows; wordplay; humor; puns; folktale variation

Filled with bovine insights and language play, this collection of cow
poems will get its share of laughs.

Now Let Me Fly: The Story of a Slave Family   PICTURE BOOK

AUTHOR/ILLUSTRATOR: Dolores Johnson

HC: Macmillan

THEMES: U.S.A., the South; freedom; slavery; folklore; family; U.S. history, pre-Civil War; African American

Wow! A look at the experience of being a slave that pulls no punches in its depiction of the grueling agonies involved. Johnson's power as a writer shines through, and she does not give up her emotional intensity or devastating portrayal of the experience until it is over, and slavery is ended.

Red Dirt Jessie   FICTION

AUTHOR: Anna Myers

HC: Walker • PB: Puffin

THEMES: Oklahoma; U.S. history, the Depression; U.S.A., the Dust Bowl

Jessie is a young girl living in the Oklahoma Dust Bowl during the Depression. This story is so rich with the sense of time and place that the reader will forget she's not there.

Search for the Shadowman   FICTION-MYSTERY

AUTHOR: Joan Lowery Nixon

HC: Delacorte • PB: Dell

THEMES: Texas; genealogy; mystery; internet; U.S. history; secrets; family history; computers

Master of the young adult mystery Nixon turns here to middle-grade readers, and delivers a thrilling novel about family secrets and the history of Texas. Andy rights a generations-old wrong through his intrepid detective work into the history of his family. If family-tree research is fascinating your kids, they will love this book.

The Secret Code Book   PICTURE BOOK NONFICTION

AUTHOR: Helen Huckle

HC: Dial

THEMES: mystery; codes; history, world; symbols; communication; secrets; detectives

From Pig Latin to secret messages between friends, codes intrigue kids. Young sleuths will find clever, mind-boggling codes that have been used over hundreds of years for sending confidential messages. Removeable code-busters are included in the back.

READING POWER

Why read? Is it just a search for knowledge? If our only goal is for everyone to be able to program the VCR and read a computer manual, then stressing only phonics and word definitions would be all there is to teaching reading. We would have a world of people who could follow directions and not much else. However, if our goal is to encourage people to think for themselves, then the teaching of reading must have higher priorities. When you nurture the questioning mind, when you allow for the prospect of disagreement or interpretation, and when you develop the power to imagine or even create—then the benefits of reading stretch beyond the obvious and reach past the possible.

As a reader you don't create the words or the story, but you provide the essential part of the equation; no story is complete until it has been read. You have the power to control the speed, to reread a page and to decide if the story works for you regardless of how hard the author worked to shape the tale. The story belongs to you as soon as you read it, and becomes no longer just the author's. You can even choose to put it down and refuse to finish it. That's power!

We often read to escape ourselves and our lives, but one of the chief reasons we read is to find ourselves. Children frequently measure stories by how closely they echo their own thoughts and feelings. They look for opportunities to identify with characters, their problems and solutions. They seek approval for themselves and their actions in books and rejoice to find it. As they grow older and their lives become more complex, reading about others who have similar concerns and conflicts gives them hope and makes them feel less alone. Finding oneself in a character or in a story is a tremendous feeling. Pride, faith, and confidence in oneself are nurtured by reading as a child reaches for independence.

Listening/Interest Level: Middle Elementary and Young Adult (M/Y). Reading Level: Middle Elementary (M).

These are the longer works, fiction and non, that make for excellent reading experiences for our M readers. The topics and concerns are complex and multivaried, with interests ranging from Greek mythology to science, and the themes in fiction ask for a reader to ponder and make choices about characters and situations.

Abel's Island
FICTION

AUTHOR/ILLUSTRATOR: William Steig

HC/PB: Farrar Straus & Giroux

THEMES: mice; survival; determination; floods; home; problem solving; islands; yearning; love

A pampered mouse learns the techniques of survival when he is swept away from home and loved ones by a flood. He lands on an island and his determined attempts to get home and return his wife's scarf are consistently thwarted. He finds he is one tough little mouse, and as he spends a year on his island foraging for food and eluding predators, he realizes how good his life was. His ultimate reunion with his wife is heartening and Steig's humorous touches help make this Newbery Honor Book a satisfying read.

Alice's Adventures in Wonderland
FICTION-FANTASY

AUTHOR: Lewis Carroll • ILLUSTRATOR: John Tenniel

HC: Morrow

THEMES: fantasy; zany; journeys; magic; strong girls; adventure

One of the great classics of childhood, though we feel it is better introduced in later years rather than younger. Dense and hard to follow in spots, the book is a far different thing from the many Disneyesque versions that have been made of it on TV and film, so be warned that it may not enchant your five year old the way the cartoon does. But when you have an inquisitive nine year old on your hands, one who thinks she is getting too smart for "baby" books, that is the time to surprise her with Carroll's masterpiece. Do not neglect to follow up with the sequel, *Through The Looking Glass.* You'll be surprised at how much you think is in Alice actually comes from the later book.

All the Colors of the Race   POETRY COLLECTION

AUTHOR: Arnold Adoff • ILLUSTRATOR: John Steptoe
HC: Lothrop
THEMES: cultural diversity; self-respect; family; individuality; African American

Adoff's poems reflect the thoughts of a young girl whose family is from a combination of races and cultures.

★ All We Needed to Say   POETRY COLLECTION

AUTHOR: Marilyn Singer • ILLUSTRATOR: Lorna Clark (photographs)
HC: Henry Holt
THEMES: individuality; school; friendship; self-respect; comparisons; teachers; point of view

Not all situations are viewed from the same perspective. That's particularly true when it comes to school. One person's favorite class can be another's least favorite. *All We Needed to Say* deals head-on with these differences. Tanya and Sophie have opposite opinions about school. Before her mom finishes her cup of coffee in the morning Tanya is out the door rushing to class because she loves to learn. Sophie is in the principal's office again for being late. Singer's poems about two friends with differing views will give comfort to young readers perplexed by their own feelings. Try reading this with your child, switching roles and seeing which one you like best.

The Alphabet From Z to A
(With Much Confusion On The Way)   PICTURE BOOK

AUTHOR: Judith Viorst • ILLUSTRATOR: Richard Hull
HC: Atheneum • PB: Aladdin
THEMES: homonyms; comparisons; alphabet; vocabulary; language; humor

Some words sound alike but are not spelled alike. Some letters have no sound at all in certain words. Viorst points out the confusion found throughout the English language. This good-humored vocabulary builder works for anyone, but will be especially appreciated by those who have struggled with English.

Ancient Ones   PICTURE BOOK NONFICTION
AUTHOR/ILLUSTRATOR: Barbara Bash
HC: Sierra Club
THEMES: nature; trees; life cycle; environment; forests

In old forests it could take over 200 years for a new Douglas fir to sprout. Informative prose and water color paintings trace the life cycle of the old growth tree and the forest itself.

Angela and Diabola   FICTION-FANTASY
AUTHOR: Lynne Reid Banks
HC/PB: Avon
THEMES: twins; sisters; babies; good vs. evil; school

Mr. and Mrs. Cuthbertson-Jones are surprised to have twins. Almost immediately they discover that one is surrounded by a pink cloud of goodness and the other is absolutely evil. Banks seems to enjoy the darkly humorous possibilities in portraying the struggle between good and evil, and in most cases, good wins, but we think it's relevant to mention that she clearly understands there is a little good and evil in all of us.

Animorphs   SCIENCE FICTION
AUTHOR: K.A. Applegate
PB: Scholastic
THEMES: science fiction; adventure; invasion; animals; change; good vs. evil; friendship; secrets; villains

More than just a popular series, this is a way that future readers of science fiction can be introduced to this exciting and challenging genre. In order to combat a takeover of Earth by a hostile race of creatures from outer space, five kids are given the ability to morph into animals at will by a dying alien. The series contains solid adventure writing that is full of action and is guaranteed to hold readers from 8 to 13.

ATTITUDE

A fifth grader came into my bookstore with his class. His attitude made it clear there wasn't anything of value there for him. He was wearing a tee-shirt with "LIFE SUCKS!" printed on the front. I said, "Whoa, that's pretty dreary!" in response to his shirt and then asked if there was anything he would like me to show him. He snickered, looking around me at his friends and said "You don't have a book about bikes do you?" I led him to a shelf that offered several titles. He mentioned that he had just modified an old Schwinn so that it was "way cool." I pulled out a book showing photos and illustrations of modified bikes. His face lit up as he settled down, book in hand, friends surrounding him, and he began pointing to pictures describing parts and paint. When it was time to go, he found me and offered a casual "thanks." As he filed past with his class, I noticed his tee-shirt had been turned inside out.

Anne of Green Gables   FICTION

AUTHOR: L.M. Montgomery

PB: Bantam

THEMES: orphans; family; strong girls; community; neighbors; Canada; adoption; farms

Matthew and Marilla Cuthbert had requested a boy orphan to be sent to help them work on their farm, not a spunky, talkative redheaded girl. But Anne wins their hearts at Green Gables farm and by the time she pleads "Oh, please, Miss Cuthbert, won't you tell me if you are going to send me away or not? I've tried to be patient all the morning, but I really feel that I cannot bear not knowing any longer," Anne has found a new home. First published in 1908, the adventures of spirited Anne Shirley continue to be requested by young readers who will find comfort in knowing that when the first one has been read, others follow: *Anne of Avonlea, Anne of the Island, Anne of Windy Poplars, Anne's House of Dreams, Anne of Ingleside, Rainbow Valley,* and *Rilla of Ingleside*.

Antics   PICTURE BOOK

AUTHOR/ILLUSTRATOR: Cathi Hepworth

HC: Putnam • PB: Paperstar

THEMES: wordplay; vocabulary; ants; alphabet; change; homonyms

In a rocking chair on the front porch sits an ancient "ANTique." A "BrilliANT" scientist mixes chemicals. Ant characters from A to Z pose to illustrate words containing "ant." The art is enchanting, and observant children will come up with some of their own.

★ Baby   FICTION

AUTHOR: Patricia MacLachlan
HC: Delacorte • PB: Dell
THEMES: adoption; loss; grief; babies; choices; homelessness; family

Twelve-year-old Larkin returns home one day to discover a baby sitting in a basket in the driveway of her family's house. The only clue to how the baby got there is a note from the child's mother saying, "This is Sophie. She is almost a year old and she is good. I cannot take care of her now, but I know she will be safe with you . . . I will come back for her one day." Larkin and her family care for the baby, knowing that it is temporary, yet allowing Sophie to fill a void that the author takes her time in revealing. The brilliance of MacLachlan's writing lies in her ability to convey the silence of people who have no words for what they are feeling. This is a powerful book about loss and redemption, and though it is well within the ability of a ten year old to read and appreciate, we like to give this book to adults as an example of the kind of astonishing writing they miss by neglecting to read children's books.

★ The Barn   FICTION

AUTHOR: Avi
HC: Orchard • PB: Avon
THEMES: gentle boys; illness; family; choices; siblings; communication; U.S. history, frontier life; farms; fate; handicaps; fathers and sons; taking action; responsibility; gifted child; wisdom; barns

An outstanding novel that will speak to anyone who has ever had to deal with an ill parent. In 1850s Oregon a ten-year-old boy is called home from school to help his older brother and sister out when their father has a stroke. The bright boy is able to communicate with his father despite his infirmity and enters into a power struggle with his siblings over the fate of the family farm. With writing that sings from the page, this is a novel to read, weep over and treasure.

This is a book I recommend to adults to read (along with Patricia MacLachlan's *Baby* and Bruce Brooks' *Midnight Hour Encores*) to show them what they are missing by not reading children's books.

RESISTERS

We read when we are ready, as it is one of the truest manifestations of our power over our own world to refuse to read. Just as you cannot make a two year old eat something that he doesn't want to, so can you not make a child/teen/adult read something that holds no interest for them. In that way, the nonreader is no different from the reader. As concerned about illiteracy as we are, the bigger problem has always been the alliterate; those who can read but choose not to. They are the ones who need to be reached, who need to learn to use the power of their own choices to say yes to the joys of reading.

The Ballad of Lucy Whipple   FICTION

AUTHOR: Karen Cushman
HC: Clarion • PB: HarperCollins
THEMES: survival; U.S. history, Westward movement; courage; California; U.S. history, Gold Rush; pioneers; strong girls

Karen Cushman's first book, *Catherine Called Birdy* won a Newbery Honor award. Her second, *The Midwife's Apprentice* won the Newbery Medal. This, her third, will not disappoint. Lucy Whipple, jaw set, shoulders back, fights for her place out west where "There is no school and no lending library, no bank, no church, no meetinghouse, no newspaper, no shopping, no parties or picnics, no eggs, no milk." You are bound to laugh, but will also gain a clear sense of what life was like for the early settlers.

The Bear's House   FICTION

AUTHOR: Marilyn Sachs
PB: Puffin
THEMES: imagination; dolls; school; family; poverty; bullies; mental illness

Fran Ellen will break your heart as she stuggles to stay on top in a world of bullies, poverty and a mentally ill mom. Her imagination provides solace when she finds a family she can live with in a classroom doll house. A sensitizing story for readers who will identify Fran as a child whose family does not fit in with society's "norm." For more of this amazing young girl, read *Fran Ellen's House*.

Belle Prater's Boy   FICTION

AUTHOR: Ruth White

HC: Farrar Straus & Giroux • PB: Dell

THEMES: U.S.A., Appalachia; mothers; friendship; family; cousins; loss; self-respect; death; mystery

"Around 5:00 a.m. on a warm Sunday morning in October 1953, my Aunt Belle left her bed and vanished from the face of the earth." The story begins with this fact. Twelve-year-old Gypsy wants to know exactly what happened. Becoming best friends with her cousin Woodrow, Aunt Belle's son, brings her closer to the truth. Readers see how differently people respond to loss. They also get a glimpse into life in a small Appalachian town through characters who are poignant, funny, sad, and inspiring. An incredibly worthwhile book.

Birthday Surprises:
Ten Great Stories to Unwrap   SHORT STORY ANTHOLOGY

EDITOR: Joanna Hurwitz

HC: Morrow

THEMES: birthdays; diversity; surprises; gifts; comparisons

Joanna Hurwitz devised the following challenge for ten popular authors of children's books: "Imagine it's your birthday and you've received lots of presents. But how would you feel if one beautifully wrapped package turned out to be empty? Would you be angry or amused, disappointed or disgusted, bitter or forgiving?" From a fairy tale and a poem to a collection of letters, the diversity of responses is intriguing.

Blitzcat   FICTION

AUTHOR: Robert Westall

PB: Scholastic

THEMES: England; cats; history, World War II; war; courage

Westall has taken day-to-day events in World War II England, added a cat's journey, and given his readers a glimpse into the lives of several people experiencing war first hand. Good historical fiction goes a long way to make young readers interested in history, and this is a prime example.

Blubber   FICTION

AUTHOR: Judy Blume

PB: Dell

THEMES: overweight; bullies; school; friendship; teasing; cruelty

A brilliant book about how rotten kids can be to each other. see: *Are You There God? It's Me, Margaret.*

The Boggart   FICTION-FANTASY

AUTHOR: Susan Cooper

HC: McElderry • PB: Aladdin

THEMES: Scotland; castles; fantasy; trickster tales; magic; ghosts; gifted child; Canada; computers

It's one thing for Emily and Jess Volnik's family to inherit a crumbly old castle in Scotland, but when an invisible, shape-changing, prank-playing spirit comes with it, it's another thing altogether. "Up in his space above the shelves, the Boggart winced at the loud young voices, and peered resentfully out past Volume One of *The Lays of Ancient Rome*. Who were these noisy disrespectful creatures with the strange accent?" This is the stuff of which classics are made: mystery, magic, mischief and an irresistible sprite that will have readers clamoring for more. For more adventures, check out *The Boggart and the Monster*.

The Book of Changes   SHORT STORY COLLECTION

AUTHOR: Tim Wynne-Jones

HC: Orchard • PB: Puffin

THEMES: change; family; friendship

A collection of irreverent and funny short stories that feature friends and families growing and changing together. Affecting and well written, many of the stories feature characters from Wynne-Jones' award-winning collection *Some of the Kinder Planets*.

Brian's Winter   FICTION

AUTHOR: **Gary Paulsen**

HC: Delacorte

THEMES: winter; survival; adventure; snow; courage; wilderness

An "imaginary" sequel to *Hatchet*. In answer to the thousands of letters he has received from readers over the years, Paulsen shows what would have happened had that book's hero, Brian, not been rescued at the end of a summer in the wilderness, but had to face a hostile Canadian winter.

AUTHOR SPOTLIGHT ON GARY PAULSEN

Gary Paulsen has done as much as anyone to create an atmosphere of cool where reading is concerned. Adventure and humor are his trademarks, along with quiet novels that seem, on the surface, to have come from the pen of a different writer than the man who gave us *Harris & Me* and *Hatchet.*

Gary was a nonreader as a boy and a young man. He knows a lot about why boys do not read and uses his knowledge to fashion books that are irresistible to that kind of child. What makes his skill so impressive is that while he attracts the kids who are on the outside of the world of reading, he does not drive away the insiders. He is a great storyteller, and we all respond to that.

He has done picture books (*Worksong, Dogsong,* and *The Tortilla Factory*) and nature-oriented nonfiction (*Father Water, Mother Woods* and *Puppies, Dogs and Blue Northers*), but he is primarily known as a novelist. His novels fall generally into three categories:

Adventure—Having written *Hatchet,* which is one of the most widely read novels for young readers published in the last 20 years, Paulsen's fame stems from his skill as a master of the survival story. In addition to *Hatchet's* sequels (*The River* and *Brian's Winter*), we hope any fan of those books will check out *The Voyage of the Frog, The Haymeadow,* and his paperback series *Gary Paulsen's World of Adventure* the next time they need a good adrenaline rush.

Humor—Laugh-out-loud, side-slapping, not-always-in-the-best-taste *Funny!* There aren't enough writers who know how to make kids laugh. His paperback series *The Culpepper Adventures,* and the novels *The Schernoff Discoveries* and *Harris & Me,* are guaranteed winners and will delight young readers—especially (but not exclusively) boys.

Quieter novels—neither gut-busting nor thrilling page-turners, these are books that grapple with many aspects of the lives of young people and the world in which they live. They cannot all be grouped together by any criteria other than the fact that they examine deeply held moral issues with an open and questioning eye. Their topics cover a lot of ground, from slavery to religious fervor, gun issues to homelessness, all with characteristic sensitivity and plenty of room for the reader to make up his own mind. Our favorites of these include: *The Cook Camp, The Monument, Dancing Carl, Nightjohn, The Tent,* and *The Winter Room.*

It's a tremendous and tremendously satisfying output, from a writer who offers up a great storytelling adventure every time, regardless of how he may make you gasp, guffaw, or think.

★ The Bridge to Terabithia   FICTION

AUTHOR: Katherine Paterson

HC/PB: HarperCollins

THEMES: death; gifted child; loss; grief; friendship; fitting in

Paterson is an author of rare power and sensitivity who could easily command a chapter of her own in any textbook on children's literature. Her affecting and brilliantly written novels are standards in classrooms and libraries and are loved passionately by children and former children the world over. We would venture to say that none is more beloved than *A Bridge to Terabithia,* the Newbery-winning story of two outsider children and their magical, life-affirming relationship. This is a moving book that reads rather easily considering the toughness of the subject matter: the devastating and sudden loss of a dear friend. This book lives inside people for years after reading it and you and your children deserve the chance to discover its beauty for yourselves. Then, when you have dried your eyes and are ready for more outstanding reading, look for these books by Paterson, each a masterpiece in its own right: *Jacob Have I Loved, Come Sing Jimmy Jo, The Great Gilly Hopkins,* and *Lyddie.*

★ Bull Run   FICTION

AUTHOR: Paul Fleischman

HC/PB: HarperCollins

THEMES: fighting; point of view; comparisons; diversity; U.S. history, Civil War

Step back in time for a look at characters, Northern and Southern, who were affected by the Battle of Bull Run. It's impossible to read this account of war without thinking about the perspectives of both sides. As a bonus, this makes for great reader's theater.

If there had been books like this available when I was a young student, I'm sure I would have been more interested in history!

But That's Another Story: Favorite Authors
Introduce Popular Genres   SHORT STORY ANTHOLOGY

EDITOR: Sandy Asher

HC: Walker

THEMES: reading; writing; authors

Children go through phases of wanting to read the same kinds of books over and over—they get onto an author or series and just won't let go.

This bothers some adults, though we tend to think it isn't a cause for concern, as we are confident in most readers' abilities to grow their tastes. However, if you have a reader who is a slave to one genre, use this book as an introduction to the different categories of fiction available to him. Thirteen writers have contributed an original short story to this collection and each is interviewed by editor Asher, to give the reader a tantalizing glimpse at what is going on in other sections of the bookstore. In addition, this is a valuable book to use with young writers, who fall prey to many of the sameness traps as young readers.

By the Great Horn Spoon   FICTION

AUTHOR: Sid Fleischman • ILLUSTRATOR: Eric Von Schmidt
HC/PB: Little Brown
THEMES: U.S. history, Westward movement; U.S. history, the Gold Rush; California; humor; hiding; adventure

Eureka! The California Gold Rush has begun, and young Jack Flagg has set out from Boston with his trusty sidekick, Praiseworthy, to seek his fortune. Young readers will have a rip roaring time with this adventurous duo.

Cat Running   FICTION

AUTHOR: Zilpha Keatley Snyder
HC: Delacorte • PB: Dell
THEMES: racing; poverty; homelessness; track and field; California; competition; prejudice; strong girls; U.S. history, the Depression; U.S.A., Dust Bowl

Set in Central California during the Great Depression, this novel nonetheless deals with many of today's issues: poverty, homelessness and prejudice. A fast-paced adventure about a strong willed runner, who is the best in her town, and a new competitor who doesn't even bother to put shoes on his feet, it will keep the pages turning.

Charlie Pippin   FICTION

AUTHOR: Candy Dawson Boyd
HC: Macmillan • PB: Puffin
THEMES: monuments; fathers and daughters; African American; peace; strong girl; death; Vietnam Veteran's Memorial; U.S. history, Vietnam War

Charlie Pippin's dad is acting crankier than usual and won't talk about what's bothering him. When eleven-year-old Charlie decides to figure things out for herself, her curiosity leads her to the Vietnam Memorial and to his past. Boyd handles this war veteran's problems with sensitivity while showing that an understanding heart can begin to heal deep scars.

Chasing Redbird   FICTION

AUTHOR: Sharon Creech
HC: HarperCollins
THEMES: coming of age; friendship; grief; death; siblings; farms; trail-blazing; camping; guilt; family life; strong girls

When thirteen-year-old Zinny discovers an overgrown trail that begins on her family farm, she decides to clear it to have time on her own away from her family, where she can think. Her aunt has died. Her uncle is acting strange. And she can't get her cousin Rose out of her mind—Rose, who died of the whooping cough she got from Zinny. Thirteen is not an easy age, especially when it's complicated by grief, guilt, and a boy named Jake. Creech shows her readers, with a touch of mystery, how one girl clears her problems along with a trail through the "whole wide-open countryside."

Children of the Dust Bowl: The True Story of the
School at Weedpatch Camp   NONFICTION

AUTHOR: Jerry Stanley • ILLUSTRATOR: (photographs)
HC/PB: Crown
THEMES: U.S.A., the Dust Bowl; U.S. history, the Depression; home-lessness; survival; getting along; prejudice

This is the true story of the children of migrant workers from Oklahoma who helped to build a school at a farm labor camp in California. A useful piece of nonfiction to have on hand when discussing Steinbeck's *The Grapes of Wrath,* as Steinbeck's personal interest in the school is detailed in Stanley's fine account of this important achievement.

The City of Gold and Lead   SCIENCE FICTION

AUTHOR: John Christopher
PB: Aladdin
THEMES: gifted child; courage; invasion; good vs. evil; science fiction

First in a classic trilogy that has served as an introduction to science fiction for generations of children. If your child is reading *Animorphs,* make sure he knows about these. Other titles are: *The Pool Of Fire* and *The White Mountains.*

City of Light, City of Dark: A Comic Book Novel   FICTION-FANTASY
AUTHOR: Avi • ILLUSTRATOR: Brian Floca
HC/PB: Orchard
THEMES: adventure; fantasy; winter; seasons; magic; comic book style;
folklore; New York; strong women; courage

We wish there were more books like this. A tale of epic proportions, told in
a black-and-white comic book format that makes for some exciting reading.
With plenty of adventure and strong characters, this mythic story of the battle for power over light and dark will appeal to accomplished readers (there
is plenty of text), but can also be used with more reluctant readers who need
a strong visual component to help them understand a complex story. If you
have a *Tin Tin* lover on your hands, make sure you give him this.

Crash   FICTION
AUTHOR: Jerry Spinelli
HC/PB: Knopf
THEMES: bullies; sports; competition; friendship

Going inside the mind of a bully isn't an easy thing, but author Spinelli
does it with unexpected results. Young readers will recognize the characters here and are bound to discuss them. You may be surprised at the
things they say, if you are lucky enough to be a part of their conversation.

The Dark Way: Stories From the
Spirit World   FOLKLORE COLLECTION
AUTHOR: **Virginia Hamilton** • ILLUSTRATOR: Lambert Davis
HC: Harcourt Brace
THEMES: folklore; African American; scary stories; ghosts

Scary, spiritual and evoking the best of around-the-fire storytelling.
Hamilton never lets us down.

Darnell Rock Reporting   FICTION
AUTHOR: **Walter Dean Myers**
HC: Delacorte • PB: Dell
THEMES: homelessness; conscience; taking action; school; newspa-
pers; community; writing

Darnell Rock is thirteen years old and he does not like school. He can't
seem to do anything right. But when the principal gives him one more
chance if he works on the school newspaper, he discovers that he can
make a difference. His articles about the homeless people in the area provide the catalyst to start a worthwhile food project in his neighborhood.

AUTHOR SPOTLIGHT ON
VIRGINIA HAMILTON

VIRGINIA Hamilton is a gifted writer—a storyteller with the heart and skill of a poet. Whether writing novels of fantasy or gritty reality, picture books or biographies, she weaves words together with such mastery that the reader is often stunned by the imagery. A demanding writer who believes strongly in the bond of language between herself and her audience, she has experimented with style and form in her quest to portray the African-American experience, and to best serve the tale she seeks to tell.

It is as a novelist that she made her mark, winning a Newbery Award for *M.C. Higgins the Great* in 1975, as well as three Newbery Honors. Her books *Zeely, Arrilla Sun Down, The House of Dies Drear,* and especially *The Planet of Junior Brown* established her as one of the great novelists for young adults. These are not "easy" books—they cannot be read frivolously or readily forgotten, and young readers may require some assistance from adults to help them to fully appreciate these books' richness.

Hamilton's mastery of language makes her novels a pleasure to read aloud, but the feeling of the spoken word is even more prevalent in Hamilton's collections of stories and folklore. In books like *The Dark Way: Stories From the Spirit World, Her Stories, In The Beginning: Creation Stories From Around the World,* and *The People Could Fly,* the retellings are so good, the writing so sure, and the feel of the time, place and culture so inviting that one need only speak the words as they are written to bring the stories to life—Hamilton has done the work for us. Even when she does not write in a dialect, the care with which she chooses her words and her judicious use of rhythm create a feel of another place when read out loud.

In her historical fiction (*Willie Bea and the Time When the Martians Landed*), science fiction (*Justice and Her Brothers, Dustland,* and *The Gathering*), biography (*Anthony Burns: The Defeat and Triumph of a Fugitive Slave*), or her other novels which defy easy categorization (*Sweet Whispers, Brothers Rush*), Hamilton delivers a brilliant reading experience and has held the lamp of her considerable talent up to illuminate the life of the African-American child for over 30 years. We long for 30 more.

Dateline: Troy
FICTION

AUTHOR: Paul Fleischman • ILLUSTRATOR: Gwen Frankfeldt & Glenn Morrow

HC: Candlewick

THEMES: ancient Greece; ancient history; Trojan War; newspapers; comparisons

Paul Fleischman is amazing. He stretches conventional style and continues to succeed in showing history, not simply explaining it. This retelling of the Trojan War is juxtaposed with contemporary news headlines and stories comparing the past with current events. There is no way readers can deny that history repeats itself. Whether interested in history or not, Fleischman gets them thinking.

The Daydreamer
FICTION-FANTASY

AUTHOR: Ian McEwan • ILLUSTRATOR: Anthony Browne

HC/PB: HarperCollins

THEMES: imagination; point of view; dreams; fantasy; individuality; daydreams

This is a book about a special child—the kind who tends to stare out the window instead of paying attention in class. He may have trouble keeping focused on the matter at hand because his imagined life is far more interesting than anything

> Reading allows the luxury of retreating from the world into a private place. It is a solo activity that can be shared, but only by invitation.

else going on. This kind of kid has a rich inner world that can sometimes get mixed up with reality, and this book shows his fantasies in all their glory. Terrific fantasy writing, sure to captivate the right kid.

Discovering the Iceman: An I Was There Book
NONFICTION

AUTHOR: Shelley Tanaka • ILLUSTRATOR: Laurie McGaw

HC: Hyperion

THEMES: human body; history, prehistory; anthropology; science; mummies

Factual, with just enough gross stuff to hold reluctant readers, this is a fascinating look at the anthropological opportunity of a lifetime—a perfectly preserved man from thousands of years ago.

Don't Open the Door After the Sun Goes Down
SHORT STORY COLLECTION

AUTHOR: Al Carusone • ILLUSTRATOR: Andrew Glass
HC/PB: Hyperion
THEMES: scary stories

Well-written scary stories that aren't gruesome. Each has a twist you don't see coming. Short fiction that you can use with readers who can't or won't read longer books.

Eating the Plates: The Pilgrim Book of Food and Manners
NONFICTION

AUTHOR: Lucille Recht Penner
HC: Simon & Schuster • PB: Aladdin
THEMES: U.S.A., New England; U.S. history, Colonial America; eating; Thanksgiving; traditions; pilgrims; food; manners

Fascinating, and full of interesting details that will keep a kid reading long after she finds the fact she is looking for. This book details the customs and food rituals of the Pilgrims.

Escape From Slavery: The Boyhood of Frederick Douglass in His Own Words
BIOGRAPHY

EDITOR/ILLUSTRATOR: Michael McCurdy • AUTHOR: Frederick Douglass
HC: Knopf
THEMES: U.S. history, the Civil War; autobiography; slavery; African American; escape; freedom

This powerful account of Frederick Douglass' life—in his own words—is likely to move readers into learning more about this extraordinary man.

> "Freedom now appeared, to disappear no more. It was heard in every sound, and seen in every thing. It was ever present to torment me with a sense of my wretched condition. I saw nothing without seeing it, I heard nothing without hearing it, and felt nothing without feeling it. It looked from every star, it smiled in every calm, breathed in every wind, and moved in every storm."
> —Frederick Douglass
> (after he finally learned to read)

Every Living Thing   SHORT STORY COLLECTION
AUTHOR: **Cynthia Rylant** • ILLUSTRATOR: S.D. Schindler
PB: Aladdin
THEMES: animals; pets; love; respect; responsibility; change

A moving and inspiring collection of stories that deal with how animals and people's lives come together.. Terrific to read aloud.

Eye Spy: A Mysterious Alphabet   PICTURE BOOK NONFICTION
AUTHOR/ILLUSTRATOR: Linda Bourke
HC/PB: Chronicle
THEMES: guessing; word play; puzzles; homonyms; vocabulary; alphabet

Treat yourself to a challenge. The format suggests that this is a book for young ones, but all I have to do is pick this book up and show how it works and the older kids are sold! Each page is a clue leading to a guessing game that is harder than it looks.

Fly! A Brief History of Flight   PICTURE BOOK NONFICTION
AUTHOR/ILLUSTRATOR: Barry Moser
HC: HarperCollins
THEMES: inventions; courage; flying; airplanes; trailblazers; history, world

A treasure of nonfiction information, well laid-out and perfectly illustrated.

TAKING FLIGHT

Readers get a lot of information from books (how to build an add-on to the deck, trace your family tree, or find the capital of Libya), but that's just the beginning of the value to be had from books. When you read, you are not limited by where you live, who your relatives are, how much money you have, or if you're the smartest or the fastest. You can travel beyond boundaries and explore the feelings and customs of unfamiliar people real or imagined. Most of us don't choose to read with such abandon, exploring all those other worlds. We choose what we read with specific tastes and needs in mind. But it's those possibilities, the knowledge that the journey is there for the taking, which are one of the chief delights of reading.

The Fragile Flag

FICTION

AUTHOR: Jane Langton

HC/PB: HarperCollins

THEMES: courage; strong g!rls; peace; fables; worry; conscience; taking action

A lot has changed in the world since Jane Langton wrote this modern-day fable of one girl's vision of peace, but no matter how dated the story becomes, it will have value until the day when there are simply no more weapons of mass destruction. Fables set in contemporary times are hard to pull off—most of us like our fantasy set in the past or in an imaginary place—but Langton's Georgie is a true visionary as well as an authentic child. A great book to read aloud as a family or in a classroom and use as a basis to discuss what can be done to work toward peace.

From the Mixed-Up Files of Mrs. Basil E. Frankweiler

FICTION

AUTHOR/ILLUSTRATOR: E.L. Konigsburg

HC: Atheneum • PB: Aladdin

THEMES: New York; running away; museums; art; humor; mystery

The Metropolitan Museum of Art seems an unlikely choice for young runaways seeking refuge, but when Claudia and Jamie sneak away from home, that is exactly where they end up. And when a question arises over the authenticity of a piece of art, they find themselves in the midst of a suspense-filled adventure. Konigsburg's Newbery Medal-winning story is fine for reading aloud, but we also recommend this for young readers ready to get lost in a good book!

A Girl From Yamhill

BIOGRAPHY

AUTHOR: Beverly Cleary

HC: Morrow • PB: Avon

THEMES: U.S. history, between the World Wars; Oregon; autobiography; authors

The early years of the life of the writer who grew up to create *Ramona the Pest* and *Henry Huggins,* told in a straightforward manner that minimizes none of the hardships. Excellent autobiographical writing that gives a sense of time and place as well as the events that shaped her life. A sequel, *My Own Two Feet,* covers her early adulthood.

Gladiator

AUTHOR/ILLUSTRATOR: Richard Watkins

HC: Houghton Mifflin

THEMES: ancient history; ancient Rome; athletes; sports; captivity; soldiers; fighting; slavery

An in-depth look at the life of the great Roman combatants, full of fascinating facts and enough gory details to intrigue the most bloodthirsty among us. Good example of how to get kids to read history by focusing on the less stuffy aspects. We guarantee that they will fight over this one.

The Glory Field

AUTHOR: **Walter Dean Myers**

HC/PB: Scholastic

THEMES: African American; slavery; U.S. history; courage; Africa; family history; ancestors; Harlem; prejudice; captivity; freedom; hardship; triumph

This is the saga of the Lewis family, which begins in 1753 Africa when Muhammad Bilal is kidnapped and taken in chains to a plantation in South Carolina. It follows the family through 1864, 1900, 1930 and 1964 to the present time in Harlem, New York. This *Roots*-like epic will capture the reader's interest not only in the characters but in the history of the African American people.

The Golem

AUTHOR: Isaac Bashevis Singer • ILLUSTRATOR: Uri Shulevitz

HC/PB: Farrar Straus & Giroux

THEMES: Jews; magic; fathers and sons; folklore; Prague; clay

Singer's longer retelling of this folktale goes more into the depth of the story—the plight of the Jews in the Prague ghetto and the inner thoughts of the conflicted rabbi—than other versions, making this an excellent book to turn to if the two picture book adaptations whet the appetite for more.

The Great Fire

AUTHOR: Jim Murphy

HC/PB: Scholastic

THEMES: U.S. history, late 19th century; Chicago; fire; disaster

Dramatic details from people who were there during the 1871 Chicago fire combine with Murphy's riveting text to create a story that holds the attention of even the most skeptical about nonfiction.

The Great Gilly Hopkins

FICTION

AUTHOR: Katherine Paterson
PB: HarperTrophy
THEMES: misbehaving; yearning; foster homes; family; survival; friendship; gifted child; anger

Galadriel Hopkins is about to enter her third foster home in less than three years, and this "difficult" eleven-year-old is not going to make things easy. Smart, brash, fearful and longing for a real home, Gilly makes a reader think about kids who strike out against the world around them. A rich, moving story.

The Greek News

PICTURE BOOK NONFICTION

AUTHOR: Anton Powell • ILLUSTRATOR: Philip Steele
HC: Candlewick
THEMES: ancient Greece; ancient history; newspapers; Greek mythology

A smashing series that takes history and brings it vividly to life with a jolt of journalism. In newspaper layout, the crucial facts of the day are presented, tabloid-style, with headlines, sidebars and plenty of illustrations. A sure-fire bet to entice nonreaders and delight history buffs. Also: *The Egyptian News, The Roman News,* and *The Aztec News.* For another angle on historical journalism, see *Dateline Troy.*

Grossology: The Science of Really Gross Things

NONFICTION

AUTHOR: Sylvia Branzei • ILLUSTRATOR: Jack Keely
HC: Planet Dexter
THEMES: science experiments; humor, gross; science; nature

Everything you've never wanted to know about scabs, snot, vomit, and dandruff. A terrific way to bring otherwise reluctant kids to an understanding of science, if you have the stomach for it!

Guests

FICTION

AUTHOR: Michael Dorris
HC/PB: Hyperion
THEMES: Native American; Pilgrims; food; change; traditions; celebrations; strangers; prejudice; U.S. history, Colonial America

A Native American boy is cautious about the visitors who are invited to join the Harvest Festival. "The guests will spoil everything, even my memory of other times. I wished they had never left wherever they came from before they came here. I wished they would return there again and forget the trail through the sea that they followed." Dorris' novel captures the feelings of a young boy who knows there must be change, in himself and in the world around him.

Harriet and the Promised Land   PICTURE BOOK NONFICTION
AUTHOR/ILLUSTRATOR: Jacob Lawrence
HC: Simon & Schuster
THEMES: Harriet Tubman; Underground Railroad; prejudice; slavery; courage; freedom; escape

It's worth its weight in art alone. Add the rhythmic verse portraying Harriet Tubman's struggle, and you'll want this gem in your library.

★ Harriet the Spy   FICTION
AUTHOR/ILLUSTRATOR: Louise Fitzhugh
HC/PB: HarperCollins
THEMES: school; friendship; family; writing; loss; secrets; revenge; lying; spying; truth; diaries

Even though she is the heroine of the book, Harriet is not particularly likable; she is flippant and often disrespectful, and is always writing down her ruthless observations about people in her notebook. She wants to be a writer, and her beloved Nurse, Ole Golly, has raised her with wisdom from classic literature, encouraging her "to thine own self be true." Ole Golly leaves to get married, saying that eleven is too old to have a nurse, and Harriet's world changes drastically. When her notebook falls into the hands of her astonished classmates, their vengeful attitudes and deliberately mean actions confuse Harriet, causing her to act similarly toward them. Harriet's parents are too busy with their own lives to be of any use to her until the situation becomes too awful to ignore.

How this all gets resolved, with hurt feelings soothed, friendships restored, parents coming to new understandings, and, most importantly, Harriet being true to herself while learning how to get along better in the world, makes for a once in a lifetime reading experience. There is no one in all of fiction quite like Harriet M. Welsch.

★ Hatchet   FICTION
AUTHOR: **Gary Paulsen**
PB: Aladdin
THEMES: survival; airplanes; solitude; resourcefulness; divorce; courage

It is entirely possible that no book in the past twenty years has grabbed so many kids as this one. It is certainly one we hear the most when talking to young readers about good books they have read. A perfect book about survival in the wilderness, featuring a boy named Brian whose heartbreak and resourcefulness you will remember for the rest of your life.

Horror Stories   ANTHOLOGY
AUTHOR: Susan Price • ILLUSTRATOR: Harry Horse
PB: Kingfisher
THEMES: scary stories; horror

Part of the *Story Library* series, this terrific selection of scary stories has a higher literary quotient than much popular horror fiction. Expose readers to good writing while still scaring the wits out of them.

The House With a Clock in Its Walls   FICTION-MYSTERY
AUTHOR: John Bellairs
PB: Puffin
THEMES: horror; mystery; adventure

Well written, though they stick close to their "formula," Bellairs' suspense filled and entertaining mystery thrillers are the perfect reads for children who are progressing fast beyond their own second or third grade reading levels but may not be emotionally ready for the more frightening horror novels the older kids are reading. In fact, these are so good that many of the fifth and sixth graders who read nothing else but adult horror become huge fans of Bellairs' work when introduced to him. There are many novels, and some of the best are: *The Trolley to Yesterday, The Vengeance of the Witch-Finder,* and *The Ghost in the Mirror.*

I Am Lavina Cumming   FICTION
AUTHOR: Susan Lowell • ILLUSTRATOR: Paul Mirocha
PB: Milkweed Editions
THEMES: California; San Francisco; family; courage; strong girls; earthquakes; coming of age; U.S. history, early 20th century

Travel back in time and meet a young girl on a train ride away from home for the first time. Ten-year-old Lavina's mother has died and her father cannot raise her properly on their Arizona ranch, so she is on her way to California to live with an aunt she has never met. This coming of age novel, set at the time of the Great San Francisco Earthquake, is sure to turn young readers into fans of historical fiction.

I Am the Mummy Heb-Nefert   PICTURE BOOK

AUTHOR: **Eve Bunting** • ILLUSTRATOR: David Christiana
HC: Harcourt Brace
THEMES: point of view; ancient history; rituals; death; memories; love; ancient Egypt; mummies; burial

This picture book is not for younger children, but it simply screams to be used for sixth-grade. Narrated from the point of view of a mummy, this story brings Ancient Egypt alive in a most unusual and intriguing way. Master storyteller Bunting is mightily aided by the awesome power of David Christiana's art.

★ The Indian in the Cupboard   FICTION-FANTASY

AUTHOR: Lynne Reid Banks • ILLUSTRATOR: Brock Cole
HC: Doubleday • PB: Avon
THEMES: Native American; little folk; magic; fantasy; adventure; friendship; toys; cowboys

Nine-year-old Omri's birthday present from his best friend is a second-hand, tiny plastic Indian. His brother's gift is an old medicine cupboard for which his mother provided a box of old keys. One is the perfect fit. At bedtime, Omri places the Indian in the cupboard, turns the lock and sleepily closes his eyes. "Just as he was dropping off to sleep his eyes snapped open. He had thought he heard a little noise . . . but no. All was

My first real, beloved, grown-up books were not the great classics many writers claim they devoured before they could digest solid food. They were the (British) Claudia books, which sucked me into the joy of total immersion when I was going on fifteen.

I'm not even ashamed. I have a feeling that if I re-read this series now, I would still love Claudia, laugh myself sick, fall in love with David and suffer a physical shock and sorrow when their son Bobby is run over and killed.

The books you love when you're young build your bones. They become part of you and never, ever leave you. That's why it's so important for people in charge of children to realize that books fill our empty spaces, and that, in all of us, these spaces come in different shapes and sizes. It follows that people read what they need.

—Lynne Reid Banks,
author of *The Indian in the Cupboard*

quiet. His eyes closed again." This gem is not simply a magical adventure. It stretches into territory that includes a young boy's sense of responsibility, moral dilemmas and the ability to give life—and take it away. Read it aloud, or give it to a fourth or fifth grader to relish. We'd hate to have it lost on very young children who could miss some important elements, never to return to experience its full pleasure. When the first volume has been devoured, readers will want to go on to others in the series, exciting adventures on their own: *The Return of the Indian, The Secret of the Indian,* and *The Mystery of the Cupboard.*

An Indian Winter
PICTURE BOOK NONFICTION

AUTHOR: Russell Freedman • ILLUSTRATOR: Karl Bodmer
HC: Holiday House
THEMES: journeys; Native American; adventure; biography; farming; dance; hunting; illness; diaries; traditions; winter; U.S. history, 19th century; U.S.A., the Midwest

Freedman tells about the experiences of a German prince, Alexander Philipp Maximilian, and a young Swiss artist as they traveled through the Missouri River Valley in 1833—recording their impressions in words and pictures. These two European adventurers offer fascinating descriptions and stories about the Indians who befriended them. Another fascinating account of Native American history can be found in Freedman's *Buffalo Hunt.*

Insides, Outsides, Loops and Lines
NONFICTION

AUTHOR: Herbert Kohl • ILLUSTRATOR: Winky Adam
PB: W. H. Freeman
THEMES: Africa; maps; games; math; drawing

Math is not all arithmetic. Those searching for an alternative can find one here in a volume filled with map making, games, drawings, designs that play with the eye, traditional patterns from Africa called lusona, and other brain-stretching challenges.

The Iron Dragon Never Sleeps
FICTION

AUTHOR: Stephen Krensky • ILLUSTRATOR: Stephen Fulweiler
PB: Dell
THEMES: friendship; Chinese; California; U.S. history, Westward movement; cultural diversity; railroad

A young girl whose father is helping to build the Central Pacific Railroad in 1867 befriends a young Chinese tea carrier. Their cultural differ-

ences, along with the depiction of life in 1867 make this a good choice
for understanding that time in California history.

It's a Girl Thing: How to Stay Healthy, Safe, and in Charge
PICTURE BOOK

AUTHOR: Mavis Jukes • ILLUSTRATOR: Debbie Tilley
HC: Houghton Mifflin
THEMES: sex; sexuality; coming of age; health; change; puberty; girls

Straightforward and funny, Jukes answers questions girls have to think
about, like buying bras, puberty and sexuality.

*I wish I'd had this book when I was a preteen. There were fasci-
nating, creative ideas going around back then. It would have been
fun finding humor in the realities of growing up, not just in what
we'd made up. If this had existed when they were younger, my
daughters would have devoured it from front to back.*

Jeremy Thatcher, Dragon Hatcher
FICTION-FANTASY

AUTHOR: Bruce Coville • ILLUSTRATOR: Gary A. Lippincott
HC: Harcourt Brace • PB: Pocket Books
THEMES: dragons; magic; responsibility; choices; love; consequences

Mr. Elives' Magic Shop is not the kind of place you can find easily. Usually it finds you, and only when you need it. And then a magical item
chooses you and the adventure begins. In later books Jennifer Murdley
learns a lesson about the true meaning of beauty from a talking toad
(*Jennifer Murdley's Toad*) and Charlie Eggleston suffers through the wise-
cracks and awful jokes of a talking skull (Yorick's, no less) on his way to
an encounter with Truth herself (*The Skull of Truth*). But in this book,
Jeremy Thatcher's destined item is a multicolored ball, an egg containing a tiny dragon that communicates with him telepathically. Raising a
mischief-loving dragon named Tiamat isn't easy, and as she grows she
teaches him more about love than he ever knew it was possible to know.
Coville has a knack for mixing realism and fantasy, laughter and tears
into a potion that makes for superb reading. This is our favorite of his
books, and it fits solidly in the canon of dragon tales after Jackie French
Koller's *Dragonling* books but before Jane Yolen's *Pit Dragon Trilogy*.

Journey FICTION

AUTHOR/ILLUSTRATOR: Patricia MacLachlan
HC: Delacorte • PB: Dell
THEMES: family; memories; abandonment; grandfathers and grandsons; farms; photographs; family history; cats; pets; memory

Reeling from the sudden exit of his mother from his life, and clinging to the hope that she will someday return (a hope neither his sister nor grandparents share), young Journey searches for a way to cope with his anger and devastating sense of loss. His grandfather has turned to photography, his grandmother to playing the flute, and his sister to relentless gardening, but there seems to be no activity that can help him master his feelings. How his remaining family members fill in the holes in both his memory and his heart and how Journey comes to realize the source of love that has always been there for him make this one of MacLachlan's most poignant works. Her spare, elegant writing is full of depth and feeling, and her ability to find light, humorous moments amid the sadness creates an atmosphere of warmth that envelops the reader. Love and a little time can heal most things, and Journey is blessed with both.

★ Joyful Noise: Poems for Two Voices POETRY COLLECTION

AUTHOR: Paul Fleischman • ILLUSTRATOR: Eric Beddows
HC/PB: HarperCollins
THEMES: sound; rhythm; insects; nature

Two voices read these poems, one the left side, the other the right. And when words exist on both sides at once, they're read together.

"I was born in a
fine old edition of Schiller

    While I started life
    in a private eye thriller

We're book lice   We're book lice
who dwell   who dwell
in these dusty bookshelves   in these dusty bookshelves."

Fleischman's poetic guide to the insect world—from Book Lice to Whirligig Beetles and House Crickets, offers more than a soaring, spinning, glimpse into bug behavior. It creates the opportunity to experience a "musical duet" perormed by two readers simultaneously. And whether you are a listener or reader, you will be richer for participating.

A book for two voices requires two readers. Reading it is a social, not a solitary pastime. All through my years at home it was my parents' habit after dinner to retire to the living room to play a game or two, games my sisters and I often joined. As with geologic eras, those years could be divided into concentration and rummy, early cribbage, Chess, double solitaire, late Cribbage, and so on. For a time, my mother copied out the cryptogram from the *Saturday Review* and raced my father in decoding it. I'm sure that those thousands of evenings, that education in the pleasures of being with others, in the joys to be found in joint amusements impossible alone, led in large part to my two-voiced books. One hand can't produce a clap, or play a game of checkers. Two can. Synergy! The television, I might add, was in a different room and seldom seemed to be on. A family watching television together isn't engaged in a cooperative activity; they're each playing solitaire.

—Paul Fleischman, author of *Joyful Noise*,
from his Newbery Medal acceptance speech

Judy Scuppernong

FICTION

AUTHOR: Brenda Seabrooke • ILLUSTRATOR: Ted Lewin
HC: Dutton • PB: Bantam
THEMES: friendship; mystery; secrets; U.S.A., the South; alcoholism;
U.S. history, the 50's

Lyrical and wistful, this brief reminiscence of a magical summer in four girls' lives is full of elation and sadness. In short prose poems that give more description than their length would indicate, it tells of three friends, Deanna, Lala, and Stacy, whose lives are changed by the freespirit Judy Sculpholm. Read this aloud to your daughters and discuss your own childhood with them.

Lassie Come Home

FICTION

AUTHOR: Eric Knight
PB: Dell
THEMES: family; lost; dogs; courage; separation; pets; England; Scotland; love

The classic boy and a dog story and the basis for countless movies and television episodes, this is a story of rare courage and heart. The reason it has lasted and become a part of our pop culture is its timelessness. You'll love reading this aloud to your family. Check out the picture book version *Eric Knight's Lassie Come Home*, by Rosemary Wells and Susan Jeffers for an introduction for younger listeners.

★ Lily's Crossing

FICTION

AUTHOR: Patricia Reilly Giff

HC: Delacorte

THEMES: U.S. history, World War II; grandmothers; refugees; fathers and daughters; taking action; courage; individuality; strong girls; friendship; separation; lying

You will never forget Lily, a heroine who ranks with Ramona Quimby and Anne of Green Gables for sheer spunkiness, as she copes with the changes World War II has brought to her life. Chief among these is the absence of her beloved father and having to live with her grandmother in Far Rockaway, NY. Headstrong and given to flights of fancy that some people think are lies, Lily is a handful, but a more loving and sympathetic portrayal of such a child would be hard to imagine. A treasure.

Lincoln in His Own Words

BIOGRAPHY

AUTHOR: Milton Meltzer • ILLUSTRATOR: Stephen Alcorn

HC: Harcourt Brace

THEMES: Abraham Lincoln; U.S. history, the Civil War; U.S. presidents; mail; speeches

Historian Meltzer has put together a fascinating collection of Lincoln's speeches, letters and writings. A brief comment at the beginning of each section helps the reader understand what was happening at that moment of Lincoln's life and highlights its historical significance.

Lizard Music

SCIENCE FICTION

AUTHOR: Daniel Pinkwater

PB: Dell

THEMES: solitude; zany; lizards; science fiction

Victor's parents go on vacation, leaving him in the care of his older sister. When she announces that she is going on a trip and leaving him home alone, he responds with all the glee that one would expect from an eleven-year-old—Yippee! He can stay up late and watch his favorite TV shows, order pizza (WITH anchovies for a change) and generally lead the sort of life all kids dream of. But wait! What is the weird, late-night TV program with the all-lizard band playing strange music? What is the lizards' connection to the increasing number of bizzare goings-on around town? And what does the mysterious Chicken Man have to do with it all? The answers are all here, delivered in quintessential Pinkwater style.

This is the book that will either turn you into a fan or leave you cold, as you will either get his sense of humor or you won't. Pinkwater's balance between secrets and revelation tends to wobble, and since he takes his time with the narrative, we can imagine that many who are not tuned into his quirky eye for detail can get weary. He can also get just a little too clever, often at the expense of anything happening in the story! However, we have found that the secret is to not resist—simply succumb and go along for the ride. When he writes in shorter format (check out his picture books and early story books) his deadpan meandering is charming. He gets more obtuse the longer his books are. We have to be in the right frame of mind for him, and when we are, he is a treasure! Look for *The Hoboken Chicken Emergency*, *Fat Men From Space* (two novels for younger readers), *Guys From Space*, and *Jolly Roger* at your bookstore or library.

Made in China: Ideas and Inventions
From Ancient China   NONFICTION

AUTHOR: Suzanne Williams • ILLUSTRATOR: Andrea Fong
HC: Pacific View Press
THEMES: trailblazing; China; ancient history; inventions; science experiments; science; maps

"You can't hunt rhinoceros in China. But once you could." So begins a fascinating account of China from 4,000 years ago to the 1500s. Don't limit this one to history projects. Any curious child will want to learn how the Chinese made salt, paper, calendars, compasses, even a seismograph to measure earthquakes. They recycled old tools, discovered natural gas, created Chinese medicine. With words and a mix of maps, photographs and drawings, this will whet the appetite of future historians and scientists.

Malcolm X: By Any Means Necessary   BIOGRAPHY

AUTHOR: **Walter Dean Myers**
HC/PB: Scholastic
THEMES: U.S. history, the 50's; U.S. history, the 60's; African American; prejudice; courage; taking action; biography; civil rights

Of the biographies we've read of Malcolm X, Walter Dean Myers' version is the best for fifth and sixth graders.

★ Maniac Magee   FICTION

AUTHOR: Jerry Spinelli

HC: Little Brown • PB: HarperCollins

THEMES: cultural diversity; track and field; tall tales; individuality; diversity; homelessness; prejudice; friendship; fables; orphans

"They say Maniac Magee was born in a dump. They say his stomach was a cereal box and his heart a sofa spring. They say he kept an eight-inch cockroach on a leash and that rats stood guard over him while he slept." That's how it starts. But Maniac Magee was not born in a dump. He was an orphan who had to make decisions for his own survival. And he was good. And he brought together people who lived on opposite sides of town, people who despised each other. He was a legend. He was the kind of legend worth reading about.

Mexico's Ancient City of Teotihuacan:
The First Metropolis In The Americas   NONFICTION

AUTHOR: Caroline Arnold • ILLUSTRATOR: Richard Hewett (photographs)

HC: Clarion

THEMES: Mexico; ancient history; cities

The story of the first big city in North America, built hundreds of years before Columbus arrived. A good combination of engaging writing, fascinating facts, and photos that will entertain children while they read for a book report. Arnold and Hewett have a knack for nonfiction, both for younger and older children, and their books have a consistently high level of quality. Their series of books about animals (*Camel, Snake, Giraffe, Koala*—all from Morrow Junior Books) are perfect for middle elementary grades.

★ Mick Harte Was Here   FICTION

AUTHOR: Barbara Park

HC/PB: Knopf

THEMES: death; safety; bicycles; family; brothers; sisters; loss; humor

This story will make you cry. It will make you laugh. It is so real that you feel you know 12-year-old Phoebe, who tells anecdotes about her quirky, fun-loving brother. There is a message here about the importance of wearing a bike helmet, but it never takes over the main theme of loss and its effect on all members of a family. Without sentimentality, Park deals with a difficult subject and turns it into a story to treasure.

Missing May

FICTION

AUTHOR: **Cynthia Rylant**
HC: Orchard • PB: Dell
THEMES: death; grief; loss; family; grandparents

Rylant's Newbery Award-winning novel. A beautiful and powerful book about death, loss, honoring our loved ones, and how we go on.

Mississippi Bridge

FICTION

AUTHOR: Mildred D. Taylor • ILLUSTRATOR: Max Ginsburg
HC: Dial • PB: Bantam
THEMES: civil rights; African American; family; prejudice; U.S.A., the South; U.S. history, the Depression

In Mississippi in the 1930s, black people couldn't ride the bus if it meant there wouldn't be enough room for white people, even if they had purchased their tickets in advance. Taylor has melded bits of history into a moving story that illustrates the injustices of segregation.

Mississippi Mud: Three Prairie Journals

PICTURE BOOK

AUTHOR: Ann Turner • ILLUSTRATOR: Robert J. Blake
HC: HarperCollins
THEMES: U.S. history, Westward movement; pioneers; point of view; siblings; courage; diaries; family; hardship

Another masterpiece from a writer who we have come to respect as one of the best historical writers alive. Learn about a family's trip west in a covered wagon from three diaries recorded within this moving and powerful picture book. One character's point of view is then compounded by the next until we get the whole picture of the trials and adventures of Amanda and her family on their way to Oregon.

Morning Girl

FICTION

AUTHOR: Michael Dorris
HC/PB: Hyperion
THEMES: Native American; U.S. history, pre-Columbus; siblings; Columbus; point of view; cultural diversity; prejudice; strong girls; coming of age; social studies

In alternating chapters, Morning Girl, a twelve-year-old Taino, and her younger brother, Star Boy, talk about their lives. "In our house, though, my brother was the footprints. He messed up the niceness for me. Just being himself, he was too loud: making jokes when he should be serious, talking when he should listen, running when he should sit, banging two rocks together for no reason except to disturb the silence . . ." Warm, carefully chosen words take the reader into the lives of these characters, helping us to understand how and why they think and feel. The powerful ending packs a wallop and will leave the reader thinking long after the last page has been turned.

Music and Drum: Voices of War and Peace, Hope and Dreams   POETRY ANTHOLOGY

EDITOR: Laura Robb • ILLUSTRATOR: Debra Lill
HC: Philomel
THEMES: war; peace; survival; fighting

". . . I saw an angel with wings pure white Breaking the rifles one by one, shattering to pieces each gun . . ." Chief Joseph, Carl Sandburg, Langston Hughes and Matti Yosef are among the poets whose voices—from all over the world—speak out about war and peace. This poignant, inspiring anthology for children and adults will move you, whether read aloud in a group or quietly alone.

My Fellow Americans: A Family Album   PICTURE BOOK NONFICTION

AUTHOR/ILLUSTRATOR: Alice Provensen
HC: Browndeer • PB: Voyager
THEMES: U.S. history; biography; heroes; cultural diversity; politics

In the Author's Note, Provensen describes her fellow Americans: ". . . its rich uncles and poor relations, its atheists and believers, its scoundrels and bigots, its gifted and compassionate . . ." This oversized album gives a sampling of the characters who make up America—from Cesar Chavez to Henry Ford, Sojourner Truth to Frank Lloyd Wright. Don't wait for a history project; these fascinating characters offer young readers a world of possibilities.

★ Nettie's Trip South   PICTURE BOOK

AUTHOR: Ann Turner • ILLUSTRATOR: Ronald Himler
HC: Macmillan • PB: Aladdin
THEMES: slavery; prejudice; U.S. history, Civil War; U.S.A., the South; sadness; diaries; mail; writing; trains; comparisons; self-respect

Based on a real diary, this powerfully moving story about slavery is told through a young Northern girl's letter to her friend. "Addie, I can't get this out of my thoughts: If we slipped into a black skin like a tight coat, everything would change." Don't be fooled by the picture-book format. Nettie's story will lead to difficult questions about a shameful time in our history. It's beautifully written, skillfully illustrated, and important.

Number the Stars   FICTION

AUTHOR: Lois Lowry
HC: Houghton Mifflin • PB: Dell
THEMES: soldiers; history, World War II; prejudice; separation; escape; Jews; friendship; Denmark; hiding; courage

Ellen Rosen and Annemarie Johansen are best friends. But their friendship leads to danger when the Nazis come to Denmark. It's 1943 and Jews are being relocated. Pretending to be a member of their family, Ellen moves in with the Johansens. This gripping story of courage and friendship is difficult to put down until the last page is turned.

On My Honor   FICTION

AUTHOR: Marion Dane Bauer
PB: Dell
THEMES: bicycles; drowning; friendship; death; conscience; responsibility; guilt; promises

Joel promises "On my honor" when his father asks him not to go anywhere except the park. But when Joel sets off with his friend Tony on their bicycles, he dares Tony to race him in a swim across the dangerous Vermillion River. Bauer's gripping novel about death, guilt, and peer pressure is also about love and overcoming impossible ordeals.

The Orphan Train Adventures   FICTION

AUTHOR: Joan Lowery Nixon
HC: Bantam • PB: Dell
THEMES: individuality; orphans; family; history; foster homes; adoption; railroad; U.S. history, 19th century

Based on historical fact, this series follows the adventures of five brothers and sisters from the orphanage to foster homes in the 19th century. Affecting and dramatic, with characters you root for and villains you despise. Titles in the series include: *A Family Apart, Caught in the Act, In the Face of Danger, A Place to Belong, Keeping Secrets, A Dangerous Promise,* and *Circle of Love.*

★ Out of the Dust

FICTION

AUTHOR: Karen Hesse

HC: Scholastic

THEMES: Oklahoma; U.S. history, the Depression; U.S.A., the Dust Bowl; coming of age; strong girls; fathers and daughters; hardship; loss; music; courage; farms; poverty; death

The hardship and loss of a Dust Bowl family is brought to life so powerfully you can feel the caked mud on the floor and the blinding sting of dust in your eyes. But more than that, it is the aching heart of Billie Jo that fills the pages of this book; as she mourns the loss of her mother and newborn brother; as she learns that she must forgive her father for his part in the accident that caused their death; as she searches for a way out of the dust and finally comes to accept the dust as part of who she is. This outstanding coming of age novel is a flip side of *The Grapes Of Wrath,* allowing us to see what happened to the families that stayed when so many were forced from their homes during one of the bleakest times in American history. Billie Jo's heart is strong, her courage inspiring, and her frailties are all too human. You will never forget her.

★ Pink and Say

PICTURE BOOK

AUTHOR/ILLUSTRATOR: Patricia Polacco

HC: Philomel

THEMES: prejudice; soldiers; courage; U.S. history, the Civil War; death; friendship; storytelling; mothers and sons; fear

Don't be fooled by its picture book format; this one is for the older child. It takes place in a time of war, deals with prejudice and is a heartwrenching, true story. Teenager Say Curtis is wounded in a fierce battle during the Civil War. Pinkus Aylee, a young black soldier, finds him and carries him to his own home. There, Pink's mother nurtures the boys until she is killed. When they try to rejoin the troops, they are captured and sent to Andersonville Prison. Pink is hanged, but Say survives to pass the story on to his own children and grandchildren. Since he has no living descendants to remember him, Polacco's book stands as a testament to the life of Pinkus Aylee.

Pop-O-Mania: How to Create Your Own Pop-Ups

NONFICTION

AUTHOR/ILLUSTRATOR: Barbara Valenta

HC: Dial

THEMES: crafts

Children even slightly interested in working with their hands will not be able to put this down. Learn to pop, flap, turn, lift or slide images like the samples on each thick paper page. There's no guessing with these instructions.

The Psychozone: Kidzilla & Other Tales   SHORT STORY COLLECTION
AUTHOR: David Lubar
PB: Tor
THEMES: horror; scary stories; comeuppance

David Lubar is a real talent! He delivers the goods to all those kids who want short, scary fiction, but his sense of humor and his lack of gratuitous violence are what put him a big cut above the schlock-meisters. Read aloud as a treat to fourth and fifth grades. When you've finished this one, try *Psychozone: The Witch's Monkey and Other Tales.*

MY KIDS ARE HOOKED ON HORROR! WHAT NOW?

Face it: R. L. Stine took thousands of children who might never have thought that reading was a cool activity, and he has turned them on to books. Sure, for a time they were hooked on *Goosebumps,* but it was also an opportunity to introduce them to more literary works that pressed the same buttons. Try this list of books out on your 3rd, 4th or 5th graders when you feel compelled to broaden their horizons:

The Psychozone: Kidzilla and Other Tales by David Lubar
Don't Give Up the Ghost edited by David Gale (Dell Yearling pb)
Don't Open the Door After the Sun Goes Down by Al Carusone (Hyperion pb)
Enter If You Dare!—Scary Stories From the Haunted Mansion by Nicholas Stephens (Disney Press pb)
Horror Stories selected by Susan Price (Kingfisher Story Library pb)
In a Messy, Messy Room and Other Scary Stories by Judith Gorog (Harper Trophy pb)

Read them aloud or let the kids have them on their own. And when they finish these and want still more, it'll be time to haul out the *Complete Works of Edgar Allan Poe* and start really scaring them with stories like *The Fall of the House of Usher* and *The Tell-Tale Heart.*

Radiance Descending   FICTION
AUTHOR: Paula Fox
HC: DK Ink
THEMES: family; Down's syndrome; brothers; anger; grandfathers

Having a brother with Down's syndrome seems a crushing burden to eleven-year-old Paul, and it fills him with anger. This book details the journey he takes in coming to terms with his feelings about his brother, guided by his patient and wise grandfather. A loving look at a family enriched by the presence of a "special" child.

Robin's Country   FICTION

AUTHOR: Monica Furlong
HC: Knopf
THEMES: adventure; history, medieval times; Robin Hood; archery; folklore; heroes; point of view; folktale variation

Glimpse into Sherwood forest through the eyes of "Dummy," a young boy who is unable to talk. Meet Marion, champion archer and protector of Robin. The reader can almost touch, smell and feel the forest, as well as the characters who bring to life the magic and mysteries of this medieval legend of Robin Hood.

Sad Underwear and Other Complications   POETRY COLLECTION

AUTHOR: Judith Viorst • ILLUSTRATOR: Richard Hull
HC: Atheneum
THEMES: humor; variety

Viorst's humor, from a child's point of view, is intertwined with truths, traumas and possibilities. "Telling a lie is called wrong. Telling the truth is called right. Except when telling the truth is called bad manners and telling a lie is called polite." There is something for every reader!

Sarah, Plain and Tall   FICTION

AUTHOR: Patricia MacLachlan
HC/PB: HarperCollins
THEMES: family; memories; separation; mail; mothers; siblings; comparisons; change; fathers; love; grief; anticipation; U.S.A., the Prairie; stepparents; single parents; U.S. history, 19th century

Only 64 pages, this novel packs a wallop! Caleb was too young when his mother died to remember her, but his sister Anna helps. Now their father has sent for a mail order bride and they wonder what life will be like when she arrives. Through letters the children first meet Sarah and when she comes from far off by the sea they are not disappointed. This tender story shows the hardships of prairie life and the value of a strong-hearted woman.

Science Experiments You Can Eat   NONFICTION

AUTHOR: Vicki Cobb • ILLUSTRATOR: David Cain

HC: HarperCollins

THEMES: science; science experiements; food; recipes

Cobb is a believer that learning comes from doing. These books are the proof in the pudding, er, the popsicle. Make one and learn about freezing temperatures. What has to happen for something to crystallize? Mix up some rock candy and find out. When you've learned your basic science principles here, read *More Science Experiments You Can Eat*, or check out her other science books co-authored with Kathy Darling: *Wanna Bet? Science Challenges to Fool You.*, *Bet You Can*, and *Bet You Can't.*

Seedfolks   FICTION

AUTHOR: Paul Fleischman

HC: HarperCollins

THEMES: cultural diversity; gardening; community; city life; taking action; immigration; point of view; prejudice; gardens

There have been stories before about people pulled together for the purpose of good. But this one in all its simplicity has staying power. A community garden is started by a young child in an empty lot behind a wasted refrigerator. Threatened by suspicion and fertilized with hope, it reminds us of the need for folks to work, to create beauty, and to be a part of a community. This one's worth more than its weight.

Sees Behind Trees   FICTION

AUTHOR: Michael Dorris

HC: Hyperion

THEMES: Native American; blindness; coming of age

So often when we learn that someone has limited eyesight we think about what they can't do. This compelling novel concentrates instead on how a young Native American boy develops other senses, earning respect from his people.

Seven Spiders Spinning   FICTION

AUTHOR: Gregory Maguire • ILLUSTRATOR: Dirk Zimmer

HC: Clarion • PB: HarperCollins

THEMES: school; spiders; teachers; Halloween; humor; spooky stories

A very funny look at the trouble seven Siberian snow spiders cause in a little town. Each has fallen in love with a different girl in Miss Earth's class, and Maguire gleefully kills off the spiders one by one as each tries to bite its beloved, all during preparation for the Halloween Pageant of Horrors. A fast pace and a classroom full of distinctly interesting children make this enjoyable even for those who don't like spiders.

Shiloh
FICTION

AUTHOR: Phyllis Reynolds Naylor
HC: Atheneum • PB: Dell
THEMES: dogs; pets; farms; family; abuse; humor; villains

When Marty finds Shiloh, a dog who has been badly mistreated by his owner, he can't keep him. After all, he belongs to someone else. And when Shiloh finds his way back to Marty, Marty makes a decision that could get him into a lot of trouble. *Shiloh* will have readers glued to the pages cheering, booing, laughing, crying and wishing for a kinder, gentler world. But this is no dreary tale: we assure you there will be smiles at the turn of the last page. There are two sequels: *Shiloh Season* and *Saving Shiloh.*

Shoebag
FICTION

AUTHOR: Mary James
HC/PB: Scholastic
THEMES: fantasy; humor; imagination; insects; school; friendship; adventure

Cockroaches are generally named for their places of birth, so Shoebag is not really unusual considering he started out as a cockroach. His mother's name is Drainboard and his father is Under The Toaster. (And speaking of names, Mary James is really writer M.E. Kerr, better known for her literary novels.) Shoebag was a happy young cockroach until one morning he woke to find he had become a human boy. What a ghastly thought. Humans could be so dirty. After all, cockroaches have to move around in human muck all the time. Original and fun, this story works read aloud or quietly alone, perhaps in the kitchen near the drainboard.

Short and Shivery
FOLKLORE COLLECTION

AUTHOR: Robert San Souci • ILLUSTRATOR: Katherine Coville
HC/PB: Doubleday
THEMES: horror; folklore; storytelling; diversity

A brilliant mix of scary stories, gathered from around the world, guaranteed to raise the hair on the back of your neck. Vivid retellings of more than 30 tales old and new make this a folklore resource as well as a great book to have at a campfire. Be sure to check out the sequels, *More Short & Shivery,* and *Even More Short & Shivery.*

Singing America: Poems That Define a Nation
POETRY ANTHOLOGY

EDITOR: Neil Philip • ILLUSTRATOR: Michael McCurdy
HC: Viking
THEMES: U.S.A.; Native American; variety; rhyme; U.S. history

More than 150 pages packed with poems that celebrate life in America. Philip's varied collection includes Emily Dickinson, Langston Hughes, and e.e. cummings as well as songs of the Pueblo and Sioux.

Skylark
FICTION

AUTHOR: Patricia MacLachlan
HC/PB: HarperCollins
THEMES: U.S.A., the prairie; family; separation; hardship; journeys; comparisons; U.S.A., New England

In the Newbery award-winning *Sarah Plain and Tall,* when Sarah came to the prairie, Anna and her brother Caleb worried that she would leave. But Sarah stayed, fell in love with and married their father. In this sequel, a drought comes to the prairie which forces Sarah to return to Maine with Anna and Caleb, leaving their father behind. Again the children worry about the future of their family. This touching sequel will not disappoint!

Smart Moves: A Kid's Guide to Self-Defense
NONFICTION

AUTHOR: Christopher Goedecke • ILLUSTRATOR: Rosemarie Hausherr (photographs)
HC: Simon & Schuster
THEMES: self-defense; peace; martial arts

A great book for the child who wants to try out martial arts—it will answer curiosity with sound advice that will also reassure the parent. The balance between the usefulness of self defense and the necessity to avoid dangerous situations is perfect.

Smelly Old History Series: Victorian Vapours, Roman Aromas, and Tudor Odours   NONFICTION

AUTHOR: Mary Dobson
PB: Oxford University Press
THEMES: history, 19th century; senses; England; history, 16th century; ancient Rome; humor, gross; ancient history

Go ahead, turn your nose up at these! Using the lighthearted and the gross to lure unsuspecting kids into scratching and sniffing a little history is the aim of this unique series, and we can already hear them now, spouting off facts about the sewage in the River Thames or the smell of a sweaty Henry the Eighth. Look, you don't have to sniff them yourself—let the kids have all the fun. But the fact is that smell played an enormously important role in the history of the world and, compared to these eras, we take a lot of our clean smells for granted. This series makes it all perfectly obvious.

Something Permanent   POETRY COLLECTION

AUTHOR: **Cynthia Rylant** • ILLUSTRATOR: Walker Evans (photographs)
HC: Harcourt Brace
THEMES: U.S.A., Appalachia; photographs; poverty; U.S. history, the Depression

Walker Evans' photographs of the people of Appalachia are some of America's greatest art. They so brilliantly tell their story, it would seem arrogant to put words to them. But in the hands of Rylant, a woman who can see herself and her family in Evans' pictures, the photos inspire poems that help the art to reach a higher level. An extraordinary achievement from a writer who continually pushes herself to better her remarkable work.

Something Rich & Strange   POETRY COLLECTION

EDITOR: Gina Pollinger • ILLUSTRATOR: Emma Chichester Clark
HC: Kingfisher
THEMES: Shakespeare

An introduction to the work of Shakespeare, focusing on his verse and poetry. Arranged thematically, this is a useful book that teachers and families will treasure.

Soul Looks Back in Wonder   POETRY ANTHOLOGY
EDITOR/ILLUSTRATOR: Tom Feelings
HC: Dial • PB: Puffin
THEMES: African American; variety

"Popcorn leaps, popping from the floor of a hot black skillet and into my mouth. Black words leap, snapping from the white page. Rushing into my eyes. Sliding into my brain which gobbles them the way my tongue and teeth chomp the buttered popcorn . . . ." Maya Angelou.

There are two good reasons to consider this gem for your library: the powerful poems by African American writers and Tom Feelings' extraordinary illustrations.

Stepping on the Cracks   FICTION
AUTHOR: Mary Downing Hahn
HC: Clarion • PB: Avon
THEMES: U.S. history, World War II; bullies; community; friendship; courage; secrets; conscience

A superb historical novel set during World War II. In addition to her outstanding portrayal of childhood during wartime, Hahn offers a thought-provoking tale about standing up for what you believe in, even when it isn't popular. This is our favorite of Hahn's books, though we are also fond of her ghost stories, *A Time for Andrew* and *Wait Till Helen Comes*, as well as her rollicking adventure novel, *The Dead Man in Indian Creek*.

Straight From the Bear's Mouth   NONFICTION
AUTHOR/ILLUSTRATOR: Bill Ross
HC: Atheneum
THEMES: nature; photosynthesis

A compulsively readable book that takes an unusual approach to the explanation of how photosynthesis works. It works! We never understood the process until we read this book. Off the wall and fun!

★ Stranded at Plimoth Plantation, 1626   NONFICTION
AUTHOR/ILLUSTRATOR: Gary Bowen
HC: HarperCollins
THEMES: U.S. history, Colonial America; color; Native American; survival; pilgrims; artists; art; rituals; courage; traditions; cultural diversity; community; orphans; new experiences; diaries

Christopher Sears is a 13-year-old orphan stranded at Plimoth Plantation while he waits for transportation to Jamestown. Every day he finds new things to describe in his journal: visits with Indians, eating pumpkins and lobsters for the first time, attending a birth or a funeral. He passes his time making woodcuts and printing them with natural dyes. With each turn of the page, the reader watches Christopher's artistic skill evolve from simple black and white woodcuts to detailed multicolored prints. We tend to stroke our hands across the cover of this book—partly because it's beautiful, and because the art and historical fiction work in perfect harmony to invite the reader in for a close-up of life in another time.

A Suitcase of Seaweed and Other Poems   POETRY COLLECTION

AUTHOR/ILLUSTRATOR: Janet Wong

HC: McElderry

THEMES: grandfathers; family; Chinese American; Korean American; cultural diversity; prejudice

" 'What you study in school?' my grandfather asks. 'Poetry,' I say, climbing high to pick a large ripe lemon off the top limb. 'Po-tree,' he says. 'It got fruit?' " Humorous and touching poems divided into three sections: Korean, Chinese, and American, reflect the cultures that make up Wong's own family. For more of Wong's poems, see: *Good Luck Gold And Other Poems.*

Sun & Spoon   FICTION

AUTHOR: **Kevin Henkes**

HC: Greenwillow

THEMES: loss; grief; family; grandparents; siblings; memory; conscience

Another deeply affecting novel from one of our most gifted writers. Dealing with the loss of his grandmother has kept Spoon's mind working double time, trying to come up with the perfect something to remember her by. He and his grandfather seem the hardest hit by Gram's death, and there is a change in their relationship that Spoon can't put into words. When he decides on the perfect thing to remember Gram by, he never considers how it might affect his grandfather. Afterward, Spoon has to take the hard path to right the wrong he created. This book explores the differing ways people grieve, and illuminates with sensitivity the fact that we often feel our pain to be unique.

Tae's Sonata
FICTION

AUTHOR: Haemi Balgassi

HC: Clarion

THEMES: Korean Americans; U.S.A., New England; coming of age; family; family store; jobs

A solid coming of age novel about a Korean girl in New England. The traditions of her culture come into conflict with her desire to be more American, causing disagreements with her parents. There is a strong sense of family and work, featuring the family owned and operated grocery store and the home as the scene of many of the novel's events.

Take Action: An Environmental Book for Kids
NONFICTION

AUTHOR: Ann Love and Jane Drake • ILLUSTRATOR: Pat Cupples

HC: Morrow Junior Books • PB: Beech Tree

THEMES: taking action; environment; animals, endangered

A practical guide to getting involved with endangered species and spaces. Filled with ideas and addresses for taking action.

Tales for the Perfect Child
SHORT STORY COLLECTION

AUTHOR: Florence Parry Heide • ILLUSTRATOR: Victoria Chess

HC: Lothrop • PB: Dell

THEMES: humor; irony; manners; family; misbehaving

We admit it: we enjoy gleefully subversive books for children, ones where they don't learn morals, or the good guy turns out to be an idiot, or the kid is allowed to get away with all sorts of stuff that makes grown-ups uneasy. If you think as we do, then this is a book you must have. Seven stories of perfectly horrid children who bend the rules, disobey, whine till they get what they want and generally act atrociously—and there isn't a single "consequence" for any of them—they all get off scot free. Funny, and perfect for reading aloud to rooms full of fourth through seventh graders who will immediately get the joke, but not for younger children, who may be able to read it, but will likely miss the point.

A Telling of the Tales
FOLKLORE COLLECTION

AUTHOR: William J. Brooke • ILLUSTRATOR: Richard Egielski

HC/PB: HarperCollins

THEMES: deadlocks; folklore; folktale variations; tall tales; fairy tales; point of view

This retelling of five classic tales filled with surprises and new insights into the personalities of familiar characters. Our favorite is entitled "The Growing Of Paul Bunyan." Here Paul Bunyan meets Johnny Appleseed. One is a planter, the other a chopper. Two folk heroes, two sides of a story. This one's great to start a talk about how two opposing sides could both be right.

Ten Little-Known Facts About Hippopotamuses: And More Little Known Facts and a Few Fibs About Other Animals
NONFICTION

AUTHOR: Douglas Little • ILLUSTRATOR: David Francis and Donna Rawlins
HC: Houghton Mifflin
THEMES: science; nature; trivia; humor

Slyly funny. Conveys tons of information about a lot of things (not just hippos) in a very clever way. For adults who have off-the-wall senses of humor and for smart aleck kids who want to impress people with fun factoids.

There's a Boy in the Girls' Bathroom
FICTION

AUTHOR: Louis Sachar
HC/PB: Knopf
THEMES: school; fitting in; bullies; self-respect; friendship; humor; lying

Bradley Chalkers doesn't fit in with the other kids in his fifth-grade class. For one thing, he's the oldest. He's also a liar and an attention-seeking bully. Fourth through eighth graders will recognize Bradley; kids like him have been in their classrooms. Funny and sometimes poignant, Sachar's work shows that friendship and understanding go a long way to help kids like Bradley Chalkers triumph over their own insecurities.

This Same Sky: A Collection of Poems From Around the World
POETRY ANTHOLOGY

EDITOR: Naomi Shihab Nye
HC: Simon & Schuster • PB: Aladdin
THEMES: cultural diversity; poets; animals; variety

129 poets from sixty-eight different countries write about people and animals. Pick out your favorite and then note the home of its poet. It may be that far across the world there is someone who thinks much like you.

★ Tuck Everlasting

FICTION

AUTHOR: Natalie Babbitt
HC/PB: Farrar Straus & Giroux
THEMES: family; aging; change; magic; choices; taking action; kidnapping

The possibility of eternal life has been pondered since the beginning of time. Who wouldn't consider it a blessing? When ten-year-old Winnie Foster discovers the spring water that could keep her from growing old, she is kidnapped by the Tuck family, who understand the harm that one taste could bring. This compelling novel, which has readers thinking about their own place in time, continues to be as popular now as it was when first published over twenty years ago.

Under the Blood Red Sun

FICTION

AUTHOR: Graham Salisbury
HC: Delacorte • PB: Dell
THEMES: friendship; prejudice; suspicion; Hawaii; U.S. history, World War II; cultural diversity; community; family; Japanese culture

Thirteen-year-old Tomizu and his best friend, Billy Davis, learn about the hardships brought on by prejudice and suspicion when the bombing of Pearl Harbor shakes up their Hawaiian homes.

The Van Gogh Cafe

FICTION

AUTHOR: **Cynthia Rylant**
HC: Harcourt Brace
THEMES: family; magic; restaurants; community; fathers and daughters

A novel in short, connected stories about a girl, her father, and the title cafe—a truly magical place.

★ The View From Saturday

FICTION

AUTHOR: E. L. Konigsburg
HC: Atheneum • PB: Aladdin
THEMES: teachers; students; friendship; diversity; school; tea parties; contests; handicaps; competition; gifted child; fitting in; rituals; cultural diversity; choices; community

Every once in a while we come across a novel that has so much texture woven within every sentence, we reread pages. This is one. A gifted teacher in a wheelchair, four students—bright, diverse and best friends—all work toward the same goal, the Academic Bowl. As good a portrait of a group of misfits forming their own community as any in fiction.

The View From the Cherry Tree   FICTION-MYSTERY
AUTHOR: Willo Davis Roberts
PB: Aladdin
THEMES: mystery; murder; family; communication

From his special perch on the cherry tree, Rob sees his neighbor murdered. And when he tells what he saw, no one pays attention. That is, no one but the murderer. Suspense will keep the pages turning.

Voices From the Fields: Children of Migrant Farmworkers Tell Their Stories   NONFICTION
AUTHOR: S. Beth Atkin
HC: Joy Street
THEMES: Mexican; gangs; California; migrant farm workers; children's writing; prejudice; jobs; poverty; change; Spanish language

Children of migrant farm workers tell their stories. A nine-year-old boy talks about the long hours in the fields. A ten-year-old describes living in crowded migrant housing. Through poetry and prose nine voices tell about gangs, discrimination, language barriers and strong family ties.

Voices From the Wild:
An Animal Sensagoria   POETRY COLLECTION
AUTHOR: David Bouchard • ILLUSTRATOR: Ron Parker
HC: Chronicle
THEMES: animals; senses; nature

A stunning collaboration! Using the wildlife paintings of Ron Parker as a springboard, poet Bouchard explores the senses of the animal kingdom. The poems come from the point of view of the animals, each claiming to have the sharpest sense of smell, sight, etc. With notes at the end of the book telling fascinating facts about each animal, this is a must for all lovers of nature and poetry.

Waiting to Waltz: A Childhood   POETRY COLLECTION
AUTHOR: Cynthia Rylant • ILLUSTRATOR: Stephen Gammell
HC: Macmillan
THEMES: towns; poverty; coming of age; U.S.A., Appalachia

A childhood rendered in poems. Rylant's first collection paints the picture of a small Appalachian town and the people who live there, as seen through the eyes of a very observant girl.

Way Home   PICTURE BOOK

AUTHOR: Libby Hawthorn • ILLUSTRATOR: Gregory Rogers
HC: Crown
THEMES: homelessness; survival; cities; cats; pets; poverty; home; dwellings; danger; resourcefulness

Way Home is a call for change, but this powerful picture book doesn't mention it once. A boy named Shane sees a frightened cat scramble up a fence. "Heeey, wild cat! Wildcat! Spitfire, Kitten Number one! I like you. Sure I do. Yeah—you're with me now, Cat . . ." He takes him around garbage cans, past boarded up buildings and broken fences, past stores, with the reader feeling the danger of a child alone on nighttime city streets. Shane protects the kitten and takes him "home" to his place. Hawthorn's conversational prose and Rogers' incredible artwork are sure to make this compelling picture of homelessness a point of discussion for older children.

The Weighty Word Book   SHORT STORY COLLECTION

AUTHOR: Paul M. Levitt, Douglas A. Burger and Elissa S. Guralnick
ILLUSTRATOR: Janet Stevens
HC: Bookmakers
THEMES: words; language; humor; puns; vocabulary; imagination; alphabet

If you mix up word meanings, this is the book for you. If you like stretching your vocabulary, making up stories, or booing at a bad pun, read this. The authors have come up with 27 stories representing challenging words—from Abasement to Zealot—each ending in a word-defining pun.

Well Wished   FICTION-FANTASY

AUTHOR: Franny Billingsley
HC: Atheneum
THEMES: magic; wishes; wisdom; adventure; friendship; love; wells; fantasy; strong girls

With wishes come responsibilities. With magic there seems always to be a catch. And there are unforeseen consequences to greedy, hasty children who wish without thinking. Nuria knows this. And yet . . . Well, surely you know what happens next. Writers have been telling us this story since the dawn of time. To the select club of Nesbit and Eager comes Franny Billingsley with her remarkable, thoughtful fantasy. Weaving elements of timeless storytelling tradition with insights fresh and bold, she has constructed an adventure that will enchant readers who will both long and fear to be in Nuria's place.

The Well   FICTION

AUTHOR: Mildred Taylor
HC: Dial • PB: Puffin
THEMES: prejudice; African American; family; wells; bullies; U.S.A., the South; community; courage

The Logan family are glad to share their water when all the wells go dry except theirs. But mean spirited Charlie, a white teenager, is intent on keeping them in their place because they are black. When ten-year-old David Logan and his proud older brother get mixed up with Charlie, tension builds, keeping the readers on edge till the end. Mildred Taylor's other books about the Logan family are *Roll of Thunder, Hear My Cry*, and *Let the Circle Be Unbroken*.

What Hearts   FICTION

AUTHOR: Bruce Brooks
HC/PB: HarperCollins
THEMES: loneliness; gifted children; stepparents; mothers and sons; depression; baseball; love; bullies; divorce

In four related short stories, Brooks shows us the development of young Asa from the crushed expectations and disappointment of his parents' divorce to his learning to accept the power of love. Along the way, he copes with his hard to like stepfather, his prone to depression mother and the fact that he is often too smart for the world around him. Full of insight, this is a novel about the difference between knowledge and understanding from one of our favorite writers.

Who Said That? Famous Americans Speak
PICTURE BOOK NONFICTION

AUTHOR: Robert Burleigh • ILLUSTRATOR: David Catrow
HC: Henry Holt
THEMES: biography; quotations; trivia; U.S. history

Young trivia seekers and Americana buffs, this is for you! Famous sayings by inventors, politicians, entertainers, and others—each accompanied by a brief biography, remind us that Americans are a diverse lot!

The Whole Story Series   FICTION

    AUTHOR: various
    HC/PB: Viking
    THEMES: variety

The Whole Story—unabridged editions of classics that have information in the sidebars filling in historical, cultural, and other background information so important to understanding the context in which these great books were written. Nothing is taken away and so much is added to the experience that this will be a boon to kids who need a little help reading these as assigned books, and will delight fans of these titles with the added information. Titles in this series include: *Heidi, The Adventures of Tom Sawyer, The Call of the Wild, Treasure Island* and *The Jungle Book*. Some folks object to altering a classic presentation in any way. We personally don't like abridged editions. When the child is ready for the book, he's ready. This series leaves nothing out and offers extra information to the children who require it. Others can ignore it.

William Shakespeare's Macbeth   FICTION

    AUTHOR: Bruce Coville • ILLUSTRATOR: Gary Kelley
    HC: Dial
    THEMES: Shakespeare; Scotland; witches; murder; fate; ambition; consequences; kings

A prose adaptation that will bring new readers to the Bard's work without sacrificing the affections of his legions of devotees. Expertly weaving Shakespeare's own text into his retelling, this tale of power, fate, and corruption will serve as a bridge to the play itself, much as his other adaptations of *A Midsummer Night's Dream* and *The Tempest* did. We can hardly wait for Coville's take on the rest of the canon!

William Shakespeare's The Tempest   FICTION

    AUTHOR: Bruce Coville • ILLUSTRATOR: Ruth Sanderson
    HC: Doubleday • PB: Dell
    THEMES: Shakespeare; magic; fathers and daughters; revenge; islands; sea; love

Making this complex and moody later play accessible to younger readers is no small feat, and writer Coville and illustrator Sanderson pull it off beautifully. Focusing on the magic, romance, and revenge aspects of the play and all but shoving aside Prospero's ruminations about his mid-life crisis, this becomes a perfect introduction to the Bard's work for fourth grade and up. And could that be author Coville serving as the model for Prospero? Coville's adaptations *William Shakespeare's Macbeth* and *William Shakespeare's A Midsummer Night's Dream* are worthy companions to this book.

Winter Poems   POETRY COLLECTION
AUTHOR: Barbara Rogasky • ILLUSTRATOR: Trina Schort Hyman
HC: Scholastic
THEMES: weather; winter; snow

Twenty-five voices combine to create a portrait of the beauty of winter—soft snow to blustery storms—from the serious to the silly. A winter collection without the mention of one holiday.

The Witches   FICTION-FANTASY
AUTHOR: Roald Dahl • ILLUSTRATOR: Quentin Blake
HC: Farrar Straus & Giroux • PB: Puffin
THEMES: witches; grandmothers; adventure; humor; taking action; good vs. evil; disguises

When it comes to children, "Squish them and squiggle them and make them disappear" is the motto of all witches. And how does one recognize a witch? Don't count on black dresses and broomsticks; those are from fairy tales, and this is no fairy tale. Dahl offers careful descriptions of these despicable creatures diguised as ladies. Young readers need not fear, for a boy with the help of his cigar-smoking grandmother saves the day. Laugh, imagine, marvel, and enjoy as Dahl creates another journey of characters—funny, disgusting and perfect for a child with a soaring imagination.

The Wolfbay Wings   FICTION
AUTHOR: Bruce Brooks
PB: HarperCollins
THEMES: hockey; sports; teams; friendship

An action-packed series about a suburban kids' hockey team. Great sports writing, full of details about the sport that will intrigue the novice and delight the insider, as well as compelling characters and situations make this a welcome addition to the shelves of sports series fiction. The two-time Newbery Honor pedigree of author (and major hockey buff) Brooks will be certain to make librarians sit up and take notice, but the kids will love them without ever having heard of the author. Titles include *Woodsie, Zip,* and *Cody*.

Wringer   FICTION

AUTHOR: Jerry Spinelli

HC: HarperCollins

THEMES: friendship; bullies; pigeons; birthdays; coming of age; peer pressure; violence; dreams; pets; courage; death

Spinelli reveals the discomfort of going along with peers who make bad choices, the thrill of being included, and the confusion that results. When boys in Palmer's city turn ten, they become wringers at the annual Family Fest. It is an honor. But Palmer is not like the others. One of the first things he knew deep inside was that he did not want to be a wringer. This is for the reader who is crossing over from the security of home to the preteen times where making the right peer choices form your future. It's heart wrenching.

A Wrinkle in Time   SCIENCE FICTION

AUTHOR: Madeleine L'Engle

HC: Farrar Straus & Giroux • PB: Dell

THEMES: time travel; gifted children; family; science fiction; love; adventure

One of the most popular novels for children ever written and a smashing combination of science fiction, adventure and a family story. Throughout the sequence of novels that begins with this book (*A Wind in the Door, A Swiftly Tilting Planet,* and *Many Waters*), we are shown the fantastic adventures of the Wallace family. As a doorway to science fiction writing, this novel is unsurpassed in its presentation of fantastic themes in a readable style, but you need not be interested in science fiction to appreciate its richness.

Challenging nonfiction and thematically wide ranging fiction and fantasy are the hallmarks of this section. These make great read aloud and discuss books for the home or classroom.

5 Novels: Alan Mendelsohn, The Boy From Mars/Slaves of Spiegel/The Last Guru/Young Adult Novel/The Snarkout Boys and the Avocado of Death
COLLECTION

AUTHOR: Daniel Pinkwater

PB: Farrar Straus & Giroux

THEMES: fantasy; gentle boys; friendship; adventure; mystery; science fiction

This is a treat for Pinkwater fans, as well as the thousands who have yet to discover him. Five novels in one volume!!!! One of the masters of novels for children, Daniel Pinkwater has made a career of never talking down to kids. He writes his books the way he sees 'em, and his readership mostly consists of intelligent kids who are interested in fantasy or science fiction, as well as anyone who likes quirky, original fiction. If you haven't read him before, this collection will serve as a terrific introduction to his style and point of view. And if, like us, you are crazy about the Snarkout Boys, there is a sequel you'll need to get: *The Snarkout Boys and the Baconburg Horror.*

★ The Adventures of Huckleberry Finn   FICTION

AUTHOR: Mark Twain • ILLUSTRATOR: Steven Kellogg

HC: Morrow

THEMES: rivers; friendship; choices; adventure; courage; taking action; humor; prejudice

This classic piece of fiction is arguably the best American novel ever written. We strongly feel that no one should grow up without meeting Huck, and this edition, with illustrations by Steven Kellogg, is our choice for the one to have on hand when the time comes to read it aloud.

★ Advice for a Frog   POETRY COLLECTION

AUTHOR: Alice Schertle • ILLUSTRATOR: Norman Green

HC: Lothrop

THEMES: animals; point of view

A great book for use with 10 to 14 year olds, though younger children needn't be left out of the fun. This sophisticated, playful book of poetry helps kids look at animals in a new light. Read the poem to the kids without telling them the title or showing the pictures. Then have them guess what the animal is. Show them Norman Green's stunning paintings and watch them congratulate themselves on their cleverness.

After the War Was Over   FICTION

AUTHOR/ILLUSTRATOR: Michael Foreman

HC: Arcade

THEMES: England; childhood; coming of age; artists; family; school; painting; jobs

A companion book to *War Boy*, this memoir of the years after World War II is notable not only for the depiction of England putting itself back together, but for its portrayal of a young artist in the making.

Alpha Beta Chowder   POETRY COLLECTION

AUTHOR: Jeanne Steig • ILLUSTRATOR: William Steig

HC/PB: HarperCollins

THEMES: wordplay; vocabulary; humor; alliteration; alphabet

One poem for each letter of the alphabet, and many of them will have you running for the dictionary! Talk about a clever way to build your vocabulary, let alone a child's! This book reads aloud very well, though some practice may be called for. It is a rare book that combines the entertaining with the educational as well as this one does.

Anne Frank: The Diary of a Young Girl
BIOGRAPHY

AUTHOR: Anne Frank

HC: Doubleday • PB: Bantam

THEMES: coming of age; diaries; autobiography; history, World War II; Anne Frank; prejudice; Holocaust; family; Jews; courage; strong girls; writing

Published all over the world, Anne Frank's account of two years in hiding during World War II has come to be a symbol of the cruelties of racism and war. Entries in her diary from Sunday, June 14, 1942, to Tuesday, August 1, 1944, tell the story of thirteen-year-old Anne, who is hidden with seven other Jews in Amsterdam, fearful of being discovered by the Nazis. It's a love story. It's raw in its honesty. It's a story that will profoundly affect young adult readers.

Anne Frank: Beyond the Diary: A Photographic Remembrance
BIOGRAPHY

AUTHOR/ILLUSTRATOR: Rian and Van Verhoeven and Ruud DerRol

HC: Viking • PB: Puffin

THEMES: history, World War II; biography; Anne Frank; prejudice; museums; Holocaust

Children who have read *The Diary of A Young Girl* and want to know more about Anne Frank will appreciate this photographic remembrance from the Anne Frank House museum in Amsterdam.

★ Black Ships Before Troy
FICTION

AUTHOR: Rosemary Sutcliff • ILLUSTRATOR: Alan Lee

HC: Delacorte

THEMES: folklore; ancient history; ancient Greece; Greek mythology; *The Iliad;* war; adventure; heroes

A brilliant retelling of the *Iliad* by the late Sutcliff, with remarkable illustrations by Alan Lee. Open this book to any page to test the writing. Written squarely on the sixth grade reading level, it is addictive reading for anyone even remotely interested in Greek mythology. Recommend it to readers looking for adventure. It stretches vocabulary, and the powerful illustrations help to move even the wary reader forward. See also:

The Wanderings of Odysseus, the companion book by the same author and illustrator.

LONG PICTURE BOOKS

Don't be afraid of picture books with long texts. Some readers, through their early teen years, need the visuals to drive them forward. Try books like:

Black Ships Before Troy (Sutcliff)
The Weaving of a Dream (Heyer)
Good Griselle (Yolen)
Excalibur (Talbott)
Charlie Drives the Stage (Kimmel)
Dippers (Nichol)
Pink and Say (Polacco)
Reading to Matthew (Vivelo)

Blue Skin of the Sea   FICTION

AUTHOR: Graham Salisbury
HC: Delacorte • PB: Dell
THEMES: Hawaii; fishing; coming of age; courage; friendship; sea; school; sharks; storms; fear of water; love

In this remarkable debut novel of stand-alone but interconnected short stories, we watch Sonny Mendoza grow up on the big island of Hawaii in the 50's and 60's. His journey from childhood through adolescence is marked by encounters with sharks, hurricanes, friendships, and his coming to terms with his fear of the sea, something quite uncommon on an island. Salisbury's portrait of island life makes it seem both exotic and familiar, and this novel will appeal to a wide range of readers.

A Bone From a Dry Sea   FICTION

AUTHOR: Peter Dickinson
HC: Delacorte • PB: Dell
THEMES: fathers and daughters; survival; archeology; strong girls; history, prehistory

Set in both ancient and contemporary times, this novel is about two girls: one lived four million years ago, the other visits the site where her father, with a team of archeologists, searches for fossil remains of ancestors. Fascinating, strong female characters.

The Book of Think

PICTURE BOOK NONFICTION

AUTHOR: Marilyn Burns • ILLUSTRATOR: Martha Weston
HC: Little Brown
THEMES: brain; learning

One of a series of books that speaks directly to kids about topics of interest to them. Informative and irreverent, the books will get them talking and reading in a way that most nonfiction cannot. Other titles include: *I Am Not a Short Adult, The I Hate Mathematics! Book,* and *This Book Is About Time.*

★ Boys Will Be

COLLECTION

AUTHOR: Bruce Brooks
HC: Henry Holt • PB: Hyperion
THEMES: fathers; bullies; reading; sports; boys

Powerful essays on the nature of manhood by this brilliant writer, who never fails to astonish. The chapter on bullies is worth the price alone. This is a book for boys, written by a man who understands about being a boy. It is also valuable for any girl or woman who wants to know more about the boys in her life.

Call Down the Moon: Poems of Music

POETRY ANTHOLOGY

EDITOR: Myra Cohn Livingston
HC: McElderry
THEMES: music; variety; musical instruments; artists; creativity; rhythm

This outstanding anthology of poems creates an excellent introduction to musical concepts, from types of music to composers to different instruments.

"One of the first books I read for pure pleasure was *Hawaii.* It took me to a place I had never been and introduced me to people I'd never met... in a time I could never visit. At times I was shocked. At times I was delighted. When I finished that book I couldn't wait to pick up another one . . . to make another journey far from my Indiana farm."
—Jim Davis, creator of *Garfield*

★ Catherine, Called Birdy   FICTION

AUTHOR: Karen Cushman
HC: Clarion • PB: HarperCollins
THEMES: diaries; history: medieval times; family; strong girls; independence

"The stars and my family align to make my life black and miserable. My mother seeks to make me a fine lady—dumb, docile, and accomplished—so I must take lady-lessons and keep my mouth closed. . . . My father, the toad, conspires to sell me like cheese to some lack-wit seeking a wife." Medieval life, as recounted in the diary of feisty, independent Birdy is funny, horrifying, and fascinating. Cushman's writing transports the reader from the present world to the world of 1290 into a life so real it's hard not to scratch for fleas with the turn of a page. When this story ends turn to *The Midwife's Apprentice*, another fabulous piece of historical fiction from Cushman—and winner of the Newbery Medal.

The Cay   FICTION

AUTHOR: Theodore Taylor
HC: Doubleday • PB: Avon
THEMES: blindness; courage; rescue; adventure; cultural diversity; prejudice; Caribbean; loss; friendship; history, World War II; survival; elderly and children

A racist boy depends upon an old black man in the aftermath of the sinking of a freighter in the Caribbean during World War II. This is a survival story, an adventure tale, and a plea for racial tolerance all rolled into one, and it reads beautifully. No wonder it has been on school reading lists for years—children respond well to this story and have been clamoring for over thirty years for a sequel. Taylor ultimately fashioned a different sort of follow-up book, *Timothy of the Cay*, that is both the story of what happened before the events of the first book and after. Read together or separately, the two books offer an unforgettable portrayal of friendship.

Chicken Soup, Boots!   PICTURE BOOK

AUTHOR/ILLUSTRATOR: Maira Kalman
HC: Viking
THEMES: careers; jobs; yearning; individuality; humor

Maira Kalman is an acquired taste, and she can go a little too far off the deep end for some people. This one is our favorite of her works: a hopeful, irreverent and self-affirming book for anyone who ever wonders what they'll be when they grow up. Use this with a teen who is struggling with what to major in at college or an adult who is facing a crossroads in her career.

Christmas in the Big House, Christmas in the Quarters
NONFICTION

AUTHOR: Patricia C. and Frederick McKissack • ILLUSTRATOR: John Thompson

HC: Scholastic

THEMES: slavery; U.S. history, pre-Civil War; Christmas; family; prejudice; comparisons; cultural diversity; traditions; jobs; community

It's 1859 in Virginia, and slaveholders and slaves ready themselves for the holidays. The McKissacks compare the two dwellings and contrast the lifestyles within. Songs, recipes and poems merge with the text to offer an inside look at how it was.

The Complete Sherlock Holmes
COLLECTION

AUTHOR: Sir Arthur Conan Doyle

HC: Doubleday

THEMES: mystery; England; adventure

This collection offers Holmes unabridged. These stories work very well when read aloud and we encourage trying them out on your nine- to twelve-year-olds at storytime. Our favorites are *The Hound of the Baskervilles* and *The Speckled Band*.

Complete Stories and Poems of Poe
COLLECTION

AUTHOR: Edgar Allan Poe

HC: Doubleday

THEMES: horror; mystery

A collection of Poe is essential to have on hand for a night when the power goes out. Better than any of the horror writers your kids are accustomed to, this guy will provide an evening of suspense and terror that will turn schlocky horror fans into Poe-heads. Read *The Tell-Tale Heart* aloud and watch them grow quiet and still as your voice gets more intense. Be sure to shriek the last line for maximum effect.

Corpses, Coffins and Crypts: A History of Burial   NONFICTION

AUTHOR: Penny Colman
HC: Henry Holt
THEMES: death; burial; cultural diversity; traditions; history, world; rituals

As much about the way the world deals with its dead as any all-dressed-in-black, morbid teenager could wish for, all in one handy volume. The research is extraordinary, the facts are presented in an organized and fascinating way, and the balance of fictional and nonfictional material invites the reader to dig right in!

Dark Thirty: Southern Tales of the Supernatural   FOLKLORE COLLECTION

AUTHOR: Patricia McKissack • ILLUSTRATOR: Brian Pinkney
HC: Knopf
THEMES: African American; U.S.A., the South; horror; folklore; storytelling; scary stories; spooky stories

An outstanding collection of stories that range from disturbing to spooky to downright terrifying. Excellent to have on hand when kids start gravitating toward scarier tales, as it not only will feed their need to be frightened but will help highlight how scary stories are a part of all our cultures.

Dear America Series   FICTION

AUTHOR: various
HC: Scholastic
THEMES: U.S. history; diaries; strong girls

A series of fictional diaries by young women written at different times in America's history. With different writers there is bound to be varying quality to the volumes, but Kathryn Lasky's Pilgrim journal *Journey to the New World: The Diary of Remember Patience Whipple, Mayflower, 1620* is superb, exemplifying the goals of this laudable attempt to bring history to life, warts and all.

When I was a child and teachers talked about Pilgrims, I imagined stiff doll-like characters dressed in crisp black and white. No mud. No dust. No life-blood. And girls? I was sure they were polite. It was a pleasure for me to find that Lasky had similar responses. She has added life to what had been a dull subject.

Other titles of note include: *The Winter of the Red Snow* by Kristiana Gregory (about the American Revolution), *I Thought My Soul Would Rise And Fly* (about the experience of slavery), and *A Picture of Freedom* (about the Civil War), both by Patricia McKissack.

December Stillness   FICTION
AUTHOR: Mary Downing Hahn
HC: Clarion • PB: Avon
THEMES: homelessness; veterans; U.S. history, Vietnam War; Vietnam Veteran's Memorial; family; fathers and daughters; libraries

A moving novel that can help answer older children's questions about the Vietnam War. When Kelly interviews a homeless Vietnam vet for a school project, her emotional involvement produces tragic results that no one could have anticipated. It is clear to the reader, and ultimately to Kelly, that she is really trying to get answers about her own father's time in the service. Hahn's skill as a writer makes the difference between a story that could have been sappy and the emotionally involving story she delivers.

★ The Devil's Arithmetic   FICTION-FANTASY
AUTHOR: **Jane Yolen**
HC: Viking • PB: Puffin
THEMES: Holocaust; time travel; Germany; Jews; adventure; captivity; courage; good vs. evil

A time-travel novel about the Holocaust that makes a gripping statement about personal response to atrocity. Hannah is tired of hearing stories about the death camps and why she should honor her Jewish heritage. When she opens the door for Elijah at the Passover Seder, she finds herself transported to 1940's Poland and learns firsthand why we must never forget the lessons of the Holocaust.

The Discovery of Dragons   PICTURE BOOK
AUTHOR/ILLUSTRATOR: Graeme Base
HC: Abrams
THEMES: dragons; scientists; fantasy; humor; trailblazing

". . . the Discovery of Dragons can in fact be credited to just three people: Bjorn of Bromme, a ninth-century Viking; Song Mei Ying, the youngest daughter of a thirteenth century Chinese silk trader; and Dr. E. F. Liebermann, an obscure mid-nineteenth-century Prussian cartographer and amphibiologist." Victorian serpentologist Rowland W. Greasebeam (a.k.a. Graeme Base) proves that dragons were discovered by the adventurers listed above. He has historical documents to prove it. Find them here along with maps and vivid colored pictures (note the story panels on the bottom of the pages.) For dragon seekers, fantasy followers and artists.

Dragon's Blood:
Volume 1 in the Pit Dragon Trilogy   FICTION-FANTASY

> AUTHOR: **Jane Yolen**
> PB: Harcourt Brace
> THEMES: fantasy; dragons; adventure

Great fantasy writing. Memorable dragons and a convincing creation of an imaginary world makes this one of the best fantasy series around. After they finish this, they will be ready for the world of adult fantasy. The remaining books in the trilogy are: *Heart's Blood* and *Sending of Dragons*.

The Egypt Game   FICTION

> AUTHOR: Zilpha Keatley Snyder
> HC: Atheneum • PB: Dell
> THEMES: ancient Egypt; costumes; obsession; mystery; traditions; rituals; friendship; games; codes

Melanie, April, and their friends are really into ancient Egypt. They hold regular meetings to act out their love of Egyptian lore, immersing themselves in the culture, from hieroglyphics to the costumes of the era. When strange things start to happen, it is only logical to connect them with the Ceremonies of the Dead and the Oracles, and the children start to wonder if things have gotten out of hand. Here is a wonderful mystery to give to a child who is completely smitten with a culture, place or time—not just Egypt.

The Face on the Milk Carton   FICTION

> AUTHOR: Caroline Cooney
> PB: Dell
> THEMES: separation; kidnapping; missing children; family; parents; mystery; secrets; truth

When Janie glanced up at the milk carton, a picture of a young girl glanced back. ". . . an ordinary little girl. Hair in tight pigtails, one against each thin cheek. A dress with a narrow white collar. The dress was white with tiny dark polka dots." The picture had been taken twelve years before. Janie recognized herself. It was impossible that her loving parents would have kidnapped her, but—there she was. There was no question. This gripping, fast-paced story will hold readers till the last page is turned. And when the reader wants to know more, the story continues in: *Whatever Happened to Janie* and *The Voice on the Radio.*

Flip-Flop Girl   FICTION
AUTHOR: Katherine Paterson
HC: Lodestar • PB: Puffin
THEMES: loss; death; siblings; grief; moving; family; friendship

When nine-year-old Vinnie's father dies, her brother Mason stops talking. Athough she too mourns the loss, it's her brother who gets the attention. When she finds out that they all have to move to her grandmother's house in Brownsville, Virginia, Vinnie decides to work on Mason. "Tell them you'll start talking and eating right if they won't make you move." Mason just stared at her. "I mean it, Mason. You'll be sorry. Nobody will feel bad for you there. You won't have this great reputation for the saddest boy that ever lived. Nobody will give a doughnut hole for you . . ." But to Brownsville they go—to a new school, new teacher, and to a rare new friendship. Newbery Medal winner Paterson has written another book about the resilience of children.

The Girl Who Dreamed Only of Geese and Other Tales of the Far North   FOLKLORE COLLECTION
AUTHOR: Howard Norman • ILLUSTRATOR: Leo and Diane Dillon
HC: Gulliver
THEMES: folklore; Inuit; journeys; snow; arctic; traditions; Canada; Alaska

A collaboration that serves as a kind of folkloric travelogue of the Inuit people and their lands. This rich collection of retold tales contains a wide variety of stories, all told in a masterly style and accompanied by the Dillons' astonishing, Inuit-inspired art.

★ The Giver   SCIENCE FICTION
AUTHOR: Lois Lowry
HC: Houghton Mifflin • PB: Dell
THEMES: utopia; taking action; courage; rituals; traditions; gifted children; community; individuality; family

One of those brilliant books that come along every few years. Winner of the Newbery Medal, it has shown up on school reading lists across the country, frequently for 5th or 6th grades. For many kids, this is too early to appreciate the ways the book makes demands upon a reader. Part of the problem lies in the fact that this is a book that begs to be discussed— it has an ending that is open to interpretation, which can frustrate readers who like their meanings clear and concise. A book that challenges readers on a variety of levels—powerful, shocking and thought-provoking, it will be read for generations as a warning against the deceptive virtues of utopian thinking.

Goddesses, Heroes, and Shamans: The Young People's Guide To World Mythology   REFERENCE
AUTHOR: David Bellingham • ILLUSTRATOR: various
HC/PB: Kingfisher
THEMES: folklore; variety; history, world; cultural diversity

The best pan-cultural look at world mythology we have found. All the Gods you've heard of are in here, as well as those that don't get much play in traditional books of this type. A valuable and fascinating resource.

★ The Golden Compass   FICTION-FANTASY
AUTHOR: Philip Pullman
HC: Knopf • PB: Ballantine
THEMES: fantasy; strong girls; witches; adventure; bears; religion; good vs. evil

Innovative, suspense-filled and multilayered, this fantasy lifts the reader into a world where adventure is the rule and original characters cause readers to wonder, "Who is this writer Philip Pullman?" He has created personal daemons to accompany their humans in one form or another throughout their lives. Pantalaimon, Lyra Belacqua's daemon, has the charm, sensibilities and loyalty that would make any of us long for a daemon of our own. And the witches? Pullman's adventure doesn't lack surprises. It challenges readers with new images and possibilities to the end where it makes clear that the second in the *His Dark Materials Trilogy* is an imperative read. The sequel: *The Subtle Knife*.

The Grey King   FICTION-FANTASY

AUTHOR: Susan Cooper
HC: Atheneum • PB: Aladdin
THEMES: fantasy; adventure; good vs. evil; England; Celtic mythology;
folklore; Wales

Book 4 in *The Dark Is Rising* Sequence, this 1976 winner of the Newbery
Medal follows Will Stanton further along on his ultimate quest to battle
it out with the forces of darkness, once and for all. See: *Over Sea, Under
Stone.*

Growing Up in Coal Country   NONFICTION

AUTHOR: Susan Campbell Bartoletti • ILLUSTRATOR: photographs
HC: Houghton Mifflin
THEMES: Pennsylvania; jobs; miners; coal; community; family; child
labor; mines; hardship; U.S. history, late 19th century; triumph

The best nonfiction writers make their subjects come vividly to life, giving a "you are there" feel to their books and a sense that they are communicating directly with the reader. Susan Campbell Bartoletti, using
the childhood stories of her husband's grandfather as inspiration, has
written a compelling account of mining life that stands with the best
nonfiction written for children. Her chapters are full of facts balanced
with personal anecdotes, all delivered in a storytelling style that is
addictively readable. The portrait she paints of life in Pennsylvania coal
country at the turn of the century focuses on childhood as well as adults,
and her account of young boys working in the mines is at turns humorous and heartbreaking. The recounting of the events leading up to and
including the strike against unfair labor practices is inspiring. This is a
great book.

The Guinness Book of World Records   REFERENCE

AUTHOR: Norris McWhirter
PB: Bantam
THEMES: trivia; comparisons

Children who swear they hate reading can often be found looking at reference and nonfiction books that pique their interests. This is the king
of all reference, and a good, safe bet to give to that militant nonreader.
Better yet, leave it in the bathroom and see if pages don't get turned
down.

SPOTLIGHT ON WALTER DEAN MYERS

WITH an ear for urban dialogue and a range of interesting and eccentric characters, Walter Dean Myers has distinguished himself with his novels both for middle grade readers and young adults. Equally adept at handing serious and lighthearted topics, Myers instills much of his writing with a sense of humor and general optimism. His positive portrayals of children and teenagers grappling with the issues of urban life offer young readers hope, role models, and exceptional reading.

This is not to say that Myers shies away from the harder issues. In books like *Scorpions, Somewhere in the Darkness,* and *Fallen Angels* he deals with gangs, drugs, war, prison, and abandonment, and these are some of the finest novels written for young adults. He has also written fiction that depicts the triumphs and hardships of 300 years of African American history—*The Glory Field* and *The Righteous Revenge of Artemis Bonner.* But it is with books such as *Hoops, Mouse Rap, Fast Sam, Cool Clyde, and Stuff,* and *Motown and Didi* that Myers has carved a niche for himself, as no one writes better about the day-to-day concerns and lives of urban black kids.

Myers writes poetry, and uses it to good advantage, whether accompanying his collection of antique photographs (*Brown Angels*), giving stylistic weight to his themes (*The Mouse Rap* cleverly uses his original rapping poetry at the beginning of each chapter), or creating a stunning full-length ode to a time and a place crucial to our understanding of Black history (*Harlem,* which has outstanding art by Myers' son, Christopher).

From time to time, Myers will write an original folk tale and offer it in picture book form. *The Story of the Three Kingdoms* (illustrated by Ashley Bryan) and *How Mr. Monkey Saw the Whole World* (illustrated by Synthia Saint James) are shining examples of Myers' rich storytelling gift.

In the world of nonfiction for young readers Myers has distinguished himself with books like *Now Is Your Time: The African American Struggle for Freedom* and *Malcolm X: By Any Means Necessary,* bringing to these works a novelist's gift for making subjects come to life and a factual narrative that reads like fiction.

We can think of no writer who has provided more compulsively readable books, spanning styles and formats, about urban life for youth of all races with an uplifting and balanced view of childhood than Walter Dean Myers.

Harlem

PICTURE BOOK

AUTHOR: **Walter Dean Myers** • ILLUSTRATOR: Christopher Myers

HC: Scholastic

THEMES: Harlem; survival; African American; U.S. history, 20th century; community; poem; city life; New York

This is one of those books where the words are so rich and the art is so powerful that you find yourself drawing it up to your chest and inhaling before going through it again. It's a history of Harlem in a poem that makes you feel the pulse of the past and of the present. "A journey on the A train that started on the banks of the Niger and has not ended."

History of the U.S.: A 10 Volume Series

NONFICTION

AUTHOR: Joy Hakim

HC/PB: Oxford University Press

THEMES: U.S. history; traditions; cultural diversity; U.S. presidents; government; immigration

A ten-book set that is by far the best history of the U.S. available for young readers. Joy Hakim writes vibrantly, finding the balance between compulsively readable and factual. Start reading any volume, on any page, and you will find information that will fascinate—you won't be able to put it down.

The Homecoming

FICTION

AUTHOR: Cynthia Voigt

HC: Atheneum • PB: Fawcett

THEMES: homelessness; courage; resourcefulness; taking action; change; gifted children; strong girls; family; journeys; siblings; determination; grandmother; relatives

A brilliant, stand-alone read, but also remarkable as the first in a sequence of novels about the Tillerman family. Dicey is the eldest of four, and due to Mama's instability she has taken on the role of the responsible one in her family. When Mama abandons them in the book's opening scene, Dicey is faced with not only providing for the immediate survival of her family, but with getting them to the only relatives they know, miles away, on foot. Dicey and her determination are inspiring, yet she is a tough person to get to know. She is balanced by the other three siblings, each a finely crafted portrayal by author Voigt. The family stays together, and their story continues in subsequent volumes:

Dicey's Song, The Runner, A Solitary Blue, Come a Stranger, On Fortune's Wheel, and *Sons From Afar.*

How to Make a Mummy Talk   NONFICTION

AUTHOR: James M. Deem • ILLUSTRATOR: True Kelley
HC: Houghton Mifflin • PB: Dell
THEMES: rituals; death; burial; mummies; ancient Egypt; ancient history

Written in a light, entertaining style, this nonfiction look at the history of mummies is a must for supplemental reading when it comes time to learn about ancient Egypt. The humorous, slightly irreverent tone and the cartoony illustrations are just the thing to entice a reluctant older reader into navigating all the text.

I Am an American: A True Story of
Japanese Internment   NONFICTION

AUTHOR: Jerry Stanley • ILLUSTRATOR: (photographs)
HC: Crown
THEMES: Japanese American; captivity; U.S. history, World War II; survival; immigration; courage; family; prejudice

Stanley's story of Japanese internment is based on interviews and personal memories. Photographs provide the visuals in this moving account of the Nomura family who were sent to Manzanar, a camp in the California desert. Stanley combines a personal story with historical information about Japanese immigration and political events before and after Pearl Harbor.

If I Were in Charge of the World . . .
And Other Worries   POETRY COLLECTION

AUTHOR: Judith Viorst • ILLUSTRATOR: Lynne Cherry
PB: Aladdin
THEMES: fairy tales; cats; humor; wishes; worry

Not interested in poetry? Show your fourth grader some of the titles in this collection. "Wicked thoughts," "Fifteen, maybe sixteen things to worry about," ". . . and although the mermaid sacrificed everything to win the love of the prince, the prince (alas) decided to wed another." Viorst knows how to tickle the funny bone with subjects kids understand and the "worries" in this collection are right on target!

The Illyrian Adventure   FICTION

AUTHOR: Lloyd Alexander
HC: Dutton • PB: Dell
THEMES: adventure; strong girls; journeys; history, early 20th century

"Miss Vesper Holly has the digestive talents of a goat and the mind of a chess master. She is familiar with half a dozen languages and can swear fluently in all of them. She understands the use of a slide rule but prefers doing calculations in her head. She does not hesitate to risk life and limb—mine as well as her own. No doubt she has other qualities as yet undiscovered. I hope not." So begins the first in a series of adventures featuring a marvelously intrepid heroine (Miss Holly), as told by her put-upon guardian, Professor Brinton Garrett. Rollicking good fun, full of historical adventure a la Indiana Jones, these are for any reader who likes page turning at a fast clip. The other titles are: *The El Dorado Adventure, The Drackenberg Adventure, The Sedera Adventure* and *The Philadelphia Adventure.*

The Invisible Ladder: An Anthology of Contemporary Poems for Young Readers   POETRY ANTHOLOGY

EDITOR: Liz Rosenberg
HC: Henry Holt
THEMES: coming of age; childhood; poets; growing up

Accompanied by memories and photos of their childhood, an eclectic mix from 40 American poets that reaches across the chasm of age and becomes a bridge to the appreciation of poetry for middle graders and teens.

Island of the Blue Dolphins   FICTION

AUTHOR: Scott O'Dell • ILLUSTRATOR: Ted Lewin
HC: Houghton Mifflin • PB: Dell
THEMES: Native American; solitude; courage; strong girls; survival; loneliness; death; loss; coming of age; islands; Channel Islands

A masterpiece, and named by the Children's Literature Association as one of the ten best American children's books ever written. Based on an actual event, here is the unforgettable story of Karana, living alone on an island for eighteen years in the aftermath of the slaughter of her tribe. Her account of the loss of her brother is heartrending, her epic adventure of survival thrilling, and her record of solitude and its effect inspiring as the reader watches her mature and come into her own as a person. When she is rescued at the book's end, it is with some sadness that she leaves the island that she made her home. O'Dell's ability to tell powerful stories in the first person is evident in this, his first of many fine books for young readers, including *Zia,* the sequel to *Island, Streams to the River, River to the Sea, Black Star, Bright Dawn, My Name Is Not Angelica,* and *The Black Pearl.*

Jip, His Story   FICTION

AUTHOR: Katherine Paterson
HC: Lodestar
THEMES: orphans; farms; Vermont; poverty; slavery; survival; Quakers; courage; prejudice; friendship; escape; resourcefulness; school; diversity

No one claimed Jip after he tumbled off a wagon onto the road, so the small boy was sent to the poor farm to live. Jip grew up taking care of the animals, doing chores, and seeing to the needs of a lunatic, all the while wondering why no one came back to claim him. Suspense builds as he and the reader get closer to finding out.

Julie of the Wolves   FICTION

AUTHOR: Jean Craighead George
HC: HarperCollins
THEMES: Inuit; San Francisco; friendship; Alaska; wilderness; courage; wolves; fathers; coming of age; adventure; strong girls

"Some slight gesture that meant nothing to her had apparently meant something to the wolf. His ears shot forward angrily and it seemed all was lost. She wanted to get up and run, but she gathered her courage and pranced closer to him." For Miyax, lost in the Alaskan wilderness with neither food nor direction, it was an act of survival. She had learned the ways of nature from her father, but things had changed. A compelling tale of courage with a deep respect for nature, this Newbery Medal-winner is the perfect choice for an animal lover with a taste for adventure. The story continues in *Julie* and *Julie's Wolf Pack.*

Kingfisher Illustrated History of the World   REFERENCE

AUTHOR: Kingfisher
HC: Kingfisher
THEMES: history, world; cultural diversity

I was the kind of kid who checked out reference books at the library to read, not to do research. If I had had this when I was 10 I would have read it cover to cover. An inviting design and good writing make this an excellent resource for homework or just to read.

Lightning Time   FICTION
AUTHOR: Douglas Rees
HC: DK Ink
THEMES: U.S. history, the Civil War; slavery; Quakers; John Brown; taking action

A compelling, firsthand, fictional account of John Brown's raid on Harper's Ferry in 1859. Though he believes in the abolition of slavery as strongly as any man, young Theodore Worth comes to realize the zeal with which Brown leads his followers may be suicidal. A great example of how history can be made riveting to the reader.

Lincoln: A Photobiography   BIOGRAPHY
AUTHOR: Russell Freedman • ILLUSTRATOR: photographs
HC/PB: Clarion
THEMES: Abraham Lincoln; biography; U.S. history, Civil War; speeches; U.S. presidents

Photographs, direct quotes from Lincoln and excerpts from his own speeches add to this fascinating Newbery Medal-winning photo biographical history of President Lincoln including his boyhood, marriage, professional life, and the presidency. Freedman is known for other intriguing photo essays, including *Franklin Delano Roosevelt* and *Eleanor Roosevelt*.

The Lost Years of Merlin   FICTION-FANTASY
AUTHOR: T.A. Barron
HC: Philomel
THEMES: King Arthur; fantasy; magic; journeys; wizards; England; Wales; coming of age; adventure; mystery; good vs. evil

"I sucked in my breath, then urged the hawk into another dive. We shot down toward the same open window as before. Wind tore at me, screaming in my ears." Action-filled images, loyal, brave, and wicked characters, and a young hero's quest for his identity make this page-turner an imaginative introduction to the boyhood of Merlin, the legendary enchanter. *The Seven Songs of Merlin* is the second in what will be a five volume epic.

Merlin: Book 3 of the Young Merlin Trilogy   FICTION-FANTASY
AUTHOR: **Jane Yolen**
HC: Harcourt Brace
THEMES: fantasy; magic; King Arthur; folklore; England; wizards

The finale delivers upon the promise of the first two books (*Passager* and *Hobby*), though we wish they were available in one volume. Terrific fantasy reading for that motivated but younger reader, as well as any Arthurian fanatic.

Midnight Hour Encores   FICTION
AUTHOR: Bruce Brooks
HC/PB: HarperCollins
THEMES: music; gifted child; U.S. history, the 60's; strong girls; fathers and daughters; journeys; secrets; coming of age; single parents

Sibilance T. Spooner (a name she made up for herself) is, at 16, a world-class cello player. Bright, articulate and possessed of a mind very much her own, she has never wanted to know her mother, never wanted to understand why she was abandoned at birth and left in the care of her father, Taxi, an unreconstructed hippie. Sib and Taxi have quite a nice life together, each respecting the other and providing the right amount of love and care to give the illusion to Sib that she is complete. Then, for reasons she chooses not to share with Taxi, she decides she would like to meet her mother. Her father, never one to do anything halfway, takes this opportunity to teach his daughter about the people who made her and the times that shaped them. This brilliant novel about love, familial bonds, secrets and self-discovery is the perfect book to give to a teenager asking "What was the big deal about the 60's, anyway?" The writing about music and what it means to people is worth the price of the book alone.

★ Nightjohn   FICTION
AUTHOR: **Gary Paulsen**
HC: Delacorte • PB: Dell
THEMES: slavery; reading; escape; literacy; U.S. history, pre-Civil War; African American; teachers

Remarkable. A portrait of slave life that focuses on learning to read as a means to escape the wretchedness of life. It pulls no punches in its portrait of the cruelty, but also shines with hope and inspiration as we watch young Sarny learn to read at the hands of the runaway slave, Nightjohn. The sequel, *Sarny,* follows her life into old age.

★ Nothing But the Truth   FICTION
AUTHOR: Avi
HC: Orchard • PB: Avon
THEMES: conscience; school; teachers; truth; point of view; patriotism

A brilliantly contrived novel about the price paid when only part of the truth is revealed. Phillip Malloy is a ninth grade student who is performing poorly in Miss Narwin's English class. His grade of a D- denies him the chance to try out for the track team, and his anger and frustration at his teacher cause him to act out during homeroom, resulting in a suspension and a major public brouhaha. The events unfold inexorably, spinning wildly out of control so quickly that reading this book is like watching a train wreck. The true genius of Avi's construction lies in the way his narrative forces the reader to choose sides in the story, while slowly coming to realize that everyone in the story is wrong because they have only part of the truth. The ending is as sad as any we have ever read, especially because if any of the main characters had stopped to consider all the sides of the situation, most of the tragedy could have been averted, which is a lot like life.

One More River   FICTION
AUTHOR: Lynne Reid Banks
HC: Morrow • PB: Avon
THEMES: change; politics; Israel; kibbutz; home; Jews; peace; jobs; community; war; Mideast; Arabs

Lesley, a wealthy fourteen-year-old cheerleader living in Canada, moves with her parents to an Israeli kibbutz where she learns about community—and about how lifetimes of discrimination affect the opportunity for peace. Lynne Reid Banks lived on a kibbutz in Israel for eight years. Her characters are believable and this powerful story offers a glimpse into the longstanding struggle between Jews and Palestinians. The sequel, *Broken Bridge,* tells what happens to the characters in *One More River,* twenty-five years later.

One World, Many Religions: The Ways We Worship   NONFICTION

AUTHOR: Mary Pope Osborne • ILLUSTRATOR: various
HC: Knopf
THEMES: religion; traditions; comparisons; rituals; faith; history, world; cultural diversity

Using more than fifty color photographs to illustrate the world's major religious faiths, Osborne describes the traditions, forms of worship and major holidays of Judaism, Christianity, Islam, Hinduism, Buddhism, Confucianism, and Taoism. This highly accessible volume includes a glossary, map, timeline and bibliograhy.

One Yellow Daffodil: A Hanukkah Story   PICTURE BOOK

AUTHOR: David Adler • ILLUSTRATOR: Lloyd Bloom
HC: Harcourt Brace
THEMES: Holocaust; Jews; Hanukkah; memories; symbols; loss; kindness

Like Patricia Palocco's *Pink & Say*, this picture book is for older children. A powerful and important addition to the canon of Holocaust literature for young people.

The Outsiders   FICTION

AUTHOR: S.E. Hinton
HC: Viking • PB: Puffin
THEMES: community; friendship; prejudice; loyalty; family; gentle boys; taking action; gangs

One of the most popular books ever written for children and on more school reading lists than any other title, this first novel by then 16-year-old Susie Hinton (that's right—S. E. stands for Susan Elizabeth) is a classic. There are few teenagers who cannot respond to the feelings of the characters, especially when they mirror their own sense of alienation.

Over Sea, Under Stone   FICTION-FANTASY

AUTHOR: Susan Cooper
HC: Harcourt Brace • PB: Aladdin
THEMES: fantasy; adventure; good vs. evil; England; Celtic mythology; folklore; Wales

Book 1 of *The Dark Is Rising* Sequence. This five-book series takes its inspiration from the great mythic history of England, weaving elements of Celtic mythology into an immensely satisfying journey into the nature of good and evil, light and dark. This is one of the great pieces of fantasy writing in the English language, and children who stay with it for the long, rewarding haul gain a basis of appreciation for Tolkien, Ursula LeGuin and almost any adult writer of fantasy we can think of. Read them in order: follow this with *The Dark Is Rising,* then *Greenwitch, The Grey King,* and finally, *Silver on the Tree.*

★ The Phantom Tollbooth   FICTION-FANTASY

AUTHOR: Norton Juster • ILLUSTRATOR: Jules Feiffer
HC/PB: Random House
THEMES: humor; adventure; cleverness; diversity; cars; dogs; imagination; journeys; zany; triumph; wisdom; math; alphabet

"There was once a boy named Milo who didn't know what to do with himself—not just sometimes but always." But when a tollbooth appeared in his room, he drove through. On the other side he jumped to the island of Conclusions, met a ticking watchdog named Tock and discovered that life wasn't boring after all. It's hard not to compare this to *Alice in Wonderland* and *The Wonderful Wizard of Oz*, where characters confront unforgettable personalities on a fantastic journey. Read it aloud and offer it as part of a permanent library.

This is a demanding book, full of clever language and allusions that can go over the heads of younger listeners. A certain amount of reading and listening experience is called for here, and I recommend it be used with children 7 and up as a read aloud. If you try this out as part of your family repertoire and it falls flat, stop. Put it away for a couple of years and bring it out again. Your children will amaze you with their ability to respond to it then. As far as reading this themselves, many adults remember this as one of their favorites from their childhood and try to give it to their own children. I don't like to be a stickler about ages, but in this case I feel strongly that there is no better way to say it: An eight year old can probably read this—an eleven year old will be more likely to love it.

Poetry From A To Z: A Guide for Young Writers   POETRY ANTHOLOGY

EDITED BY: Paul B. Janeczko
HC: Atheneum
THEMES: variety; writing; poets

For beginning poets, Janeczko offers suggestions, samples and ideas. His selected poems include a wide range that will appeal to personalities across the board. We've noticed that he publishes three kinds of poetry books: collections of his own work (see *Brickyard Summer*), anthologies of carefully selected gems (see *I Feel A Little Jumpy Around You*) and selections like this one which combines poems with his thoughts to offer teens poetry insights.

Prairie Songs   FICTION

AUTHOR: Pam Conrad • ILLUSTRATOR: Darryl S. Zudeck
HC/PB: HarperCollins
THEMES: U.S.A., the prairie; pioneers; death; family; friendship

Louisa loves the quiet life of the Nebraska prairie, and is thrilled when Emmeline, the doctor's wife, comes all the way from New York City to live nearby. But Emmeline is not used to the solitude, and finally goes mad. A gripping story from a young girl's perspective of the beauty and pain of life on the prairie.

Princess Nevermore   FICTION-FANTASY

AUTHOR: Dian Curtis Regan
HC/PB: Scholastic
THEMES: fantasy; strong girls; princesses; love; escape; adventure; comparisons; strangers

Taking the familiar tale of a princess who longs for life outside of her kingdom and giving it a new twist, author Regan weaves a clever fantasy novel that will delight girls who are on the cusp of their own life choices but secretly desire the chance to escape. Lighthearted observations of contemporary life from the point of view of outsider Princess Quinn make for an enchanting, romantic, adventuresome read that kids will revel in, then pass on to their best friends.

★ The Prydian Chronicles   FICTION-FANTASY

AUTHOR: Lloyd Alexander
HC: Dutton • PB: Dell
THEMES: fantasy; adventure; journeys; courage; heroes; coming of age

As good as fantasy writing gets. In the course of five books (*The Book of Three, The Black Cauldron, The Castle of Llyr, Taran Wanderer,* and *The High King*) we hear of the adventures of Taran, the assistant Pig Keeper who wants to be a hero. Taking his cue from Welsh mythology but creating a broader canvas uniquely his own, Alexander fills his pages with enough wonderful adventure, thrills, laughter and heartbreak for several lifetimes, but such is the nature of fantasy. We recommend that *The Chronicles of Prydain* be introduced to young readers after *The Chronicles of Narnia* but before Tolkien, though whenever you begin this quintet you need to be prepared to stay with it for the long haul, as you will find yourself craving more as each book comes to an end.

★ Red Scarf Girl: A Memoir of the Cultural Revolution
BIOGRAPHY

AUTHOR: Ji-Li Jiang
HC: HarperCollins
THEMES: China; history; autobiography; courage; coming of age; family; jobs; school; bullies; hardship

A moving account of a Chinese family and their troubles during the upheaval of the late 60's. Young Ji-Li is bright and motivated, and has a comfortable life—her future seems assured. When Mao begins to persecute the educated and the well-to-do, her family is set upon by neighbors and friends, and Jiang's remembrances carry all the weight of similar accounts, such as *The Diary of Anne Frank*. A courageous young girl, now grown to womanhood, gives the world her childhood to stand as a testament against cruelty and inhumanity.

Redwall
FICTION-FANTASY

AUTHOR: Brian Jacques • ILLUSTRATOR: Gary Chalk
HC: Philomel • PB: Berkley
THEMES: diversity; knights; fighting; magic; fantasy; weapons; adventure

This enormously popular series shows no signs of waning and can be recommended confidently for any age child who is interested in a long and involved fantasy. Imagine medieval England, with all its pageantry, chivalry, sorcery and swordplay. Now imagine that all the characters are small, furry animals. With a cast that includes mice, ferrets, rats and hedgehogs, this is a look at class and ethnicity, rodent-style. Great, absorbing adventure, and when kids get started on one volume, they want to keep going, so have several on hand to stay ahead of the voracious Redwall reader your child will surely become. The subsequent titles, in order, are *Mossflower, Mattimeo, Mariel of Redwall, Salamandastron, Martin the Warrior, The Bellmaker, Outcast of Redwall,* and *Pearls of Lutra*.

Roll of Thunder, Hear My Cry   FICTION

AUTHOR: Mildred Taylor

HC: Dial • PB: Puffin

THEMES: courage; family; pride; U.S. history, the Depression; independence; strong girls; gifted children; prejudice; U.S.A., the South

It's an uphill battle for Cassie and her family, whose love for their land and strong family ties strengthen them against rural Southern racism during the Depression. In her author's note, Taylor describes how her history was passed from generation to generation, "a history of great-grandparents and of slavery and of the days following slavery; of those who lived still not free, yet who would not let their spirits be enslaved. From my father the story-teller I learned to respect the past, to respect my own heritage and myself." And like her father, Taylor has passed a story on to us, allowing a glimpse into the time of night riders, burnings, and public humiliation, when personal respect and family strength provide the power for survival. For further stories in the life of this remarkable family, see: *Let The Circle Be Unbroken* and *The Well*.

> My father was a master storyteller. He could tell a fine old story that made me hold my sides with rolling laughter and sent happy tears down my cheeks, or a story of stark reality that made me shiver and be grateful for my own warm, secure surroundings. He could tell stories of beauty and grace, stories of gentle dreams, and paint them as vividly as any picture with splashes of character and dialogue. His memory detailed every event of ten or forty years or more before, just as if it had happened yesterday.
>
> —Mildred Taylor, from the Author's Notes to *Roll of Thunder, Hear My Cry*

Save Queen of Sheba   FICTION

AUTHOR: Louise Moeri

PB: Puffin

THEMES: U.S. history, Westward movement; survival; courage; Oregon; pioneers; Native American; brothers; sisters; adventure

"A huge greenish black fly was crawling slowly over his hand. The fly was so close to his eyes, for his hand lay tossed up on the dirt just a few inches from his face, that King David could see every leg as it moved, the iridescent wings flick, the big bulbous eyes. He wondered why he did not move his hand and brush the fly away . . ." An attack on their wagon train has killed everyone except David and his young sister. Now they must venture ahead to find their parents on their own, and David is hurt. Here's a breath-catching story that will get the attention of adventure seekers.

There are times when "grabbers" like this one come in handy. When I've been introduced as a storyteller in a 7th grade English class and face a row of passive, slumped figures, legs stretched forward arms folded, daring me to read aloud, I read the first chapter and close the book. The slumpers change position, and a few will make their way to the library to finish what I've started.

Singer to the Sea God
FICTION

AUTHOR: Vivian Alcock
HC: Delacorte • PB: Dell
THEMES: Greek mythology; ancient Greece; coming of age; adventure; journeys; music; singing; friendship; strong girls; gentle boys; sisters

Using the legend of Perseus and Medusa as a springboard, this is the epic tale of Phaidon and his quest to be reunited with his sister Cleo, who has been turned to stone. With the sweep and magic of great storytelling, there is enough adventure here to satisfy most readers, and enough about the Greeks and their lives to make this a useful book for supplemental reading when the time comes to learn about this period of history.

Skin Deep and Other Teenage Reflections
POETRY COLLECTION

AUTHOR: Angela Shelf Medearis • ILLUSTRATOR: Michael Bryant
HC: Macmillan
THEMES: African American; coming of age; school; friendship

"I wear these dark glasses because they're really cool (and because I don't want you to see the fear in my eyes) . . ." Sad, funny, moving, this collection of contemporary poetry will hit the spot—even for the teenager who finds reading difficult.

A Solitary Blue
FICTION

AUTHOR: Cynthia Voigt
HC/PB: Scholastic
THEMES: family; loneliness; love; abandonment; music; mothers and sons; friendship; school; solitude

A must for emotionally sensitive teens and the ones who love them. Jeff moves from a supporting role in *Dicey's Song* to the lead in this book, and his story is compassionately told. As fine a tale of teen loneliness and redemption as one could wish for.

Stones in Water   FICTION

AUTHOR: Donna Jo Napoli
HC: Dutton
THEMES: history, World War II; prejudice; coming of age; Italy; escape; friendship; hardship; hope; courage; determination

Samuel and Roberto are watching a movie in their hometown of Venice, Italy, when they are abducted by German soldiers and forced to work in a World War II Labor Camp. Roberto's attempts to keep secret the fact that his friend is Jewish will haunt you for weeks after you finish reading. It's a story about war and survival. It's a page turner.

The Story Library Series   ANTHOLOGY

EDITORS: various
PB: Kingfisher
THEMES: variety

The Story Library consists of volumes of collected writings, each organized around a particular theme; horses, growing up, mystery and horror are among those covered. The selections are short—some are excerpts from longer works, others are short stories. In every case the editors have chosen a terrifically interesting mix of writers and style. The British are more prominent than the Americans, but then, this series originates in England. The caliber of the writing is always high, making this an excellent way to introduce thematically-challenged young readers to a variety of writers while still feeding their need to be slaves to one particular category. Titles include: *Horse Stories, Growing Up Stories, Horror Stories, Fantasy Stories,* and *Mystery Stories.*

Sworn Enemies   FICTION

AUTHOR: Carol Matas
HC: Bantam • PB: Dell
THEMES: Russia; history, 19th century; Jews; kidnapping; hardship; soldiers; conscription

In the late 1800s Russia filled their military quotas by hiring kidnappers to kidnap Jewish boys. This suspense-filled story is about Aaron, who ends up in the same battalion as his kidnapper.

To Be a Slave   NONFICTION
AUTHOR: Julius Lester, compiler • ILLUSTRATOR: Tom Feelings
PB: Scholastic
THEMES: slavery; African American; U.S. history, pre-Civil War; prejudice; captivity; freedom

Still as powerful as when it was originally published in 1968, Lester's oral history of slavery is all the more remarkable for being the first of such works for young readers. Slave narratives are used almost exclusively, with Lester intruding only to connect or amplify, and Feelings' art adds depth to this important piece of American history.

The True Confessions of Charlotte Doyle   FICTION
AUTHOR: Avi
HC: Orchard • PB: Avon
THEMES: history, the 19th century; boats; sea; journeys; adventure; courage; strong girls; survival

Beginning with "An Important Warning" the story of Charlotte Doyle captures its reader from the start. "Not every thirteen-year-old girl is accused of murder, brought to trial, and found guilty. But I was just such a girl, and my story is worth relating even if it did happen years ago. Be warned, however . . . if strong ideas and action offend you, read no more." The terrible captain and mutinous crew were on the Seahawk, crossing the Atlantic Ocean in 1832. And there was one passenger, Charlotte Doyle. This is her riveting story.

Uncanny   SHORT STORY COLLECTION
AUTHOR: Paul Jennings
HC: Viking • PB: Puffin
THEMES: horror; variety

Australian Jennings has a sense for the bizzare and a knack for delivering it in a pull-the-rug-out-from-under-you style. A writer we love to recommend to 5th grade and up, especially those who cannot seem to get enough of horror. When those kids exhaust themselves on what is available in the children's section of the bookstore or library, they often seek out adult writers like King and Koontz. Steer them to Jennings if you can, and you'll have them reading stuff just as twisted but still geared for their age and sensibilities. Besides, it would be a shame to miss such a good storyteller as this, no matter how old you get. His collections just keep on coming, and they all start with "Un": *Unbearable, Uncovered, Unbelievable, Undone, Unmentionable,* and *Unreal.*

Walk Two Moons
FICTION

AUTHOR: Sharon Creech

HC/PB: HarperCollins

THEMES: comparisons; journeys; mothers and daughters; fathers and daughters; grandparents; Native American; loss; grief; death; mystery

In chapters that shift back and forth through time, Salamanca Hiddle tells the story of the loss of her mother and how she learned the value of the Native American saying "Don't judge a man until you've walked two moons in his moccasins." Creech takes her time with the revelations, and there are a lot of them by the end, so the reader spends much of the time waiting for the answers to many of the book's mysteries, but the characters are so engaging that the contrivances of the plot hardly matter. Sal's wisdom is hard-earned and she makes an unforgettable heroine.

The Wanderings of Odysseus: The Story of the Odyssey
FICTION

AUTHOR: Rosemary Sutcliff • ILLUSTRATOR: Alan Lee

HC: Delacorte

THEMES: Greek mythology; ancient Greece; folklore; adventure; sailing; sea; monsters; boats; journeys; *The Odyssey*

A spirited retelling of *The Odyssey* by the team that gave us *Black Ships Before Troy.* A great way to introduce this epic tale to young readers.

War Boy: A Country Childhood
PICTURE BOOK

AUTHOR/ILLUSTRATOR: Michael Foreman

HC: Arcade

THEMES: England; childhood; history, World War II; soldiers; family; war

In this extraordinary book, Michael Foreman tells of growing up on the south coast of England during World War II. *War Boy* deals better with the subject of children continuing to live as children during wartime than any book we can think of. The picture-book format may mislead some into thinking this book is for young children, but the audience is decidedly older, more fifth grade and up. Making his very personal memories into a story of universal interest, the author/illustrator tells it like it was, holding back little of the experience simply because this is a book for children. Some of the British vernacular may be a bit alien, but it is decidedly worth the trouble and will serve as an excellent introduction to rural English culture. The sequel, *After The War Was Over*, covers the ten years after the war and deals with the author's coming of age.

★ The Watsons Go to Birmingham, 1963   FICTION
AUTHOR: Christopher Paul Curtis
HC: Delacorte • PB: Dell
THEMES: prejudice; violence; family; African American; U.S. history, the 60's; civil rights; humor; friendship; U.S.A., the South

It made us laugh out loud and then it made us cry. Curtis' exceptional novel tells of how the struggle for civil rights affects one family, all seen through the eyes of ten-year-old Kenny, the middle child in a family known as "The Weird Watsons." Rich with character and detail of life in both the North and South during the early 60's, this is as good a first novel as we have read.

★ The Westing Game   FICTION
AUTHOR: Ellen Raskin
HC: Dutton • PB: Puffin
THEMES: mystery; detectives; contests; puzzles; wordplay

Sam Westing left a will. Now his heirs must follow clues to find his murderer. The problem is, only two people have all the clues, and you (if you choose to read this puzzle mystery) will be one of them. We don't recommend that you read this while the TV is on; Raskin's demanding game will require all your attention.

What Jamie Saw   FICTION
AUTHOR: Carolyn Coman
HC: Front Street • PB: Puffin
THEMES: abuse; escape; family; stepparents

Though this is about a younger child, the intensity of the writing makes this a book for older readers. Coman's Newbery Honor book is a devastating look at the horrors of a neglected and abused childhood. Powerful and disturbing, but full of hope.

Where the Red Fern Grows

FICTION

AUTHOR: Wilson Rawls
HC: Doubleday • PB: Dell
THEMES: friendship; loss; death; pets; faith; dogs; determination; Oklahoma; country life; family; hunting

We defy you to read this beloved classic without crying! The story of Billy and his faithful hunting dogs Old Dan and Little Ann has moved legions of ten-, eleven-, and twelve-year-olds to tears, not to mention their parents and teachers. A rich sense of place and time—the Ozarks during the Depression—and the loving depiction of Bill's family make this a book to treasure.

"What snapped me out of my surly adolescence and moved me on were books that let me live other people's lives. I got to visit the Dust Bowl and London and the Civil War and Rhodesia . . . When I picked up *Martha Quest*, a novel set in southern Africa, it jarred open a door that was right in front of me. I found I couldn't close it.
—Barbara Kingsolver, author, from her essay, "How Mr. Dewey Decimal Saved My Life"

Where Will This Shoe Take You?: A Walk Through the History of Footwear

NONFICTION

AUTHOR: Laurie Lawlor
HC: Walker
THEMES: history, world; feet; shoes; clothes; comparisons; cultural diversity

A history of the world, told through footwear. Fascinating, and the kind of book to have on hand for a unique book report.

World Mythology Series

FOLKLORE COLLECTION

AUTHOR: various • ILLUSTRATOR: various
HC: Peter Bedrick
THEMES: folklore; history, world; variety

A treasure for those who love folklore! This series of illustrated collections of stories from world mythology is the best and most comprehensive we have seen. Excellent selections and retellings combined with strong research make these books teens will return to again and again. Titles include *Angels Prophets Rabbis and Kings From the Stories of the Jewish People, Heroes Monsters & Other Worlds From Russian Mythology,*

Warriors Gods & Spirits From Central & South American Mythology, and *Gods and Pharaohs From Egyptian Mythology.*

Zel FICTION

AUTHOR: Donna Jo Napoli
HC: Dutton
THEMES: history, medieval times; princes; love; family; witches; captivity; courage; mothers and daughters; folktale variations

An astonishing retelling of the Rapunzel tale from the point of view of the witch, Rapunzel, and her prince. Full of magic and heightened emotion, this is a fresh new look at a story, similar to Napoli's *The Magic Circle* in its intensity. By retelling tales in depth, the author shows us that no one is all good or evil, and in this case that the witch who locked her daughter in a tower was powerless to do otherwise. A terrific opportunity to discuss how stories get told and how what we hear depends on who is doing the telling.

These books, mostly fiction, can be read by our upper M's, but call for a level of maturity that is more often found in our Y's. Just because a child can read a book does not automatically mean she must. You and your reader will have plenty to talk about here—we advocate reading with them the books that may benefit from an adult perspective.

The Acorn People   FICTION

AUTHOR: Ron Jones

HC: Dell • PB: Bantam

THEMES: camp; handicaps; determination; encouragement; death

Without sentimentality, Ron Jones tells the true story of the kids at Camp Wiggin, kids dependent on wheelchairs, ramps and rails. With heart-tugging determination that sends them up Lookout Mountain, into the pool and on stage to perform, these kids take on camp. There is humor here, but nothing about this story is cute—in fact, it is downright straightforward in its realistic portrayal of these kids' lives. Readers will turn the last page, a lump in their throats, with the profound understanding that they have been touched in a way that will last them throughout their lives.

> " . . . the only way children learn to read is by reading. We cannot send them mixed messages—read, but oh, God! don't read *that!*—and expect them to become genuine readers."
> —Dorothy M. Broderick, "Editorial," THE VOYA (Voice of Youth Advocates) READER

Beyond the Western Sea   FICTION

AUTHOR: Avi

HC: Orchard • PB: Avon

THEMES: escape; adventure; England; Ireland; wealth; poverty; courage; history, 19th century; immigration

Book 1 in the two-part adventure *The Escape From Home* will send readers searching for Book 2, *Lord Kirkle's Money*. It's hard not to think of a Dickens novel here, where three youths, 11 to 15, fight to survive in the dank alleys of England's Liverpool in the 1850s. Maura O'Connell is the oldest and she and her brother have fled from the cruel poverty of Ireland to find a life in England. Sir Laurence Kirkle, only 11, has left his wealthy home to seek justice in the brutal world outside. Fast paced, with no chapter lasting longer than two pages, and with enough adventure and suspense to keep the pages turning.

Brickyard Summer   POETRY COLLECTION

AUTHOR: Paul B. Janeczko

HC: Orchard

THEMES: city life; courage; poverty; friendship; coming of age

"Spider always wore sunglasses but we knew he wasn't blind, not the way he moved match to Marlboro, raked a comb through his hair, and smirked . . . leaning against the hood of his glossy black Impala." Two boys, just out of eighth grade, observe life around them in their poor neighborhood. Janeczko makes pictures so clearly with his words, readers find familiarity in the streets and the lives surviving there.

Cool Salsa: Bilingual Poems on Growing Up Latino in the United States   POETRY ANTHOLOGY

EDITOR: Lori Carlson

HC/PB: Henry Holt

THEMES: Spanish language; Hispanic; growing up; bilingual; coming-of-age

Covering the wide range of Latino experience, this is a wonderful anthology of poems from voices well known and new, each presented in Spanish and English.

The Cuckoo's Child   FICTION

AUTHOR: Suzanne Freeman
HC: Greenwillow • PB: Hyperion
THEMES: separation; siblings; family; grief; loss; belonging; change;
aunts; hope; anxiety

When word comes that their parents are lost at sea, Mia and her sisters
leave Lebanon and return to their home in America to live with their
aunt. While her sisters seem to face the loss and adjust to their new
lives, Mia wavers between hope, anxiety, and despair. This deeply moving—sometimes funny—novel introduces a heroine who finds herself,
along with the strength to get through a heartbreaking experience.

Dear Mr. Sprouts   FICTION

AUTHOR: Errol Broome
HC: Knopf
THEMES: Australia; self-respect; environment; love; confidence; mail;
writing

Set in Australia, and told through letters between two people con-
fronting personal struggle. One plants a forest, only to have to defend it
against a fire. The other overcomes her self-consciousness and fulfills
her dream to be a writer. "Believe in yourself" is the message here.

Deathwatch   FICTION

AUTHOR: Robb White
PB: Dell
THEMES: survival; resourcefulness; desert; hunting; adventure; truth

One of our favorite books to give to the boy who refuses to read anything. Ben is alone in the desert, wearing only his shorts, with no water
or food, and is being pursued by a madman with a gun. How he got into
that predicament is revealed in the first three chapters, with the chase
taking up the better part of the book. Courageous Ben knows the desert
well—he grew up here—and his survival techniques are plausible and
clever. His evil pursuer, Madec, is a fast-talking, self-justifying sociopath
who thinks he has the answer to everything. Will Ben escape? And if he
does, how will he convince the authorities of the truth of what really
happened? You just have to read it to find out . . .

My niece Patty was in the sixth grade when she asked me to read
a book she complained her teacher was "making her read." She

hated it. "Why would I read a book you hate?" I responded. My twelve-year-old daughter was there and offered to read it. It was Deathwatch. *The entire time she read that book she complained, "I hate this book Mom, you've got to read it!" When she finished it, she handed it over. I read it. I hated it and took it to work and asked the staff to read it. They too "hated" it and have been recommending it ever since. Sometimes a book is so gripping, it makes the reader breathless with frustration at not being able to step in to change the action. This is one. Read it. Maybe you too will hate it.*

The Earthsea Quartet   FICTION-FANTASY
AUTHOR: Ursula LeGuin
PB: Bantam
THEMES: responsibility; choices; dragons; gifted children; magic; wizards; coming of age; fantasy

A four-book meditation on the effects and uses of power, this outstanding piece of fantasy writing has been acclaimed in the adult as well as children's arena. Many bookstores keep these in the science fiction section, not with the children's books. Darker than you might expect, but it ranks at the very top of the list of world building fantasy. Dragons, wizards, magic—it's all here, ready and waiting for the young reader done with Susan Cooper's *The Dark Is Rising* sequence and *The Hobbit* but not yet ready for *The Lord of the Rings*. The order of the books is: *The Wizard of Earthsea, The Tombs of Atuan, The Farthest Shore,* and *Tehanu*.

The Forestwife   FICTION
AUTHOR: Theresa Tomlinson
HC: Orchard • PB: Dell
THEMES: history: medieval life; Robin Hood; herbs; point of view; healing; strong girls; hunting

We know Robin Hood's story, but this tale gives us Marian's point of view along with a dose of medieval times. A hunter, a solver of mysteries, and a healer, Marian learns which herbs to use as a cure and which plants work best for making dyes. This is no passive Marian waiting around in the forest to be rescued!

★ Freak the Mighty   FICTION
AUTHOR: Rodman Philbrick
HC/PB: Scholastic
THEMES: bullies; gifted children; courage; friendship; handicaps; imagination; teamwork; computers

Two boys—misfits—combine themselves into a single entity to take on the world. This compassionate, wise and funny book will appeal to the outcast lurking in most adolescents and deserves to be a classic, along side of *The Outsiders* and *Maniac Magee.*

★ A Girl Named Disaster   FICTION
AUTHOR: Nancy Farmer
HC: Orchard • PB: Puffin
THEMES: Africa; courage; strong girls; rivers; survival; adventure; journeys; animals; boats; maps; ancestors; grandmothers; traditions

Nhamo is eleven years old when she sets off alone on the Musengezi River to find her father. She has far to travel and the danger of starvation and drowning are ever present. Farmer has included maps of her voyage, a cast of characters, a glossary of African words, and a brief history of Zimbabwe, Mozambique and the beliefs of the Shona. This is no textbook. It is a spellbinding adventure that offers curious readers answers with a turn of the page.

★ The Hobbit   FICTION-FANTASY
AUTHOR: J.R.R. Tolkien
HC: Houghton Mifflin • PB: Ballantine
THEMES: fantasy; adventure; courage; maps; community; fighting; good vs. evil; little folk

"In a hole in the ground there lived a hobbit. Not a nasty, dirty, wet hole, filled with the ends of worms and an oozy smell, nor yet a dry, bare, sandy hole with nothing in it to sit down on or to eat: it was a hobbit-hole, and that means comfort." Hobbits are tiny, sociable little people who like parties, feastings, and peace and quiet in their lives. They live in a land called The Shire, found between the River Brandywind and the Far Downs. This is a story about the Hobbits and about one Bilbo Baggins, who traveled far from home and brought back the One Ring of Power along with adventure to the Hobbits' once peaceful world. *The Hobbit* is the prequel to Tolkien's trilogy, *The Lord of the Rings.* Though this introduction to Tolkien's fantasy world is a perfect book to read aloud as a family when the children hit 8, the subsequent volumes take a leap in terms of sophistication and may be better off left for discovery in the early teens. We have always felt that *The Hobbit* is a children's book and the other three are not, but you and your child will need to make that decision for your family.

THE TREK FROM "X-FILES" TO HAWTHORNE

"The funny thing about how critical discussion of books in schools kills the joy of reading for so many people is that the critical impulse is alive and well. Don't believe me? Check out any online newsgroup for any science fiction show. "X-Files," "Babylon 5," "Trek," "Highlander," whatever—they all have their gosh-wow fanboys and their unthinking idiots, but the big name fans are the ones who chew up the themes, analyze the structure, point out subtle clues to the plot or bits of characterization, thrash out the moral implications, discuss what the show is doing in relation to the conventions of its genre, etc.

"So what's the difference? Why does the same sixteen-year-old who devotes hours of his life to analyzing the "X-Files" in greater depth than any teacher would ever require skim through *The Scarlet Letter* and crib his paper on it from Cliff's Notes? Part of it is that nobody made him watch the "X-Files." It's his own discovery. *The Scarlet Letter* has been force-fed him before he was ready for it. The minute someone says: "You must," the human impulse is to sit back, fold the arms, and say, "You're not the boss of me." Also, there's no received wisdom to overcome about a current TV show or a brand-new book or comic. You don't need to fear getting a failing grade because you disagree with your teacher about which parts of "Jose Chung's *From Outer Space*" are most nearly true in the context of the series, but you might well hesitate to take the side of the whale in *Moby Dick* if the teacher insists that the whale is evil. Asking a teenager to develop his own critical ideas in the face of the pressure to conform that a classroom provides is asking for trouble. Also, if a fan has nothing to say about an episode, he can keep quiet. No one on the newsgroup will think less of him if he isn't inspired to speak.

"Teachers must see that this critical impulse exists even in their dull-eyed classes occasionally. And they must hear the fan in their classes talking over the latest developments in B-5, or eagerly passing around the most recent Miles Vorkosigan adventure so they can talk about the implications for Our Hero's ongoing identity crisis. It must be painful to see this enthusiasm and critical acumen dry up and blow away when faced with Hawthorne and Shakespeare. Possibly bringing in new books geared for YA audiences would help; but I think the fault isn't in the material, but in the classroom practice. The mere fact that they're getting a grade and that they have to put an opinion on paper whether they've formed one or not is a killer all by itself. And what the best thing is to do about that, I don't have any idea. If I did, I guess I'd be a teacher."

—Peni Griffin, author of
Vikki Vanishes, Hobkin, and *Switching Well*

Hobkin   FICTION-FANTASY

AUTHOR: Peni R. Griffin

HC: McElderry

THEMES: abuse; little folk; running away; sisters; Texas; home; fantasy

Mixing elements of fantasy with realistic, almost traumatic situations is a specialty of Griffin's, and this book works extremely well as a book about how we all can use a little help to heal. Liza and Kay flee an abusive stepfather, winding up in a small Texas town masquerading as rightful residents of an empty farmhouse. It just so happens that there IS a resident, a magical brownie named Hobkin. With stylish humor, Griffin makes this unusual mix work. Other books where she creates similar magic are:*Vikki Vanishes, A Dig in Time, Margo's House,* and *Switching Well.*

I Feel a Little Jumpy Around You: A Book of Her Poems and His Poems Collected in Pairs   POETRY ANTHOLOGY

EDITORS: Naomi Shihab Nye and Paul Janeczko

HC: Simon & Schuster

THEMES: variety; family; relationships; love

Pairing poems by over 150 poets according to gender and theme, this volume takes a look at the many ways men and women relate and express themselves. This treasure trove is remarkable not only for the poetry but for the way we are asked to consider each selection. A valuable acheivement by editors Nye and Janeczko!

The Magic Circle   FICTION

AUTHOR: Donna Jo Napoli

HC: Dutton • PB: Puffin

THEMES: fairy tales; strong women; folktale variations; healing; witches; mothers and daughters; history, medieval times

A powerful, thought-provoking and illuminating book to give to an intuitive reader ready for a challenge—and to adults who fit this category. Feminists, eco-warriors, mystics, shamans and witches will find it right-on in its depiction of the price women paid for knowledge in the Middle Ages. Warning! The jacket copy gives the plot away. Hide it. Allow yourself the delicious moment of recognition when you find out that you've been reading the untold side of a familiar tale.

Make Lemonade   FICTION

AUTHOR: Virginia Euwer Wolff
HC: Henry Holt • PB: Scholastic
THEMES: poverty; teenage mothers; coming of age; determination; friendship; family

Fourteen-year-old LaVaughn is determined to go to college and not end up like Jolly, the 17-year-old mother of the two children she baby-sits. This is a portrait of two young women who assist each other in getting their lives on track and an unblinking look at the lives of families in the grip of the cycle of urban poverty. A positive and hopeful ending that is a touch bittersweet adds just the right dose of reality. For another look at teenage motherhood, look for Rita Williams-Garcia's *Like Sisters on the Homefront.*

★ Memoirs of a Bookbat   FICTION

AUTHOR: **Kathryn Lasky**
HC/PB: Harcourt Brace
THEMES: reading; coming of age; strong girls; religion; sisters; individuality; friendship; taking action; censorship; judging; self-respect

Prepare to have your love of reading be used in ways you never dreamed possible. Telling the story of a fundamentalist family that works to ban books from schools through the eyes of their book-loving oldest daughter is an inspired idea. As she grows, we know what she is reading, and our memories of childhood favorites are stroked fondly. But as her family becomes more set upon making it impossible for other people to read books they find offensive, we begin to feel our personal memories being attacked. This is a hard look from the inside at how intolerance and unquestioning fundamentalism can destroy not only communities but families. You may cheer at the ending, as we did, or you may be bothered by it. But there is no question that Lasky uses her power over words to make us think—something the book banners would like to control.

A Place to Call Home   FICTION

AUTHOR: Jackie French Koller
HC: Atheneum • PB: Aladdin
THEMES: coming of age; strong girls; orphans; cultural diversity; secrets; family

As a young girl struggles to keep her family together despite all odds, she must also come to terms with her biracial heritage. Affecting and poignant.

Virtual War   FICTION-SCIENCE FICTION

AUTHOR: Gloria Skurzynski

HC: Simon & Schuster

THEMES: war; virtual reality; future; courage; faith; friendship; strong girls; problem solving; computers; teamwork

Sure to have a lot of kid appeal, this futuristic look at war waged via computers offers no easy answers but plenty of opportunity for discussion about the nature and purpose of war. Genetically engineered and raised from birth to be the perfect cyber fighting machine, fourteen-year-old Corgan slowly learns that the things his country's leaders have been telling him weren't all true. Teamed up with a girl his age who is a whiz at cracking codes and a mutant boy who is expert at strategy, he learns to question authority and wonder about how he fits into the computer controlled society. This is a good book to read in conjunction with *The Giver,* another look at a possible future, and will certainly be a bridge to more adult science fiction for many readers.

The Weekend Was Murder   FICTION-MYSTERY

AUTHOR: Joan Lowery Nixon

HC: Delacorte • PB: Dell

THEMES: mystery; games; contests; detectives; writing; creativity; murder; authors

A mystery weekend, complete with fictional murder, clues, and suspects, turns deadly when an actual murder occurs. Nixon's skill as a plotter serves her readers well, and this is just one in a long line of satisfying, challenging mysteries from one of the most honored writers in the genre. Four-time winner of the Edgar Award, given by the Mystery Writers of America for the best children's mystery of the year, Nixon has written dozens of books that have become favorites of thriller, horror and mystery lovers. Some of our favorites are: *The Seance, A Candidate for Murder, The Other Side of Dark,* and *The Kidnapping of Christina Lattimore,* but by all means do not be limited to our list. Any book with Joan Lowery Nixon's name on it is a fair bet to be a crackling good read.

Westmark   FICTION

AUTHOR: Lloyd Alexander

HC: Dutton • PB: Dell

THEMES: war; adventure; courage; heroes; peace; fighting; soldiers

Book 1 of the Westmark Trilogy, an accomplished feat of storytelling! In three books, Alexander details the course of a war raging through his imaginary land of Westmark, which looks a lot like 17th-century Europe. This is epic fiction at its best, and there is some awfully fine writing about the nature of war here, as well as strong, believable characters of both sexes. Book 2 is *The Kestrel,* and Book 3 is *The Beggar Queen.*

My stepsister Paula announced upon graduating from high school that she was so glad, because "I never have to read another book again, as long as I live!" My grandmother nearly had a heart attack. What she heard was an emphasis on the word "never." Paula's emphasis was on "have to." The process of reading had been made so odious to her, with no adult around to shepherd her through the tough times (we who turn to literature early and often are true anomalies and frequently do so in a solitary fashion) that she associated all reading with everything she loathed about school. She is now a preschool teacher and the mother of four and, like so many others, she came to reading for pleasure in her own good time.

PART FIVE

Books for Middle School Readers and Young Adults

For middle school readers and older, these books can feature mature subject matters and often bridge the gap between young adult books and adult fiction.

3 NBS of Julian Drew   FICTION

AUTHOR: James M. Deem

HC: Houghton Mifflin • PB: Avon

THEMES: courage; school; abuse; diaries; mental illness; language; mothers and sons; stepparents; captivity

This book challenges the reader from the start with its use of code in Julian's writing (NB = notebook), and it rarely lets up. It's a stunning piece of writing about a badly abused teen who may also be mentally disturbed. Compelling and full of well plotted revelations, it is a rewarding and affecting read.

The Adrian Mole Diaries   FICTION

AUTHOR: Sue Townsend

PB: Avon

THEMES: humor; coming of age; embarrassment; diaries; writing; worry; England; dogs; family; school

At times in this hilarious book, you feel so deeply for poor Adrian that you ache—but that doesn't stop you from laughing. This very British and spot-on account of male adolescence is a delight to read, though your own teenager will probably die of embarrassment if he thinks you know all this about him.

I cannot prove this, but I'll bet you anything that kids who join gangs do not have books in their lives. It has always seemed to me that children who are read to and who read for themselves have a healthy ability to deal with strong, even disturbing, feelings. Could it be possible that children who have been deprived of that joy lack such inner strength and may feel that they have to search for a more concrete way to show their personal power—frequently resulting in violent expression? I'm not sure, but though it might be over-simplifying the problem, I believe a person willing to read to these children could have a strong effect on their lives. Why not books instead of guns? It sure couldn't hurt.

Am I Blue? Coming Out From the Silence   ANTHOLOGY

EDITOR: Marion Dane Bauer
HC/PB: HarperCollins
THEMES: gay and lesbian; coming of age; self-respect; diversity; sexuality

A collection of stories of interest to gay and lesbian youth, chosen with care by editor and contributor Bauer. Rich in viewpoints, this is an essential collection for any library and will give comfort to teens afraid or confused by their feelings as well as to their more confident peers.

Baby Be-Bop   FICTION

AUTHOR: Francesca Lia Block
HC/PB: HarperCollins
THEMES: gay and lesbian; diversity; fantasy; love; Los Angeles

Growing up gay has often been mishandled in young adult fiction, but this book is outstanding and treats the subject with respect. This continuation of the cycle of novels begun with *Weetzie Bat* stands on its own as a coming of age romance for gay teens.

★ Beyond the Divide   FICTION

AUTHOR: **Kathryn Lasky**
PB: Aladdin
THEMES: strong girls; coming of age; pioneers; U.S. history, Westward movement; violence; Amish; hardship; loss; fathers and daughters

Meribah is questioning her Amish ways—her world view has become too broad to live in such a repressive society, so she leaps at the chance to travel west by covered wagon with her father instead of waiting behind with the women. In this harrowing coming of age novel, Meribah starts off as a girl in Pennsylvania, but ends up a woman in the Oregon territory, experiencing hardship, violence, and loss on the path to a hard-earned maturity.

Blood and Chocolate   FICTION

AUTHOR: Annette Curtis Klause
HC: Delacorte
THEMES: werewolves; horror; love; death; belonging; change; fitting in; loss; family; independence

A fabulous horror read for the sophisticated teen. Vivian is trying to cope with the loss of her father and a move to a new neighborhood. Her extended family is constantly at war with itself and she feels the need to withdraw from "family" matters and try to fit in in her new surroundings. This is all made much more difficult by the fact that Vivian and her family are werewolves. A thought-provoking and compulsively readable thriller that will enthrall the teen reader who loves adult horror, especially if they are already fans of Klause's *The Silver Kiss,* one of our favorite vampire novels.

The Buffalo Tree   FICTION

AUTHOR: Adam Rapp
HC: Front Street • PB: HarperCollins
THEMES: friendship; dreams; yearning; coming of age; bullies; cruelty; violence; mothers and sons; captivity; death; survival; redemption; triumph

With haunting imagery and a slang vocabulary that takes some getting used to, this novel of life in a detention facility for troubled boys is heavy going, but it is a rich and rewarding reading experience. Though it is a work of rare power, there are echoes of three masterpieces of fiction that it is helpful to acknowledge, seeing as how they are often required reading in high school: The friendship between Sura and Coley Jo is heartbreakingly portrayed, reminiscent of the relationship between George and Lenny in *Of Mice and Men;* the disturbing, almost unreal quality to the writing about Sura's dreams and nighttime fantasies will remind readers of Chief Bromden's hallucinations in *One Flew Over the Cuckoo's Nest;* and the use of jargon unfamiliar to the reader at first encounter is a device used to great effect, similar to the street slang in *A Clockwork Orange,* though in this case there is no glossary in the back of the book—the reader gains understanding of the language through continued exposure, much as in an immersion foreign language course. All these things come together to create an unforgettable book about survival, redemption, and beating the system.

Children of the River   FICTION

AUTHOR: Linda Crew
HC: Delacorte • PB: Dell
THEMES: Cambodia; immigration; fitting in; Oregon; friendship; traditions; social studies; cultural diversity; refugees; school; strong girls; escape

Sundara escaped from Cambodia with her aunt's family during the war, leaving her mother, father, sister, brother and friends behind. She was thirteen years old. It's now four years later in Oregon, U.S.A, and Sundara is trying desperately to fit in a world where social expectations and home life continually clash. A sensitive story about a young girl's loyalty to her people and past, and her struggle to find a place in her present.

The Chocolate War   FICTION

AUTHOR: Robert Cormier
HC: Knopf • PB: Dell
THEMES: school; bullies; competition; cruelty; boxing; courage; taking action; chocolate; defeat; contests

Oftentimes in books for children, the struggle between good and evil is played out in fantasy terms of witches, demons, dragons, and sorcerers. Young adult fiction can bring the reader face to face with more commonplace evil, featuring real people in real situations. One of the most influential writers in this genre is Robert Cormier, and *The Chocolate War* is one of his bleakest and most memorable novels. Set in a Catholic high school in working class New England, it offers two vivid characterizations of evil in Archie Goodwin, the master manipulator and power behind the secret society called The Vigils, and his sometime ally sometime nemesis Brother Leon, the sadistic and ambitious teacher who is the story's catalyst. The hero of the book, poor Jerry Renault becomes victim to these two via an innocuous sounding fundraising contest to sell boxes of chocolates, thereby learning that the answer to the question "Do I dare disturb the universe?" is: Only if you are willing to pay the price. Cormier is a writer of rare skill, whose willingness to explore themes of abuse of power, cruelty, violence, and the nature of evil dovetails quite neatly with that moment in teen's lives when they realize that life is not only not fair, but it often doesn't come close.

The Crossing   FICTION

AUTHOR: **Gary Paulsen**

HC: Orchard • PB: Dell

THEMES: Mexico; self-respect; friendship; mental illness; soldiers; poverty; homelessness; alcoholism; survival; orphans

Manny Bustos is an orphan, and at fourteen years old he is fighting to survive in the border town of Juarez, Mexico. Robert S. Locke is a sergeant and a Vietnam vet. He is stationed across the border at Fort Bliss, Texas. Locke drinks alcohol to hide the sound of the friends in his mind who cry for help. This is a story of their meeting and friendship with a final blend of sadness and hope. It's a story that will stick with the young adult fortunate enough to read it.

TOO TOUGH A SUBJECT TO READ?

I remember someone mentioning to Gary Paulsen that The Crossing *contained difficult subject matter for a twelve year old. His response was that it was OK if it happens to a twelve year old, but we don't want one to read about it. He got me thinking. Twelve year olds are savvy. They know that homelessness is rough, that drugs aren't healthy, and that kids get abused. Keeping them from reading tough subjects isn't going to help them deal with those issues. It may be just the opposite. A well-written book on a difficult subject can help a child sort through hard situations.*

Damned Strong Love: The True Story of
Willi G. and Stephan K.   NONFICTION

AUTHOR: Lutz Van Dijk

HC: Henry Holt

THEMES: Jews; love; soldiers; cultural diversity; Holocaust; history, World War II; gay and lesbian; Germany

Based on a true story, this is a potent story of a doomed love between a Jewish boy and a soldier in Germany during World War II.

Earth-Shattering Poems

POETRY ANTHOLOGY

EDITOR: Liz Rosenberg
HC: Henry Holt
THEMES: love; death; sadness; fate; hardship

Got a highly sensitive teen on your hands? One deep in the throes of desperation? Have you lost the ability to communicate with this child? Then try leaving this collection of poetry where he can find it. Here is a book filled with poem-sized doses of love, death, tragedy, inexorable fate, agony, loss and despair enough to give a month of journal entry material to even the most downtrodden wannabe poet. Lousy lives can sometimes yield terrific poetry, and this collection, brought to us from the same woman who gave us *The Invisible Ladder,* contains some of the best, most intense writing around. For another shattering, poetic experience, look for *Pierced by the Rays of the Sun,* edited by Ruth Gordon.

Earthshine

FICTION

AUTHOR: Theresa Nelson
HC: Orchard • PB: Dell
THEMES: fathers and daughters; AIDS; gay and lesbian; strong girls; survival; faith; illness; journeys; miracles; love

A personal look at a devastating issue. Slim's father is dying of AIDS and she would do anything within reason to save him from his fate. When a solution beyond reason comes along, in the person of a faith healer and self-proclaimed miracle man, she wavers. With the help of her friend Isaiah, she comes to accept the possibility of miracles. The journey that follows is one not only through the mountains but through the heart of this brave and loving young girl.

Eva

FICTION-SCIENCE FICTION

AUTHOR: Peter Dickinson
HC: Delacorte • PB: Dell
THEMES: science fiction; gifted children; monkeys; strong girls; secrets; mishaps; ethics

A thought-provoking piece of "what-if" fiction that will challenge and disturb. Injured in an accident and unable to see, Eva can tell from the way people speak to her that her condition is worse than she has been told. She knows something is wrong, but cannot figure it out. When it is revealed that she has had her brain transplanted into the body of a monkey, it is almost as horrifying for the reader as it is for her. This is a book kids will talk about for years after having read it, as it brings into play all the ethical, moral, practical, and philosophical questions anyone would have in such a situation, in a thrilling style that leaves the reader's head spinning. An absolutely brilliant book!

A Fate Totally Worse Than Death FICTION
AUTHOR: Paul Fleischman
HC: Candlewick
THEMES: parodies; humor; horror; school

A screamingly funny parody of teen horror novels that is so clever, the intended audience may not realize they are being made fun of.

Help Wanted: Short Stories About
Young People Working SHORT STORY ANTHOLOGY
AUTHOR: Anita Silvey
HC: Little Brown
THEMES: jobs; coming of age; cultural diversity; variety

With contributions by such noted authors as Tim Wynne-Jones, Ray Bradbury, and Norma Fox Mazer, this is a diverse look at teenagers and their jobs. A great read to have on hand for job hunting time.

I Am the Cheese FICTION
AUTHOR: Robert Cormier
HC: Knopf • PB: Dell
THEMES: journeys; gifted children; mystery; bicycles; secrets; separation; government; memories

One of the darkest, most paranoid novels you or your teen will likely read, and a masterpiece of suspense writing. Bleak seems to be the mood Cormier favors, and it is sometimes hard for adult educators and parents to understand his ability to enthrall a teen audience. Chances are they have also tried very hard to suppress memories of how wretched some parts of the teen years were for them. When you are low, it is a great comfort to have a writer like Cormier to turn to, as he reinforces several key teen beliefs: "They ARE all out to get me," and "Life is not fair," while simultaneously letting you wallow in the life of someone who has it worse off than you.

I Had Seen Castles   FICTION

AUTHOR: **Cynthia Rylant**
HC/PB: Harcourt Brace
THEMES: U.S. history, World War II; veterans; soldiers; memories

War as seen from a soldier on the front lines in World War II. Devastating. If only this could be given to all military enlistees before they sign on the dotted line.

I Hadn't Meant to Tell You This   FICTION

AUTHOR: Jacqueline Woodson
HC: Delacorte • PB: Dell
THEMES: African American; prejudice; school; friendship; incest; fathers and daughters; love; cultural diversity; loss

In Chauncey, Ohio, prosperous black families live on one side of town and poor whites on another. People pretty well stay where they belong. Then Lena Bright, a white girl, becomes friends with Marie, who is popular and black. Friends share secrets, and when Marie discovers that Lena's father is abusing her, she is stuck with some hard knowledge and a dilemma about what to do. Difficult family situations, racism and class prejudice, the tough subject of sexual abuse, and the strength of friendship are well-handled here by Woodson's sensitive and powerful writing.

Ice   FICTION

AUTHOR: Phyllis Reynolds Naylor
HC: Atheneum • PB: Aladdin
THEMES: fathers and daughters; mothers and daughters; self-respect; coming of age; grandmothers; family; farms; comparisons; solitude; anger

Thirteen-year-old Chrissa is angry. Her father has been gone for three years, and her mom won't explain why he left. This has not been a pleasant time for her mother, either. "We're not going to go on like this . . ." her mother said one morning at breakfast. "I'm sending you to live with Gram for a year." Chrissa's life changes from the city to the country and in her quest for her father's whereabouts, she discovers her own strengths. Feeling misunderstood and alone during the teenage years and communicating only through monosyllabic utterances is not unusual. This poignant story of a girl's move from isolation and anger to self-understanding will hold fascination for teens who identify with Chrissa as well as for the ones with friends who act like her.

★ Ironman   FICTION

AUTHOR: Chris Crutcher

HC: Greenwillow • PB: Dell

THEMES: coming of age; bullies; sports; forgiveness; anger; fathers and sons; school; friendship; strong girls; determination; encouragement; self-respect; triumph; track and field

With Crutcher writing in top form, *Ironman* features many of the hall-marks of his previous books: Bo Brewster has a real problem with anger, and he's smart enough to know it but not smart enough not to do anything about it. He has one of the truly wretched fathers of all time, and their emotional battlefield has grown too small to hold all Bo's rage, so it has started to spill out into the rest of his life, getting him booted off the football team and nearly expelled from school. Channeling all his energies into becoming a triathelete isn't the solution he hoped it would be, and it is only with the help of Mr. Nak, his Anger Management Group, and his new girlfriend, Shelly, that Bo is able to triumph over his father, his anger, and himself. You will laugh, you will cry, you will cheer, and you will learn the definition of mercy.

Let me just get this out of the way right now: Chris Crutcher is a god, and I am not the only one who thinks it. There is no better companion to have for a teenage boy navigating the waters of anger, coming of age, sports, and screwed-up families than this amazing storyteller. Talk about a writer having an effect on his audience? I think Crutcher's books save lives. He reaches right down into the pits of despair where many of his characters live and he gives them, and by extension the reader, hope and triumph. Not that he is a goody-goody—far from it, but every book of his has at least one wrenching, cathartic moment that presents the main character with a choice, and for me the choice always comes down to, "You can either live this way, or you can rise above it." Crutcher's people almost always learn the value of rising above it.

Not schooled in the world of literature (he claims never to have read kids' books until after he had written one), Crutcher writes from what he knows, and his work as a therapist and a teacher is evident in both the subjects he chooses and how he handles them. You will find vulgar language and violent situations in his books, much as you would find in any high school in America. You will find deplorable parents and noble teachers, long-suffering parents and teachers who are idiots. But most of all, you will find teenagers who learn to "own their own shit" (to use a Crutcheresque turn of phrase) on the treacherous road to adulthood. He is the best there is at this kind of honest, uplifting writing, and has earned the respect of librarians, teachers, parents, and booksellers, but I suspect that respect means little compared to how much he treasures the response of the teens who read his work. He knows his audience and writes solely for them. Like I said, he's a god.

Join In: Multiethnic Short Stories By Outstanding Writers for Young Adults
SHORT STORY ANTHOLOGY

EDITOR: Donald R. Gallo
HC: Delacorte • PB: Dell
THEMES: cultural diversity; prejudice; getting along

Seventeen stories written especially for this collection reflecting a wide range of ethnic and cultural backgrounds and the concerns of teens growing up in a multicultural society.

Killing Mr. Griffin
FICTION-MYSTERY

AUTHOR: Lois Duncan
PB: Dell
THEMES: murder; Shakespeare; teachers; school; guilt; secrets

One of the most gripping thrillers we have read. The plan was to teach Mr. Griffin a lesson by kidnapping and scaring him. No one thought of it as more than a prank, getting back at a teacher who made life too hard by demanding that kids actually learn something in his English class. But when Mr. Griffin dies right in front of his captors as a result of their prank, the scramble to cover up the deed goes awry. Using the best elements of mystery fiction, and stirring in a little horror in a high school setting is a recipe for reading that Duncan practically invented. Her books *Ransom, I Know What You Did Last Summer, The Stranger in the Mirror,* and *Daughters of Eve* are classics in the genre, and any teen who loves a good page turner has probably already found out about her. She distinguishes herself from the pack of teen horror writers (Duncan imitators, all!) with her dazzling writing. In *Killing Mr. Griffin,* her use of Shakespeare's works to comment on the story is deeply affecting and illustrates the difference between a potboiler and literature.

Kinship
FICTION

AUTHOR: Trudy Krisher
HC: Delacorte
THEMES: coming of age; fathers and daughters; family; U.S.A., the South; reunion; single parents; relatives; U.S. history, the 60's

Set in 1961, this novel of the south follows Krisher's debut *Spite Fences*, and features a supporting character from that book. Fifteen-year-old Pert has to come to terms with the father who has walked into her life for the first time and in the process learns the true meaning of kin.

Kissing the Witch
FICTION

AUTHOR: Emma Donoghue
HC: HarperCollins
THEMES: point of view; strong women; gay and lesbian; folktale variations

Classic folktales retold with a real edge and often a lesbian slant. If you can deal with the idea of Cinderella running off with the Fairy Godmother instead of the Prince, then this is the book for you. All the stories are connected, many in unusual ways, making this a book for comparison and discussion.

Letters From the Inside
FICTION

AUTHOR: John Marsden
HC: Houghton Mifflin • PB: Dell
THEMES: captivity; coming of age; abuse; pen pals; Australia; secrets; lying; friendship; mail

A disturbing and compulsively readable novel of the pen-pal friendship of two girls, full of secrets and revelations. Halfway through the book you begin to wonder if everything is as the girls claim, and by the book's stunning conclusion you may find yourself thinking you missed a part, but trust us—it's all there. The reader must decide for herself what the real story is.

Mary Wolf
FICTION

AUTHOR: Cynthia D. Grant
HC: Atheneum
THEMES: homelessness; alcoholism; strong girls; community; violence; choice; poverty; resourcefulness; coming of age

A powerful portrait of a family's agonizing slide into the depths of homelessness. Amid the disintegration of her life, Mary finds herself having to be the "adult" and the results are devastating.

The Pigman   FICTION

AUTHOR: Paul Zindel
HC: HarperCollins • PB: Bantam
THEMES: high school; playing tricks; loss; grief; responsibility; friendship; loneliness

John and Lorraine are two smart-alec, misfit teens who spend a lot of their time playing tricks on the unsuspecting. When they encounter simple, guileless, lonely Mr. Angelo Pignati, he seems too easy a target. But the Pigman has charms they never suspected and they form an unlikely trio. Over time secrets are revealed and tragedy strikes and the reader learns along with John and Lorraine a heartbreaking lesson. This groundbreaking novel is as fresh today as it was when it was first published in 1968, and is rightfully thought of as one of the first true young adult novels.

★ Rats Saw God   FICTION

AUTHOR: Rob Thomas
HC: Simon & Schuster • PB: Aladdin
THEMES: school; fathers and sons; betrayal; change; writing; family; love

A blisteringly honest look at high school life. Steve York is angry, smarting from a betrayal he is trying to forget by breaking the world record for staying stoned. Too intelligent to be throwing away his life, he is given a challenge by his counselor to write a 100-page paper, the only way he can salvage his English grade and graduate on time. What comes pouring out is an account of his last three years, told in a voice both hilarious and full of pain. This is one terrific read and we highly recommend it to parents and teachers of teenagers as well as the teens themselves. Thomas's next two books, *Slave Day* and *Doing Time: Notes From the Undergrad*, are almost as brilliant as this one.

Remembering the Good Times   FICTION

AUTHOR: Richard Peck
HC: Delacorte • PB: Dell
THEMES: suicide; gifted children; death; loss; grief; friendship

We have to give away the plot of this book in order to tell you why we feel it is important. Peck skillfully creates the relationship of three teens, Buck, Trav, and Kate, with his customary insight and humor. Buck narrates the story of their friendship and the reader comes to know these three bright teens and their journey toward adulthood. When toward the novel's end Trav commits suicide, it comes out of the blue, without any of the usual literary foreshadowing. The reader is stunned, as are Kate, Buck and everyone else in their community. This may be Peck's most powerful novel, though we also think highly of *The Last Safe Place on Earth,* which deals with religious fundamentalism and community standards in a head-on style.

Shabanu-Daughter of the Wind   FICTION

AUTHOR: Suzanne Fisher Staples
HC/PB: Knopf
THEMES: Pakistan; desert; strong girl; social studies; coming of age; family

When she comes of age, Shabanu has been promised to a rich land owner to settle a feud. Teenage readers, wherever they live, will feel the strength and suffering of a spirited young girl faced with a future where her options have been chosen for her. The sequel, *Haveli,* tells of Shabanu's life as a young mother, and the continued struggles she has with rigid customs and ancient laws.

Staples' respect for the culture, with its close family ties and struggle for survival on the Pakistani desert, were so richly described that when I finished reading Shabanu, *I longed for a pet camel.*

Slave Day   FICTION

AUTHOR: Rob Thomas
HC: Simon & Schuster
THEMES: African American; comparisons; contests; taking action; prejudice; traditions; point of view; high school; friendship; teachers; fitting in; judging; slavery

It's Slave Day at Robert E. Lee High School. Eight characters participate in the tradition of auctioning off students and faculty as slaves for a day. This will get older readers thinking about race, class and tradition, and is sure to be discussed by them as they recognize the characters and their similarities to their own lives.

WHERE WOULD I BE WITHOUT LIBRARIES?

By the time I started the ninth grade I was attending my eleventh school. We moved a lot, and I remember every library at every school I attended. My first school had no library, only a "book room," and by the time I left there (midway through third grade) I had read every book in it that was of interest to me. After two more moves in third and fourth grades, I spent my fifth and sixth grade years at a brand-new school, and I was proud to know that my name would be the first one on so many library cards. The libraries at the three junior high schools I went to were lifesavers, and I spent enormous amounts of time there, especially the one in Gaithersburg, MD. It was open until 5 PM every day after school and, as I lived nearby and was a latchkey kid, I preferred to spend my time there reading than at home (except for *Dark Shadows*—I never missed it!). The public libraries were a treat to go to, as they were usually too far away from my house. Then we moved (again!) to California in March of my eighth grade year. I was devastated and surly and hated my new school. I spent two periods a day in the library, reading the entire works of Madeleine L'Engle and others.

My high school years were all spent at the same school, and I knew every nook and cranny of that library. The librarian was the mother of a friend of mine and when I was a senior she allowed me to go through a drawer in her office of books she had acquired but couldn't put out in the stacks for various reasons. Through her I discovered Brautigan, Ferlinghetti, Ginsberg and Vonnegut.

During the same time, we lived far away from the school and the nearest branch library was 30 miles away, but we had the Bookmobile!!!!!! Twice a week I would walk the mile and a half down to where it parked and I would fill up on what they had and badger the librarian for other titles. You could ask them for books and the next week they would *bring them to you!* My only regret was that a lot of the reference books I wanted to get my hands on could not be checked out. So, I rode the bus all the way into downtown San Diego (it took about an hour) and went to the big main library. I thought it was heaven! I spent hours in the recordings area, checking out Broadway shows whose soundtracks I didn't own and works by composers I had never heard of (I discovered Villa-Lobos, Ives and Hindemith this way) taking them into the private rooms and listening! I was forever asking the reference librarian for some huge atlas or compendium and having her (*always* a her) lug it down off some high shelf and watch me as I merrily plopped myself down in a chair at a table and read the damn thing. I never looked stuff up, wasn't trying to do research. I just wanted to read and absorb. The staff knew me and my tastes after a few months of this and would try to interest me in more obscure tomes of arcane knowledge (weather, mining, invertebrates, folklore, flags, whatever . . .), and they were never surprised when I took the book and read through it. This panned out nicely when, years later, I appeared on *Jeopardy!* and won four games. I always use that anecdote to illustrate to impressionable youth the value of reading.

★ Soda Jerk   POETRY COLLECTION

AUTHOR: **Cynthia Rylant** • ILLUSTRATOR: Peter Catalanotto

HC: Orchard • PB: Beech Tree

THEMES: coming of age; jobs; yearning; secrets; fitting in; wisdom; gentle boys; towns

How Rylant knows what she knows about adolescent males is beyond me, but she is dead-on accurate in her portrait of teen yearnings. A novel in prose poems of the life of a seventeen-year-old boy in Cheston, Virginia. This is my favorite of her books and I read it aloud to teens and adults when I get the chance.

I want to make it clear that this is not just a "boy" book. It's great reading and girls will recognize the soda jerk—it will give them some idea of how he thinks. And while we're at it, this goes for Bruce Brooks' Boys Will Be, *too!*

Spite Fences   FICTION

AUTHOR: Trudy Krisher

HC: Delacorte • PB: Dell

THEMES: U.S.A., the South; prejudice; civil rights; taking action; conscience; point of view; photography; secrets; coming of age; mothers and daughters; strong girls; U.S. history, the 60's

In the summer of 1960, Maggie Pugh comes to realize that everything she thought she knew about life in Kinship, Georgia, is wrong. Witness to a horrendous act of bigoted cruelty, she must decide how to live with the knowledge of what she saw and whether or not to take action. Her decisions rip wide open the seething, festering wound of racism and she finds herself standing on the opposite side of an abyss from her family and most of the whites in town. Maggie has true courage, and this inspiring book is a testament to doing what you know is right, even when it is unpopular.

Staying Fat for Sarah Byrnes   FICTION

AUTHOR: Chris Crutcher
HC: Greenwillow • PB: Dell
THEMES: friendship; bullies; swimming; abuse; betrayal; step families; promises; loyalty; fitting in; overweight

Always a good writer, Crutcher ascends to new heights in this outstanding novel about the bonds of friendship and the boundaries of loyalty. Sometimes people will not ask for help, even if they desperately need it. Sometimes promises made sincerely prove to be difficult to keep. The turbulence of the teen years is portrayed affectingly in this story of a boy and girl, two outcasts, whose devotion is challenged by their reaction to changes in their lives. Anyone who has been through something similar will sympathize—how wonderful to have this available for teens who are in the throes. Other amazing titles by this brilliant author include: *Stotan, Chinese Handcuffs, Athletic Shorts,* and *Ironman.*

Talking Peace: A Vision for the Next Generation   NONFICTION

AUTHOR: Jimmy Carter
HC: Dutton
THEMES: peace; U.S. presidents; problem solving; getting along; social studies; history, World War II; disagreements; politics

To help understand the causes and cures for conflict, President Carter has written this highly accessible book for young adults. We recommend it not only for solutions to the large political process of peace, but for working through the daily conflicts often found in a teenager's life.

Twelve Shots: Outstanding Short Stories About Guns   SHORT STORY ANTHOLOGY

EDITOR: Harry Mazer
HC: Delacorte
THEMES: guns; violence; friendship; choices; consequences

With contributions from authors like Walter Dean Myers, Chris Lynch, Rita Williams-Garcia, and Nancy Werlin, this outstanding anthology of original short stories will get any group of teens talking about the ways guns affect our lives.

The NRA will probably not like this book, but let 'em write their own anthology.

Weetzie Bat

FICTION-FANTASY

AUTHOR: Francesca Lia Block
HC/PB: HarperCollins
THEMES: Los Angeles; humor; fantasy; love; magic; friendship

Francesa Lia Block writes of a Los Angeles that exists in a teenager's fairy tale in this magical sequence of novels for older teens that begins with *Weetzie Bat*. Because she deals straightforwardly with the dicier topics in teens' lives (sex and substance abuse occur in her books, just as in real life), she is not an author blithely to give to a child who may not be ready. But when they are ready, the adventures of Weetzie, Dirk and the gang will enchant readers in a way that no other writing for that age can. Highly recommended. Other titles include: *Witch Baby, Missing Angel Juan,* and *Baby Be-Bop.*

Appendix One: Tricky Situations and Frequently Asked Questions

We each get asked many of the same questions. We offer our responses here:

Q: I have a seven year old and a four year old. What books can I read to them both?

A: Look for books that tell a story with both words and pictures so there is plenty to see, notice and do. Young ones enjoy challenging an older sibling to find things on the page. For starters, try these:

Puzzling Day at Castle McPelican (Anderson)
The Mysterious Tadpole (Kellogg)
Officer Buckle and Gloria (Rathmann)
Piggie Pie (Palatini)

Go For Action and Humor:
Possum Come a Knockin (Van Laan)
Pigs In the Mud (Plourde)
The Day Jimmy's Boa Ate the Wash (Noble)
The Three-Legged Cat (Mahy)

Q: My toddler gets fidgety and wants to turn the pages faster than I can read the story.

A: Let her. Don't make the reading experience a struggle for control. Figure out what's going on. Is it the story (not interesting?) or a need to move on because she's excited? If it's the latter, try having her tell YOU the story. Some toddlers have a hard time waiting. If that's the case, use books with fewer words on each page and build up to longer stories. There is nothing wrong with keeping up with her by leaving out some of the words.

Q: My ten year old's soccer team practices three days a week and on Saturdays. By the time he finishes his paper route, eating dinner and doing his homework, there is no time for reading.

A: Usually, time spent reading is time taken away from something else. Is there time for TV? Is there time for computer play? !f you believe reading is important, then you will find the time.

Q: My four year old is starting to be afraid of the dark, but he wants me to read him stories about monsters. Is this a good idea?

A: Yes, because reading and listening to scary stories help manage fears. Children usually look for things they need in their stories and it is a sign of emotional intelligence that your child seeks out a story solution to things that frighten him.

Try these:

There Is a Nightmare in My Closet (Mayer)
There's a Monster Under My Bed (Howe)
The Monster Bed (Willis)
Where the Wild Things Are (Sendak)

Q: My preschooler is too rough to have his own books. He still rips the pages.

A: Divide books into two stacks: HIS to do with what he likes, and OURS which are to be treasured. You can get his books at garage sales, library sales and used bookstores. He needs to learn to respect books and these are the ones he learns on. Read to him from both stacks, but put OURS away for together time.

Q: What do you recommend I do to help my baby become a good reader?

A: Don't push it. Babies have no business reading, so don't try and teach them. A baby's job is to explore—frequently with their mouths, so as Valerie always says, "Give them books that are nontoxic." We could cite a host of experts on the subject of getting your child ready to read . One thing they all agree on is that a child will read when she is ready. A steady dose of stories will help her along, but won't make her read any sooner than she wants to.

Q: My son is finally reading, but he only wants to read the same series over and over. I'm concerned because he won't read better books.

A: Sameness is comforting. If your son is reading for pleasure, don't worry too much about what he is reading. A lot of great readers started off with Nancy Drew and the Hardy Boys. Make other books available to him. Give him the opportunity to go to the library and bookstore and make his own choices. He'll move on when he's ready.

Q: I'm a single parent. I work full time as well as drive the kids to their respective meetings, events, and practices. As much as I'd like to read aloud to my children, I'm exhausted by the end of the day.

A: On those days when you're worn out, have your children read to you. If they aren't yet reading, on high energy days tape yourself reading stories and save them. There are also fine wordless books a nonreader can "read" aloud to you. Be sure you don't trade these in for read alone times. A big value here is time, spent close.

Q: I can't get my child interested in reading.

A: You can't make a child read. If you make it into a big deal—a standoff—you are probably going to lose. All you can really do is make sure that the opportunities for reading are there and that the books are available. If she is not interested in reading herself, at least give her the experience of being read to.

Q: It's time for my child to be introduced to books explaining sex. Every time I bring one out to read with him, he bolts. Any suggestions?

A: Get a copy of *It's Perfectly Normal* (Harris). Leave it where he can find it on his own. *After several self-conscious sessions attempting to read the appropriate books about sex to my daughters, I put* Where Did I Come From? *(Mayle) in their bedroom. That night I could hear them sharing a bunk pointing at pictures and laughing hysterically. I thought—at least they are hysterical over facts—which is more than I could say for my experiences at that age.*

Q: My daughter wants me to read the same book to her repeatedly. I've gotten so I want to hide it. Help!

A: If it's because you are tired of the story, that's one issue. If you just don't like it, that is another. You are not a gateway to a story with no opinions of your own. If the story bores you, offends you, fails to engage you or simply doesn't hold up under countless readings, don't read it.

Part of the joy of reading together is shared pleasure. When you don't like a story, you're not fooling your child. Say, "I don't want to read that. You read that one on your own later. It drives me crazy." Then pick up a book you love and read that instead.

Q: Authors put their agendas into the books they write. I'm not always comfortable with those agendas.

A: Who doesn't have an agenda? As a parent, yours may be selecting books that reinforce your values. If you have read a book, and decided that your child is not ready for the issues it presents, or that it does not echo your values, don't share that book. However, when it comes time to face the challenges life presents, remember that a book will be waiting.

Q: My fifth grader is reading at a third-grade reading level. Can you suggest titles that will interest him?

A: First of all, look for books that are not frighteningly thick, where the chapters and the description are short and the text is a reasonable size. These should work:

Gary Paulsen's series: *The Culpeppers* and *World of Adventure*
Stone Fox (Gardiner)
Poetry collections by Shel Silverstein, Jeff Moss, Jack Prelutsky, and Kalli Dakos

Some kids need visuals:
Dogzilla by Dav Pilkey
any nonfiction titles from DK Publishing
City of Light, City of Dark: A Comic Book Novel (Avi)
Amelia's Notebook (Moss)
Amazon Diary (Talbott)

It may be that while there is no problem reading individual words, a sea of words without enough breaks is frustrating. Try these:
The Dragonling (Koller) . . . and other books in this series
anything by Matt Christopher.

Short story collections offer the feeling of accomplishment that reading can provide, but with fewer pages per story:
Every Living Thing (Rylant)
In a Messy Messy Room and Other Scary Stories (Gorog)

The Random House Book of Sports Stories
The Macmillan Book of Baseball Stories

Read aloud to your older sons and daughters. Often we abandon kids who need our help, deciding that because they are old enough to read on their own, they no longer need us. Children struggling with reading at school need the comfort and reward of a good story read aloud at home.

Q: How do you share books with your kids that reinforce your values?

A: Take a look at the themes and categories at the end of this book. Choose titles that match your concerns. Don't make reading aloud into a lesson. Good stories speak for themselves. Kids can smell a moral a mile away and tend to run in the other direction.

Q: What about books with medals and gold seals on them? What do they mean?

A: There are many awards given to recognize books that have rated praise or merit, and publishers will put a gold medal on the cover of a book if they think it will generate sales. The most important awards are the Newbery Medal, given by the American Library Association for the most distinguished novel for children in a given year, the Caldecott Medal, which is awarded to the most distinguished picture book, and the Coretta Scott King Award, given to a novel and a picture book each year that is by an African American author. Each award also can have Honor books, which are similar to runners-up, and these titles, along with the award winners, receive a great deal of attention from publishers, booksellers, and librarians each year.

Appendix Two:
Themes

Want to know if there's a good book about dogs? Is your child having trouble adjusting to a move, a new school, or other problems? Looking for a story that will give comfort, teach a lesson, or make a point? Look here. This index of nearly 1,000 themes is designed to help you make a connection between your child and books using interests, situations, and issues as a guide.

We chose books because we liked them and not because they fit a particular theme, so some themes have only a few titles, while some others have many. Even if a theme only had one book, we mention it if we think it can be of interest or use. Most of the themes are self-explanatory, but when we felt there was a need for a description we added one. We encourage using these themes as a starting place for those who need them or as a more in-depth reference for others. We're sure there are ways to use them we haven't considered, and we look forward to hearing from readers about how you use them.

In order by theme, with an alphabetical listing of the books for each:

abandonment
Eleanor
Hansel and Gretel
Journey
Mean Margaret
Pole Dog
Solitary Blue

aborigines
Burnt Stick

abuse
3 NBS of Julian Drew
Hobkin

Letters From the Inside
Shiloh
Staying Fat for Sarah Byrnes
What Jamie Saw

actors and acting
Bard of Avon
Grandpa's Face
Onstage and Backstage at the Night
    Owl Theater
Pretend You're a Cat
Show Time at the Polk Street
    School
Starring First Grade

Adams, John
Young John Quincy

Adams, John Quincy
Young John Quincy

adoption
Allison
Animal Family
Anne of Green Gables
Baby
Good Griselle
Let's Talk About It: Adoption
Mean Margaret
Orphan Train Adventures
Rainbabies
Saving Sweetness
Shaker Boy
Stellaluna
Tell Me Again About the Night I Was
    Born
Through Moon and Stars and Night
    Skies

adventure
5 Novels by Daniel Pinkwater
Adventures of Captain Underpants
Adventures of Huckleberry Finn
Adventures of Tintin
Ali, Child of the Desert
Alice's Adventures in Wonderland
Amazon Diary
Animorphs
Barefoot
Beyond the Western Sea
BFG
Black Ships Before Troy
Borrowers
Brian's Winter
By the Great Horn Spoon
Cat in the Hat
Caves and Caverns
Cay
Chocolate Fever
Chronicles of Narnia
City of Light, City of Dark
Cloudland
Clown
Commander Toad in Space
Complete Sherlock Holmes
Culpepper Adventures
Curious George

Deathwatch
Devil's Arithmetic
Don Quixote
Dragonling
Dragon's Blood
East O' the Sun and West O' the Moon
Edward and the Pirates
Five Children and It
Free Fall
Gary Paulsen's World of Adventure
Girl Named Disaster
Golden Compass
Good, the Bad, and the Goofy
Grey King
Grey Lady and the Strawberry
    Snatcher
Gulliver's Adventures in Lilliput
Half Magic
Harris and Me
Hobbit
House With a Clock in Its Walls
Illyrian Adventure
In the Driver's Seat
Indian in the Cupboard
Indian Winter
Julie of the Wolves
King of the Wind
Knight's Castle
Lost Years of Merlin
Magic School Bus in the Time of the
    Dinosaurs
Meanwhile . . .
Mouse and the Motorcycle
Nicholas Pipe
Over Sea, Under Stone
Paddle-to-the-Sea
Phantom Tollbooth
Pirate's Handbook
Princess Nevermore
Prydain Chronicles
Redwall
Robin's Country
Santa Calls
Save Queen of Sheba
Seven-Day Magic
Shoebag
Shortcut
Singer to the Sea God
Story About Ping
Stuart Little
Sweetwater Run
Tale of Peter Rabbit

Tales of King Arthur Series
True Confessions of Charlotte Doyle
Tuesday
Wanderings Of Odysseus
Well Wished
Westmark
Where the Wild Things Are
Whipping Boy
Will's Mammoth
Wings: A Tale of Two Chickens
Witches
Wonderful Wizard of Oz
Wrinkle in Time
Zeke Pippin
Zoom! Zoom! Zoom! I'm Off to the
    Moon

Africa
A Is for Africa
Ancestor Tree
Ashanti to Zulu
Boundless Grace
Bringing the Rain to Kapiti Plain
Fire Children
Flying Tortoise
Fortune-Tellers
Galimoto
Girl Named Disaster
Glory Field
Insides, Outsides, Loops, and Lines
Learning to Swim in Swaziland
Lion's Whiskers
Masai and I
Misoso
Mufaro's Beautiful Daughters
Nanta's Lion
Oh, No, Toto!
One Night
Pulling the Lion's Tail
Ring of Tricksters
River That Went to the Sky
Talking Walls
When Africa Was Home
Where Are You Going, Manyoni?
Why Mosquitoes Buzz in People's
    Ears

African American
Adventures of High John the
    Conqueror
All the Colors of the Race
Alvin Ailey

Amazing Grace
Barefoot
Black Snowman
Bo Rabbit Smart for True
Brown Angels
Brown Honey in Broomwheat Tea
Celebration!
Charlie Pippin
Chicken Sunday
Children's Book of Kwanzaa
Coming Home
Creation
Dark Thirty
Dark Way
Dear Willie Rudd
Escape From Slavery
Everett Anderson's Goodbye
Front Porch Stories at the One-Room
    School
Glass Bottle Tree
Glory Field
Harlem
Headless Haunt and Other African-
    American
Her Stories
Hired Hand
Honey, I Love and Other Poems
I Hadn't Mean to Tell You This
I Have a Dream
In Daddy's Arms I Am Tall
Jazz: My Music, My People
Jojo's Flying Side Kick
Leagues Apart
Ma Dear's Aprons
Mac and Marie and the Train Toss
    Surprise
Malcolm X: By Any Means Necessary
Masai and I
Meet Danitra Brown
Minty
Mississippi Bridge
More Than Anything Else
Mysterious Thelonious
Nathaniel Talking
Nightjohn
Now Let Me Fly
Pass It On
Patchwork Quilt
People Could Fly
Peter's Chair
Real McCoy
Ring of Tricksters

Rolling Store
Seven Candles for Kwanzaa
Skin Deep and other Teenage
    Reflections
Slave Day
Smoky Night
Snowy Day
Soul Looks Back in Wonder
Sweet Clara and the Freedom
    Quilt
Sweet Words So Brave
Tales of Uncle Remus
Tar Beach
To Be a Slave
Uncle Jed's Barbershop
Wagon
Watson's Go to Birmingham, 1963
Well
When Jo Louis Won the Title
White Socks Only
Wilma Unlimited
Working Cotton

African culture
Black Snowman
Misoso
Mufaro's Beautiful Daughters
River That Went to the Sky

African words
Girl Named Disaster
Where Are You Going, Manyoni?

aging
Clown of God
Fruit and Vegetable Man
It's So Nice to Have a Wolf Around
    the House
Miss Rumphius
Peppermint Race
Rosalie
Supergrandpa
Toby
Tuck Everlasting
Verdi
Waiting for the Whales
Wilfred Gordon McDonald
    Partridge

AIDS
Earthshine
Tiger Flowers

air
Elements series

airplanes
First Flight
Flight
Fly! A Brief History of Flight
Hatchet
I'll See You in My Dreams
Richard Scarry's Cars and Trucks and
    Things
Stephen Biesty's Incredible Cross-
    Sections
Through Moon and Stars and Night
    Skies

airports
First Flight
Fly Away Home
Gila Monsters Meet You at the
    Airport

Alaska
Eagle's Gift
Girl Who Dreamed Only of Geese
Julie of the Wolves
Seasons and Someone

alcoholism
Crossing
Judy Scuppernong
Mary Wolf

aliens
Company's Coming
Here Come the Aliens

alligators
All About Alligators
Nutshell Library
Wide-Mouthed Frog

alliteration
A My Name Is Alice
Alison's Zinnia
Alpha Beta Chowder
Animalia
Aster Aardvarks's Alphabet Adventures
Away From Home
Busy Buzzing Bumblebees
Colors Around Us
Some Smug Slug

alphabet
26 Letters and 99 Cents
A Is for Africa
A My Name Is Alice
ABC Mystery
Alison's Zinnia
Alpha Beta Chowder
Alphabet From Z to A
Animalia
Antics
Ashanti to Zulu
Aster Aardvarks's Alphabet Adventures
Away From Home
Bamboo Hats and a Rice Cake
Chicka Chicka Boom Boom
D Is for Doufu
Eating the Alphabet
Eight Hands Round
Eye Spy: A Mysterious Alphabet
Flora McDonnell's ABC
Gathering the Sun
Graphic Alphabet
Halloween ABC
Handmade Alphabet
Handsigns
Handtalk
Jeremy Kooloo
K Is for Kiss Goodnight
Martha Speaks
Miss Bindergarten Gets Ready for
    Kindergarten
Nutshell Library
Old Black Fly
On Market Street
Phantom Tollbooth
Spice Alphabet Book
Weighty Word Book
Z Was Zapped

Amazon
Amazon Diary
Great Kapok Tree
Inside the Amazing Amazon

American history (see: U.S. History)

Amish
Beyond the Divide

ancestors
Fox Song
Girl Named Disaster

Glass Bottle Tree
Glory Field
New Hope
Pablo Remembers

ancient Egypt
Cleopatra
Egypt Game
How to Make a Mummy Talk
I Am the Mummy Heb-Nefert
Kingfisher Book of the Ancient
    World

ancient Greece
Black Ships Before Troy
Dateline: Troy
D'Aulaire's Book of Greek Myths
Greek News
Kingfisher Book of the Ancient World
Librarian Who Measured the Earth
Singer of the Sea God
Wanderings of Odysseus

ancient history
Black Ships Before Troy
Cleopatra
Dateline: Troy
D'Aulaire's Book of Greek Myths
Dragon's Robe
Gladiator
Greek News
How to Make a Mummy Talk
I Am the Mummy Heb-Nefert
Kingfisher Book of the Ancient World
Made in China
Maples in the Mist
Mexico's Ancient City of Teotihuacan
Piece of String Is a Wonderful Thing
Popcorn Book
Silk Route
Smelly Old History Series
Story of Money

ancient Rome
Gladiator
Kingfisher Book of the Ancient World
Smelly Old History Series

angels
Good Griselle
High Rise Glorious Skittle Skat
    Roarious Sky Pie Angel Food Cake

anger
Allison
Black Snowman
Everett Anderson's Goodbye
Feelings
First Strawberries
Great Gilly Hopkins
Ice
Ironman
Lilly's Purple Plastic Purse
Radiance Descending
Spinky Sulks
There's a Party at Mona's Tonight
War with Grandpa

animal babies
I Love You as Much
If You Were Born a Kitten
Owl Babies
Pinky Is a Baby Mouse
Time for Bed

animal defenses
And So They Build
Toad
What Do You Do When Something
    Wants to Eat You?

animal tracks
How to Be a Nature Detective
In the Woods: Who's Been Here

animals, endangered
Eyes of Gray Wolf
Great Kapok Tree
Hey! Get Off Our Train
My Visit to the Zoo
Sato and the Elephants
Take Action
Whaling Days

animals, farm
Babe, the Gallant Pig
Barn Dance!
Barnyard Dance!
Big Red Barn
Cow Buzzed
Cow that Went Oink
Fair!
Farm Morning
Farmer Duck
Hattie and the Fox

Hunting the White Cow
Midnight Farm
Old MacDonald Had a Farm
Ornery Morning
Parents in the Pigpen, Pigs in the
    Tub
Piggie Pie
Pigs in the Mud in the Middle of the
    Rud
Sitting on the Farm
Very Busy Spider
What a Wonderful Day to Be a Cow
Year at Maple Hill Farm

animals, general
A My Name Is Alice
And So They Build
Animal Dads
Animalia
Animorphs
Annie and the Wild Animals
As the Crow Flies
Badger's Parting Gifts
Barefoot
Bay Shore Park
Beauty of the Beast
Before I Go to Sleep
Big Cats
Biggest, Strongest, Fastest
Bringing the Rain to Kapiti Plain
Brown Bear, Brown Bear, What Do
    You See?
Christmas Tree Tangle
Cinder-Eyed Cats
Clap Your Hands
Every Living Thing
Extremely Weird Animal Defenses
Fables
Fire in the Forest
Fire Race
Flora McDonnell's ABC
From Head to Toe
Fuzzy Yellow Ducklings
Girl Named Disaster
Girl Who Loved Wild Horses
Gobble, Growl, Grunt
Henny Penny
Here Is the Tropical Rain Forest
"Hi, Pizza Man!"
Home Sweet Home
House Is a House for Me
How to Be a Nature Detective

Hush! A Thai Lullaby
I Don't Care, Said the Bear
I Want to Be a Veterinarian
I Went to the Zoo
I Went Walking
In the Desert
In the Next Three Seconds
In the Tall, Tall Grass
In the Woods: Who's Been Here
Inside the Amazing Amazon
Jumanji
Jump!
Keepers of the Earth
Kratts' Creatures: Our Favorite Creatures
Lion Named Shirley Williamson
Listen to the Desert
Little Red Ant and the Great Big
    Crumb
Meet the Marching Smithereens
Meet the Orchestra
Mitten
My Visit to the Aquarium
My Visit to the Zoo
Noah's Ark
Number One Number Fun
Once There Was a Bull . . . (Frog)
Peck Slither and Slide
Piles of Pets
Pretend You're a Cat
Rats on the Range and Other Stories
Saint Francis
Santa's Favorite Story
Sing a Song of Popcorn
Snake Is Totally Tail
Some Smug Slug
Splash!
Squash and a Squeeze
Stories From Firefly Island
Tales Alive
Talking Like the Rain
Teddy Bear's Picnic
This Is the Hat
This Same Sky
Time for Bed
Time to Sleep
To Market, To Market
Toad or Frog, Swamp or Bog
Today Is Monday
Tumble Bumble
Turtle in July
Voices From the Wild
Welcome to the Green House

What Do You Do When Something
    Wants to Eat You?
When Hunger Calls
When I'm Sleepy
Where Are You Going, Manyoni?
Where's Spot
Whittler's Tale
Who Says a Dog goes Bow-Wow?
Wide-Mouthed Frog
Wind Says Goodnight
Wombat Divine
World Is Full of Babies!
World of Christopher Robin
World of Pooh

anticipation
At the Crossroads
Company's Coming
"Hi, Pizza Man!"
Monster at the End of this Book
Sarah, Plain and Tall
When Will I Read?

ants
Antics
Little Red Ant and the Great Big Crumb
One Hundred Hungry Ants
Those Amazing Ants

apples
Apple Pie Tree
Folks Call Me Appleseed John
Life and Times of the Apple

Arabs
Neve Shalom Wahat Al-Salam: Oasis
    of Peace
One Night
One More River

archeology
Bone From a Dry Sea

archery
Forestwife
Robin Hood and Little John
Robin's Country

architects and architecture
And So They Build
House Is a House for Me
Rome Antics

Round Buildings, Square Buildings
   and Buildings That Wiggle Like a
   Fish
Stephen Biesty's Incredible Cross-
   Sections

Arctic
Girl Who Dreamed Only of Geese
Mama, Do You Love Me?
Santa Calls
Small Tall Tale from the Far, Far
   North
Winter White

art
All I See
Appelemando's Dreams
Art Dog
Bill Peet: An Autobiography
Celebrate America in Poetry and
   Art
Celebrating America
Cherries and Cherry Pits
Color
Come Look With Me
Draw 50 Series
Easter Egg Farm
Ed Emberley's Big Purple Drawing
   Book
Emma
Fantastic Drawings of Danielle
From the Mixed-Up Files of Mrs. Basil
   E. Frankweiler
Gentleman and the Kitchen Maid
Getting to Know the World's Great
   Artists
Grandfather Tang's Story
Hands
Harold and the Purple Crayon
I Spy Two Eyes
Incredible Ned
Linnea in Monet's Garden
Max Makes a Million
Mouse Paint
My Painted House, My Friendly
   Chicken, & Me
Navajo: Visions and Voices Across the
   Mesa
No Good in Art
Paper Dragon
Quilt Story
Sato and the Elephants

Stranded at Plimoth Plantation, 1626
Tales Alive
Visiting the Art Museum
Zoom

artists
After the War Was Over
All I See
Art Dog
Bill Peet: An Autobiography
Call Down the Moon
Christmas Miracle of Jonathan
   Toomey
Dawn (Bang)
Easter Egg Artists
Elijah's Angel
Fantastic Drawings of Danielle
From Sea to Shining Sea
Gentleman and the Kitchen Maid
Getting to Know the World's Great
   Artists
Gift of Driscoll Lipscomb
Greatest Table
I Have a Dream
I Spy Two Eyes
Kite Flier
Linnea in Monet's Garden
Little Painter of Sabana Grande
Painter
Paper Dragon
Rechenka's Eggs
Sing a Song of Popcorn
Stranded at Plimoth Plantation, 1626
Wonderful Towers of Watts

Asia
Through Moon and Stars and Night
   Skies

astronauts
Zoom! Zoom! Zoom! I'm Off to the Moon

astronomy
Earth, Sky, and Beyond
Star Walk
Starry Messenger

athletes
Gladiator
Lives of the Athletes
Teammates
Wilma Unlimited

aunts
Cuckoo's Child
James and the Giant Peach
Last Dragon
My Great-Aunt Arizona
So Much

Australia
Burnt Stick
Dear Mr. Sprouts
Letters From the Inside
Possum Magic
Talking Walls
Wombat Divine
Wombat Stew

authors
Author: A True Story
Author's Day
Bard of Avon
Bill Peet: An Autobiography
But That's Another Story
Charles Dickens: The Man Who Had
    Great Expectations
Coming Home
Dear Mr. Henshaw
Emily
From Pictures to Words
Girl From Yamhill
How a Book Is Made
In Flight With David McPhail
Lives of the Writers
Peppermint Race
Sweet Words So Brave
Weekend Was Murder

autobiography
Anne Frank: The Diary of a Young Girl
Author: A True Story
Escape From Slavery
Girl From Yamhill
In Flight With David McPhail
Red Scarf Girl

Aztec
All of You Was Singing

babies
Angela and Diabola
Animal Dads
Baby
Blanket

Dressing
Ginger
Good Dog, Carl
Happy Birth Day
Hush Little Baby
Hush! A Thai Lullaby
I Can
If You Were Born a Kitten
Mean Margaret
More, More, More, Said the Baby
Mrs. Mustard's Baby Faces
New Baby
Smudge
So Much
Tell Me Again About the Night I Was
    Born
Welcoming Babies
When I Was Little
White on Black
World Is Full of Babies!
Za-Za's Baby Brother

baby animals (see: animal
    babies)

babysitters (see: child care)

bad days
Absolutely, Positively Alexander
Felix's Hat
Mean Soup
Voyage to the Bunny Planet

bakers
Baker's Dozen
Gardener
In the Night Kitchen
Tony's Bread

baking
Arthur's Christmas Cookies
Baker's Dozen
Gardener
Gingerbread Boy
Goody O'Grumpity
High Rise Glorious Skittle Skat
    Roarious Sky Pie Angel Food Cake
How to Make an Apple Pie and See
    the World
In the Night Kitchen
Thunder Cake
Too Many Pumpkins

ballet
Angelina Ballerina
Dance, Tanya
Lili Backstage
Max
Noel the First

balloons
Goodnight Moon
Harvey Potter's Balloon Farm
Three in a Balloon

bands
Five Live Bongos
Mama Don't Allow
Meet the Marching Smithereens

barns
Barn (Avi)
Barn (Atwell)
Barn Dance!
Barnyard Dance!
Big Red Barn
Parents in the Pigpen, Pigs in the Tub

baseball
Baseball Saved Us
Bats About Baseball
Casey at the Bat
Extra Innings
Game of Catch
Leagues Apart
Max
Teammates
What Hearts

baths
Five Minutes Peace
King Bidgood's in the Bathtub
Raggly, Scraggly, No-Soap, No-Scrub
    Girl

bats
Arthur's Camp-Out
Great Ball Game
House That Drac Built
Is Your Mama a Llama?
Mean Margaret
Stellaluna

beaches
At the Beach

Bear Called Paddington
Castle Builder
Riptide
Until I Saw the Sea

beads
One Small Blue Bead
String of Beads

bears
Animal Family
Bear Called Paddington
Bear That Heard Crying
Blueberries for Sal
Don't Laugh, Joe
Golden Compass
Goldilocks and the Three Bears
I Don't Care, Said the Bear
Jump!
Little Bear
Little Mouse, the Red Ripe Straw-
    berry, and the Big Hungry
    Bear
Swamp Angel
Time to Sleep
Where's My Teddy?
World of Pooh

beavers
Beaver at Long Pond

beds
How Big Is a Foot?

bedtime
Bedtime for Frances
Before I Go to Sleep
Can't You Sleep, Little Bear?
Goodnight Moon
Hush! A Thai Lullaby
K Is for Kiss Goodnight
Midnight Farm
Monster Bed
Napping House
Papa!
Time for Bed
When I'm Sleepy
Wind Says Goodnight

bees
Apple Pie Tree
Bee Tree

In Enzo's Splendid Gardens
In the Tall, Tall Grass
Life and Times of the Honeybee
Pioneer Sampler
World of Pooh

Beethoven
All I See

belonging
Blood and Chocolate
Cuckoo's Child
Little Blue and Little Yellow
Pee Wee Scouts series
Smudge

betrayal
Adopted by the Eagles
Rats Saw God
Staying Fat for Sarah Byrnes

bilingual (contains some foreign words
     or all text is in both languages)
Abuela
Arroz con Leche
Bamboo Hats and a Rice Cake
Bread Is for Eating
Calling the Doves
Cool Salsa
Cow that Went Oink
De Colores
Fabulous Fireworks Family
Gathering the Sun
Grandmother's Nursery Rhymes
Listen to the Desert
Margaret and Margarita
My First Book of Proverbs
Piñata Maker
Who Says a Dog Goes Bow-Wow?

Bible stories
Creation
Noah's Ark
One Wintry Night

bicycles
Delphine
I Am the Cheese
Mick Harte Was Here
On My Honor
Red Racer
Supergrandpa

biography
Alvin Ailey
Anne Frank: Beyond the Diary
Bard of Avon
Bill Peet: An Autobiography
Buddha
Calling the Doves
Charles Dickens: The Man Who Had
     Great Expectations
Children's Book of Kwanzaa
Cleopatra
Close Your Eyes So You Can See
Coming Home
El Chino
Eleanor
Finding Providence
Flight
Folks Call Me Appleseed John
Grandma Essie's Covered Wagon
Grass Sandals
Her Stories
Indian Winter
Last Princess
Librarian Who Measured the Earth
Lincoln: A Photobiography
Lives of the Athletes
Lives of the Musicians
Lives of the Writers
Malcolm X: By Any Means
     Necessary
Minty
Mistakes That Worked
More Than Anything Else
My Fellow Americans
Only Opal
Picture Book Biography Series
Rattlesnake Dance
Real McCoy
Saint Francis
Starry Messenger
Sweetwater Run
Teammates
Who Said That?
Will You Sign Here, John Hancock?
Wilma Unlimited
Young John Quincy

birds
Adopted by the Eagles
Apple Pie Tree
Bird's Body
Birdsong

Chickens Aren't the Only Ones
Days of the Blackbird
Finster Frets
Flying Tortoise
Girl Who Loved Wild Horses
Grandmother's Pigeon
Hawk, I'm Your Brother
Miro in the Kingdom of the Sun
My Visit to the Zoo
Nine in One Grr! Grr!
Nuts to You
Raven
Rome Antics
Secret Garden
Smudge
Stellaluna
Stuart Little
Time Flies
Wringer

birth
Happy Birth Day
If You Were Born a Kitten
On the Day You Were Born
Tell Me Again About the Night I Was
    Born
World Is Full of Babies!

birthdays
All About Alfie
Barnyard Dance!
Birthday for Frances
Birthday Surprises
Days With Frog and Toad
Hooray, a Piñata!
Make a Wish Molly
Mr. Rabbit and the Lovely Present
On the Day You Were Born
So Much
Wringer

blindness
Cay
Sees Behind Trees
Seven Blind Mice

boats
All Dads on Deck
Cinder-Eyed Cats
Dawn (Bang)
Dawn (Shulevitz)
Floating House

Fool of the World and the Flying Ship
Girl Named Disaster
Gulliver's Adventures in Lilliput
Little Ships
Little Toot
Maggie B
Paddle-to-the-Sea
Pirate's Handbook
Polar the Titanic Bear
Stephen Biesty's Incredible Cross-Sections
Story About Ping
True Confessions of Charlotte Doyle
Wanderings of Odysseus

bones
Bone From a Dry Sea
Bone Poems
Dem Bones

books
Amber on the Mountain
Bee Tree
From Pictures to Words
Half Magic
Hog-Eye
How a Book Is Made
I Like Books
In Flight With David McPhail
Knight's Castle
Library
Library Dragon
Pop-O-Mania
Poppleton
Seven-Day Magic

boredom
Cat in the Hat
Jumanji

Boston
Make Way for Ducklings

boxing
Chocolate War
When Jo Louis Won the Title

boys (Shhhhhhhh! Boys only!)
Boys Will Be

boys, gentle (mild mannered boys in non-aggressive roles)
5 Novels by Daniel Pinkwater

All About Alfie
All Dads on Deck
Barn (Avi)
Boy Who Dreamed of an Acorn
Dear Mr. Henshaw
Max
Nathaniel Talking
Oliver Button Is a Sissy
Outsiders
Salamander Room
Shy Charles
Singer to the Sea God
Soda Jerk
Story of Ferdinand
Today I'm Going Fishing With My
     Dad
William's Doll
Willy the Wimp

brain
Book of Think

bravery (see courage)

bread
Bread Is for Eating
Tony's Bread

breakfast (see: meals)

bridges
Mississippi Bridge
Tar Beach
Three Billy Goats Gruff
Toll Bridge Troll

brothers
Absolutely, Positively Alexander
All the Lights in the Night
Folks Call Me Appleseed John
I'll Fix Anthony
Julius, the Baby of the World
Maggie B
Max's Dragon Shirt
Mick Harte Was Here
Peter's Chair
Radiance Descending
Rhymes for Annie Rose
Santa Calls
Save Queen of Sheba
Waiting for the Evening Star
William's Doll

Wreck of the Zanzibar
Young Larry

Brown, John
Lightning Time

Buddhism
Buddha

bugs
Bugs (Greenberg)
Bugs! (Parker)
How Many Bugs in a Box?
Jack's Garden
Tumble Bumble

buildings
Mike Mulligan & His Steam Shovel
Round Buildings, Square Buildings and
     Buildings That Wiggle Like a Fish
Stephen Biesty's Incredible Cross-
     Sections
Tar Beach

bullfighting
El Chino
Story of Ferdinand

bullies (not only found on the play-
     ground, also among adults from
     all walks of life)
Angel Child, Dragon Child
Araboolies of Liberty Street
Bear's House
Big Bad Bruce
Blubber
Bootsie Barker Bites
Boys Will Be
Buffalo Tree
Chocolate War
Christmas Menorahs
Clay Boy
Crash
Fin M'Coul, the Giant of Knockmany
     Hill
Freak the Mighty
Hazel's Amazing Mother
How to Lose All Your Friends
Ironman
John Patrick Norman McHennessy,
     the Boy Who Was Always
     Late

Mean Margaret
Meet Danitra Brown
Monster Mama
Rat and the Tiger
Red Scarf Girl
Rolling Harvey Down the Hill
Staying Fat for Sarah Byrnes
Stepping on the Cracks
There's a Boy in the Girls'
    Bathroom
Three Billy Goats Gruff
Tortoise and the Hare
Well
White Socks Only
Willy the Wimp
Wringer
Zeke Pippin

bulls
Story of Ferdinand

burial
Bone From a Dry Sea
Corpses, Coffins, and Crypts
How to Make a Mummy Talk
I Am the Mummy Heb-Nefert

buses
Richard Scarry's Cars and Trucks and
    Things that Go
Wheels on the Bus

busybodies
Owen

butterflies
I Wish I Were a Butterfly
Monarchs

cake
Good O'Grumpity
High Rise Glorious Skittle Skat
    Roarious Sky Pie Angel Food
    Cake
In the Night Kitchen

California
Ballad of Lucy Whipple
By the Great Horn Spoon
California, Here We Come!
Calling the Doves
Cat Running

I Am Lavina Cumming
Iron Dragon Never Sleeps
Island of the Blue Dolphins
Rainbow Bridge
Voices From the Fields
Working Cotton

Cambodia
Children of the River
Who Belongs Here?

camels
Ali, Child of the Desert
Arabian Nights: Three Tales

camping
Acorn People
Arthur's Camp-Out
Camp Ghost Away
Chasing Redbird
Cowboy Country
Just Me and My Dad

Canada
Anne of Green Gables
Boggart
Dippers
Girl Who Dreamed Only of
    Geese
Josepha
Loup Garou
Man Called Raven
Owls in the Family
Paddle-to-the-Sea

candy
Charlie and the Chocolate Factory
Jelly Beans for Sale
Peppermint Race

captivity (includes internment and
    concentration camps)
3 NBS of Julian Drew
Baseball Saved Us
Bracelet
Buffalo Tree
Devil's Arithmetic
Gladiator
Glory Field
I Am an American
Letters From the Inside
Misty of Chincoteague

Rapunzel
Rose Blanche
To Be a Slave
Zel

careers
Bill Peet: An Autobiography
Chicken Soup, Boots
I Want to Be a Dancer
Richard Scarry's What Do People Do
    All Day
Worksong

Caribbean
Cat's Purr
Cay
Down by the River
Faithful Friend
Ring of Tricksters

cars
Adventures of Taxi Dog
Cadillac
Galimoto
Go, Dog. Go!
In the Driver's Seat
Phantom Tollbooth
Richard Scarry's Cars and Trucks and
    Things that Go
Sheep in a Jeep

carvers
Sato and the Elephants

castles
Boggart
Castle Builder
Castle in the Attic
King Arthur's Camelot
Nutcracker
Puzzling Day at Castle MacPelican
Stephen Biesty's Incredible Cross-
    Sections

caterpillars
Girl Who Loved Caterpillars
In the Tall, Tall Grass
Very Hungry Caterpillar

cathedrals
Good Griselle
Rome Antics

Catholicism
Clown of God
Saint Francis

cats
Allison
Angel for Solomon Singer
Angus and the Cat
Beautiful Feast for a Big King Cat
Blitzcat
Bunnicula
Cat's Purr
Catwings
Chato's Kitchen
Christmas Tree Tangle
Cinder-Eyed Cats
Cricket in Times Square
Ginger
Hannah and Jack
I Am the Dog, I Am the Cat
If I Were in Charge of the World
Jeremy Kooloo
Journey
Millions of Cats
Old Ladies Who Liked Cats
Scary, Scary Halloween
Smoky Night
Tenth Good Thing About Barney
Three-Legged Cat
Tight Times
Town Mouse, Country Mouse
Way Home

caves
Caves and Caverns

celebrations
Baby Sister for Frances
Celebration!
Celebrations
Cherokees
Children's Book of Kwanzaa
Classic Poems to Read Aloud
Day of the Dead
Fabulous Fireworks Family
Festivals
Fiesta
Guests
Happy New Year! Kung-Hsi Fa-Ts'ai!
Hooray, a Piñata!
I'm in Charge of Celebrations
Keeping Quilt

Make a Wish Molly
Molly's Pilgrim
Piñata Maker
Read-Aloud Rhymes for the Very
    Young
Seven Candles for Kwanzaa
Somebody Loves You, Mr. Hatch
Star Mother's Youngest Child
Teeny Weeny Zucchinis
Three Bears Holiday Rhyme Book
Welcoming Babies
When Zaydeh Danced on Eldridge
    Street
Wombat Divine

Celtic mythology
Grey King
Over Sea, Under Stone

censorship
Memoirs of a Bookbat

centipedes
Bugs (Parker)
James and the Giant Peach

change
Absolutely, Positively Alexander
Always Prayer Shawl
Amelia's Road
Ancestor Tree
Animorphs
Antics
Barn
Bay Shore Park
Blanket
Blood and Chocolate
Book of Changes
Chalk Doll
Charlotte's Web
Cheyenne Again
Chocolate Fever
Cinderella's Rat
Cloudy With a Chance of Meatballs
Color
Cuckoo's Child
Dawn (Bang)
Dinosaurs Divorce
Egg Is an Egg
Every Living Thing
Fanny's Dream
Fireflies, Peach Pies & Lullabyes

Fruit and Vegetable Man
Gather Up Gather In
Giant
Gila Monsters Meet You at the Air-
    port
Go Away, Big Green Monster
Go Away, Dog
Great Piratical Rumbustification
Guests
Homecoming
Homeplace
House for a Hermit Crab
If Your Name Was Changed at Ellis
    Island
Imogene's Antlers
Is That You, Winter?
Is This a House for Hermit Crab?
It's a Girl Thing
It's Perfectly Normal
It's So Nice to Have a Wolf Around
    the House
January Rides the Wind
John Henry
Julius, the Baby of the World
Kid in the Red Jacket
Library Dragon
Lifetimes
Little Blue and Little Yellow
Little House
Little House on the Prairie
Mike Mulligan & His Steam Shovel
Mouse Paint
Navajo: Visions and Voices Across the
    Mesa
Oh, the Places You'll Go!
One More River
Piggybook
R. E. M.
Rapunzel
Rats Saw God
Sarah, Plain and Tall
Shaker Boy
Shrinking of Treehorn
Somebody Loves You, Mr. Hatch
Something From Nothing
Squash and a Squeeze
Stellaluna
Stone Soup
Story of Little Babaji
Sun Song
Swan Stories
Sylvester and the Magic Pebble

Ten Mile Day and the Building
  of the Transcontinental
  Railroad
Thirteen
Thunder at Gettysburg.
Tight Times
Toby
Tuck Everlasting
Tucker Pfeffercorn
Velveteen Rabbit
Verdi
Very Hungry Caterpillar
Voices From the Fields
What You Know First
When Africa Was Home
When the Monkeys Came Back
When the Whippoorwill Calls
Who Said Red?
Yonder

characteristics (books about distinc-
  tive, identifiable features)
Biggest, Strongest, Fastest
Owl Eyes
People
Snake Is Totally Tail

chases
Barefoot
Donna O'Neeshuck Was Chased by
  Some Cows
Gingerbread Boy
Grey Lady and the Strawberry
  Snatcher
Suddenly!

Chelm
Chanukkah in Chelm
Feather Merchants

Chicago
Great Fire

chickens
Charlie the Chicken
Chicken Man
Chickens Aren't the Only
  Ones
Don't Count Your Chicks
Easter Egg Farm
Minerva Louise at School
My Hen Is Dancing

My Painted House, My Friendly
  Chicken, & Me
Wings: A Tale of Two Chickens

childcare
All About Alfie
Animal Dads
Good Dog, Carl
Shy Charles

childhood
After the War Was Over
Brown Angels
Chalk Doll
Fun! No Fun!
Growing Up in Coal Country
I Saw Esau
Invisible Ladder
Polar Express
Roxaboxen
War Boy
When I Was Little
When I Was Nine
World of Pooh

children's art
Dear World

children's writing
Dear World
Learning to Swim in Swaziland
Voices From the Fields

China
Arabian Nights: Three Tales
D Is for Doufu
Dragon's Robe
Empty Pot
Grandfather Tang's Story
Lon Po Po
Made in China
Maples in the Mist
Paper Dragon
Red Scarf Girl
Silk Route
Story About Ping
Talking Walls
Weaving of a Dream
Yeh-Shen: A Cinderella Story from China

Chinese American
Cleversticks

El Chino
I Hate English
Iron Dragon Never Sleeps
Last Dragon
Spotlight on Laurence Yep
Suitcase Full of Seaweed and other
    Poems
Ten Mile Day and the Building of the
    Transcontinental Railroad

Chinese culture
Happy New Year! Kung-Hsi Fa-Ts'ai!
Last Dragon
Ten Mile Day and the Building of the
    Transcontinental Railroad

Chinese language
At the Beach

Chinese New Year
Happy New Year! Kung-Hsi Fa-Ts'ai!
Last Dragon

chocolate
Charlie and the Chocolate Factory
Chocolate Fever
Chocolate Touch
Chocolate War

choices (decisions, turning points,
    and being put on the spot)
Adventures of Huckleberry Finn
Baby
Barn (Avi)
Castle Builder
Earthsea Quartet
Everybody Needs a Rock
Jeremy Thatcher, Dragon Hatcher
Jeremy's Decision
Mary Wolf
Mufaro's Beautiful Daughters
Tight Times
Tuck Everlasting
Twelve Shots
View From Saturday

chopsticks
Cleversticks
How My Parents Learned to Eat

Christianity
Child's First Bible

Close Your Eyes So You Can See
One Wintry Night
Saint Francis
Santa's Favorite Story

Christmas
Arthur's Christmas Cookies
Baker's Dozen
Christmas Alphabet
Christmas House
Christmas in the Big House, Christ-
    mas in the Quarters
Christmas Miracle of Jonathan
    Toomey
Christmas Tree Tangle
Elijah's Angel
Frog and Toad All Year
Gingerbread Doll
Harvey Slumfenburger's Christmas
    Present
Hilary Knight's The Twelve Days of
    Christmas
Marvin's Best Christmas Present Ever
Mr. Willowby's Christmas Tree
Night Before Christmas
Noel the First
Nutcracker
One Wintry Night
Polar Express
Santa Calls
Santa's Favorite Story
Santa's Short Suit Shrunk and Other
    Christmas Tongue Twisters
Star Mother's Youngest Child
Stories By Firelight
Tales of Trotter Street
Too Many Tamales
Tree of Cranes
Twelve Days of Christmas
Velveteen Rabbit
Wombat Divine

Christmas carols
Hilary Knight's The Twelve Days of
    Christmas
Twelve Days of Christmas

Christmas trees
Christmas House
Christmas Tree Tangle
Mr. Willowby's Christmas Tree
Tree of Cranes

cities
Ben's Trumpet
Gingerbread Boy
I Like the Music
Little House
Mexico's Ancient City of Teotihuacan
Philharmonic Gets Dressed
Richard Scarry's Busy Town
Rome Antics
Story of Babar
Way Home

city life
Brickyard Summer
Cricket in Times Square
Gardener
Harlem
House on East 88th Street
Metropolitan Cow
On Sally Perry's Farm
Rolling Harvey Down the Hill
Seedfolks
Tight Times
Town Mouse, Country Mouse
Witch Way to the Country
Year on My Street

civil rights
Dear Willie Rudd
I Have a Dream
Malcolm X: By Any Means Necessary
Mississippi Bridge
Spite Fences
Watson's Go to Birmingham, 1963
White Socks Only

clapping
Clap Your Hands

clay
Clay Boy
Fire Children
Golem (Wisniewski)
Golem (Singer)
Golem: A Giant Made of Mud
Owl Eyes
When Clay Sings

Cleopatra
Cleopatra

cleverness (includes outsmarting the enemy)
Adventures of High John the Conqueror
All About Alfie
Aunt Nancy and Old Man Trouble
Chato's Kitchen
Counting Crocodiles
Do Not Open
Gentleman and the Kitchen Maid
Hansel and Gretel
Hershel and the Hanukkah Goblins
King Bidgood's in the Bathtub
King Snake
Little Mouse, the Red Ripe Strawberry, and the Big Hungry Bear
Liza Lou and the Yeller Belly Swamp
Mailing May
Mama Don't Allow
Marvin's Best Christmas Present Ever
Meanwhile . . .
Mysterious Tadpole
Nate the Great
One Grain of Rice
Paper Dragon
Phantom Tollbooth
Rikki-Tikki-Tavi
Sam and the Tigers
Saving Sweetness
Spoon for Every Bite
Stephanie's Ponytail
Stone Soup
Story of Little Babaji
Sweet Clara and the Freedom Quilt
Three Little Javelinas
Toll-Bridge Troll
Tops and Bottoms
Wombat Stew

clothing
Bit by Bit
Dressing
Froggy Gets Dressed
Maisy Goes Swimming
Mitten
Where Does It Go?
Where Will This Shoe Take You?

clouds
Cloudland
Mendel's Ladder

clowns
Clown

clubs
Pee Wee Scouts series

coal
Growing Up in Coal Country
In Coal Country
Mama Is a Miner

cocoons
Monarchs
Very Hungry Caterpillar

codes
Egypt Game
Secret Code Book

collecting
Captain Snap and the Children of
    Vinegar Lane
Galimoto
On Sally Perry's Farm
Sally Arnold
Wonderful Towers of Watts

color
Blue Hat, Green Hat
Brown Bear, Brown Bear, What Do
    You See?
Color
Colors Around Us
Colors Everywhere
Easter Egg Artists
Frederick
Freight Train
Gift of Driscoll Lipscomb
Growing Colors
Hailstones and Halibut Bones
How a Book Is Made
I Went Walking
Little Blue and Little Yellow
Lunch
Mouse Paint
Mr. Rabbit and the Lovely Present
Mysterious Thelonious
Night Sounds, Morning Colors
Of Colors and Things
Seven Blind Mice
Stranded at Plimoth Plantation,
    1626

What Am I?
Who Said Red?

Columbus
Corn Is Maize
Follow the Dream
Morning Girl

comeuppance
Araboolies of Liberty Street
Big David, Little David
Bootsie Barker Bites
Charlie and the Chocolate Factory
Faithful Friend
Fin M'Coul, the Giant of Knockmany
    Hill
Hired Hand
John Patrick Norman McHennessy,
    the Boy Who Was Always Late
Just Rewards
King's Equal
Man Who Could Call Down Owls
Matilda
My Place in Space
Psychzone: Kidzilla and Other Tales
Spoon for Every Bite
Tale of Ali Baba and the Forty
    Thieves
White Socks Only

comfort
Blanket
Can't You Sleep, Little Bear?
Cozy Book
Dancing With the Wind
Emma
Felix's Hat
Grandfather Twilight
Hush! A Thai Lullaby
Mama, Do You Love Me?
Monster Bed
Owen
Runaway Bunny
Something From Nothing
Time for Bed
Voyage to the Bunny Planet
When the Big Dog Barks
You Hold Me and I'll Hold You

comic book style
Adventures of Tintin
City of Light, City of Dark

Don Quixote
Meanwhile . . .

coming of age
Adrian Mole Diaries
After the War Was Over
Am I Blue?
Anne Frank: The Diary of a Young
    Girl
Are You There God? It's Me, Margaret
Beyond the Divide   •
Blue Skin of the Sea
Bone Man
Boy Who Dreamed of an Acorn
Brickyard Summer
Buddha
Buffalo Tree
Chasing Redbird
Cool Salsa
Day of Ahmed's Secret
Eagle's Gift
Earthsea Quartet
Giant
Help Wanted
I Am Lavina Cumming
Ice
Invisible Ladder
Ironman
Island of the Blue Dolphins
It's a Girl Thing
Julie of the Wolves
Kinship
Kite Flier
Letters From the Inside
Lost Years of Merlin
Make Lemonade
Mary Wolf
Memoirs of a Bookbat
Midnight Hour Encores
Moonstick
Morning Girl
Out of the Dust
Place to Call Home
Prydain Chronicles
Rapunzel
Red Scarf Girl
Sees Behind Trees
Shabanu
Singer to the Sea God
Skin Deep and other Teenage Reflec-
    tions
Soda Jerk

Spite Fences
Stones in Water
Tae's Sonata
Thunder at Gettysburg
Waiting to Waltz
Wringer

communication
All I See
Amelia Bedelia
Angel Child, Dragon Child
Barn (Avi)
Bats About Baseball
Chatting
Communication
Cow that Went Oink
Dear World
Dogs
Feelings
Forgotten Door
Handmade Alphabet
Handsigns
Handtalk
Hattie and the Fox
Jolly Postman
Margaret and Margarita
Meteor!
Outsiders
Pass the Fritters, Critters
Puff . . . Flash . . . Bang!
Ruby Mae Has Something to Say
Say Hola to Spanish
Secret Code Book
View From the Cherry Tree

community
All About Alfie
Anne of Green Gables
Appelemando's Dreams
Araboolies of Liberty Street
Badger's Parting Gifts
Bein' With You This Way
Ben's Trumpet
Christmas in the Big House,
    Christmas in the Quarters
Christmas Menorahs
Darnell Rock Reporting
Dippers
Dragonling
Farmer Duck
Front Porch Stories at the One-Room
    School

Fruit and Vegetable Man
Giver
Green Truck Garden Giveaway
Growing Up in Coal Country
Harlem
Hobbit
Homer Price
I Got a Family
Kid in the Red Jacket
Last Dragon
Little House on the Prairie
Little Painter of Sabana Grande
Little Ships
Mary Wolf
Meteor!
My Map Book
My Painted House, My Friendly
    Chicken, & Me
Nate the Great
Old Mother Hubbard and Her Won-
    derful Dog
One More River
Paper Dragon
Pink Paper Swans
Rattlebone Rock
Richard Scarry's Busy Town
Roxaboxen
See You Around, Sam
Seedfolks
Shaker Boy
Somebody Loves You, Mr. Hatch
Someday a Tree
Stepping on the Cracks
Stone Soup
Stranded at Plimoth Plantation, 1626
Supergrandpa
Tacky the Penguin
Tales of Trotter Street
Thunder at Gettysburg
Uncle Jed's Barbershop
Under the Blood Red Sun
Van Gogh Cafe
View From Saturday
Well
When Africa Was Home
World of Pooh
Year on My Street

comparisons (includes contrasts and
    differences)
All About Alligators
All the Places to Love

All We Needed to Say
Allison
Alphabet From Z to A (with Much
    Confusion Along the Way)
Amber on the Mountain
Banging Book
Biggest, Strongest, Fastest
Birthday Surprises
Blueberries for Sal
Bull Run
Butter Battle Book
Chester's Way
Children Just Like Me
Christmas in the Big House, Christ-
    mas in the Quarters
Cleversticks
Colors Everywhere
Dancing Feet
Dateline: Troy
Dawn (Shulevitz)
Earl's Too Cool for Me
Earrings!
East O' the Sun and West O' the Moon
Egg Is an Egg
Elijah's Angel
Enormous Egg
Everybody Needs a Rock
Fantastic Drawings of Danielle
Fast, Slow, High, Low
Fortunately
Frogs
Fun! No Fun!
Gila Monsters Meet You at the Air-
    port
Girls to the Rescue
Go, Dog. Go!
Goldilocks and the Three Bears
Grandfather's Journey
Great Ball Game
Green Eggs and Ham
Guess How Much I Love You
Guinness Book of World Records
Hands
House Is a House for Me
How Much Is a Million?
I Am the Dog, I Am the Cat
Ice
If You Were Born a Kitten
In the Next Three Seconds
Margaret and Margarita
Masai and I
Math Start Series

May I Bring A Friend?
My Song Is Beautiful
My Visit to the Zoo
Nana Upstairs and Nana Downstairs
Navajo: Visions and Voices Across the Mesa
Nettie's Trip South
One World, Many Religions
Our Granny
Parents in the Pigpen, Pigs in the Tub People
Peter Spier's Rain
Princess Nevermore
Puffins Climb, Penguins Rhyme
Quick as a Cricket
Sarah, Plain and Tall
Shortcut
Sisters
Skylark
Slave Day
Somewhere in the World Right Now
Splash!
Stellaluna
String of Beads
Stupids Step Out
Sun Song
Toad or Frog, Swamp or Bog
Today I'm Going Fishing With My Dad
Town Mouse, Country Mouse
Until I Met Dudley
Verdi
Walk Two Moons
We Are a Rainbow
We're Back!
What's What?
When I Was Little
Where Will This Shoe Take You?
Where's That Insect?
Whipping Boy
White on Black
Who Belongs Here?
Witch Way to the Country
Worksong
World Is Full of Babies!

competition
Atlanta's Race
Babe, the Gallant Pig
Big David, Little David
Bookworm Buddies
Cat Running
Chestnut Cove

Chocolate War
Crash
Don't Fidget a Feather
Great Ball Game
Noel the First
Peppermint Race
Rolling Harvey Down the Hill
Stone Fox
Strega Nona
Ten Mile Day and the Building of the Transcontinental Railroad
Tortoise and the Hare
View From Saturday

computers
The Boggart
Cyber.Kdz Series
Freak the Mighty
Search for the Shadowman
Virtual War

concentration camps (see: captivity)

concepts (helping define a child's understanding of basic relationships between objects: size, color, shape, etc.)
Colors Around Us
Colors Everywhere
Crash! Bang! Boom!
Fast, Slow, High, Low
Fuzzy Yellow Ducklings
Goldilocks and the Three Bears
How Much Is a Million?
I Can
Little Blue and Little Yellow
Lunch
Mouse Paint
Of Colors and Things
Splash!
String of Beads
Very Hungry Caterpillar
What Am I?
What's What?
Where Does It Go?

confidence
Dear Mr. Sprouts
Emma
I, Houdini
Just Me and My Dad
Some Smug Slug

conflict and resolution (getting along)
Angus and the Cat
Bootsie Barker Bites
Children of the Dust Bowl
Game of Catch
How to Lose All Your Friends
Join In
Luka's Quilt
People Who Hugged Trees
Smoky Night
Talking Peace
Three Little Wolves and the Big Bad Pig
War with Grandpa

connections (Just as a follows b in our alphabet, the pages of these books are linked—through rhyme, connecting art, specific words, puzzles or games encouraging the reader to anticipate the turn of the next page.)
Alison's Zinnia
An Egg Is an Egg
Cow Buzzed
Free Fall
Jack's Garden
Jeremy Kooloo
Mordant's Wish
Mr. Willowby's Christmas Tree
My Family Tree
My Little Sister Ate One Hare
My Place in Space
Night Becomes Day
Old Ladies Who Liked Cats
Once There Was a Bull . . . (Frog)
Runaway Bunny
Thirteen
Time to Sleep

conscience (includes: doing the right thing)
Darnell Rock Reporting
Day's Work
Fragile Flag
Great Kapok Tree
It's So Nice to Have a Wolf Around the House
Lilly's Purple Plastic Purse
Nothing But the Truth
On My Honor

Rose Blanche
Spite Fences
Stepping on the Cracks
Sun and Spoon
Too Many Tamales

conscription
Stones in Water
Sworn Enemies

consequences
Banging Book
Jeremy Thatcher, Dragon Hatcher
Jumanji
Lilly's Purple Plastic Purse
Little Red Riding Hood
Ornery Morning
Red Riding Hood
Shortcut
Tale of Peter Rabbit
Too Many Tamales
Twelve Shots
William Shakespeare's Macbeth

constellations
Star Walk
Tales Alive

contests
Big Bazoohley
Charlie and the Chocolate Factory
Chestnut Cove
Chocolate War
Homer Price
How to Eat Fried Worms
Slave Day
View From Saturday
Weekend Was Murder
Westing Game

contrasts (see: comparisons)

cooking
Everybody Cooks Rice
Miracle of the Latkes
Mud Pies and Other Recipes
Pancakes for Breakfast
Piggie Pie
Popcorn Book
Spice Alphabet Book
Too Many Pumpkins
Too Many Tamales

cooperation
Albert's Play
Chestnut Cove
Day's Work
Did You See What I Saw?
Fire Race
Fool of the World and the Flying
    Ship
Great Ball Game
Here Comes Henny
Hunting the White Cow
Moans and Groans and Dinosaur
    Bones
Mouse and Mole and the Year-Round
    Garden
Neve Shalom Wahat Al-Salam: Oasis
    of Peace
Ornery Morning

copy cats
Ruby the Copycat
Stephanie's Ponytail

corn
Corn Is Maize
Dragonfly's Tale

costumes
Away From Home
Egypt Game
Lili Backstage
Real-Skin Rubbermonster Mask
When the Goblins Came Knocking
Who Said Boo?

counting
1 Is One
12 Ways to Get to 11
26 Letters and 99 Cents
500 Hats of Bartholomew
    Cubbins
Barnyard Dance!
Benny's Pennies
Big Red Barn
Counting Crocodiles
Don't Count Your Chicks
Hippos Go Berserk
How Many Bugs in a Box?
How Much Is a Million?
I Spy Two Eyes
Jelly Beans for Sale
Math Start Series

My Little Sister Ate One Hare
Nutshell Library
One Gaping, Wide-Mouthed, Hopping
    Frog
Piggies
Puzzling Day at Castle MacPelican
Ten Sly Piranhas
Twelve Days of Christmas
Zin! Zin! Zin! A Violin

country life
Amber on the Mountain
Barn Dance!
Blue Hill Meadows
Gardener
Little House
Regular Flood of Mishap
Town House, Country Mouse
Waiting for the Evening Star
What a Wonderful Day to Be a Cow
When the Whippoorwill Calls
Where the Red Fern Grows
Witch Way to the Country
Yonder

courage (includes bravery)
3 NBS of Julian Drew
500 Hats of Bartholomew Cubbins
Adventures of Huckleberry Finn
Ali, Child of the Desert
All About Alfie
All the Lights in the Night
Amazon Diary
Anne Frank: The Diary of a Young
    Girl
Around the World in a Hundred
    Years
Arthur's Loose Tooth
Babe, the Gallant Pig
Ballad of Lucy Whipple
Ballad of the Pirate Queens
Barefoot
Beyond the Western Sea
Birdie's Lighthouse
Blitzcat
Blue Skin of the Sea
Bone Man
Bootsie Barker Bites
Boy and the Cloth of Dreams
Brave Irene
Brian's Winter
Brickyard Summer

Burnt Stick
Cay
Charlotte's Web
Chocolate War
Christmas Menorahs
Chronicles of Narnia
City of Gold and Lead
City of Light, City of Dark
Come a Tide
Delphine
Devil's Arithmetic
Do Not Open
Dragonling
Drinking Gourd
Edward and the Pirates
Fly Away Home
Fly! A Brief History of Flight
Fragile Flag
Freak the Mighty
Gary Paulsen's World of Adventure
Get on Board
Ghost Dance
Giant
Girl Named Disaster
Giver
Glory Field
Grandmother Bryant's Pocket
Hansel and Gretel
Harriet and the Promised Land
Hatchet
Hattie and the Fox
Heckedy Peg
Hershel and the Hanukkah Goblins
Hobbit
Homecoming
I Am an American
I Am Lavina Cumming
If Your Name Was Changed at Ellis
    Island
Island of the Blue Dolphins
Jack and the Beanstalk
James and the Giant Peach
Jip, His Story
Jojo's Flying Side Kick
Julie of the Wolves
Lassie Come Home
Last Princess
Lily's Crossing
Lion's Whiskers
Little House on the Prairie
Little Ships
Little Toot

Loup Garou
Malcolm X: By Any Means Necessary
Minty
Mirette on the High Wire
Miro in the Kingdom of the Sun
Mississippi Mud
Monster Mama
Noah's Ark
Number of Stars
One Night
Out of the Dust
Paper Dragon
Pee Wee Pool Party
People Who Hugged Trees
Peppe the Lamp Lighter
Pink and Say
Prydain Chronicles
Real McCoy
Red Scarf Girl
Roll of Thunder, Hear My Cry
Sadako
Sadako and the Thousand Paper
    Cranes
Saint George and the Dragon
Save Queen of Sheba
Scared Silly
Seven Brave Women
Shepherd Boy
Shy Charles
Stellaluna
Stepping on the Cracks
Stone Fox
Stones in Water
Stranded at Plimoth Plantation, 1626
Sweet Clara and the Freedom Quilt
They're Off!
Tom Thumb
True Confessions of Charlotte Doyle
Very Scary
Virtual War
Well
Westmark
White Dynamite and Curly Kidd
Wonderful Wizard of Oz
Wringer
Zel

cousins
Bell Prater's Boy
So Much
Story of Babar
Too Many Tamales

cowboys
Cowboy Country
Indian in the Cupboard
Just Like My Dad
White Dynamite and Curly Kidd

cows
Donna O'Neeshuck Was Chased by
    Some Cows
How Now Brown Cow
Hunting the White Cow
Is Your Mama a Llama?
Nell Nuggett and the Cow Caper
When the Bluebell Sang

coyotes
Coyote
Coyote in Love
Fire Race
Tale of Rabbit and Coyote
Three Little Javelinas

crabs
House for a Hermit Crab
Is This a House for Hermit Crab?

crafts
Captain Snap and the Children of
    Vinegar Lane
Children's Book of Kwanzaa
Dragonfly's Tale
Eight Hands Round
Fox Song
Galimoto
Hands
Keepers of the Earth
Kite Flier
On Sally Perry's Farm
Pink Paper Swans
Pop-O-Mania
Quilt Story
Sally Arnold
String of Beads
Tales Alive
When Clay Sings
Wonderful Towers of Watts
Woodlore

creation
All of You Was Singing
Cherokees
Creation

Dance of the Sacred Circle
Fire Children
Golem
In the Beginning
Owl Eyes
Rainbow Bridge

creativity
Appelemando's Dreams
Art Dog
Call Down the Moon
Captain Snap and the Children of
    Vinegar Lane
Cherries and Cherry Pits
Christmas Miracle of Jonathan Toomey
Easter Egg Farm
Emma
Five Live Bongos
From Pictures to Words
Hands
Harold and the Purple Crayon
How a Book Is Made
Incredible Ned
Little Painter of Sabana Grande
Lives of the Musicians
Lives of the Writers
Magic Fan
Max Makes a Million
Mistakes That Worked
My Painted House, My Friendly
    Chicken, & Me
Mysterious Thelonious
Paper Dragon
Rechenka's Eggs
Sing, Sophie!
Thirteen
Weekend Was Murder
Wonderful Towers of Watts

crickets
Cricket in Times Square
Growing Colors
Very Quiet Cricket

crocodiles
All About Alligators
Counting Crocodiles
House on East 88th Street

cruelty
Blubber
Buffalo Tree

Chocolate War
Cyber.Kdz Series
James and the Giant Peach
Matilda
Mean Margaret
Mufaro's Beautiful Daughters
Sootface
Tucker Pfeffercorn

cultural diversity (books that fea-
  ture two or more cultures in rela-
  tion to or contrast with each other)
Abiyoyo
Acorn Tree & Other Folktales
All the Colors of the Race
Allison
American Girl Series
Araboolies of Liberty Street
Bein' With You This Way
Cay
Chicken Sunday
Children Just Like Me
Children of the River
Christmas in the Big House, Christ-
  mas in the Quarters
Circling the Globe
Cleversticks
Corpses, Coffins, and Crypts
Cyber.Kdz Series
Damned Strong Love
Dear World
Earth, Fire, Water, Air
El Chino
Elijah's Angel
Everybody Cooks Rice
Festivals
Fire Children
Friends and Amigos Series
From Sea to Shining Sea
Fruit and Vegetable Man
Giants!
Goddesses, Heroes, and Shamans
Grandfather's Journey
Green Tales
Handmade Alphabet
Help Wanted
History of the US
How My Parents Learned to Eat
I Hadn't Mean to Tell You This
In the Beginning
Iron Dragon Never Sleeps
Join In

K Is for Kiss Goodnight
Kingfisher Illustrated History of the
  World
Last Princess
Little Folk
Lives of the Athletes
Lives of the Musicians
Lives of the Writers
Make a Wish Molly
Maniac Magee
Market!
Masai and I
Mermaid Tales From Around the
  World
Molly's Pilgrim
More, More, More, Said the Baby
Morning Girl
My Fellow Americans
My House Has Stars
My Song Is Beautiful
Neve Shalom Wahat Al-Salam: Oasis
  of Peace
Nursery Tales Around the World
One World, Many Religions
People
Pink Paper Swans
Sacred Places
Seedfolks
Shoes, Shoes, Shoes
Silver Pony
Skip Across the Ocean
Smoky Night
Soon, Annala
South and North, East and West
Stranded at Plimoth Plantation, 1626
String of Beads
Suitcase Full of Seaweed and Other
  Poems
Tales Alive
Talking Walls
Teammates
This Same Sky
Through Moon and Stars and Night
  Skies
Tortilla Factory
Treasury of Mermaids
Treasury of Princesses
Tree of Cranes
Tree of Dreams
True Lies
Under the Blood Red Sun
View From Saturday

We Are a Rainbow
When Africa Was Home
Where Will This Shoe Take You?
Who Belongs Here?
Who Says a Dog Goes Bow-Wow?
Worksong

cumulative story (a story that builds
    upon itself, layer by layer)
Bit by Bit
Bringing the Rain to Kapiti Plain
Brown Bear, Brown Bear, What Do
    You See?
By the Light of the Halloween Moon
Hattie and the Fox
Henny Penny
House That Drac Built
I Went to the Zoo
I'll See You When the Moon Is Full
In Enzo's Splendid Gardens
Jack's Garden
My Little Sister Ate One Hare
Napping House
Old Devil Wind
One Gaping, Wide-Mouthed, Hopping
    Frog
Sitting on the Farm
This Is the Hat
Today Is Monday
Tree in the Wood
Wind Says Goodnight

curiosity
Angus and the Cat
Curious George
Eeny, Meeny, Miney Mole
Ginger
Max and Ruby's First Greek Myth:
    Pandora's
Minerva Louise at School
When Zaydeh Danced on Eldrige
    Street

customs (see: traditions)

dance
Alvin Ailey
Angelina Ballerina
Barn Dance!
Cinder-Eyed Cats
Dance, Tanya
Dancing Feet

Day of the Dead
Eagle's Gift
Four Story Mistake
Ghost Dance
I Want to Be a Dancer
Indian Winter
Lili Backstage
Max
Noel the First
Nutcracker
Oliver Button Is a Sissy
Pulling the Lion's Tail
Raggly, Scraggly, No-Soap, No-Scrub
    Girl
When Zaydeh Danced on Eldridge Street

dancers
Alvin Ailey
I Want to Be a Dancer
Lili Backstage

danger
Story About Ping
Way Home

Darwin, Charles
Old Ladies Who Liked Cats

Day of the Dead
Day of the Dead
Fiesta
Pablo Remembers

daydreams
Daydreamer
Don't Count Your Chicks
I'll See You in My Dreams

days of the week
Ma Dear's Aprons
Today Is Monday

daytime
Big Red Barn
Dawn (Shulevitz)
Night Sounds, Morning Colors
Sun Song
Twilight Comes Twice

deadlocks (or stalemates)
Butter Battle Book
Telling of the Tales

deafness
Handmade Alphabet
Handsigns
Handtalk

death
Acorn People
Annie and the Old One
Badger's Parting Gifts
Belle Prater's Boy
Blood and Chocolate
Bridge to Terabithia
Buffalo Tree
Charlie Pippin
Charlotte's Web
Chasing Redbird
Corpses, Coffins, and Crypts
Dead Bird
Earth-Shattering Poems
Everett Anderson's Goodbye
Fireflies, Peach Pies & Lullabies
Fish in His Pocket
Flip-Flop Girl
Grandad Bill's Song
How to Make a Mummy Talk
I Am the Mummy Heb-Nefert
I'll Always Love You
Island of the Blue Dolphins
Jim's Dog Muffins
Lifetimes
Mick Harte Was Here
Missing May
Nana Upstairs and Nana
    Downstairs
Old Pig
On My Honor
Only Opal
Out of the Dust
Pink and Say
Prairie Songs
Remembering the Good Times
Sadako
Sadako and the Thousand Paper
    Cranes
Tenth Good Thing About Barney
Tiger Flowers
Tough Boris
Waiting for the Whales
Walk Two Moons
Where the Red Fern Grows
Wringer
You Hold Me and I'll Hold You

Declaration of Independence
Will You Sign Here, John Hancock?
Young John Quincy

defeat
Cheyenne Again
Chocolate War

definitions
Frank and Ernest
Geography From A to Z
Hole Is to Dig

denial
Everett Anderson's Goodbye\

Denmark
Number the Stars

dentists
Doctor DeSoto

desert
Alejandro's Gift
Ali, Child of the Desert
Amigo
Arabian Nights: Three Tales
Deathwatch
Hawk, I'm Your Brother
I'm in Charge of Celebrations
In the Desert
Listen to the Desert
One Night
One Small Blue Bead
Roxaboxen
Shabanu
Three Little Javelinas
When Clay Sings

detectives
Encyclopedia Brown Series
Secret Code Book
Weekend Was Murder
Westing Game

determination
Abel's Island
Acorn People
Amazing Grace
Angelina Ballerina
Brave Irene
Casey at the Bat

Charlie Drives the Stage
El Chino
Galimoto
Girl Who Loved Caterpillars
Harvey Slumfenburger's Christmas
    Present
Homecoming
Ironman
John Henry
Leagues Apart
Lion's Whiskers
Little Toot
Make Lemonade
Moonstruck
Real McCoy
Ruby Mae Has Something to Say
Stone Fox
Stones in Water
Supergrandpa
They're Off!
Tortoise and the Hare
Uncle Jed's Barbershop
Very Busy Spider
Way West
Where the Red Fern Grows

diaries (includes journals)
3 NBS of Julian Drew
Adrian Mole Diaries
Amelia's Notebook
Anne Frank: The Diary of a Young
    Girl
Birdie's Lighthouse
Catherine, Called Birdy
Communication
Dear America Series
Harriet the Spy
Indian Winter
Mississippi Mud
Nettie's Trip South
Only Opal
Stranded at Plimoth Plantation,
    1626
Way West
Wreck of the Zanzibar

differences (see: comparisons)

difficult times (see: bad days)

dingos
Wombat Stew

dinosaurs
Bone Poems
Chickens Aren't the Only Ones
Dinosaurs!: Strange and Wonderful
Enormous Egg
Jeremy's Decision
Magic School Bus in the Time of the
    Dinosaurs
Moans and Groans and Dinosaur
    Bones
Time Flies
We're Back!

disabilities (see: handicaps)

disagreements
First Strawberries
Let's Be Enemies
Luka's Quilt
No Fighting, No Biting!
Talking Peace

disaster
Come a Tide
Great Fire
Hill of Fire
I Am Lavina Cumming
Polar the Titanic Bear

discipline
John Patrick Norman McHennessy
Oink

disguises
Babushka Baba Yaga
Big Al
Great White Man-Eating Shark
Piggie Pie
There's a Party at Mona's Tonight
Wings: A Tale of Two Chickens
Witches

disobeying
Heckedy Peg
Little Red Riding Hood
Oh, No, Toto!
Red Riding Hood
Tale of Peter Rabbit

diversity
All Dads on Deck
All the Places to Love

Am I Blue?
Baby Be-Bop
Big Al
Birthday Surprises
Bull Run
Chester's Way
Company's Coming
Cow that Went Oink
Cyber.Kdz Series
Dancing Feet
Everybody Needs a Rock
Family Reunion
Friends
Frog in Love
Gardener
Great Ball Game
House Is a House for Me
It's Perfectly Normal
Jip, His Story
K Is for Kiss Goodnight
Let's Talk About It: Adoption
Little Blue and Little Yellow
Maniac Magee
May I Bring a Friend?
Metropolitan Cow
Miss Bindergarten Gets Ready for
   Kindergarten
Our Granny
People
Phantom Tollbooth
Philharmonic Gets Dressed
Redwall
Sally Arnold
Short and Shivery
Spice Alphabet Book
String of Beads
Town Mouse, Country Mouse
View From Saturday
Wilfred Gordon McDonald Partridge
Wonderful Towers of Watts

divorce
Dinosaurs Divorce
Hatchet
What Hearts

doctors
Chocolate Fever
Dear Dr. Sillybear

dogs
A Boy, a Dog, and a Frog

Adrian Mole Diaries
Adventures of Taxi Dog
Angus and the Cat
Art Dog
Bunnicula
Christmas Tree Tangle
Courtney
Dogs
Dogteam
Dogzilla
Eric Knight's Lassie Come Home
Faith and the Electric Dog
Go Away, Dog
Go, Dog. Go!
Good Dog, Carl
Henry and Mudge
Henry Huggins
Hobyahs
I Am the Dog, I Am the Cat
I'll Always Love You
It's Hard to Read a Map With a Beagle
   on Your Lap
Jim's Dog Muffins
Lassie Come Home
Martha Speaks
Marvin Redpost: Alone in His
   Teacher's House
My Dog Never Says Please
Nate the Great
Officer Buckle and Gloria
Old Mother Hubbard and Her Won-
   derful Dog
Phantom Tollbooth
Pole Dog
Riptide
Rosalie
Shiloh
Smudge
Some Swell Pup
Speak!
Star Mother's Youngest Child
Stone Fox
Three Stories You Can Read to Your Dog
Toby
What's What?
When the Big Dog Barks
Where the Red Fern Grows
Where's Spot?

dolls
Allison
Bear's House

Hazel's Amazing Mother
Is That You, Winter?
Mennyms
Mud Pies and Other Recipes
William's Doll

Down's syndrome
Be Good to Eddie Lee
Radiance Descending

dragonflies
Bugs (Parker)
Dragonflies
Dragonfly's Tale

dragons
Castle Builder
Demi's Dragons and Fantastic
    Creatures
Discovery of Dragons
Dove Isabeau
Dragonling
Dragons Are Singing Tonight
Dragon's Blood
Dragon's Robe
Earthsea Quartet
Happy New Year! Kung-Hsi Fa-Ts'ai!
Jeremy Thatcher, Dragon Hatcher
Komodo
Last Dragon
Library Dragon
Minstrel and the Dragon Pup
My Father's Dragon
Paper Bag Princess, The
Paper Dragon
Saint George and the Dragon

drawing
At the Beach
Cherries and Cherry Pits
Draw 50 Series
Ed Emberley's Big Purple Drawing
    Book
Fantastic Drawings of Danielle
Harold and the Purple Crayon
Insides, Outsides, Loops, and Lines
My Map Book
No Good in Art

dreams (the kind while you sleep—
    otherwise, see yearning)
Appelemando's Dreams

Boy and the Cloth of Dreams
Boy Who Dreamed of an Acorn
Buffalo Tree
Daydreamer
Frederick
Free Fall
Friends
Hey! Get Off Our Train
I'll Fix Anthony
In the Night Kitchen
Morgan's Dream
R. E. M.
Saint Patrick and the Peddler
Tree of Dreams
Voyage to the Bunny Planet
Wringer

dressing
Blue Hat, Green Hat
Dressing
Froggy Gets Dressed
Jesse Bear, What Will You Wear?
Maisy Goes Swimming
Philharmonic Gets Dressed

driving
In the Driver's Seat
Cadillac

drought
Bringing the Rain to Kapiti Plain
Dragon's Robe
Out of the Dust
Red Dirt Jessie

drowning
On My Honor

ducks
Don't Fidget a Feather
Make Way for Ducklings
Story About Ping
Three in a Balloon

dusk
Grandfather's Twilight
Twilight Comes Twice

Dutch, the
Anne Frank: Beyond the Diary
Anne Frank: Diary of a Young Girl
Baker's Dozen

dwellings
House Is a House for Me
My House Has Stars
Dakota Dugout
Sod Houses on the Great Plains
Seasons and Someone
Round Buildings, Square Buildings
    and Buildings That Wiggle Like a
    Fish
Way Home

Earth, the
Big Big Book for Our Planet
Earth, Sky, and Beyond
Earthdance
Elements Series
Old Turtle
On the Day You Were Born

Easter
Country Bunny and the Little Gold
    Shoes
Easter Egg Artists
Easter Egg Farm
Rechenka's Eggs

Easter bunny
Country Bunny and the Little Gold
    Shoes

eating
Blueberries for Sal
Bread and Jam for Frances
Clay Boy
Eating the Plates
Everybody Cooks Rice
How My Parents Learned to Eat
My Little Sister Ate One Hare
Never Take a Pig to Lunch
Very Hungry Caterpillar

eggs
Chicken Man
Chicken Sunday
Chickens Aren't the Only
    Ones
Easter Egg Artists
Easter Egg Farm
Enormous Egg
Green Eggs and Ham
Pancakes for Breakfast
Rechenka's Eggs

Egypt
Day of Ahmed's Secret
Talking Walls

elderly and children
Ancestor Tree
Cay
Elijah's Angel
Fireflies, Peach Pies & Lullabies
Miss Rumphius
Miz Berlin Walks
Other Way to Listen
Pink Paper Swans
Sally Arnold
Star Mother's Youngest Child
Tales of Trotter Street
Wilfred Gordon McDonald Partridge
Worry Stone

electricity
Ben and Me

elephants
17 Kings & 42 Elephants
Sato and the Elephants
Seven Blind Mice
Story of Babar

elves (see: little folk)

embarrassment
Adrian Mole Diaries
Badger's Bring Something Party
Elbert's Bad Word
Monster at the End of this Book
Red Racer
When Jo Louis Won the Title

emigration (see: immigration)

emotions
Badger's Bring Something Party
Dinosaurs Divorce
Feelings
Gardener
Grandad Bill's Song
Grandpa's Face
Mean Soup
Mrs. Mustard's Baby Faces

emus
Wombat Stew

encouragement (people on your side, support)
Acorn People
Ironman
Jospha
Teammates

England
Adrian Mole Diaries
After the War Was Over
Bard of Avon
Beyond the Western Sea
Blitzcat
Borrowers
Castle in the Attic
Charles Dickens: Man Who Had Great Expectations
Complete Sherlock Holmes
Eric Knight's Lassie Come Home
Grey King
How My Parents Learned to Eat
King Arthur's Camelot
Knight's Castle
Lassie Come Home
Little Ships
Lost Years of Merlin
Mennyms
Merlin
Over Sea, Under Stone
Robin Hood & Little John
Saint George and the Dragon
Secret Garden
Smelly Old History Series
Tales of King Arthur Series
War Boy
Wreck of the Zanzibar

environment (includes ecology and care of the planet)
Alejandro's Gift
Ancient Ones
Bay Shore Park
Big Big Book for Our Planet
Brother Eagle, Sister Sky
Dear Mr. Sprouts
Dear World
Earthdance
Elements Series
Everglades
Giants in the Land
Great Kapok Tree
Green Tales
Here Is the Tropical Rain Forest
Hey! Get Off Our Train
In the Next Three Seconds
Keepers of the Earth
Little House
Lorax
Man Called Raven
Okino and the Whales
Old Turtle
On the Day You Were Born
People Who Hugged Trees
Salamander Room
Someday a Tree
Take Action
Welcome to the Green House
Whaling Days
When the Monkeys Came Back

envy
Earl's Too Cool for Me
Just Rewards
Ruby the Copycat
Weaving of a Dream

Eratosthenes
Librarian Who Measured the Earth

escape
All the Lights in the Night
Barefoot
Beyond the Western Sea
Borrowers
Children of the River
Drinking Gourd
Escape From Slavery
Get on Board
Good Night, Gorilla
Harriet and the Promised Land
I, Houdini
Jip, His Story
Loup Garou
Minty
Nightjohn
Number the Stars
Princess Nevermore
Stone in Water
Sweet Clara and the Freedom Quilt
What Jamie Saw

Europe
Anno's Journey

Everglades
Everglades

exercise
From Head to Toe
Yummers!

extinction
Bone From a Dry Sea
Bone Poems
Will's Mammoth

fables
Fables
Fragile Flag
Hey! Get Off Our Train
Maniac Magee
Misoso
Tortoise and the Hare

faces
Fish Faces
Mrs. Mustard's Baby Faces

fairies
Book of Little Folk
Five Children and It
Little Folk
Velveteen Rabbit
Weaving of a Dream

fairs
Babe, the Gallant Pig
Charlotte's Web
Fair!
That Kookoory!

fairy tales
Arabian Nights: Three Tales
Baba Yaga and Vasalisa the Brave
Blue Fairy Book
Brocaded Slipper and Other Viet-
    namese Tales
Cinder Edna
East O' the Sun and West O' the Moon
If I Were in Charge of the World
Jolly Postman
King's Equal
Korean Cinderella
Ladybird Favorite Tales Series
Lon Po Po
Magic Circle

Mufaro's Beautiful Daughters
Rainbow Fairy Book
Red Riding Hood
Rumplestiltskin
Stinky Cheese Man and Other Fairly
    Stupid Tales
Swan Stories
Telling of the Tales
Tooth Fairy's Tale
Treasury of Princesses

faith
All the Lights in the Night
Always Prayer Shawl
Clown of God
Earthshine
Hershel and the Hannukkah Goblins
Miracle of the Latkes
Noah's Ark
One World, Many Religions
Polar Express
Secret Garden
Virtual War
Where the Red Fern Grows

fame
Enormous Egg
Mr. Popper's Penguins
Nothing But the Truth
When Bluebell Sang

family (Families come in all shapes
    and sizes. Find yours reflected in
    this list.)
A Is for Africa
Adrian Mole Diaries
After the War Was Over
Airmail to the Moon
All the Colors of the Race
All the Places to Love
Allison
All-of-a-Kind Family
Amazing Grace
Amber Brown Is Not a Crayon
Anastasia Krupnik
Angel Child, Dragon Child
Animal Family
Anne Frank: Diary of a Young Girl
Anne of Green Gables
Are You There God? It's Me, Margaret
Baby
Baby Sister for Frances

Barn (Avi)
Baseball Saved Us
Bear's House
Bedtime for Frances
Bee Tree
Belle Prater's Boy
Benny's Pennies
Best Friends for Frances
Birdie's Lighthouse
Blood and Chocolate
Blue Hill Meadows
Book of Changes
Borrowers
Brown Honey in Broomwheat
 Tea
Bunnicula
Bunyans
Calling the Doves
Catherine, Called Birdy
Celebration!
Charlotte's Web
Chasing Redbird
Chester's Way
Chicken Man
Chicken Sunday
Children Just Like Me
Chocolate Fever
Christmas House
Christmas in the Big House, Christ-
 mas in the Quarters
Christmas Miracle of Jonathan
 Toomey
Come a Tide
Cricket in Times Square
Cuckoo's Child
Dakota Dugout
Day With Wilbur Robinson
December Stillness
Dinner at Alberta's
Dinosaurs Divorce
Dragonling
Earrings!
Face on the Milk Carton
Fair!
Family Reunion
Fanny's Dream
Felix's Hat
Five Children and It
Five Live Bongos
Five Minutes Peace
Flip-Flop Girl
Four Story Mistake

Front Porch Stories at the One-Room
 School
Gardener
Gingerbread Doll
Giver
Glass Bottle Tree
Grandmother's Pigeon
Great Gilly Hopkins
Greatest Table
Growing Up in Coal Country
Guess How Much I Love You
Half Magic
Happy Hocky Family
Harriet the Spy
Henry Huggins
Hey World, Here I Am!
High Rise Glorious Skittle Skat Roari-
 ous Sky Pie Angel Food Cake
Homecoming
Homeplace
Honey, I Love and Other Poems
Hooray for Me
House on East 88th Street
Hunting the White Cow
I Am an American
I Am Lavina Cumming
I Feel a Little Jumpy Around You
I Got a Family
I, Houdini
Ice
In Coal Country
In Daddy's Arms I Am Tall
It's a Spoon, Not a Shovel
James and the Giant Peach
Journey
Julius, the Baby of the World
K Is for Kiss Goodnight
Keeping Quilt
Kinship
Knight's Castle
Lassie Come Home
Let's Eat
Let's Talk About It: Adoption
Little Bear
Little Blue and Little Yellow
Little House on the Prairie
Lotus Seed
Louella Mae, She's Run Away!
Ma Dear's Aprons
Mac and Marie and the Train Toss
 Surprise
Make Lemonade

Mama Don't Allow
Mama Is a Miner
Martha Speaks
Marvin's Best Christmas Present Ever
Matilda
Max Makes a Million
Mennyms
Meteor!
Mick Harte Was Here
Missing May
Mississippi Bridge
Mississippi Mud
Misty of Chinocoteague
Monster Mama
Morgan's Dream
Mufaro's Beautiful Daughters
My Dog Never Says Please
My Family Tree
My Father's Dragon
My Grandma Has Black Hair
My Great-Aunt Arizona
My Life With the Wave
Nana Upstairs and Nana Downstairs
Nathaniel Talking
Night Before Christmas
Noisy Nora
Now Let Me Fly
Old Black Fly
Once There Were Giants
Orphan Train Adventures
Outsiders
Owen
Owls in the Family
Ox-Cart Man
Pablo Remembers
Painter
Parents in the Pigpen, Pigs in the Tub
Patchwork Quilt
Peacebound Trains
Peppe the Lamp Lighter
Peter Spier's Rain
Piggybook
Pigs in the Mud in the Middle of the
    Rud
Pioneer Sampler
Place to Call Home
Possum Come a-Knockin'
Prairie Songs
Radiance Descending
Raggly, Scraggly, No-Soap, No-Scrub
    Girl
Rain

Ramona the Pest
Rats Saw God
Red Scarf Girl
Regular Flood of Mishap
Relatives Came
Roll of Thunder, Hear My Cry
Rosalie
Sadako
Sadako and the Thousand Paper
    Cranes
Sarah, Plain and Tall
See You Around, Sam
Sewing Quilts
Shabanu
Shaker Boy
She'll Be Comin' Round the Mountain
Shiloh
Shrinking of Treehorn
Sisters
Skylark
So Much
Solitary Blue
Spinky Sulks
Story About Ping
Story of Babar
Stuart Little
Stupids Step Out
Suitcase Full of Seaweed and other
    Poems
Sun and Spoon
Sylvester and the Magic Pebble
Tae's Sonata
Take Action
Tale of Peter Rabbit
Tales for the Perfect Child
Tales of Trotter Street
Talking Like the Rain
Tar Beach
Tell Me Again About the Night I Was
    Born
Tiger Flowers
Tight Times
Tom and Pippo Books
Too Many Tamales
Tuck Everlasting
Uncle Jed's Barbershop
Under the Blood Red Sun
Van Gogh Cafe
Very Scary
View From the Cherry Tree
Visiting the Art Museum
Wagon

War Boy
Watson's Go to Birmingham, 1963
Wednesday Surprise
Well
What Jamie Saw
What You Know First
When Africa Was Home
When Jo Louis Won the Title
When We Married Gary
Where the Red Fern Grows
World of Christopher Robin
Wreck of the Zanzibar
Wrinkle in Time
You Hold Me and I'll Hold You
Za-Za's Baby Brother
Zeke Pippin
Zel

family history
Children's Book of Kwanzaa
Glory Field
Grandma Essie's Covered Wagon
Homeplace
Journey
New Hope
Patchwork Quilt
Search for the Shadowman
Seven Brave Women
This Land Is My Land
Wish You Were Here
Yonder

family store
Fruit and Vegetable Man
Tae's Sonata

fantasy
5 Novels by Daniel Pinkwater
Alice's Adventures in Wonderland
Animalia
Baby Be-Bop
BFG
Big Bad Bruce
Boggart
Burnt Toast on Davenport Street
Catwings
Charlie and the Chocolate Factory
Chronicles of Narnia
City of Light, City of Dark
Cloudland
Cloudy With a Chance of Meatballs
Courtney

Day With Wilbur Robinson
Daydreamer
Demi's Dragons and Fantastic
    Creatures
Dippers
Discovery of Dragons
Dove Isabeau
Dragonling
Dragon's Blood
Earthsea Quartet
East O' the Sun and West O' the Moon
Elbert's Bad Word
Faith and the Electric Dog
Five Children and It
Golden Compass
Grandmother's Pigeon
Grey King
Gulliver's Adventures in Lilliput
Half Magic
Harvey Potter's Balloon Farm
Hobbit
Hobkin
Hoover's Bride
If . . .
Imogene's Antlers
Indian in the Cupboard
James and the Giant Peach
Lost Years of Merlin
Lunch
Meanwhile . . .
Mennyms
Merlin
Minstrel and the Dragon Pup
Monster Motel
Moonstruck
Mud Pies and Other Recipes
My Father's Dragon
My Life With the Wave
Night Before Christmas
Nutcracker
Over Sea, Under Stone
Princess Nevermore
Prydain Chronicles
Redwall
Rootabaga Stories
Seven-Day Magic
Shoebag
Silver Pony
Tar Beach
Tooth Fairy's Tale
Tuesday
Weaving of a Dream

Weetzie Bat
Well Wished
Where the Wild Things Are
Wing Shop
Wonderful Wizard of Oz
World of Christopher Robin
Young Guinevere

farmers
Babe, the Gallant Pig
Corn Is Maize
Harvey Potter's Balloon Farm
Hill of Fire
Josepha
Old MacDonald Had A Farm
Ornery Morning
Tale of Peter Rabbit
When Bluebell Sang

farming
Corn Is Maize
Indian Winter
Life and Times of the Apple
Life and Times of the Peanut
Tortilla Factory

farms
All the Places to Love
Anne of Green Gables
Babe, the Gallant Pig
Barn (Atwell)
Barnyard Dance!
Big Red Barn
Calling the Doves
Charlotte's Web
Chasing Redbird
Cow Buzzed
Cow that Went Oink
Day Jimmy's Boa Ate the Wash
Donna O'Neeshuck Was Chased By
    Some Cows
Easter Egg Farm
Enormous Egg
Farm Morning
Farmer Duck
Good Times on Grandfather Moun-
    tain
Harvey Potter's Balloon Farm
Hattie and the Fox
Henny Penny
Homeplace
Hunting the White Cow

Ice
Jip, His Story
Josepha
Journey
Midnight Farm
My Hen Is Dancing
Number One Number Fun
Oink
Old MacDonald Had a Farm
On Sally Perry's Farm
Ornery Morning
Out of the Dust
Parents in the Pigpen, Pigs in the Tub
Piggie Pie
Shiloh
Silver Pony
Sitting on the Farm
Stone Fox
Tale of Peter Rabbit
That Kookoory!
Three in a Balloon
Very Busy Spider
What a Wonderful Day to Be a Cow
When Bluebell Sang
Year at Maple Hill Farm
Yonder

fate
Barn (Avi)
Bone Man
Earth-Shattering Poems
William Shakespeare's Macbeth

fathers
All Dads on Deck
Animal Dads
At the Crossroads
Boys Will Be
Everett Anderson's Goodbye
I'll See You When the Moon Is Full
In Daddy's Arms I Am Tall
Julie of the Wolves
More, More, More, Said the Baby
Papa!
Sarah, Plain and Tall
So Much
William's Doll

fathers and daughters
Beyond the Divide
Birdie's Lighthouse
Bone From a Dry Sea

Boundless Grace
Casey at the Bat
Charlie Pippin
Days of the Blackbird
December Stillness
Earthshine
Fantastic Drawings of Danielle
Farm Morning
Hands
I Hadn't Mean to Tell You This
Ice
Kinship
Lily's Crossing
Mailing May
Midnight Hour Encores
Ornery Morning
Out of the Dust
Painter
Papa, Please Get the Moon for Me
Tony's Bread
Van Gogh Cafe
Walk Two Moons
Wednesday Surprise
White Dynamite and Curly
    Kidd
William Shakespeare's Tempest

fathers and sons
Abiyoyo
Ali, Child of the Desert
Barn (Avi)
Big David, Little David
Can't You Sleep, Little Bear?
Edward and the Pirates
Fly Away Home
Golem(Wisniewski)
Golem (Singer)
Guess How Much I Love You
Heroes
Ironman
Jeremy's Decision
Just Like My Dad
Just Me and My Dad
Kite Flier
Leo the Late Bloomer
Rats Saw God
Today I'm Going Fishing With My
    Dad
Wall

fear of flying
First Flight

fear of monsters
Monster Bed
My Mama Says There Aren't Any
    Zombies . . .
Papa!
Scary, Scary Halloween
There's a Nightmare in My Closet

fear of new things
Delphine
Gila Monsters Meet You at the Air-
    port
House for a Hermit Crab
When the Big Dog Barks

fear of separation
I'll See You When the Moon Is Full
Owl Babies

fear of storms
Thunder Cake

fear of strangers
Stone Soup
When the Big Dog Barks

fear of the dark
Camp Ghost Away
Can't You Sleep, Little Bear?
Ghost-Eye Tree
Midnight Farm
Monster Bed
Scary, Scary Halloween
There's a Nightmare in My Closet

fear of water
Blue Skin of the Sea

fear, general
Arthur's Camp-Out
Big Al
Feelings
Grandpa's Face
I Don't Care, Said the Bear
Little Mouse, the Red Ripe Straw-
    berry, and the Big Hungry Bear
Little Toot
Pink and Say
Real-Skin Rubbermonster Mask
Sewing Quilts
Sylvester and the Magic Pebble
Where's My Teddy?

Who Is the Beast?
Zilla Sasparilla and the Mud Baby

feelings, hurt
Luka's Quilt
Spinky Sulks

feet
Barefoot
Dancing Feet
Where Will This Shoe Take You?

festivals
Festivals
Fiesta
Rechenka's Eggs
Yeh-Shen: A Cinderella Story from
    China

fighting
Bull Run
Gladiator
Hobbit
Millions of Cats
Music and Drum
No Fighting, No Biting!
Redwall
Saint George and the Dragon
Westmark

fingerplay
Piggies
Too Many Rabbits

fire
Elements Series
Fire in the Forest
Fire Race
Great Fire

fireflies
Fireflies, Peach Pies & Lullabies
In the Tall, Tall Grass

first grade
First Grade Takes a Test

fish
Big Al
Chickens Aren't the Only Ones
Cinder-Eyed Cats

Fish Faces
Higgins Bend Song and Dance
My Visit to the Aquarium
Smudge
Ten Sly Piranhas

fishing
All Dads on Deck
Blue Skin of the Sea
Higgins Bend Song and Dance
Just Me and My Dad
Today I'm Going Fishing With My
    Dad

fitting in (and the problems of not
    fitting in)
Allison
Badger's Bring Something Party
Beast in Ms. Rooney's Room
Big Al
Blood and Chocolate
Bridge to Terabithia
Children of the River
Forgotten Door
Game of Catch
Heroes
House on East 88th Street
Molly's Pilgrim
Slave Day
Soda Jerk
Staying Fat for Sarah Byrnes
There's a Boy in the Girl's
    Bathroom
View From Sturday
We're Back!
Wombat Divine

floods
Abel's Island
Come a Tide
Noah's Ark

flowers
Birdsong
Empty Pot
Girl Who Loved Wild Horses
Jack's Garden
Linnea in Monet's Garden

flying
Abuela
Catwings

Faith and the Electric Dog
First Flight
Flight
Fly! A Brief History of Flight
Flying Tortoise
Fool of the World and the Flying Ship
Hawk, I'm Your Brother
I'll See You in My Dreams
Tar Beach
Three in a Balloon
Wing Shop

folk art
A Is for Africa
Eight Hands Round
Rechenka's Eggs
When Clay Sings

folklore (includes myths, tales, folktales, and legends)
Acorn Tree & Other Folktales
Adventures of High John the Conqueror
Alice Nizzy Nazzy
All of You Was Singing
Anansi and the Moss-Covered Rock
Arabian Nights
Arabian Nights: Three Tales
Arrow to the Sun
Atalanta's Race
Baba Yaga and Vasalisa the Brave
Baker's Dozen
Big Men, Big Country
Bit by Bit
Black Ships Before Troy
Black Snowman
Blue Fairy Book
Bo Rabbit Smart for True
Bone Man
Book of Little Folk
Brocaded Slipper and Other
 Vietnamese Tales
Caps for Sale
Cat's Purr
Chanukkah in Chelm
Cherokees
City of Light, City of Dark
Clay Boy
Clown of God
Come Look With Me
Coyote
Coyote in Love

Dance of the Sacred Circle
Dancing With the Wind
Dark Thirty
Dark Way
D'Aulaire's Book of Greek Myths
Dawn (Bang)
Demi's Dragons and Fantastic
 Creatures
Don't Count Your Chicks
Dove Isabeau
Down by the River
Dragonflies
Dragonfly's Tale
Eagle's Gift
Earth, Fire, Water, Air
Empty Pot
Fables
Faithful Friend
Feather Merchants
Fiesta
Fin M'Coul, Giant of Knockmany Hill
Fire Children
Fire Race
Flying Tortoise
Folks Call Me Appleseed John
Fool of the World and the Flying Ship
Fortune-Tellers
From Sea to Shining Sea
Giants!
Gift of Wali Dad
Gingerbread Boy
Girl Who Dreamed Only of Geese
Girl Who Loved Caterpillars
Girls to the Rescue
Goddesses, Heroes, and Shamans
Golden Carp and Other Tales from
 Vietnam
Goldilocks and the Three Bears
Golem (Wisniewski)
Golem (Singer)
Golem: A Giant Made of Mud
Grandfather Tang's Story
Great Ball Game
Great Pirate Activity Book
Green Tales
Grey King
Hansel and Gretel
Henny Penny
Her Stories
Here Comes the Storyteller
Hershel and the Hanukkah Goblins
Hired Hand

Hobyahs
In the Beginning
Jack and the Beanstalk
John Henry
Jump!
Just Rewards
Katya's Book of Mushrooms
King Arthur's Camelot
Korean Cinderella
Ladybird Favorite Tales Series
Larger Than Life
Lion's Whiskers
Little Folk
Little Red Ant and the Great Big
    Crumb
Little Red Riding Hood
Lon Po Po
Loup Garou
Magic Fan
Man Called Raven
Man Who Could Call Down Owls
Max and Ruby's First Greek Myth:
    Pandora's Box
Mendel's Ladder
Merlin
Mermaid Tales from Around the
    World
Miro in the Kingdom of the Sun
Misoso
Mitten
Mufaro's Beautiful Daughters
Nine in One Grr! Grr!
Now Let Me Fly
Nursery Tales Around the World
One Grain of Rice
Over Sea, Under Stone
Owl Eyes
Paper Dragon
People Could Fly
People Who Hugged Trees
Phantom Hitchhiker
Pirates Handbook
Punga, the Goddess of Ugly
Rainbow Bridge
Rainbow Fairy Book
Rapunzel
Rattlesnake Dance
Red Riding Hood
Ring of Tricksters
River That Went to the Sky
Robin Hood & Little John
Robin's Country

Rumplestiltskin
Saint George and the Dragon
Saint Patrick and the Peddler
Sally Ann Thunder Ann Whirlwind
    Crockett
Scary Stories to Tell in the Dark
Seven Blind Mice
Short and Shivery
Sleeping Ugly
Small Tall Tale from the Far, Far
    North
Soap! Soap! Don't Forget the Soap!
Something From Nothing
South and North, East and West
Spoon for Every Bite
Strega Nona
Swamp Angel
Swan Stories
Tale of Ali Baba and the Forty
    Thieves
Tale of Rabbit and Coyote
Tales Alive
Tales of King Arthur Series
Tales of Uncle Remus
Talking Eggs
Tatterhood and the Goblins
Telling of the Tales
Thirteen Moons on Turtles Back
Three Billy Goats Gruff
Tom Thumb
Tony's Bread
Tortoise and the Hare
Treasury of Mermaids
Treasury of Princesses
Tree of Dreams
True Lies
True Story of the Three Little Pigs
Tucker Pfeffercorn
Uninvited Guest and Other Jewish
    Holiday Tales
Wanderings of Odysseus
Weaving of a Dream
When Stories Fell Like Shooting Stars
Why Mosquitoes Buzz in People's Ears
World Mythology Series
Worry Stone

folk songs
De Colores
Gonna Sing My Head Off!
Hush Little Baby
Tree in the Wood

folktale variations (twisted and fractured adaptations as well as versions from differing cultures of well-known tales)
Alice Nizzy Nazzy
Baba Yaga and Vasalisa the Brave
Brocaded Slipper and Other Vietnamese Tales
Chicken Little
Chocolate Touch
Cinder Edna
Cinderella's Rat
Each Peach Pear Plum
Fanny's Dream
Girls to the Rescue
How Now Brown Cow
Jolly Postman
Kissing the Witch
Korean Cinderella
Little Red Cowboy Hat
Liza Lou and the Yeller Belly Swamp
Magic Circle
Moonstruck
Mufaro's Beautiful Daughters
Old Mother Hubbard and Her Wonderful Dog
Onstage and Backstage at the Night Owl Theater
Piggie Pie
Robin's Country
Sam and the Tigers
Sleeping Ugly
Sootface
Stinky Cheese Man and Other Fairly Stupid Tales
Talking Eggs
Telling of the Tales
Three Blind Mice Mystery
Three Little Javelinas
Three Little Wolves and the Big Bad Pig
Tucker Pfeffercorn
Yeh-Shen: A Cinderella Story from China
Yo, Hungry Wolf!
Zel

folktales (see: folklore)

food
Baker's Dozen
Bread and Jam for Frances
Bread Is for Eating
Charlie and the Chocolate Factory
Cloudy With a Chance of Meatballs
Corn Is Maize
Eating the Plates
Everybody Cooks Rice
Greatest Table
Green Eggs and Ham
Guests
Happy New Year! King-Hsi Fa-Ts'ai!
Heckedy Peg
Hi, Pizza Man!
Let's Eat
Lunch
Market!
Mouse Mess
Never Take a Pig to Lunch
Of Colors and Things
Oh, No, Toto!
On Market Street
Possum Magic
Science Experiments You Can Eat
Sitting on the Farm
Stone Soup
Teddy Bear's Picnic
To Market, To Market
Today Is Monday
Tortilla Factory
Yummers!

food chain
What Do You Do When Something Wants to Eat You?
When Hunger Calls

fools
Channukah in Chelm
Feather Merchants
Fool of the World and the Flying Ship
Hobyahs
Stupids Step Out

forests
Ancient Ones
Dogteam
Fire in the Forest
Grandfather Twilight
In the Woods: Who's Been Here
Little Red Riding Hood
People Who Hugged Trees
Red Riding Hood
Where's My Teddy?

forgiveness
Ironman
Lilly's Purple Plastic Purse
Out of the Dust

foster homes
Great Gilly Hopkins
Orphan Train Adventures

foxes
Doctor DeSoto
Don't Fidget a Feather
Jump!
Wings: A Tale of Two Chickens
Winter White

France
Good Grisselle
Talking Walls

Frank, Anne
Anne Frank: Beyond the Diary
Anne Frank: Diary of a Young Girl

freedom
Celebration!
Escape From Slavery
Glory Field
Harriet and the Promised Land
Now Let Me Fly
Sweet Clara and the Freedom Quilt
To Be a Slave
Wagon

friendship
5 Novels by Daniel Pinkwater
Adopted by the Eagles
Adventures of Captain Underpants
Adventures of Huckleberry Finn
Adventures of Taxi Dog
Ali, Child of the Desert
All We Needed to Say
Amber Brown Is Not a Crayon
Amber on the Mountain
Amelia's Notebook
Angel Child, Dragon Child
Angel for Solomon Singer
Angelina Ballerina
Animorphs
Annie and the Wild Animals
Annie Bananie
Appelemando's Dreams

Arthur's Pen Pal
Baby Sister for Frances
Badger's Bring Something Party
Badger's Parting Gifts
Bargain for Frances
Be Good to Eddie Lee
Bein' With You This Way
Belle Prater's Boy
Ben and Me
Best Friends for Frances
BFG
Big Al
Blubber
Blue Skin of the Sea
Book of Changes
Borrowers
Boy, a Dog, and a Frog
Bracelet
Brickyard Summer
Bridge to Terabithia
Buffalo Tree
Butterfly Jar
Cat's Purr
Cay
Charlotte's Web
Chasing Redbird
Chester's Way
Chestnut Cove
Chicken Sunday
Children of the River
Chronicles of Narnia
Clown
Cow that Went Oink
Cozy Book
Crash
Cricket in Times Square
Crossing
Culpepper Adventures
Cyber.Kdz Series
Day With Wilbur Robinson
Did You See What I Saw?
Don't Fidget a Feather
Don't Read This Book, Whatever You
    Do
Dragonling
Earl's Too Cool For Me
Egypt Game
Elijah's Angel
Eric Knight's Lassie Come Home
Faithful Friend
Farmer Duck
Feelings

First Grade Takes a Test
Flip-Flop Girl
Freak the Mighty
Friends
Friends and Amigos Series
Frog and Toad Are Friends
Frog in Love
Fun! No Fun!
Gary Paulsen's World of
    Adventure
George & Martha
Gift of Driscoll Lipscomb
Go Away, Dog
Great Gilly Hopkins
Growing Colors
Gulliver's Adventures in Lilliput
Gus and Grandpa
Hannah and Jack
Harriet the Spy
Harris and Me
Henry and Mudge
Henry Huggins
Heroes
Hey World, Here I Am!
Hooray, a Piñata!
House for a Hermit Crab
House on East 88th Street
How to Lose All Your Friends
I Hadn't Mean to Tell You This
I Never Did That Before
If You're Not Here, Please Raise Your
    Hand
Indian in the Cupboard
Iron Dragon Never Sleeps
Ironman
It's a Spoon, Not a Shovel
It's So Nice to Have a Wolf Around
    the House
Jip, His Story
Josepha
Judy Scuppermong
Julie of the Wolves
Kid in the Red Jacket
Kids of the Polk Street School
Let's Be Enemies
Letters From the Inside
Lily's Crossing
Little Blue and Little Yellow
Make a Wish Molly
Make Lemonade
Mangaboom
Maniac Magee

Marvin Redpost: Alone in His
    Teacher's House
Max Makes a Million
May I Bring a Friend?
Meet Danitra Brown
Memoirs of a Bookbat
Metropolitan Cow
Mirette on the High Wire
Miss Rumphius
Miz Berlin Walks
Mouse and Mole and the Year-Round
    Garden
Mouse and the Motorcycle
My Life With the Wave
My Song Is Beautiful
Mysterious Tadpole
Number the Stars
Officer Buckle and Gloria
On My Honor
Outsiders
Pee Wee Scouts series
Pigman
Pink and Say
Pink Paper Swans
Poppleton
Prairie Songs
Ramona the Pest
Rat and the Tiger
Remembering the Good Times
Rolling Store
Ruby the Copycat
Sadako
Sadako and the Thousand Paper
    Cranes
Sally Arnold
Santa Calls
Secret Garden
Shoebag
Sideways Stories From Wayside
    School
Silver Pony
Singer to the Sea God
Skin Deep and other Teenage Reflec-
    tions
Slave Day
Solitary Blue
Somebody Loves You, Mr. Hatch
Staying Fat for Sarah Byrnes
Stepping on the Cracks
Stones in Water
Story of Babar
Tacky the Penguin

Tales of Trotter Street
Teammates
There's a Boy in the Girl's Bathroom
There's a Party at Mona's Tonight
Three Hat Day
Tumble Bumble
Twelve Shots
Under the Blood Red Sun
View From Sturday
Virtual War
Watsons Go to Birmingham, 1963
We Are a Rainbow
Well Wished
When Africa Was Home
Where the Red Fern Grows
Wilfred Gordon McDonald Patridge
Wolfbay Wings
Wonderful Wizard of Oz
World of Christopher Robin
World of Pooh
Worry Stone
Wringer
Year on My Street
Young Larry

frogs
Boy, a Dog, and a Frog
Chickens Aren't the Only Ones
Frogs
Frogs in Clogs
In the Small, Small Pond
Mysterious Tadpole
One Gaping, Wide-Mouthed, Hopping
    Frog
Tuesday
Wide-Mouthed Frog

fruit
Blueberries for Sal
Cherries and Cherry Pits
Eating the Alphabet
Fruit and Vegetable Man
Grey Lady and the Strawberry
    Snatcher
Growing Colors
Lunch
What Am I?

frustration
Allison
Author: A True Story
I Hate English

Monster at the End of this Book
Noisy Nora

funerals
Fireflies, Peach Pies & Lullabies
You Hold Me and I'll Hold You

future
Fortune-Tellers
In the Next Three Seconds
Oh, the Places You'll Go!

Galileo
Starry Messenger

games
Anno's Math Games
Down by the River
Egypt Game
Fun! No Fun!
Great Ball Game
Great Pirate Activity Book
Insides, Outsides, Loops, and Lines
Jumanji
Weekend Was Murder

gangs
Outsiders
Scorpions (Myers Spotlight)
Voices From the Fields

gardeners
Carrot Seed
Elbert's Bad Word
Gardener

gardening
Alison's Zinnia
Carrot Seed
Empty Pot
From Seed to Plant
Gardener
Green Truck Garden Giveaway
It's Pumpkin Time!
Jack's Garden
Life and Times of the Honeybee
Miss Rumphius
Mouse and Mole and the Year-Round
    Garden
On Sally Perry's Farm
Seedfolks
Tales Alive

Teeny Weeny Zucchinis
Too Many Pumpkins
Tops and Bottoms
What About Ladybugs?

gardens
Gardener
Growing Colors
I Wish I Were a Butterfly
Jack's Garden
Linnea in Monet's Garden
Oliver's Vegetables
On Sally Perry's Farm
Secret Garden
Seedfolks
Snail's Spell
Summer of Stanley

gargoyles
Good Griselle

gay and lesbian
Am I Blue?
Baby Be-Bop
Damned Strong Love
Earthshine
Kissing the Witch

geese
Dawn (Bang)
Don't Fidget a Feather
Rechenka's Eggs

gender roles
Amazing Grace
Arthur's Pen Pal
Girl Who Loved Caterpillars
Girls to the Rescue
Mama Is a Miner
Max
Paper Bag Princess, The
Piggybook
William's Doll

genealogy
Homeplace
My Family Tree
Search for the Shadowman
Seven Brave Women

generosity
Baker's Dozen

Gardener
Gift of Wali Dad
Peppermint Race

geography
Anno's Journey
Around the World in a Hundred Years
As the Crow Flies
Away From Home
Bunyans
Circling the Globe
Fire Children
Geography From A to Z
How to Make an Apple Pie and See
    the World
Learning to Swim in Swaziland
Librarian Who Measured the Earth
Life and Times of the Peanut
Livingstone Mouse
Monarchs
My House Has Stars
My Visit to the Zoo
Paddle-to-the-Sea
Puzzle Maps USA
Sacred Places
Silver Pony
Skip Across the Ocean
Somewhere in the World Right
    Now
South and North, East and West
Wish You Were Here

geology
Caves and Caverns

Germany
Damned Strong Love
Devil's Arithmetic
Rumplestiltskin
Talking Walls

germs
Cow Buzzed

getting dressed (see: dressing)

getting even (see: revenge)

ghosts
Boggart
Dark Way
Ghost-Eye Tree

Headless Haunt and Other African-
    American Ghost Stories
Rattlebone Rock
Scary, Scary Halloween
Tog the Ribber, or Granny's Tale

giants
Abiyoyo
BFG
Delphine
Fin M'Coul, Giant of Knockmany Hill
Giant
Giants!
Jack and the Beanstalk
Mangaboom

gifted child
Anastasia Krupnik
Archibald Frisby
Barn (Avi)
Boggart
Bridge to Terabithia
City of Gold and Lead
Earthsea Quartet
Eva
Forgotten Door
Freak the Mighty
Girl Who Loved Caterpillars
Giver
Great Gilly Hopkins
Homecoming
I Am the Cheese
Matilda
Midnight Hour Encores
Nate the Great
Remembering the Good Times
Roll of Thunder, Hear My Cry
Sweet Clara and the Freedom Quilt
View From Sturday
What Hearts
Wrinkle in Time

gifts (includes presents)
Arthur's Christmas Cookies
Badger's Bring Something Party
Badger's Parting Gifts
Birthday for Frances
Birthday Surprises
Chicken Sunday
Clown of God
Company's Coming
Delphine

Gift of Wali Dad
How Big Is a Foot?
Josepha
Looking for Atlantis
Madeline
Marvin's Best Christmas Present Ever
Mr. Popper's Penguins
Mr. Rabbit and the Lovely Present
Night Before Christmas
Papa, Please Get the Moon for Me
Polar Express
Star Mother's Youngest Child
Wednesday Surprise
Welcoming Babies
Whale's Song
Wilfred Gordon McDonald Partridge

girls (Shhhhh! Girls Only)
It's a Girl Thing

girls, strong (girls as spirited charac-
    ters showing determination, self-
    reliance, and/or courage)
Airmail to the Moon
Alice's Adventures in Wonderland
Amazing Grace
Amber Brown Is Not a Crayon
Amber on the Mountain
American Girl Series
Anastasia Krupnik
Anne Frank: Diary of a Young Girl
Anne of Green Gables
Atalanta's Race
Ballad of Lucy Whipple
Beyond the Divide
BFG
Birdie's Lighthouse
Bone From a Dry Sea
Bootsie Barker Bites
Boundless Grace
Brave Irene
Captain Abdul's Pirate School
Casey at the Bat
Cat Running
Catherine, Called Birdy
Charlie Drives the Stage
Charlie Pippin
Chasing Redbird
Chester's Way
Children of the River
Cinder Edna
Dance, Tanya

Dawn (Bang)
Dear America Series
Delphine
Earthshine
Eloise
Eva
Forestwife
Fragile Flag
Gentleman and the Kitchen Maid
Girl Named Disaster
Girl Who Loved Caterpillars
Girls to the Rescue
Golden Compass
Her Stories
Homecoming
I Am Lavina Cumming
I'll See You in My Dreams
Illyrian Adventure
Imogene's Antlers
Ironman
Island of the Blue Dolphins
Jojo's Flying Side Kick
Julie of the Wolves
Julius, the Baby of the World
King's Equal
Library
Lilly's Purple Plastic Purse
Lily's Crossing
Little Red Riding Hood
Little Ships
Liza Lou and the Yeller Belly Swamp
Lon Po Po
Madeline
Maggie B
Mary Wolf
Matilda
Meet Danitra Brown
Memoirs of a Bookbat
Midnight Hour Encores
Mirette on the High Wire
Miro in the Kingdom of the Sun
Morning Girl
Nanta's Lion
Neil Nuggett and the Cow Caper
Nicholas Pipe
Once There Were Giants
Out of the Dust
Paper Bag Princess, The
People Who Hugged Trees
Place to Call Home
Princess Nevermore
Roll of Thunder, Hear My Cry

Rose Blanche
Sally Ann Thunder Ann Whirlwind
   Crockett
Saving Sweetness
Secret Garden
Shabanu
Sing, Sophie!
Singer to the Sea God
Sleeping Ugly
Spite Fences
Stephanie's Ponytail
Tatterhood and the Goblins
True Confessions of Charlotte Doyle
Virtual War
Well Wished
Wonderful Wizard of Oz
Wreck of the Zanzibar
Young Guinevere
Zee

goats
Christmas Tree Tangle
One Night
Summer of Stanley
Three Billy Goats Gruff

God
Creation
Old Turtle
One Wintry Night

good deeds
Brave Irene
Miracle of the Latkes
Silver Pony

good vs. evil
Angela and Diabola
Animorphs
BFG
Chronicles of Narnia
City of Gold and Lead
Devil's Arithmetic
Golden Compass
Grey King
Hobbit
Hobyahs
Lost Years of Merlin
Over Sea, Under Stone
Santa Calls
Sootface
Witches

government
Buck Stops Here
History of the US
I Am the Cheese
Look Out Washington, DC!
Money, Money, Money
Young John Quincy

grandfathers
Cowboy Country
Day With Wilbur Robinson
Grandad Bill's Song
Jojo's Flying Side Kick
Lili Backstage
Looking for Atlantis
Oliver's Vegetables
Radiance Descending
Rolling Store
Stone Fox
Suitcase Full of Seaweed and other
    Poems
Supergrandpa
Tomas and the Library Lady
Wall

grandfathers and granddaughters
Grandpa's Face
Sweet Words So Brave
Waiting for the Whales
When Jo Louis Won the Title
When Zaydeh Danced on Eldridge
    Street

grandfathers and grandsons
Always Prayer Shawl
Charlie and the Chocolate Factory
Dawn (Shulevitz)
Day's Work
Grandfather's Journey
Gus and Grandpa
Journey
War with Grandpa

grandmothers
Abuela
Amazing Grace
Babushka Baba Yaga
Bone Man
Boundless Grace
Bunny Money
Cadillac
Chicken Sunday

Coming Home
Dear Rebecca, Winter Is Here
Girl Named Disaster
Glass Bottle Tree
Grandma Essie's Covered Wagon
Grandmother's Nursery Rhymes
Grandmother's Pigeon
Hannah and Jack
Homecoming
Ice
Lily's Crossing
Little Red Riding Hood
Lotus Seed
More, More, More, Said the Baby
My Grandma Has Black Hair
Nana Upstairs and Nana Downstairs
Napping House
Oh, No, Toto!
Old Pig
One Night
Our Granny
Patchwork Quilt
Pigs in the Mud in the Middle of the Rud
Possum Magic
Red Riding Hood
So Much
Tog the Ribber, or Granny's Tale
Train to Grandma's
Whale's Song
Witches

grandmothers and granddaughters
Annie and the Old One
Fox Song
I Like the Music
Little Red Cowboy Hat
Luka's Quilt
Thunder Cake
Wednesday Surprise
Wish You Were Here

grandmothers and grandsons
Bats About Baseball
Boy and the Cloth of Dreams
William's Doll

grandparents
Grandmother Bryant's Pocket
Homeplace
Missing May
Sun and Spoon
Walk Two Moons

grasshoppers
James and the Giant Peach

graveyards
Corpses, Coffins, and Crypts
Rattlebone Rock

Great Plains (Canada)
Josepha

greed
Chocolate Touch
Clay Boy
Dragon's Robe
Just Rewards
Mufaro's Beautiful Daughters
Tale of Ali Baba and the Forty
    Thieves
Weaving of a Dream

Greek mythology
Atalanta's Race
Black Ships Before Troy
D'Aulaire's Book of Greek Myths
Greek News
Max and Ruby's First Greek Myth:
    Pandora's Box
Wanderings of Odysseus

grief
Baby
Badger's Parting Gifts
Bridge to Terabithia
Chasing Redbird
Christmas Miracle of Jonathan
    Toomey
Cuckoo's Child
Fireflies, Peach Pies & Lullabies
Flip-Flop Girl
I'll Always Love You
Jim's Dog Muffins
Missing May
Nathaniel Talking
Old Pig
Pigman
Remembering the Good Times
Sarah, Plain and Tall
Sun and Spoon
Tenth Good Thing About Barney
Tiger Flowers
Toby
Tough Boris

Walk Two Moons
Wall
You Hold Me and I'll Hold You

growing up
All-of-a-Kind Family
Arthur's Honey Bear
Cool Salsa
Invisible Ladder
It's Perfectly Normal
Look to the North
Once There Were Giants
Owen
When I Was Little

guessing (books that allow the reader
    to guess what is hiding or coming
    next)
Away From Home
Christmas Alphabet
Colors Around Us
Everyday Mysteries
Eye Spy: A Mysterious Alphabet
Guess What?
In the Next Three Seconds
Is Your Mama a Llama?
Mac and Marie and the Train Toss
    Surprise
Mysteries of Harris Burdick
Of Colors and Things
Once There Was a Bull . . . (Frog)
Peck Slither and Slide
Rumplestiltskin
Shortcut
What Am I?
What's What?
Where Does It Go?
Where's Spot
Yikes! Your Body Up Close
Z Was Zapped

guilt
Chasing Redbird
Fish in His Pocket
Killing Mr. Griffin
On My Honor

Gullah
Bo Rabbit Smart for True

guns
Twelve Shots

habitats
All About Alligators
And So They Build
Beaver at Long Pond
Birdsong
Gray Wolf, Red Wolf
House Is a House for Me
How to Be a Nature Detective
In the Woods: Who's Been Here
Inside the Amazing Amazon
Is This a House for Hermit Crab?
Livingstone Mouse
Lizard in the Sun
My Visit to the Zoo
Those Amazing Ants
When I'm Sleepy
When the Monkeys Came Back

hair
Rapunzel
Stephanie's Ponytail

Halloween
By the Light of the Halloween Moon
Halloween ABC
House That Drac Built
It's Pumpkin Time!
Old Devil Wind
Rattlebone Rock
Scary, Scary Halloween
See You Around, Sam
Seven Spiders Spinning
Six Creepy Sheep
Velcome!
Very Scary
When the Goblins Came Knocking
Who Said Boo?

hamsters
I, Houdini

Hancock, John
Will You Sign Here, John Hancock?

handicaps (includes disabilities)
Acorn People
Author: A True Story
Barn (Avi)
Be Good to Eddie Lee
Bee Tree
Freak the Mighty
View From Sturday

Hanukkah
All the Lights in the Night
Chanukkah in Chelm
Christmas Menorahs
Elijah's Angel
Hershel and the Hanukkah Goblins
Miracle of the Latkes
One Yellow Daffodil
Uninvited Guest and Other Jewish
    Holiday Tales

hardship
Beyond the Divide
Earth-Shattering Poems
Eric Knight's Lassie Come Home
Glory Field
Growing Up in Coal Country
Mississippi Mud
Out of the Dust
Peacebound Trains
Red Scarf Girl
Skylark
Stones in Water
Sworn Enemies
Tight Times
Way West

Harlem
Coming Home
Glory Field
Harlem
Sweet Words So Brave

harvest
It's Pumpkin Time!
Teeny Weeny Zucchinis
Tops and Bottoms

hats
500 Hats of Bartholomew Cubbins
Caps for Sale
Felix's Hat
Finster Frets
This Is the Hat
Three Hat Day
Three-Legged Cat

Hawaii
Blue Skin of the Sea
Last Princess
Luka's Quilt
Under the Blood Red Sun

healing (alternative medicine)
Forestwife
Grandmother Bryant's Pocket
Katya's Book of Mushrooms
Magic Circle
Miro in the Kingdom of the Sun

health
Body Atlas
Cow Buzzed
In the Next Three Seconds
It's a Girl Thing
It's Perfectly Normal

herbs
Forestwife
Grandmother Bryant's Pocket

heroes
Art Dog
Black Ships Before Troy
Come Look With Me
D'Aulaire's Book of Greek
    Myths
Flight
Heroes
Homer Price
John Henry
My Fellow Americans
Prydain Chronicles
Robin's Country
Santa Calls
Tales of King Arthur Series
Westmark

hibernation
Straight From the Bear's
    Mouth
Time to Sleep

hiding
By the Great Horn Spoon
Do You See a Mouse?
Number the Stars
Where's Spot

Hispanic
Chato's Kitchen
Cool Salsa
Three Little Javelinas
Tomas and the Library Lady
Too Many Tamales

history, 16th century
Around the World in a Hundred Years
Smelly Old History Series

history, 19th century
Beyond the Western Sea
Charles Dickens: Man Who Had Great
    Expectations
Smelly Old History Series
Sworn Enemies
True Confessions of Charlotte Doyle

history, early 20th century
Illyrian Adventure

history, the Age of Exploration
Follow the Dream

history, general (includes world spe-
    cific, not U.S. specific)
Circling the Globe
Corpses, Coffins, and Crypts
Fly! A Brief History of Flight
Goddesses, Heroes, and Shamans
Golden Carp and Other Tales from
    Vietnam
Great Pirate Activity Book
In the Beginning . . .
Kingfisher Book of the Ancient
    World
Kingfisher Illustrated History of the
    World
Life and Times of the Apple
Life and Times of the Peanut
Misoso
Mistakes That Worked
One World, Many Religions
Piece of String Is a Wonderful Thing
Pirates Handbook
Red Scarf Girl
River That Went to the Sky
Secret Code Book
Silk Route
Where Will This Shoe Take You?
World Mythology Series

history, medieval times
Castle Builder
Catherine, Called Birdy
Forestwife
Knight's Castle
Magic Circle

Robin's Country
Rumplestiltskin
Strega Nona
Young Guinevere
Zel

history, pre-history
Bone From a Dry Sea
Discovering the Iceman

history, the Renaissance
Clown of God
Rapunzel

history, World War II
Anne Frank: Beyond the Diary
Anne Frank: Diary of a Young Girl
Blitzcat
Cay
Damned Strong Love
Little Ships
Number the Stars
Rose Blanche
Stones in Water
Talking Peace
Under the Blood Red Sun
War Boy

Hmong
Nine in One Grr! Grr!

hockey
Wolfbay Wings

holidays
Celebration!
Celebrations
Festivals
Fiesta
Kids of the Polk Street School
Three Bears Holiday Rhyme
    Book
Uninvited Guest and Other Jewish
    Holiday Tales

Holocaust, the
Anne Frank: Beyond the Diary
Anne Frank: Diary of a Young Girl
Damned Strong Love
Devil's Arithmetic
One Yellow Daffodil
Rose Blanche

home
Abel's Island
Amelia's Road
And So They Build
Children Just Like Me
Clown
Dakota Dugout
Fly Away Home
Forgotten Door
Hobkin
Is This a House for Hermit
    Crab?
Little House
Make Way for Ducklings
My Place in Space
One More River
Painter
Richard Scarry's Busy Town
Smudge
Sod Houses on the Great Plains
Town Mouse, Country Mouse
War with Grandpa
Way Home
When the Whippoorwill Calls
Wing Shop
Wonderful Wizard of Oz

homelessness
Baby
Cat Running
Children of the Dust Bowl
Clown
Crossing
Darnell Rock Reporting
December Stillness
Fly Away Home
Homecoming
Maniac Magee
Mary Wolf
Way Home

homesickness
Camp Ghost Away
Cloudland
When Africa Was Home
Wing Shop

honesty (see: truth)

honey
Life and Times of the Honeybee
World of Pooh

hope
Cuckoo's Child
Lotus Seed
Old Turtle
Stones in Water

hopes (see: yearning)

horror
Blood and Chocolate
Complete Stories and Poems of Poe
Dark Thirty
Fate Totally Worse Than Death
Headless Haunt and Other African-
    American Ghost Stories
Horror Stories
House With a Clock in Its Walls
Psychzone: Kidzilla and other Tales
Scary Stories to Tell in the Dark
Short and Shivery
Uncanny

horses
Cowboy Country
Dance of the Sacred Circle
Girl Who Loved Wild Horses
Just Like My Dad
King of the Wind
Misty of Chincoteague
Neil Nuggett and the Cow Caper
Paul Revere's Ride
Silver Pony
Sweetwater Run
They're Off!

hospitals
Happy Birth Day
I'll See You in My Dreams
Madeline

hotels
Do You See a Mouse?
Eloise

houses
House Is a House for Me
Little House
My House Has Stars
Tales of Trotter Street

Hughes, Langston
Coming Home

human body
Body Atlas
Dem Bones
Discovering the Iceman
It's Perfectly Normal
My Map Book
Yikes! Your Body Up Close

humor
Adventures of Huckleberry Finn
Airmail to the Moon
Alpha Beta Chowder
Alphabet From Z to A (with Much
    Confusion Along the Way)
Amber Brown Is Not a Crayon
Amelia Bedelia
Amelia's Notebook
Angelina Ballerina
Are You There God? It's Me,
    Margaret
Art Dog
Arthur's Camp-Out
Aunt Nancy and Old Man Trouble
Author's Day
Bats About Baseball
Best of Michael Rosen
Big Bazoohley
Blue Hat, Green Hat
Bumps in the Night
Bunnicula
Bunny Money
Bunyans
Busy Buzzing Bumblebees
Butterfly Jar
By the Great Horn Spoon
Cadillac
Captain Abdul's Pirate School
Channukah in Chelm
Chato's Kitchen
Chester's Way
Chicken Soup, Boots
Chocolate Moose for Dinner
Classic Poems to Read Aloud
Company's Coming
Complete Nonsense of Edward Lear
Day Jimmy's Boa Ate the Wash
Day With Wilbur Robinson
Dear Dr. Sillybear
Dear Mr. Blueberry
Doctor DeSoto
Dogzilla
Don Quixote

Donna O'Neeshuck Was Chased By
    Some Cows
Don't Laugh, Joe
Earl's Too Cool For Me
Elbert's Bad Word
Eloise
Fate Totally Worse Than Death
Feather Merchants
Felix's Hat
Finster Frets
Fortune-Tellers
Froggy Gets Dressed
From the Mixed-Up Files of Mrs. Basil
    E. Frankweiler
George & Martha
Go Hang a Salami! I'm a Lasagna
    Hog!
Good, the Bad, and the Goofy
Happy Hocky Family
Henry Huggins
Here Come the Aliens
Hey! Get Off Our Train
Higgins Bend Song and Dance
Hilary Knight's Twelve Days of
    Christmas
Hippos Go Berserk
Hole Is to Dig
Homer Price
Hoover's Bride
How Now Brown Cow
If I Were in Charge of the World
Imogene's Antlers
In the Driver's Seat
It's a Spoon, Not a Shovel
Julius, the Baby of the World
Kid in the Red Jacket
Library
Lives of the Athletes
Lives of the Musicians
Lives of the Writers
Livingstone Mouse
Martha Speaks
Marvin Redpost: Alone in His
    Teacher's House
Math Curse
Max
May I Bring a Friend?
Mean Margaret
Mick Harte Was Here
Minerva Louise at School
Monster at the End of this Book
Monster Bed

Mouse and the Motorcycle
Mrs. Mustard's Baby Faces
Mrs. Piggle-Wiggle
My Grandma Has Black Hair
My Mama Says There Aren't Any
    Zombies . . .
Never Take a Pig to Lunch
Officer Buckle and Gloria
Oink
Old Black Fly
Old Man and His Door
Old Mother Hubbard and Her Won-
    derful Dog
Once There Was a Bull . . . (Frog)
Our Granny
Owls in the Family
Papa, Please Get the Moon for Me
Phantom Tollbooth
Piggie Pie
Possum Come a-Knockin'
Ramona the Pest
Rat and the Tiger
Rats on the Range and Other Stories
Red Racer
Rootabaga Stories
Sad Underwear and other
    Complications
Santa's Short Suit Shrunk and Other
    Christmas Tongue Twisters
Saving Sweetness
Scared Silly
Seven Spiders Spinning
Shiloh
Shoebag
Shrinking of Treehorn
Sideways Stories From Wayside
    School
Snake Is Totally Tail
Soap! Soap! Don't Forget the Soap!
Something Big Has Been Here
Squash and a Squeeze
Stinky Cheese Man and Other Fairly
    Stupid Tales
Stupids Step Out
Suddenly!
Tales for the Perfect Child
Tales of Uncle Remus
Tell Me Again About the Night I Was
    Born
Ten Little-Known Facts About Hippos
Ten Sly Piranhas
There's a Boy in the Girls' Bathroom

Three Stories You Can Read to Your
    Dog
Three-Legged Cat
To Market, To Market
True Story of the Three Little
    Pigs
Until I Met Dudley
Walking the Bridge of Your Nose
Watsons Go to Birmingham, 1963
Weetzie Bat
Weighty Word Book
We're Back!
Where the Sidewalk Ends
Wide-Mouthed Frog
Witch Way to the Country
Witches
Yummers!

humor, adolescent
Adventures of Captain Underpants
Culpepper Adventures
Harris and Me
Velcome!

humor, gross
Bugs! (Greenberg)
Grossology
How to Eat Fried Worms
My Little Sister Ate One Hare
Slugs
Smelly Old History Series
Yikes! Your Body Up Close

hunger
Annie and the Wild Animals
Greatest Table
Piggie Pie
Stone Soup
Very Hungry Caterpillar
When Hunger Calls

hunters
Adopted by the Eagles
Animal Family
Story of Babar

hunting
Deathwatch
Forestwife
Indian Winter
Nanta's Lion
Where the Red Fern Grows

Idaho
Mailing May

Iliad
Black Ships Before Troy

illness
Barn
Brave Irene
Chocolate Fever
Days of the Blackbird
Dippers
Earthshine
Fireflies, Peach Pies & Lullabies
I'll See You in My Dreams
Indian Winter
Madeline
Miro in the Kingdom of the Sun
Patchwork Quilt
Sadako
Sadako and the Thousand Pager
    Cranes
Secret Garden
Tiger Garden
Tiger Flowers
Velveteen Rabbit
Wilma Unlimited

illustrators
From Pictures to Words
How a Book Is Made
In Flight With David McPhail
Speak!

imagination (these titles tweak a
    child's imagination, showing no
    end to the possibilities of fantasy,
    pretending, and/or original
    thinking)
Abuela
Amazing Grace
And to Think That I Saw It on
    Mulberry Street
Appelemando's Dreams
As the Crow Flies
Bears's House
Before I Go to Sleep
BFG
Big David, Little David
Castle Builder
Cherries and Cherry Pits
Cinder-Eyed Cats

Daydreamer
Earthdance
Edward and the Pirates
Fantastic Drawings of Danielle
Follow the Dream
Freak the Mighty
Frederick
Harold and the Purple Crayon
Here Come the Aliens
Hi, Pizza Man!
House Is House for Me
I Like Books
I Want to Be
If . . .
Incredible Ned
Is That You, Winter?
John Patrick Norman McHennessy,
   Boy Who Was Always Late
June Is a Tune Jumps on a Stair
Lizard in the Sun
Masai and I
Meanwhile . . .
Monster Motel
Mr. Rabbit and the Lovely Present
My Mama Says There Aren't Any
   Zombies . . .
Mysteries of Harris Burdick
On Market Street
On Sally Perry's Farm
Phantom Tollbooth
R. E. M.
Rootabaga Stories
Roxaboxen
Runaway Bunny
Secret Garden
She'll Be Comin' Round the
   Mountain
Shoebag
Sing, Sophie!
Snail's Spell
Stories From Firefly Island
Tar Beach
Tog the Ribber, or Granny's
   Tale
Tooth Fairy's Tale
Tuesday
Until I Met Dudley
Voyage to the Bunny Planet
Weighty Word Book
When I'm Sleepy
Whittler's Tale
Will's Mammoth

World of Pooh
Would You Rather . . . ?

immigration (includes emigration)
All the Lights in the Night
Always Prayer Shawl
Angel Child, Dragon Child
Beyond the Western Sea
Children of the River
Grandfather's Journey
History of the US
I Am an American
I Hate English
If Your Name Was Changed at Ellis
   Island
Josepha
Keeping Quilt
Lotus Seed
Make a Wish Molly
Molly's Pilgrim
New Hope
Peacebound Trains
Peppe the Lamp Lighter
Seedfolks
Soon, Annala
Who Belongs Here?

Incas
Miro in the Kingdom of the
   Sun

incest
I Hadn't Meant to Tell You This

independence
Blood and Chocolate
Catherine, Called Birdy
Eeny, Meeny, Miney Mole
I Can
Miss Rumphius
Roll of Thunder, Hear My Cry
Story About Ping

India
Buddha
Gift of Wali Dad
One Grain of Rice
People Who Hugged Trees
Rikki-Tikki-Tavi
Seven Blind Mice
Story of Little Babaji
Talking Walls

Indiana
Floating House

individuality
All the Colors of the Race
All the Places to Love
All We Needed to Say
Archibald Frisby
Boy Who Dreamed of an Acorn
Brown Honey in Broomwheat Tea
Carrot Seed
Chicken Soup, Boots
Cinder Edna
Cow that Went Oink
Daydreamer
Eeny, Meeny, Miney Mole
Emily
Everybody Needs a Rock
Fantastic Drawings of Danielle
First Grade Takes a Test
Girl Who Loved Caterpillars
Giver
Harvey Potter's Balloon Farm
Hip Cat
Jeremy's Decision
Lily's Crossing
Maniac Magee
Memoirs of a Bookbat
Miss Rumphius
My Grandma Has Black Hair
Oh, the Places You'll Go!
Oliver Button Is a Sissy
Orphan Train Adventures
Sisters
Story of Ferdinand
Tacky the Penguin
Tatterhood and the Goblins
Three Hat Day
Town Mouse, Country Mouse
Wonderful Towers of Watts

Indonesia
Komodo

infinity
Zoom

insects
Bay Shore Park
Bugs (Parker)
Dragonflies
Fire Race

Girl Who Loved Wild Horses
Hush! A Thai Lullaby
I Wish I Were a Butterfly
Jack's Garden
Joyful Noise
My Visit to the Zoo
Nuts to You
Old Black Fly
Shoebag
Turtle in July
Very Quiet Cricket
What About Ladybugs?
Where's That Insect?
Why Mosquitoes Buzz in People's Ears
Wind Says Goodnight

internet
Cyber.Kdz Series
Search for the Shadowman

internment, Japanese (see: captivity)

Inuit
Eagle's Gift
Girl Who Dreamed Only of Geese
Julie of the Wolves
On Mother's Lap
Seasons and Someone
Small Tall Tale from the Far, Far
   North

invasion
Animorphs
City of Gold and Lead

inventions
Ben and Me
Fly! A Brief History of Flight
Made in China
Mistakes That Worked
Piece of String Is a Wonderful Thing
Real McCoy
Way Things Work

Ireland
Beyond the Western Sea
Fin M'Coul, Giant of Knockmany Hill
Saint Patrick and the Peddler

Irish Americans
Ten Mile Day and the Building of the
   Transcontinental Railroad

islands
Abel's Island
Island of the Blue Dolphins
Last Princess
William Shakespeare's Tempest

Israel
All the Lights in the Night
Chicken Man
Neve Shalom Wahat Al-Salam: Oasis
    of Peace
One More River
Talking Walls

Italy
Clown of God
Days of the Blackbird
Rome Antics
Saint Francis
Starry Messenger
Stones in Water
Strega Nona
Tony's Bread

ivory
Sato and the Elephants

Jamaica
Chalk Doll

Japan
Allison
Bamboo Hats and a Rice Cake
Girl Who Loved Caterpillars
Grandfather's Journey
Grass Sandals
How My Parents Learned to Eat
Magic Fan
Okino and the Whales
Sadako
Sadako and the Thousand Paper
    Cranes
Sato and the Elephants
Tree of Cranes

Japanese American
Baseball Saved Us
Bracelet
Grandfather's Journey
Heroes
I Am an American

Pink Paper Swans
Under the Blood Red Sun

jazz
Ben's Trumpet
Hip Cat
Jazz: My Music, My People
Mysterious Thelonious

jealousy
Birthday for Frances
Cat's Purr
Feelings
Julius, the Baby of the World
Lion Named Shirley Williamson
Madeline
New Baby
Noel the First
Noisy Nora
On Mother's Lap
Peter's Chair

Jesus
Close Your Eyes So You Can See
One Wintry Night
Santa's Favorite Story

jewelry
Earrings!
String of Beads

Jews
All the Lights in the Night
Always Prayer Shawl
Anne Frank: Diary of a Young Girl
Chanukkah in Chelm
Chicken Man
Damned Strong Love
Devil's Arithmetic
Golem (Wisniewski)
Golem (Singer)
Golem: A Giant Made of Mud
Hershel and the Hanukkah Goblins
Keeping Quilt
Make a Wish Molly
Miracle of the Latkes
Molly's Pilgrim
Neve Shalom Wahat Al-Salam: Oasis
    of Peace
Number the Stars
One More River
One Yellow Daffodil

Sworn Enemies
When Zaydeh Danced on Eldridge
    Street

jobs
Adventures of High John the
    Conqueror
After the War Was Over
Amelia Bedelia
Art Dog
At the Crossroads
Bats About Baseball
Bill Peet: An Autobiography
Bread Is for Eating
Chicken Man
Chicken Soup, Boots
Christmas in the Big House, Christ-
    mas in the Quarters
Cinder Edna
Clown of God
Country Bunny and the Little Gold
    Shoes
Cowboy Country
Day of Ahmed's Secret
Day's Work
El Chino
Farmer Duck
Fly Away Home
Frank and Ernest
Fruit and Vegetable Man
Growing Up in Coal Country
Harvey Slumfenburger's Christmas
    Present
Help Wanted
I Want to Be a Dancer
I Want to Be a Veterinarian
In Coal Country
In Daddy's Arms I Am Tall
Jeremy's Decision
John Henry
Ma Dear's Aprons
Mama Is a Miner
Market!
Max Makes a Million
Mike Mulligan & His Steam Shovel
One More River
Omery Morning
Ox-Cart Man
Painter
Paperboy
Peppe the Lamp Lighter
Piggybook

Real McCoy
Red Scarf Girl
Richard Scarry's Busy Town
Richard Scarry's What Do People Do
    All Day?
Soda Jerk
Tae's Sonata
Ten Mile Day and the Building of the
    Transcontinental Railroad
Tight Times
Tortilla Factory
Uncle Jed's Barbershop
Very Busy Spider
Voices From the Fields
Working Cotton
Workson
Yeh-Shen: A Cinderella Story from
    China
Young Larry

journals (see: diaries)

journeys
17 Kings & 42 Elephants
Alice's Adventures in Wonderland
All the Lights in the Night
Anno's Journey
Around the World in a Hundred Years
As the Crow Flies
Cinder-Eyed Cats
Eagle's Gift
Earthshine
Eleanor
Eric Knight's Lassie Come Home
Folks Call Me Appleseed John
Girl Named Disaster
Girl Who Dreamed Only of Geese
Grandfather's Journey
Grass Sandals
Homecoming
I Am the Cheese
Illyrian Adventure
Indian Winter
Lost Years of Merlin
Midnight Hour Encores
Miss Rumphius
Mufaro's Beautiful Daughters
Oh, the Places You'll Go!
Paddle-to-the-Sea
Phantom Tollbooth
Polar Express
Prydain Chronicles

R. E. M.
Rome Antics
Saint Patrick and the Peddler
Silk Route
Singer to the Sea God
Skylark
Small Tall Tale from the Far, Far
      North
True Confessions of Charlotte Doyle
Walk Two Moons
Wanderings of Odysseus
Way West
Where the Wild Things Are
Wonderful Wizard of Oz
Would You Rather . . . ?

joy
Eagle's Gift
Feelings

Judaism
All-of-a-Kind Family
Always Prayer Shawl
Elijah's Angel
Golem (Singer)
Miracle of the Latkes
Something From Nothing
Uninvited Guest and Other Jewish
      Holiday Tales
When Zaydeh Danced on Eldridge
      Street

judging (as in judging others)
Company's Coming
Courtney
Earl's Too Cool for Me
Memoirs of a Bookbat
Mufaro's Beautiful Daughters
Slave Day
Supergrandpa

juggling
Clown of God

jumping rope
A My Name Is Alice
Down by the River

jungles
17 Kings & 42 Elephants
Amazon Diary
Inside the Amazing Amazon

Jumanji
Who Is the Beast?

kangaroos
Is Your Mama a Llama?
World of Pooh

kibbutz
Chicken Man
One More River

kidnapping
Face on the Milk Carton
Sworn Enemies
Tuck Everlasting
Whipping Boy

kindergarten
Big David, Little David
Miss Bindergarten Gets Ready for
      Kindergarten

kindness
Country Bunny and the Little Gold
      Shoes
Days of the Blackbird
Dragonfly's Tale
Gardener
One Yellow Daffodil
Sootface
Stone Fox
Talking Eggs

King Arthur
King Arthur's Camelot
Lost Years of Merlin
Merlin
Tales of King Arthur Series
Young Guinevere

kings
17 Kings & 42 Elephants
500 Hats of Bartholomew
      Cubbins
How Big Is a Foot?
King Bidgood's in the Bathrub
May I Bring a Friend?
Mufaro's Beautiful Daughters
Story of Babar
William Shakespeare's Macbeth
Yeh-Shen: A Cinderella Story from
      China

kitchens
In the Night Kitchen
Mouse Mess

kites
Ben and Me
Days With Frog and Toad
Kite Flier

kittens (see: cats)

knights
Castle Builder
Castle in the Attic
Don Quixote
King Arthur's Camelot
Knight's Castle
Redwall
Saint George and the Dragon
Tales of King Arthur Series
Tom Thumb

koalas
Wombat Stew

komodo dragons
Komodo

Korea
Korean Cinderella
Peacebound Trains

Korean American
Smoky Night
Suitcase Full of Seaweed and other
    Poems
Tae's Sonata

Kwanzaa
Children's Book of Kwanzaa
Seven Candles for Kwanzaa

ladybugs
James and the Giant Peach
Time to Sleep
What About Ladybugs?

language (books that use words
    and communication in
    ways that are of special
    note)
3 NBS of Julian Drew

Alphabet from Z to A (with Much
    Confusion Along the Way)
Chocolate Moose for Dinner
Cow that Went Oink
D Is for Doufu
First Things First
Frank and Ernest
Frogs in Clogs
Go Hang a Salami! I'm a Lasagna
    Hog!
Graphic Alphabet
Handtalk
Jesse Bear, What Will You Wear?
Josepha
Librarian Who Measured the Earth
Macmillan Dictionary for Children
Many Luscious Lollipops
Martha Speaks
Small Talk
Walking the Bridge of Your Nose
Weighty Word Book
Who Says a Dog Goes Bow-Wow?

language, learning
I Hate English

laziness
Farmer Duck
Hired Hand

legends (see: folklore)

lemmings
Winter White

lessons
Beautiful Feast for a Big King Cat
Big Bad Bruce
Fables
Flying Tortoise
Froggy Gets Dressed
Great White Man-Eating Shark
Nathaniel Talking
Piggybook
Small Green Snake
Squash and a Squeeze
Toll-Bridge Troll
Town Mouse, Country Mouse
War with Grandpa

librarians
Great Piratical Rumbustification

Librarian Who Measured the Earth
Library Dragon
Tomas and the Library Lady

libraries
Bookworm Buddies
December Stillness
Library Dragon
Peppermint Race
Poppleton
Tomas and the Library Lady

life cycle
Ancient Ones
Charlotte's Web
Fire in the Forest
Giants in the Land
Gray Wolf, Red Wolf
Into the Sea
Lifetimes
Look to the North
Monarchs
Tree Is Growing
Yonder

lighthouses
Birdie's Lighthouse

lightning
Ben and Me

limericks
Complete Nonsense of Edward Lear

Lincoln, Abraham
Lincoln in His Own Words
Lincoln: A Photobiography

Lindbergh, Charles
Flight

lions
Big Cats
Lion Named Shirley Williamson
Nanta's Lion
Pulling the Lion's Tail

listening
Communication
Miro in the Kingdom of the Sun
Other Way to Listen
Pink Paper Swans

literacy
Amber on the Mountain
Day of Ahmed's Secret
Josepha
More Than Anything Else
Nightjohn
Wednesday Surprise
Whipping Boy

little folk (includes elves and lep-
    rechauns)
Book of Little Folk
Borrowers
Gulliver's Adventures in Lilliput
Hobbit
Hobkin
Indian in the Cupboard
Little Folk
Rainbabies
Rumplestiltskin
Tom Thumb

lizards
Komodo
Lizard in the Sun
Lizard Music

llamas
Is Your Mama a Llama?

loneliness
Alejandro's Gift
Amigo
Angel for Solomon Singer
Babushka Baba Yaga
Big Al
Christmas Miracle of Jonathan
    Toomey
Dear Mr. Henshaw
Island of the Blue Dolphins
Millions of Cats
Pigman
Solitary Blue
Star Mother's Youngest Child
Sylvester and the Magic Pebble
Three Hat Day
Waiting for the Whales
What Hearts
Worry Stone

Los Angeles
Baby Be-Bop

Chato's Kitchen
Smoky Night
Weetzie Bat

loss
Annie Bananie
Baby
Badger's Parting Gifts
Belle Prater's Boy
Beyond the Divide
Blood and Chocolate
Bridge to Terabithia
Butterfly Jar
Cay
Christmas Miracle of Jonathan
    Toomey
Cuckoo's Child
Everett Anderson's Goodbye
Felix's Hat
Fireflies, Peach Pies & Lullabies
Flip-Flop Girl
Grandmother Bryant's Pocket
Harriet the Spy
I Hadn't Mean to Tell You This
I'll Always Love You
I'll See You in My Dreams
Island of the Blue Dolphins
Jim's Dog Muffins
Kite Flier
Lifetimes
Mick Harte Was Here
Missing May
Nana Upstairs and Nana Downstairs
Nathaniel Talking
Old Pig
One Yellow Daffodil
Out of the Dust
Pigman
Remembering the Good Times
Sun and Spoon
Tenth Good Thing About Barney
Tiger Flowers
Tough Boris
Walk Two Moons
Where the Red Fern Grows
You Hold Me and I'll Hold You

lost (and finally, found)
Ali, Child of the Desert
Are You My Mother?
Bear That Heard Crying
Goldilocks and the Three Bears

Hazel's Amazing Mother
Lassie Come Home
Lost in the Museum
Louella Mae, She's Run Away!
Max's Dragon Shirt
Mitten

Louisiana
Loup Garou

love
Abel's Island
Baby Be-Bop
Blood and Chocolate
Blue Hill Meadows
Blue Skin of the Sea
Charlotte's Web
Coyote in Love
Damned Strong Love
Dear Mr. Sprouts
Don Quixote
Dove Isabeau
Earth-Shattering Poems
Earthshine
East O' the Sun and West O' the Moon
Enormous Egg
Every Living Thing
Feelings
Frog in Love
Gentleman and the Kitchen Maid
Grandpa's Face
Guess How Much I Love You
High Rise Glorious Skittle Skat Roari-
    ous Sky Pie Angel Food Cake
Honey, I Love and Other Poems
Hoover's Bride
I Am the Mummy Heb-Nefert
I Feel a Little Jumpy Around You
I Got a Family
I Hadn't Mean to Tell You This
I Love You as Much
I'll Always Love You
Is That You, Winter?
It's Perfectly Normal
Jeremy Thatcher, Dragon Hatcher
Lassie Come Home
Lifetimes
Lion's Whiskers
Looking for Atlantis
Ma Dear's Aprons
Mama, Do You Love Me?
More, More, More, Said the Baby

Nathaniel Talking
Nicholas Pipe
Princess Nevermore
Rapunzel
Rats Saw God
Runaway Bunny
Sarah, Plain and Tall
So Much
Solitary Blue
Somebody Loves You, Mr. Hatch
Tales of King Arthur Series
Tell Me Again About the Night I Was
    Born
Three Hat Day
Through Moon and Stars and Night
    Skies
Velveteen Rabbit
Weetzie Bat
Welcoming Babies
Well Wished
What Hearts
William Shakespeare's The Tempest
Wrinkle in Time
Zel

loyalty
Faithful Friend
Hobyahs
Outsiders
Staying Fat for Sarah Byrnes

luck
Fortunately
In the Dinosaur's Paw
Saint Patrick and the Peddler

lullabies
Hush Little Baby
Hush! A Thai Lullaby
I Love You as Much
Skip Across the Ocean

lying
Harriet the Spy
Letters From the Inside
Liar Liar Pants on Fire
Lily's Crossing
There's a Boy in the Girls' Bathroom
True Lies

lynx
Animal Family

machines
Mike Mulligan & His Steam Shovel
Until I Met Dudley
Way Things Work

magic
Abiyoyo
Alice's Adventures in Wonderland
Anansi and the Moss-Covered Rock
Appelemando's Dreams
Arabian Nights
Aunt Nancy and Old Man Trouble
Baker's Dozen
Boggart
Castle in the Attic
Cinderella's Rat
Cinder-Eyed Cats
City of Light, City of Dark
Classic Poems to Read Aloud
Don Quixote
Dove Isabeau
Earthsea Quartet
East O' the Sun and West O' the Moon
Elbert's Bad Word
Emma
Faithful Friend
Five Children and It
Gift of Wali Dad
Glass Bottle Tree
Golem (Wisniewski)
Golem (Singer)
Golem: A Giant Made of Mud
Grandmother's Pigeon
Half Magic
Harvey Potter's Balloon Farm
Heckedy Peg
High Rise Glorious Skittle Skat Roari-
    ous Sky Pie Angel Food Cake
Hired Hand
Indian in the Cupboard
Jack and the Beanstalk
Jeremy Thatcher, Dragon Hatcher
Jumanji
Knight's Castle
Little Folk
Lost Years of Merlin
Magic Fan
Merlin
Meteor!
Mysteries of Harris Burdick
Nicholas Pipe
Possum Magic

Rainbabies
Rapunzel
Redwall
Secret Garden
Seven-Day Magic
Sootface
Strega Nona
Swan Stories
Sylvester and the Magic Pebble
Talking Eggs
Talking Like the Rain
Thirteen
Tuck Everlasting
Van Gogh Cafe
Velveteen Rabbit
Weaving of a Dream
Weetzie Bat
Well Wished
White Socks Only
Whittler's Tale
William Shakespeare's The Tempest
Wonderful Wizard of Oz
Young Guinevere
Zee
Zeke Pippin

magicians
Abiyoyo
Burnt Toast on Davenport Street

mail
Captain Abdul's Pirate School
Communication
Dear Mr. Blueberry
Dear Mr. Henshaw
Dear Mr. Sprouts
Dear Rebecca, Winter Is Here
Dear Willie Rudd
Dear World
Fortunately
Frog and Toad Are Friends
Gardener
Hannah and Jack
Jolly Postman
Letters From the Inside
Lincoln in His Own Words
Mailing May
Nettie's Trip South
Polar the Titanic Bear
Sarah, Plain and Tall
Somebody Loves You, Mr. Hatch
Stringbean's Trip to the Shining Sea

Sweetwater Run
They're Off!
Wish You Were Here

mail carrier
Jolly Postman
Mailing May
One Gaping, Wide-Mouthed, Hopping
   Frog
Somebody Loves You, Mr. Hatch

mammoths
Way Things Work
Will's Mammoth

manners
Dinner at Alberta's
Eating the Plates
Here Comes Henny
How My Parents Learned to Eat
It's a Spoon, Not a Shovel
Let's Eat
May I Bring a Friend?
Mrs. Piggle-Wiggle
My Dog Never Says Please
Owl Eyes
Pass the Fritters, Critters
Tales for the Perfect Child

Maori
Punga, the Goddess of Ugly

maps (about maps and/or books that
   use them to support a story)
Around the World in a Hundred Years
As the Crow Flies
Book of North American Owls
Cherokees
Circling the Globe
Cleopatra
Girl Named Disaster
Hobbit
Insides, Outsides, Loops, and Lines
Komodo
Made in China
My Map Book
Paddle-to-the-Sea
Puzzle Maps USA
Silk Route
Small Tall Tale from the Far, Far
   North
Sweet Clara and the Freedom Quilt

markets
Market!
Oh, No, Toto!
On Market Street
Ox-Cart Man
Rolling Store

marriage
Burnt Toast on Davenport Street
Fanny's Dream
Mufaro's Beautiful Daughters

martial arts
Arthur's Pen Pal
Jojo's Flying Side Kick
Smart Moves

math
12 Ways to Get to 11
17 Kings & 42 Elephants
26 Letters and 99 Cents
Anno's Math Games
Benny's Pennies
Bunny Money
Counting Crocodiles
Don't Count Your Chicks
Grandfather Tang's Story
How Big Is a Foot?
How Much Is a Million?
I'll See You When the Moon Is Full
In the Next Three Seconds
Insides, Outsides, Loops, and Lines
Jelly Beans for Sale
Librarian Who Measured the Earth
Math Curse
Math Start Series
Number One Number Fun
One Gaping, Wide-Mouthed, Hopping
    Frog
One Grain of Rice
One Hundred Hungry Ants
Phantom Tollbooth
Splash!
Starry Messenger
String of Beads
Ten Sly Piranhas
Zin! Zin! Zin! A Violin

meals
Chato's Kitchen
Dinner at Alberta's
Everybody Cooks Rice

Five Minutes Peace
Let's Eat
Pancakes for Breakfast
Pass the Fritters, Critters
Raggly, Scraggly, No-Soap, No-Scrub
    Girl
Sitting on the Farm
Today Is Monday

measurement
How Big Is a Foot?
How Much Is a Million?

memories
Badger's Parting Gifts
Chalk Doll
Day of the Dead
Dear Willie Rudd
Fireflies, Peach Pies & Lullabies
Fun! No Fun!
Grandad Bill's Song
Grandfather's Journey
I Am the Cheese
I Am the Mummy Heb-Nefert
I Had Seen Castles
Journey
One Yellow Daffodil
Patchwork Quilt
Peacebound Trains
Polar the Titanic Bear
Rain
Roxaboxen
Sarah, Plain and Tall
When I Was Little
When I Was Nine
Wilfred Gordon McDonald Partridge

memory
Bracelet
Journey
Soap! Soap! Don't Forget the Soap!
Sun and Spoon
Through Moon and Stars and Night
    Skies
When I Was Nine
Wilfred Gordon McDonald Partridge

mental illness
3 NBS of Julian Drew
Bear's House
Crossing
What Hearts

mentors
Fantastic Drawings of Danielle
Gift of Driscoll Lipscomb
Looking for Atlantis

mermaids
Animal Family
Mermaid Tales from Around the
    World
Nicholas Pipe
Treasury of Mermaids

Mexican (the people)
Amelia's Road
Calling the Doves
Day's Work
Voices From the Fields

Mexican American
Fiesta
Gathering the Sun
My First Book of Proverbs

Mexican culture
Fiesta
Too Many Tamales

Mexico
Calling the Doves
Crossing
Day of the Dead
De Colores
Fabulous Fireworks Family
Faith and the Electric Dog
Hill of Fire
Hooray, a Piñata!
Little Red Ant and the Great Big
    Crumb
Mexico's Ancient City of Teotihuacan
My First Book of Proverbs
Old Man and His Door
Pablo Remembers
Piñata Maker
Spoon for Every Bite
Tale of Rabbit and Coyote
Talking Walls
Tortilla Factory

mice
Abel's Island
Beautiful Feast for a Big King Cat
Ben and Me

Chato's Kitchen
Cricket in Times Square
Do You See a Mouse?
Doctor DeSoto
Fool of the World and the Flying Ship
Frederick
I Don't Care, Said the Bear
I'll See You When the Moon Is Full
King Snake
Little Mouse, the Red Ripe Straw-
    berry, and the Big Hungry Bear
Livingstone Mouse
Lunch
Mouse and the Motorcycle
Mouse Mess
Mouse Paint
Seven Blind Mice
Smudge
Stuart Little
Three Blind Mice Mystery
Town Mouse, Country Mouse
Turtle in July

Middle East
Arabian Nights
Arabian Nights: Three Tales
King of the Wind
One More River
Silk Route
Tale of Ali Baba and the Forty
    Thieves

migrant farmworkers
Amelia's Road
Calling the Doves
Gathering the Sun
Tomas and the Library Lady
Voices From the Fields
Working Cotton

milk
In the Night Kitchen
Pancakes for Breakfast

minerals
String of Beads

miners
At the Crossroads
Growing Up in Coal Country
In Coal Country
Mama Is a Miner

mines
At the Crossroads
Growing Up in Coal Country
Mama Is a Miner

miracles
Charlotte's Web
Earthshine
Meteor!
Miracle of the Latkes
Rechenka's Eggs

misbehaving
Charlie and the Chocolate
    Factory
Elbert's Bad Word
Great Gilly Hopkins
Miss Nelson Is Missing
My Dog Never Says Please
Nutshell Library
Ornery Morning
Small Green Snake
Tales for the Perfect Child

mischief
Caps for Sale
Cat in the Hat
Eloise
Good Night, Gorilla
Hush! A Thai Lullaby
Just Me and My Dad
Madeline
Miss Nelson Is Missing
Nutshell Library
Oh, No, Toto!
Small Green Snake
Where the Wild Things
    Are
Whipping Boy

mishaps
Eva
In Enzo's Splendid Gardens
Officer Buckle and Gloria
Regular Flood of Mishap
Sheep in a Jeep
Willy the Wimp

mistaken identity
Author's Day
Three-Legged Cat
Toad or Frog, Swamp or Bog

mistakes
Amelia Bedelia
Aunt Eater Loves a Mystery
Blue Hat, Green Hat
Mistakes That Worked
Ramona the Pest
Regular Flood of Mishap

misunderstanding
Amelia Bedelia
Bumps in the Night
Chicken Little
Josepha
Minerva Louise at School
White Socks Only

moles
Eeny, Meeny, Miney Mole
Mordant's Wish

Monet, Claude
Linnea in Monet's Garden

money
26 Letters and 99 Cents
Absolutely, Positively Alexander
Benny's Pennies
Big Bazoohley
Bunny Money
Count Your Money with the Polk
    Street School
Jelly Beans for Sale
Money, Money, Money
Story of Money
Teeny Weeny Zucchinis

mongooses
Rikki-Tikki-Tavi

monkeys and apes
Caps for Sale
Counting Crocodiles
Curious George
Eva
I Like Books
When the Monkeys Came Back
Willy the Wimp

monsters
Barnyard Dance!
Do Not Open
Dogzilla

Go Away, Big Green Monster
Golem (Wisniewski)
Golem: A Giant Made of Mud
Grey Lady and the Strawberry
   Snatcher
Hershel and the Hanukkah Goblins
Hobyahs
House That Drac Built
Liza Lou and the Yeller Belly Swamp
Monster at the End of This Book
Monster Mama
My Mama Says There Aren't Any
   Zombies . . .
Mysterious Tadpole
Scared Silly
Scary, Scary Halloween
There's a Nightmare in My Closet
Wanderings of Odysseus
Where the Wild Things Are

Montana
Christmas Menorahs

months
January Rides the Wind
June Is a Tune That Jumps on a Stair
Nutshell Library

monuments
Charlie Pippin
Wall
Wonderful Towers of Watts

moon
Can't You Sleep, Little Bear?
I'll See You When the Moon Is Full
Just Rewards
Papa, Please Get the Moon for Me
Rainbabies
Thirteen Moons on Turtle's Back
Zoom! Zoom! Zoom! I'm Off to the
   Moon

morning
Dawn (Shulevitz)
Farm Morning
Good Morning Pond
Paperboy
Twilight Comes Twice

Mother Goose
James Marshall's Mother Goose

Moonstruck
My Very First Mother Goose

mothers
Are You My Mother?
Beautiful Feast for a Big King Cat
Belle Prater's Boy
Chalk Doll
Chocolate Touch
Country Bunny and the Little Gold
   Shoes
Five Minutes Peace
Good Griselle
Hazel's Amazing Mother
Heckedy Peg
Here Comes Henny
Hush Little Baby
Hush! A Thai Lullaby
I Love You as Much
Make Way for Ducklings
Mama, Do You Love Me?
More, More, More, Said the Baby
My Mama Says There Aren't Any
   Zombies . . .
Oink
Owl Babies
Papa!
Piggybook
Runaway Bunny
Sarah, Plain and Tall
Small Green Snake
So Much
Stellaluna
Welcome Little Baby

mothers and daughters
Angel Child, Dragon Child
Blueberries for Sal
Dippers
Hands
High Rise Glorious Skittle Skat
   Roarious Sky Pie Angel Food
   Cake
Ice
Magic Circle
Mama Is a Miner
Mr. Rabbit and the Lovely Present
Quilt Story
Rapunzel
Spite Fences
Walk Two Moons
Zel

mothers and sons
3 NBS of Julian Drew
Buffalo Tree
Burnt Stick
Don't Laugh, Joe
Edward and the Pirates
Egg Is an Egg
Froggy Gets Dressed
Leo the Late Bloomer
Ma Dear's Aprons
Mean Soup
Monster Mama
Pink and Say
Polar the Titanic Bear
Solitary Blue
Tree of Cranes
Weaving of a Dream
What Hearts
Young Larry
Zilla Sasparilla and the Mud Baby

motorcycles
Mouse and the Motorcycle
Richard Scarry's Cars and Trucks and
   Things that Go

moving
Absolutely, Positively Alexander
Amelia's Notebook
Amelia's Road
Annie Bananie
Faith and the Electric Dog
Flip-Flop Girl
Gila Monsters Meet You at the Air-
   port
House for a Hermit Crab
Is This a House for Hermit Crab?
Kid in the Red Jacket
Quilt Story
We Are a Rainbow
What You Know First
When the Whippoorwill Calls

Mozart
Muffin Fiend

mud
Mud Pies and Other Recipes
Peter Spier's Rain
Pigs in the Mud in the Middle of the
   Rud
Zilla Sasparilla and the Mud Baby

muffins
Muffin Fiend
Young Larry

multicultural (see cultural diversity)

mummies
Discovering the Iceman
How to Make a Mummy Talk
I Am the Mummy Heb-Nefert

murder
Killing Mr. Griffin
View From the Cherry Tree
Weekend Was Murder
William Shakespeare's Macbeth

museum
Anne Frank: Beyond the Diary
Art Dog
Bone Poems
Celebrate America in Poetry and Art
Come Look With Me
From the Mixed-Up Files of Mrs. Basil
   E. Frankweiler
Gentleman and the Kitchen Maid
Lost in the Museum
Moans and Groans and Dinosaur Bones
My Visit to the Aquarium
Time Flies
Visiting the Art Museum
We're Back!

mushrooms
Katya's Book of Mushrooms

music
Abiyoyo
All I See
All of You Was Singing
Arroz con Leche
Barn Dance!
Ben's Trumpet
Bread Is for Eating
Call Down the Moon
De Colores
Dem Bones
Five Live Bongos
From Sea to Shining Sea
Gonna Sing My Head Off!
Good Times on Grandfather Mountain
Hip Cat

I Like the Music
Jazz: My Music, My People
Jeremy's Decision
Lives of the Musicians
Maestro Plays
Mama Don't Allow
Meet the Marching Smithereens
Meet the Orchestra
Midnight Hour Encores
Muffin Fiend
Mysterious Thelonious
Nathaniel Talking
Nutcracker
On the Day You Were Born
Out of the Dust
Peppermint Race
Philharmonic Gets Dressed
Sally Arnold
She'll Be Comin' Round the Mountain
Sing, Sophie!
Singer to the Sea God
Solitary Blue
Tales Alive
Teddy Bear's Picnic
Twelve Days of Christmas
Wheels on the Bus
Zeke Pippin
Zin! Zin! Zin! A Violin

musical instruments
Philharmonic Gets Dressed
Meet the Marching Smithereens
Meet the Orchestra
Zin! Zin! Zin! A Violin
Ben's Trumpet
Peppermint Race
Call Down the Moon
Arthur's Pen Pal

musicians
Ben's Trumpet
Jazz: My Music, My People
Meet the Marching Smithereens
Meet the Orchestra

mystery
5 Novels by Daniel Pinkwater
ABC Mystery
Adventures of Tintin
Aunt Eater Loves a Mystery
Belle Prater's Boy
Bunnicula

Castle in the Attic
Cinder-Eyed Cats
Complete Sherlock Holmes
Complete Stories and Poems of Poe
Cyber.Kdz Series
Dippers
East O' the Sun and West O' the Moon
Egypt Game
Encyclopedia Brown Series
Face on the Milk Carton
From the Mixed-Up Files of Mrs. Basil
     E. Frankweiler
House With a Clock in Its Walls
I Am the Cheese
In a Messy, Messy Room and Other
     Scary Stories
Judy Scuppernong
Jumanji
Lost Years of Merlin
Miss Nelson Is Missing
Muffin Fiend
Mysteries of Harris Burdick
Nate the Great
Puzzling Day at Castle MacPelican
Search for the Shadowman
Secret Code Book
Talking Eggs
Three Blind Mice Mystery
View From the Cherry Tree
Walk Two Moons
Weekend Was Murder
Westing Game

myths (see: folklore)

names
Alison's Zinnia
Chrysanthemum (see Henkes spot-
     light)
If Your Name Was Changed at Ellis
     Island
Lion Named Shirley Williamson
When Jo Louis Won the Title

nations
Children Just Like Me
Circling the Globe
Dear World

Native American
Adopted by the Eagles
Annie and the Old One

Arrow to the Sun
Bone Man
Boy Who Dreamed of an Acorn
Brother Eagle, Sister Sky
Cherokees
Cheyenne Again
Corn Is Maize
Coyote
Coyote in Love
Dance of the Sacred Circle
Did You Hear Wind Sing Your Name?
Dragonfly's Tale
Everglades
Fire Race
First Strawberries
Follow the Dream
Fox Song
Ghost Dance
Girl Who Loved Wild Horses
Great Ball Game
Guests
Hawk, I'm Your Brother
House Is a House for Me
I'm in Charge of Celebrations
Indian in the Cupboard
Indian Winter
Island of the Blue Dolphins
Keepers of the Earth
Man Called Raven
Moonstick
Morning Girl
Navajo: Visions and Voices Across the
    Mesa
One Small Blue Bead
Other Way to Listen
Owl Eyes
Paddle-to-the-Sea
Rainbow Bridge
Rattlesnake Dance
Raven
Save Queen of Sheba
Sees Behind Trees
Shepherd Boy
Singing America
Sootface
Stone Fox
Stranded at Plimoth Plantation, 1626
String of Beads
Thirteen Moons on Turtle's Back
This Land Is My Land
Walk Two Moons
Way West

When Clay Sings
Worry Stone

nature

Alejandro's Gift
All About Alligators
Ancient Ones
Annie and the Old One
Bay Shore Park
Beauty of the Beast
Beaver at Long Pond
Big Blue Whale
Big Cats
Bird's Body
Body Atlas
Bone Poems
Book of North American Owls
Brother Eagle, Sister Sky
Chickens Aren't the Only Ones
Classic Poems to Read Aloud
Did You Hear Wind Sing Your Name?
Dragonflies
Dragonfly's Tale
Earth, Fire, Water, Air
Elements Series
Extremely Weird Animal Defenses
Eyes of Gray Wolf
Fox Song
Frogs
Girl Who Loved Caterpillars
Gray Wolf, Red Wolf
Grossology
Have You Seen Trees?
Hawk, I'm Your Brother
Home Sweet Home
House for a Hermit Crab
How to Be a Nature Detective
Hush Little Baby (Long)
If You Were Born a Kitten
I'm in Charge of Celebrations
In the Desert
In the Tall, Tall Grass
In the Woods: Who's Been Here
Inside the Amazing Amazon
Into the Sea
Is This a House for Hermit Crab?
January Rides the Wind
Joyful Noise
Katya's Book of Mushrooms
Keepers of the Earth
Kratt's Creatures: Our Favorite Crea-
    tures

Life and Times of the Apple
Life and Times of the Honeybee
Lizard in the Sun
Look to the North
Lorax
Magic School Bus in the Time of the
    Dinosaurs
Man Called Raven
Moonstick
My Hen Is Dancing
My House Has Stars
My Visit to the Zoo
Okino and the Whales
Old Ladies Who Liked Cats
Old Turtle
On the Day You Were Born
One Night
Only Opal
Other Way to Listen
Outside and Inside Snakes
Pinky Is a Baby Mouse
Rattlesnake Dance
Salamander Room
Skip Across the Ocean
Snail's Spell
Snake Is Totally Tail
Straight From the Bear's Mouth
Ten Little-Known Facts About Hippos
Those Amazing Ants
Toad
Toad or Frog, Swamp or Bog
Too Many Rabbits
Tree in the Wood
Tree Is Growing
Tree Is Nice
Turtle in July
Voices From the Wild
Volcano: The Eruption and Healing of
    Mount St. Helens
What About Ladybugs?

navigation
Drinking Gourd
Flight
Sweet Clara and the Freedom Quilt

neighbors
Anne of Green Gables
Araboolies of Liberty Street
Bein' With You This Way
Best Friends for Frances
Chicken Sunday

Everybody Cooks Rice
Gardener
Green Truck Garden Giveaway
Henry Huggins
Homer Price
Hooray for Me
House for a Hermit Crab
Kid in the Red Jacket
Last Dragon
Miracle of the Latkes
Owen
Pancakes for Breakfast
Pink Paper Swans
Ramona the Pest
Red Racer
See You Around, Sam
Somebody Loves You, Mr. Hatch
Spoon for Every Bite
Tales of Trotter Street
Year on My Street

new baby
All-of-a-Kind Family
Baby Sister for Frances
Happy Birth Day
Julius, the Baby of the
    World
Let's Eat
New Baby
Noisy Nora
On Mother's Lap
Peter's Chair
Tales of Trotter Street
Welcome Little Baby
Welcoming Babies
World Is Full of Babies!
Za-Za's Baby Brother

new experiences
Beast in Ms. Rooney's Room
Delphine
Did You See What I Saw?
First Grade Takes a Test
Green Eggs and Ham
I Never Did That Before
Miss Bindergarten Gets Ready for
    Kindergarten
Oliver's Vegetables
Stellaluna
Stranded at Plimoth Plantation,
    1626
Watch Out Man Eating Snake

New Mexico
Fiesta
Talking Walls

New York
Adventures of Taxi Dog
All-of-a-Kind Family
Angel for Solomon Singer
Baker's Dozen
City of Light, City of Dark
Cricket in Times Square
Eloise
Fiesta
From the Mixed-Up Files of Mrs. Basil
    E. Frankweiler
Gila Monsters Meet You at the Air-
    port
Harlem
House on East 88th Street
James and the Giant Peach
Soon, Annala
Tar Beach
We're Back!
When Zaydeh Danced on Eldridge
    Street

newspapers
Darrell Rock Reporting
Dateline: Troy
Greek News

night
Big Red Barn
Cinder-Eyed Cats
Dogteam
Good Night, Gorilla
Goodnight Moon
Grandfather Twilight
Night Sounds, Morning Colors
Twilight Comes Twice
Wind Says Goodnight

nightmares
Boy and the Cloth of Dreams
There's a Nighmare in My Closet

noise
Banging Book
Crash! Bang! Boom!
Five Minutes Peace
Gobble, Growl, Grunt
Poems Go Clang!

Norway
East O' the Sun and West O' the
    Moon
Tatterhood and the Goblins

numbers
1 Is One
12 Ways to Get to 11
Barnyard Dance!
Benny's Pennies
How Many Bugs in a Box?
How Many, How Many, How
    Many?
How Much Is a Million?
I Spy Two Eyes
Math Start Series
Midnight Farm
Number One Number Fun
One Gaping, Wide-Mouthed, Hopping
    Frog
One Hundred Hungry Ants
One to Ten Pop-Up Surprises!
Twelve Days of Christmas

nurses
Dear Dr. Sillybear

obsession
Chocolate Fever
Cuckoo's Child
Egypt Game
Library
Spoon for Every Bite
Three Hat Day

Odyssey, the
Wanderings of Odysseus

Ohio
In Coal Country

Oklahoma
Out of the Dust
Red Dirt Jessie
Where the Red Fern Grows

old age (see: elderly)

onomatopoeia
Banging Book
Poems Go Clang!
Rain Talk

opossums
Don't Laugh, Joe
Liza Lou and the Yeller Belly Swamp
Possum Come a-Knockin'
Possum Magic

optimism
Aunt Nancy and Old Man Trouble
Chicken Man
Gardener
Good Times on Grandfather
    Mountain

orchestras
I Like the Music
Jeremy's Decision
Maestro Plays
Meet the Orchestra
Philharmonic Gets Dressed

Oregon
Children of the River
Girl From Yamhill
Only Opal
Save Queen of Sheba
Way West

orphans
Anne of Green Gables
BFG
Crossing
Eleanor
Hobyahs
Jip, His Story
Madeline
Maniac Magee
Orphan Train Adventures
Place to Call Home
Saving Sweetness
Secret Garden
Story of Babar
Stranded at Plimoth Plantation, 1626

outer space
Commander Toad in Space
Here Come the Aliens
My Place in Space
Planets
Star Walk
Zoom! Zoom! Zoom! I'm Off to the
    Moon

overweight
Blubber
Staying Fat for Sarah Byrnes

owls
Book of North American Owls
Man Who Could Call Down Owls
Owl Babies
Owl Eyes
Owls in the Family
Town Mouse, Country Mouse
Turtle in July

oxen
Ox-Cart Man

paint
Little Painter of Sabana Grande
Mouse Paint

painting
After the War Was Over
All I See
Fantastic Drawings of Danielle
Little Painter of Sabana Grande

paintings
ABC Mystery
Celebrate America in Poetry and Art
Celebrating America
Come Look With Me
Gentleman and the Kitchen Maid
Getting to Know the World's Great
    Artists
I Spy Two Eyes
Linnea in Monet's Garden
Painter
Visiting the Art Museum

Pakistan
Shabanu

palindromes
Go Hang a Salami! I'm a Lasagna Hog!

parents (see also mothers or fathers)
Edward and the Pirates
Face on the Milk Carton
Papa!
Rainbabies
Shy Charles
When the Big Dog Barks

Paris
Fantastic Drawings of Danielle
Good Griselle
Linnea in Monet's Garden
Madeline

parodies
Dogzilla
Fate Totally Worse Than Death
Happy Hocky Family

parties
All About Alfie
Badger's Bring Something Party
Go, Dog. Go!
Great Piratical Rumbustification
Hooray, a Piñata!
Make a Wish Molly
So Much
There's a Party at Mona's Tonight

parts of speech
Alphabet From Z to A (with Much
    Confusion Along the Way)
Antics
Chocolate Moose for Dinner
Eye Spy: A Mysterious
    Alphabet
Hailstones and Halibut Bones
Maestro Plays
Many Luscious Lollipops
Peck Slither and Slide
Puffins Climb, Penguins Rhyme
Quick as a Cricket
Walking the Bridge of Your Nose
Where Does It Go?

Passover
Make a Wish Molly
Uninvited Guest and Other Jewish
    Holiday Tales

patience
At the Crossroads
Carrot Seed
Dawn (Bang)
Gift of Driscoll Lipscomb
Good Griselle
Grandmother Bryant's Pocket
How a Book Is Made
Pulling the Lion's Tail
Runaway Bunny

Soon, Annala
Uncle Jed's Barbershop

patriotism
Nothing But the Truth
Under the Blood Red Sun

peace
Big Book for Our Planet
Charlie Pippin
Fragile Flag
Ghost Dance
Music and Drum
Neve Shalom Wahat Al-Salam: Oasis
    of Peace
Old Turtle
One More River
Peacebound Trains
Rose Blanche
Ruby Mae Has Something to Say
Sadako
Sadako and the Thousand Paper
    Cranes
Saint Francis
Seven Brave Women
Smart Moves
Story of Ferdinand
Talking Peace
Westmark
When Stories Fell Like Shooting
    Stars

peaches
James and the Giant Peach

peanuts
Life and Times of the Peanut

peddlers
Caps for Sale

peek-a-boo
Each Peach Pear Plum
Pat the Bunny

peer pressure
Wringer

pen pals
Arthur's Pen Pal
Communication
Letters From the Inside

penguins
Mr. Popper's Penguins
Puffins Climb, Penguins Rhyme
Tacky the Penguin

Pennsylvania
Growing Up in Coal Country

performing
Albert's Play
Amazing Grace
Lili Backstage
Mike Mulligan & His Steam Shovel
Onstage and Backstage at the Night
    Owl Theater

perseverance
Author: A True Story
Brave Irene
Carrot Seed
Good Times on Grandfather Mountain

perspective
Zoom

Peru
Talking Walls

pet care
I Want to Be a Veterinarian
Some Swell Pup

photographs, magnification
Drop of Water
Yikes! Your Body Up Close

photosynthesis
Straight From the Bear's Mouth

picnics
Family Reunion
Here Comes Henny
One Hundred Hungry Ants
Tar Beach
Teddy Bear's Picnic

pies
How to Make an Apple Pie and See
    the World

pigs
Babe, the Gallant Pig
Charlotte's Web
Christmas Tree Tangle
Hog-Eye
Louella Mae, She's Run Away!
Oink
Old Pig
Piggybook
Suddenly!
Three Blind Mice Mystery
Three Little Javelinas
Three Little Wolves and the Big Bad
    Pig
True Story of the Three Little Pigs

pilgrims
Eating the Plates
Goody O'Grumpity
Guests
Molly's Pilgrim
Stranded at Plimoth Plantation, 1626

piñatas
Hooray, A Piñata!
Piñata Maker

pioneers
Ballad of Lucy Whipple
Beyond the Divide
Big Men, Big Country
Floating House
Grandma Essie's Covered Wagon
Mississippi Mud
Only Opal
Pioneer Sampler
Prairie Songs
Quilt Story
Save Queen of Sheba
Sewing Quilts
Way West

pirates
Ballad of the Pirate Queens
Captain Abdul's Pirate School
Great Pirate Activity Book
Great Piratical Rumbustification
Pirate's Handbook
Tough Boris

planets
On the Day You Were Born
Planets
Star Walk

plants (fiction and nonfiction with
    an emphasis on flowers and veg-
    etation)
Bay Shore Park
From Seed to Plant
Here Is the Tropical Rain Forest
Jack's Garden
Keepers of the Earth
Linnea in Monet's Garden
Lotus Seed
Nuts to You
Spice Alphabet Book
Welcome to the Green House

platypus
Wombat Stew

playing
Did You See What I Saw?
Galimoto
Heroes
I Never Did That Before
I Saw Esau
Mud Pies and Other Recipes
Peter Spier's Rain
Rat and the Tiger
Roxaboxen
Snowy Day

playing tricks
Adventures of Captain Underpants
Bargain for Frances
Big David, Little David
Cat's Purr
Fortune-Tellers
Good Night, Gorilla
Great White Man-Eating Shark
Matilda
Pigman
Possum Come a-Knockin'
Rumplestiltskin
Toll-Bridge Troll

plays
Albert's Play
Amazing Grace
Show Time at the Polk Street School
Z Was Zapped

poem
Casey at the Bat
Earthdance

Goody O'Grumpity
Harlem
Heartland
Night Before Christmas
Paul Revere's Ride
Tog the Ribber, or Granny's Tale
Tyger

poetry
Celebrate America in Poetry and
    Art
Celebrating America
Classic Poems to Read Aloud
From Sea to Shining Sea
Hailstones and Halibut Bones
Pass It On
Stories by Firelight
Sweet Corn

poets
Bard of Avon
Calling the Doves
Coming Home
Frederick
Grass Sandals
Invisible Ladder
Max Makes a Million
Poetry From A to Z
Random House Book of Poetry for
    Children
This Same Sky

point of view (a list of books
    that encourage the reader to
    see things from a different
    angle)
Adventures of Huckleberry
    Finn
All I See
All We Needed to Say
As the Crow Flies
Bull Run
Christmas House
Daydreamer
Everyday Mysteries
Forestwife
Graphic Alphabet
I Am the Dog, I Am the Cat
I Am the Mummy Heb-Nefert
If You're Not Here, Please Raise Your
    Hand
Kissing the Witch

Math Curse
Mississippi Mud
Monster Mama
Moonstruck
Morgan's Dream
Morning Girl
My Map Book
Nanta's Lion
Nothing But the Truth
Punga, the Goddess of Ugly
Robin's Country
Seedfolks
Seven Blind Mice
Shortcut
Shrinking of Treehorn
Slave Day
Sleeping Ugly
Snail's Spell
Spite Fences
Stupids Step Out
Telling of the Tales
Thirteen
True Lies
Turtle in July
Zoom

polar bears
Winter White
Young Larry

police
Officer Buckle and Gloria

Polish American
Soon, Annala

politics
Buck Stops Here
My Fellow Americans
One More River
Talking Peace

ponds
Beaver at Long Pond
Good Morning Pond
I Wish I Were a Butterfly
In the Small, Small Pond
Splash!

Pony Express
Sweetwater Run
They're Off!

popcorn
Corn Is Maize
Popcorn Book

possums (see: opossums)

postman (see: mail carrier)

poverty
Bear's House
Beyond the Western Sea
Black Snowman
Brickyard Summer
Cat Running
Clown
Crossing
Fly Away Home
Gingerbread Doll
Hansel and Gretel
Jip, His Story
Make Lemonade
Mary Wolf
Out of the Dust
Something Permanent
Voices From the Fields
Waiting to Waltz
Way Home
Wonderful Towers of Watts

Prague
Golem (Wiesniewski)
Golem (Singer)
Golem: A Giant Made of Mud

prairie dogs
Amigo

prayer
Home Sweet Home
Old Turtle

predators
Toad
What Do You Do When Something
    Wants to Eat You?
When Hunger Calls

predictable (these titles allow a child
    to anticipate what will happen at
    the turn of a page)
Hush! A Thai Lullaby
I'll See You When the Moon Is Full

Is Your Mama a Llama?
Louella May, She's Run Away!
Night Becomes Day

preferences
Green Eggs and Ham
Today I'm Going Fishing With My
    Dad

prehistoric animals
Bone Poems
Magic School Bus in the Time of the
    Dinosaurs
Will's Mammoth

prejudice
Adventures of Huckleberry Finn
Amazing Grace
Anne Frank: Beyond the Diary
Anne Frank: The Diary of a Young
    Girl
Araboolies of Liberty Street
Baseball Saved Us
Big Al
Bracelet
Cat Running
Cay
Children of the Dust Bowl
Christmas in the Big House,
    Christmas in the Quarters
Christmas Menorahs
Dear Willie Rudd
Dragonling
Drinking Gourd
Glory Field
Guests
Harriet and the Promised Land
Heroes
I Am an American
I Hadn't Mean to Tell You This
I Have a Dream
Jip, His Story
Join In
Leagues Apart
Malcolm X: By Any Means Necessary
Maniac Magee
Metropolitan Cow
Mississippi Bridge
Morning Girl
Nettie's Trip South
Number the Stars
Outsiders

Pink and Say
Real McCoy
Roll of Thunder, Hear My Cry
Seedfolks
Slave Day
Spite Fences
Stones in Water
Suitcase Full of Seaweed and other
    Poems
Teammates
To Be a Slave
Under the Blood Red Sun
Voices From the Fields
Watsons Go to Birmingham, 1963
We Are a Rainbow
Well
White Socks Only
Who Belongs Here?

presents (see: gifts)

pretending
Amazing Grace
From Head to Toe
Mennyms
Pretend You're a Cat

pride
Black Snowman
Celebration!
Fruit and Vegetable Man
One Night
Roll of Thunder, Hear My Cry
Spinky Sulks
Uncle Jed's Barbershop
When Jo Louis Won the Title

princes
King's Equal
Tatterhood and the Goblins
Whipping Boy
Zel

princesses
King's Equal
Last Princess
Paper Bag Princess, The
Princess Nevermore
Treasury of Princesses

problem solving
Abel's Island

Allison
Amelia's Road
Angel Child, Dragon Child
Big Bazoohley
Bit by Bit
Clown
Cow that Went Oink
Cyber.Kdz Series
Day's Work
Dead Bird
Dear Dr. Sillybear
Elbert's Bad Word
Finster Frets
First Strawberries
Gentleman and the Kitchen Maid
Hannah and Jack
How to Lose All Your Friends
Hunting the White Cow
I'll See You in My Dreams
Incredible Ned
Jumanji
Mailing May
Math Curse
Math Start Series
Mean Soup
Mendel's Ladder
Mike Mulligan & His Steam
    Shovel
Mr. Popper's Penguins
Mrs. Piggle-Wiggle
Ornery Morning
Owen
Pigs in the Mud in the Middle of the
    Rud
Piles of Pets
Pink Paper Swans
Spinky Sulks
Sylvester and the Magic Pebble
Talking Peace
There's a Nightmare in My Closet
Too Many Pumpkins
Virtual War
War with Grandpa
Wonderful Towers of Watts
Zeke Pippin

promises
Harvey Slumfenburger's Christmas
    Present
Mailing May
On My Honor
Staying Fat for Sarah Byrnes

proverbs
First Things First
My First Book of Proverbs

puberty
It's a Girl Thing
It's Perfectly Normal

pueblo
Arrow to the Sun

puffins
Mama, Do You Love Me?
Puffins Climb, Penguins Rhyme

pumpkins
It's Pumpkin Time!
Scary, Scary Halloween
Too Many Pumpkins

punctuation
Librarian Who Measured the Earth

puns
Art Dog
Bunyans
Dogzilla
How Now Brown Cow
Velcome!
Walking the Bridge of Your Nose
Weighty Word Book

puzzles
Anno's Math Games
Eye Spy: A Mysterious Alphabet
Grandfather Tang's Story
Great Pirate Activity Book
Peck Slither and Slide
Puzzle Maps USA
Puzzling Day at Castle MacPelican
Westing Game

Quakers
Jip, His Story
Lightning Time

Quebec
Talking Walls

queens
How Big Is a Foot?
King Bidgood's in the Bathtub

May I Bring a Friend?
Tatterhood and the Goblins

quiet
Five Minutes Peace
Home Sweet Home
Secret Places

quilts
Eight Hands Round
Keeping Quilt
Luka's Quilt
Patchwork Quilt
Quilt Story
Sewing Quilts
Sweet Clara and the Freedom Quilt

quotations
Who Said That?

rabbits
Bunnicula
Bunny Money
Easter Egg Artists
Jump!
Smudge
Tale of Peter Rabbit
Tale of Rabbit and Coyote
Tortoise and the Hare
Velveteen Rabbit

racing
Atalanta's Race
Cat Running
Dogteam
King of the Wind
Shortcut
Supergrandpa
Tortoise and the Hare

railroad
Freight Train
Iron Dragon Never Sleeps
John Henry
Mailing May
Orphan Train Adventures
Ten Mile Day and the Building of the
    Transcontinental Railroad

rain
Bringing the Rain to Kapiti Plain
Here Is the Tropical Rain Forest

Mendel's Ladder
Peter Spier's Rain
Rain
Rain Talk
Rainy Day
Windsongs and Rainbows

rain forest
Great Kapok Tree
Here Is the Tropical Rain
    Forest
Inside the Amazing Amazon
My Visit to the Aquarium
Welcome to the Green House
When the Monkeys Came Back

rainbows
Rainbow Bridge
Windsongs and Rainbows

ranches
Cowboy Country
Just Like My Dad

rats
Cat's Purr
Cinderella's Rat

ravens
Man Called Raven
Raven

readiness
Cleversticks
Edward the Unready
Leo the Late Bloomer
Owen
Philharmonic Gets Dressed

reading
Amber on the Mountain
Bee Tree
Bookworm Buddies
Boys Will Be
But That's Another Story
Communication
Day of Ahmed's Secret
Edward and the Pirates
Great Piratical Rumbustification
Half Magic
Hog-Eye
How a Book Is Made

I Like Books
Kids of the Polk Street School
Knight's Castle
Library
Library Dragon
Memoirs of a Bookbat
More Than Anything Else
Nightjohn
Peppermint Race
Poppleton
Seven-Day Magic
Three Stories You Can Read to Your
    Dog
Tomas and the Library Lady
Wednesday Surprise
When Will I Read?
Wings: A Tale of Two Chickens

rebus
Bamboo Hats and a Rice Cake

recipes
Apple Pie Tree
Children's Book of Kwanzaa
Everybody Cooks Rice
Goody O'Grumpity
How to Make an Apple Pie and See
    the World
Miracle of the Latkes
Mud Pies and Other Recipes
Pancakes for Breakfast
Pioneer Sampler
Popcorn Book
Science Experiments You Can
    Eat
Thunder Cake

recycling
Mr. Willowby's Christmas Tree

redemption
Buffalo Tree
Christmas Miracle of Jonathan
    Toomey
Chronicles of Narnia
Good Griselle

refugees
Children of the River
Lily's Crossing
Lotus Seed
Who Belongs Here?

regret
Dear Willie Rudd
Lilly's Purple Plastic Purse

relatives
Family Reunion
Homecoming
Homeplace
Homer Price
Hooray for Me
Kinship
Little House on the Prairie
My Family Tree
Relatives Came
So Much

religion
Buddha
Chicken Sunday
Child's First Bible
Clown of God
Creation
Elijah's Angel
Golden Compass
Memoirs of a Bookbat
One World, Many Religions
Sacred Places
Saint Francis
Shaker Boy
Talking Walls

repetition
Anansi and the Moss-Covered Rock
Bit by Bit
Blueberries for Sal
Brown Bear, Brown Bear, What Do
    You See?
Fortunately
Froggy Gets Dressed
Good Night, Gorilla
Harvey Slumfenburger's Christmas
    Present
Hattie and the Fox
Hilary Knight's The Twelve Days of
    Christmas
House Is a House for Me
House That Drac Built
I Went Walking
If You're Not From the Prairie
King Bidgood's in the Bathtub
Millions of Cats
My Little Sister Ate One Hare

One Gaping, Wide-Mouthed, Hopping
    Frog
Pigs in the Mud in the Middle of the
    Rud
Sitting on the Farm
Twelve Days of Christmas
Very Busy Spider
Very Quiet Cricket
Wheels on the Bus

rescue
Cay
Christmas Tree Tangle
Hazel's Amazing Mother
Heckedy Peg
Little Ships
Summer of Stanley
Wombat Stew

resourcefulness
Deathwatch
Fin M'Coul, the Giant of Knockmany
    Hill
Gardener
Gingerbread Doll
Hatchet
Homecoming
Jip, His Story
King Bidgood's in the Bathtub
Mary Wolf
Mike Mulligan & His Steam Shovel
Mr. Popper's Penguins
Rumplestiltskin
Way Home

respect
500 Hats of Bartholomew Cubbins
Every Living Thing
When Stories Fell Like Shooting Stars

responsibility
Barn (Avi)
Bookworm Buddies
Brother Eagle, Sister Sky
Day's Work
Earthsea Quartet
Enormous Egg
Every Living Thing
Fish in His Pocket
Fruit and Vegetable Man
Half Magic
Jeremy Thatcher, Dragon Hatcher

Knight's Castle
Marvin Redpost: Alone in His
    Teacher's House
Miss Rumphius
On My Honor
Pigman
Seven-Day Magic
Whipping Boy

restaurants
Angel for Solomon Singer
Frank and Ernest
Homer Price
In Enzo's Splendid Gardens
Van Gogh Cafe

reunion
Family Reunion
Kinship
Relatives Came

revenge
Harriet the Spy
I'll Fix Anthony
Man Who Could Call Down Owls
Slugs
William Shakespeare's The Tempest

Revere, Paul
Paul Revere's Ride

Rhode Island
Finding Providence

rhyme
1 Is One
A My Name Is Alice
Adventures of Taxi Dog
Amigo
And to Think That I Saw It on Mul-
    berry Street
Arroz con Leche
Aster Aardvarks's Alphabet Adven-
    tures
Barn Dance!
Beautiful Feast for a Big King Cat
Before I Go to Sleep
Best of Michael Rosen
Big Bear's Treasury
Big Red Barn
Buck Stops Here
Bugs! (Greenberg)

Butter Battle Book
Butterfly Jar
By the Light of the Halloween Moon
Cadillac
California, Here We Come!
Calling the Doves
Cat in the Hat
Chicka Chicka Boom Boom
Child's Garden of Verses
Christmas House
Christmas Tree Tangle
Cinder-Eyed Cats
Clap Your Hands
Complete Nonsense of Edward Lear
Cozy Book
Donna O'Neeshuck Was Chased By
    Some Cows
Down by the River
Each Peach Pear Plum
Earl's Too Cool for Me
Frogs in Clogs
Good Morning Pond
Grandmother's Nursery Rhymes
Halloween ABC
Have You Seen Trees?
House Is a House for Me
House That Drac Built
How Many, How Many, How Many?
Hush! A Thai Lullaby
I Don't Care, Said the Bear
I Love You as Much
I Saw Esau
I Went to the Zoo
I'm in Charge of Celebrations
In Enzo's Splendid Gardens
In the Tall, Tall Grass
Is Your Mama a Llama?
It's Hard to Read a Map With a Beagle
    on Your Lap
James Marshall's Mother Goose
Jesse Bear, What Will You Wear?
Jolly Postman
Library
Lorax
Louella Mae, She's Run Away!
Madeline
Many Luscious Lollipops
Miss Bindergarten Gets Ready for
    Kindergarten
Mouse Mess
Mr. Willowby's Christmas Tree
My Very First Mother Goose

Napping House
Nathaniel Talking
Never Take a Pig to Lunch
Noisy Nora
Oh, The Places You'll Go!
Old Mother Hubbard and Her Won-
    derful Dog
On Market Street
On Sally Perry's Farm
One Hundred Hungry Ants
Piece of String Is a Wonderful
    Thing
Piggies
Poems Go Clang!
Possum Come a-Knockin'
Pretend You're a Cat
Random House Book of Poetry for
    Children
Rattlebone Rock
Read-Aloud Rhymes for the Very
    Young
Rhymes for Annie Rose
Say Hola to Spanish
Scary, Scary Halloween
Seven Blind Mice
Sheep in a Jeep
Sing a Song of Popcorn
Sing, Sophie!
Singing America
Sitting on the Farm
Six Creepy Sheep
Skip Across the Ocean
Slugs
Something Big Has Been Here
Squash and a Squeeze
Sweet Corn
Talking Like the Rain
This Is the Hat
Three Bears Holiday Rhyme Book
Three in a Balloon
Time for Bed
To Market, To Market
Tree in the Wood
Walking the Bridge of Your Nose
What's What?
Where the Sidewalk Ends
Where's My Teddy?
Who Said Boo?
Who Said Red?
World of Christopher Robin
Yo, Hungry Wolf!
You Be Good and I'll Be Night

Zoom! Zoom! Zoom! I'm Off to the Moon

rhythm (books where the rhythm exerts a powerful pull on the reader)
17 Kings & 42 Elephants
Bein' With You This Way
Call Down the Moon
Chicka Chicka Boom Boom
Dancing Feet
Five Live Bongos
Frogs in Clogs
Grandmother's Nursery Rhymes
Hip Cat
I Like the Music
I Saw Esau
If You're Not From the Prairie
Joyful Noise
Meet the Marching Smithereens
Nathaniel Talking
On Sally Perry's Farm
Possum Come a-Knockin'
Ten Sly Piranhas
This Is the Hat
Today Is Monday
White Dynamite and Curly Kidd
Yo, Hungry Wolf!

rice
Everybody Cooks Rice
One Grain of Rice

riddles
Colors Around Us
Grandmother's Nursery Rhymes
How Many, How Many, How Many?
Toll-Bridge Troll
Walking the Bridge of Your Nose

rituals
Cherokees
Chicken Sunday
Corpses, Coffins, and Crypts
Day of the Dead
Dead Bird
Dragonling
Egypt Game
Farm Morning
Giver
How to Make a Mummy Talk
I Am the Mummy Heb-Nefert

K Is for Kiss Goodnight
One World, Many Religions
Pablo Remembers
Sacred Places
Stranded at Plimoth Plantation, 1626
View From Sturday
Welcoming Babies

rivers
Adventures of Huckleberry Finn
Girl Named Disaster
My Visit to the Aquarium
Story About Ping
Zilla Sasparilla and the Mud Baby

Robin Hood
Forestwife
Robin Hood & Little John
Robin's Country

rocks
Anansi and the Moss-Covered Rock
Everybody Needs a Rock
Sylvester and the Magic Pebble

Rome
Rome Antics

roosters
That Kookoory!
Three in a Balloon

running away
From the Mixed-Up Files of Mrs. Basil E. Frankweiler
Hobkin
Runaway Bunny
Saving Sweetness
See You Around, Sam
Zeke Pippin

Russia
Always Prayer Shawl
Baba Yaga and Vasalisa the Brave
Babushka Baba Yaga
Bit by Bit
Clay Boy
Fool of the World and the Flying Ship
Keeping Quilt
Miracle of the Latkes
Molly's Pilgrim
Sworn Enemies

Russian Americans
Chicken Sunday
Make a Wish, Molly

sadness
Earth-Shattering Poems
Feelings
Nettie's Trip South

safety
Make Way for Ducklings
Mick Harte Was Here
Officer Buckle and Gloria

sailing
Maggie B
Pirate's Handbook
Wanderings of Odysseus

saints
Saint Francis

salamanders
Salamander Room

San Francisco
Fiesta
I Am Lavina Cumming
Julie of the Wolves

Santa Claus
Harvey Slumfenburger's Christmas
    Present
Night Before Christmas
Polar Express
Santa Calls
Santa's Favorite Story

scary stories and poems (chilling,
    and sometimes horrifying)
Bone Man
Dark Thirty
Dark Way
Don't Open the Door After the Sun
    Goes Down
Headless Haunt and Other African-
    American Ghost Stories
Horror Stories
In a Messy, Messy Room and Other
    Scary Stories
Phantom Hitchhiker
Psychzone: Kidzilla and Other Tales

Scary Stories to Tell in the Dark
Sing a Song of Popcorn
Tog the Ribber, or Granny's Tale

school
3 NBS of Julian Drew
Adrian Mole Diaries
Adventures of Captain Underpants
After the War Was Over
All We Needed to Say
Amber Brown Is Not a Crayon
Amelia's Notebook
Angel Child, Dragon Child
Angela and Diabola
Angelina Ballerina
Author's Day
Bear's House
Bee Tree
Blubber
Blue Skin of the Sea
Captain Abdul's Pirate School
Children Just Like Me
Children of the River
Chocolate War
Cleversticks
Cyber.Kdz Series
Darnell Rock Reporting
Did You See What I Saw?
Don't Read This Book, Whatever You
    Do
Emma
Fate Totally Worse Than Death
First Grade Takes a Test
Fish in His Pocket
Friends and Amigos Series
Front Porch Stories at the One-Room
    School
Harriet the Spy
Hey World, Here I Am!
I Hadn't Mean to Tell You This
I Hate English
If You're Not Here, Please Raise Your
    Hand
Ironman
Jip, His Story
John Patrick Norman McHennessy,
    The Boy Who Was Always Late
Josepha
Kid in the Red Jacket
Kids of the Polk Street School
Killing Mr. Griffin
Library Dragon

Lilly's Purple Plastic Purse
Madeline
Marvin Redpost: Alone in His
    Teacher's House
Math Curse
Matilda
Minerva Louise at School
Miss Bindergarten Gets Ready for
    Kindergarten
Miss Nelson Is Missing
Molly's Pilgrim
Nothing But the Truth
Officer Buckle and Gloria
Pee Wee Scouts series
Pigman
Ramona the Pest
Rats Saw God
Red Scarf Girl
Ruby the Copycat
Seven Spiders Spinning
Shoebag
Sideways Stories From Wayside
    School
Skin Deep and other Teenage Reflec-
    tions
Slave Day
Solitary Blue
Stephanie's Ponytail
Tales of Trotter Street
There's a Boy in the Girl's Bathroom
Toll-Bridge Troll
View From Saturday
Where Are You Going, Manyoni?

science
All About Alligators
Animal Dads
Archibald Frisby
Beyond Amazing
Body Atlas
Bone Poems
Bugs
Chickens Aren't the Only Ones
Corn Is Maize
Dear Mr. Blueberry
Dem Bones
Discovering the Iceman
Dragonflies
Earth, Fire, Water, Air
Earth, Sky, and Beyond
Enormous Egg
Good Morning Pond

Grossology
House for a Hermit Crab
I'll See You When the Moon Is Full
In the Beginning . . .
Inside the Amazing Amazon
Into the Sea
Is This a House for Hermit Crab?
Kingfisher Science Encyclopedia
Learning to Swim in Swaziland
Life and Times of the Apple
Life and Times of the Honeybee
Made in China
Magic School Bus in the Time of the
    Dinosaurs
Mouse and Mole and the Year-Round
    Garden
My Hen Is Dancing
Old Ladies Who Liked Cats
Outside and Inside Snakes
Papa, Please Get the Moon for Me
Popcorn Book
Science Experiments You Can Eat
Snail's Spell
Star Walk
Starry Messenger
Ten Little-Known Facts About Hippos
Those Amazing Ants
Too Many Rabbits
Until I Met Dudley
Volcano: The Eruption and Healing of
    Mount St. Helens
Way Things Work
Where's That Insect?
Yikes! Your Body Up Close

science experiments
Beyond Amazing
Drop of Water
Grossology
Made in China
Science Experiments You Can Eat

science fiction
5 Novels by Daniel Pinkwater
Adventures of Tintin
Animorphs
City of Gold and Lead
Commander Toad in Space
Eva
Forgotten Door
Lizard Music
Wrinkle in Time

scientists
Discovery of Dragons
Enormous Egg
Starry Messenger

Scotland
Boggart
Eric Knight's Lassie Come Home
Lassie Come Home
Mysterious Tadpole
Puzzling Day at Castle MacPelican
William Shakespeare's Macbeth

sculpture
Celebrate America in Poetry and Art
Getting to Know the World's Great
    Artists

sea
At the Beach
Big Al
Birdie's Lighthouse
Blue Skin of the Sea
Into the Sea
Is This a House for Hermit Crab?
Maggie B
My Life With the Wave
Nicholas Pipe
Paddle-to-the-Sea
True Confessions of Charlotte Doyle
Until I Saw the Sea
Wanderings Of Odysseus
William Shakespeare's The Tempest
Wreck of the Zanzibar

seals
Is Your Mama a Llama?

searches
Are You My Mother?
Each Peach Pear Plum
Livingstone Mouse
Stellaluna
Stuart Little
Where's Spot

searching game (In these books the
    reader Is encouraged through
    clues and/or pictures to make a
    game out of searching for an
    object or character.)
Animalia

Do You See a Mouse?
Each Peach Pear Plum
I Spy Series
Looking for Atlantis
Louella Mae, She's Run Away!
My Life With the Wave
Puzzling Day at Castle MacPelican
Where's That Insect?

seasons
Apple Pie Tree
City of Light, City of Dark
Classic Poems to Read Aloud
Did You Hear Wind Sing Your Name?
Eeny, Meeny, Miney Mole
Frog and Toad All Year
Gather Up Gather In
It's Pumpkin Time!
January Rides the Wind
June Is a Tune That Jumps on a Stair
Look to the North
Moonstick
Nutshell Library
Ox-Cart Man
Seasons and Someone
Thirteen Moons on Turtle's Back
Three Bears Holiday Rhyme Book
Turtle in July
Year at Maple Hill Farm
Year on My Street
Yonder

secrets
Animorphs
Are You There God? It's Me, Margaret
Borrowers
Cinderella's Rat
Dawn (Bang)
Day of Ahmed's Secret
Eva
Face on the Milk Carton
Harriet the Spy
High Rise Glorious Skittle Skat Roari-
    ous Sky Pie Angel Food Cake
I Am the Cheese
Judy Scuppernong
Killing Mr. Griffin
Letters From the Inside
Man Who Could Call Down Owls
Midnight Hour Encores
Mouse and the Motorcycle
Place to Call Home

Search for the Shadowman
Secret Code Book
Secret Garden
Soda Jerk
Spite Fences
Stepping on the Cracks

self-defense
Smart Moves

self-respect (books that show characters dealing with Issues of pride and self confidence)
Absolutely, Positively Alexander
All Dads on Deck
All the Colors of the Race
All We Needed to Say
Am I Blue?
Amazing Grace
Badger's Bring Something Party
Baseball Saved Us
Belle Prater's Boy
Black Snowman
Brown Honey in Broomwheat Tea
Butterfly Jar
Carrot Seed
Charlotte's Web
Cleversticks
Crossing
Cyber.Kdz Series
Dear Mr. Sprouts
Earl's Too Cool For Me
Emma
Fortunately
Hey World, Here I Am!
Hooray for Me
I Hate English
I Want to Be
I Wish I Were a Butterfly
I, Houdini
Ice
If You're Not Here, Please Raise Your Hand
Ironman
Kid in the Red Jacket
King's Equal
Leo the Late Bloomer
Little Red Ant and the Great Big Crumb
Magic Fan
Matilda
Meet Danitra Brown

Memoirs of a Bookbat
Miss Rumphius
My Map Book
Nettie's Trip South
Noel the First
Oh, the Places You'll Go!
Oliver Button Is a Sissy
Quick as a Cricket
Ruby Mae Has Something to Say
Ruby the Copycat
Shy Charles
Somebody Loves You, Mr. Hatch
Teammates
There's a Boy in the Girl's Bathroom
There's a Nightmare in My Closet
Uncle Jed's Barbershop
Verdi
Voyage to the Bunny Planet
What a Wonderful Day to Be a Cow
Who Is the Beast?
William's Doll
Wonderful Wizard of Oz

senses
Cozy Book
Fuzzy Yellow Ducklings
Gather Up Gather In
Night Sounds, Morning Colors
Pat the Bunny
Seven Blind Mice
Smelly Old History Series
Voices From the Wild
Windsongs and Rainbows

separation
All the Lights in the Night
Angel Child, Dragon Child
Cuckoo's Child
Face on the Milk Carton
Gardener
Hannah and Jack
I Am the Cheese
Kite Flier
Lassie Come Home
Lily's Crossing
Number the Stars
Peacebound Trains
Rapunzel
Sarah, Plain and Tall
Skylark
Waiting for the Evening Star

sewing
Bit by Bit
Hands

sexuality
Am I Blue?
It's a Girl Thing
It's Perfectly Normal

Shakers
Shaker Boy

Shakespeare
Bard of Avon
Killing Mr. Griffin
Something Rich and Strange
William Shakespeare's Macbeth

shapes
Grandfather Tang's Story
Puzzle Maps USA
What Am I?
White on Black

sharing
Benny's Pennies
Cat's Purr
Ginger
Green Truck Garden Giveaway
Let's Be Enemies
Mr. Willowby's Christmas Tree
Rat and the Tiger
War with Grandpa

sharks
Blue Skin of the Sea
Great White Man-Eating Shark

sheep
Babe, the Gallant Pig
Sheep in a Jeep
Shepherd Boy
Six Creepy Sheep
Three in a Balloon

shepherds
Shepherd Boy

shoes
All About Alfie
Frogs in Clogs
Shoes, Shoes, Shoes

Where Will This Shoe Take You?

shopping
Bear Called Paddington
Bunny Money
Market!
Max's Dragon Shirt
On Market Street
To Market, To Market

shyness
Emily
Shy Charles
Willy the Wimp

siblings
Absolutely, Positively Alexander
Anastasia Krupnik
Angela and Diabola
Baby Sister for Frances
Barn (Avi)
Birthday for Frances
Bunny Money
Chasing Redbird
Chronicles of Narnia
Cinderella's Rat
Cuckoo's Child
Dance, Tanya
Dinner at Alberta's
Dragonfly's Tale
Felix's Hat
Five Children and It
Flip-Flop Girl
Four Story Mistake
Ghost-Eye Tree
Homecoming
I'll Fix Anthony
Jeremy's Decision
Maggie B
Max's Dragon Shirt
Mean Margaret
Mississippi Mud
Morning Girl
New Baby
No Fighting, No Biting!
Noisy Nora
On Mother's Lap
Peter Spier's Rain
Peter's Chair
Santa Calls
Sarah, Plain and Tall
Sisters

Summer of Stanley
Sun and Spoon
Watch Out Man Eating Snake
Wreck of the Zanzibar
Za-Za's Baby Brother

sign language
Communication
Handmade Alphabet
Handsigns
Handtalk

signs and signals
Communication
Puff . . . Flash . . . Bang!

silk
Silk Route

singing
Chicken Man
Day of the Dead
Eagle's Gift
Sing, Sophie!
Singer to the Sea God
When Bluebell Sang

single parents
Boundless Grace
Christmas Miracle of Jonathan
    Toomey
Country Bunny and the Little Gold
    Shoes
Dear Mr. Henshaw
Fly Away Home
Half Magic
Kinship
Kite Flier
Ma Dear's Aprons
Midnight Hour Encores
Monster Mama
Peppermint Race
Sarah, Plain and Tall
Zilla Sasparilla and the Mud Baby

sisters
All About Alfie
All-of-a-Kind Family
Angela and Diabola
Arthur's Loose Tooth
Baby Sister for Frances
Birthday for Frances

Eeny, Meeny, Miney Mole
Hobkin
Lon Po Po
Maggie B
Max's Dragon Shirt
Memoirs of a Bookbat
On Mother's Lap
Peter's Chair
Ramona the Pest
Rhymes for Annie Rose
Santa Calls
Save Queen of Sheba
Singer to the Sea God
Sisters
Soon, Annala
Sootface

skating
Mr. Popper's Penguins

skunks
Mean Margaret
Time to Sleep

sky
Cloudland
Earth, Sky, and Beyond

slang
Buffalo Tree
Frank and Ernest

slavery
Adventures of High John the
    Conqueror
Barefoot
Black Snowman
Celebration!
Christmas in the Big House,
    Christmas in the Quarters
Drinking Gourd
Escape From Slavery
Get on Board
Gladiator
Glory Field
Harriet and the Promised Land
Jip, His Story
Lightning Time
Minty
Nettie's Trip South
Nightjohn
Now Let Me Fly

Slave Day
Sweet Clara and the Freedom Quilt
Sweet Words So Brave
To Be a Slave
Wagon

sleep
Napping House
When I'm Sleepy

slugs
Bugs (Parker)
Slugs
Some Smug Slug

snails
Snail's Spell
Time to Sleep

snakes
Arthur's Camp-Out
Chickens Aren't the Only Ones
Day Jimmy's Boa Ate the Wash
King Snake
Mean Margaret
Outside and Inside Snakes
Possum Magic
Rattlesnake Dance
Rikki-Tikki-Tavi
Small Green Snake
Turtle in July
Verdi

snow
Black Snowman
Brave Irene
Brian's Winter
Dogteam
Froggy Gets Dressed
Girl Who Dreamed Only of Geese
In the Dinosaur's Paw
In the Snow: Who's Been Here
Is That You, Winter?
Mitten
Snowy Day
Will's Mammoth
Winter Poems
Winter White

solar system
Earth, Sky, and Beyond
Planets

soldiers
Crossing
Damned Strong Love
Gladiator
Heroes
I Had Seen Castles
Number the Stars
Nutcracker
Pink and Say
Rose Blanche
Stone Soup
Sworn Enemies
War Boy
Westmark

solitude
Allison
Angel for Solomon Singer
Captain Snap and the Children of
    Vinegar Lane
Christmas Miracle of Jonathan
    Toomey
Eleanor
Five Minutes Peace
Great Ball Game
Hatchet
Ice
Island of the Blue Dolphins
Lizard Music
Only Opal
Rapunzel
Secret Places
Solitary Blue
Stellaluna
War with Grandpa
Zee

solstice
Dear Rebecca, Winter Is Here

songs
Abiyoyo
Arroz con Leche
Bread Is for Eating
Dem Bones
Down by the River
From Sea to Shining Sea
Get on Board
Gonna Sing My Head Off!
Hilary Knight's The Twelve Days of
    Christmas
Hush Little Baby

Mysterious Thelonious
Old MacDonald Had a Farm
She'll Be Comin' Round the Mountain
Sing, Sophie!
Sitting on the Farm
Talking Like the Rain
Teddy Bear's Picnic
Twelve Days of Christmas
Welcoming Babies
Wheels on the Bus
When Bluebell Sang

sound
Crash! Bang! Boom!
Gobble, Growl, Grunt
In the Tall, Tall Grass
Joyful Noise
Listen to the Desert
Night Sounds, Morning Colors
Poems Go Clang!
Rain Talk
Very Quiet Cricket
Why Mosquitoes Buzz in People's
     Ears

soup
Martha Speaks
Nutshell Library
Stone Soup
To Market, To Market

South Africa
Abiyoyo
At the Crossroads
My Painted House, My Friendly
     Chicken, & Me

Spain
El Chino

Spanish (the language)
Abuela
Arroz con Leche
Bread Is for Eating
Calling the Doves
Cool Salsa
De Colores
Fabulous Fireworks Family
Gathering the Sun
Grandmother's Nursery
     Rhymes
Listen to the Desert

Little Red Ant and the Great Big
     Crumb
Margaret and Margarita
My First Book of Proverbs
Old Man and His Door
Voices From the Fields
We Are a Rainbow

Spanish words
Alice Nizzy Nazzy
Chato's Kitchen
Day's Work
Fiesta
Friends and Amigos Series
Here Comes the Storyteller
Say Hola to Spanish
Tale of Rabbit and Coyote

speeches
Creation
I Have a Dream
Lincoln in His Own Words
Lincoln: A Photobiography
Ruby Mae Has Something to Say

spelling
Handtalk
Macmillan Dictionary for Children

spices
Spice Alphabet Book

spiders
Bugs (Parker)
Charlotte's Web
Chickens Aren't the Only Ones
I Wish I Were a Butterfly
James and the Giant Peach
Seven Spiders Spinning
Very Busy Spider

spooky stories (lightly scary and not
     violent)
Bumps in the Night
By the Light of the Halloween Moon
Dark Thirty
Ghost-Eye Tree
Guess What?
Halloween ABC
Hershel and the Hanukkah Goblins
Hobyahs
House That Drac Built

Monster Motel
Old Devil Wind
Seven Spiders Spinning
Six Creepy Sheep
Velcome!

sports
Boys Will Be
Crash
Gladiator
Ironman
Lives of the Athletes
Red Hot Hightops
Wilma Unlimited
Wolfbay Wings

Spring
Did You Hear Wind Sing Your Name?
Eeny, Meeny, Miney Mole
From Seed to Plant

spying
Harriet the Spy

squirrels
Mean Margaret
Nuts to You
Smudge

stagecoaches
Charlie Drives the Stage

stalemate (see: deadlocks)

stars
Coyote in Love
Drinking Gourd
My House Has Stars
Starry Messenger

step families
Baba Yaga and Vasalisa the Brave
Boundless Grace
Cinder Edna
Staying Fat for Sarah Byrnes
When We Married Gary
Yeh-Shen: A Cinderella Story from
    China

stepparents
3 NBS of Julian Drew
Lion's Whiskers

Pulling the Lion's Tail
Sarah, Plain and Tall
What Hearts
What Jamie Saw
When We Married Gary

storms
Ali, Child of the Desert
Ben and Me
Blue Skin of the Sea
Brave Irene
Do Not Open
Gulliver's Adventures in Lilliput
Peter Spier's Rain
Rain
Rainy Day
Thunder Cake
Way West
Windsongs and Rainbows

storytelling
Amazing Grace
Ancestor Tree
Arabian Nights
Black Snowman
Calling the Doves
Clay Boy
Close Your Eyes So You Can See
Cloudy With a Chance of Meatballs
Dancing With the Wind
Dark Thirty
Eagle's Gift
Everglades
Frederick
Front Porch Stories at the One-Room
    School
Grandfather Tang's Story
Grandma Essie's Covered Wagon
Headless Haunt and Other African-
    American Ghost Stories
Here Comes the Storyteller
Hog-Eye
John Henry
King Snake
Larger Than Life
Max and Ruby's First Greek Myth:
    Pandora's Box
Miz Berlin Walks
Mysteries of Harris Burdick
Nursery Tales Around the World
Patchwork Quilt
People Could Fly

Pink and Say
River That Went to the Sky
Santa's Favorite Story
Short and Shivery
Stories by Firelight
Swan Stories
Tog the Ribber, or Granny's Tale
Tomas and the Library Lady
Whale's Song
Whittler's Tale
Will's Mammoth
Worry Stone

strangers
Guests
Heckedy Peg
Princess Nevermore
Raggly, Scraggly, No-Soap, No-Scrub
    Girl
Winter White

strawberries
First Strawberries
Grey Lady and the Strawberry
    Snatcher
Little Mouse, the Red Ripe Straw-
    berry, and the Big Hungry Bear

string
Piece of String Is a Wonderful Thing

stubbornness
Ornery Morning
Too Many Pumpkins

stuffed animals
Tom and Pippo Books
Velveteen Rabbit
Where's My Teddy?
World of Pooh

suicide
Remembering the Good Times

Summer
Camp Ghost Away
Pee Wee Pool Party
Relatives Came

sun
Arrow to the Sun
First Strawberries

Raven
Sun Song
Windsongs and Rainbows
Winter White

surprises
Birthday Surprises
Charlie Drives the Stage
Charlie the Chicken
Cinderella's Rat
Enormous Egg
Good Night, Gorilla
Mac and Marie and the Train Toss
    Surprise
Monster at the End of This Book
So Much
Suddenly!
Wednesday Surprise

survival
Abel's Island
Ballad of Lucy Whipple
Bone From a Dry Sea
Brian's Winter
Buffalo Tree
Cay
Chato's Kitchen
Children of the Dust Bowl
Crossing
Deathwatch
Earthshine
Girl Named Disaster
Great Gilly Hopkins
Hansel and Gretel
Harlem
Hatchet
Hattie and the Fox
I Am an American
Island of the Blue Dolphins
James and the Giant Peach
Jip, His Story
King Snake
Music and Drum
One Night
Polar the Titanic Bear
Riptide
Save Queen of Sheba
Seasons and Someone
Stranded at Plimoth Plantation, 1626
True Confessions of Charlotte Doyle
Way Home
Way West

suspicion
Baseball Saved Us
Under the Blood Red Sun

swamps
Liza Lou and the Yeller Belly Swamp
Mama Don't Allow

swans
Is Your Mama a Llama?
Swan Stories

Sweden
Supergrandpa

swimming
Frog and Toad Are Friends
Great White Man-Eating Shark
Maisy Goes Swimming
Pee Wee Pool Party
Riptide
Staying Fat for Sarah Byrnes
Young Larry

symbols
Children's Book of Kwanzaa
Communication
Eight Hands Round
Elijah's Angel
Keeping Quilt
Money, Money, Money
One Yellow Daffodil
Secret Code Book

taking action (includes doing the
    right thing and taking a stand)
Adventures of Huckleberry Finn
Araboolies of Liberty Street
Art Dog
Ballad of the Pirate Queens
Barn
Big Bazoohley
Captain Snap and the Children of
    Vinegar Lane
Chocolate War
Christmas Menorahs
Darnell Rock Reporting
Dear Willie Rudd
Fragile Flag
Giver
Great Kapok Tree
Green Truck Garden Giveaway

Heroes
Homecoming
Last Princess
Lightning Time
Lilly's Purple Plastic Purse
Lily's Crossing
Lorax
Malcolm X: By Any Means Necessary
Memoirs of a Bookbat
Mendel's Ladder
Miss Rumphius
Nicholas Pipe
Okino and the Whales
Outsiders
People Who Hugged Trees
Peppe the Lamp Lighter
Pole Dog
Rose Blanche
Ruby Mae Has Something to Say
Seedfolks
Slave Day
Someday a Tree
Spite Fences
Take Action
Teammates
Tuck Everlasting
When the Monkeys Came Back
Witches

talent
Babe, the Gallant Pig
Courtney
Emma
Mirette on the High Wire

tall tales
Big Men, Big Country
Bo Rabbit Smart for True
Bunyans
Come Look With Me
Folks Call Me Appleseed John
Giants!
Higgins Bend Song and Dance
John Henry
Larger Than Life
Maniac Magee
Raggly, Scraggly, No-Soap, No-Scrub
    Girl
Sally Ann Thunder Ann Whirlwind
    Crockett
Small Tall Tale from the Far, Far
    North

Swamp Angel
Telling of the Tales

tangrams
Grandfather Tang's Story

tardiness
John Patrick Norman McHennessy,
    The Boy Who Was Always Late

tea parties
Bargain for Frances
May I Bring a Friend?
Mud Pies and Other Recipes
View From Saturday

teachers
All We Needed to Say
Don't Read This Book, Whatever You
    Do
Emma
I Hate English
If You're Not Here, Please Raise Your
    Hand
John Patrick Norman McHennessy,
    The Boy Who Was Always Late
Josepha
Kids of the Polk Street School
Killing Mr. Griffin
Lilly's Purple Plastic Purse
Marvin Redpost: Alone in His
    Teacher's House
Matilda
Mirette on the High Wire
Miss Bindergarten Gets Ready for
    Kindergarten
Miss Nelson Is Missing
My Great-Aunt Arizona
Nightjohn
Nothing But the Truth
Ruby the Copycat
Seven Spiders Spinning
Sideways Stories From Wayside
    School
Slave Day
View From Saturday

teachers, substitute
Miss Nelson Is Missing

teams
Baseball Saved Us

Leagues Apart
Red Hot Hightops
Teammates
Wolfbay Wings

teamwork
Dancing With the Wind
Freak the Mighty
Light, Action, Land-Ho!
Officer Buckle and Gloria
On Sally Perry's Farm
Virtual War

teasing
Arrow to the Sun
Beautiful Feast for a Big King
    Cat
Blubber
Caps for Sale
Cow that Went Oink
Cyber.Kdz Series
Game of Catch
Gingerbread Boy
Heroes
Molly's Pilgrim
Oliver Button Is a Sissy
Red Racer
Story of Ferdinand
Tortoise and the Hare

teddy bears
First Flight
Polar the Titanic Bear
Teddy Bear's Picnic
Where's My Teddy?

teenage mothers
Make Lemonade

teeth
Airmail to the Moon
Arthur's Loose Tooth
Doctor DeSoto

tests
First Grade Takes a Test

Texas
Hobkin
Search for the Shadowman

Thailand
Hush! A Thai Lullaby

Thanksgiving
Eating the Plates
Molly's Pilgrim

theater
Away From Home
Bard of Avon
Bear Called Paddington
Grandpa's Face
Light, Action, Land-Ho!
Lili Backstage
Show Time at the Polk Street School

theft
ABC Mystery
Art Dog
Grey Lady and the Strawberry
    Snatcher

thunder
Sing, Sophie!
Thunder Cake

tidepools
My Visit to the Aquarium

tigers
Big Cats
Nine in One Grr! Grr!
Sam and the Tigers
Story of Little Babaji
Tyger
Who Is the Beast?

time
I'll See You When the Moon Is Full
Moonstick
Somewhere in the World Right Now
Sun Song
Talking Like the Rain
Twilight Comes Twice
Verdi

time travel
Devil's Arithmetic
Good, the Bad, and the Goofy
Knight's Castle
We're Back!
Wrinkle in Time

Titanic
Polar the Titanic Bear

toads
Commander Toad in Space
Frogs
Toad

toddlers
Mean Margaret
More, More, More, Said the Baby
Tom and Pippo Books

tongue twisters
Aster Aardvark's Alphabet
    Adventures
Busy Buzzing Bumblebees
Santa's Short Suit Shrunk and Other
    Christmas Tongue Twisters
Six Sick Sheep
Walking the Bridge of Your Nose

tooth fairy
Airmail to the Moon
Tooth Fairy's Tale

tortillas
Tortilla Factory

tortoises
Flying Tortoise
Stories From Firefly Island
Tortoise and the Hare

touch
Fuzzy Yellow Ducklings
Pat the Bunny
Very Busy Spider

towns
Homer Price
Mike Mulligan & His Steam Shovel
New Hope
Richard Scarry's Busy Town
Soda Jerk
Waiting to Waltz

toys
Clown
Galimoto
Indian in the Cupboard
Nutcracker

Of Colors and Things
Velveteen Rabbit
Where Does It Go?
William's Doll

track and field
Atalanta's Race
Cat Running
Ironman
Maniac Magee
Wilma Unlimited

trade
Silk Route

traditions (includes customs)
A Is for Africa
All-of-a-Kind Family
Always Prayer Shawl
Ancestor Tree
Ashanti to Zulu
Baker's Dozen
Bee Tree
Cherokees
Children of the River
Christmas in the Big House,
    Christmas in the Quarters
Corpses, Coffins, and Crypts
Day of the Dead
Dragonling
Eating the Plates
Egypt Game
Fabulous Fireworks Family
Fair!
Girl Named Disaster
Girl Who Dreamed Only of Geese
Giver
Golden Carp and Other Tales from
    Vietnam
Guests
Happy New Year! Kung-Hsi Fa-Ts'ai!
Hershel and the Hanukkah Goblins
History of the US
Hooray, a Piñata!
How My Parents Learned to Eat
Indian Winter
Luka's Quilt
Make a Wish Molly
Misoso
Molly's Pilgrim
One World, Many Religions
Pablo Remembers

Sacred Places
Seasons and Someone
Seven Candles for Kwanzaa
Slave Day
Stranded at Plimoth Plantation, 1626
Tree of Cranes
Welcoming Babies

trailblazing (includes being first and
    getting there first)
Alvin Ailey
Around the World in a Hundred Years
Ben and Me
Chasing Redbird
Discovery of Dragons
Eeny, Meeny, Miney Mole
Flight
Fly! A Brief History of Flight
Follow the Dream
In the Beginning . . .
Made in China
New Hope
Small Tall Tale from the Far, Far North

trains
Bear Called Paddington
Charlie Drives the Stage
Freight Train
Hey! Get Off Our Train
Mac and Marie and the Train Toss
    Surprise
Moans and Groans and Dinosaur
    Bones
Nettie's Trip South
Peacebound Trains
Polar Express
Real McCoy
Richard Scarry's Cars and Trucks and
    Things that Go
Stephen Biesty's Incredible Cross-
    Sections
Train to Grandma's
Waiting for the Evening Star

transportation
Freight Train
Richard Scarry's Cars and Trucks and
    Things that Go
Wheels on the Bus

travel
Away From Home

Easter Egg Artists
Fortunately
How to Make an Apple Pie and See
    the World
Kidding Around Washington DC
Linnea in Monet's Garden
Look Out Washington, DC!
Madeline
Miss Rumphius
Moans and Groans and Dinosaur
    Bones
Relatives Came
Stringbean's Trip to the Shining Sea
Three-Legged Cat
Through Moon and Stars and Night
    Skies
Train to Grandma's
Wish You Were Here

treasure
Looking for Atlantis
Tale of Ali Baba and the Forty
    Thieves

trees
Ancestor Tree
Ancient Ones
Apple Pie Tree
Chicka Chicka Boom Boom
Ghost-Eye Tree
Giants in the Land
Have You Seen Trees?
Mr. Willowby's Christmas Tree
People Who Hugged Trees
Someday a Tree
Tree in the Wood
Tree Is Growing
Tree Is Nice
When the Monkeys Came Back

trick-or-treat
Very Scary
When the Goblins Came Knocking
Who Said Boo?

trickster tales
Adventures of High John the Con-
    queror
Anansi and the Moss-Covered Rock
Aunt Nancy and Old Man Trouble
Bo Rabbit Smart for True
Boggart

Coyote
Fire Race
Flying Tortoise
Jump!
Nine in One Grr! Grr!
Raven
Ring of Tricksters
Stone Soup
Tale of Rabbit and Coyote
Tales of Uncle Remus
Tops and Bottoms
Winter White

triumph
Alice Nizzy Nazzy
Author: A True Story
Babe, the Gallant Pig
Big Bazoohley
Buffalo Tree
Chato's Kitchen
Clay Boy
Glory Field
Growing Up in Coal Country
Hattie and the Fox
Hobyahs
Ironman
Jack and the Beanstalk
John Patrick Norman McHennessy,
    The Boy Who Was Always Late
Liza Lou and the Yeller Belly Swamp
Mama Don't Allow
Mysterious Tadpole
Nell Nuggett and the Cow Caper
Paper Dragon
Phantom Tollbooth
Piggie Pie
Rat and the Tiger
Rikki-Tikki-Tavi
Sam and the Tigers
Story of Little Babaji
Tacky the Penguin
That Kookoory!
Three Little Wolves and the Big Bad
    Pig
Tops and Bottoms
Tortoise and the Hare
Wilma Unlimited

trivia (includes fascinating facts)
Guinness Book of World Records
In the Next Three Seconds
Lives of the Athletes

Ten Little-Known Facts About Hippos
Who Said That?

Trojan War
Black Ships Before Troy
Dateline: Troy

trolls
Three Billy Goats Gruff
Toll-Bridge Troll

trucks
Dear Mr. Henshaw
Richard Scarry's Cars and Trucks and
    Things that Go
Tales of Trotter Street

truth (includes honesty)
Big Bazoohley
Day's Work
Deathwatch
Empty Pot
Face on the Milk Carton
Harriet the Spy
John Patrick Norman McHennessy,
    The Boy Who Was Always Late
Liar Liar Pants on Fire
Nothing But the Truth
Poppleton
True Lies
When Stories Fell Like Shooting Stars

Tubman, Harriet
Harriet and the Promised Land
Minty

turtles
Into the Sea
Mordant's Wish
Old Turtle
Thirteen Moons on Turtle's Back
Time to Sleep
Turtle in July
Wreck of the Zanzibar

twilight
Grandfather Twilight
Twilight Comes Twice

U.S. history, 19th century
Indian Winter
Orphan Train Adventures

Ox-Cart Man
Sarah, Plain and Tall

U.S. history, 20th century
Harlem

**U.S. history, between the World
    Wars**
Girl From Yamhill

U.S. history, Civil War
Bull Run
Celebration!
Escape From Slavery
Lightning Time
Lincoln in His Own Words
Lincoln: A Photobiography
Nettie's Trip South
Pink and Say
Thunder at Gettysburg
Wagon

U.S. history, Colonial America
Baker's Dozen
Bear That Heard Crying
Ben and Me
Eating the Plates
Finding Providence
Giants in the Land
Goody O'Grumpity
Grandmother Bryant's Pocket
Guests
Hired Hand
Stranded at Plimoth Plantation, 1626
Whaling Days

U.S. history, early 20th century
All-of-a-Kind Family
Flight
I Am Lavina Cumming
Only Opal
Roxaboxen
Waiting for the Evening Star

U.S. history, frontier life
Barn (Avi)
Big Men, Big Country
Cheyenne Again
Dakota Dugout
Floating House
Little House on the Prairie
Only Opal

rians
Be a Veterinarian

ild, Dragon Child
Slipper and Other
hamese Tales
arp and Other Tales from
1am
ed

Veterans Memorial
ippin
r Stillness

ese culture
arp and Other Tales from
1am

hs
ls

Boy

ne Divide
ree
lf
ight
tle Wolves and the Big Bad

1ots
Go to Birmingham, 1963

Meadows
hincoteague

eality
ar

craggly, No-Soap, No-Scrub

Came

ry (standout combinations
rds that turn text into an art

form and words into vocabulary
  stretchers)
Alpha Beta Chowder
Alphabet From Z to A (with Much
  Confusion Along the Way)
Animalia
Antics
Color
Dragons Are Singing Tonight
Drop of Water
Eating the Alphabet
Eye Spy: A Mysterious Alphabet
Frank and Ernest
Freight Train
Frogs in Clogs
Go Hang a Salami! I'm a Lasagna
  Hog!
Hole Is to Dig
House That Drac Built
Lunch
Macmillan Dictionary for
  Children
Maestro Plays
Number One Number Fun
Peck Slither and Slide
Puffins Climb, Penguins Rhyme
Richard Scarry's Best Word Book
  Ever
Say Hola to Spanish
Six Sick Sheep
Some Smug Slug
String of Beads
Tog the Ribber, or Granny's Tale
Weighty Word Book
What a Wonderful Day to Be a Cow
Where Does It Go?
Windsongs and Rainbows
Woodlore
Z Was Zapped
Zin! Zin! Zin! A Violin

volcanoes
Hill of Fire
Volcano: The Eruption and Healing of
  Mount St. Helens

wagers
Good Griselle
How to Eat Fried Worms

Wales
Grey King

Pioneer Sampler
Sewing Quilts
Sod Houses on the Great Plains
Sweetwater Run
Way West

U.S. history, general
American Girl Series
Barn (Atwell)
Buck Stops Here
California, Here We Come!
Celebrate America in Poetry and Art
Celebrating America
Cherokees
Come Look With Me
Dear America Series
Eight Hands Round
From Sea to Shining Sea
Glory Field
History of the U.S.
Homeplace
Look Out Washington, DC!
Money, Money, Money
My Fellow Americans
New Hope
Picture Book Biography Series
Search for the Shadowman
Seven Brave Women
Singing America
Sweet Words So Brave
Who Said That?

U.S. history, late 19th century
Eleanor
Great Fire
Growing Up in Coal Country

U.S. history, pre-Civil War
Adventures of High John the Con-
  queror
Barefoot
Christmas in the Big House,
  Christmas in the Quarters
Drinking Gourd
Nightjohn
Now Let Me Fly
Sweetwater Run
They're Off!
To Be a Slave

U.S. history, pre-Columbus
Corn Is Maize

Morning Girl
One Small Blue Bead
When Clay Sings

U.S. history, Reconstruction
Ma Dear's Aprons

U.S. history, the 20's
Mr. Popper's Penguins

U.S. history, the 50's
Judy Scuppernong
Malcolm X: By Any Means Necessary

U.S. history, the 60's
Kinship
Malcolm X: By Any Means Necessary
Midnight Hour Encores
Spite Fences
Watson's Go to Birmingham, 1963

**U.S. history, the American Revo-
  lution**
Ben and Me
Paul Revere's Ride
Will You Sign Here, John Hancock?
Young John Quincy

U.S. history, the Depression
Cat Running
Children of the Dust Bowl
Gardener
Gingerbread Doll
In Coal Country
Mississippi Bridge
Out of the Dust
Red Dirt Jessie
Roll of Thunder, Hear My Cry
Something Permanent
When I Was Nine

U.S. history, the Gold Rush
Ballad of Lucy Whipple
By the Great Horn Spoon

U.S. history, the Old West
Charlie Drives the Stage
Nell Nuggett and the Cow Caper

U.S. history, Vietnam War
Charlie Pippin
December Stillness

U.S. history, Westward movement
Ballad of Lucy Whipple
Beyond the Divide
By the Great Horn Spoon
Dakota Dugout
Iron Dragon Never Sleeps
Little House on the Prairie
Mississippi Mud
Save Queen of Sheba
Sewing Quilts
Ten Mile Day and the Building of the
     Transcontinental Railroad
Way West

U.S. history, World War II
Baseball Saved Us
Bracelet
I Am an American
I Had Seen Castles
Lily's Crossing
Stepping on the Cracks
Summer of Stanley

U.S. Presidents
Buck Stops Here
History of the U.S.
Lincoln in His Own Words
Lincoln: A Photobiography
Talking Peace

U.S.A., Appalachia
Airmail to the Moon
Belle Prater's Boy
Come a Tide
My Great-Aunt Arizona
Sally Arnold
Soap! Soap! Don't Forget the Soap!
Something Permanent
Waiting to Waltz

U.S.A., general
Celebrate America in Poetry and Art
Celebrating America
Fair!
Gonna Sing My Head Off!
How My Parents Learned to Eat
Singing America

U.S.A., New England
Birdie's Lighthouse
Eating the Plates
Grandmother Bryant's Pocket

Jip, His Story
Ox-Cart Man
Paul Revere's Ride
Skylark
Tae's Sonata

U.S.A., the Dust Bowl
Cat Running
Children of the Dust Bowl
Out of the Dust
Red Dirt Jessie

U.S.A., the Midwest
Homer Price
Indian Winter

U.S.A., the Pacific Northwest
Raven

U.S.A., the Prairie
Dakota Dugout
Heartland
If You're Not From the Prairie
Little House on the Prairie
Prairie Songs
Sarah, Plain and Tall
Sewing Quilts
Skylark
Sod Houses on the Great Plains
What You Know First

U.S.A., the South
Dark Thirty
Dear Willie Rudd
Judy Scuppernong
Jump!
Kinship
Mississippi Bridge
Nettie's Trip South
Now Let Me Fly
Roll of Thunder, Hear My Cry
Spite Fences
Tucker Pfeffercorn
Watson's Go to Birmingham, 1963
Well

U.S.A., the Southeast
Bo Rabbit Smart for True

U.S.A., the Southwest
Alice Nizzy Nazzy
Coyote

Dragonfly's Tale
Here Comes the Storyteller
I'm in Charge of Celebrations
Little Red Cowboy Hat
One Small Blue Bead
Shepherd Boy
Spoon for Every Bite
Three Little Javelinas
When Clay Sings

U.S.A., the States
Birdsong
Puzzle Maps USA
Wish You Were Here

U.S.A., the West
Cowboy Country
Gila Monsters Meet You at the Air-
     port
Saving Sweetness
Stringbean's Trip to the Shining
     Sea
They're Off!

Ukraine
Mitten
Rechenka's Eggs

uncles
Gardener
Heroes
I'll See You in My Dreams
Mac and Marie and the Train Toss
     Surprise
Secret Garden
So Much
Tiger Flowers

Underground Railroad
Barefoot
Drinking Gourd
Get on Board
Harriet and the Promised Land
Minty

United Nations
Children Just Like Me
Dear World
Ruby Mae Has Something to Say

utopia
Giver

Valentin
Bee My V
Somebody

vampires
Bunnicula
Silver Kiss

variety (c
     ries,
Big Bear's
Call Dow
Celebratio
Child's Ga
Dinosaurs
Don't Rea
     Do
Goddesses
Help Wan
I Feel a Li
Poetry Fro
Random H
     Child
Sad Under
Singing Ar
Small Talk
Something
Soul Looks
Story Libr
This Same
Uncanny
Where the
Whole Stor
World Myt

vegetables
Bunnicula
Carrot See
Eating the
From Seed
Fruit and
Growing C
Lunch
Oliver's Ve
String of B
Tale of Pet
To Market,
Tops and B

veterans
December
I Had Seen

veteri
I Want
Rosali

Vietn
Angel
Broca
     V
Golde
     V
Lotus

Vietn
Charli
Decer
Wall

Vietn
Golde
     V

villai
Anim
Santa
Shilo
Whip

viole
Beyor
Buffa
Mary
Smok
Three
     I
Twel
Watso
Wrin

Virgi
Blue
Misty

virtu
Virtu

visit
Ragg
     C
Relat

voca

Lost Years of Merlin
Over Sea, Under Stone

walls
Talking Walls
Wall

war
Always Prayer Shawl
Black Ships Before Troy
Blitzcat
Butter Battle Book
Ghost Dance
Grandfather's Journey
Gulliver's Adventures in
    Lilliput
Heroes
Lotus Seed
Music and Drum
One More River
Peacebound Trains
Rose Blanche
Sadako
Sadako and the Thousand Paper
    Cranes
Thunder at Gettysburg
Virtual War
Waiting for the Evening Star
War Boy
War with Grandpa
Westmark

Washington, DC
Kidding Around Washington DC
Look Out Washington, DC!
Talking Walls

water
Drop of Water
Elements Series

way things work, the
Round Buildings, Square Buildings
    and Buildings That Wiggle Like a
    Fish
Until I Met Dudley
Way Things Work

wealth
Beyond the Western Sea
Gift of Wali Dad
Just Rewards

One Grain of Rice
Spoon for Every Bite

weapons
Butter Battle Book
Redwall

weasels
That Kookoory!

weather
Bringing the Rain to Kapiti Plain
Cloudy With a Chance of
    Meatballs
Dancing With the Wind
Gather Up Gather In
In the Next Three Seconds
Mendel's Ladder
Rain
Rainy Day
Sing a Song of Popcorn
Snowy Day
Talking Like the Rain
Windsongs and Rainbows
Winter Poems
Year at Maple Hill Farm

weaving
Dragon's Robe
Fox Song
Weaving of a Dream

weddings
Keeping Quilt
When We Married Gary

wells
Well
Well Wished

werewolves
Blood and Chocolate
Loup Garou

whales
Big Blue Whale
Dear Mr. Blueberry
Mama, Do You Love Me?
Okino and the Whales
Waiting for the Whales
Whale's Song
Whaling Days

wilderness
Brian's Winter
Julie of the Wolves

wind
Dancing With the Wind
Windsongs and Rainbows

wings
Wing Shop

winter
Annie and the Wild Animals
Brian's Winter
City of Light, City of Dark
Dear Rebecca, Winter Is Here
Dogteam
In the Dinosaur's Paw
In the Snow: Who's Been Here
Indian Winter
Is That You, Winter?
Mitten
Night Before Christmas
One Wintry Night
Stories By Firelight
Time to Sleep
Winter Poems

wisdom
500 Hats of Bartholomew Cubbins
Badger's Parting Gifts
Barn (Avi)
Bone Man
Charlotte's Web
Country Bunny and the Little Gold
    Shoes
Fox Song
Grandmother Bryant's Pocket
One Night
Paper Dragon
Phantom Tollbooth
Pulling the Lion's Tail
Soda Jerk
Well Wished
Wilfred Gordon McDonald Partridge
Winter White
Zilla Sasparilla and the Mud Baby

wishes
Burnt Toast on Davenport Street
Five Children and It
If I Were in Charge of the World

Maggie B
Mordant's Wish
Rainbabies
Sylvester and the Magic Pebble
Well Wished

witches
Alice Nizzy Nazzy
Baba Yaga and Vasalisa the Brave
Babushka Baba Yaga
Big Bad Bruce
Golden Compass
Guess What?
Hansel and Gretel
Heckedy Peg
Liza Lou and the Yeller Belly
    Swamp
Magic Circle
Piggie Pie
Scary, Scary Halloween
Strega Nona
Talking Eggs
William Shakespeare's Macbeth
Witch Way to the Country
Witches
Wonderful Wizard of Oz
Zel

wizards
Earthsea Quartet
Elbert's Bad Word
Lost Years of Merlin
Merlin
Wonderful Wizard of Oz

wolves
Eyes of Gray Wolf
Gray Wolf, Red Wolf
Hog-Eye
It's So Nice to Have a Wolf Around
    the House
Julie of the Wolves
Little Red Riding Hood
Lon Po Po
Look to the North
Loup Garou
Mama, Do You Love Me?
Red Riding Hood
Suddenly!
Three Blind Mice Mystery
Three Little Wolves and the Big Bad
    Pig

True Story of the Three Little Pigs
Yo, Hungry Wolf!

wombats
Wombat Divine
Wombat Stew

women, independent (women
    across the ages who have made
    their mark in a man's world)
Aunt Nancy and Old Man Trouble
Ballad of the Pirate Queens
City of Light, City of Dark
Cleopatra
Come Look With Me
Country Bunny and the Little Gold
    Shoes
Do Not Open
Fanny's Dream
Fin M'Coul, The Giant of Knockmany
    Hill
Kissing the Witch
Ma Dear's Aprons
Magic Circle
Mama Is a Miner
Mangaboom
Miss Rumphius
Raggly, Scraggly, No-Soap, No-Scrub
    Girl
Seven Brave Women
Swamp Angel
Tale of Ali Baba and the Forty
    Thieves
Way West
When the Monkeys Came Back
Wilma Unlimited

woodchucks
Mean Margaret
Time to Sleep

woodworking
Christmas Miracle of Jonathan
    Toomey
Good Times on Grandfather Moun-
    tain
Hands
Whittler's Tale
Woodlore

wordless (and nearly wordless books)
Anno's Journey

Boy, a Dog, and a Frog
Clown
Colors Everywhere
Free Fall
Good Dog, Carl
Grey Lady and the Strawberry
    Snatcher
Handmade Alphabet
Noah's Ark
Pancakes for Breakfast
Peter Spier's Rain
R. E. M.
Silver Pony
Stories by Firelight
Thirteen
Time Flies
Tuesday
Will's Mammoth
Zoom

wordplay (Books that lend them-
    selves to having a good time with
    language: puns, tongue twisters,
    alliterations and creative combi-
    nations).
Alpha Beta Chowder
Amelia Bedelia
Animalia
Antics
Bats About Baseball
Best of Michael Rosen
Busy Buzzing Bumblebees
Butterfly Jar
Chocolate Moose for Dinner
Cloudy With a Chance of Meatballs
Dear Dr. Sillybear
Eye Spy: A Mysterious Alphabet
First Things First
Fortune-Tellers
Frogs in Clogs
Go Hang a Salami! I'm a Lasagna
    Hog!
Here Comes Henny
Hi, Pizza Man!
How Now Brown Cow
Jeremy Kooloo
Livingstone Mouse
Minerva Louise at School
My First Book of Proverbs
Night Becomes Day
Old Man and His Door
Once There Was a Bull . . . (Frog)

Piggie Pie
Puffins Climb, Penguins Rhyme
Quick as a Cricket
Small Green Snake
Snake Is Totally Tail
Walking the Bridge of Your Nose
Westing Game
Who Says a Dog Goes Bow-Wow?
Witch Way to the Country

words
Elbert's Bad Word
Macmillan Dictionary for Children
Richard Scarry's Best Word Book Ever
Weighty Word Book

work (see jobs)

worms
How to Eat Fried Worms
James and the Giant Peach
Rainy Day

worry
Adrian Mole Diaries
Cuckoo's Child
Delphine
Finster Frets
Fish in His Pocket
Fragile Flag
If I Were in Charge of the World
Mama Is a Miner

writing
Adrian Mole Diaries
Anne Frank: The Diary of a Young
    Girl
Arthur's Pen Pal
Author: A True Story
Bill Peet: An Autobiography
But That's Another Story
Communication
Cyber.Kdz Series
Darnell Rock Reporting
Day of Ahmed's Secret
Dear Mr. Blueberry
Dear Mr. Henshaw
Dear Mr. Sprouts
Dear Rebecca, Winter Is Here
Dear Willie Rudd
Dear World
Emily

From Pictures to Words
Grass Sandals
Hannah and Jack
Harriet the Spy
Hey World, Here I Am!
How a Book Is Made
In Flight With David McPhail
Max Makes a Million
More Than Anything Else
Nettie's Trip South
Poetry From A to Z
Polar the Titanic Bear
Rats Saw God
Stringbean's Trip to the Shining Sea
Sweet Words So Brave
Weekend Was Murder
Wish You Were Here

Yanomami
Amazon Diary

yearning (hopes, wishes, dreams,
    desires, aspirations, and wants it!)
Abel's Island
Amigo
Angel for Solomon Singer
At the Crossroads
Ben's Trumpet
Chicken Soup, Boots
Country Bunny and the Little Gold Shoes
Earrings!
El Chino
Fanny's Dream
Fly Away Home
Grandmother Bryant's Pocket
Great Gilly Hopkins
Maggie B
Max Makes a Million
Max's Dragon Shirt
Soda Jerk
White Dynamite and Curly Kidd
William Shakespeare's Macbeth

Yiddish
Bit by Bit

young and old (see: elderly and children)

zany (absurd characters, preposter-
    ous situations, and/or a ridicu-
    lous or silly story)
Alice's Adventures in Wonderland

Day With Wilbur Robinson
Happy Hocky Family
Hoover's Bride
Lizard Music
Math Curse
Max Makes a Million
Night Becomes Day
Parents in the Pigpen, Pigs in the Tub
Phantom Tollbooth
Sideways Stories From Wayside School

Stinky Cheese Man and Other Fairly Stupid Tales
True Story of the Three Little Pigs

zombies
Faithful Friend

zoos
Good Night, Gorilla
I Went to the Zoo
Lion Named Shirley Williamson
My Visit to the Zoo

Index

A Is for Africa (Onyefulu), 170
A My Name Is Alice (Bayer), 267
Aardema, Verna
    Bringing the Rain to Kapiti Plain,
      85
    Misoso: Once Upon a Time Tales
      From Africa, 339-40
    Why Mosquitoes Buzz in People's
      Ears, 196
The ABC Mystery (Cushman), 74
Abel's Island (Steig), 442
Abiyoyo (Seeger), 74
Absolutely, Positively Alexander
    (Viorst), 74
Abuela (Dorros), 75
The Acorn People (Jones), 526
The Acorn Tree & Other Folktales
    (Rockwell), 170
Ada, Alma Flor, Gathering the Sun:
    An Alphabet in Spanish and
    English,28
Adams, Adrienne, Easter Egg Artists,
    95
Adams, Winky, Insides, Outsides,
    Loops and Lines, 465
Adler, David
    Chanukkah in Chelm, 274
    One Yellow Daffodil: A Hanukkah
      Story, 514
    Picture Book Biography series, 301
Adoff, Arnold, All the Colors of the
    Race, 443
Adopted by the Eagles: A Plains Story
    of Friendship and Treachery
    (Goble), 313
The Adrian Mole Diaries (Townsend),
    539
The Adventures of the Bailey School
    Kids (Dadey and Jones), 120
The Adventures of Captain
    Underpants (Pilkey), 267-68
The Adventures of High John the
    Conqueror (Sanfield), 313
The Adventures of Huckleberry Finn
    (Twain), 494
The Adventures of Pinnochio
    (Collodi), 355
The Adventures of Taxi Dog (Barracca
    and Barracca), 170-71
The Adventures of Tintin (Herge),
    381
Advice for a Frog (Schertle), 494
After the War Was Over (Foreman),
    494
Agee, Jon

Go Hang a Salami! I'm a Lasagna
    Hog!, 357
    Mean Margaret, 338
Agell, Charlotte, Dancing Feet,92-93
Ahlberg, Janet and Allan
    Each Peach Pear Plum, 94
    The Jolly Postman or Other People's
      Letters, 182
Airmail to the Moon (Birdseye), 207,
    244, 313-14
Akintola, Ademola, The River That
    Went to the Sky, 419
Alan Mendelsohn, The Boy From
    Mars (Pinkwater), 493
Alarcon, Karen Beaumont, Louella
    Mae, She's Run Away!, 125
Albert, Richard, Alejandro's Gift, 75
Albert's Play (Tryon), 75
Alborough, Jez, Where's My Teddy?,
    165
Alcock, Vivian, Singer to the Sea God,
    519
Alcorn, Stephen, Lincoln In His Own
    Words, 469
Alderson, Brian, The Arabian Nights,
    383
Alejandro's Gift (Albert), 75
Alexander, Lloyd
    The Fortune-Tellers, 284
    The Illyrian Adventure, 509
    The Prydian Chronicles, 516-17
    Westmark, 534-35
Ali, Abira, The Big Bazoohley, 271
Ali, Child of the Desert (London), 255
Alice Nizzy Nazzy: The Witch of
    Santa Fe (Johnston), 229
Alice's Adventures in Wonderland
    (Carroll), 355, 442-43
Aliki
    Communication, 90
    Corn Is Maize: The Gift of the
      Indians, 90
    Feelings, 96
    How a Book Is Made, 404
    Hush Little Baby, 112
    My Visit to the Aquarium, 134-35
    My Visit to the Zoo, 189
    Welcome Little Baby, 163
Alison's Zinnia (Lobel), 24
All About Alfie (Hughes), 75-76
All About Alligators (Arnosky), 171
All I See (Rylant), 171, 374
All-of-a-Kind Family (Taylor), 382
All of You Was Singing (Lewis), 230
All the Colors of the Race (Adoff), 443

All the Lights In the Night (Levine),
    314
All the Places to Love (MacLachlan),
    171
All Those Secrets of the World (Yolen),
    55
All We Needed to Say (Singer), 443
Allard, Harry
    Bumps in the Night, 199
    It's So Nice to Have a Wolf Around
      the House, 181
    Miss Nelson Is Missing!, 358
    The Stupids Step Out, 360
    There's a Party at Mona's Tonight,
      19
Allen, Jonathan
    The Great White Man-Eating
      Shark: A Cautionary Tale, 289
    The Three-Legged Cat, 225
Allen, Thomas B.
    In Coal Country, 292
    Sewing Quilts, 263
Alley, R.W.
    Family Reunion, 283
    Who Said Boo?, 72
Allison (Say), 255
Alpha Beta Chowder (Steig), 494-95
The Alphabet From Z to A (With
    Much Confusion On The Way)
    (Viorst), 443-44
Altman, Linda Jacobs, Amelia's
    Road, 314
Alvin Ailey (Pinkney), 314
The Always Prayer Shawl
    (Oberman), 268
Am I Blue? Coming Out From the
    Silence (Bauer), 540
Amazing Grace (Hoffman), 210
Amazon Diary: Jungle Adventures of
    Alex Winters (Talbott and
    Greenberg), 232, 382
Amber Brown Is Not a Crayon
    (Danziger), 268
Amber on the Mountain (Johnston),
    268
Amelia Bedelia (Parish), 76-77, 120
Amelia's Notebook (Moss), 435
Amelia's Road (Altman), 314
American Dragon: Twenty-five Asian
    American Voices (Yep), 350
The American Girl series, 314-15
Ames, Lee J., Draw 50 series, 393
Amigo (Baylor), 269
Amoss, Berthe, The Loup Garou,
    296

Anansi and the Moss-Covered Rock
(Kimmel), 77
Anastasia Krupnik (Lowry), 315
The Ancestor Tree (Echewa), 250
Ancient Ones (Bash), 444
Ancona, George
  Fiesta, 397
  *Handtalk: An ABC of Finger
    Spelling and Sign Language*, 13-
    14
  *Pablo Remembers: The Fiesta of the
    Day of the Dead*, 341-42
  Piñata Maker/El Piñatero, 144
And So They Build (Kitchen), 24
*And to Think That I Saw It On
  Mulberry Street* (Seuss), 77
Andersen, Bethanne, *Seven Brave
  Women*, 376
Andersen, Hans Christian, *The
  Swan Stories*, 423
Anderson, Lena, *Linnea In Monet's
  Garden*, 336-37
Anderson, Scoular, *A Puzzling Day
  at Castle MacPelican*, 38
Andrews, Sylvia, *Rattlebone Rock*,
  192
The Angel and the Soldier Boy
  (Collington), 359
An Angel for Solomon Singer
  (Rylant), 269, 374
Angela and Diabola (Banks), 444
Angel Child, Dragon Child (Surat),
  243
Angelina Ballerina (Holabird), 171
Angelou, Maya, *My Painted House,
  My Friendly Chicken, & Me*, 34
Angus and the Cat (Flack), 78
Angus and the Ducks (Flack), 355
Animal Dads (Collard), 78
The Animal Family (Jarrell), 382
Animalia (Base), 42-44
Animorphs (Applegate), 444
*Anna Banana: 101 Jump-Rope
  Rhymes* (Calmenson and Cole),
  220
Anne Frank: Beyond the Diary
  (Verhoeven, Verhoeven, and
  DerRol), 495
*Anne Frank: The Diary of a Young
  Girl* (Frank), 495
Anne of Green Gables (Montgomery),
  445
Annie Bananie (Komaiko), 9-10
Annie and the Old One (Miska), 218,
  256
Annie and the Wild Animals (Brett),
  24-25
Anno, Mitsumasa
  Anno's Journey, 10, 359
  *Anno's Math Games, Volumes I, II,
    And III*, 256
Anno's Journey (Anno), 10, 359
*Anno's Math Games, Volumes I, II,
  And III* (Anno), 256
*Anthony Burns: The Defeat and
  Triumph of a Fugitive Slave*
  (Hamilton), 455
Antics (Hepworth), 445-46
Appelbaum, Diana, *Giants in the
  Land*, 398
Appelemando's Dream (Polacco), 78
Apple, Margot
  The Chocolate Touch, 322
  Just Like My Dad, 118
  Sheep in a Jeep, 150
Apple Pie Tree (Hall), 78

Applegate, K.A., *Animorphs*, 444
The Arabian Nights (Alderson), 383
Arabian Nights: Three Tales
  (Lattimore), 315-16
The Araboolies of Liberty Street
  (Swope), 207, 316
Archambault, John
  Barn Dance!, 82
  *A Beautiful Feast for a Big King
    Cat*, 172-73
  Chicka Chicka Boom Boom, 88, 355
  The Ghost-Eye Tree, 101
  White Dynamite & Curly Kidd,
    352-53
Archibald Frisby (Chesworth), 78-79
Are You My Mother? (Eastman), 79
Are You There God? It's Me, Margaret
  (Blume), 435-36
Argent, Kerry, *Wombat Divine*, 167-
  68
Armstrong, Jennifer, *The Whittler's
  Tale*, 353
Arnold, Caroline, *Mexico's Ancient
  City of Teotihuacan*, 471
Arnold, Katya, *Katya's Book of
  Mushrooms*, 406
Arnold, Tedd, *My Dog Never Says
  Please*, 134
Arnosky, Jim, *All About Alligators*,
  171
Around the World in 80 Days
  (Verne), 355
Around the World in a Hundred Years
  (Fritz), 436
Arrilla Sun Down (Hamilton), 455
Arrow to the Sun (McDermott), 80
*Arroz Con Leche: Popular Songs and
  Rhymes From Latin America*
  (Delacre), 230
Art Dog (Hurd), 198
Arthur's Camp-Out (Hoban), 80
Aruego, Jose, *Leo the Late Bloomer*,
  121-22
*As the Crow Flies: A First Book of
  Maps* (Hartman), 80
Ashanti to Zulu: African Traditions
  (Musgrove), 230
Asher, Sandy, *But That's Another
  Story*, 451-52
Ashley, Bernard, *Cleversticks*, 89
Asking About Sex and Growing Up
  (Cole), 220
Aster Aardvark's Alphabet Adventures
  (Kellogg), 316
Atalanta's Race: A Greek Myth
  (Climo), 383
At the Beach (Lee), 256
At the Crossroads (Isadora), 256-57
Atkin, S. Beth, *Voices From the Fields*,
  487
Atwater, Richard and Florence, *Mr.
  Popper's Penguins*, 355, 388, 414
Atwell, Debby, *Barn*, 257
Auch, Mary Jane, *The Easter Egg
  Farm*, 325-26
Aunt Eater Loves a Mystery
  (Cushman), 80-81
Aunt Nancy and Old Man Trouble
  (Root), 172
Author: A True Story (Lester), 269
Author's Day (Pinkwater), 269
Avashai, Susan, *When the Big Dog
  Barks*, 165
Avi
  The Barn, 446
  Beyond the Western Sea, 527

*City of Light, City of Dark: A
  Comic Book Novel*, 454
*Finding Providence: The Story of
  Roger Williams*, 120, 251
Nothing But the Truth, 513
*The True Confessions of Charlotte
  Doyle*, 521
Away From Home (Lobel), 211
Aylesworth, Jim, *Old Black Fly*, 190,
  244

Baba Yaga and Vasilisa the Brave
  (Mayer), 270
Babbitt, Natalie, *Tuck Everlasting*,
  486
Babe, the Gallant Pig (King-Smith),
  316-17, 388
Babushka Baba Yaga (Polacco), 172
Baby (MacLachlan), 446
Baby Be-Bop (Block), 540
Baby Bear's Bedtime Book (Yolen), 55
A Baby Sister for Frances (Hoban),
  81
Bacon, Paul, *Teammates*, 308
Badger's Bring Something Party
  (Oram), 230
Badger's Parting Gifts (Varley), 172,
  218
Bahti, Tom, *When Clay Sings*, 379
Baker, Keith
  The Magic Fan, 126
  Who Is the Beast?, 166
Baker, Kent, *Finster Frets*, 233-34
*The Baker's Dozen: A Saint Nicholas
  Tale* (Shepard), 81
Balan, Brice, *Cyber.Kdz* series, 436-37
Balgassi, Haemi
  Peacebound Trains, 416
  Tae's Sonata, 484
The Ballad of Lucy Whipple
  (Cushman), 447
The Ballad of the Pirate Queens
  (Yolen), 55, 383
*Bamboo Hats and a Rice Cake: A Tale
  Adapted from Japanese Folklore*,
  81-82
Bancroft, Catherine, *Felix's Hat*, 202
Bang, Molly
  Dawn, 364
  Delphine, 200
  *The Grey Lady and the Strawberry
    Snatcher*, 204, 359
The Banging Book (Grossman), 82
Banks, Lynne Reid
  Angela and Diabola, 444
  I, Houdini, 332
  The Indian in the Cupboard, 464-65
  One More River, 513
Bannerman, Helen, *The Story of
  Little Babaji*, 154
Banyai, Istvan
  R.E.M., 17, 359
  Re-Zoom, 359
  Zoom, 23, 359
*Bard of Avon: The Story of William
  Shakespeare* (Stanley and
  Vennema), 317
*Barefoot: Escape on the Underground
  Railroad* (Edwards), 257
Barn (Atwell), 257
The Barn (Avi), 446
Barn Dance! (Martin and
  Archambault), 82
Barnard, Bryn, *Bay Shore Park: The
  Death and Life of an
  Amusement Park*, 383

Barner, Bob
Benny's Pennies, 83
Dem Bones, 214
Barnyard Dance! (Boynton), 63
Baron, Richard, Here Comes the
Storyteller, 331
Barracca, Debra and Sal, The
Adventures of Taxi Dog, 170-71
A Barrel of Laughs, a Vale of Tears,
245
Barrett, Judi
Cloudy With a Chance of
Meatballs, 275
A Snake Is Totally Tail, 263
Barrett, Ron, Cloudy With a Chance
of Meatballs, 275
Barron, T.A., The Lost Years of
Merlin, 511-12
Barry, Robert, Mr. Willowby's
Christmas Tree, 133
Bartlett, Alison, Oliver's Vegetables,
190
Bartoletti, Susan Campbell, Growing
Up in Coal Country, 505
Barton, Byron, Gila Monsters Meet
You at the Airport, 216
Barton, Harriett, Geography From A
To Z: A Picture Glossary, 287
Bartone, Alisa, Peppe the Lamplighter,
301
Base, Graeme
Animalia, 42-44
The Discovery of Dragons, 501-2
Baseball Saved Us (Mochizuki), 270
Bash, Barbara, Ancient Ones, 444
Batki, Laszlo, King Arthur's Camelot:
A Popup Castle & Four
Storybooks, 50-51
Bats About Baseball (Little and
MacKay), 270
Bats: Nightfliers (Maestro), 234
Bauer, Marion Dane
Am I Blue? Coming Out From the
Silence, 540
If You Were Born a Kitten, 115
On My Honor, 218, 474
Baum, L. Frank, The Wonderful
Wizard of Oz, 354, 355, 388
Bay Shore Park: The Death and Life
of an Amusement Park
(Crenson), 383
Bayer, Jane, A My Name Is Alice, 267
Baylor, Byrd
Amigo, 269
Everybody Needs a Rock, 283
Hawk, I'm Your Brother, 290
I'm in Charge of Celebrations, 367
One Small Blue Bead, 299
The Other Way to Listen, 372
When Clay Sings, 379
Be Good to Eddie Lee (Fleming), 211
A Bear Called Paddington (Bond),
317, 388
The Bear That Heard Crying (Kinsey-
Warnock and Kinsey), 318
The Bear's House (Sachs), 245, 447
A Beautiful Feast for a Big King Cat
(Martin and Archambault),
172-73
The Beauty of the Beast (Prelutsky),
44
Beaver at Long Pond (George and
George), 211
Bedard, Michael, Emily, 395
Beddows, Eric, Joyful Noise: Poems
for Two Voices, 467

The Bee Tree (Polacco), 231
Before I Go to Sleep (Hood), 82
Begay, Shonto
The Boy Who Dreamed of an
Acorn, 319
Navajo: Visions and Voices Across
the Mesa, 414-15
Begin-Callanan, Maryjane, Before I
Go to Sleep, 82
Beier, Ellen, The Blue Hill Meadows,
272
Bein' With You This Way (Nikola-
Lisa), 231
Bellairs, John, The House With a
Clock in Its Walls, 463
Belle Prater's Boy (White), 448
Bellingham, David, Goddesses,
Heroes, and Shamans, 504
Bemelmans, Ludwig, Madeline, 125
Ben and Me (Lawson), 436
Beneduce, Ann Keay, Gulliver's
Adventures in Lilliput, 297
Benjamin, Floella, Skip Across the
Ocean, 151-52
Benny's Pennies (Brisson), 83
Ben's Trumpet (Isadora), 198-99
Benson, Patrick, Owl Babies, 141
Berenzy, Alix, Into the Sea, 293
Berger, Barbara, Grandfather
Twilight, 103
Bernardin, James
Big Men, Big Country, 318
Dancing With the Wind, 213
Giants! Stories From Around the
World, 328
Little Folk: Stories From Around the
World, 410
Bernhard, Durga, Dragonfly, 177
Berry, James, Classic Poems to Read
Aloud, 46
The Best of Michael Rosen (Rosen),
25
Beyond Amazing: Six Spectacular
Science Pop-Ups (Young), 436
Beyond the Burning Time (Lasky),
409
Beyond the Divide (Lasky), 409, 540-
41
Beyond the Western Sea (Avi), 527
The BFG (Dahl), 384
Biesty, Stephen, Stephen Biesty's
Incredible Cross-Sections, 423
Big Al (Clements), 83
Big Bad Bruce (Peet), 173
The Big Bazoohley (Carey), 271
Big Bear's Treasury: A Children's
Anthology, 173
Big Blue Whale (Davies), 318
The Big Book for Our Planet (Durell),
44
Big Cats (Simon), 271
Big David, Little David (Hinton), 173-
74
Big Men, Big Country: A Collection of
American Tall Tales (Walker),
318, 388
The Big Red Barn (Brown), 83
Biggest Boy (Henkes), 184
Biggest, Strongest, Fastest (Jenkins),
271-72
Bill Peet: An Autobiography (Peet),
384
Billingsley, Franny, Well Wished,
488-89
Binch, Caroline
Amazing Grace, 210

Boundless Grace, 361-62
Down by the River, 233
Birchman, David F., The Raggly
Scraggly, No-Soap, No-Scrub
Girl, 417
Birdie's Lighthouse (Hopkinson), 384
A Bird's Body (Cole), 220, 272
Birdseye, Debbie, She'll Be Comin'
Round the Mountain, 150
Birdseye, Tom
Airmail to the Moon, 207, 244, 313-
14
A Regular Flood of Mishap, 237
She'll Be Comin' Round the
Mountain, 150
Soap! Soap! Don't Forget The Soap!:
Appalachian Folktale, 193
Birdsong (Wood), 231
Birthday Surprises: Ten Great Stories
to Unwrap (Hurwitz), 448
Bit by Bit (Sanfield), 83, 84
Bjork, Christina, Linnea In Monet's
Garden, 336-37
Bjorkman, Steve, I Hate English, 180
Black Ships Before Troy (Sutcliff),
245, 495-96
The Black Snowman (Mendez), 272
Blake, Quentin
The Best of Michael Rosen, 25
The BFG, 384
Clown, 199-200, 359
The Great Piratical
Rumbustification, 400
Matilda, 337-38
The Witches, 491
Blake, Robert
Mississippi Mud: Three Prairie
Journals, 472
Riptide, 303
Blake, William, The Tyger, 427
The Blanket (Burningham), 63
Blathwayt, Benedick, Stories From
Firefly Island, 347
Blegvad, Erik
Mud Pies and Other Recipes: A
Cookbook for Dolls, 187-88
The Tenth Good Thing About
Barney, 157
Blitzcat (Westall), 448
Blizzard, Gladys, Come Look With
Me: Enjoying Art With Children,
323
Block, Francesca Lia
Baby Be-Bop, 540
Weetzie Bat, 555
Blood and Chocolate (Klause), 541
Bloom, Lloyd
One Yellow Daffodil: A Hanukkah
Story, 514
Yonder, 379
Blubber (Blume), 448-49
A Blue-Eyed Daisy (Rylant), 374
The Blue Fairy Book (Lang), 44-45
Blue Hat, Green Hat (Boynton), 64
The Blue Hill Meadows (Rylant),
272
Blue Skin of the Sea (Salisbury), 496
Blueberries for Sal (McCloskey), 25
Blume, Judy
Are You There God? It's Me,
Margaret, 449-50
Blubber, 448-49
Blythe, Gary, The Whale's Song, 40
Bo Rabbit Smart for True Tall Tales
From the Gullah (Jaquith), 231-
32

Bode, Janet, *Death Is Hard to Live With*, 218

Bodecker, N.M.
Half Magic, 401
The Knight's Castle, 407
Seven-Day Magic, 420-21

Bodmer, Karl, *An Indian Winter*, 465

The Body Atlas (Parker), 385

The Boggart (Cooper), 449

Bon, Pierre, *Earth, Sky and Beyond*, 325

Bond, Felicia
The Big Red Barn, 83
If You Give a Mouse a Cookie, 114-15
Tumble Bumble, 70

Bond, Michael, *A Bear Called Paddington*, 317, 388

A Bone From a Dry Sea (Dickinson), 496

The Bone Man: A Native American Modoc Tale (Simms), 385

Bone Poems (Moss), 318-19

The Book of Changes (Wynne-Jones), 449

Book of Little Folk: The Faery Stories & Poems From Around the World, 45

The Book of North American Owls (Sattler), 385

The Book of Think (Burns), 497

Booth, George, *Possum Come A-Knockin'*, 192

Bootman, Colin, *Oh, No, Toto!*, 34

Bootsie Barker Bites (Bottner), 84, 207

Borden, Louise, *Little Ships*, 410-11

The Borrowers (Norton), 385-86, 388

Bottner, Barbara, *Bootsie Barker Bites*, 84, 207

Bouchard, David
If You're Not From the Prairie, 332-33
Voices From the Wild: An Animal Sensagoria, 487

Boulton, Jane, *Only Opal: The Diary of a Young Girl*, 415

Boundless Grace (Hoffman), 361-62

Bourke, Linda, *Eye Spy: A Mysterious Alphabet*, 458

Bowen, Gary, *Stranded at Plimoth Plantation, 1626*, 482-83

The Boy and the Cloth of Dreams (Koralek), 319

A Boy, a Dog, and a Frog (Mayer), 84, 359

The Boy Who Dreamed of an Acorn (Casler), 319

The Boy Who Swallowed Snakes (Yep), 350

Boyd, Candy Dawson, *Charlie Pippin*, 452-53

Boynton, Sandra
Barnyard Dance!, 63
Blue Hat, Green Hat, 64
Hippos Go Berserk, 14

Boys Will Be (Brooks), 497

The Bracelet (Uchida), 272-73

Bradby, Marie, *More Than Anything Else*, 187

Branzei, Sylvia, *Grossology: The Science of Really Gross Things*, 461

Brave Irene (Steig), 85, 207

The Bravest Dog Ever: The True Story of Balto (Standiford), 120

Brazell, Derek, *Cleversticks*, 89

Bread Is for Eating (Gershator), 85

Brenner, Barbara, *Where's That Insect?*, 352

Brenner, Fred, *The Drinking Gourd: A Story of the Underground Railroad*, 259

Brett, Jan
Annie and the Wild Animals, 24-25
Goldilocks and the Three Bears, 102
The Mitten, 186-87
Scary, Scary Halloween, 149
Town Mouse Country Mouse, 195
The Twelve Days of Christmas, 40

Brian's Winter (Paulsen), 449, 450

Brickyard Summer (Janeczko), 527

The Bridge to Terabithia (Paterson), 218, 288, 451

Brinckloe, Julie, *Sideways Stories From Wayside School*, 345

Bringing the Rain to Kapiti Plain (Aardema), 85

Brink, Carol Ryrie, *Goody O'Grumpity*, 216

Brisson, Pat, *Benny's Pennies*, 83

The Brocaded Slipper and Other Vietnamese Tales (Vuong), 273, 354

Brodie, James Michael, *Sweet Words So Brave*, 424

Brooke, William J., *A Telling of the Tales*, 484-85

Brooks, Bruce
Boys Will Be, 497
Midnight Hour Encores, 512
What Hearts, 489
The Wolfbay Wings, 491-92

Brooks, Ron, *Old Pig*, 206

Broome, Errol, *Dear Mr. Sprouts*, 528

Brother Eagle, Sister Sky: A Message From Chief Seattle (Seattle), 386

Brothers Rush (Hamilton), 245, 455

Brott, Ardyth, *Jeremy's Decision*, 15

Brown, Craig McFarland, *The Ornery Morning*, 191

Brown, Jane Clark, *Marvin's Best Christmas Present Ever*, 205

Brown, Kathryn
Eeny, Meeny, Miney Mole, 95
Tough Boris, 160

Brown, Laurie Krasny, *Dinosaurs Divorce*, 177

Brown, Marc
Dinosaurs Divorce, 177
Read-Aloud Rhymes for the Very Young, 146-47
Scared Silly, 149
Visiting the Art Museum, 310

Brown, Marcia, *Stone Soup*, 153-54

Brown, Margaret Wise
The Big Red Barn, 83
The Dead Bird, 11, 218
Goodnight Moon, 103, 355
The Runaway Bunny, 148

Brown, Ruth, *Toad*, 20

Brown Angels: An Album of Pictures and Verse (Myers), 386, 506

Brown Bear, Brown Bear, What Do You See? (Martin), 85-86

Brown Honey in Broomwheat Tea (Thomas), 362

Browne, Anthony
The Daydreamer, 456
I Like Books, 113
Piggybook, 373
Willy the Wimp, 209

Bruchac, Joseph
The First Strawberries: A Cherokee Story, 326-27
Fox Song, 327
The Great Ball Game: A Muskogee Story, 234
Keepers of the Earth, 406
Thirteen Moons on Turtle's Back, 426

Bryan, Ashley, *The Cat's Purr*, 174

Bryant, Michael
Bein' With You This Way, 231
Skin Deep and Other Teenage Reflections, 519

Buchanan, George, *The Great Pirate Activity Book*, 330

Buck, Nola, *Santa's Short Suit Shrunk & Other Christmas Tongue Twisters*, 149

The Buck Stops Here: Presidents of the United States (Provensen), 362

Buddha (Demi), 362

Buehner, Caralyn
Fanny's Dream, 283-84, 354
It's a Spoon, Not a Shovel, 181

Buehner, Mark
The Adventures of Taxi Dog, 170-71
Fanny's Dream, 283-84, 354
Harvey Potter's Balloon Farm, 234
It's a Spoon, Not a Shovel, 181
My Life With the Wave, 188

The Buffalo Tree (Rapp), 541-42

Bugs (Parker and Wright), 174

Bugs! (Greenberg), 273

Bull Run (Fleischman), 451

Bumps in the Night (Allard), 199

Bunnicula (Howe and Howe), 319-20

Bunny Cakes (Wells), 128

Bunny Money (Wells), 86

Bunting, Eve, 278
Cheyenne Again, 278, 389
A Day's Work, 277
Fly Away Home, 244, 278, 365
I Am the Mummy Heb-Nefert, 278, 464
The Man Who Could Call Down Owls, 369
Moonstick: The Seasons of the Sioux, 370-71
Our Sixth Grade Sugar Babies, 278
St. Patrick's Day in the Morning, 278
Scary, Scary Halloween, 149
Smoky Night, 278, 304-5
Someday a Tree, 377
Train to Somewhere, 278
A Turkey for Thanksgiving, 278
The Valentine Bears, 278
The Wall, 278, 378
The Wednesday Surprise, 278, 378

The Bunyans (Wood), 363

Burger, Douglas A., *The Weighty Word Book*, 488

Burleigh, Robert
Flight, 284
Who Said That? Famous Americans Speak, 489-90

Burnett, Frances Hodgson, *The Secret Garden*, 345, 355

Burningham, John
The Blanket, 63
Cloudland, 89
Courtney, 276
Harvey Slumfenburger's Christmas Present, 106-7
Hey! Get Off Our Train, 108

John Patrick Norman McHennessy, 293-94

Would You Rather...?, 168

Burns, Marilyn, *The Book of Think*, 497

Burnt Stick (Hill), 320

Burnt Toast on Davenport Street (Egan), 273

Burroughes, Joanna, *My Grandma Has Black Hair*, 15-16

Burton, Albert, *Windsongs and Rainbows*, 227

Burton, Virginia Lee
　The Little House, 123-24
　Mike Mulligan and His Steam Shovel, 15, 355

Busy Buzzing Bumblebees and Other Tongue Twisters (Schwartz), 86

But I'll Be Back Again (Rylant), 374

But That's Another Story: Favorite Authors Introduce Popular Genres, 451-52

Butler, Jerry, *Sweet Words So Brave*, 424

The Butter Battle Book (Seuss), 363

The Butterfly Jar (Moss), 25

Butterworth, Oliver, *The Enormous Egg*, 395

By the Great Horn Spoon (Fleischman), 452

By the Light of the Halloween Moon (Stutson), 86

Byard, Carole
　The Black Snowman, 272
　Working Cotton, 266

Cadillac (Temple), 86-87

Caduto, M., *Keepers of the Earth*, 406

Cain, David, *Science Experiments You Can Eat*, 478

Calder, Nancy Edwards, *The Christmas House*, 322

California, Here We Come! (Ryan), 232

Call Down the Moon: Poems of Music (Livingston), 497

Calling the Doves/El Canto De Las Palomas (Herrera), 273-74

Calmenson, Stephanie
　Anna Banana: 101 Jump-Rope Rhymes, 220
　Give a Dog a Bone, 220
　Pat-A-Cake and Other Play Rhymes, 220
　Pin the Tail on the Donkey and Other Party Games, 220

Cannon, Annie, *You Hold Me and I'll Hold You*, 228

Cannon, Janell
　Stellaluna, 193, 234
　Verdi, 161

Can't You Sleep, Little Bear? (Waddell), 87, 207

Canyon, Christopher, *Did You Hear Wind Sing Your Name?*, 176

Capote, Truman, *A Christmas Memory*, 37

Caps for Sale: A Tale of a Peddler, Some Monkeys, & Their Monkey Business (Slobodkina), 87, 355

Captain Abdul's Pirate School (McNaughton), 274

Captain Snap & the Children of Vinegar Lane (Schotter), 25-26

Capucilli, Alyssa Satin, *Good Morning Pond*, 102-3

Card, Michael, *Close Your Eyes So You Can See*, 323

Carey, Peter, *The Big Bazoohley*, 271

Carle, Eric
　Brown Bear, Brown Bear, What Do You See?, 85-86
　From Head to Toe, 100
　A House for a Hermit Crab, 110
　Papa, Please Get the Moon for Me, 141
　Today Is Monday, 160
　The Very Busy Spider, 162
　The Very Hungry Caterpillar, 162, 355
　The Very Quiet Cricket, 162

Carlson, Lori, *Cool Salsa*, 527

Carlson, Nancy, *How to Lose All Your Friends*, 112

Carlstrom, Nancy White
　Jesse Bear, What Will You Wear?, 66
　Who Said Boo?, 72

Carmi, Giora, *The Miracle of the Potato Latkes*, 130

Carpenter, Nancy, *Masai and I*, 262

Carrick, Carol, *Whaling Days*, 311

Carrick, Donald
　Rosalie, 147
　The Wednesday Surprise, 378

Carroll, Lewis, *Alice's Adventures in Wonderland*, 355, 442-43

The Carrot Seed (Krauss), 88

Carson, Jo, *You Hold Me and I'll Hold You*, 218, 228

Carter, David A., *How Many Bugs in a Box?*, 111

Carter, Gail
　The Glass Bottle Tree, 399
　Mac and Marie and the Train Toss Surprise, 221

Carter, Jimmy, *Talking Peace: A Vision for the Next Generation*, 554

Carusone, Al, *Don't Open the Door After the Sun Goes Down*, 457, 476

Casey at the Bat (Thayer), 88

Casilla, Robert, *The Little Painter of Sabana Grande*, 337

Casler, Leigh, *The Boy Who Dreamed of an Acorn*, 429

The Castle in the Attic (Winthrop), 320

Castle Builder (Nolan), 174

The Cat in the Hat (Seuss), 199

Cat Running (Snyder), 452

Catalanotto, Peter
　All I See, 171
　An Angel for Solomon Singer, 269
　Mama Is a Miner, 297
　My House Has Stars, 134
　The Painter, 191-92
　The Rolling Store, 18
　Soda Jerk, 5, 553

Catherine, Called Birdy (Cushman), 245, 498

Catling, Patrick Skene, *The Chocolate Touch*, 322

Catrow, David, *Who Said That? Famous Americans Speak*, 489-90

A Cat's Body (Cole), 220

The Cat's Purr (Bryan), 174

Catwings (LeGuin), 320-21

Cauley, Lorinda Bryan, *Clap Your Hands*, 89

Caves and Caverns (Gibbons), 211-12

The Cay (Taylor), 498

Cazet, Denys
　A Fish in His Pocket, 215
　Frosted Glass, 207

Cecil, Randy
　Dear Dr. Sillybear, 176
　Little Red Cowboy Hat, 185

Celebrate America in Poetry and Art (Panzer), 45

Celebrating America: A Collection of Poems & Images of the American Spirit, 45

Celebration! (Thomas), 363

Celebrations (Livingston), 386-87

Cepeda, Joe, *The Old Man & His Door*, 138

Chalk, Gary, *Redwall*, 517

The Chalk Doll (Pomerantz), 321

Chamberlain, Margaret, *A Piece of String Is a Wonderful Thing*, 342

Chanukkah in Chelm (Adler), 274

Chapman, Cheryl, *Pass the Fritters, Critters*, 142

Charles, N.N., *What Am I? Looking Through Shapes at Apples and Grapes*, 71

Charles Dickens: The Man Who Had Great Expectations (Stanley and Vennema), 387

Charlie the Chicken (Denchfield), 64

Charlie and the Chocolate Factory (Dahl), 321

Charlie Drives the Stage (Kimmel), 387

Charlie Pippin (Boyd), 452-53

Charlip, Remy
　The Dead Bird, 11
　Fortunately, 202-3
　Handtalk: An ABC of Finger Spelling and Sign Language, 13-14
　Hooray for Me, 110
　Thirteen, 56

Charlotte's Web (White), 355, 387-88

Chasing Redbird (Creech), 453

Chato's Kitchen (Soto), 232

Chatting (Hughes), 64

Chee, Cheng-Khee, *Old Turtle*, 16

Cheese, Choe, *Walking the Bridge of Your Nose*, 429

Chen, Tony, *A Child's First Bible*, 232

The Cherokees (Sneve), 274-75

Cherries and Cherry Pits (Williams), 175

Cherry, Lynne
　The Great Kapok Tree, 330
　If I Were in Charge of the World...And Other Worries, 508
　The Snail's Spell, 152
　When I'm Sleepy, 164

Chess, Victoria
　Rolling Harvey Down the Hill, 373
　Slugs, 376-77
　Tales for the Perfect Child, 484
　Ten Sly Piranhas: A Counting Story in Reverse, 225

Chester's Way (Henkes), 175, 184

Chestnut Cove (Egan), 275

Chesworth, Michael D., *Archibald Frisby*, 78-79

Cheyenne Again (Bunting), 278, 389

Chicka Chicka Boom Boom (Martin and Archambault), 88, 355

Chicken Little (Kellogg), 26
Chicken Man (Edwards), 88-89
Chicken Soup, Boots! (Kalman), 498-99
Chicken Sunday (Polacco), 26
Chickens Aren't the Only Ones (Heller), 199
Child of the Owl (Yep), 350
Children of the Dust Bowl: The True Story of the School at Weedpatch Camp, 453
Children Just Like Me: Unique Celebration of Children Around the World, 46
Children of the River (Crew), 542
Children's Book of Kwanzaa, A Guide to Celebrating The Holiday (Johnson), 389
A Child's Christmas in Wales (Thomas), 37
A Child's First Bible (Stoddard), 232
A Child's Garden of Verses (Stevenson), 212
Chocolate Fever (Smith), 321
A Chocolate Moose for Dinner (Gwynne), 258
The Chocolate Touch (Catling), 322
The Chocolate War (Cormier), 542-43
Choldenko, Gennifer, *Moonstruck*, 298
Chorao, Kay
    My Mama Says There Aren't Any Zombies, Ghosts, or Things, 188-89
    Number One Number Fun, 189
Christiana, David
    Good Griselle, 439
    I Am the Mummy Heb-Nefert, 464
    A Tooth Fairy's Tale, 194
The Christmas Alphabet (Sabuda), 10
A Christmas Carol (Dickens), 37
The Christmas House (Turner), 322
Christmas in the Big House, Christmas in the Quarters (McKissack), 499
A Christmas Memory (Capote), 37
The Christmas Menorahs: How a Town Fought Hate (Cohn), 389-90
The Christmas Miracle of Jonathan Toomey (Wojciechowski), 37, 389
The Christmas Tree Tangle (Mahy), 26-27
Christopher, John, *The City of Gold and Lead*, 453
Christopher, Matt, *Red Hot Hightops*, 344
The Chronicles of Narnia (Lewis), 355, 390
Chrysanthemum (Henkes), 184
Cinder Edna (Jackson), 322, 354
The Cinder-Eyed Cats (Rohmann), 11
Cinderella's Rat (Meddaugh), 275, 354
Circling the Globe (Grabham), 390
The City of Dragons (Yep), 350
The City of Gold and Lead (Christopher), 453
City of Light, City of Dark: A Comic Book Novel (Avi), 454
Clap Your Hands (Cauley), 89
Clark, Emma Chichester
    The Minstrel and the Dragon Pup, 221-22
    Something Rich & Strange, 481

Clark, Lorna, *All We Needed to Say*, 443
Clarke, Margaret Courtney, *My Painted House, My Friendly Chicken, & Me*, 34
Classic Poems to Read Aloud (Berry), 46
Clay, Wil, *The Real McCoy: The Life of an African-American Inventor*, 343-44
Clay Boy (Ginsburg), 212
Cleary, Beverly
    Dear Mr. Henshaw, 392
    A Girl From Yamhill, 459
    Henry Huggins, 331
    The Mouse and the Motorcycle, 235
    Ramona the Pest, 343, 355
Clements, Andrew, *Big Al*, 83
Cleopatra (Stanley), 391
Cleversticks (Ashley), 89
Clifton, Lucille, *Everett Anderson's Goodbye*, 11-12, 218
Climo, Shirley
    Atalanta's Race: A Greek Myth, 383
    Egyptian Cinderella, 354
    The Irish Cinderlad, 354
    The Korean Cinderella, 294, 354
    Little Red Ant and the Great Big Crumb-A Mexican Fable, 185
    A Treasury of Mermaids, 349
    A Treasury of Princesses, 349
Close Your Eyes So You Can See: Stories of Children in the Life of Jesus, 323
Cloud Eyes (Lasky), 408
Cloudland (Burningham), 89
Cloudy With a Chance of Meatballs (Barrett), 275
Clouse, Nancy
    Pink Paper Swans, 263
    Puzzle Maps U.S.A., 417
Clown (Blake), 199-200, 359
The Clown of God (dePaola), 363-64
Coalson, Glo, *On Mother's Lap*, 139
Cobb, Vicki, *Science Experiments You Can Eat*, 478
Coerr, Eleanor
    Sadako, 303
    Sadako and the Thousand Paper Cranes, 420
Cogancherry, Helen, *The Floating House*, 397
Cohen, Barbara
    Make a Wish Molly, 337
    Molly's Pilgrim, 340
    Robin Hood & Little John, 224
Cohen, Daniel, *The Phantom Hitchhiker*, 342
Cohen, Miriam, *The First Grade Takes a Test*, 97
Cohn, Amy, *From Sea to Shining Sea*, 47, 388
Cohn, Janice, *The Christmas Menorahs: How a Town Fought Hate*, 389-90
Cole, Brock, *The Indian in the Cupboard*, 464-65
Cole, Henry
    Barefoot: Escape on the Underground Railroad, 257
    Jack's Garden, 181
    Livingstone Mouse, 124
    Some Smug Slug, 208
Cole, Joanna, 220
    Anna Banana: 101 Jump-Rope Rhymes, 220

Asking About Sex and Growing Up, 220
A Bird's Body, 220, 272
A Cat's Body, 220
A Dog's Body, 220
Give a Dog a Bone, 220
How I Was Adopted, 220
The Magic School Bus in the Time of the Dinosaurs, 221
The New Baby at Your House, 220
Pat-A-Cake and Other Play Rhymes, 220
Pin the Tail on the Donkey and Other Party Games, 220
The Read-Aloud Treasury, 220
Ready...Set...Read!, 120, 220
Six Sick Sheep, 151
Your New Potty, 220
Coleman, Evelyn
    The Glass Bottle Tree, 399
    White Socks Only, 431
Collard, Sneed B., III, *Animal Dads*, 78
Collins, Heather, *A Pioneer Sampler*, 301
Colman, Penny, *Corpses, Coffins and Crypts: A History of Burial*, 500
Colon, Raul
    Celebration!, 363
    Tomas and the Library Lady, 427
Color (Heller), 323
Colors Around Us: A Lift-the-Flap Surprise Book (Rotner and Woodbull), 89-90
Colors Everywhere (Hoban), 90, 359
Coltman, Paul, *Tog the Ribber, or, Granny's Tale*, 426
Coman, Carolyn, *What Jamie Saw*, 523
Come Look With Me: Enjoying Art With Children (Blizzard), 323
Come a Tide (Lyon), 212-13
Coming Home (Cooper), 276
Commander Toad in Space (Yolen), 200
Commander Toad series (Yolen), 55
Communication (Aliki), 90
Company's Coming (Yorinks), 258
The Complete Nonsense of Edward Lear (Lear), 27
The Complete Sherlock Holmes (Doyle), 499
Complete Stories and Poems of Poe (Poe), 499
Complete Works of Edgar Allan Poe (Poe), 476
Conrad, Pam, *Prairie Songs*, 516
Contrary Mary (Jeram), 207
The Cook Camp (Paulsen), 450
Cooke, Trish, *So Much*, 19
Cool Salsa: Bilingual Poems on Growing Up Latino in the U.S., 527
Cooney, Barbara
    Eleanor, 282
    Emily, 395
    Miss Rumphius, 370
    Only Opal: The Diary of a Young Girl, 415
    Ox-Cart Man, 141
    Roxaboxen, 375
Cooney, Caroline, *The Face on the Milk Carton*, 502-3
Cooper, Floyd
    Be Good to Eddie Lee, 211

Brown Honey in Broomwheat Tea, 362
Coming Home, 276
The Girl Who Loved Caterpillars, 101-2
Grandpa's Face, 104
Ma Dear's Aprons, 337
Meet Danitra Brown, 298
Miz Berlin Walks, 413
Pass It On: African American Poetry for Children, 53
Pulling the Lion's Tail, 416
When Africa Was Home, 227
Cooper, Kay, *Too Many Rabbits & Other Fingerplays,* 70
Cooper, Melrose, *I Got a Family,* 217
Cooper, Susan
The Boggart, 449
The Grey King, 505
Over Sea, Under Stone, 514-15
Corentin, Philippe, *Papa!,* 141, 207
Cormier, Robert
The Chocolate War, 542-43
I Am the Cheese, 545
Corn Is Maize: The Gift of the Indians (Aliki), 90
Cornell, Laura
Annie Bananie, 9-10
Earl's Too Cool for Me, 94-95
Tell Me Again About the Night I Was Born, 157
When I Was Little: A Four-Year-Old's Memoir of Her Youth, 164
Corpses, Coffins and Crypts: A History of Burial (Colman), 500
Costello, Robert B., *The Macmillan Dictionary for Children,* 51
Cote, Nancy, *Fireflies, Peach Pies & Lullabies,* 284
Counting Crocodiles (Sierra), 91
The Country Bunny and the Little Gold Shoes (Heyward), 91
A Couple of Kooks and Other Stories About Love (Rylant), 374
Coursen, Valerie, *Mordant's Wish,* 132, 207
Courtney (Burningham), 276
Cousins, Lucy
Maisy Goes Swimming, 66-67
Za-Za's Baby Brother, 169
Coville, Bruce
Jeremy Thatcher, Dragon Hatcher, 466
William Shakespeare's Macbeth, 490
William Shakespeare's The Tempest, 490-91
Coville, Katherine, *Short and Shivery,* 479-80
The Cow Buzzed (Zimmerman and Zimmerman), 175
The Cow That Went Oink (Most), 91, 207
Cowan, Catherine, *My Life With the Wave,* 188
Cowboy Country (Scott), 391
Coyote: A Trickster Tale From the American Southwest (McDermott), 175
Coyote in Love (Dwyer), 213
The Cozy Book (Hoberman), 175-76
Craft, Kinuko, *Baba Yaga and Vasilisa the Brave,* 270
Craig, Helen, *Angelina Ballerina,* 171
Crash (Spinelli), 454
Crash! Bang! Boom! (Spier), 91-92

The Creation (Johnson), 46
Creech, Sharon
Chasing Redbird, 453
Walk Two Moons, 522
Crenson, Victoria, *Bay Shore Park,* 383
Crew, Linda, *Children of the River,* 542
Crews, Donald, *Freight Train,* 99
The Cricket in Times Square (Selden), 388, 391
The Crossing (Paulsen), 245, 543
Crutcher, Chris
Ironman, 547-48
Staying Fat for Sarah Byrnes, 245, 554
Cruz, Ray, *Absolutely, Positively Alexander,* 74
The Cuckoo's Child (Freeman), 528
The Culpepper Adventures (Paulsen), 276, 450
Cupples, Pat, *Take Action: An Environmental Book for Kids,* 484
Curious George (Rey), 92
Curry, Barbara K., *Sweet Words So Brave,* 424
Curtis, Christopher Paul, *The Watsons Go to Birmingham, 1963,* 523
Curtis, Jamie Lee
Tell Me Again About the Night I Was Born, 157
When I Was Little: A Four-Year-Old's Memoir of Her Youth, 164
Curtis, Munzee, *When the Big Dog Barks,* 165
Cushman, Doug
The ABC Mystery, 74
Aunt Eater Loves a Mystery, 80-81
Mouse and Mole and the Year-Round Garden, 187
Cushman, Karen
The Ballad of Lucy Whipple, 447
Catherine, Called Birdy, 245, 498
Cut From the Same Cloth (San Souci), 324, 388
Cyber.Kdz series (Balan), 436-37

D Is For Doufu: An Alphabet Book of Chinese Culture (Krach), 47
Dadey, Debbie, *Adventures of the Bailey School Kids,* 120
Dahl, Roald
The BFG, 384
Charlie and the Chocolate Factory, 321
James and the Giant Peach, 334
Matilda, 337-38
The Witches, 491
Dakos, Kalli
Don't Read This Book, Whatever You Do, 324-25
If You're Not Here, Please Raise Your Hand, 333
Dakota Dugout (Turner), 276-77
Dale, Penny, *Once There Were Giants,* 206
Damned Strong Love: The True Story of Willi G. and Stephan K. (Van Dijk), 543
Dance of the Sacred Circle (Rodanas), 324
Dance, Tanya (Gauch), 92
Dancing Carl (Paulsen), 450

Dancing Feet (Agell), 92-93
Dancing With the Wind (Orser), 213
Daniel, Alan
Big David, Little David, 173-74
Bunnicula, 319-20
Danny and the Dinosaur (Hoff), 120
Danziger, Paula, *Amber Brown Is Not a Crayon,* 268
Dark Thirty: Southern Tales of the Supernatural (McKissack), 500
The Dark Way: Stories From the Spirit World (Hamilton), 454, 455
Darling, Louis
The Enormous Egg, 395
The Mouse and the Motorcycle, 235
Ramona the Pest, 343
Darnell Rock Reporting (Myers), 454-56
Dasent, George W., *East o' the Sun and West o' the Moon,* 394
Dateline: Troy (Fleischman), 456
D'Aulaire, Ingri and Edgar Parin
D'Aulaire's Book of Greek Myths, 391-92
Don't Count Your Chicks, 94
D'Aulaire's Book of Greek Myths (D'Aulaire and D'Aulaire), 391-92
Davies, Nicola, *Big Blue Whale,* 318
Davis, Lambert, *The Dark Way: Stories From the Spirit World,* 454
Davol, Marguerite W., *The Paper Dragon,* 36
Dawn (Bang), 364
Dawn (Shulevitz), 11
Day, Alexandra
Frank and Ernest, 286
Good Dog, Carl, 204, 359
Day, Nancy Raines, *The Lion's Whiskers: An Ethiopian Folktale,* 295
The Day of Ahmed's Secret (Heide), 93
Day of the Dead (Johnston), 176
The Day of the Dead: A Mexican-American Celebration (Hoyt-Goldsmith), 392
The Day Jimmy's Boa Ate the Wash (Noble), 277
A Day With Wilbur Robinson (Joyce), 207, 277
The Daydreamer (McEwan), 456
Day's of the Blackbird: A Tale of Northern Italy (dePaola), 214
Days of the Dead (Lasky), 408
A Day's Work (Bunting), 277
De Colores and Other Latin-American Folksongs for Children (Orozco), 47
The Dead Bird (Brown), 11, 218
Dear America series, 500-1
Dear Dr. Sillybear (Regan), 176
Dear Mr. Blueberry (James), 93
Dear Mr. Henshaw (Cleary), 392
Dear Mr. Sprouts (Broome), 528
Dear Rebecca, Winter Is Here (George), 324
Dear Willie Rudd (Gray), 279
Dear World: How Children Around the World Feel About Our Environment, 47
Death Is Hard to Live With (Bode), 218
Deathwatch (White), 528-29
deBrunhoff, Jean, *The Story of Babar the Little Elephant,* 306-7

December Stillness (Hahn), 501
Deedy, Carmen Agra, *The Library Dragon*, 219
Deem, James M., *How to Make a Mummy Talk*, 508
  3 NBS of Julian Drew, 539
Degen, Bruce
  A Beautiful Feast for a Big King Cat, 172-73
  Commander Toad in Space, 200
  Jesse Bear, What Will You Wear?, 66
  The Magic School Bus in the Time of the Dinosaurs, 221
deGroat, Diane, *Pinky Is a Baby Mouse and Other Baby Animal Names*, 37
Delacre, Lulu, *Arroz Con Leche*, 230
Delf, Brian, *In the Beginning . . .*, 333-34
Delphine (Bang), 200
Delton, Judy, *Pee Wee Scouts* series, 120, 142
Dem Bones (Barner), 214
Demarest, Chris
  The Butterfly Jar, 25
  Today I'm Going Fishing With My Dad, 266
Demi
  Bamboo Hats and a Rice Cake, 81-82
  Buddha, 362
  Demi's Dragons and Fantastic Creatures, 364
  The Empty Pot, 201
  Grass Sandals: The Travels of Basho, 288-89
  Happy New Year! Kung-Hsi Fa-Ts'ai!, 290
  One Grain of Rice: A Mathematical Folktale, 299
Demi's Dragons and Fantastic Creatures (Demi), 364
Demuth, Patricia Brennan
  The Ornery Morning, 191, 207
  Those Amazing Ants, 56
Denchfield, Nick, *Charlie the Chicken*, 64
Dengler, Marianna, The Worry Stone, 379
Denise, Christopher, *The Fool of the World and the Flying Ship*, 397-98
Dennis, Wesley, *Misty of Chincoteague*, 413
Denslow, W.W., *The Wonderful Wizard of Oz*, 354
dePaola, Tomie
  Alice Nizzy Nazzy: The Witch of Santa Fe, 229
  The Clown of God, 363-64
  Days of the Blackbird: A Tale of Northern Italy, 214
  Fin M'Coul, the Giant of Knockmany Hill, 28
  The Legend of the Poinsettia, 219
  Nana Upstairs & Nana Downstairs, 135, 218
  Oliver Button Is a Sissy, 247
  Pancakes for Breakfast, 16-17
  The Popcorn Book, 144
  The Quilt Story, 145
  Strega Nona, 155
  The Tale of Rabbit and Coyote, 194
  Tony's Bread, 226

Deraney, Michael J., *Molly's Pilgrim*, 340
deRegniers, Beatrice Schenk
  May I Bring a Friend?, 129
  Sing a Song of Popcorn, 54-56
DerRol, Ruud, *Anne Frank: Beyond the Diary*, 495
The Devil's Arithmetic (Yolen), 55, 501
Dewdney, Anna, *The Peppermint Race*, 254
Dewey, Jennifer Owings, *Rattlesnake Dance*, 418
DeZutter, Hank, *Who Says a Dog Goes Bow-Wow?*, 21
Diaz, David
  Smoky Night, 304-5
  Wilma Unlimited, 312
Dickens, Charles, *A Christmas Carol*, 37
Dickinson, Peter
  A Bone From a Dry Sea, 496
  Eva, 544-45
Did You Hear Wind Sing Your Name?: An Oneida Song of Spring (Orie), 176
Did You See What I Saw?: Poems About School (Winters), 93
Dillon, Leo & Diane
  Ashanti to Zulu: African Traditions, 230
  The Girl Who Dreamed Only of Geese & Other Tales, 503
  Her Stories, 402
  Honey, I Love and Other Love Poems, 403
  The People Could Fly, 416
  What Am I? Looking Through Shapes at Apples and Grapes, 71
  Why Mosquitoes Buzz in People's Ears, 196
Dinner at Alberta's (Russell), 279
Dinosaurs Divorce (Brown and Brown), 177
Dinosaurs!: Strange and Wonderful (Pringle), 392
Dippers (Nichol), 393
DiSalvo-Ryan, Dyanne, *Friends and Amigos Series*, 286
Discovering the Iceman: An I Was There Book (Tanaka), 456-57
The Discovery of Dragons (Base), 501-2
Do Not Open (Turkle), 177
Do You See a Mouse? (Waber), 93
Dobson, Mary, *Smelly Old History* series, 481
Doctor De Soto (Steig), 200
Dodds, Dayle Ann, *Sing Sophie!*, 224-25
Dodson, Bert, *Supergrandpa*, 307
Dogs (Gibbons), 214-15
A Dog's Body (Cole), 220
Dogsong (Paulsen), 450
Dogteam (Paulsen), 279
Dogzilla (Pilkey), 364-65
Dolphin, Laurie and Ben, *Neve Shalom Wahat Al-Salam: Oasis of Peace*, 340-41
Don Quixote (Williams), 280
Donaldson, Julia, *A Squash and a Squeeze*, 153
Doney, Todd L.W., *January Rides the Wind: A Book of Months*, 32
Donna O'Neeshuck Was Chased by Some Cows (Grossman), 94

Donnelly, Marlene Hill, *How to Be a Nature Detective*, 111
Donoghue, Emma, *Kissing the Witch*, 549
Don't Count Your Chicks (D'aulaire and D'aulaire), 94
Don't Fidget a Feather (Silverman), 207, 232, 233
Don't Give Up the Ghost (Gale, ed.), 476
Don't Laugh, Joe (Kasza), 94
Don't Open the Door After the Sun Goes Down (Carusone), 457, 476
Don't Read This Book, Whatever You Do (Dakos), 324-25
Dooley, Norah, *Everybody Cooks Rice*, 250
Dorris, Michael
  Guests, 461-62
  Morning Girl, 472-73
  Sees Behind Trees, 478
Dorros, Arthur
  Abuela, 75
  A Tree Is Growing, 349
Double Trouble Squared (Lasky), 409
Douglass, Frederick, *Escape From Slavery*, 457
Dove Isabeau (Yolen), 55, 325
Down by the River: Afro-Caribbean Rhymes, Games, and Songs for Children, 233
Downing, Julie, *Soon, Annala*, 346
Doyle, Arthur Conan, Sir, *The Complete Sherlock Holmes*, 499
Dragon Cauldron (Yep), 350
Dragon of the Lost Sea (Yep), 350
The Dragon Prince (Yep), 350
Dragon Steel (Yep), 350
Dragon War (Yep), 350
Dragonfly (Bernhard), 177
Dragonfly's Tale (Rodanas), 258
The Dragonling (Koller), 280
The Dragons Are Singing Tonight (Prelutsky), 233
Dragon's Blood: Volume 1 in the Pit Dragon Trilogy (Yolen), 502
Dragon's Gate (Yep), 350
The Dragon's Robe (Lattimore), 280
Dragonwings (Yep), 350
Drake, Gary, *The Morgan's Dream*, 414
Drake, Jane, *Take Action: An Environmental Book for Kids*, 484
Draw 50 series (Ames), 393
Dressing (Oxenbury), 65
The Drinking Gourd: A Story of the Underground Railroad (Monjo), 259
A Drop of Water (Wick), 393
Du Bois, William Pene, *William's Doll*, 167
Duncan, Lois, *Killing Mr. Griffin*, 548
Duncan, Robert, *Amber on the Mountain*, 268
Dunphy, Madeleine, *Here Is the Tropical Rain Forest*, 180
Durell, Ann, *The Big Book for Our Planet*, 44
Dust for Dinner (Turner), 120
Dustland (Hamilton), 455
Dwyer, Mindy, *Coyote in Love*, 213
Dyer, Jane
  Talking Like the Rain: A First Book of Poems, 194

The Three Bears Holiday Rhyme Book, 158
Time for Bed, 69

Each Peach Pear Plum (Ahlberg and Ahlberg), 94
Eager, Edward
  Half Magic, 401
  The Knight's Castle, 407
  Seven-Day Magic, 420-21
The Eagle's Gift (Martin), 393-94
Earl's Too Cool for Me (Komaiko), 94-95, 207
Earrings! (Viorst), 121, 207, 281
Earth, Fire, Water, Air (Hoffman), 325
Earth, Sky and Beyond: A Journey Through Space (Verdet), 325
Earthdance (Ryder), 27
The Earthsea Quartet (LeGuin), 529
Earth-Shattering Poems (Rosenberg, ed.), 544
Earthshine (Nelson), 544
East o' the Sun and West o' the Moon (Dasent, translation), 394
Easter Egg Artists (Adams), 95
The Easter Egg Farm (Auch), 325-26
Eastman, P.D.
  Are You My Mother?, 79
  Go, Dog. Go!, 102, 120
Eating the Alphabet: Fruits & Vegetables From A to Z (Ehlert), 95
Eating the Plates: The Pilgrim Book of Food and Manners (Penner), 457
Echewa, Obinkaram, *The Ancestor Tree*, 250
Ed Emberley's Big Purple Drawing Book (Emberley), 259
Edelson, Wendy, *The Baker's Dozen: A Saint Nicholas Tale*, 81
Edward in Deep Water (Wells), 128
Edward and the Pirates (McPhail), 27
Edward Unready for School (Wells), 121, 128
Edward Unready for a Sleep Over (Wells), 121
Edward Unready for Swimming (Wells), 121
Edwards, Michelle, *Chicken Man*, 88-89
Edwards, Pamela Duncan
  Barefoot: Escape on the Underground Railroad, 257
  Livingstone Mouse, 124
  Some Smug Slug, 207, 208
Edward's Overwhelming Overnight (Wells), 128
Eeny, Meeny, Miney Mole (Yolen), 55, 95
Egan, Tim
  Burnt Toast on Davenport Street, 273
  Chestnut Cove, 275
  Metropolitan Cow, 298
An Egg Is an Egg (Weiss), 96
Egielski, Richard
  The Gingerbread Boy, 101
  A Telling of the Tales, 484-85
The Egypt Game (Snyder), 502
Egyptian Cinderella (Climo), 354
Ehlert, Lois
  Chicka Chicka Boom Boom, 88
  Eating the Alphabet: Fruits & Vegetables From A to Z, 95

Hands, 105
Nuts to You, 137
Ehrlich, Amy, *Parents in the Pigpen, Pigs in the Tub*, 373
Eight Hands Round: A Patchwork Alphabet (Paul), 281
El Chino (Say), 282
Elbert's Bad Word (Wood), 201
Eleanor (Cooney), 282
The Elements series (Robbins), 394
Elijah's Angel: A Story for Chanukah and Christmas (Rosen), 282
Eloise (Thompson), 394-95
Elya, Susan Middleton, *Say Hola to Spanish*, 237
Emberley, Ed
  Ed Emberley's Big Purple Drawing Book, 259
  Go Away, Big Green Monster!, 102
Emberley, Michael
  Happy Birth Day, 106
  It's Perfectly Normal, 49
Emily (Bedard), 395
Emma's Rug (Say), 259
The Emperor and the Kite (Yolen), 55
The Empty Pot (Demi), 201
Encounter (Yolen), 55
Encyclopedia Brown Series (Sobol), 282-83
Enderle, Judith
  Nell Nuggett and the Cow Caper, 136
  Six Creepy Sheep, 151
The Enormous Egg (Butterworth), 395
Enright, Elizabeth
  The Four Story Mistake, 437
  Zee, 356
Enter If You Dare!: Scary Stories From the Haunted Mansion (Stephens), 476
Erdrich, Louise, *Grandmother's Pigeon*, 204
Eric Knight's Lassie Come Home (Wells), 335
Ernst, Lisa Campbell, *When Bluebell Sang*, 164
Escape From Slavery: Boyhood of Frederick Douglass in His Own Words, 457
Esterl, Arnica, *Okino and the Whales*, 190
Eva (Dickinson), 544-45
Evans, Leslie, *The Spice Alphabet Book*, 305
Evans, Walker, *Something Permanent*, 481
Everett Anderson's Goodbye (Clifton), 11-12, 218
Everglades (George), 326
Everitt, Betsy, *Mean Soup*, 129, 207, 265
Every Living Thing (Rylant), 374, 458
Everybody Cooks Rice (Dooley), 250
Everybody Needs A Rock (Baylor), 283
Everyday Mysteries (Wexler), 326
Extra Innings: Baseball Poems (Hopkins, selections by), 395
Extremely Weird Animal Defenses (Lovett), 395-96
Eye Spy: A Mysterious Alphabet (Bourke), 458
The Eyes of Gray Wolf (London), 177

Fables (Lobel), 201-2

The Fabulous Firework Family (Flora), 178
The Face on the Milk Carton (Cooney), 502-3
Fadden, J.K., *Keepers of the Earth*, 406
Fain, Kathleen, *Handsigns: A Sign Language Alphabet*, 13
Fair! (Lewin), 28
Faith and the Electric Dog (Jennings), 326
The Faithful Friend (San Souci), 396
Falla, Dominique, *Woodlore*, 58
Fallen Angels (Myers), 506
Family Reunion (Singer), 283
Fanelli, Sara, *My Map Book*, 205
Fanny's Dream (Buehner), 283-84, 354
The Fantastic Drawings of Danielle (McClintock), 260
Farm Morning (McPhail), 202
Farmer, Nancy, *A Girl Named Disaster*, 530
Farmer Duck (Waddell), 96
Farnsworth, Bill
  The Christmas Menorahs: How a Town Fought Hate, 389-90
  Sally Arnold, 304
Fast Sam, Cool Clyde, and Stuff (Myers), 506
A Fate Totally Worse Than Death (Fleischman), 545
Father Water, Mother Woods (Paulsen), 450
Faulkner, Keith, *The Wide-Mouthed Frog: A Pop-Up Book*, 166-67
The Feather Merchants and Other Tales of the Fools of Chelm (Sanfield), 396
Feelings, Tom
  Moja Means One, 355
  Soul Looks Back in Wonder, 482
  To Be a Slave, 521
Feelings (Aliki), 96
Feiffer, Jules
  Meanwhile . . ., 369
  The Phantom Tollbooth, 515
Felix's Hat (Bancroft), 202
Festivals (Livingston), 365
Fiammenghi, Gioia, *Chocolate Fever*, 321
Fieser, Stephen, *The Silk Route: 7,000 Miles of History*, 346
Fiesta (Ancona), 397
Fin M'Coul, the Giant of Knockmany Hill (dePaola), 28
Finding Providence: The Story of Roger Williams (Avi), 120, 251
Fine, Howard, *Piggie Pie*, 222-23
A Fine White Dust (Rylant), 374
Finster Frets (Baker), 233-34
Fiore, Peter, *Dear Willie Rudd*, 279
The Fire Children: A West African Creation Tale (Maddern), 178
Fire in the Forest: A Cycle of Growth and Renewal (Pringle), 437
Fire Race: A Karuk Coyote Tale About How Fire Came to the People, 178
Fireflies, Peach Pies & Lullabies (Kroll), 218, 284
First Flight (McPhail), 97
The First Grade Takes a Test (Cohen), 97
The First Strawberries: A Cherokee Story (Bruchac), 326-27

First Things First (Fraser), 97

Firth, Barbara, *Can't You Sleep, Little Bear?*, 87

Fish Faces (Wu), 98

A Fish in His Pocket (Cazet), 215

Fisher, Leonard Everett
  Celebrations, 386-87
  Festivals, 365

Fitzhugh, Louise, *Harriet the Spy*, 462

Five Children and It (Nesbit), 437

The 500 Hats of Bartholomew Cubbins (Seuss), 361

Five Live Bongos (Lyon), 178

Five Minutes Peace (Murphy), 98

5 Novels (Pinkwater collection), 493

Flack, Marjorie
  Angus and the Cat, 78
  Angus and the Ducks, 355
  The Country Bunny and the Little Gold Shoes, 91
  The Story About Ping, 154

Fleischman, Paul
  Bull Run, 451
  Dateline: Troy, 456
  A Fate Totally Worse Than Death, 545
  Joyful Noise: Poems for Two Voices, 467
  Seedfolks, 251, 478

Fleischman, Sid
  By the Great Horn Spoon, 452
  The Whipping Boy, 430-31

Fleming, Denise
  In the Tall, Tall Grass, 116-17
  Lunch, 205
  Time to Sleep, 159

Fleming, Virginia, *Be Good to Eddie Lee*, 211

Fletcher, Ralph, *Twilight Comes Twice*, 227

Flight (Burleigh), 284

Flip-Flop Girl (Paterson), 503

The Floating House (Sanders), 397

Floca, Brian, *City of Light, City of Dark: A Comic Book Novel*, 454

Flora, James, *The Fabulous Firework Family*, 178

Flora McDonnell's ABC (McDonnell), 98

Florczak, Robert
  Birdsong, 231
  The Rainbow Bridge, 417

Florian, Douglas, *Very Scary*, 70-71
  Monster Motel, 340

Flournoy, Valerie, *The Patchwork Quilt*, 263

Fly Away Home (Bunting), 244, 278, 365

Fly! A Brief History of Flight (Moser), 458

The Flying Tortoise: An Igbo Tale (Mollel), 260

Folks Call Me Appleseed John (Glass), 397

Follow the Dream (Sis), 327

Fong, Andrea, *Made in China: Ideas and Inventions From Ancient China*, 470

The Fool of the World and the Flying Ship (Denise), 397-98

Ford, H.J., *The Blue Fairy Book*, 44-45

Foreman, Michael
  After the War Was Over, 494
  The Arabian Nights, 383

Little Ships: The Heroic Rescue at Dunkirk in WW II, 410-11
  War Boy: A Country Childhood, 522-23

Forest of Dreams (Wells), 128

The Forestwife (Tomlinson), 529

The Forgotten Door (Key), 327

Fornari, Giuliano, *The Body Atlas*, 385

Fortnum, Peggy, *A Bear Called Paddington*, 317

Fortunately (Charlip), 202-3

The Fortune-Tellers (Alexander), 284

The Four Story Mistake (Enright), 437

Fowler, Jim, *I'll See You When the Moon Is Full*, 114

Fowler, Susi Gregg, *I'll See You When the Moon Is Full*, 114

Fox, Mem
  Guess What?, 13
  Hattie & the Fox, 107
  Possum Magic, 144
  Time for Bed, 69, 355
  Tough Boris, 160
  Wilfred Gordon McDonald Partridge, 21-22, 265
  Wombat Divine, 167-68

Fox, Paula, *Radiance Descending*, 476-77

Fox Song (Bruchac), 327

The Fragile Flag (Langton), 459

Frampton, David
  Miro in the Kingdom of the Sun, 370
  Whaling Days, 311

Francis, David, *Ten Little-Known Facts About Hippopotamuses*, 485

Frank, Anne, *Anne Frank: The Diary of a Young Girl*, 495

Frank and Ernest (Day), 286

Frankenberg, Robert, *Owls in the Family*, 415-16

Frankfeldt, Gwen, *Dateline: Troy*, 456

Franklin, Kristine L.
  Shepherd Boy, 192
  When the Monkeys Came Back, 312

Fraser, Betty
  The Cozy Book, 175-76
  First Things First, 97
  A House Is a House for Me, 111

Fraser, Mary Ann, *Ten Mile Day & Building of Transcontinental Railroad*, 348

Frasier, Debra, *On the Day You Were Born*, 35-36

Frazee, Marla, *That Kookoory!*, 238

Freak the Mighty (Philbrick), 529-30

Freddy the Detective (Brooks), 388

Frederick (Lionni), 98-99

Free Fall (Wiesner), 12, 359

Freedman, Russell
  An Indian Winter, 465
  Lincoln: A Photobiography, 511

Freeman, Suzanne, *The Cuckoo's Child*, 528

Freight Train (Crews), 99

French, Vivian, *Oliver's Vegetables*, 190

Friedman, Ina R., *How My Parents Learned to Eat*, 111

Friends (Heine), 99

Friends and Amigos series (Giff), 286

Fritz, Jean

Around the World in a Hundred Years, 436
  Will You Sign Here, John Hancock?, 353

Fritz and the Mess Fairy (Wells), 128

Froehlich, Margaret Walden, *That Kookoory!*, 238

Frog in Love (Velthuijs), 100

Frog and Toad books (Lobel), 120

Frog and Toad Are Friends (Lobel), 99-100

Froggy Gets Dressed (London), 100

Frogs (Gibbons), 215

Frogs in Clogs (Samton), 203

From Head to Toe (Carle), 100

From the Mixed-Up Files of Mrs. Basil E. Frankweiler (Konigsburg), 459

From Pictures to Words: A Book About Making A Book (Stevens), 365

From Sea to Shining Sea (Cohn, ed.), 47, 388

From Seed to Plant (Gibbons), 215

Front Porch Stories at the One-Room School (Tate), 438

Frosted Glass (Cazet), 207

A Fruit and Vegetable Man (Schotter), 203

Fulweiler, Stephen, *The Iron Dragon Never Sleeps*, 465-66

Fun! No Fun! (Stevenson), 286

Funny (Paulsen), 450

Furlong, Monica, *Robin's Country*, 477

Fuzzy Yellow Ducklings (Van Fleet), 65

Gaber, Susan
  Bit By Bit, 83
  Good Times on Grandfather Mountain, 12-13
  Small Talk: A Book of Short Poems, 422
  Zee, 356

Gag, Wanda, *Millions of Cats*, 130

Galdone, Paul, *Henny Penny*, 107-8

Gale, David, *Don't Give Up the Ghost*, 476

Galimoto (Williams), 100-1

Gallo, Donald R., *Join In*, 548

A Game of Catch (Wilbur), 438

Gammell, Stephen
  Airmail to the Moon, 313-14
  Come a Tide, 212-13
  Is That You, Winter?, 14-15
  Monster Mama, 33
  Old Black Fly, 190
  The Relatives Came, 373
  Scary Stories to Tell in the Dark, 420
  Thunder at Gettysburg, 308
  Waiting to Waltz: A Childhood, 487-88
  Will's Mammoth, 22
  The Wing Shop, 228

Gannett, Ruth, *My Father's Dragon*, 222, 388

Gantschev, Ivan, *Santa's Favorite Story*, 149

Garcia, Jerry, *The Teddy Bears Picnic*, 157

Gardella, Tricia, *Just Like My Dad*, 118

The Gardener (Stewart), 203

Gardiner, John Reynolds, *Stone Fox*, 346-47

Garland, Sherry, *The Lotus Seed*, 251

Garns, Allen, *Gonna Sing My Head Off!: American Folk Songs for Children*, 48

Gary Paulsen's World of Adventure series (Paulsen), 398, 450

Gates, Donald, *The Summer of Stanley*, 307

Gates, Frieda, *Owl Eyes*, 300-1

Gather Up, Gather In: A Book of Seasons (Helldorfer), 286-87

The Gathering (Hamilton), 455

Gathering the Sun: An Alphabet in Spanish and English (Ada), 28

Gauch, Patricia Lee
  Dance, Tanya, 92
  Thunder at Gettysburg, 308

Geisert, Arthur, *Oink*, 138

Gelman, Rita, *I Went to the Zoo*, 113

The Gentleman and the Kitchen Maid (Stanley), 398

Geography From A To Z: A Picture Glossary (Knowlton), 287

George, Jean Craighead
  Dear Rebecca, Winter Is Here, 324
  Everglades, 326
  Julie of the Wolves, 510
  Look to the North: A Wolf Pup Diary, 296

George, Lindsay Barrett
  Beaver at Long Pond, 211
  In the Woods: Who's Been Here?, 117
  Secret Places, 304

George, William T., *Beaver at Long Pond*, 211

George and Martha (Marshall), 12

Gerig, Sybil Graber, *The Worry Stone*, 379

Geringer, Laura, *A Three Hat Day*, 308

Gershator, David, *Bread Is for Eating*, 85

Gerstein, Mordicai, *The Giant*, 439

Get on Board: The Story of the Underground Railroad (Haskins), 438

Get Ready, Get Set, Read! series, 120

Geter, Tyrone, *White Socks Only*, 431

Getting to Know the World's Great Artists series (Venezia), 398

Ghantschev, Ivan, *The Train to Grandma's*, 160

The Ghost Dance (McLerran), 328

The Ghost-Eye Tree (Martin and Archambault), 101

The Giant (Gerstein), 439

Giants in the Land (Appelbaum), 398

Giants! Stories From Around the World (Walker), 328

Gibbons, Gail
  Caves and Caverns, 211-12
  Dogs, 214-15
  Frogs, 215
  From Seed to Plant, 215
  The Planets, 223
  Puff...Flash...Bang! A Book About Signals, 223

Giff, Patricia Reilly
  Friends and Amigos series, 286
  The Kids of the Polk Street School series, 119, 120
  Lily's Crossing, 469
  New Kids at the Polk Street School series, 120

The Gift of Driscoll Lipscomb (Yamaka), 287

The Gift of Sarah Barker (Yolen), 55

The Gifts of Wali Dad: A Tale of India and Pakistan (Shepard), 287

Gila Monsters Meet You at the Airport (Sharmat), 216

Gilchrist, Jan Spivey, *Nathaniel Talking*, 372

Gillman, Alec
  The Green Truck Garden Giveaway, 289
  Toad or Frog, Swamp or Bog, 264

Gilman, Phoebe, *Something From Nothing*, 153

Ginger (Voake), 101

The Gingerbread Boy (Egielski), 101

The Gingerbread Doll (Tews), 179

Ginsburg, Max, *Mississippi Bridge*, 472

Ginsburg, Mirra, *Clay Boy*, 212

A Girl Named Disaster (Farmer), 530

The Girl Who Cried Flowers and Other Tales (Yolen), 55

The Girl Who Dreamed Only of Geese and Other Tales of the Far North, 503

The Girl Who Loved Caterpillars: A Twelfth Century Tale, From Japan, 101-2

The Girl Who Loved Wild Horses (Goble), 328

A Girl From Yamhill (Cleary), 459

Girls to the Rescue (Lansky), 328

Give a Dog a Bone (Calmenson and Cole), 220

The Giver (Lowry), 503-4

Gladiator (Watkins), 460

Glass, Andrew
  Don't Open the Door After the Sun Goes Down, 457
  Folks Call Me Appleseed John, 397
  Larger Than Life, 407
  She'll Be Comin' Round the Mountain, 150
  Soap! Soap! Don't Forget The Soap!, 193
  Sweetwater Run, 348

The Glass Bottle Tree (Coleman), 399

Gliori, Debi, *Poems Go Clang!: A Collection of Noisy Verse*, 37

The Glory Field (Myers), 245, 460, 506

Go Away, Big Green Monster! (Emberley), 102

Go Away, Dog (Nodset), 243, 244

Go, Dog. Go! (Eastman), 102, 120

Go Hang a Salami! I'm a Lasagna Hog! (Agee), 357

Goble, Paul
  Adopted by the Eagles, 313
  The Girl Who Loved Wild Horses, 328

Goddesses, Heroes, and Shamans: Young People's Guide to World Mythology, 504

Godkin, Celia, *What About Ladybugs?*, 238

Goedecke, Christopher, *Smart Moves: A Kid's Guide to Self-Defense*, 480

Goembel, Ponder, *"Hi, Pizza Man!"*, 109

The Golden Carp and Other Tales From Vietnam (Vuong), 399

The Golden Compass (Pullman), 504

Goldilocks and the Three Bears (Brett), 102

The Golem (Singer), 460

Golem (Wisniewski), 288

Golem: A Giant Made of Mud (Podwal), 399

Golenbock, Peter, *Teammates*, 308

Gonna Sing My Head Off!: American Folk Songs for Children (Krull), 48

Gonzalez, Ralfka & Ana, *My First Book of Proverbs*, 371

The Good, the Bad, and the Goofy (Scieszka), 399

Good-Bye Curtis (Henkes), 184

Good Dog, Carl (Day), 204, 359

Good Griselle (Yolen), 55, 439

Good Morning Pond (Capucilli), 102-3

Good Night, Gorilla (Rathmann), 103

Good Times on Grandfather Mountain (Martin), 12-13

Goodman, Vivienne, *Guess What?*, 13

Goodnight Moon (Brown), 103, 355

Goody O'Grumpity (Brink), 216

Gorbaty, Norman, *Earthdance*, 27

Gorey, Edward, *The Shrinking of Treehorn*, 421

Gorog, Judith
  In a Messy, Messy Room & Other Scary Stories, 404-5, 476
  Zilla Sasparilla and the Mud Baby, 312

Gottlieb, Dale, *I Got a Family*, 217

Grabham, Sue, *Circling the Globe*, 390

Grace, Catherine O'Neil, *I Want to Be a Veterinarian*, 332

Graham, Ruth Bell, *One Wintry Night*, 53

Graham-Barber, Lynda, *Toad or Frog, Swamp or Bog*, 264

Gramatky, Hardie, *Little Toot*, 124

Grandad Bill's Song (Yolen), 179, 218

Grandfather Tang's Story (Tompert), 260

Grandfather Twilight (Berger), 103

Grandfather's Journey (Say), 288

Grandma Essie's Covered Wagon (Williams), 329

Grandmother Bryant's Pocket (Martin), 400

Grandmother's Nursery Rhymes/Las Nanas De Abuelita (Jaramillo), 179

Grandmother's Pigeon (Erdrich), 204

Grandpa's Face (Greenfield), 104

Granstorm, Brita, *The World Is Full of Babies!*, 168

Grant, Cynthia D., *Mary Wolf*, 549

The Graphic Alphabet (Pelletier), 400

Grass Sandals: The Travels of Basho (Spivak), 288-89

Gray, Libba Moore
  Dear Willie Rudd, 279
  Small Green Snake, 152

Gray Wolf, Red Wolf (Patent), 330

The Great Ball Game: A Muskogee Story (Bruchac), 234

The Great Fire (Murphy), 460

The Great Gilly Hopkins (Paterson), 461

The Great Kapok Tree (Cherry), 330

The Great Pirate Activity Book (Robins), 330

The Great Piratical Rumbustification
(Mahy), 400
*The Great White Man-Eating Shark: A
Cautionary Tale* (Mahy), 289
The Greatest Table (Rosen), 48
The Greek News (Powell), 461
Green, Norman, *Advice for a Frog*,
494
Green Eggs and Ham (Seuss), 104,
120
Green Tales (Tanaka), 400-1
The Green Truck Garden Giveaway
(Martin), 289
Greenberg, David
Bugs!, 273
Slugs, 244, 376-77
Greenberg, Mark, *Amazon Diary:
The Jungle Adventures of Alex
Winters*, 382
Greene, Carol, *The Old Ladies Who
Liked Cats*, 138
Greene, Jeffrey, *The Rain*, 17
Greenfield, Eloise
Grandpa's Face, 104
*Honey, I Love and Other Love
Poems*, 403
Nathaniel Talking, 372
Greenstein, Elaine, *Mendel's Ladder*,
252
Greenwood, Barbara, *A Pioneer
Sampler*, 301
Gregory, Valiska, *When Stories Fell
Like Shooting Stars*, 20-21
The Grey King (Cooper), 505
*The Grey Lady and the Strawberry
Snatcher* (Bang), 204, 359
Grifalconi, Ann
Everett Anderson's Goodbye, 11-12
*The Lion's Whiskers: An Ethiopian
Folktale*, 295
Griffin, Peni R., *Hobkin*, 532
Grimes, Nikki, *Meet Danitra Brown*,
298
Grisman, David, *The Teddy Bears
Picnic*, 157
Grossman, Bill
The Banging Book, 82
*Donna O'Neeshuck Was Chased by
Some Cows*, 94
My Little Sister Ate One Hare, 188,
244
*Grossology: The Science of Really
Gross Things* (Branzei), 461
Growing Colors (McMillan), 104
Growing Up in Coal Country
(Bartoletti), 505
Gruenberg, Hannah, *Felix's Hat*, 202
Guarino, Deborah, *Is Your Mama a
Llama?*, 117
Guback, Georgia, *Luka's Quilt*, 296-
97
Guess How Much I Love You
(McBratney), 104-5, 207
Guess What? (Fox), 13
Guests (Dorris), 461-62
Guevara, Susan, *Chato's Kitchen*,
232
Guiberson, Brenda Z., *Into the Sea*,
293
The Guinness Book of World Records
(McWhirter), 505
Gulliver's Adventures in Lilliput
(Swift), 289
Guralnick, Elissa A., *The Weighty
Word Book*, 488
Gus and Grandpa (Mills), 105

Gwynne, Fred, *A Chocolate Moose
for Dinner*, 258

Haas, Irene, *The Maggie B.*, 125-26
Hague, Michael
The Rainbow Fairy Book, 54
Rootabaga Stories, Part One, 237
Hahn, Mary Downing
December Stillness, 501
Stepping on the Cracks, 482
Hailstones and Halibut Bones
(O'Neill), 401
Hakim, Joy, *History of the U.S.: A 10
Volume Series*, 507
Hale, Christy, *The Ancestor Tree*, 250
Hale, James Graham, *Through Moon
and Stars and Night Skies*, 158-
59
Half Magic (Eager), 401
Hall, Donald
I Am the Dog, I Am the Cat, 261
Ox-Cart Man, 141
Hall, Zoe
Apple Pie Tree, 78
It's Pumpkin Time!, 181
Halloween ABC (Merriam), 290
Hallworth, Grace, *Down by the River*,
233
Hally, Greg, *Once There Was a
Bull . . . (Frog)*, 140
Halperin, Wendy Anderson
Homeplace, 260-61
Hunting the White Cow, 112
Halpern, Shari
Apple Pie Tree, 78
It's Pumpkin Time!, 181
Hamilton, Virginia, 455
Anthony Burns, 455
Arrilla Sun Down, 455
Brothers Rush, 245, 455
*The Dark Way: Stories From the
Spirit World*, 454, 455
Dustland, 455
The Gathering, 455
Her Stories, 402, 455
The House of Dies Drear, 455
In the Beginning, 405, 455
Justice and Her Brothers, 455
M.C. Higgins the Great, 455
The People Could Fly, 388, 416,
455
The Planet of Junior Brown, 455
A Ring of Tricksters, 418-19
Sweet Whispers, 245, 455
*Willie Bea and the Time When the
Martians Landed*, 455
Zeely, 455
The Handmade Alphabet (Rankin),
357-58
Hands (Ehlert), 105
*Handsigns: A Sign Language
Alphabet* (Fain), 13
*Handtalk: An ABC of Finger Spelling
and Sign Language* (Fain), 13-14
Hannah and Jack (Nethery), 105
Hansel and Gretel (Marshall), 106
Happy Birth Day (Harris), 106
The Happy Hocky Family (Smith), 14
Happy New Year! Kung-Hsi Fa-Ts'ai!
(Demi), 290
Harlem (Myers), 506, 507
Harness, Cheryl
The Night Before Christmas, 52
*They're Off! The Story of the Pony
Express*, 349
Young John Quincy, 356

Harold and the Purple Crayon
(Johnson), 106
Harriet and the Promised Land
(Lawrence), 462
Harriet the Spy (Fitzhugh), 462
Harriet's Recital (Carlson), 207
Harris, H. Robie
Happy Birth Day, 106
It's Perfectly Normal, 49
Harris, Jim, *The Three Little
Javelinas*, 377
Harris, Joel, *Jump! The Adventures of
Brer Rabbit*, 50
Harris and Me (Paulsen), 401-2, 450
Harry the Dirty Dog (Zion), 120
Hartman, Gail, *As the Crow Flies: A
First Book of Maps*, 80
Harvey, Amanda, *Zilla Sasparilla
and the Mud Baby*, 312
Harvey, Roland, *My Place in Space*,
189
Harvey Potter's Balloon Farm (Nolen),
234
*Harvey Slumfenburger's Christmas
Present* (Burningham), 106-7
Haseley, Dennis, *Kite Flier*, 407
Haskins, James
*Get on Board: The Story of the
Underground Railroad*, 438
*The Headless Haunt & Other African-
American Ghost Stories*, 439
Hatchet (Paulsen), 450, 462-63
Hattie & the Fox (Fox), 107
*The Haunted House: A Collection of
Original Stories* (Yolen), 55
Hausherr, Rosemarie, *Smart Moves:
A Kid's Guide to Self-Defense*,
480
Have You Seen Trees? (Oppenheim),
179
Havill, Juanita, *Sato and the
Elephants*, 344
Hawk, I'm Your Brother (Baylor), 290
Hawkes, Kevin
*By the Light of the Halloween
Moon*, 86
*The Librarian Who Measured the
Earth*, 407
My Little Sister Ate One Hare, 188
Hawthorn, Libby, *Way Home*, 488
Hayes, Ann
Meet the Marching Smithereens,
186
Meet the Orchestra, 186
*On Stage & Backstage at the Night
Owl Theater*, 140, 354
Hayes, Joe
Here Comes the Storyteller, 331
A Spoon for Every Bite, 377
The Haymeadow (Paulsen), 450
Haynes, Max, *In the Driver's Seat*, 66
Hays, Michael
Abiyoyo, 74
*K Is for Kiss Good Night: A
Bedtime Alphabet*, 66
Hazel's Amazing Mother (Wells), 107,
128
Hazen, Barbara Shook, *Tight Times*,
159
*The Headless Haunt & Other African-
American Ghost Stories*
(Haskins), 439
Hearne, Betsy, *Seven Brave Women*,
376
Heartland (Siebert), 402
Heckedy Peg (Wood), 28-29, 244

Heide, Florence Parry
  The Day of Ahmed's Secret, 93
  The Shrinking of Treehorn, 421
  Tales for the Perfect Child, 484
Heidi (Spyri), 355
Heine, Helme, *Friends,* 99
Helldorfer, M.C., *Gather Up, Gather
    In: A Book of Seasons,* 286-87
Heller, Ruth
  Chickens Aren't the Only Ones, 199
  Color, 323
  The Korean Cinderella, 294
  Many Luscious Lollipops, 358
*Help Wanted: Short Stories About
    Young People Working* (Silvey),
    545
Hendershot, Judith, *In Coal
    Country,* 292
Henkes, Kevin, 184
  Biggest Boy, 184
  Chester's Way, 175, 184
  Chrysanthemum, 184
  Good-Bye Curtis, 184
  Julius, the Baby of the World, 184,
    207, 244, 294
  Lilly's Purple Plastic Purse, 183,
    184, 207
  Once Around the Block, 184
  Owen, 184, 191
  Protecting Marie, 184
  Sun & Spoon, 184, 265, 483-84
  Words of Stone, 184
Henny Penny (Galdone), 107-8
Henry, Marguerite
  King of the Wind, 406
  Misty of Chincoteague, 388, 413
Henry Huggins (Cleary), 331
Henry and Mudge (Rylant), 108, 374
Henterly, Jamichael, *Young
    Guinevere,* 355-56
Hepworth, Cathi, *Antics,* 445-46
Her Stories (Hamilton), 402, 455
Here Come the Aliens (McNaughton),
    204
Here Comes Henny (Pomerantz), 108
Here Comes the Storyteller (Hayes),
    331
Here Is the Tropical Rain Forest
    (Dunphy), 180
Herge, *The Adventures of Tintin,* 381
Heroes (Mochizuki), 366
Herrera, Juan Felipe, *Calling the
    Doves/El Canto De Las Palomas,*
    273-74
Hershel and the Hanukkah Goblins
    (Kimmel), 366
Hesse, Karen, *Out of the Dust,* 475
Hewett, Richard, *Mexico's Ancient
    City of Teotihuacan,* 471
Hewitt, Joan, *Rosalie,* 147
Hewitt, Kathryn
  Lives of the Athletes, 411
  Lives of the Musicians, 411
  Lives of the Writers, 411-12
Hey! Get Off Our Train
    (Burningham), 108
Hey World, Here I Am! (Little), 402
Heyer, Carol, *Dinosaurs!: Strange
    and Wonderful,* 392
Heyer, Marilee, *The Weaving of a
    Dream,* 429
Heyman, Ken, *Shoes Shoes Shoes,* 18
Heyward, Du Bose, *The Country
    Bunny and the Little Gold Shoes,*
    91
"Hi, Pizza Man!" (Walter), 109

Higgins Bend Song and Dance
    (Martin), 290-91
*The High Rise Glorious Skittle Skat
    Roarious Sky Pie Angel Food
    Cake* (Willard), 403
*Hilary Knight's The Twelve Days of
    Christmas* (Knight), 109
Hill, Anthony, *Burnt Stick,* 320
Hill, Eric, *Where's Spot?,* 166
Hill of Fire (Lewis), 246
Hillenbrand, Will
  Counting Crocodiles, 91
  The House That Drac Built, 180
  *The Tale of Ali Baba and the Forty
    Thieves,* 424
Himler, Ronald
  The Cherokees, 274-75
  Dakota Dugout, 276-77
  A Day's Work, 277
  Fly Away Home, 365
  Nettie's Trip South, 473-74
  One Small Blue Bead, 299
  *Sadako and the Thousand Paper
    Cranes,* 420
  Someday a Tree, 377
  The Wall, 378
Hindley, Judy, *A Piece of String Is a
    Wonderful Thing,* 342
Hines, Anna Grossnickle
  When the Goblins Came Knocking,
    71
  When We Married Gary, 165
Hinton, S.E.
  Big David, Little David, 173-74
  The Outsiders, 514
Hip Cat (London), 403
Hippos Go Berserk (Boynton), 14
*The Hired Hand, An African-
    American Folktale* (San Souci),
    291
Hiroshima: A Novella (Yep), 350
Hirst, Robin and Sally, *My Place in
    Space,* 189
Hisako, Aoki, *Santa's Favorite Story,*
    149
*History of the U.S.: A 10 Volume
    Series* (Hakim), 507
Ho, Minfong
  Hush! A Thai Lullaby, 217
  *Maples in the Mist: Children's
    Poems From the Tang Dynasty,*
    261
Hoban, Lillian
  Arthur's Camp-Out, 80
  A Baby Sister for Frances, 81
  The First Grade Takes a Test, 97
  I Never Did That Before, 180-81
Hoban, Russell
  A Baby Sister for Frances, 81
  Dinner at Alberta's, 279
Hoban, Tana
  Colors Everywhere, 90, 359
  Of Colors and Things, 68
  26 Letters and 99 Cents, 73
  White On Black, 68, 72
The Hobbit (Tolkien), 355, 530
Hoberman, Mary Ann
  The Cozy Book, 175-76
  A House Is a House for Me, 111
  My Song Is Beautiful, 222
Hobkin (Griffin), 532
The Hobyahs (San Souci), 291
Hodges, Margaret
  Saint George and the Dragon, 375
  Saint Patrick and the Peddler, 375-
    76

Hoff, Syd, *Danny and the Dinosaur,*
    120
Hoffman, E.T.A., *The Nutcracker,* 52
Hoffman, Mary
  Amazing Grace, 210
  Boundless Grace, 361-62
  Earth, Fire, Water, Air, 325
  My Grandma Has Black Hair, 15-
    16
Hog-Eye (Meddaugh), 109
Holabird, Katharine, *Angelina
    Ballerina,* 171
*A Hole Is to Dig: A First Book of First
    Definitions* (Krauss), 109
Holling, Holling Clancy, *Paddle-to-
    the-Sea,* 342
Hom, Nancy, *Nine-In-One Grr! Grr!,*
    136
Home Sweet Home (Marzollo), 110
The Homecoming (Voigt), 507-8
Homeplace (Shelby), 260-61
Homer Price (McCloskey), 331, 355
Honey, I Love and Other Love Poems
    (Greenfield), 359
Hood, Thomas, *Before I Go to Sleep,*
    83
Hoops (Myers), 506
Hooray, a Piñata! (Kleven), 110
Hooray for Me (Charlip), 110
Hoover's Bride (Small), 403
Hop on Pop (Seuss), 120
Hopkins, Lee Bennett
  Extra Innings: Baseball Poems, 395
  Small Talk: A Book of Short Poems,
    422
Hopkinson, Deborah
  Birdie's Lighthouse, 384
  Sweet Clara and the Freedom Quilt,
    348
Horror Stories (Price), 463, 476
Horse, Harry, *Horror Stories,* 463
A House for a Hermit Crab (Carle),
    110
A House Is a House for Me
    (Hoberman), 111
The House of Dies Drear (Hamilton),
    455
The House on East 88th Street
    (Waber), 216
The House That Drac Built (Sierra),
    180
The House With a Clock in Its Walls
    (Bellairs), 463
Houston, Gloria, *My Great-Aunt
    Arizona,* 246
*How Beastly! A Menagerie of
    Nonsense Poems* (Yolen), 55
How Big Is a Foot? (Myller), 291-92
How I Was Adopted (Cole), 220
How a Book Is Made (Aliki), 404
How Many Bugs in a Box? (Carter),
    111
How Many, How Many, How Many
    (Walton), 246
*How Mr. Monkey Saw the Whole
    World* (Myers), 506
How Much Is a Million? (Schwartz),
    366-67
How My Parents Learned to Eat
    (Friedman), 111
How Now, Brown Cow? (Schertle),
    439
How to Be a Nature Detective
    (Selsam), 111
How to Eat Fried Worms (Rockwell),
    292

How to Lose All Your Friends
(Carlson), 112
How to Make an Apple Pie and See
the World (Priceman), 292
How to Make a Mummy Talk
(Deem), 508
Howard, Elizabeth, Mac and Marie
and the Train Toss Surprise, 221
Howard, Jane, When I'm Sleepy, 164
Howe, Deborah, Bunnicula, 319-20
Howe, James
Bunnicula, 319-20
I Wish I Were a Butterfly, 114, 207
Howell, Troy, Mermaid Tales From
Around the World, 338-39
Hoyt-Goldsmith, Diane, The Day of
the Dead, 392
Hubbard, Woodleigh, Hip Cat, 403
Huck, Charlotte, Secret Places, 304
Huckle, Helen, The Secret Code
Book, 440
Hudson, Wade, Pass It On: African
American Poetry for Children, 53
Hugh Pine (de Wetering), 388
Hughes, Shirley
All About Alfie, 75-76
Chatting, 64
Rhymes for Annie Rose, 69
Stories by Firelight, 56
Tales of Trotter Street, 225
Hull, Richard
The Alphabet From Z to A, 443-44
Sad Underwear and Other
Complications, 477
Hunting the White Cow (Seymour),
112
Hurd, Clement
Goodnight Moon, 103
The Runaway Bunny, 148
Hurd, Thacher
Art Dog, 198
Mama Don't Allow, 126
Hurwitz, Joanna, Birthday Surprises:
Ten Great Stories to Unwrap,
448
Hush Little Baby (Aliki), 112
Hush Little Baby (Long), 112
Hush! A Thai Lullaby (Ho), 217
Hyman, Trina Schart
The Fortune-Tellers, 284
Hershel and the Hanukkah Goblins,
366
Little Red Riding Hood, 32-33
Saint George and the Dragon, 375
Star Mother's Youngest Child, 38
Tight Times, 159
Will You Sign Here, John Hancock?,
353
Winter Poems, 491

I Am an American: A True Story of
Japanese Internment (Stanley),
508
I Am the Cheese (Cormier), 545
I Am the Dog, I Am the Cat (Hall),
261
I Am Lavina Cumming (Lowell), 463-
64
I Am the Mummy Heb-Nefert
(Bunting), 278, 464
I Can (Oxenbury), 66
I Can Read series, 119
I Don't Care, Said the Bear (West),
112-13
I Feel a Little Jumpy Around You
(Nye and Janeczko, ed.), 532

I Got a Family (Cooper), 217
I Had Seen Castles (Rylant), 374, 546
I Hadn't Meant to Tell You This
(Woodson), 546
I Hate English (Levine), 180
I Have an Aunt on Marlborough Street
(Lasky), 408
I Have a Dream (King, Jr.), 48
I, Houdini (Banks), 332
I Like Books (Browne), 113
I Like the Music (Komaiko), 29
I Love You as Much . . . (Melmed),
113
I Never Did That Before (Moore),
180-81
I Saw Esau (Opie and Opie), 29, 31
I Spy Two Eyes: Numbers in Art
(Micklethwait), 332
I Want to Be (Moss), 48-49
I Want to Be a Dancer (Maze), 404
I Want to Be a Veterinarian (Maze
and Grace), 332
I Went to the Zoo (Gelman), 113
I Went Walking (Williams), 113
I Wish I Were a Butterfly (Howe),
114, 207
Ice (Naylor), 546
Ichikawa, Satomi, Dance, Tanya, 92
If . . . (Perry), 14
If I Were in Charge of the World . . .
And Other Worries (Viorst), 508
If You Give a Mouse a Cookie
(Numeroff), 114-15
If You Were Born a Kitten (Bauer),
115
If Your Name Was Changed at Ellis
Island (Levine), 333
If You're Not From the Prairie
(Bouchard), 332-33
If You're Not Here, Please Raise Your
Hand (Dakos), 333
I'll Always Love You (Wilhelm), 217,
218
I'll Fix Anthony (Viorst), 114
I'll See You in My Dreams (Jukes),
358
I'll See You When the Moon Is Full
(Fowler), 114
The Illyrian Adventure (Alexander),
509
I'm in Charge of Celebrations
(Baylor), 367
Imogene's Antlers (Small), 217
In a Messy, Messy Room & Other
Scary Stories (Gorog), 404-5,
476
In Coal Country (Hendershot), 292
In Daddy's Arms I Am Tall: African
Americans Celebrating Their
Fathers, 49
In Enzo's Splendid Gardens (Polacco),
115
In Flight With David McPhail: A
Creative Autobiography
(McPhail), 293
In the Beginning . . . (Platt), 333-34
In the Beginning: Creation Stories
From Around the World
(Hamilton), 405, 455
In the Desert (Schwartz), 115-16
In the Driver's Seat (Haynes), 66
In the Next Three Seconds (Morgan),
405
In the Night Kitchen (Sendak), 116
In the Tall, Tall Grass (Fleming), 116-
17

In the Woods: Who's Been Here?
(George), 117
Incredible Ned (Maynard), 31-32
The Indian in the Cupboard (Banks),
464-65
An Indian Winter (Freedman), 465
Ingpen, Robert, Lifetimes: The
Beautiful Way to Explain Death
to Children, 32
Innocenti, Roberto
The Nutcracker, 52
Rose Blanche, 375
Inside the Amazing Amazon
(Lessem), 251
Insides, Outsides, Loops and Lines
(Kohl), 465
Into the Sea (Guiberson), 293
The Invisible Ladder: Anthology of
Contemporary Poems for Young
Readers, 509
The Irish Cinderlad (Climo), 354
The Iron Dragon Never Sleeps
(Krensky), 465-66
Ironman (Crutcher), 547-48
I Spy Mystery (Marzollo), 31
Is That You, Winter? (Gammell), 14-
15
Is This a House for Hermit Crab?
(McDonald), 117
Is Your Mama a Llama? (Guarino),
117
Isaacs, Anne, Swamp Angel, 193, 244
Isaacson, Philip M., Round Buildings,
Square Buildings, 419
Isadora, Rachel
At the Crossroads, 256-57
Ben's Trumpet, 198-99
Lili Backstage, 122
Max, 127
Island of the Blue Dolphins (O'Dell),
509-10
It's a Girl Thing: How to Stay
Healthy, Safe, and in Charge
(Jukes), 466
It's Hard to Read a Map With a Beagle
on Your Lap (Singer), 293
It's Perfectly Normal (Harris), 49
It's Pumpkin Time! (Hall), 181
It's So Nice to Have a Wolf Around the
House (Allard), 181
It's a Spoon, Not a Shovel (Buehner),
181

Jabar, Cynthia
Good Morning Pond, 102-3
How Many, How Many, How
Many, 246
Jack and the Beanstalk (Kellogg), 367
Jack's Garden (Cole), 181
Jackson, Ellen, Cinder Edna, 322,
354
Jacques, Brian, Redwall, 517
Jaffe, Nina, The Uninvited Guest &
Other Jewish Holiday Tales,
309
James, Mary, Shoebag, 479
James, Simon, Dear Mr. Blueberry,
93
James and the Giant Peach (Dahl),
334
James Marshall's Mother Goose
(Marshall), 15
Jane Yolen's Old MacDonald
Songbook, 55
Janeczko, Paul B.
Brickyard Summer, 527

I Feel a Little Jumpy Around You, 532

Poetry From A to Z, 515-16

January Rides the Wind: A Book of Months (Otten), 32

Janulewicz, Mike, *Yikes! Your Body, Up Close,* 432

Jaquith, Priscilla, *Bo Rabbit Smart for True Tall Tales,* 231-32

Jaramillo, Nelly, *Grandmother's Nursery Rhymes/Las Nanas De Abuelita,* 179

Jarrell, Randall, *The Animal Family,* 382

Jazz: My Music, My People (Monceaux), 50

Jeffers, Susan
  Brother Eagle, Sister Sky: A Message From Chief Seattle, 386
  Eric Knight's Lassie Come Home, 335
  The Midnight Farm, 129
  Waiting for the Evening Star, 429

Jelly Beans for Sale (McMillan), 117-18

Jenkins, Steve
  Animal Dads, 78
  Biggest, Strongest, Fastest, 271-72
  What Do You Do When Something Wants to Eat You?, 208-9

Jennings, Patrick, *Faith and the Electric Dog,* 326

Jennings, Paul, *Uncanny,* 521-22

Jeram, Anita
  Contrary Mary, 207
  Guess How Much I Love You, 104-5
  My Hen Is Dancing, 222

Jeremy Kooloo (Mahurin), 218

Jeremy Thatcher, Dragon Hatcher (Coville), 466

Jeremy's Decision (Brott), 15

Jesse Bear, What Will You Wear? (Carlstrom), 66

Jiang, Ji-Li, *Red Scarf Girl: A Memoir of the Cultural Revolution,* 517

Jip, His Story (Paterson), 510

John, Helen, *All-of-a-Kind Family,* 382

John Henry (Lester), 182

John Patrick Norman McHennessy: The Boy Who Was Always Late, 293-94

Johnson, Angela, *The Rolling Store,* 18

Johnson, Cathy, *A Rainy Day,* 302

Johnson, Crockett
  The Carrot Seed, 88
  Harold and the Purple Crayon, 106

Johnson, Dolores
  The Children's Book of Kwanzaa, 389
  Now Let Me Fly: The Story of a Slave Family, 440

Johnson, James Weldon, *The Creation,* 46

Johnson, Larry, *When Jo Louis Won the Title,* 311

Johnson, Lonni Sue, *A Snake Is Totally Tail,* 263

Johnson, Paul Brett, *Saint Patrick and the Peddler,* 375-76

Johnson, Steve, *The Salamander Room,* 148

Johnston, Tony
  Alice Nizzy Nazzy: The Witch of Santa Fe, 229

Amber on the Mountain, 268
  Day of the Dead, 176
  The Quilt Story, 145
  The Tale of Rabbit and Coyote, 194
  Very Scary, 70-71
  The Wagon, 266
  Yonder, 379

Join In: Multiethnic Short Stories By Outstanding Writers, 548

Jojo's Flying Side Kick (Pinkney), 182

The Jolly Postman or Other People's Letters (Ahlberg and Ahlberg), 182

Jonas, Ann, *Splash!,* 153

Jones, Charlotte Foltz, *Mistakes That Worked,* 412

Jones, Jan Naimo, *Make a Wish Molly,* 337

Jones, Marcia T., *Adventures of the Bailey School Kids,* 120

Jones, Ron, *The Acorn People,* 526

Joosse, Barbara M., *Mama, Do You Love Me?,* 185

Jorgensen, David, *Wind Says Good Night,* 167

Josepha: A Prairie Boy's Story (McGugan), 405-6

Josey, Rod and Kira, *In the Next Three Seconds,* 405

Journey (MacLachlan), 467

Joyce, William
  A Day With Wilbur Robinson, 207, 277
  Santa Calls, 37, 420

Joyful Noise: Poems for Two Voices (Fleischman), 467

Joyner, Jerry, *Thirteen,* 56

Judkis, Jim
  Let's Talk About It: Adoption, 122
  The New Baby, 67

Judy Scuppernong (Seabrooke), 468

Jukes, Mavis
  I'll See You in My Dreams, 358
  It's a Girl Thing, 466

Julie of the Wolves (George), 510

Julius, the Baby of the World (Henkes), 184, 207, 244, 294

Jumanji (Van Allsburg), 367-68

Jump! The Adventures of Brer Rabbit (Harris), 50

June Is a Tune That Jumps On a Stair (Wilson), 118

The Jungle Book (Kipling), 355

Junie B. Jones series (Park), 120

Just Like My Dad (Gardella), 118

Just Me and My Dad (Mayer), 118

Just Rewards (Sanfield), 118-19

Just So Stories (Kipling), 355

Juster, Norton, *The Phantom Tollbooth,* 515

Justice and Her Brothers (Hamilton), 455

K Is for Kiss Good Night: A Bedtime Alphabet (Sardegna), 66

Kalman, Maira
  Chicken Soup, Boots!, 498-99
  Max Makes a Million, 412

Karas, G. Brian
  Don't Read This Book, Whatever You Do, 324-25
  If You're Not Here, Please Raise Your Hand, 333
  Saving Sweetness, 304

Karlin, Bernie, *12 Ways to Get to 11,* 73

Karlins, Mark, *Mendel's Ladder,* 254

Kasza, Keiko
  Don't Laugh, Joe, 94
  Rat and the Tiger, 146

Katya's Book of Mushrooms (Arnold), 406

Keats, Ezra Jack
  Peter's Chair, 143
  The Snowy Day, 152

Keely, Jack, *Grossology: The Science of Really Gross Things,* 461

Keepers of the Earth: Native American Stories & Environmental Activities, 406

The Keeping Quilt (Polacco), 218-19

Kelley, Gary, *William Shakespeare's Macbeth,* 490

Kelley, True
  How to Make a Mummy Talk, 508
  Three Stories You Can Read to Your Dog, 248-49

Kellogg, Steven
  A My Name Is Alice, 267
  The Adventures of Huckleberry Finn, 494
  Aster Aardvark's Alphabet Adventures, 316
  Chicken Little, 26
  The Day Jimmy's Boa Ate the Wash, 277
  How Much Is a Million?, 366-67
  Is Your Mama a Llama?, 117
  Jack and the Beanstalk, 367
  The Mysterious Tadpole, 372
  Parents in the Pigpen, Pigs in the Tub, 373
  Sally Ann Thunder Ann Whirlwind Crockett, 376

Kennedy, X.J. and Dorothy, *Talking Like the Rain: A First Book of Poems,* 194

Kerins, Anthony, *The Christmas Tree Tangle,* 26-27

Kessler, Cristina, *One Night: A Story From the Desert,* 341

Key, Alexander, *The Forgotten Door,* 327

The Kid in the Red Jacket (Park), 334

Kidding Around Washington, D.C. (Levy), 334-35

The Kids of the Polk Street School series (Giff), 119, 120

Kiesler, Kate, *Twilight Comes Twice,* 227

Killing Mr. Griffin (Duncan), 548

Kim, Joung Un, *The Gift of Driscoll Lipscomb,* 287

Kimber, Murray, *Josepha: A Prairie Boy's Story,* 405-6

Kimmel, Eric
  Anansi and the Moss-Covered Rock, 77
  Charlie Drives the Stage, 387
  Hershel and the Hanukkah Goblins, 366
  The Tale of Ali Baba and the Forty Thieves, 424

Kindersley, Anabel, *Children Just Like Me,* 46

Kindersley, Barnabas, *Children Just Like Me,* 46

King, Bob, *Sitting on the Farm,* 151

King, Jr., Martin Luther, *I Have a Dream,* 48

King Arthur's Camelot: A Popup Castle and Four Storybooks (Rojany), 50

King Bidgood's in the Bathtub (Wood), 121
King Snake (Slotboom), 182
King of the Wind (Henry), 406
Kingfisher
  Kingfisher Illustrated History of the World, 510-11
  Kingfisher Science Encyclopedia, 406
  The Kingfisher Book of the Ancient World (Martell), 335
Kingfisher Illustrated History of World (Kingfisher), 510-11
Kingfisher Science Encyclopedia (Kingfisher), 406
The King's Equal (Paterson), 294
King-Smith, Dick, *Babe, the Gallant Pig*, 316-17, 388
Kinsey, Helen, *The Bear That Heard Crying*, 318
Kinsey-Warnock, Natalie
  The Bear That Heard Crying, 318
  The Summer of Stanley, 307
Kinship (Krisher), 548-49
Kipling, Rudyard
  The Jungle Book, 355
  Just So Stories, 355
  Rikki-Tikki-Tavi, 303, 355
Kissing the Witch (Donoghue), 549
Kitchen, Bert
  And So They Build, 24
  When Hunger Calls, 40
Kite Flier (Haseley), 407
Kiuchi, Tatsuro
  The Eagle's Gift, 393-94
  The Lotus Seed, 251
  The Seasons and Someone, 345
Klause, Annette Curtis, *Blood and Chocolate*, 541
Kleven, Elisa
  Abuela, 75
  De Colores and Other Latin-American Folksongs for Children, 47
  Hooray, a Piñata!, 110
Klutz's Kids' Back Seat Survival Guide, 50
Knight, Amelia Stewart, *The Way West: Journal of a Pioneer Woman*, 310-11
Knight, Christopher, *Monarchs*, 413
Knight, Eric, *Lassie Come Home*, 128, 468
Knight, Hilary
  Eloise, 394-95
  Hilary Knight's The Twelve Days of Christmas, 109
  Mrs. Piggle-Wiggle, 340
Knight, Margy Burns
  Talking Walls, 348
  Welcoming Babies, 163
  Who Belongs Here? An American Story, 431
The Knight's Castle (Eager), 407
Knowlton, Jack, *Geography From A To Z: A Picture Glossary*, 287
Kohl, Herbert, *Insides, Outsides, Loops and Lines*, 465
Koller, Jackie French
  The Dragonling, 280
  A Place to Call Home, 533
Komaiko, Leah
  Annie Bananie, 9-10
  Earl's Too Cool for Me, 94-95, 207
  I Like the Music, 29
  On Sally Perry's Farm, 190-91

Komodo (Sis), 261
Konigsburg, E.L.
  From the Mixed-Up Files of Mrs. Basil Frankweiler, 459
  The View From Saturday, 486-87
Koralek, Jenny, *The Boy and the Cloth of Dreams*, 319
The Korean Cinderella (Climo), 294, 354
Koshkin, Alexander, *Atalanta's Race: A Greek Myth*, 383
Kostner, Jill, *Shepherd Boy*, 192
Kovalski, Maryann, *I Went to the Zoo*, 113
Krach, Maywan Shen, *D Is For Doufu: An Alphabet Book of Chinese Culture*, 47
Krasny, Laurie, *Visiting the Art Museum*, 310
Kratt, Martin and Chris, *Kratts' Creatures: Our Favorite Creatures*, 234-35
Kratts' Creatures: Our Favorite Creatures (Kratt and Kratt), 234-35
Kraus, Robert, *Leo the Late Bloomer*, 121-22
Krauss, Ruth
  The Carrot Seed, 88
  A Hole Is to Dig: A First Book of First Definitions, 109
Krensky, Stephen
  The Iron Dragon Never Sleeps, 465-66
  The Three Blind Mice Mystery, 158
Krisher, Trudy
  Kinship, 548-49
  Spite Fences, 553-54
Kroll, Virginia
  Fireflies, Peach Pies & Lullabies, 218, 284
  Masai and I, 262
  Pink Paper Swans, 263
  The Seasons and Someone, 345
Krull, Kathleen
  Gonna Sing My Head Off!, 48
  Lives of the Athletes, 411
  Lives of the Musicians, 411
  Lives of the Writers, 285, 411-12
  Wilma Unlimited, 312
  Wish You Were Here: Emily's Guide to the 50 States, 353-54
Krupinski, Loretta
  Dear Rebecca, Winter Is Here, 324
  The Old Ladies Who Liked Cats, 138
Krush, Beth and Joe, *The Borrowers*, 385-86
Kuhn, Dwight, *In the Desert*, 115-16
Kunhardt, Dorothy, *Pat the Bunny*, 68
Kurtz, Jane
  Miro in the Kingdom of the Sun, 370
  Pulling the Lion's Tail, 416
Kuskin, Karla, *The Philharmonic Gets Dressed*, 143

Lacey, Carol, *Winter White*, 41
Laden, Nina, *My Family Tree: A Bird's Eye View*, 299
Ladybird Favorite Tales Series, 121
LaFave, Kim, *Bats About Baseball*, 270
LaMarche, Jim
  Grandmother's Pigeon, 204

The Rainbabies, 145-46
Lamb, Susan Condie, *My Great-Aunt Arizona*, 246
Lambert, Jonathan, *The Wide-Mouthed Frog: A Pop-Up Book*, 166-67
Lang, Andrew
  The Blue Fairy Book, 44-45
  The Rainbow Fairy Book, 54
  The Red Fairy Book, 355
Langton, Jane, *The Fragile Flag*, 459
The Language of Doves (Wells), 128
Lansky, Bruce, *Girls to the Rescue*, 328
Larger Than Life: The Adventures of American Legendary Heroes (San Souci), 407
Laser, Michael, *The Rain*, 17
Lasky, Kathryn, 408-9
  Beyond the Burning Time Railroad, 409
  Beyond the Divide, 409, 540-41
  Cloud Eyes, 408
  Days of the Dead, 408
  Double Trouble Squared, 409
  I Have an Aunt on Marlborough Street, 408
  The Librarian Who Measured the Earth, 407, 408
  Lunch Bunnies, 408
  Marven of the Great North Woods, 408
  Memoirs of a Bookbat, 409, 533
  Monarchs, 408, 413
  The Most Beautiful Roof in the World, 408
  Night Journey, 409
  Sea Swan, 408
  Searching for Laura Ingalls: A Reader's Journey, 408
  Shadows in the Water, 409
  She's Wearing a Dead Bird on Her Head!, 408
  Sugaring Time, 408
  True North: A Novel of the Underground Railroad, 409
  A Voice in the Wind, 409
Lassie Come Home (Knight), 128, 468
The Last Dragon (Nunes), 295
The Last Guru (Pinkwater), 493
The Last Princess: The Story of Princess Ka'iulani of Hawaii (Stanley), 335
Lattimore, Deborah Nourse
  Arabian Nights: Three Tales, 315-16
  The Dragon's Robe, 280
  Punga, the Goddess of Ugly, 343
Lauber, Patricia, *Volcano: The Eruption & Healing of Mount St. Helens*, 428
Lavallee, Barbara, *Mama, Do You Love Me?*, 185
Lawlor, Laurie, *Where Will This Shoe Take You?*, 524
Lawrence, Jacob, *Harriet and the Promised Land*, 462
Lawson, Robert
  Ben and Me, 436
  The Story of Ferdinand, 154
Leaf, Munro, *The Story of Ferdinand*, 154, 355
Leagues Apart: The Men & Times of the Negro Baseball Leagues (Ritter), 335-36

Lear, Edward, *The Complete Nonsense of Edward Lear*, 27
Learning to Swim in Swaziland (Leigh), 246
Lee, Alan
  Black Ships Before Troy, 495-96
  The Wanderings of Odysseus: The Story of the Odyssey, 522
Lee, Dom
  Baseball Saved Us, 270
  Heroes, 366
Lee, Huy Voun, *At the Beach*, 256
Leer, Rebecca, *A Spoon for Every Bite*, 377
The Legend of the Poinsettia (dePaola), 219
LeGuin, Ursula
  Catwings, 320-21
  The Earthsea Quartet, 529
Leigh, Nila, *Learning to Swim in Swaziland*, 246
Leigh, Tom, *Bone Poems*, 318-19
L'Engle, Madeleine, *A Wrinkle in Time*, 492
Lennox, Elsie, *The Phantom Hitchhiker*, 342
Leo the Late Bloomer (Kraus), 121-22
Lessac, Frane
  The Chalk Doll, 321
  The Fire Children: A West African Creation Tale, 178
  The Wonderful Towers of Watts, 431-32
Lessem, Don, *Inside the Amazing Amazon*, 251
Lesser, Carolyn, *What a Wonderful Day to Be a Cow*, 163
Lester, Helen
  Author: A True Story, 269
  Tacky the Penguin, 156
Lester, Julius
  John Henry, 182
  Sam and the Tigers, 148
  The Tales of Uncle Remus, 425
  To Be a Slave, 521
Let Me Read series (Wesley), 120
Let's Be Enemies (Udry), 122
Let's Eat (Zamorano), 182-83
Let's Talk About It: Adoption (Rogers), 122
Letters From the Inside (Marsden), 549
Letting Swift River Go (Yolen), 55
Levine, Arthur A., *All the Lights In the Night*, 314
Levine, Ellen
  I Hate English, 180
  If Your Name Was Changed at Ellis Island, 333
Levine, Joe, *My Place in Space*, 189
Levinson, Riki, *Soon, Annala*, 346
Levitt, Paul M., *The Weighty Word Book*, 488
Levy, Debbie, *Kidding Around Washington, D.C.*, 334-35
Lewin, Betsy, *Yo, Hungry Wolf!*, 432
Lewin, Ted
  Ali, Child of the Desert, 255
  The Always Prayer Shawl, 268
  Cowboy Country, 391
  The Day of Ahmed's Secret, 93
  Fair!, 28
  Island of the Blue Dolphins, 509-10
  Judy Scuppernong, 468
  Market, 33
  Peppe the Lamplighter, 301

Lewis, C.S., *The Chronicles of Narnia*, 355, 390
Lewis, Richard, *All of You Was Singing*, 230
Lewis, Thomas P., *Hill of Fire*, 246
The Librarian Who Measured the Earth (Lasky), 407, 408
The Library (Stewart), 183
The Library Dragon (Deedy), 219
The Life and Times of the Apple (Micucci), 336
The Life and Times of the Honeybee (Micucci), 336
The Life and Times of the Peanut (Micucci), 336
Lifetimes: The Beautiful Way to Explain Death to Children, 32, 218
Lightburn, Ron, *Waiting for the Whales*, 378
Lightning Time (Rees), 511
Lili Backstage (Isadora), 122
Lill, Debra, *Music and Drum: Voices of War and Peace, Hope and Dreams*, 473
Lilly's Purple Plastic Purse (Henkes), 183, 184, 207
Lily's Crossing (Giff), 469
Lincoln, Margarette, *The Pirate's Handbook*, 343
Lincoln: A Photobiography (Freedman), 511
Lincoln in His Own Words (Meltzer), 469
Lindberg, Reeve, *The Midnight Farm*, 129
Linnea In Monet's Garden (Bjork), 336-37
A Lion Named Shirley Williamson (Waber), 123
Lionni, Leo
  Frederick, 98-99
  Little Blue and Little Yellow, 123
The Lion's Whiskers: An Ethiopian Folktale (Day), 295
Lippincott, Gary A., *Jeremy Thatcher, Dragon Hatcher*, 466
Lisker, Emily, *Just Rewards*, 118-19
Listen to the Desert (Oye El Desierto) (Mora), 185
Little, Douglas, *Ten Little-Known Facts About Hippopotamuses*, 485
Little, Jean
  Bats About Baseball, 270
  Hey World, Here I Am!, 402
Little Bear (Minarik), 120, 123
Little Blue and Little Yellow (Lionni), 123
Little Critter books (Mayer), 120
The Little Engine That Could (Piper), 355
Little Folk: Stories From Around the World (Walker), 410
The Little House (Burton), 123-24
The Little House in the Big Woods (Wilder), 355
The Little House on the Prairie (Wilder), 355
The Little Mouse, the Red Ripe Strawberry, & the Big Hungry Bear (Wood), 124
The Little Painter of Sabana Grande (Markun), 337
The Little Red Ant and the Great Big Crumb-A Mexican Fable (Climo), 185

Little Red Cowboy Hat (Lowell), 185
Little Red Riding Hood (Hyman), 32-33
Little Ships: The Heroic Rescue at Dunkirk in World War II (Borden), 410-11
Little Toot (Gramatky), 124
Littlechild, George
  A Man Called Raven, 297
  This Land Is My Land, 39
Litzinger, Rosanne, *Louella Mae, She's Run Away!*, 125
Lives of the Athletes: Thrills, Spills (Krull), 411
Lives of the Musicians: Good Times, Bad Times (Krull), 411
Lives of the Writers: Comedies, Tragedies (Krull), 285, 411-12
Livingston, Myra Cohn
  Call Down the Moon: Poems of Music, 497
  Celebrations, 386-87
  Festivals, 365
Livingstone Mouse (Edwards), 124
Liza Lou and the Yeller Belly Swamp (Mayer), 207, 295
Lizard in the Sun: A Just for the Day Book (Ryder), 296
Lizard Music (Pinkwater), 469-70
Lloyd, Megan
  A Regular Flood of Mishap, 237
  Too Many Pumpkins, 308-9
Lobel, Anita
  Alison's Zinnia, 24
  Away From Home, 211
  Mangaboom, 51-52
  On Market Street, 139
Lobel, Arnold
  Fables, 201-2
  Frog and Toad books, 120
  Frog and Toad Are Friends, 99-100
  I'll Fix Anthony, 114
  On Market Street, 139
  The Random House Book of Poetry for Children, 236
  A Three Hat Day, 308
Locker, Thomas, *Thirteen Moons on Turtle's Back*, 426
Lockhart, Lynne, *Cadillac*, 86
Lofts, Pamela, *Wombat Stew*, 22
Lon Po Po, *A Red-Riding Hood Story From China* (Young), 219-21
London, Jonathan
  Ali, Child of the Desert, 255
  The Eyes of Gray Wolf, 177
  Fire Race, 178
  Froggy Gets Dressed, 100
  Hip Cat, 403
  Thirteen Moons on Turtle's Back, 426
Long, Sylvia
  Alejandro's Gift, 75
  Fire Race, 178
  Hush Little Baby, 112
Longfellow, Henry Wadsworth, *Paul Revere's Ride*, 53
Look to the North: A Wolf Pup Diary (George), 296
Looking for Atlantis (Thompson), 412
Lopez, Loretta, *Say Hola to Spanish*, 237
The Lorax (Seuss), 368
The Lost Garden (Yep), 350
The Lost Years of Merlin (Barron), 511-12
The Lotus Seed (Garland), 251

Louella Mae, She's Run Away!
(Alarcon), 125
Louie, Ai-Ling, *Yeh-Shen: A
Cinderella Story From China,*
354
The Loup Garou (Amoss), 296
Love, Ann, *Take Action: An
Environmental Book for Kids,*
484
Lovett, Sarah, *Extremely Weird
Animal Defenses,* 395-96
Lowell, Susan
I Am Lavina Cumming, 463-64
Little Red Cowboy Hat, 185
The Three Little Javelinas, 377
Lowry, Lois
Anastasia Krupnik, 315
The Giver, 503-4
Number the Stars, 474
See You Around, Sam, 345
Lubar, David, *The Psychozone:
Kidzilla & Other Tales,* 476
Luka's Quilt (Guback), 296-97
Lunch (Fleming), 205
Lunch Bunnies (Lasky), 408
Lynch, P.J.
*The Christmas Miracle of Jonathan
Toomey,* 389
*East o' the Sun and West o' the
Moon,* 394
Lyon, George Ella
Come a Tide, 212-13
Five Live Bongs, 178
Mama Is a Miner, 297

Ma Dear's Aprons (McKissack),
337
*Mac and Marie and the Train Toss
Surprise* (Howard), 221
Macaulay, David
Rome Antics, 419
Shortcut, 421
The Way Things Work, 57-58
McBratney, Sam, *Guess How Much I
Love You,* 104-5, 207
MacCarthy, Patricia, *17 Kings & 42
Elephants,* 9
McClintock, Barbara, *The Fantastic
Drawings of Danielle,* 260
McCloskey, Robert
Blueberries for Sal, 25
Homer Price, 331, 355
Make Way for Ducklings, 33, 355
McClure, Gillian, *Tog the Ribber, or,
Granny's Tale,* 426
McCully, Emily Arnold
How to Eat Fried Worms, 292
Mirette on the High Wire, 131
McCurdy, Michael
*The Bone Man: A Native American
Modoc Tale,* 385
Escape From Slavery, 457
Giants in the Land, 398
*Singing America: Poems That
Define a Nation,* 480
*The Way West: Journal of a Pioneer
Woman,* 310-11
McDermott, Gerald
Arrow to the Sun, 80
*Coyote: Trickster Tale From the
American Southwest,* 175
*Raven: A Trickster Tale from the
Pacific Northwest,* 146
MacDonald, Betty, *Mrs. Piggle-
Wiggle,* 340
McDonald, Megan

Is This a House for Hermit Crab?,
117
My House Has Stars, 134
MacDonald, Suse
*Nanta's Lion: A Search-and-Find
Adventure,* 135
Peck, Slither, and Slide, 142
Who Says a Dog Goes Bow-Wow?,
21
McDonnell, Flora, *Flora McDonnell's
ABC,* 98
McDuff and the Baby (Wells), 128
McDuff Comes Home (Wells), 128
McDuff Moves In (Wells), 128
McEwan, Ian, *The Daydreamer,* 456
McFarlane, Sheryl, *Waiting for the
Whales,* 218, 378
McGaw, Laurie
*Discovering the Iceman: An I Was
There Book,* 456-57
Polar the Titanic Bear, 302
McGough, Roger, *Until I Met Dudley:
How Everyday Things Really
Work,* 428
McGugan, Jim, *Josepha: A Prairie
Boy's Story,* 405-6
McGuire, Richard, *Night Becomes
Day,* 136
McIntosh, Jon, *Witch Way to the
Country?,* 167
Mackain, Bonnie, *One Hundred
Hungry Ants,* 247
MacKay, Claire, *Bats About Baseball,*
270
McKissack, Frederick, *Christmas in
the Big House,* 499
McKissack, Patricia
Christmas in the Big House, 499
*Dark Thirty: Southern Tales of the
Supernatural,* 500
Ma Dear's Aprons, 337
MacLachlan, Patricia
All the Places to Love, 171
Baby, 446
Journey, 467
Sarah, Plain and Tall, 251, 477
Skylark, 480
What You Know First, 378-79
McLerran, Alice
The Ghost Dance, 328
Roxaboxen, 375
McMillan, Bruce
Growing Colors, 104
Jelly Beans for Sale, 117-18
Puffins Climb, Penguins Rhyme,
223
*The Macmillan Dictionary for
Children* (Costello), 51
McMullan, Jim, *Noel the First,* 247
McNaughton, Colin
Captain Abdul's Pirate School, 274
Here Come the Aliens, 204
Suddenly!, 155
McPhail, David
Edward and the Pirates, 27
Farm Morning, 202
First Flight, 97
*In Flight With David McPhail: A
Creative Autobiography,* 293
Night Sounds, Morning Colors, 34
Sisters, 19
McWhirter, Norris, *The Guinness
Book of World Records,* 505
Maddern, Eric, *The Fire Children: A
West African Creation Tale,* 178
Made in China: Ideas and Inventions

From Ancient China (Williams),
470
Madeline, (Bemelmans), 125
Maestro, Betsy and Guillio
Bats: Nightfliers, 234
The Story of Money, 423
The Maestro Plays (Martin), 125
Magaril, Mikhail, *The Feather
Merchants and Other Tales,* 396
The Maggie B. (Haas), 125-26
The Magic Circle (Napoli), 532
The Magic Fan (Baker), 126
*The Magic School Bus in the Time of
the Dinosaurs* (Cole), 221
Magic Tree House series (Osborne),
120
Maguire, Gregory, *Seven Spiders
Spinning,* 478-79
Mahurin, Tim, *Jeremy Kooloo,* 218
Mahy, Margaret
The Christmas Tree Tangle, 26-27
*The Great Piratical
Rumbustification,* 400
*The Great White Man-Eating
Shark: A Cautionary Tale,* 289
17 Kings & 42 Elephants, 9, 244
The Three-Legged Cat, 225
Mai, Vo-Dinh
Angel Child, Dragon Child, 243
*The Brocaded Slipper and Other
Vietnamese Tales,* 273
Mailing May (Tunnell), 368-69
Maisy Goes Swimming (Cousins), 66-
67
Major, John, *The Silk Route: 7,000
Miles of History,* 346
Make Lemonade (Wolff), 533
Make Way for Ducklings
(McCloskey), 33, 355
Make a Wish Molly (Cohen), 337
Maland, Nick, *Big Blue Whale,* 182
Malcolm X: By Any Means Necessary
(Myers), 470, 506
Malone, Nola Langner, *Earrings!,* 281
Mama, Do You Love Me? (Joosse),
185
Mama Don't Allow (Hurd), 126
Mama Is a Miner (Lyon), 297
A Man Called Raven (Van Camp),
297
The Man Who Could Call Down Owls
(Bunting), 369
The Man Who Tricked a Ghost (Yep),
350
The Man in the Woods (Wells), 128
Manders, John, *King Snake,* 182
Mangaboom (Pomerantz), 51-52
Maniac Magee (Spinelli), 245, 471
Manning, Mick, *The World Is Full of
Babies!,* 168
Manson, Christopher, *The Tree in the
Wood: An Old Nursery Song,*
160-61
Many Luscious Lollipops (Heller),
358
*Maples in the Mist: Children's Poems
From the Tang Dynasty* (Ho),
261
Marcellino, Fred, *The Story of Little
Babaji,* 154
Marchesi, Stephen, *Close Your Eyes
So You Can See,* 323
Margaret and Margarita (Reiser), 186
Mariconda, Barbara, *Witch Way to
the Country?,* 167
Market! (Lewin), 33

Markle, Sandra
  Outside and Inside Snakes, 341
  A Rainy Day, 302
Markun, Patricia, *The Little Painter of Sabana Grande*, 337
Marsden, John, *Letters From the Inside*, 549
Marshall, Bob, *Fire in the Forest: A Cycle of Growth and Renewal*, 437
Marshall, James
  Bumps in the Night, 199
  Dinner at Alberta's, 279
  George and Martha, 12
  Hansel and Gretel, 106
  It's So Nice to Have a Wolf Around the House, 181
  James Marshall's Mother Goose, 15
  Miss Nelson Is Missing!, 358
  Old Mother Hubbard and Her Wonderful Dog, 139
  Rats on the Range and Other Stories, 17
  Red Riding Hood, 17-18
  The Stupids Step Out, 360
  There's a Party at Mona's Tonight, 19
  Wings: A Tale of Two Chickens, 40-41
  Yummers, 23
Martchenko, Michael
  Jeremy's Decision, 15
  The Paper Bag Princess, 36
  Stephanie's Ponytail, 208
Martell, Hazel Mary, *The Kingfisher Book of the Ancient World*, 335
Martha Quest, 524
Martha Speaks (Meddaugh), 254
Martin, Bill, Jr.
  Barn Dance!, 82
  A Beautiful Feast for a Big King Cat, 172-73
  Brown Bear, Brown Bear, What Do You See?, 85-86
  Chicka Chicka Boom Boom, 88, 355
  The Ghost-Eye Tree, 101
  The Maestro Plays, 125
  Old Devil Wind, 190
  White Dynamite & Curly Kidd, 352-53
Martin, Jacqueline Briggs
  Good Times on Grandfather Mountain, 12-13
  Grandmother Bryant's Pocket, 400
  The Green Truck Garden Giveaway, 289
  Higgins Bend Song and Dance, 290-91
Martin, Rafe
  The Eagle's Gift, 393-94
  Will's Mammoth, 22, 359
Martinez, Ed, *Too Many Tamales*, 309
Marven of the Great North Woods (Lasky), 408
Marvin Redpost: Alone in His Teacher's House (Sachar), 262
Marvin's Best Christmas Present Ever (Paterson), 205
Mary Wolf (Grant), 549
Marzollo, Jean
  Home Sweet Home, 110
  I Spy Mystery, 31
  Pretend You're a Cat, 144-45
  Sun Song, 155-56
Masai and I (Kroll), 262

Matas, Carol, *Sworn Enemies*, 520
Math Curse (Scieszka), 244, 369
Math Start series (Murphy), 126-27
Mathers, Petra, *Grandmother Bryant's Pocket*, 400
Mathis, Melissa Bay
  Grandad Bill's Song, 179
  What a Wonderful Day to Be a Cow, 163
Matilda (Dahl), 337-38
Max (Isadora), 127
Max Makes a Million (Kalman), 412
Max and Ruby's First Greek Myth: Pandora's Box (Wells), 127
Max's Bath (Wells), 128
Max's Bedtime (Wells), 128
Max's Birthday (Wells), 128
Max's Dragon Shirt (Wells), 128, 129
Max's Ride (Wells), 128
May I Bring a Friend? (deRegniers), 129
Mayer, Marianna, *Baba Yaga and Vasilisa the Brave*, 270
Mayer, Mercer
  A Boy, a Dog, and a Frog, 84, 359
  Just Me and My Dad, 118
  Little Critter books, 120
  Liza Lou and the Yeller Belly Swamp, 207, 295
  There's a Nightmare in My Closet, 157-58
Mayhew, James, *The Boy and the Cloth of Dreams*, 319
Maynard, Bill, *Incredible Ned*, 31-32
Maze, Stephanie
  I Want to Be a Dancer, 404
  I Want to Be a Veterinarian, 332
Mazer, Anne, *The Salamander Room*, 148
Mazer, Harry, *Twelve Shots: Outstanding Short Stories About Guns*, 554-55
M.C. Higgins the Great (Hamilton), 455
Meade, Holly
  Hush! A Thai Lullaby, 217
  Small Green Snake, 152
  This Is the Hat: A Story in Rhyme, 158
Mean Margaret (Seidler), 338
Mean Soup (Everitt), 129, 207, 265
Meanwhile . . . (Feiffer), 369
Meddaugh, Susan
  Cinderella's Rat, 275, 354
  Hog-Eye, 109
  Martha Speaks, 254
Medearis, Angela Shelf, *Skin Deep and Other Teenage Reflections*, 519
Medlicott, Mary, *The River That Went to the Sky*, 419
Medlock, Scott, *Extra Innings: Baseball Poems*, 395
Meet Danitra Brown (Grimes), 298
Meet the Marching Smithereens (Hayes), 186
Meet the Orchestra (Hayes), 186
Meisel, Clemesha, *The Cow Buzzed*, 175
Meisel, Paul
  Busy Buzzing Bumblebees and Other Tongue Twisters, 86
  Go Away, Dog, 243
Mellonie, Bryan, *Lifetimes: Beautiful Way to Explain Death to Children*, 32

Melmed, Laura Krauss
  I Love You as Much . . . , 113
  The Rainbabies, 145-46
Meltzer, Milton, *Lincoln In His Own Words*, 469
Memoirs of a Bookbat (Lasky), 409, 533
Mendel's Ladder (Karlins), 254
Mendez, Phil, *The Black Snowman*, 272
The Mennyms (Waugh), 338
Merkin, Richard, *Leagues Apart*, 335-36
Merlin: Book 3 of the Young Merlin Trilogy (Yolen), 512
Mermaid Tales From Around the World (Osborne), 338-39
Merriam, Eve
  Halloween ABC, 290
  12 Ways to Get to 11, 73
  You Be Good and I'll Be Night, 169
Merrill, Jean, *The Girl Who Loved Caterpillars*, 101-2
The Merry Adventures of Robin Hood (Pyle), 355
Meteor! (Polacco), 370
Metropolitan Cow (Egan), 298
Mexico's Ancient City of Teotihuacan: First Metropolis in the Americas, 471
Mick Harte Was Here (Park), 218, 471
Micklethwait, Lucy, *I Spy Two Eyes: Numbers in Art*, 332
Micucci, Charles
  The Life and Times of the Apple, 336
  The Life and Times of the Honeybee, 336
  The Life and Times of the Peanut, 336
The Midnight Farm (Lindberg), 129
Midnight Hour Encores (Brooks), 512
Migdale, Lawrence, *The Day of the Dead: A Mexican-American Celebration*, 392
Mike Mulligan and His Steam Shovel (Burton), 15, 355
Mikolaycak, Charles, *The Man Who Could Call Down Owls*, 369
Miller, Cameron, *Woodlore*, 58
Miller, Margaret, *Where Does It Go?*, 71-72
Miller, Mary Beth, *Handtalk: ABC of Finger Spelling and Sign Language*, 13-14
Miller, Sara Swan, *Three Stories You Can Read to Your Dog*, 248-49
Millions of Cats (Gag), 130
Mills, Claudia, *Gus and Grandpa*, 105
Mills, Lauren
  Book of Little Folk, 45
  Tatterhood and the Hobgoblins: A Norwegian Folktale, 426
Milne, A.A.
  Winnie the Pooh, 355
  World of Christopher Robin, 196-97
  The World of Pooh, 197
Milord, Susan, *Tales Alive: Ten Multicultural Folktales with Activities*, 425
Minarik, Else Holmelund
  Little Bear, 120, 123
  No Fighting, No Biting!, 137
Minerva Louise at School (Stoeke), 130
Minor, Wendell

Everglades, 326
Heartland, 402
The Minstrel and the Dragon Pup
    (Sutcliff), 221-22
Minty: A Story of Young Harriet
    Tubman (Schroeder), 339
The Miracle of the Potato Latkes
    (Penn), 130
Miranda, Anne, To Market, to Market,
    159, 207
Mirette on the High Wire (McCully),
    131
Miro in the Kingdom of the Sun
    (Kurtz), 370
Mirocha, Paul, I Am Lavina
    Cumming, 463-64
Miska, Miles, Annie and the Old One,
    218, 256
Misoso: Once Upon a Time Tales
    From Africa (Aardema), 339-40
Miss Bindergarten Gets Ready for
    Kindergarten (Slate), 131
Miss Nelson Is Missing! (Allard), 358
Miss Rumphius (Cooney), 370
Missing May (Rylant), 218, 374, 472
Mississippi Bridge (Taylor), 472
Mississippi Mud: Three Prairie
    Journals (Turner), 472
Mistakes That Worked (Jones), 412
Misty of Chincoteague (Henry), 388,
    413
Mitchell, Judith, The Dragonling, 280
Mitchell, Margaree, Uncle Jed's
    Barbershop, 351-52
The Mitten (Brett), 186-87
Miz Berlin Walks (Yolen), 55, 413
Mochizuki, Ken
    Baseball Saved Us, 270
    Heroes, 366
Moeri, Louise
    Save Queen of Sheba, 518-19
    Star Mother's Youngest Child, 37,
    38
Moffatt, Judith, Too Many Rabbits &
    Other Fingerplays, 70
Moja Means One (Feelings), 355
Mollel, Tololwa, The Flying Tortoise:
    An Igbo Tale, 260
Molly's Pilgrim (Cohen), 340
Monarchs (Lasky), 408, 413
Monceaux, Morgan, Jazz: My Music,
    My People, 50
Money, Money, Money: Meaning of
    the Art & Symbols on U.S. Paper
    Money (Parker), 413-14
Monjo, F.N., The Drinking Gourd: A
    Story of the Underground
    Railroad, 259
The Monster Bed (Willis), 132
The Monster at the End of This Book
    (Stone), 131
Monster Mama (Rosenberg), 33, 244,
    265
Monster Motel (Douglas), 340
Montgomery, L.M., Anne of Green
    Gables, 445
Montresor, Beni, May I Bring a
    Friend?, 129
The Monument (Paulsen), 450
Moog-Moog Space Barber (Teague),
    207
Moonstick: The Seasons of the Sioux
    (Bunting), 370-71
Moonstruck: True Story of the Cow
    Who Jumped Over the Moon
    (Choldenko), 298

Moore, Clement C., The Night Before
    Christmas, 52
Moore, Lilian, I Never Did That
    Before, 180-81
Mora, Francisco X.
    Listen to the Desert (Oye El
    Desierto), 185
    Little Red Ant & the Great Big
    Crumb-A Mexican Fable, 185
Mora, Pat
    Listen to the Desert (Oye El
    Desierto), 185
    Tomas and the Library Lady, 427
Mordant's Wish (Coursen), 132, 207
More, More, More, Said the Baby: 3
    Love Stories (Williams), 132
More Than Anything Else (Bradby),
    187
Morgan, Mary, Hannah and Jack,
    105
Morgan, Rowland, In the Next Three
    Seconds, 405
The Morgan's Dream (Singer), 414
Morin, Paul
    Fox Song, 327
    The Ghost Dance, 328
Morning Girl (Dorris), 472-73
Morpurgo, Michael, The Wreck of the
    Zanzibar, 432
Morris, Ann, Shoes Shoes Shoes, 18
Morris' Disappearing Bag (Wells), 128
Morrow, Glenn, Dateline: Troy, 456
Moser, Barry
    Dippers, 393
    Fly! A Brief History of Flight, 458
    A Game of Catch, 438
    I Am the Dog, I Am the Cat, 261
    In the Beginning: Creation Stories
    From Around the World, 405
    Jump! The Adventures of Brer
    Rabbit, 50
    A Ring of Tricksters, 418-19
    Tucker Pfeffercorn, 351
    What You Know First, 378-79
Moss, Jeff
    Bone Poems, 318-19
    The Butterfly Jar, 25
Moss, Lloyd, Zin! Zin! Zin! A Violin,
    197
Moss, Marissa, Amelia's Notebook,
    449
Moss, Thylias, I Want to Be, 48-49
Most, Bernard, The Cow That Went
    Oink, 91, 207
The Most Beautiful Roof in the World
    (Lasky), 408
Motown and Didi (Myers), 506
Mouse Mess (Riley), 133
Mouse and Mole and the Year-Round
    Garden (Cushman), 187
The Mouse and the Motorcycle
    (Cleary), 235
Mouse Paint (Walsh), 133
Mouse Rap (Myers), 506
Mowat, Farley, Owls in the Family,
    415-16
Moxley, Sheila, Skip Across the
    Ocean, 151-52
Mr. Popper's Penguins (Atwater and
    Atwater), 355, 388, 414
Mr. Putter and Tabby books (Rylant),
    374
Mr. Rabbit and the Lovely Present
    (Zolotow), 133
Mr. Willowby's Christmas Tree
    (Barry), 133

Mrs. Mustard's Baby Faces
    (Wattenberg), 67
Mrs. Piggle-Wiggle (MacDonald), 340
Mud Pies and Other Recipes: A
    Cookbook for Dolls (Winslow),
    187-88
Mufaro's Beautiful Daughters
    (Steptoe), 52
The Muffin Fiend (Pinkwater), 298-
    99
Mullins, Patricia, Hattie & the Fox,
    107
Munoz, William, Gray Wolf, Red
    Wolf, 330
Munsch, Robert
    The Paper Bag Princess, 36
    Stephanie's Ponytail, 208
Munsinger, Lynn
    Bugs!, 273
    Tacky the Penguin, 156
    The Three Blind Mice Mystery, 158
Murphy, Chuck, One to Ten Pop-Up
    Surprises, 16
Murphy, Jill, Five Minutes Peace, 98
Murphy, Jim, The Great Fire, 460
Murphy, Stuart J., Math Start series,
    126-27
Musgrove, Margaret, Ashanti to Zulu:
    African Traditions, 230
Music and Drum: Voices of War and
    Peace, Hope and Dreams (Robb),
    473
My Dog Never Says Please
    (Williams), 134
My Family Tree: A Bird's Eye View
    (Laden), 299
My Father's Dragon (Gannett), 222,
    388
My Fellow Americans: A Family
    Album (Provensen), 473
My First Book of Proverbs/Mi Primer
    Libro De Dichos, 371
My Grandma Has Black Hair
    (Hoffman), 15-16
My Great-Aunt Arizona (Houston),
    246
My Hen Is Dancing (Wallace), 222
My House Has Stars (McDonald),
    134
My Life With the Wave (Cowan),
    188
My Little Sister Ate One Hare
    (Grossman), 188, 244
My Mama Says There Aren't Any
    Zombies, Ghosts, Vampires, or
    Things, 188-89
Map Book (Fanelli), 205
My Painted House, My Friendly
    Chicken, & Me (Angelou), 34
My Place in Space (Hirst and Hirst),
    189
My Song Is Beautiful: Poems and
    Pictures in Many Voices
    (Hoberman), 222
My Very First Mother Goose (Opie),
    128, 134
My Visit to the Aquarium (Aliki), 134-
    35
My Visit to the Zoo (Aliki), 189
Myers, Anna, Red Dirt Jessie, 440
Myers, Christopher, Harlem, 507
Myers, Walter Dean
    Brown Angels: An Album of
    Pictures and Verse, 386, 506
    Darnell Rock Reporting, 454-56
    Fallen Angels, 506

Fast Sam, Cool Clyde, and Stuff, 506

The Glory Field, 245, 460, 506

Harlem, 506, 507

Hoops, 506

How Mr. Monkey Saw the Whole World, 506

Malcolm X: By Any Means Necessary, 470, 506

Motown and Didi, 506

Mouse Rap, 506

Now Is Your Time, 506

The Righteous Revenge of Artemis Bonner, 506

Scorpions, 506

Somewhere in the Darkness, 506

The Story of the Three Kingdoms, 506

Myller, Rolf, *How Big Is a Foot?,* 291-92

The Mysteries of Harris Burdick (Van Allsburg), 43, 371

The Mysterious Tadpole (Kellogg), 372

Mysterious Thelonious (Raschka), 34

Nana Upstairs & Nana Downstairs (dePaola), 135, 218

Nanta's Lion: A Search-and-Find Adventure (MacDonald), 135

Napoli, Donna Jo

The Magic Circle, 532

Stones in Water, 520

Zel, 525

The Napping House (Wood), 135, 355

Narahashi, Keiko

Rain Talk, 145

What's What? A Guessing Game, 163

Who Said Red?, 166

Natchev, Alexi, *The Hobyahs,* 291

Nate the Great (Sharmat), 120, 135-36

Nathaniel Talking (Greenfield), 372

Navajo: Visions and Voices Across the Mesa (Begay), 414-15

Naylor, Phyllis Reynolds

Ice, 546

Shiloh, 479

Nell Nuggett and the Cow Caper (Enderle and Tessler), 136

Nelson, Theresa, *Earthshine,* 544

Nesbit, E.

Five Children and It, 437

The Railway Children, 388

Nethery, Mary, *Hannah and Jack,* 105

Nettie's Trip South (Turner), 473-74

Neve Shalom Wahat Al-Salam: Oasis of Peace (Dolphin and Dolphin), 340-41

Never Take a Pig To Lunch: and Other Poems About the Fun of Eating (Westcott), 235

The New Baby (Rogers), 67

The New Baby at Your House (Cole), 220

New Hope (Sorensen), 262

New Kids at the Polk Street School series (Giff), 120

Nichol, Barbara, *Dippers,* 393

Nicholas Pipe (San Souci), 415

Nicholson, William, *The Velveteen Rabbit,* 428

Night Becomes Day (McGuire), 136

The Night Before Christmas (Moore), 52

Night Journey (Lasky), 409

Night Sounds, Morning Colors (Wells), 34, 128

Nightjohn (Paulsen), 251, 450, 512-13

Nikola-Lisa, W., *Bein' With You This Way,* 231

Nine-In-One Grr! Grr!: A Folktale from the Hmong People of Laos (Xiong), 136

Nixon, Joan Lowery

The Orphan Train Adventures, 474

Search for the Shadowman, 440

The Weekend Was Murder, 534

No Fighting, No Biting! (Minarik), 137

Noah's Ark (Spier), 16

Noble, Trina Hakes, *The Day Jimmy's Boa Ate the Wash,* 277

Nodset, Joan L., *Go Away, Dog,* 243, 244

Noel the First (McMullan), 247

Noisy Nora (Wells), 128, 137

Nolan, Dennis

Castle Builder, 174

Dove Isabeau, 325

The Gentleman and the Kitchen Maid, 398

Nolen, Jerdine, *Harvey Potter's Balloon Farm,* 234

Norman, Howard, *The Girl Who Dreamed Only of Geese and Other Tales,* 503

Norton, Mary, *The Borrowers,* 385-86, 388

Nothing But the Truth (Avi), 513

Now Everybody Really Hates Me, 265

Now Is Your Time: The African American Struggle for Freedom (Myers), 506

Now Let Me Fly: The Story of a Slave Family (Johnson), 440

Number One Number Fun (Chorao), 189

Number the Stars (Lowry), 474

Numeroff, Laura, *If You Give a Mouse a Cookie,* 114-15

Nunes, Susan, *The Last Dragon,* 295

Nursery Tales Around the World (Sierra), 236

The Nutcracker (Hoffman), 52

Nuts to You (Ehlert), 137

Nutshell Library (Sendak), 137-38

Nye, Naomi Shihab

I Feel a Little Jumpy Around You, 532

This Same Sky, 485

Oberman, Sheldon, *The Always Prayer Shawl,* 268

O'Brien, Anne Sibley

Talking Walls, 348

Welcoming Babies, 163

Who Belongs Here? An American Story, 431

O'Brien, John

Mistakes That Worked, 412

Six Creepy Sheep, 151

True Lies: 18 Tales for You to Judge, 427

O'Dell, Scott, *Island of the Blue Dolphins,* 509-10

Of Colors and Things (Hoban), 68

Officer Buckle and Gloria (Rathmann), 205-6

Oh the Places You'll Go! (Seuss), 35

Oh, No, Toto! (Tchana), 34

Oink (Geisert), 138

Okino and the Whales (Esterl), 190

Old Black Fly (Aylesworth), 190, 244

Old Devil Wind (Martin), 190

The Old Ladies Who Liked Cats (Greene), 138

Old MacDonald Had a Farm (Rounds), 16

The Old Man & His Door (Soto), 138

Old Mother Hubbard and Her Wonderful Dog (Marshall), 139

Old Pig (Wild), 206

Old Turtle (Wood), 16

The Old Woman Who Named Things (Rylant), 374

Oliver Button Is a Sissy (dePaola), 247

Oliver's Vegetables (French), 190

O'Malley, Kevin

Chanukkah in Chelm, 274

Cinder Edna, 322

Velcome!, 310

On Christmas Eve (Collington), 359

On the Day You Were Born (Frasier), 35-36

On Market Street (Lobel), 139

On Mother's Lap (Scott), 139

On My Honor (Bauer), 218, 474

On Sally Perry's Farm (Komaiko), 190-91

Once Around the Block (Henkes), 184

Once There Was a Bull . . . (Frog) (Walton), 140

Once There Were Giants (Waddell), 206

1 Gaping Wide-Mouthed Hopping Frog (Tryon), 140

One Grain of Rice: A Mathematical Folktale (Demi), 299

One Hundred Hungry Ants (Pinczes), 247

One Is One (Tudor), 73

One More River (Banks), 513

One Night: A Story From the Desert (Kessler), 341

One Small Blue Bead (Baylor), 299

One to Ten Pop-Up Surprises! (Murphy), 16

One Wintry Night (Graham), 53

One World, Many Religions: The Ways We Worship (Osborne), 514

One Yellow Daffodil: A Hanukkah Story (Adler), 514

O'Neill, Mary, *Hailstones and Halibut Bones,* 401

Only Opal: The Diary of a Young Girl (Whiteley and Boulton), 415

Onstage & Backstage at the Night Owl Theater (Hayes), 140, 354

Onyefulu, Ifeoma, *A Is for Africa,* 170

Opie, Iona

I Saw Esau, 31

My Very First Mother Goose, 128, 134

Opie, Peter, *I Saw Esau,* 31

Oppenheim, Joanne, *Have You Seen Trees?,* 179

Oram, Hiawyn, *Badger's Bring Something Party,* 230

Orie, Sandra De Coteau, *Did You Hear Wind Sing Your Name?,* 176

The Ornery Morning (Demuth), 191, 207

Orozco, Jose-Luis, *De Colores & Other Latin-American Folksongs*, 47

The Orphan Train Adventures (Nixon), 474

Orser, Sheldon, *Dancing With the Wind*, 213

Osborne, Mary Pope
Magic Tree House series, 120
Mermaid Tales From Around the World, 338-39
One World, Many Religions: The Ways We Worship, 514

Otero, Ben, *The Headless Haunt & Other African-American Ghost Stories*, 439

The Other Way to Listen (Baylor), 372

Otten, Charlotte F., *January Rides the Wind: A Book of Months*, 32

Oubrerie, Clement, *It's Hard to Read a Map With a Beagle on Your Lap*, 293

Our Granny (Wild), 140

Our Sixth Grade Sugar Babies (Bunting), 278

Out of the Dust (Hesse), 475

Outside Inside Book of Bats, 234

Outside and Inside Snakes (Markle), 341

The Outsiders (Hinton), 514

Over Sea, Under Stone (Cooper), 514-15

Owen (Henkes), 184, 191

Owl Babies (Waddell), 141

Owl Eyes (Gates), 300-1

Owl Moon (Yolen), 55

Owls in the Family (Mowat), 415-16

Ox-Cart Man (Hall), 141

Oxenbury, Helen
Dressing, 65
Farmer Duck, 96
I Can, 66
So Much, 19
The Three Little Wolves & the Big Bad Pig, 39
Tom and Pippo Books, 69-70

Pablo Remembers: The Fiesta of the Day of the Dead (Ancona), 341-42

Paddle-to-the-Sea (Holling), 342

The Painter (Catalanotto), 191-92

Palatini, Margie, *Piggie Pie*, 222-23

Pallotta, Jerry, *The Spice Alphabet Book*, 305

Pamall, Peter, *Annie and the Old One*, 256

Pancakes for Breakfast (dePaola), 16-17

Panzer, Nora, *Celebrate America in Poetry and Art*, 45

Papa! (Corentin), 141, 207

Papa, Please Get the Moon for Me (Carle), 141

The Paper Bag Princess (Munsch), 36

The Paper Dragon (Davol), 36

The Paperboy (Pilkey), 206-8

Parents in the Pigpen, Pigs in the Tub (Ehrlich), 373

Parish, Peggy, *Amelia Bedelia*, 76-77, 120

Park, Barbara
Junie B. Jones series, 120
The Kid in the Red Jacket, 334
Mick Harte Was Here, 218, 471

Parker, Nancy Winslow
Bugs, 174
Here Comes Henny, 108
Money, Money, Money, 413-14

Parker, Robert Andrew, *Grandfather Tang's Story*, 260

Parker, Ron, *Voices From the Wild: An Animal Sensagoria*, 487

Parker, Steve, *The Body Atlas*, 385

Parkins, David, *Aunt Nancy and Old Man Trouble*, 172

Parmenter, Wayne, *If Your Name Was Changed at Ellis Island*, 333

Parnall, Peter
Everybody Needs a Rock, 283
Hawk, I'm Your Brother, 290
I'm in Charge of Celebrations, 367
The Other Way to Listen, 372

Pass the Fritters, Critters (Chapman), 142

Pass It On: African American Poetry for Children (Hudson), 53

Pat-A-Cake and Other Play Rhymes (Calmenson and Cole), 220

Pat the Bunny (Kunhardt), 68

The Patchwork Quilt (Flournoy), 263

Patent, Dorothy Hinshaw, *Gray Wolf, Red Wolf*, 330

Paterson, Katherine
The Bridge to Terabithia, 218, 288, 451
Flip-Flop Girl, 503
The Great Gilly Hopkins, 461
Jip, His Story, 510
The King's Equal, 294
Marvin's Best Christmas Present Ever, 205

Paul, Ann Whitford, *Eight Hands Round: A Patchwork Alphabet*, 281

Paul Revere's Ride (Longfellow), 53

Paulsen, Gary, 450
Brian's Winter, 449, 450
The Cook Camp, 450
The Crossing, 245, 543
The Culpepper Adventures, 276, 450
Dancing Carl, 450
Dogsong, 450
Dogteam, 279
Father Water, Mother Woods, 450
Funny, 450
Gary Paulsen's World of Adventure series, 398, 450
Harris and Me, 401-2, 450
Hatchet, 450, 462-63
The Haymeadow, 450
The Monument, 450
Nightjohn, 251, 450, 512-13
Puppies, Dogs and Blue Northers, 450
The River, 450
The Schernoff Discoveries, 450
The Tent, 450
The Tortilla Factory, 160, 450
The Voyage of the Frog, 450
The Winter Room, 450
Worksong, 22-23, 450

Paulsen, Ruth
Dogteam, 279
The Tortilla Factory, 160, 450
Worksong, 22-23, 450

Peacebound Trains (Balgassi), 416

Peck, Richard, *Remembering the Good Times*, 550-51

Peck, Slither, and Slide (MacDonald), 142

Pedersen, Judy, *Gather Up, Gather In: A Book of Seasons*, 286-87

Pee Wee Scouts series (Delton), 120, 142

Peet, Bill
Big Bad Bruce, 173
Bill Peet: An Autobiography, 384

Pelletier, David, *The Graphic Alphabet*, 400

Penn, Malka, *The Miracle of the Potato Latkes*, 130

Penner, Lucille Recht, *Eating the Plates*, 457

People (Spier), 53

The People Could Fly (Hamilton), 388, 416, 455

The People Who Hugged Trees: An Environmental Folk Tale (Rose), 236

Peppe the Lamplighter (Bartone), 301

The Peppermint Race (Regan), 254

Perry, Sarah, *If...*, 14

Peter Pan (Barrie), 355

Peter Spier's Rain (Spier), 143, 359

Peter's Chair (Keats), 143

The Phantom Hitchhiker (Cohen), 342

The Phantom Tollbooth (Juster), 515

Philbrick, Rodman, *Freak the Mighty*, 529-30

The Philharmonic Gets Dressed (Kuskin), 143

Philip, Neil, *Singing America: Poems That Define a Nation*, 480

Picture Book Biography series (Adler), 301

A Piece of String Is a Wonderful Thing (Hindley), 342

Piggie Pie (Palatini), 222-23

Piggies (Wood and Wood), 68

Piggins (Yolen), 55

Piggybook (Browne), 373

The Pigman (Zindel), 550

Pigs in the Mud in the Middle of the Rud (Plourde), 143-44

Pilkey, Dav
The Adventures of Captain Underpants, 267-68
Dogzilla, 364-65
The Paperboy, 206-8

Pin the Tail on the Donkey and Other Party Games (Calmenson and Cole), 220

Piñata Maker/El Piñatero (Ancona), 144

Pinczes, Elinor, *One Hundred Hungry Ants*, 247

Pink Paper Swans (Kroll), 263

Pink and Say (Polacco), 475

Pinkney, Andrea Davis
Alvin Ailey, 314
Seven Candles for Kwanzaa, 224

Pinkney, Brian
Alvin Ailey, 314
Dark Thirty: Southern Tales of the Supernatural, 500
The Faithful Friend, 396
Jojo's Flying Side Kick, 182
Seven Candles for Kwanzaa, 224

Pinkney, Jerry
Cut From the Same Cloth, 324
The Hired Hand, An African-American Folktale, 291
I Want to Be, 48-49

John Henry, 182
Minty: A Story of Young Harriet Tubman, 339
The Patchwork Quilt, 263
Pretend You're a Cat, 144-45
Rikki-Tikki-Tavi, 303
Sam and the Tigers, 148
The Talking Eggs, 307
Turtle in July, 227
Pinkwater, Daniel
  Alan Mendelsohn, The Boy From Mars, 493
  Author's Day, 269
  5 Novels (collection), 493
  The Last Guru, 493
  Lizard Music, 469-70
  The Muffin Fiend, 298-99
  Slaves of Spiegel, 493
  The Snarkout Boys and the Avocado of Death, 493
  Young Adult Novel, 493
  Young Larry, 379-80
Pinkwater, Jill, *Young Larry,* 379-80
A Pinky Is a Baby Mouse and Other Baby Animal Names (Ryan), 37
A Pioneer Sampler: Daily Life of a Pioneer Family in 1840 (Greenwood), 301
The Pirate's Handbook: How to Become a Rogue of the High Seas (Lincoln), 343
The Pit Dragon Trilogy (Yolen), 55
Place, Francois, *The Wreck of the Zanzibar,* 432
A Place to Call Home (Koller), 533
The Planet of Junior Brown (Hamilton), 455
The Planets (Gibbons), 223
Platt, Richard
  In the Beginning. . . , 333-34
  Stephen Biesty's Incredible Cross-Sections, 423
Plecas, Jennifer, *Rattlebone Rock,* 192
Plourde, Lynn, *Pigs in the Mud in the Middle of the Rud,* 143-44
Podwal, Mark, *Golem: A Giant Made of Mud,* 399
Poe, Edgar Allan
  Complete Stories and Poems of Poe, 499
  Complete Works of Edgar Allan Poe, 476
Poems Go Clang!: A Collection of Noisy Verse (Gliori), 37
Poetry From A to Z: A Guide for Young Writers (Janeczko), 515-16
Polacco, Patricia
  Appelemando's Dream, 78
  Babushka Baba Yaga, 172
  The Bee Tree, 231
  Casey at the Bat, 88
  Chicken Sunday, 26
  In Enzo's Splendid Gardens, 115
  The Keeping Quilt, 218-19
  Meteor!, 370
  Pink and Say, 475
  Rechenka's Eggs, 302-3
  Thunder Cake, 264
The Polar Express (Van Allsburg), 37
Polar the Titanic Bear (Spedden), 302
Pole Dog (Seymour), 302
Pollinger, Gina, *Something Rich & Strange,* 481
Pomerantz, Charlotte
  The Chalk Doll, 321
  Here Comes Henny, 108

Mangaboom, 51-52
The Popcorn Book (dePaola), 144
Pop-O-Mania: How to Create Your Own Pop-Ups (Valenta), 475-76
Poppleton (Rylant), 247
Porfirio, Guy, *The Raggly Scraggly, No-Soap, No-Scrub Girl,* 417
Possum Come A-Knockin' (Van Laan), 192
Possum Magic (Fox), 144
Potter, Beatrix, *The Tale of Peter Rabbit,* 156-57, 355
Powell, Anton, *The Greek News,* 461
Prairie Songs (Conrad), 516
Prelutsky, Jack
  The Beauty of the Beast, 44
  The Dragons Are Singing Tonight, 233
  The Random House Book of Poetry for Children, 236
  Read-Aloud Rhymes for the Very Young, 146-47
  Rolling Harvey Down the Hill, 373
  Something Big Has Been Here, 305
Pretend You're a Cat (Marzollo), 144-45
Price, Susan, *Horror Stories,* 463, 476
Priceman, Marjorie
  How to Make an Apple Pie and See the World, 292
  When Zaydeh Danced on Eldridge Street, 165
  Zin! Zin! Zin! A Violin, 197
Princess Nevermore (Regan), 516
Pringle, Laurence
  Dinosaurs!: Strange and Wonderful, 392
  Fire in the Forest: A Cycle of Growth and Renewal, 437
Protecting Marie (Henkes), 184
Provensen, Alice
  The Buck Stops Here: Presidents of the United States, 362
  My Fellow Americans: A Family Album, 473
  The Year at Maple Hill Farm, 168
Provensen, Martin, *The Year at Maple Hill Farm,* 168
The Prydian Chronicles (Alexander), 516-17
The Psychozone: Kidzilla & Other Tales (Lubar), 476
Puff...Flash...Bang! A Book About Signals (Gibbons), 223
Puffins Climb, Penguins Rhyme (McMillan), 223
Pulling the Lion's Tail (Kurtz), 416
Pullman, Philip, *The Golden Compass,* 504
Punga, the Goddess of Ugly (Lattimore), 343
Puppies, Dogs and Blue Northers (Paulsen), 450
Puzzle Maps U.S.A. (Clouse), 417
A Puzzling Day at Castle MacPelican (Anderson), 38

Quattlebaum, Mary, *A Year on My Street,* 209
Quick as a Cricket (Wood), 145
The Quilt Story (Johnston), 145
Quinlan, Patricia, *Tiger Flowers,* 264

Radiance Descending (Fox), 476-77
Radunsky, Vladimir, *The Maestro Plays,* 125

Rael, Elsa Okan, *When Zaydeh Danced on Eldridge Street,* 165
The Raggly Scraggly, No-Soap, No-Scrub Girl (Birchman), 417
The Railway Children (Nesbit), 388
The Rain (Laser), 17
Rain Talk (Serfozo), 145
The Rainbabies (Melmed), 145-46
The Rainbow Bridge (Wood), 417
The Rainbow Fairy Book (Lang), 54
The Rainbow People (Yep), 350
A Rainy Day (Markle), 302
Ramona the Pest (Cleary), 343, 355
Rand, Ted
  Barn Dance!, 82
  The Bear That Heard Crying, 318
  The Ghost-Eye Tree, 101
  Mailing May, 368-69
  Paul Revere's Ride, 53
  White Dynamite & Curly Kidd, 352-53
The Random House Book of Poetry for Children (Prelutsky), 236
Rankin, Laura, *The Handmade Alphabet,* 357-58
Ransom, Candice F., *When the Whippoorwill Calls,* 430
Ransome, James
  All the Lights In the Night, 314
  The Creation, 46
  Sweet Clara and the Freedom Quilt, 348
  Uncle Jed's Barbershop, 351-52
  The Wagon, 266
Rapp, Adam, *The Buffalo Tree,* 541-42
Rapunzel (Zelinsky), 355, 418
Raschka, Chris, *Mysterious Thelonious,* 34
Raskin, Ellen, *The Westing Game,* 523
Rat and the Tiger (Kasza), 146, 207
Rathmann, Peggy
  Bootsie Barker Bites, 84
  Good Night, Gorilla, 103
  Officer Buckle and Gloria, 205-6
  Ruby the Copycat, 147
Rats on the Range and Other Stories (Marshall), 147
Rats Saw God (Thomas), 550
Rattlebone Rock (Andrews), 192
Rattlesnake Dance: True Tales, Mysteries, and Rattlesnake Ceremonies (Dewey), 418
Raven: A Trickster Tale from the Pacific Northwest (McDermott), 146
Rawlins, Donna, *Ten Little-Known Facts About Hippopotamuses,* 485
Rawls, Wilson, *Where the Red Fern Grows,* 524
Ray, David, *Robin Hood & Little John,* 224
Ray, Jane, *Earth, Fire, Water, Air,* 325
Ray, Mary Lyn, *Shaker Boy,* 421
Raynor, Mary, *Babe, The Gallant Pig,* 316-17
Read-Aloud Rhymes for the Very Young (Prelutsky), 146-47
Read-Aloud Treasury (Cole), 220
Ready . . . Set . . . Read! (Cole), 120, 220
The Real McCoy: The Life of an African-American Inventor (Towle), 343-44
Rechenka's Eggs (Polacco), 302-3

Red Dirt Jessie (Myers), 440
The Red Fairy Book (Zang), 355
Red Hot Hightops (Christopher), 344
The Red Racer (Wood), 248
Red Riding Hood (Marshall), 17-18
Red Scarf Girl: A Memoir of the
   Cultural Revolution (Jiang), 517
Redwall (Jacques), 517
Rees, Douglas, Lightning Time, 511
Regan, Dian Curtis
   Dear Dr. Sillybear, 176
   The Peppermint Race, 254
   Princess Nevermore, 516
Regan, Laura
   Sun Song, 155-56
   Welcome to the Green House, 430
A Regular Flood of Mishap
   (Birdseye), 237
Reid, Margarette S., A String of
   Beads, 155
Reiser, Lynn, Margaret and
   Margarita, 186
The Relatives Came (Rylant), 373,
   374
R.E.M. (Banyai), 17, 359
Remembering the Good Times (Peck),
   550-51
Remkiewicz, Frank
   Froggy Gets Dressed, 100
   Incredible Ned, 31-32
Rey, H.A., Curious George, 92
Re-Zoom (Banyai), 359
Rhymes for Annie Rose (Hughes), 69
Richard Scarry's Best Word Book Ever
   (Scarry), 147
Riddell, Chris
   The Swan Stories, 423
   Until I Met Dudley: How Everyday
   Things Really Work, 428
The Righteous Revenge of Artemis
   Bonner (Myers), 506
Rikki-Tikki-Tavi (Kipling), 303, 355
Riley, Linnea, Mouse Mess, 133
A Ring of Tricksters (Hamilton), 418-
   19
Ringgold, Faith, Tar Beach, 38-39
Ripplinger, Henry, If You're Not From
   the Prairie, 332-33
Riptide (Weller), 303
Ritter, Lawrence, Leagues Apart,
   335-36
The River (Paulsen), 450
The River That Went to the Sky:
   Twelve Tales by African
   Storytellers, 419
Robb, Laura, Music and Drum: Voices
   of War and Peace, Hope and
   Dreams, 473
Robbins, Ken, The Elements series,
   394
Roberts, Will Davis, The View From
   the Cherry Tree, 487
Robin Hood & Little John (Cohen),
   224
Robins, Deri, The Great Pirate
   Activity Book, 330
Robin's Country (Furlong), 477
Robinson, Aminah Brenda, Elijah's
   Angel: Story for Chanukah &
   Christmas, 282
Rochelle, Belinda, When Jo Louis
   Won the Title, 311
Rockwell, Anne, The Acorn Tree &
   Other Folktales, 170
Rockwell, Thomas, How to Eat Fried
   Worms, 292

Rodanas, Kristina
   Dance of the Sacred Circle, 324
   Dragonfly's Tale, 258
Rogasky, Barbara, Winter Poems, 491
Rogers, Fred
   Let's Talk About It: Adoption, 122
   The New Baby, 67
Rogers, Gregory, Way Home, 488
Rogers, Jacqueline, Five Live Bongos,
   178
Rohmann, Eric
   The Cinder-Eyed Cats, 11
   Time Flies, 19-20, 359
Rojany, Lisa, King Arthur's Camelot:
   A Popup Castle & Four
   Storybooks, 50-51
Roll of Thunder, Hear My Cry
   (Taylor), 518
Rolling Harvey Down the Hill
   (Prelutsky), 373
The Rolling Store (Johnson), 18
Rome Antics (Macaulay), 419
Ronato, Michael, Tales Alive: Ten
   Multicultural Folktales with
   Activities, 425
Root, Barry
   The Araboolies of Liberty Street,
   316
   Old Devil Wind, 190
Root, Kimberly Bulcken
   Birdie's Lighthouse, 384
   In a Messy, Messy Room & Other
   Scary Stories, 404-5
   The Toll-Bridge Troll, 226
   When the Whippoorwill Calls, 430
Root, Phyllis, Aunt Nancy and Old
   Man Trouble, 172
Rootabaga Stories, Part One
   (Sandburg), 237, 355
Rosalie (Hewitt), 147
Rose, Deborah Lee, The People Who
   Hugged Trees, 236
Rose Blanche (Innocenti), 375
Rosen, Michael
   The Best of Michael Rosen, 25
   Elijah's Angel: A Story for
   Chanukah and Christmas, 282
   The Greatest Table, 48
   South and North, East and West,
   238
   Speak!, 422
   Walking the Bridge of Your Nose,
   429
Rosenberg, Liz
   Earth-Shattering Poems, 544
   The Invisible Ladder, 509
   Monster Mama, 33, 244, 265
Ross, Bill, Straight From the Bear's
   Mouth, 482
Ross, Tony, Amber Brown Is Not a
   Crayon, 268
Roth, Robert, When the Monkeys
   Came Back, 312
Roth, Susan L.
   The Great Ball Game: A Muskogee
   Story, 234
   Pass the Fritters, Critters, 142
Rothman, Michael
   Here Is the Tropical Rain Forest,
   180
   Inside the Amazing Amazon, 251
   Lizard in the Sun: A Just for the
   Day Book, 296
Rotner, Shelley, Colors Around Us: A
   Lift-the-Flap Surprise Book, 89-
   90

Round Buildings, Square Buildings, &
   Buildings That Wiggle Like a
   Fish, 419
Rounds, Glen
   Charlie Drives the Stage, 387
   Old MacDonald Had a Farm, 16
   Sod Houses on the Great Plains,
   305
Rowe, John A., Smudge, 38
Roxaboxen (McLerran), 375
Ruby the Copycat (Rathmann), 147
Ruby Mae Has Something to Say
   (Small), 303
Ruffins, Reynold, Misoso: Once Upon
   a Time Tales From Africa, 339-
   40
Rumpelstiltskin (Zelinsky), 224
The Runaway Bunny (Brown), 148
Ryan, Cheryl, Sally Arnold, 304
Ryan, Pam Munoz
   California, Here We Come!, 232
   Pinky Is a Baby Mouse and Other
   Baby Animal Names, 37
Rydell, Katy, Wind Says Good Night,
   167
Ryder, Joanne
   Earthdance, 27
   Lizard in the Sun: A Just for the
   Day Book, 296
   The Snail's Spell, 152
   Winter White, 41
Rylant, Cynthia, 374
   All I See, 171, 374
   An Angel for Solomon Singer, 269,
   374
   A Blue-Eyed Daisy, 374
   The Blue Hill Meadows, 272
   But I'll Be Back Again, 374
   A Couple of Kooks and Other
   Stories About Love, 374
   Every Living Thing, 374, 458
   A Fine White Dust, 374
   Henry and Mudge, 108, 374
   I Had Seen Castles, 374, 546
   Missing May, 218, 374, 472
   Mr. Putter and Tabby books, 374
   The Old Woman Who Named
   Things, 374
   Poppleton, 247
   The Relatives Came, 373, 374
   Soda Jerk, 5, 374, 553
   Something Permanent, 374, 481
   The Van Gogh Cafe, 374, 486
   Waiting to Waltz: A Childhood, 374,
   487-88
   When I Was Young in the
   Mountains, 374

Sabuda, Robert
   The Christmas Alphabet, 10
   The Paper Dragon, 36
Sachar, Louis
   Marvin Redpost: Alone in His
   Teacher's House, 262
   Sideways Stories From Wayside
   School, 345
   There's a Boy in the Girls'
   Bathroom, 485
Sachs, Marilyn, The Bear's House,
   245, 447
Sacred Places (Yolen), 54, 55
Sad Underwear and Other
   Complications (Viorst), 477
Sadako (Coerr), 303
Sadako and the Thousand Paper
   Cranes (Coerr), 420

Sadowski, Wiktor, *Grandma Essie's Covered Wagon*, 329

Saflund, Brigitta, *The People Who Hugged Trees*, 236

Saint Francis (Wildsmith), 344

Saint George and the Dragon (Hodges), 375

Saint Patrick and the Peddler (Hodges), 375-76

St. Patrick's Day in the Morning (Bunting), 278

Saito, Manabu, *The Golden Carp and Other Tales From Vietnam*, 399

The Salamander Room (Mazer), 148

Salem, Kay, *California, Here We Come!*, 232

Salisbury, Graham
  Blue Skin of the Sea, 496
  Under the Blood Red Sun, 486

Sally Ann Thunder Ann Whirlwind Crockett (Kellogg), 376

Sally Arnold (Ryan), 304

Sam and the Tigers (Lester), 148

Samton, Sheila White, *Frogs in Clogs*, 203

San Souci, Daniel
  The Gifts of Wali Dad: A Tale of India and Pakistan, 287
  Sootface: An Ojibwa Cinderella Story, 354, 422

San Souci, Robert
  Cut From the Same Cloth, 324, 388
  The Faithful Friend, 396
  The Hired Hand, An African-American Folktale, 291
  The Hobyahs, 291
  Larger Than Life, 407
  Nicholas Pipe, 415
  Short and Shivery, 479-80
  Sootface: An Ojibwa Cinderella Story, 354, 422
  The Talking Eggs, 307, 354
  Young Guinevere, 355-56

Sanchez, Enrique O., *Amelia's Road*, 314

Sandburg, Carl, *Rootabaga Stories, Part One*, 237, 355

Sanders, Scott Russell, *The Floating House*, 397

Sanderson, Ruth
  A Treasury of Princesses, 349
  William Shakespeare's The Tempest, 490-91

Sandford, John, *Moonstick: The Seasons of the Sioux*, 370-71

Sandin, Joan, *Hill of Fire*, 246

Sanfield, Steve
  The Adventures of High John the Conqueror, 313
  Bit by Bit, 83, 84
  The Feather Merchants and Other Tales, 396
  Just Rewards, 118-19

Santa Calls (Joyce), 37, 420

Santa's Favorite Story (Hisako and Gantschev), 149

Santa's Short Suit Shrunk and Other Christmas Tongue Twisters (Buck), 149

Sarah, Plain and Tall (MacLachlan), 251, 477

Sardegna, Jill, *K Is for Kiss Good Night: A Bedtime Alphabet*, 66

Sato and the Elephants (Havill), 344

Sattler, Helen, *The Book of North American Owls*, 385

Savadier, Elivia
  Grandmother's Nursery Rhymes/Las Nanas De Abuelita, 179
  The Uninvited Guest & Other Jewish Holiday Tales, 309

Save Queen of Sheba (Moeri), 518-19

Saving Sweetness (Stanley), 304

Say, Allen
  Allison, 255
  El Chino, 282
  Emma's Rug, 259
  Grandfather's Journey, 288
  How My Parents Learned to Eat, 111
  Tree of Cranes, 161

Say Hola to Spanish (Elya), 237

Scared Silly (Brown), 149

Scarry, Richard, *Richard Scarry's Best Word Book Ever*, 147

Scary, Scary Halloween (Bunting), 149

Scary Stories to Tell in the Dark: Collected From American Folklore (Schwartz), 420

Schaffer, Amanda, *How Now, Brown Cow?*, 439

Scheffler, Axel, *A Squash and a Squeeze*, 153

The Schernoff Discoveries (Paulsen), 450

Schertle, Alice
  Advice for a Frog, 494
  How Now, Brown Cow?, 439

Schindelman, Joseph, *Charlie and the Chocolate Factory*, 321

Schindler, S.D.
  Catwings, 320-21
  Don't Fidget a Feather, 233
  Every Living Thing, 458
  Is This a House for Hermit Crab?, 117
  Those Amazing Ants, 56
  A Tree Is Growing, 349

Schmidt, Karen Lee, *You Be Good and I'll Be Night*, 169

Schoenherr, Ian, *One Night: A Story From the Desert*, 341

Schoenherr, John, *Pigs in the Mud in the Middle of the Rud*, 143-44

Schotter, Roni
  Captain Snap & the Children of Vinegar Lane, 25-26
  A Fruit and Vegetable Man, 203

Schroeder, Alan, *Minty: A Story of Young Harriet Tubman*, 339

Schuett, Stacey
  I'll See You in My Dreams, 358
  Somewhere in the World Right Now, 238

Schwartz, Alvin
  Busy Buzzing Bumblebees and Other Tongue Twisters, 86
  Scary Stories to Tell in the Dark, 420

Schwartz, Amy, *Wish You Were Here: Emily's Guide to the 50 States*, 353-54

Schwartz, Carol, *Where's That Insect?*, 352

Schwartz, David
  How Much Is a Million?, 366-67
  In the Desert, 115-16
  Supergrandpa, 307

Science Experiments You Can Eat (Cobb), 478

Scieszka, Jon
  The Good, the Bad, and the Goofy, 399
  Math Curse, 244, 369
  The Stinky Cheese Man and Other Fairly Stupid Tales, 306
  The True Story of the Three Little Pigs, 351

Scorpions (Myers), 506

Scott, Ann Herbert
  Cowboy Country, 391
  On Mother's Lap, 139

Sea Swan (Lasky), 408

Seabrooke, Brenda, *Judy Scuppernong*, 468

Search for the Shadowman (Nixon), 440

Searching for Laura Ingalls: A Reader's Journey (Lasky), 408

The Seasons and Someone (Kroll), 345

Seattle, Chief, *Brother Eagle, Sister Sky: A Message From Chief Seattle*, 386

The Secret Code Book (Huckle), 440

The Secret Garden (Burnett), 345, 355

Secret Places (Huck), 304

See You Around, Sam (Lowry), 345

Seedfolks (Fleischman), 251, 478

Seeger, Pete, *Abiyoyo*, 74

Sees Behind Trees (Dorris), 478

Seidler, Tor, *Mean Margaret*, 338

Selden, George, *The Cricket in Times Square*, 388, 391

Selsam, Millicent E., *How to Be a Nature Detective*, 111

Seltzer, Isadore, *Tree of Dreams: Ten Tales From the Garden of Night*, 351

Sendak, Matthew, *Some Swell Pup, or Are You Sure You Want a Dog?*, 264

Sendak, Maurice
  The Animal Family, 382
  A Hole Is to Dig: A First Book of First Definitions, 109
  I Saw Esau, 31
  In the Night Kitchen, 116
  Let's Be Enemies, 122
  Little Bear, 123
  Mr. Rabbit and the Lovely Present, 133
  No Fighting, No Biting!, 137
  Nutshell Library, 137-38
  Some Swell Pup, or Are You Sure You Want a Dog?, 264
  Where the Wild Things Are, 21, 244, 355

Serfozo, Mary
  Rain Talk, 145
  What's What? A Guessing Game, 163
  Who Said Red?, 166

Seuss, Dr.
  And to Think That I Saw It On Mulberry Street, 77
  The Butter Battle Book, 363
  The Cat in the Hat, 199
  The 500 Hats of Bartholomew Cubbins, 361
  Green Eggs and Ham, 104, 120
  Hop on Pop, 120
  The Lorax, 368
  Oh, the Places You'll Go!, 35

Seven Blind Mice (Young), 150

Seven Brave Women (Hearne), 376
Seven Candles for Kwanzaa (Pinkney), 224
Seven-Day Magic (Eager), 420-21
Seven Spiders Spinning (Maguire), 478-79
17 Kings & 42 Elephants (Mahy), 9, 244
Sewall, Marcia
  Captain Snap & the Children of Vinegar Lane, 25-26
  Stone Fox, 346-47
Sewing Quilts (Turner), 263
Seymour, Tres
  Hunting the White Cow, 112
  Pole Dog, 302
Shabanu-Daughter of the Wind (Staples), 551
Shadows in the Water (Lasky), 409
Shadows of the Night, 234
Shaker Boy (Ray), 421
Shannon, David
  The Ballad of the Pirate Queens, 383
  The Bunyans, 363
  Nicholas Pipe, 415
  Sacred Places, 54
Shannon, George, *True Lies: 18 Tales for You to Judge*, 427
Sharmat, Marjorie Weinman
  Gila Monsters Meet You at the Airport, 216
  Nate the Great, 120, 135-36
Sharp, N.L., *Today I'm Going Fishing With My Dad*, 266
Shaw, Alison, *Until I Saw the Sea: A Collection of Seashore Poems*, 57
Shaw, Nancy, *Sheep in a Jeep*, 150
Sheep in a Jeep (Shaw), 150
Shelby, Anne, *Homeplace*, 260-61
Sheldon, Dyan, *The Whale's Song*, 40
She'll Be Comin' Round the Mountain (Birdseye and Birdseye), 150
Shepard, Aaron
  The Baker's Dozen: A Saint Nicholas Tale, 81
  The Gifts of Wali Dad: A Tale of India and Pakistan, 287
Shepard, Ernest H.
  World of Christopher Robin, 196-97
  The World of Pooh, 197
Shepherd Boy (Franklin), 192
She's Wearing a Dead Bird on Her Head! (Lasky), 408
Shiloh (Naylor), 479
Shoebag (James), 479
Shoes Shoes Shoes (Morris), 18
Short and Shivery (San Souci), 479-80
Shortcut (Macaulay), 421
The Shrinking of Treehorn (Heide), 421
Shulevitz, Uri
  Dawn, 11
  The Golem, 460
Shy Charles (Wells), 150, 207
Sideways Stories From Wayside School (Sachar), 345
Siebel, Fritz, *Amelia Bedelia*, 76-77
Siebert, Diane, *Heartland*, 402
Sierra, Judy
  Counting Crocodiles, 91
  The House That Drac Built, 180
  Nursery Tales Around the World, 236
Silent Night (Wells), 128

The Silk Route: 7,000 Miles of History (Major), 346
Silva, Simon, *Gathering the Sun: An Alphabet in Spanish and English*, 28
Silver Pony (Ward), 43, 359
Silverman, Erica, *Don't Fidget a Feather*, 207, 232, 233
Silverstein, Shel, *Where the Sidewalk Ends: Poems and Drawings*, 430
Silvey, Anita, *Help Wanted: Short Stories About Young People Working*, 545
Simmons, Elly, *Calling the Doves/El Canto De Las Palomas*, 273-74
Simms, Laura, *The Bone Man: A Native American Modoc Tale*, 385
Simon, Seymour
  Big Cats, 271
  Star Walk, 306
Simont, Marc
  Nate the Great, 135-36
  The Philharmonic Gets Dressed, 143
  A Tree Is Nice, 161
Sims, Blanche, *The Kids of the Polk Street School* series, 119
Sing a Song of Popcorn: Every Child's Book of Poems (deRegniers, ed.), 54-56
Sing Sophiel (Dodds), 224-25
Singer, Isaac Bashevis, *The Golem*, 460
Singer, Marilyn
  All We Needed to Say, 443
  Family Reunion, 283
  It's Hard to Read a Map With a Beagle on Your Lap, 293
  The Morgan's Dream, 414
  Turtle in July, 227
Singer to the Sea God (Alcock), 519
Singing America: Poems That Define a Nation (Philip), 480
Sis, Peter
  The Dragons Are Singing Tonight, 233
  Follow the Dream, 327
  Komodo, 261
  A Small Tall Tale From the Far Far North, 346
  Starry Messenger: Galileo Galilei, 422-23
  The Whipping Boy, 430-31
Sisters (McPhail), 19
Sitting on the Farm (King), 151
Six Creepy Sheep (Enderle and Tessler), 151
Six Sick Sheep (Cole), 151
Skin Deep and Other Teenage Reflections (Medearis), 519
Skip Across the Ocean: Nursery Rhymes From Around the World (Benjamin), 151-52
Skurzynski, Gloria, *Virtual War*, 534
Skylark (MacLachlan), 480
Slate, Joseph, *Miss Bindergarten Gets Ready for Kindergarten*, 131
Slave Day (Thomas), 551
Slaves of Spiegel (Pinkwater), 493
Slavin, Bill, *Sitting on the Farm*, 151
Sleep Rhymes Around the World (Yolen), 55
Sleeping Ugly (Yolen), 55, 421
Slobodkina, Esphyr, *Caps for Sale*, 87, 355

Slotboom, Wendy, *King Snake*, 182
Slugs (Greenberg), 244, 376-77
Small, David
  Company's Coming, 258
  The Gardener, 203
  Hoover's Bride, 403
  Imogene's Antlers, 217
  The Library, 183
  Ruby Mae Has Something to Say, 303
Small Green Snake (Gray), 152
Small Talk: A Book of Short Poems, 422
A Small Tall Tale From the Far Far North (Sis), 346
Smart Moves: A Kid's Guide to Self-Defense (Goedecke), 480
Smelly Old History Series: Victorian Vapours, Roman Aromas, Tudor Odours, 481
Smith, Cat Bowman
  On Sally Perry's Farm, 190-91
  A Year on My Street, 209
Smith, Jessie Willcox, *A Child's Garden of Verses*, 212
Smith, Joseph A., *Clay Boy*, 212
Smith, Lane
  The Good, the Bad, and the Goofy, 399
  Halloween ABC, 290
  The Happy Hocky Family, 14
  Math Curse, 369
  The Stinky Cheese Man and Other Fairly Stupid Tales, 306
  The True Story of the Three Little Pigs, 351
Smith, Robert Kimmel
  Chocolate Fever, 321
  The War With Grandpa, 265, 429
Smoky Night (Bunting), 278, 304-5
Smollin, Mike, *The Monster at the End of This Book*, 131
Smudge (Rowe), 38
The Snail's Spell (Ryder), 152
A Snake Is Totally Tail (Barrett), 263
The Snarkout Boys and the Avocado of Death (Pinkwater), 493
Sneed, Brad, *Higgins Bend Song and Dance*, 290-91
Sneve, Virginia Driving Hawk, *The Cherokees*, 274-75
The Snowy Day (Keats), 152
Snyder, Zilpha Keatley
  Cat Running, 452
  The Egypt Game, 502
So, Meilo, *The Beauty of the Beast*, 44
So Much (Cooke), 19
Soap! Soap! Don't Forget The Soap!: An Appalachian Folktale (Birdseye), 193
Sobol, Donald, *Encyclopedia Brown Series*, 282-83
Sod Houses on the Great Plains (Rounds), 305
Soda Jerk (Rylant), 5, 374, 553
Soentpiet, Chris
  The Last Dragon, 295
  More Than Anything Else, 187
  Peacebound Trains, 416
Sofilas, Mark, *Burnt Stick*, 320
A Solitary Blue (Voigt), 519-20
Soman, David, *Pole Dog*, 302
Some Smug Slug (Edwards), 207, 208
Some Swell Pup, or Are You Sure You Want a Dog? (Sendak and Sendak), 264

Somebody Loves You, Mr. Hatch (Spinelli), 152-53

Someday a Tree (Bunting), 377

Something Big Has Been Here (Prelutsky), 305

Something From Nothing (Gilman), 153

Something Permanent (Rylant), 374, 481

Something Rich & Strange (Pollinger), 481

Somewhere in the Darkness (Myers), 506

Somewhere in the World Right Now (Schuett), 238

Soon, Annala (Levinson), 346

Sootface: An Ojibwa Cinderella Story (San Souci), 354, 422

Sorensen, Henri
  I Love You as Much . . . , 113
  New Hope, 262

Soto, Gary
  Chato's Kitchen, 232
  The Old Man & His Door, 138
  Too Many Tamales, 309

Soul Looks Back in Wonder (Feelings), 482

South and North, East and West: The Oxfam Book of Children's Stories, 238

Speak! Children's Book Illustrators Brag About Their Dogs (Rosen), 422

Spedden, Daisy, *Polar the Titanic Bear*, 302

The Spice Alphabet Book: Herbs, Spices, and Other Natural Flavors, 305

Spier, Peter
  Crash! Bang! Boom!, 91-92
  Noah's Ark, 16
  People, 53
  Peter Spier's Rain, 143, 359

Spinelli, Eileen, *Somebody Loves You, Mr. Hatch*, 152-53

Spinelli, Jerry
  Crash, 454
  Maniac Magee, 245, 471
  Wringer, 492

Spinky Sulks (Steig), 265, 305-6

Spirin, Gennady, *Gulliver's Adventures in Lilliput*, 289

Spite Fences (Krisher), 553-54

Spivak, Dawnine, *Grass Sandals: The Travels of Basho*, 288-89

Splash! (Jonas), 153

A Spoon for Every Bite (Hayes), 377

Spuril, Barbara, *The Flying Tortoise: An Igbo Tale*, 260

A Squash and a Squeeze (Donaldson), 153

Stack, Catherine, *Gus and Grandpa*, 105

Stammen, JoEllen McAllister, *If You Were Born a Kitten*, 115

Standiford, Natalie, *The Bravest Dog Ever: The True Story of Balto*, 120

Stanley, Diane
  Bard of Avon: The Story of William Shakespeare, 317
  Charles Dickens: The Man Who Had Great Expectations, 387
  Cleopatra, 391
  The Gentleman and the Kitchen Maid, 398

The Last Princess, 335

Saving Sweetness, 304

Sleeping Ugly, 421

Stanley, Fay, *The Last Princess*, 335

Stanley, Jerry
  Children of the Dust Bowl, 454
  I Am an American: A True Story of Japanese Internment, 508

Staples, Suzanne Fisher, *Shabanu-Daughter of the Wind*, 551

Star Mother's Youngest Child (Moeri), 37, 38

Star Walk (Simon), 306

Start to Read series, 120

Starry Messenger: Galileo Galilei (Sis), 422-23

Staying Fat for Sarah Byrnes (Crutcher), 245, 554

Steele, Philip, *The Greek News*, 461

Steig, Jeanne, *Alpha Beta Chowder*, 494-95

Steig, William
  Abel's Island, 442
  Alpha Beta Chowder, 494-95
  Brave Irene, 85, 207
  Doctor De Soto, 200
  Spinky Sulks, 265, 305-6
  Sylvester and the Magic Pebble, 156
  Zeke Pippin, 228

Stellaluna (Cannon), 193, 234

Step into Reading series, 119

Stephanie's Ponytail (Munsch), 208

Stephen Biesty's Incredible Cross-Sections (Platt), 423

Stephens, Nicholas, *Enter If You Dare!*, 476

Stepping on the Cracks (Hahn), 482

Steptoe, Javaka, *In Daddy's Arms I Am Tall*, 49

Steptoe, John
  All the Colors of the Race, 443
  Mufaro's Beautiful Daughters, 52

Stevens, Janet
  Anansi and the Moss-Covered Rock, 77
  From Pictures to Words: A Book About Making A Book, 365
  The Three Billy Goats Gruff, 194
  To Market, To Market, 159
  Tops and Bottoms, 195
  The Tortoise and the Hare, 195
  The Weighty Word Book, 488

Stevenson, Harvey, *As the Crow Flies: A First Book of Maps*, 80

Stevenson, James
  Fun! No Fun!, 286
  Something Big Has Been Here, 305
  Sweet Corn: Poems, 423
  When I Was Nine, 311

Stevenson, Robert Louis
  A Child's Garden of Verses, 212
  Treasure Island, 355

Stevenson, Sucie, *Henry and Mudge*, 108

Stewart, Sarah
  The Gardener, 203
  The Library, 183

Stillman, Susan, *Windsongs and Rainbows*, 227

The Stinky Cheese Man and Other Fairly Stupid Tales (Scieszka), 306

Stock, Catherine
  Galimoto, 100-1
  Where Are You Going, Manyoni?, 352

Stoddard, Sandol, *A Child's First Bible*, 232

Stoeke, Janet Morgan, *Minerva Louise at School*, 130

Stone, Jon, *The Monster at the End of This Book*, 131

Stone Fox (Gardiner), 346-47

Stone Soup (Brown), 153-54

Stones in Water (Napoli), 520

Stories by Firelight (Hughes), 56

Stories From Firefly Island (Blathwayt), 347

The Story About Ping (Flack), 154

The Story of Babar the Little Elephant (deBrunhoff), 306-7

The Story of Doctor Doolittle (Lofting), 355

The Story of Ferdinand (Leaf), 154, 355

The Story Library series, 520

The Story of Little Babaji (Bannerman), 154

The Story of Money (Maestro and Maestro), 423

The Story of the Three Kingdoms (Myers), 506

Straight From the Bear's Mouth (Ross), 482

Stranded at Plimoth Plantation, 1626 (Bowen), 482-83

Strega Nona (dePaola), 155

A String of Beads (Reid), 155

Stringbean's Trip to the Shining Sea (Williams), 347

Stuart Little (White), 347

The Stupids Step Out (Allard), 360

Stutson, Caroline, *By the Light of the Halloween Moon*, 86

Suddenly! (McNaughton), 155

Sugaring Time (Lasky), 408

A Suitcase of Seaweed and Other Poems (Wong), 483

Sullivan, Barbara, *Marvin Redpost: Alone in His Teacher's House*, 262

The Summer of Stanley (Kinsey-Warnock), 307

Sun Song (Marzollo), 155-56

Sun & Spoon (Henkes), 184, 265, 483-84

Supergrandpa (Schwartz), 307

Surat, Michele Maria, *Angel Child, Dragon Child*, 243

Sutcliff, Rosemary
  Black Ships Before Troy, 245, 495-96
  The Minstrel and the Dragon Pup, 221-22
  The Wanderings of Odysseus, 522

Swamp Angel (Isaacs), 193, 244

The Swan Stories (Andersen), 423

Sweet Clara and the Freedom Quilt (Hopkinson), 348

Sweet Corn: Poems (Stevenson), 423

Sweet Whispers (Hamilton), 245, 455

Sweet Words So Brave: The Story of African American Literature (Curry and Brodie), 424

Sweetwater Run (Glass), 348

Swift, Jonathan, *Gulliver's Adventures in Lilliput*, 289

Swope, Sam
  The Araboolies of Liberty Street, 207, 316
  Katya's Book of Mushrooms, 406

Sworn Enemies (Matas), 520

Sylvester and the Magic Pebble (Steig), 156

Tabor, Nancy Maria Grande, *We Are a Rainbow*, 162-63
Tacky the Penguin (Lester), 156
Tae's Sonata (Balgassi), 484
Take Action: An Environmental Book for Kids (Love and Drake), 484
Talbott, Hudson
  Amazon Diary: The Jungle Adventures of Alex Winters, 232, 382
  Tales of King Arthur series, 425
  We're Back!: A Dinosaur's Story, 195-96
The Tale of Ali Baba and the Forty Thieves (Kimmel), 424
The Tale of Peter Rabbit (Potter), 156-57, 355
The Tale of Rabbit and Coyote (Johnston), 194
Tales Alive: Ten Multicultural Folktales with Activities (Milord), 425
Tales of King Arthur series (Talbott), 425
Tales for the Perfect Child (Heide), 484
Tales of Trotter Street (Hughes), 225
The Tales of Uncle Remus (Lester), 425
The Talking Eggs (San Souci), 307, 354
Talking Like the Rain: A First Book of Poems (Kennedy and Kennedy), 194
Talking Peace: A Vision for the Next Generation (Carter), 554
Talking Walls (Knight), 348
Tanaka, Beatrice, *Green Tales*, 400-1
Tanaka, Shelley, *Discovering the Iceman: An I Was There Book*, 456-57
Tar Beach (Ringgold), 38-39
Tate, Eleanora, *Front Porch Stories at the One-Room School*, 438
Tatterhood and the Hobgoblins: A Norwegian Folktale (Mills), 426
Taylor, Mildred
  Mississippi Bridge, 472
  Roll of Thunder, Hear My Cry, 518
  The Well, 489
Taylor, Sydney, *All-of-a-Kind Family*, 382
Taylor, Theodore, *The Cay*, 498
Tchana, Katrin Hyman, *Oh, No, Toto!*, 34
Teague, Mark
  Moog-Moog Space Barber, 207
  Poppleton, 247
Teammates (Golenbock), 308
The Teddy Bears Picnic (Garcia and Grisman), 157
Tell Me Again About the Night I Was Born (Curtis), 157
A Telling of the Tales (Brooke), 484-85
Temple, Charles, *Cadillac*, 86-87
Temple, Lannis, *Dear World*, 47
Ten Little-Known Facts About Hippopotamuses (Little), 485
The Ten Mile Day & the Building of the Transcontinental Railroad (Fraser), 348
Ten Sly Piranhas: A Counting Story in Reverse (Wise), 225

Tenniel, John, *Alice's Adventures in Wonderland*, 442-43
The Tent (Paulsen), 450
The Tenth Good Thing About Barney (Viorst), 157, 218
Tessler, Stephanie G.
  Nell Nuggett and the Cow Caper, 136
  Six Creepy Sheep, 151
Tews, Susan, *The Gingerbread Doll*, 179
That Kookoory! (Froehlich), 238
Thayer, Ernest Lawrence, *Casey at the Bat*, 88
There's a Boy in the Girls' Bathroom (Sachar), 485
There's a Nightmare in My Closet (Mayer), 157-58
There's a Party at Mona's Tonight (Allard), 19
They're Off!: The Story of the Pony Express (Harness), 349
Thirteen (Charlip and Joyner), 56
Thirteen Moons on Turtle's Back: A Native American Year of Moons (Bruchac and London), 264
This Is the Hat: A Story in Rhyme (Van Laan), 158
This Land Is My Land (Littlechild), 39
This Same Sky: A Collection of Poems From Around the World (Nye, ed.), 485
Thomas, Dylan, *A Child's Christmas in Wales*, 37
Thomas, Jane Resh, *Celebration!*, 363
Thomas, Joyce Carol, *Brown Honey in Broomwheat Tea*, 362
Thomas, Rob
  Rats Saw God, 550
  Slave Day, 551
Thompson, Colin, *Looking for Atlantis*, 412
Thompson, John, *Christmas in the Big House, Christmas in the Quarters*, 514
Thompson, Karmen
  Meet the Marching Smithereens, 186
  Meet the Orchestra, 186
  Onstage & Backstage at the Night Owl Theater, 140
Thompson, Kay, *Eloise*, 394-95
Thornton, Peter, *Everybody Cooks Rice*, 250
Those Amazing Ants (Demuth), 56
Three in a Balloon (Wilson), 158
The Three Bears Holiday Rhyme Book (Yolen), 55, 158
The Three Billy Goats Gruff (Stevens), 194
The Three Blind Mice Mystery (Krensky), 158
A Three Hat Day (Geringer), 308
The Three-Legged Cat (Mahy), 225
The Three Little Javelinas (Lowell), 377
The Three Little Wolves & the Big Bad Pig (Trivizas), 39
3 NBS of Julian Drew (Deem), 539
Three Stories You Can Read to Your Dog (Miller), 248-49
Through the Hidden Door (Wells), 128

Through Moon and Stars and Night Skies (Turner), 158-59
Thunder Cake (Polacco), 264
Thunder at Gettysburg (Gauch), 308
Tiegreen, Alan
  Pee Wee Scouts series, 142
  Six Sick Sheep, 151
Tiger Flowers (Quinlan), 264
Tight Times (Hazen), 159
*Tilley, Debbie, *It's a Girl Thing*, 466
Time for Bed (Fox), 69, 355
Time to Sleep (Fleming), 159
Time Flies (Rohmann), 19-20, 359
To Be a Slave (Lester, compiler), 521
To Market, to Market (Miranda), 159, 207
Toad (Brown), 20
Toad or Frog, Swamp or Bog (Graham-Barber), 264
Toby (Wild), 360
Today I'm Going Fishing With My Dad (Sharp), 266
Today Is Monday (Carle), 160
Toddy, Irving, *Cheyenne Again*, 389
Tog the Ribber, or, Granny's Tale (Coltman), 426
Tolkien, J.R.R., *The Hobbit*, 355, 530
The Toll-Bridge Troll (Wolff), 226
Tom and Pippo Books (Oxenbury), 69-70
Tom Thumb (Watson), 39-40
Tomas and the Library Lady (Mora), 427
Tomlinson, Theresa, *The Forestwife*, 529
Tompert, Ann
  Bamboo Hats and a Rice Cake, 81-82
  Grandfather Tang's Story, 260
Tongues of Jade (Yep), 350
Tony's Bread (dePaola), 226
Too Many Pumpkins (White), 308-9
Too Many Rabbits & Other Fingerplays (Cooper), 70
Too Many Tamales (Soto), 309
A Tooth Fairy's Tale (Christiana), 194
Tops and Bottoms (Stevens), 195
The Tortilla Factory (Paulsen), 160, 450
The Tortoise and the Hare (Stevens), 195
Tough Boris (Fox), 160
Towle, Wendy, *The Real McCoy: Life of an African-American Inventor*, 343-44
Town Mouse Country Mouse (Brett), 195
Townsend, Sue, *The Adrian Mole Diaries*, 539
The Train to Grandma's (Ghantschev), 160
Train to Somewhere (Bunting), 278
Treasure Island (Stevenson), 355
A Treasury of Mermaids: Mermaid Tales From Around the World (Climo), 349
A Treasury of Princesses (Climo), 349
A Tree Is Growing (Dorros), 349
A Tree Is Nice (Udry), 161, 355
The Tree in the Wood: An Old Nursery Song (Manson), 160-61
Tree of Cranes (Say), 161
Tree of Dreams: Ten Tales From the Garden of Night (Yep), 351
Trivizas, Eugene, *The Three Little Wolves & the Big Bad Pig*, 39

The True Confessions of Charlotte Doyle (Avi), 521
True Lies: 18 Tales for You to Judge (Shannon), 427
True North: A Novel of the Underground Railroad (Lasky), 409
The True Story of the Three Little Pigs (Scieszka), 351
Truesdell, Sue
  Donna O'Neeshuck Was Chased by Some Cows, 94
  Hey World, Here I Am!, 402
  Santa's Short Suit Shrunk, 149
Tryon, Leslie
  Albert's Play, 75
  1 Gaping Wide-Mouthed Hopping Frog, 140
Tseng, Jean and Mou-sien
  Have You Seen Trees?, 179
  Maples in the Mist, 261
  Sato and the Elephants, 344
  A Treasury of Mermaids, 349
Tuck Everlasting (Babbitt), 486
Tucker Pfeffercorn (Moser), 351
Tudor, Tasha
  A Child's Garden of Verses, 212
  1 Is One, 73
  The Secret Garden, 345
Tuesday (Wiesner), 20, 359
Tumble Bumble (Bond), 70
Tunnell, Michael O., Mailing May, 368-69
A Turkey for Thanksgiving (Bunting), 278
Turkle, Brinton, Do Not Open, 177
Turner, Ann
  The Christmas House, 322
  Dakota Dugout, 276-77
  Mississippi Mud: Three Prairie Journals, 472
  Nettie's Trip South, 473-74
  Sewing Quilts, 263
  Through Moon and Stars and Night Skies, 158-59
Turtle in July (Singer), 227
Twain, Mark, The Adventures of Huckleberry Finn, 494
The Twelve Days of Christmas (Brett), 40
Twelve Shots: Outstanding Short Stories About Guns (Mazer), 554-55
12 Ways to Get to 11 (Merriam), 73
26 Letters and 99 Cents (Hoban), 73
Twilight Comes Twice (Fletcher), 227
The Tyger (Blake), 427

Uchida, Yoshiko, The Bracelet, 272-73
Udry, Janice May
  Let's Be Enemies, 122
  A Tree Is Nice, 161, 355
Uncanny (Jennings), 521-22
Uncle Jed's Barbershop (Mitchell), 351-52
Under the Blood Red Sun (Salisbury), 486
Understood Betsy (Canfield), 355
The Uninvited Guest & Other Jewish Holiday Tales (Jaffe), 309
Until I Met Dudley: How Everyday Things Really Work (McGough), 436
Until I Saw the Sea: A Collection of Seashore Poems (Shaw), 57

Utzinger, Roseanne, Sing Sophie!, 224-25

Vagin, Vladimir, The King's Equal, 294
Valenta, Barbara, Pop-O-Mania: How to Create Your Own Pop-Ups, 475-76
The Valentine Bears (Bunting), 278
Van Allsburg, Chris
  Jumanji, 367-68
  The Mysteries of Harris Burdick, 43, 371
  The Polar Express, 37
  The Z Was Zapped: A Play in Twenty-Six Acts, 43, 360
Van Camp, Richard, A Man Called Raven, 297
Van Dijk, Lutz, Damned Strong Love, 543
Van Fleet, Matthew, Fuzzy Yellow Ducklings, 65
The Van Gogh Cafe (Rylant), 374, 486
Van Laan, Nancy
  Possum Come A-Knockin', 192
  This Is the Hat: A Story in Rhyme, 158
Van Zyle, Jon, The Eyes of Gray Wolf, 177
Varley, Susan
  Badger's Bring Something Party, 230
  Badger's Parting Gifts, 172, 218
  The Monster Bed, 132
Vasilieu, Valerie, The Whittler's Tale, 353
Vaughan, Marcia K., Wombat Stew, 22
Velasquez, Eric, Front Porch Stories at the One-Room School, 438
Velcome! (O'Malley), 310
Velthuijs, Max, Frog in Love, 100
The Velveteen Rabbit (Williams), 428
Venezia, Mike, Getting to Know the World's Great Artists series, 398
Vennema, Peter
  Bard of Avon: The Story of William Shakespeare, 317
  Charles Dickens: The Man Who Had Great Expectations, 387
Venti, Anthony Bacon, Around the World in a Hundred Years, 436
Verdet, Jean-Pierre, Earth, Sky and Beyond: A Journey Through Space, 325
Verdi (Cannon), 161
Verhoeven, Rian and Van, Anne Frank: Beyond the Diary, 495
The Very Busy Spider (Carle), 162
The Very Hungry Caterpillar (Carle), 162, 355
The Very Quiet Cricket (Carle), 162
Very Scary (Johnston), 70-71
Vidal, Beatrix, Bringing the Rain to Kapiti Plain, 85
The View From the Cherry Tree (Roberts), 487
The View From Saturday (Konigsburg), 486-87
Viorst, Judith
  Absolutely, Positively Alexander, 74
  The Alphabet From Z to A, 443-44
  Earrings!, 121, 207, 281

If I Were in Charge of the World...And Other Worries, 508
I'll Fix Anthony, 114
My Mama Says There Aren't Any Zombies, or Things, 188-89
Sad Underwear and Other Complications, 477
The Tenth Good Thing About Barney, 157, 218
Virtual War (Skurzynski), 534
Visiting the Art Museum (Krasny and Brown), 310
Vitale, Stefano
  Nursery Tales Around the World, 236
  When Stories Fell Like Shooting Stars, 20-21
Vivas, Julie
  I Went Walking, 113
  Let's Eat, 182-83
  Our Granny, 140
  Possum Magic, 144
  Wilfred Gordon McDonald Partridge, 21-22
Voake, Charlotte, Ginger, 101
A Voice in the Wind (Lasky), 409
Voices From the Fields (Atkins), 487
Voices From the Wild: An Animal Sensagoria (Bouchard), 487
Voigt, Cynthia
  The Homecoming, 507-8
  A Solitary Blue, 519-20
Vojtech, Anna, The First Strawberries: A Cherokee Story, 326-27
Volcano: The Eruption & Healing of Mount St. Helens (Lauber), 428
Von Schmidt, Eric, By the Great Horn Spoon, 452
Voyage to the Bunny Planet (Wells), 20, 128, 265
The Voyage of the Frog (Paulsen), 450
Vozar, David, Yo, Hungry Wolf!, 432
Vuong, Lynette
  The Brocaded Slipper and Other Vietnamese Tales, 273, 354
  The Golden Carp and Other Tales From Vietnam, 399

Waber, Bernard
  Do You See a Mouse?, 93
  The House on East 88th Street, 216
  A Lion Named Shirley Williamson, 123
Waddell, Martin
  Can't You Sleep, Little Bear?, 87, 207
  Farmer Duck, 96
  Once There Were Giants, 206
  Owl Babies, 141
The Wagon (Johnston), 266
Waiting for the Evening Star (Wells), 128, 429
Waiting for the Whales (McFarlane), 218, 378
Waiting to Waltz: A Childhood (Rylant), 374, 487-88
Waldman, Neil, The Tyger, 427
Walk Two Moons (Creech), 522
Walker, Paul Robert
  Big Men, Big Country, 318, 388
  Giants! Stories From Around the World, 328
  Little Folk: Stories From Around the World, 410

Walking the Bridge of Your Nose
(Rosen), 429
The Wall (Bunting), 278, 378
Wallace, Karen, My Hen Is Dancing,
222
Wallner, Alexandra, Picture Book
Biographies, 309
Wallner, John
Hailstones and Halibut Bones, 401
Picture Book Biography series, 301
Walsh, Ellen, Mouse Paint, 133
Walter, Virginia, "Hi, Pizza Man!",
109
Walton, Rick
How Many, How Many, How
Many, 246
Once There Was a Bull...(Frog), 140
The Wanderings of Odysseus: The
Story of the Odyssey (Sutcliff),
522
War Boy: A Country Childhood
(Foreman), 522-23
The War With Grandpa (Smith), 265,
429
Ward, Lynd, Silver Pony, 43, 359
Washburn, Lucia, Look to the North:
A Wolf Pup Diary, 296
Watkins, Richard, Gladiator, 460
Watling, James, Finding Providence:
The Story of Roger Williams,
251
Watson, Richard Jesse
High Rise Glorious Skittle Skat
Roarious Sky Pie, 403
One Wintry Night, 53
Tom Thumb, 39-40
The Watsons Go to Birmingham, 1963
(Curtis), 523
Wattenberg, Jane, Mrs. Mustard's
Baby Faces, 67
Waugh, Sylvia, The Mennyms, 338
Way Home (Hawthorn), 488
The Way Things Work (Macaulay),
57-58
The Way West: Journal of a Pioneer
Woman (Knight), 310-11
We Are a Rainbow (Tabor), 162-63
The Weaving of a Dream (Heyer),
429
The Wednesday Surprise (Bunting),
278, 378
The Weekend Was Murder (Nixon),
534
Weetzie Bat (Block), 555
The Weighty Word Book (Levitt,
Burger, and Guralnick), 488
Weird Parents (Wood), 207
Weiss, Nicki, An Egg Is an Egg, 96
Welcome Little Baby (Aliki), 163
Welcome to the Green House (Yolen),
430
Welcoming Babies (Knight), 163
The Well (Taylor), 489
Well Wished (Billingsley), 488-89
Weller, Frances Ward, Riptide, 303
Wells, Rosemary, 128
Bunny Cakes, 128
Bunny Money, 86
Edward in Deep Water, 128
Edward Unready for School, 121,
128
Edward Unready for a Sleep Over,
121
Edward Unready for Swimming,
121

Edward's Overwhelming Overnight,
128
Eric Knight's Lassie Come Home,
335
Forest of Dreams, 128
Fritz and the Mess Fairy, 128
Hazel's Amazing Mother, 107, 128
The Language of Doves, 128
McDuff and the Baby, 128
McDuff Comes Home, 128
McDuff Moves In, 128
The Man in the Woods, 128
Max and Ruby's First Greek Myth:
Pandora's Box, 127
Max's Bath, 128
Max's Bedtime, 128
Max's Birthday, 128
Max's Dragon Shirt, 128, 129
Max's Ride, 128
Morris' Disappearing Bag, 128
My Very First Mother Goose, 128,
134
Night Sounds, Morning Colors, 34,
128
Noisy Nora, 128, 137
Shy Charles, 150, 207
Silent Night, 128
Through the Hidden Door, 128
Voyage to the Bunny Planet, 20,
128, 265
Waiting for the Evening Star, 128,
429
When No One Was Looking, 128
We're Back!: A Dinosaur's Story
(Talbott), 195-96
Wesley, Addison, Let Me Read series,
120
Wesley, Dennis, King of the Wind,
406
West, Colin, I Don't Care, Said the
Bear, 112-13
Westall, Robert, Blitzcat, 448
Westcott, Nadine Bernard, Never
Take a Pig To Lunch, 235
The Westing Game (Raskin), 523
Westman, Barbara, I Like the Music,
29
Westmark (Alexander), 534-35
Weston, Martha
The Book of Think, 497
Did You See What I Saw?: Poems
About School, 93
Wexler, Jerome
A Bird's Body, 272
Everyday Mysteries, 326
The Whale's Song (Sheldon), 40
Whaling Days (Carrick), 311
What About Ladybugs? (Godkin), 238
What Am I? Looking Through Shapes
at Apples and Grapes (Charles),
71
What Do You Do When Something
Wants to Eat You? (Jenkins),
208-9
What Hearts (Brooks), 489
What Jamie Saw (Coman), 523
What a Wonderful Day to Be a Cow
(Lesser), 163
What You Know First (MacLachlan),
378-79
Whatley, Bruce, The Teddy Bears
Picnic, 157
What's What? A Guessing Game
(Serfozo), 163
The Wheels on the Bus (Zelinsky),
164

When Africa Was Home (Williams),
227
When Bluebell Sang (Ernst), 164
When Clay Sings (Baylor), 379
When Hunger Calls (Kitchen), 40
When I Was Little: A Four-Year-Old's
Memoir of Her Youth (Curtis),
164
When I Was Nine (Stevenson), 311
When I Was Young in the Mountains
(Rylant), 374
When I'm Sleepy (Howard), 164
When Jo Louis Won the Title
(Rochelle), 311
When No One Was Looking (Wells),
128
When Stories Fell Like Shooting Stars
(Gregory), 20-21
When the Big Dog Barks (Curtis), 165
When the Goblins Came Knocking
(Hines), 71
When the Monkeys Came Back
(Franklin), 312
When the Whippoorwill Calls
(Ransom), 430
When We Married Gary (Hines), 165
When Zaydeh Danced on Eldridge
Street (Rael), 165
Where Are You Going, Manyoni?
(Stock), 352
Where Does It Go? (Miller), 71-72
Where the Red Fern Grows (Rawls),
524
Where the Sidewalk Ends: Poems and
Drawings (Silverstein), 430
Where the Wild Things Are (Sendak),
21, 244, 355
Where Will This Shoe Take You?: A
Walk Through the History of
Footwear (Lawlor), 524
Where's My Teddy? (Alborough), 165
Where's Spot? (Hill), 166
Where's That Insect? (Brenner), 352
The Whipping Boy (Fleischman),
430-31
Whipple, Laura, Celebrating America,
45
White, E.B.
Charlotte's Web, 355, 387-88
Stuart Little, 347
White, Linda, Too Many Pumpkins,
308-9
White, Michael P., The Library
Dragon, 219
White, Robb, Deathwatch, 528-29
White, Ruth, Belle Prater's Boy, 448
White Dynamite & Curly Kidd
(Martin and Archambault),
352-53
White On Black (Hoban), 68, 72
White Socks Only (Coleman), 431
Whiteley, Opal, Only Opal: The
Diary of a Young Girl, 415
The Whittler's Tale (Armstrong), 353
Who Belongs Here? An American
Story (Knight), 431
Who Is the Beast? (Baker), 166
Who Said Boo? (Carlstrom), 72
Who Said Red? (Serfozo), 166
Who Said That? Famous Americans
Speak (Burleigh), 489-90
Who Says a Dog Goes Bow-Wow?
(DeZutter), 21
The Whole Story series, 490
Why Mosquitoes Buzz in People's Ears
(Aardema), 196

Wick, Walter, *A Drop of Water*, 393
   I Spy Mystery, 31
The Wide-Mouthed Frog: A Pop-Up Book (Faulkner), 166-67
Wiese, Kurt, *The Story About Ping*, 154
Wiesner, David
   Free Fall, 12, 359
   Kite Flier, 407
   Tuesday, 20, 359
Wilbur, Richard, *A Game of Catch*, 438
Wild, Margaret
   Old Pig, 206
   Our Granny, 140
   Toby, 360
Wilder, Laura Ingalls
   The Little House in the Big Woods, 355
   The Little House on the Prairie, 410
Wildsmith, Brian, *Saint Francis*, 344
Wilfred Gordon McDonald Partridge (Fox), 21-22, 265
Wilhelm, Hans, *I'll Always Love You*, 217, 218
Will You Sign Here, John Hancock? (Fritz), 353
Willard, Nancy, *The High Rise Glorious Skittle Skat Roarious Sky Pie*, 403
William Shakespeare's Macbeth (Coville), 490
William Shakespeare's The Tempest (Coville), 490-91
Williams, David, *Grandma Essie's Covered Wagon*, 329
Williams, Garth
   Amigo, 269
   Charlotte's Web, 387-88
   The Cricket in Times Square, 391
   The Little House on the Prairie, 410
   Stuart Little, 347
Williams, Jennifer, *Stringbean's Trip to the Shining Sea*, 347
Williams, Karen Lynn
   Galimoto, 100-1
   When Africa Was Home, 227
Williams, Marcia, *Don Quixote*, 280
Williams, Margery, *The Velveteen Rabbit*, 428
Williams, Sherley Anne, *Working Cotton*, 266
Williams, Sue, *I Went Walking*, 113
Williams, Suzanne
   Made in China: Ideas & Inventions From Ancient China, 470
   My Dog Never Says Please, 134
Williams, Vera
   Cherries and Cherry Pits, 175
   Hooray for Me, 110
   More, More, More, Said the Baby: 3 Love Stories, 132
   Stringbean's Trip to the Shining Sea, 347
William's Doll (Zolotow), 167
Willie Bea and the Time When the Martians Landed (Hamilton), 455
Willis, Jeanne, *The Monster Bed*, 132
Will's Mammoth (Martin), 22, 359
Willy the Wimp (Browne), 209
Wilma Unlimited: How Wilma Rudolph Became the World's Fastest Woman, 312
Wilson, Janet, *Tiger Flowers*, 264

Wilson, Sarah
   June Is a Tune That Jumps On a Stair, 118
   Three in a Balloon, 158
Wimmer, Mike
   All the Places to Love, 171
   Flight, 284
The Wind in the Willows (Grahame), 355
Wind Says Good Night (Rydell), 167
Windsongs and Rainbows (Burton), 227
The Wing Shop (Woodruff), 228
Wings: A Tale of Two Chickens (Marshall), 40-41
Winnie the Pooh (Milne), 355
Winslow, Marjorie, *Mud Pies and Other Recipes: A Cookbook for Dolls*, 187-88
Winter, Jeanette
   Day of the Dead, 176
   Eight Hands Round: A Patchwork Alphabet, 281
   A Fruit and Vegetable Man, 203
   Shaker Boy, 421
Winter Poems (Rogasky), 491
The Winter Room (Paulsen), 450
Winter White (Ryder), 41
Winters, Kay, *Did You See What I Saw?: Poems About School*, 93
Winthrop, Elizabeth, *The Castle in the Attic*, 320
Wise, William, *Ten Sly Piranhas: A Counting Story in Reverse*, 225
Wish You Were Here: Emily's Guide to the 50 States (Krull), 353-54
Wisniewski, David, *Golem*, 288
Witch Way to the Country? (Mariconda), 167
The Witches (Dahl), 491
Wojciechowski, Susan, *The Christmas Miracle of Jonathan Toomey*, 37, 389
The Wolfbay Wings (Brooks), 491-92
Wolff, Ashley
   Goody O'Grumpity, 216
   Home Sweet Home, 110
   Miss Bindergarten Gets Ready for Kindergarten, 131
   A String of Beads, 155
Wolff, Patricia Rae, *The Toll-Bridge Troll*, 226
Wolff, Virginia Euwer, *Make Lemonade*, 533
Wombat Divine (Fox), 167-68
Wombat Stew (Vaughan), 22
The Wonderful Towers of Watts (Zelver), 431-32
The Wonderful Wizard of Oz (Baum), 354, 355, 388
Wong, Janet, *A Suitcase of Seaweed and Other Poems*, 483
Wood, Audrey
   Birdsong, 231
   The Bunyans, 363
   Elbert's Bad Word, 201
   Heckedy Peg, 28-29, 244
   King Bidgood's in the Bathtub, 121
   Little Mouse, the Red Ripe Strawberry, & the Big Hungry Bear, 124
   The Napping House, 135, 355
   Piggies, 68
   Quick as a Cricket, 145
   The Rainbow Bridge, 417
   The Red Racer, 248

Wood, C., *Keepers of the Earth*, 406
Wood, Don
   Elbert's Bad Word, 201
   Heckedy Peg, 28-29, 244
   King Bidgood's in the Bathtub, 121
   The Little Mouse, the Red Ripe Strawberry, & the Big Hungry Bear, 124
   The Napping House, 135, 355
   Piggies, 68
   Quick as a Cricket, 145
Wood, Douglas, *Old Turtle*, 16
Woodbull, Anne, *Colors Around Us: A Lift-the-Flap Surprise Book*, 89-90
Woodlore (Miller and Falla), 58
Woodruff, Elvira, *The Wing Shop*, 228
Woodson, Jacqueline, *I Hadn't Meant to Tell You This*, 546
Words of Stone (Henkes), 184
Working Cotton (Williams), 266
Worksong (Paulsen), 22-23, 450
World of Christopher Robin (Milne), 196-97
The World Is Full of Babies!: How All Sorts of Babies Grow and Develop, 168
World Mythology series, 524-25
The World of Pooh (Milne), 197
The Worry Stone (Dengler), 379
Would You Rather . . . ? (Burningham), 168
The Wreck of the Zanzibar (Morpurgo), 432
Wright, Joan R., *Bugs*, 174
Wringer (Spinelli), 492
A Wrinkle in Time (L'Engle), 492
Wu, Norbert, *Fish Faces*, 98
Wynne-Jones, Tim, *The Book of Changes*, 449

Xiong, Blia, *Nine-In-One Grr! Grr!*, 136

Yaccarino, Dan, *Zoom! Zoom! Zoom! I'm Off to the Moon*, 169
Yalowitz, Paul
   Moonstruck, 298
   Nell Nuggett and the Cow Caper, 138
   Somebody Loves You, Mr. Hatch, 152-53
Yamaka, Sara, *The Gift of Driscoll Lipscomb*, 287
Yardley, Joanna, *The Bracelet*, 272-73
The Year at Maple Hill Farm (Provensen and Provensen), 168
A Year on My Street (Quattlebaum), 209
Yearling First Choice Chapter Books, 120
Yeh-Shen: A Cinderella Story From China (Louie), 354
Yep, Laurence, 350
   American Dragon: Twenty-five Asian American Voices, 350
   The Boy Who Swallowed Snakes, 350
   Child of the Owl, 350
   The City of Dragons, 350
   Dragon Cauldron, 350
   Dragon of the Lost Sea, 350
   The Dragon Prince, 350
   Dragon Steel, 350

Dragon War, 350
Dragon's Gate, 350
Dragonwings, 350
Hiroshima: A Novella, 350
The Lost Garden, 350
The Man Who Tricked a Ghost, 350
The Rainbow People, 350
Tongues of Jade, 350
Tree of Dreams: Ten Tales From the Garden of Night, 351
Yikes! Your Body, Up Close (Janulewicz), 432
Yo, Hungry Wolf! (Vozar), 432
Yolen, Jane, 55
  All Those Secrets of the World, 55
  Baby Bear's Bedtime Book, 55
  The Ballad of the Pirate Queens, 55, 383
  Commander Toad in Space, 200
  Commander Toad series, 55
  The Devil's Arithmetic, 55, 501
  Dove Isabeau, 55, 325
  Dragon's Blood: Volume 1 in the Pit Dragon Trilogy, 502
  Eeny, Meeny, Miney Mole, 55, 95
  The Emperor and the Kite, 55
  Encounter, 55
  The Gift of Sarah Barker, 55
  The Girl Who Cried Flowers and Other Tales, 55
  Good Griselle, 55, 439
  Grandad Bill's Song, 179, 218
  The Haunted House: A Collection of Original Stories, 55
  How Beastly! A Menagerie of Nonsense Poems, 55
  Jane Yolen's Old MacDonald Songbook, 55
  Letting Swift River Go, 55
  Merlin: Book 3 of the Young Merlin Trilogy, 512
  Miz Berlin Walks, 55, 413
  Owl Moon, 55

Piggins, 55
The Pit Dragon Trilogy, 55
Sacred Places, 54, 55
Sleep Rhymes Around the World, 55
Sleeping Ugly, 55, 421
The Three Bears Holiday Rhyme Book, 55, 158
Welcome to the Green House, 430
The Young Merlin Trilogy, 55
Yonder (Johnston), 379
Yorinks, Arthur, *Company's Coming*, 258
Yoshi, *Big Al*, 83
You Be Good and I'll Be Night (Merriam), 169
You Hold Me and I'll Hold You (Carson), 218, 228
Young, Ed
  All of You Was Singing, 230
  Bo Rabbit Smart for True Tall Tales From the Gullah, 231-32
  I Wish I Were a Butterfly, 114
  Lon Po Po, A Red-Riding Hood Story From China, 219-21
  Sadako, 303
  Seven Blind Mice, 150
  Yeh-Shen: A Cinderella Story From China, 354
Young, Jay, *Beyond Amazing: Six Spectacular Science Pop-Ups*, 436
Young, Noela, *Toby*, 360
Young Adult Novel (Pinkwater), 493
Young Guinevere (San Souci), 355-56
Young John Quincy (Harness), 356
Young Larry (Pinkwater), 379-80
The Young Merlin Trilogy (Yolen), 55
Your New Potty (Cole), 220
Yummers (Marshall), 23

The Z Was Zapped: A Play in Twenty-Six Acts (Van Allsburg), 43, 360
Zallinger, Jean Day, *The Book of North American Owls*, 385

Zamorano, Ana, *Let's Eat*, 182-83
Zawadzki, Marek, *Okino and the Whales*, 190
Za-Za's Baby Brother (Cousins), 169
Zee (Enright), 356
Zeely (Hamilton), 455
Zeke Pippin (Steig), 228
Zel (Napoli), 525
Zelinsky, Paul O.
  Dear Mr. Henshaw, 392
  Rapunzel, 355, 418
  Rumpelstiltskin, 224
  Swamp Angel, 193
  The Wheels on the Bus, 164
Zelver, Patricia, *The Wonderful Towers of Watts*, 431-32
Zhang, Hongbin, *D Is For Doufu: An Alphabet Book of Chinese Culture*, 47
Zilla Sasparilla and the Mud Baby (Gorog), 312
Zimmer, Dirk, *Seven Spiders Spinning*, 478-79
Zimmerman, Andrew and David, *The Cow Buzzed*, 175
Zimmerman, Robert, *The Banging Book*, 82
Zimmermann, H. Werner, *Finster Frets*, 233-34
Zin! Zin! Zin! A Violin (Moss), 197
Zindel, Paul, *The Pigman*, 550
Zion, Gene, *Harry the Dirty Dog*, 120
Zipping Zapping Zooming Bats, 234
Zolotow, Charlotte
  Mr. Rabbit and the Lovely Present, 133
  William's Doll, 167
Zoom (Banyai), 23, 359
Zoom! Zoom! Zoom! I'm Off to the Moon (Yaccarino), 169
Zudeck, Darryl S., *Prairie Songs*, 516